THE COMPLETE BOOK OF THE DOG

THE COMPLETE BOOK OF THE DOG

Foreword by Charles Cruft

General Editor

Joyce Robins

HAMLYN

ACKNOWLEDGEMENTS

The publishers wish to thank the following photographers and agencies for their kind permission to reproduce their photographs in this publication:

Alton Anderson; AFIP, A M Berenger; Animal Graphics; Animal Photography; Animals Unlimited; Ardea; K Barkleigh-Shute; S C Bisserot; M Buzzini; Hanson Carroll; Bruce Coleman; Ann Cumbers; A Hamilton-Rowan; Michael Holford; Jacana; Octopus Group Picture Library; Dick Polak; Diane Pearce; Pictor; Anne Roslin-Williams; Michael Serlick; Spectrum; Tony Stone Worldwide; Guy Trouillet; US Customs; Mireille Vautier; Zefa Picture Library.

Published in 1991 by The Hamlyn Publishing Group Limited
a division of the Octopus Publishing Group,
Michelin House, 81 Fulham Road, London SW3 6RB

This book makes use of material from the following books published by Octopus Books Limited:– *Sit!*, 1982; *The Encyclopedia of the Dog*, 1981; *The Beauty of Dogs*, 1979 and *The World Encyclopedia of Dogs*, 1977.

ISBN 0 600 570 770

Produced by Mandarin Offset

Printed and bound in Hong Kong

CONTENTS

FOREWORD 6

1 INTRODUCING THE DOG 8

Evolution . Domestication . Development of breeding . Senses . Communication . The skeleton . Muscles and nerves . Respiration . Teeth and digestion . Reproduction . Instincts and behaviour .

2 CHOOSING A DOG 20

Dog or bitch . Two dogs or one . Puppy or adult dog . Pedigree or mongrel . Which breed . Long or shorthaired . Family dogs . Guard dogs . Amount of exercise . Breed drawbacks . Where to find your dog . Choosing from the litter

3 BREEDS OF THE WORLD 32

An A–Z of more than 150 breeds from all over the world

4 THE NEW PUPPY 110

Dogproofing your home . Equipment . Collecting your puppy . Children and puppies . Introduction to other pets . Diet . Puppy health . Learning its name . Early lessons . Play . Collars and leads . Grooming . House-training . Car travel . Dogs and the law . Responsible dog ownership .

5 TRAINING AND OBEDIENCE 126

Joining a class . Check chains . Training sessions . 'Come!' . The release word . 'Heel!' and 'Sit' . 'Sit and Stay' . 'Wait!' and 'Come' . 'Down and stay' . 'Leave!' . The retrieve . Tricks . Curing bad habits . Aggression . Climbing on furniture . Pulling . Wandering . Mounting . Phobias . Destructive dogs . Barking . Jumping up . Stealing food . Chasing cats . Chasing vehicles . Digging holes . Resentment of handling . Urinating indoors . Car travel . Fights .

6 CARE OF THE DOG 146

Food . Special grooming . Nails . Anal sacs and glands . Baths . Health and sickness . Signs of a healthy dog . Giving medication . First aid . Consulting a veterinary surgeon . A–Z of ailments . The older dog . Travelling . Boarding .

7 BREEDING 166

Preparations . Mating . Gestation . Whelping . The litter . Weaning . Hand-rearing puppies .

8 SHOWING 178

Show organisation . Show judging . Preparing for showing . Handling . The show day . Obedience competitions . Field trials .

INDEX 188

FOREWORD

It is with great pleasure that I am in the happy position of writing the Foreword to THE COMPLETE BOOK OF THE DOG. It is not only an extremely comprehensive book, but also gives simple and explicit guidance from the very beginning for the potential dog owner.

My grandfather Charles Cruft made a great contribution to the dog world when, in 1891, he founded the now world-famous international dog show. While I am fortunate enough to have a name well known in the dog world, I can supplement this inheritance by a wealth of experience, acquired over the last sixty years, in most things relating to dogs.

During the last war I was directing the training of German Shepherd guard and search dogs at the first Royal Air Force Dog School near Cheltenham. This gave me a deep interest in the field and, back in civilian life, I continued training guard dogs for industry. On the lighter side, I organised the frolics of the first Labrador puppy to find himself confronted with a toilet roll. Another interesting departure was the schooling of the Staffordshire Bull Terrier, which took the part of Bill Sykes's dog in David Lean's film of *Oliver Twist*.

How can you describe in print the immense pleasure to be derived from owning a dog, which gives so much in return for so little? Just see a blind person skilfully led through the street by a guide dog and give a word of admiration to the owner: you will be sent away in a happy frame of mind.

Rearing a new puppy is very like bringing up a child, except with a puppy you have some choice in the matter. But do think carefully before you acquire your puppy and never make that important decision just because the little creature is appealing. Remember that a dog has feelings like you and a change of ownership (let alone the abandonment of a pet) may be disastrous to the poor animal.

I can only wish that sixty years ago, when I was very short of experience, THE COMPLETE BOOK OF THE DOG had been available.

CHARLES CRUFT

INTRODUCING THE DOG

The dog has always had a special place in man's affections; the relationship between the two goes back for thousands of years, with dogs being bred first for their usefulness as hunters, drovers and guards and later, by careful selection, for their distinctive looks and value in the show ring. You will get more out of your relationship with your pet if you understand the basic design of the dog, how its body works, the benefits of its highly developed sense of smell and hearing, and how its instincts and patterns of behaviour are related.

The dog was the first wild animal domesticated by man and it has been his constant companion for thousands of years. Its basic nature makes it uniquely adaptable to the needs of man; it is essentially a pack animal, happily living under the dominance of a pack leader and ready to accept its human family as a substitute pack and its owner as the leader. The dog is an enthusiast, always keen to join in family activities, unquestioning in its loyalty and totally reliable in giving companionship and returning affection. Its ready submission to its owner means that it is easier to train than other animals; in fact, it eagerly welcomes training and man has been able to breed dogs for guarding, hunting, fighting, haulage, and as eyes for the blind and ears for the deaf. Since man's early days as a nomad hunter, the dog has earned its place as his best friend.

Dogs readily accept man as the substitute pack leader and so are easily trainable to fulfill a variety of roles.

Evolution

Despite their huge range of shapes and sizes, all dogs belong to the same species, *canis familiaris*. The many breeds we know today are the result of selective breeding by man. The earliest ancestor of the *canidae* family, to which the dog belongs, along with other carnivores such as wolves, jackals and foxes, was the small carnivorous mammal called *Miacis*. This was a long-bodied, short-legged, tree-climbing animal rather like today's polecat, which flourished about 40 million years ago, during the late Eocene and early Oligocene periods. Various transitional forms evolved from *Miacis* until, some 10–20 million years ago, the forerunners of present-day *canidae* existed: first *Cynodictus*, with five toes, partly webbed, then *Tomarctus*, a primitive form of dog with longer jaws. About one million years ago, the forms we know as wolves, jackals and coyotes were already developing.

Scientists have never produced certain proof of the dog's immediate ancestor. In the nineteenth century Charles Darwin, among others, held that the wolf and the golden jackal, might have given rise to the domestic dog, with some degree of cross-breeding. Certain breeds, it was argued, displayed a high degree of wolf ancestry, while others displayed mainly jackal ancestry. However, this theory has since been discredited and it is now generally accepted that the wolf alone is the dog's direct ancestor and that domestication of certain breeds of wolf probably happened in various geographical sites – North America, China and Africa as well as the Middle East – at around the same time, and this could help to explain some of the variations seen between today's breeds of dogs.

The origins of the dog have been the subject of much argument among the experts but it is now generally accepted that it is descended from the wolf.

DOMESTICATION

The earliest fossil finds of domestic dogs date from about 12,000 years ago and include finds from Iraq and northern Israel. There are several other dog fossils dating from about 8,000 to over 10,000 years ago, from such widespread sites as Idaho in the United States, Turkey, Czechoslovakia and Yorkshire, England. However, the exact process of domestication is still a subject for debate among scientists.

It is possible that the relationship between dog and man first developed on a basis of mutual advantage. They were both hunting the same prey and though man was no match for the wolves as a hunter, he would have been able to drive them from their kill and enjoy the benefit of their stalking and killing skills. In turn, the wolves may have learned to exploit food discarded by man, as well as hunting the rats and other species that might have lived on grain stored by man. Tamer individuals, or cubs that grew up around humans, might have been tolerated for their use in keeping down vermin and were then befriended by man. Dogs and men might then have become hunting companions, co-operating in the gathering of food.

Another possibility is that dogs were pets or companions rather than working animals right from the start. Cubs orphaned when their mothers were killed by predators, or by man, might have been brought home as playthings for children, who brought them up much as today's youngsters might bring up an orphaned fox or badger. The working uses of the dog may have grown out of the understanding that developed between the children and their pets.

An alternative theory is that the early domestic dogs were kept as guards rather than hunters. Their superior senses of smell and hearing could have alerted man to the presence of wild animals or other

Wall paintings in the tomb of Rameses VI in the Valley of the Kings in Egypt show hunting dogs similar to modern greyhounds.

humans that might threaten his campsite. This may explain why barking is common behaviour for the domestic dog but not for the wolf. Once man began keeping cattle and sheep, the dog's guarding skills would have been extended to protecting the flocks.

Whatever the details of domestication, it seems obvious that in time, the offspring of the wolf came to live in close association with man, learning to respond to his moods, fit in with his ways and obey his commands, eventually turning into the reliable worker and companion of modern times.

Development of Breeding

Once the process of domestication had begun, man was able to breed dogs for a variety of uses. As long ago as 4000 BC the civilizations of the Middle East were breeding dogs with some care and selectivity. Egyptian murals of this period show several types of greyhounds: one has upright bat ears like the modern Ibizan Hound, while another has the small drop ear and the feathering of the modern Saluki. There is a theory that some type of greyhound, one of the ancestors of the Afghan Hound, reached Afghanistan along the trade routes of the ancient world between the Middle East and China. It was discovered there by British military men in the late nineteenth century and introduced to the western world.

The greyhound family were at their most successful in desert countries where the hot, still air makes for bad scenting conditions but visibility is excellent. This suits all types of greyhounds, since they hunt by sight rather than scent and use speed to overtake their prey. For this reason, they are also known as gazehounds.

Early Assyrian wall paintings portray a much larger, heavier Mastiff-like dog with a wrinkled head and curled tail. These were apparently used for hunting lions and were taken into battle by their Assyrian masters in 625 BC. The Greeks knew of the heavy, robust Molussus dog, also a Mastiff-type, that became famous for its courage and ferocity in tackling wild boar in the sixth century BC. Dogs of this type may have reached Britain with the Phoenician traders who came to buy tin. By the time the Romans invaded Britain, the British Mastiff was sufficiently impressive for several to be sent back to Rome to fight in gladiatorial contests.

The Middle Eastern peoples had no use for hounds that hunt by scent and the scent hounds evolved in cooler, milder climates, where the thickness of vegetation would prevent a sight hound from seeing the game. From the time of the peak of Greek civilization through to the Middle Ages in Europe, hunting with packs of scent hounds was a passion with the nobility.

Spaniels are the oldest of the gundog breeds and were widely used in medieval times to find and spring birds for the falconers' hawks, or flushing

birds into a net for huntsmen.

Not all dogs were bred for their usefulness; many of the toy breeds have histories as long and well-documented as the more utilitarian varieties. Small dogs, though scorned by sportsmen, have been coveted and cosseted throughout the civilized world. The mummified remains of very small dogs have been found in Egyptian tombs. A tiny, long-coated dog was known in Malta in the time of the Phoenicians, and the Maltese seems to have existed in much its present form at the time of the Apostle Paul. In AD 100 the Chinese were breeding 'pai' dogs, described as short-legged, short-mouthed dogs which belonged under the table. The earliest of the flat-faced Chinese dogs to reach Europe was the Pug, brought home by Dutch and Portuguese traders in the sixteenth century; the first Pekingese seen in the western world came as part of the booty when the French and English troops sacked the Imperial Palace in Peking in 1860.

Many of the working breeds of the past, as opposed to the hunting dogs, have an undocumented history, for they did not attract the attention of artists and writers. We know that the vermin-hunting terriers, the cattle-droving dogs and the sheepdogs have been in existence for centuries, but we know little about their appearance before the nineteenth century.

Although some dogs have been bred over so many centuries, it was not until the advent of dog shows and the formation of the Kennel Club in Britain in 1873 and in other countries shortly afterwards that pedigrees as records of ancestry became the universal practice. The Kennel Club's first positive action was to organize a stud book and to rule that only registered dogs were allowed to enter its shows. The purpose of this was to eliminate some of the unscrupulous practices and confusion that reigned at the early shows.

The Bayeux Tapestry, depicting the Norman Conquest, is one of the many pieces of artistic evidence showing that man has been breeding dogs for selected purposes for hundreds of years.

Senses

To the dog, the most important sense is that of smell; it is estimated that its sense of smell is at least 100 times better than ours. Man has always put the dog's superior sense of smell to his own use and dogs have been trained to locate a wide variety of objects, from edible fungi such as truffles, to explosives or hidden drugs in a cargo. A dog concentrating on a track may become so absorbed in following its nose that it falls over the object of its search before its eyes register the find. As so much of its knowledge of the world is gained through its nose, the dog adapts very well to the handicap of blindness and its owner may not realize that a pet is losing its sight. A blind dog can still retrieve a ball, apparently locating it by smell and sound.

The dog's hearing is also better than ours and it is more sensitive to some sounds, specially those at high frequencies; hence the use of 'silent' dog whistles, audible to the dog but not to humans. Dogs seem to detect nuances of voice that humans are unaware of, so that a nervous person saying 'Good boy' may be conveying more about his fear than his good intentions to the dog. Most dogs can distinguish the sound of their owner's car from a medley of other traffic noises and this ability of the animal to hear an approach long before the sound is perceptible to human ears makes them valuable as sentries, watch dogs and border patrol guards. This acute hearing means that some dogs are 'sound shy', meaning that they are nervous or afraid of some noises and need a good deal of training before they become indifferent to the feared noise.

There is some controversy over whether dogs are colour-blind or not; it seems likely that they see only in black and white. They cannot move their eyeballs in the sockets as freely as humans but compensate for this by the longer, more mobile neck and they move their heads more frequently. They have better peripheral vision than ours, giving a larger visual field. It is movement that attracts a dog's attention to a distant object but it is remarkably difficult to point out a stationary object to a dog. The way a dog's eye lights up in the glare of car headlights is an indication of the animal's ability to make the best use of available light and see well in dim conditions. Light is reflected from a layer at the back of the animal's eye and passes twice through the light-sensitive retina, thus doubling sensitivity.

Communication

Dogs use body signals, sounds and chemical smells in communicating with one another. The position of ears and tails indicates a great deal about a dog's mood. Two strange male dogs will approach one another with a jaunty step, heads and tails held high. Nervous dogs will make themselves appear smaller by crouching slightly and laying back their ears; they hold their tails tightly between their legs and will not allow another dog to sniff their rear. The aggressive dog, on the other hand, makes itself seem larger by raising the hair on the back of its neck and along its spine. The dog will be tense and stiff and it will fix its opponent with an intimidating glare. A stare is usually a threat signal and if an owner stares at a dog it will usually look away and become submissive, perhaps rolling on its back.

The use of smell is very important. When two dogs first meet they usually smell each others' faces

The dog's sense of smell is far superior to that of humans. It is so highly developed that a dog can be trained to detect hidden drugs or explosives.

This German Shepherd shows that it has sensed a friendly presence; its ears are pricked and moving round in the direction of a sound and its nose has picked up a scent.

and then their hindquarters. A male dog cocks its leg to mark prominent objects while out walking in order to mask the smell of dogs that have passed recently and claim the territory as its own. Scratching with the back feet, seen mainly in male dogs after defecation, leaves a chemical signal, known as a pheromone, from special glands between the toes. Faeces may be used as scent markers and a dog has anal glands that secrete a mixture of chemicals.

Sounds used include barking, whining and howling. Barking is usually to gain attention, perhaps as an excited greeting or a request for a game. Whining, often heard when a dog is left alone, is a distress call aimed at the owner and is hardly ever used towards another dog. Howling is probably a warning sound used to protect a territory.

The Skeleton

The dog's basic skeletal structure remains the same in a tiny Chihuahua or a huge St Bernard though the size and thickness of individual bones varies from breed to breed.

Many dogs have skulls that differ little from their wild ancestors. However, in the short-faced breeds, the jaws are considerably shortened and the curvature of the cheekbones increased, giving the appearance of a greater width of skull: this shape is known as brachycephalic. In some of the breeds, such as the Bulldog, the lower jaw is slightly longer than the upper, causing the lower teeth to meet outside the upper set, a condition known as 'undershot'.

The neck has seven vertebrae, known as the cervical vertebrae. The first (the atlas) allows the head to nod up and down and the second (the axis) allows the head to rotate. The remainder of the neck vertebrae permit the dog to bend its neck to look behind much more efficiently than a human being. Behind the neck are 13 thoracic vertebrae which protect the spinal cord and support the ribs. The seven lumbar vertebrae support the abdomen and lead to the sacrum, which usually consists of three vertebrae fused together. The sacrum supports the pelvic girdle and the hind limbs. The number of tail bones varies greatly according to breed.

The thoracic vertebrae, the ribs and sternum form what is commonly known as the rib-cage, which encloses the heart and two lungs. It is particularly deep and roomy in the racing breeds, such as the Greyhounds. The heart of a racing Greyhound is measurably larger than that of a dog of similar size not subjected to so much exertion.

The structure of the shoulder, particularly the relationship between the shoulder blade (scapula) and upper arm (humerus), determines what kind of movement the dog has. Many breeds require the forelegs to move straight forward parallel to each other, covering the maximum of ground with the most efficiency. In this case the ideal is a shoulder blade at an angle of 45 degrees to the perpendicular, with the upper arm at right angles to it. The 'straight' front required by some terrier breeds is

The skeleton is made up of two parts: the axial skeleton comprises the skull and spinal column and the appendicular skeleton comprises the shoulders, pelvic girdle and the limbs.

The skeleton

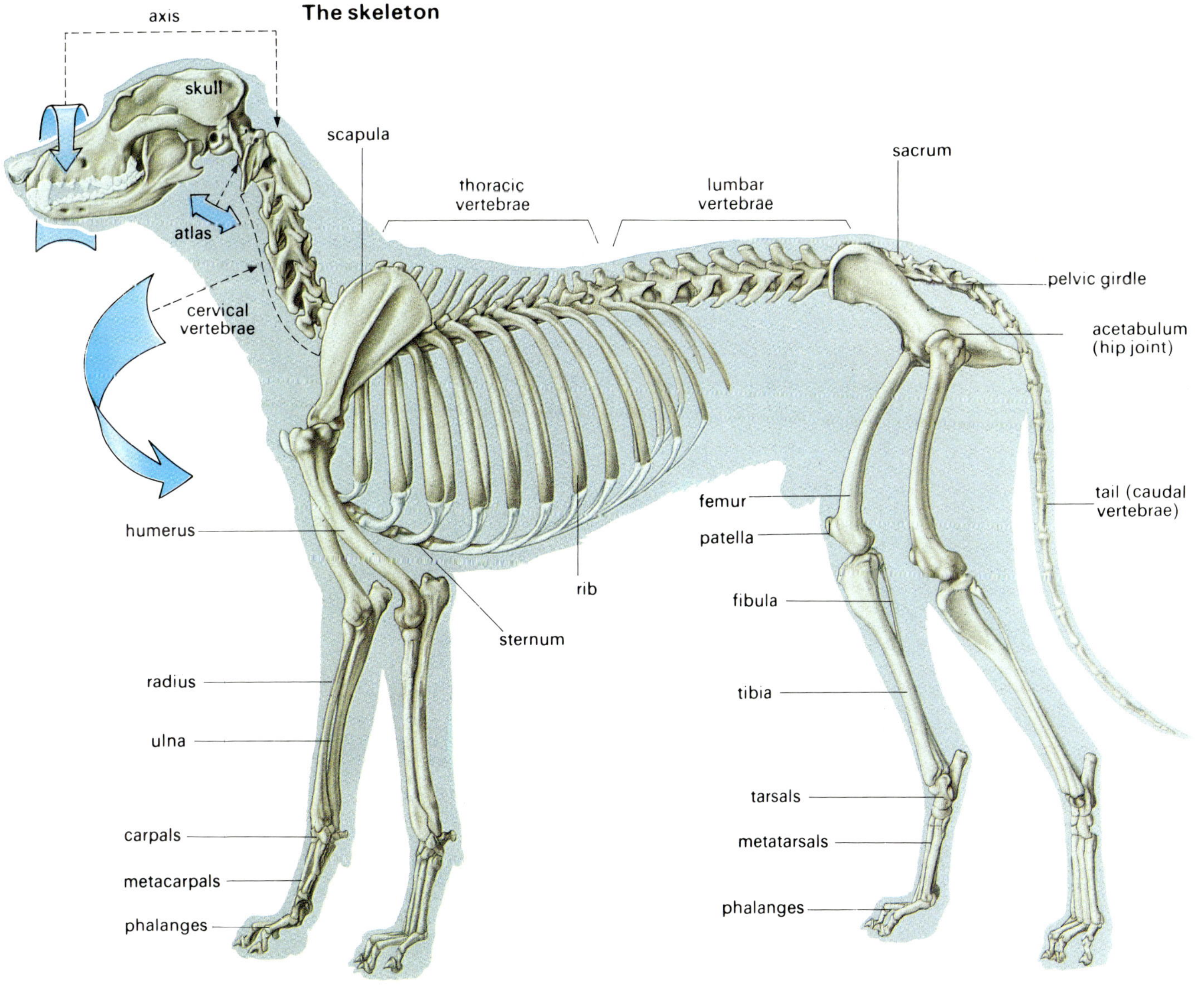

The action of the muscles in extending and contracting can be seen in the action of the racing Greyhound, a dog designed for great speed.

achieved by a short upper arm which brings the elbow of the dog up above the line of the brisket. Conversely, many of the racing breeds have a very long upper arm.

In the very short-legged dog, the leg bones have been shortened by selective breeding, rather than reducing the size of the animal, so that the result is quite a large dog set very low to the ground, for example Dachshunds and Basset Hounds. The long back comes from the length of rib cage and loin.

Muscles and Nerves

The dog's skeleton is covered by layers of muscles and these provide the complex system necessary for the precise control of movement. Muscles always act in pairs or groups in which some contract to bend a joint while others contract to straighten a joint. Muscles are richly supplied wth blood vessels and nerves. The nerves carry messages to and from the brain, which contains the majority of nerve cells within the body. Messages from the brain control functions: for instance, instructing a muscle to contract or a gland to discharge its contents. Messages to the brain inform it of what is happening all over the body. If, for example, the dog's skin is inflamed, a message indicating pain will be transmitted to the animal's brain, which may then 'instruct' a leg to scratch the area concerned. If a nerve is seriously damaged the message will not get through and the result will be loss of feeling and motor paralysis.

Respiration

Air is drawn in through the dog's nose and down the trachea, or wind-pipe. From the trachea the air

This Deerhound is cooling itself by panting, which causes evaporation and therefore loss of excess heat.

passes through the bronchi and bronchioles, which are extensions of the trachea and which gradually reduce in diameter, and finally into the air sacs in the lungs. These sacs have a rich supply of tiny blood vessels called capillaries which absorb the oxygen from the air and release waste carbon dioxide from the blood into the air sacs. This waste gas is then expelled when the dog breathes out.

The technique of panting, by which the dog regulates its body temperature, is connected with the respiratory system. Cold air is drawn in over the tongue and passed out again, taking with it moisture. It thus reduces the dog's body heat by evaporation.

Teeth and Digestion

The dog has two sets of teeth in its lifetime. There are 28 milk teeth which appear at 3–5 weeks of age; then these are pushed out by the adult teeth which begin appearing at about four months, though the time varies between breeds with large dogs teething rather earlier than the toy breeds. There are 42 permanent teeth: the lower jaw has six incisors, two canines, eight premolars and six molars and the upper jaw has two less molars. The last premolar of the upper jaw and the first molar of the lower jaw are modified into 'carnassial' teeth, a type found only in carnivores. The sharp edges of these teeth slide over one another like scissor blades. These teeth can best be seen in action when a dog gnaws meat from a bone, using the side of its mouth.

Food is roughly chopped by the teeth and softened with the help of saliva secreted by the three pairs of salivary glands that empty into the mouth. It then passes down the oesophagus, or food pipe, into the stomach. There, acids and enzymes work on the food, preparing it for passage through the pylorus, a ring-shaped muscle around the hind end of the stomach and into the small intestine where useful parts of the diet are absorbed into the bloodstream. After all the nutrients have been extracted the remainder of the food moves into the large intestine, where excess fluid is removed and faeces are formed before elimination through the rectum.

The main task of the liver, the largest single organ in the body, is to aid the digestion of food taken

The dog's adult teeth replace the milk teeth of the puppy when it is about four months old.

Dentition

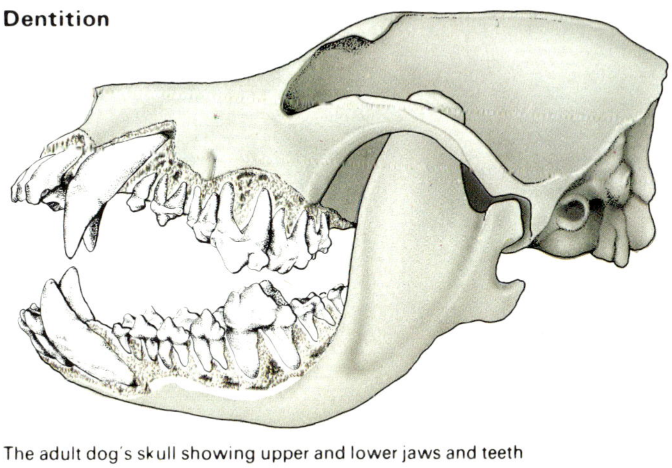

The adult dog's skull showing upper and lower jaws and teeth

The last premolar of the upper jaw and the first molar of the lower jaw are modified into carnassial teeth, a type found only in carnivores. The sharp edges of these teeth slide over each other like scissor blades. These teeth can best be seen in action when a dog gnaws meat from a bone using the side of its mouth.

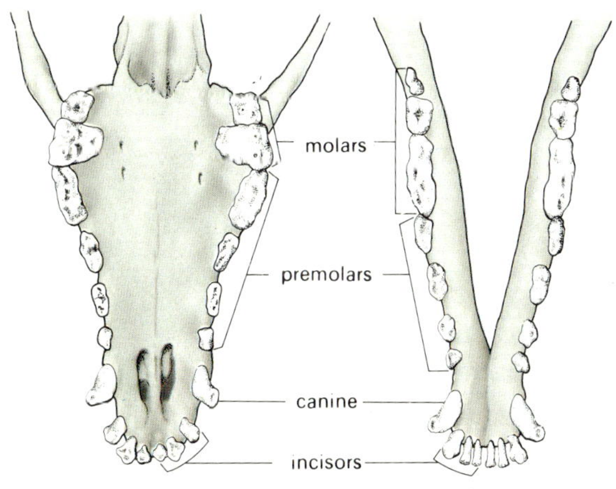

upper jaw seen from below

lower jaw seen from above

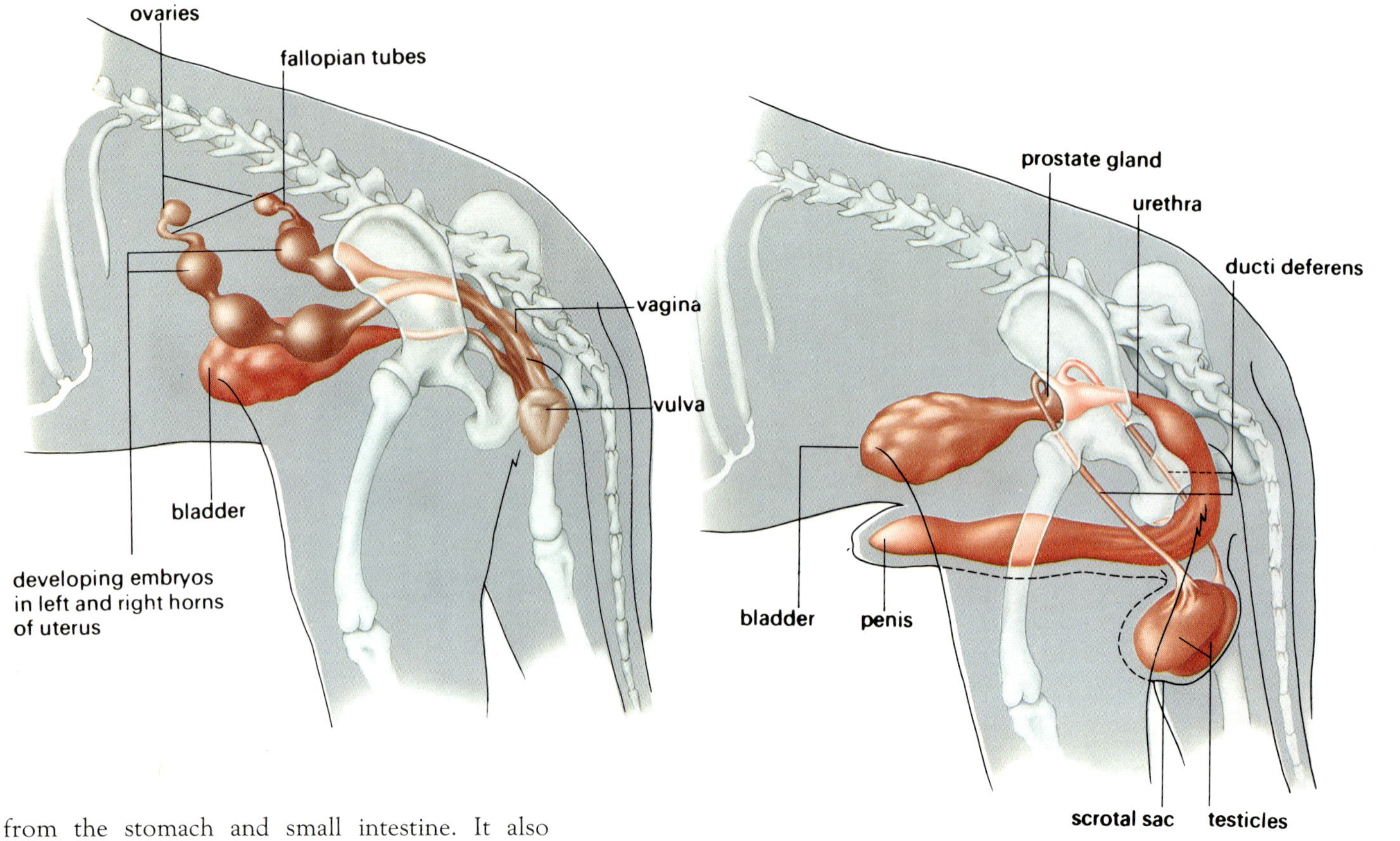

The illustrations above show the male and female reproductive organs which enable puppies to be conceived, carried and born after a dog and bitch have mated successfully. The horns of the uterus in the female show the bulges of the developing embryos.

from the stomach and small intestine. It also produces bile, which assists in the digestive process and is stored in the gall-bladder. The kidneys act as a sophisticated filter, ridding the blood of waste products and toxic substances, passed through the ureters to the bladder in the form of urine.

Reproduction

The male dog is easily distinguished from the female by its external genitals: the penis and the two testicles, where the sperm is stored, ready to be ejaculated at mating. Of the bitch's reproductive organs, only the slit of the vulva, the end of the genital canal, is visible. The other organs of the reproductive system are the vagina (into which the penis is inserted), the cervix (a valve-like construction between the vagina and the uterus) and the uterus itself, which has two 'arms' or horns, each leading to a fallopian tube and an ovary. Each ovary produces female hormones and eggs.

Most bitches come into season or heat twice a year. A season lasts about 21 days, beginning with the discharge of a fluid, opaque at first, then stained with blood. This happens when the walls of the uterus prepare to receive fertilized eggs. After 10 to 14 days the discharge loses its colour; this is when the eggs produced by the ovaries are liberated and flow into the fallopian tubes ready for fertilization and eventual implantation.

At mating, seminal fluid is released via the dog's penis and the sperms in the fluid travel towards the cervix, which opens to allow them to pass into the uterus and from there to the fallopian tubes where the eggs are stored. Mating will only succeed if male sperms fertilize the eggs; then the fertilized eggs travel to the uterus and attach themselves to its walls. The embryos that form will develop into puppies which will be expelled through the vagina after about 63 days.

Instincts and Behaviour

Some of the dog's most basic instincts result in behaviour that is useful in its relationship with man. Chief among these is the pack instinct. The dog is a highly sociable animal and in the wild, dogs would live as a group, remaining close together, doing the same sort of thing at the same time and observing a set hierarchy. Therefore the dog is content with its position in a human family, where the owner dominates. However, there is one aspect of pack behaviour that is often overlooked. It is easy for man to take over as pack leader for his dogs – but only if he is capable of leading. Nearly anyone can train a submissive dog but a dominant dog needs a dominant trainer. Within a household, a dog will often obey some members of the family and not others.

Fear is instinctive in the wild dog and is necessary to its survival but in a domestic dog, nervousness makes it less predictable, more difficult to train and control. Nerves and fear probably account for many of the dog bites suffered by children. Some dogs, for example, are easily frightened by a child rushing up with outstretched arms and misinterpret this friendly gesture as an attack. On the occasions where a dog bites its owner, it is often because the dog fears that it will be hurt and decides to attack first.

The dog's predatory instincts have been turned to good account in the hunting dogs. In pets it means that dogs will enjoy chasing balls and sticks but they also love to chase cats or rabbits. The herding instinct is only a slight deviation from the hunting instinct and in some dogs, like the Border Collie, it is strong enough to make it attempt to herd anything that moves, such as the ducks on the local pond.

Instinctive protective behaviour can be useful to the human owner and is seen at its most extreme in trained guard dogs. Even a peaceful family pet will often defend its territory strenuously. Tradesmen who wear a distinctive uniform are often on the receiving end of this behaviour: if they retreat when a dog barks or rushes towards the gate, the dog will regard this as a victory and will be encouraged to threaten even more fiercely when it next sees the uniform.

The dog's natural instincts can be put to use by man. Aggression can be useful in a guard dog and only a brave, or foolhardy, trespasser would ignore the menacing stance of the dog pictured below. The Golden Retriever (below left) makes a valuable companion on a pheasant shoot.

CHOOSING A DOG

There are so many types of dog that you will be spoiled for choice but taking a dog into your home should never be a spur of the moment decision. You will need to be sure that its size, temperament and energy level suits your family's way of life, so that you can enjoy many happy years together. You will have to consider whether you want a pet or a show dog, whether your home needs a watchdog or your children a protector. Once you find a litter of suitable puppies, you will want to be sure of picking a healthy specimen.

Taking a dog into your home brings many pleasures and benefits; it also brings responsibilities. It will be dependent on you for years to come and you will be in charge of its well-being for the span of its life. No dog should have to change an established home for a new one unless unforeseen circumstances make it unavoidable. You will be responsible for its behaviour at all times, as no pet should be allowed to roam unsupervised. You should only consider taking on a dog if everyone in the family wants one and you are sure that you can care for it over a long period. It should never be simply a child's plaything, to be over-indulged as a puppy then, when it is no longer a furry little bundle, neglected in favour of a new toy.

Your choice of dog will depend on your lifestyle and on what you expect to get from your pet. It is no use thinking about a Great Dane or St Bernard if you live in a flat or a mobile home; these dogs need plenty of room and once they spread themselves across the hearthrug, you may end up with nowhere to put your feet. You may want a dog primarily as a watchdog, or as a playmate for your children, or a cuddly armful to share your evenings in front of the television. There is little point in choosing a Pekingese if you want a companion on long country walks or a Golden Retriever if you want a guard dog to strike fear into the hearts of would-be burglars.

Before looking for a particular dog you must be sure that you can house and care for it properly. Companionship is high on the list of the dog's own needs and the happiest of dogs are those that spend most of their time with their owners, especially if they can participate in their activities in some way. If everyone in the household is at work for eight hours a day, or you spend most of your evenings and weekends out with friends, you would be wise to choose a more independent pet, a cat for instance.

A dog means extra expense, so calculate the amount you will need to spend on food, vaccinations, grooming equipment, collars and leads, baskets and bowls. There will also be veterinary fees over the years and perhaps boarding and training fees. On the whole, large dogs cost more and produce more waste, which may be a real problem for town dwellers; on the other hand, you may feel much safer walking a large dog at night through city streets.

Apart from size, you will need to decide whether to have a dog or a bitch, puppy or adult, pedigree or mongrel and how much time you are willing and able to spend on exercise and grooming.

The right dog can be a protector, a playmate and a faithful companion from puppyhood to old age.

Dog or Bitch

Dogs and bitches do differ in temperament and a bitch may be more suitable as a family pet as the relationship between the male dog and its owner can become very intense. Male dogs are often bolder and more independent by nature, and may also be more aggressive and eager to roam. The male dog kept as a pet should be kept away from sexual temptation; it is a great mistake to allow him to mate a bitch as he may become disorientated and begin to wander. He may start marking out a territory in the home and become aggressive with other male dogs. Dogs used for stud work are specially trained from a young age and lead a completely different style of life from a pet. Though it is possible to castrate a male dog by a simple operation, this is not usually advised as it changes the animal's personality. A castrated dog will be less active and is liable to become overweight unless its diet is carefully monitored. It will probably be less protective and may lose its instinct to guard the home.

Bitches are often more affectionate and home-loving, needing less discipline but they have the disadvantage of coming into season twice a year. Each time there is a three-week period when the bitch is 'on heat'; this begins with a blood-stained discharge from the vagina which changes to straw colour at about the tenth day. During this time, she is very attractive to males who will track her down by her scent and may haunt your house and annoy you and your neighbours. The bitch will be eager to find a mate so she will escape if given the slightest opportunity and this may happen even before you realize she is on heat. If you do not want your bitch to have puppies, you will need to take great care, securing doors, gates and windows so that it is impossible for her to get out.

The alternative is to have her spayed, a major operation involving removal of the ovaries and the uterus. The spayed bitch will not have any further heats and cannot produce an unwanted litter. She will keep her female character and continue to be a home-loving pet but you may have to watch her diet if she shows signs of putting on too much weight. Your veterinary surgeon will advise on the best age for spaying; some favour around five months, well before the first 'season', others prefer to wait until the first heat has passed, believing that this cuts the risk of side effects, such as obesity.

Two Dogs or One

Though the human family takes the place of the pack for the dog, it is beneficial to have more than one dog wherever possible. They will keep one another company if you are out a good deal and they will be less dependent on you for games. Dogs needing a good deal of exercise can run off their excess energy together without exhausting their owners.

Two bitches will usually get along well together with only an occasional squabble. If you plan to keep two male dogs in the household, choose one of the more placid-natured breeds as some males, particularly those of the terrier groups, are inclined

Two puppies brought into the family at the same time will play and exercise together and form a firm and lasting friendship.

A dog can provide valuable companionship for an elderly person but it should be carefully chosen for a quiet nature and the need for a minimum of exercise.

to fight. Keeping a dog and a bitch will mean problems when the bitch is in season, unless she has been spayed.

PUPPY OR ADULT DOG

It is normally more satisfactory to buy a puppy rather than a full-grown dog as a family pet. Of course, you will have to tackle housetraining and basic training as well as vaccinations but as the puppy grows up it will fit readily into your home life.

Taking an older dog can present difficulties; its habits and patterns of behaviour are already formed. However, some dogs really need new homes, through no fault of their own. Sometimes owners die or emigrate or someone in the house becomes allergic and a healthy, well-behaved dog may find itself in need of a new owner. Occasionally a breeder has a young dog, kept because of its showing potential, which has been well trained and cared for but has to find a new owner because it has not lived up to its early promise. For an elderly person, who might find a lively puppy too much of a handful, or a busy household with children of various ages and a great deal of coming and going, an adult dog may be a more suitable pet.

If you take a dog from a pound or shelter, beware of sentimentality. A pair of brown eyes gazing out from a pen may be appealing but, sadly, some dogs have been passed from hand to hand, perhaps because of serious behaviour problems, and may be difficult to rehabilitate. It is unwise to take such a dog unless you are sure that you can devote a great deal of time and patience to training and care. Some people have a knack of rescuing 'incorrigible' dogs but it is a special skill and not everyone can be successful. Remember that you will be doing an abandoned dog no favours if you take it in, only to find that you are unable to cope and have to return it several weeks later, adding another upheaval to its already unsatisfactory life.

Pedigree or Mongrel

When you buy a pedigree puppy, you can be sure of its eventual adult size, shape, coat length and texture, as well as having a fair idea of its temperament, suitability for your lifestyle and the amount of time you will have to spend on grooming and exercise. With a mongrel, all these things are a gamble. Mongrel puppies may be very cheap to buy but may cost just as much to keep as a pedigree dog of the same size. Many mongrels prove to be intelligent and make good family dogs. As they are cross-bred they rarely show any hereditary defects and it is sometimes possible to buy first-cross puppies, either from a mis-mating or from a mating that was intended to combine the characteristics of both breeds. Such puppies may combine the best traits of both parents, in which case the results can be delightful but you need to be aware that they could combine the less desirable characteristics.

Which Breed

Try to look at some adults of any breed that attracts you and talk to the owners about possible problems before buying a puppy. Generalizations about breed characteristics can be very misleading as there are always exceptions but knowledge of the breed's original use may be a guide to the usual temperament you can expect. For instance, the gundog's original role was to find game for the sportsman but to refrain from chasing it, so they had to be extremely obedient. Most gundogs, therefore, are amenable to discipline but they also have plenty of energy and stamina that needs an outlet. Few gundogs make good guard dogs but most of them are superb with children.

The greyhound family make gentle and dignified house dogs but the instinct to chase and kill can be triggered off by the sight of a small, moving object in the distance, and once in pursuit of anything they are virtually unstoppable. The scent hounds, like the Basset or Beagle, originally bred to live and work in packs, are surprisingly sociable, friendly and non-aggressive types. However, they can be obstinate and conveniently deaf when following their own interests. Sight hounds like the Afghan can be very aloof and retain a strong hunting instinct.

The Bulldog may look ferocious but it makes a lovable, intelligent and trainable family pet and is very good with children.

Long haired dogs, like this Rough Collie, need frequent and careful grooming, so prospective owners should take this into account.

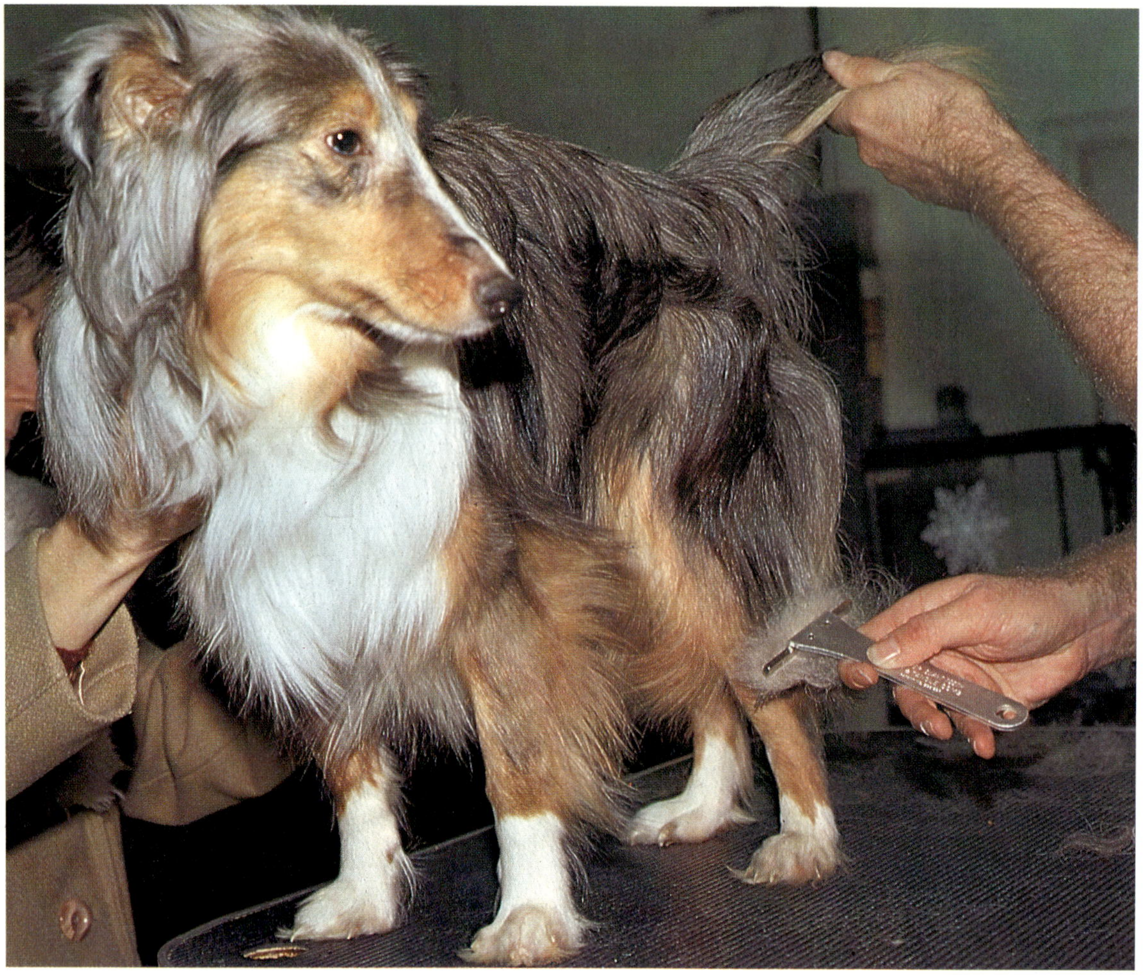

Dogs can be important to a child and Border Terriers (above right) make affectionate family pets.

Even in the White House the English Springer Spaniel Millie (below right) belonging to President Bush and his wife Barbara, claims pride of place after producing six puppies.

The terriers are very varied in appearance; many are named after the regions in which they were originally developed to hunt and kill vermin. They are all basically similar in temperament – very quick, agile and alert with fast reactions that cause them to snap first and ask questions later. They can also be noisy and excitable.

The giant breeds are expensive to keep and need a great deal of space. Though they do not need as much exercise as many of the smaller, lighter breeds, their bulk makes them unsuitable for many modern homes. Toy dogs, on the other hand, can fit into the most compact home and are often very good watch dogs. They make lively and amusing companions, so long as they are not spoilt by their owners.

The Spitz breeds are usually bold, hardy, adaptable dogs with strong wills. One or two of the Spitz breeds tend to be rather noisy.

Some breeds enjoy more robust health than others. This is because the basic dog shape is that of a medium-sized dingo type of animal and the further the breeds deviate from the norm, the more likely it becomes that the exaggeration of proportion represents a health risk to the dog. Giant breeds or those with large heads and very flattened muzzles tend to have a shorter life span than other breeds. Miniature sizes or very long backs, heavily wrinkled faces, protruding or very small eyes – all these can be weaknesses from a health point of view. Serious dog breeders are always well aware of the strengths and defects of their chosen breeds and take both health and temperament into account when planning their breeding programme.

Long or Shorthaired

Too many owners have fallen in love with a shaggy Old English Sheepdog or a silky Afghan on the TV screen, only to find that the splendid appearance is the result of long and painstaking grooming, which does not fit into their busy lives. Many of the longhaired breeds need daily grooming but with others, a short session once a week is sufficient. Among the breeds needing minimum grooming are: Basenji, Basset Hound, Beagle, Bloodhound, Boston Terrier, Boxer, Bulldog, Bull Terrier, Corgi, Smoothhaired Dachshund, Dalmatian, Doberman Pinscher, Labrador Retriever, Miniature Pinscher, Norfolk Terrier, Papillon, Pug, Staffordshire Bull Terrier, Weimaraner, Whippet.

Whether you choose a long or a shorthaired

animal, remember that almost all dogs will moult in spring and autumn. Long hairs look more obvious on your upholstery but short hairs can be even more difficult to remove sometimes. The only way round this is to choose a breed that does not moult: these include Poodles, Bedlington Terriers and Kerry Blue Terriers.

Family Dogs

Most dogs that grow up with a family will get on well with the children of the household, though it is important that children are taught never to tease an animal. However, a placid breed is a better choice than an excitable one that can get too carried away with rough and noisy games. Taking on a puppy when there is a toddler in the house is not really fair to either of them. The child will be too young to appreciate what will hurt or frighten the dog and the puppy may get carried away in a rough and tumble and hurt the child unintentionally.

Breeds with the reputation of being affectionate family dogs, good with children, include: Pointer, Golden Retriever, Labrador Retriever, English Setter, Cocker Spaniel, Basset Hound, Beagle, Finnish Spitz, Border Terrier, West Highland White Terrier, Cavalier King Charles Spaniel, Border Collie, Schipperke, Shih Tzu.

Some breeds, including Pekingese, Chihuahua and Scottish Terrier are less likely to make good pets for children, and Afghans react badly to teasing. Most Poodles prefer older children.

Guard Dogs

You may like the idea of a dog that will warn of intruders and scare away burglars but do not forget that a domestic watchdog is very different from a guard dog, which will attack if necessary.

The breeds famous for their guarding potential need a high standard of training and so do their handlers. Untrained or under-trained guard dogs can be rather like carrying round a loaded gun it can go off with disastrous results. A well-trained Doberman Pinscher can make an excellent guard and companion but needs careful handling and firm discipline. They are powerful, muscular dogs with a strong sense of loyalty. The German Shepherd has a reputation as a 'one-man' dog though it has sometimes earned a bad reputation because in the wrong hands it can become dangerous; it is essentially a working dog and becomes very frustrated if given nothing to do. The Rottweiler first became known to the world as a German police and army dog and the power and strength of the breed is evident. It is a fearless and highly intelligent dog but, again, it needs expert training and skilled handling.

Other, less potentially ferocious breeds may be more suitable for a suburban neighbourhood. Though not usually thought of as guard dogs,

Dalmatians have a long tradition in this field; at one time they were used as war dogs and in the nineteenth century their normal duty was as carriage guards. The Great Dane looks the part and its awe-inspiring appearance and deep-throated bark would scare away all but the very bold or foolhardy.

Many small breeds do a good job as watchdogs, such as the small, tailless Schipperke, once used on Flemish canal barges to repel boarders. They are active, bustling, vigilant little dogs and their shrill piercing bark gives obvious warning of strangers. The happy little Lhasa Apso makes a courageous little guard and is quick to give a warning.

AMOUNT OF EXERCISE

Unless you are a keen walker and you live in an area where your dog has the opportunity to run free as part of its regular exercise, do not choose the muscular, active dogs that need a great deal of exercise. The Labrador Retriever, Border Collie or Dalmatian, for instance, need at least an hour's exercise a day and fare best if half of it is at the gallop!

All dogs appreciate a change of scene and fresh air but among the breeds that can manage with just a daily game with their owners are: Chihuahua, Chinese Crested Dog, Griffon, King Charles Spaniel, Lhasa Apso, Maltese, Miniature Pinscher, Papillon, Pekingese, Pomeranian, Pug, Shih Tzu, Yorkshire Terrier.

The rough haired Lakeland Terrier needs careful brushing and trimming.

Some dogs need a great deal of exercise to keep in the peak of condition and a sedate walk around the block will not be sufficient.

BREED DRAWBACKS

Some popular dogs have particular problems from the point of view of ownership and it is important to consider whether or not these will cause you trouble:

Weimaraner: easily bored, can become destructive
Basset Hound: tends to roam
Irish Wolfhound: may be over-protective
Airedale Terrier: may be over-protective

Fox Terrier, Kerry Blue Terrier, Irish Terrier, Sealyham Terrier, Boxer, Doberman Pinscher: like to fight

Basenji, Scottish Terrier, Rough Collie, Doberman Pinscher, Shetland Sheepdog, Welsh Corgi, Lhasa Apso, Schnauzer: dislike or are suspicious of strangers

The Labrador Retriever is one of the most popular dogs in the USA: it is bright, alert, friendly and easily trained to obedience standards.

Where to Find your Dog

Puppies, both pedigree and mongrel, are often offered for sale through the classified advertisements in local newspapers, or 'For Sale' cards in shops or stores. Veterinary surgeons in your locality may know of available litters and specialist magazines covering the dog world will usually carry particulars of breeders who are likely to have puppies for sale. If you have decided on a particular breed, you can obtain the addresses of local breeders from the breed society. Your local library should be able to find the address for you; otherwise contact the head office of your Kennel Club. The secretaries of breed societies usually work on a voluntary basis, so send your request in writing, enclosing a large, stamped addressed envelope.

It is always best to obtain your puppy direct from the breeder, if possible. You will then be able to see the conditions in which the dogs are kept and get advice from the breeder on diet, exercise and so on. You will also get a much better idea of the likely temperament of your puppy if you see the mother and watch the puppies playing together. Most breeders are concerned about the future welfare of their puppies and will want to make sure that they are going to the right sort of home. Normally, they will be pleased to advise on any problems that arise after you have taken the puppy home.

Pet shops or dealers, who buy in many different breeds and offer them for sale, are not the best places to buy your pet. When puppies come from several different places and are kept in close proximity the chances of infection are much higher. The puppies may be stressed by long journeys and may be handled by several strangers in the course of a day. None of this contributes to their well-being. If you do buy from a pet shop or from a dealer, make sure that the establishment is scrupulously clean, that it is staffed by knowledgeable, caring people and that all the puppies look healthy. If you see any signs of diarrhoea, discharge from the eyes or noses on any puppies, not just the one you are thinking of buying – do not consider buying. If a puppy becomes ill after you have taken it home and made it part of the family, you will go through a great deal of worry and unhappiness, and no refund or replacement can make up for the sadness of losing a pet.

Choosing from the Litter

Choosing a puppy from the litter is not as simple as it sounds and you should take care not to allow sentimentality to cloud your judgment. Virtually all puppies are irresistibly attractive and it is easy to buy on impulse, so before you go shopping for your dog you should make contingency plans and stick to them rigidly. Do *not* take any family, friends, or children with you: it is easy to be swayed into buying a puppy for the wrong reasons.

The smallest and weakest pup may look the most appealing, but it might require a great deal of attention and veterinary help during rearing. It is quite a good idea to choose the puppy that first comes to you (if it is of the right sex). You should be able to handle it without the puppy showing fear or aggression. The puppies in the litter should look healthy and clean and not smell too 'doggy'. There should be no signs of discharge from the eyes or nostrils (some breeders may try to excuse these symptoms by saying they are due to sawdust or bedding). The ears should be spotless inside and the teeth should be sharp and white. The breath should smell sweet. Healthy puppies are plump, but without the extreme pot-bellied effect that could indicate a heavy worm burden. The skin should be very mobile and seemingly too large for the puppy's frame. The skin should be clean without any sign of soreness or redness anywhere, particularly under

the belly or between the thighs, and there should be no black specks indicating the presence of fleas. Look under the tail for any staining – a sign of diarrhoea – and examine the umbilicus area for any sign of a hernia. Make sure that you see your chosen puppy running around and that it moves correctly. If you arrive during the litter's sleep period, be prepared to wait until the pups have had a chance to wake up properly – after a long sleep it takes some minutes before their natural bounce returns.

Buying a pup with a pedigree does not necessarily mean that you acquire a show dog. If you do eventually hope to show or breed, you must make this quite clear to the breeder from the outset. High-quality puppies with show potential may cost several times more than a pedigree pup of only pet potential. It is in the breeder's interests to sell you the puppy most suitable for your needs. If you just want a healthy, happy pet, do not pay the extra money for one that excels in all physical features; it is equally pointless to buy a standard puppy if you hope to win top prizes.

If you do decide to go in for a show dog, you may have to wait longer for your puppy. The reason is that the breeder may decide that he needs to 'run on' several of the puppies for a few months before he will be able to be certain that they are of show standard. Naturally, this will increase the purchase price, but it is worth it if you want to win in competition.

It would be hard to choose from this litter of irresistible English Cocker Spaniel puppies but you should check each animal carefully before making your final selection.

BREEDS OF THE WORLD

Dogs come in all shapes and sizes and colours, from the glamorous little pets like the Shih Tzu to hardy working animals like the Samoyed. They may be as tiny as the Chihuahua or as large as the Great Dane; they may have the extraordinary corded coats of the Komondor and the Puli or no coats at all, like the Chinese Crested Dog. Each country has its own traditional dogs and its own domestic favourites. This section describes a wide range of breeds from all corners of the world, with details of their origins, their original uses, their appearance and temperament.

Breeds of the World

Each breed has a detailed standard, covering every facet of its appearance, but these vary from one country to another so the descriptions in this section are designed to give an overall picture of the look of each dog, as well as its origins and temperament. If you wish to show your dog, you will need to contact your kennel club for full details.

Ideal sizes and weights are prescribed for the breeds by each kennel club and these also vary, so in the following pages, dogs are graded according to average heights – small (up to 38 cm, 15 in), large (over 56 cm, 22 in) and medium – as a general guide for prospective owners. Specific figures are only given if the breed is especially large, small or heavy.

For showing purposes, breeds are divided into groups, as follows: American Kennel Club (AKC): Sporting; Hounds; Working; Terriers; Toys; Non-Sporting; Herding. Kennel Club in Britain (KC): Hound; Terrier; Gundog; Toy; Utility; Working. Australian National Kennel Club (ANKC): Terrier; Toy; Gundog; Hound; Working; Non-Sporting. The Fédération Cynologique Internationale, which governs dog shows in Europe and some Latin American countries, has its own groupings; these are mentioned in this section only when the dogs concerned are not registered in Britain or the USA.

Glossary

Brindle: fine even mixture of black hairs with hairs of a lighter colour.
Cropped ears: ears cut at the top so that they stand erect. In some countries, including Britain, this operation is illegal.
Docked tail: tail shortened by surgery.
Hound colour: white, tan or black.
Grizzle: bluish-grey.
Pied: large patches of two or more colours.
Points: the ears, face, legs and tail of a contrasting colour.
Undershot: where lower incisors lie in front of the upper ones when the jaw is closed.
Spitz: hardy dogs originating in the far north where they were bred for working under rigorous conditions.
Wheaten: pale yellow or fawn colour.

▲ **Affenpinscher**

▼ **Afghan Hound**

A

AFFENPINSCHER

Origins. Dogs which look very like the modern breed are to be seen in many paintings dating from the fourteenth century, but it was not until the turn of this century that the breed attracted enough attention in Germany, its country of origin, to be scheduled at shows.

Characteristics. Facially the Affenpinscher resembles a monkey and has some of that animal's mischievousness and humour. The face is flat with round dark eyes. The teeth fit closely together and many dogs are slightly undershot. The ears are small and pointed, in the USA they may be cropped. The body is short, compact and square with a docked tail.

Group. Toy.

Size. Small.

Coat. *Colour:* Usually black. *Texture:* Short and dense, hard and wiry.

The head should carry a good crop of whiskers.

AFGHAN HOUND

Origins. This is a coursing hound from two distinct types, now almost entirely intermingled, from the mountains and plains of Afghanistan, its country of origin. Afghans were first imported into Britain in 1894 and into North America in 1926.

Characteristics. A dignified hound, but capable of playing the wilful fool. The movement of the Afghan should be smooth and springy with considerable style. The dog gives the impression of strength and dignity. The head is long and lean, the body strong and deep.

Group. Hound.

Size. Large: average 71 cm (28 in).

Coat. *Colour:* Various. *Texture:* Long and fine.

AIREDALE TERRIER

Origins. The Airedale is by far the largest of the terriers and for that reason is sometimes referred to

◀ **Airedale Terrier**

as the King of Terriers. In fact, the breed's size makes it something of an oddity and probably, both in origin and function, it owes as much to the hound group as it does to the terrier. The breed was developed to combine some of the capabilities of both terrier and hound, terrier characteristics being inherited from the Old English Rough-Coated Black and Tan Terrier, and hound characteristics, including size, from the Otter Hound. The breed's size, courage and intelligence make it an excellent guard and police dog.

Characteristics. The Airedale's character is shown by the expression of the eyes and by the carriage of the ears and tail. The head is long and flat, the jaws deep, powerful, strong and muscular. The eyes are dark, small, with a look of keenness and intelligence, the neck muscular, set into long, well-laid-back shoulders. The back is short, strong and level, the chest is deep but not broad. The tail is carried gaily.

Group. Terrier.

Size. Large.

Coat. *Colour:* Black or dark grizzle with tan head and legs. *Texture:* Hard, dense and wiry.

Alaskan Malamute

Origins. First used as a sledge dog by the Mahlemut people in Alaska, its country of origin, the Malamute is one of the northern Spitz breeds and the largest of the sledge dogs. These dogs are very tough, capable of great feats of endurance and will survive in conditions to which other dogs would quickly succumb.

Characteristics. A powerful and substantially built dog with deep chest and strong, compact body. The head is strong and like a wolf's with a distinctive white cap or mask. The ears are pricked, the eyes alert and wolf-like. The tail, as in all Spitz breeds, is carried over the back and is thickly plumed. The dog is affectionate, friendly, loyal, an excellent guard and formidable fighter when roused.

Group. Working.

Size. Large.

Coat. *Colour:* Usually various shades of grey with white underbodies, legs, feet and part of the face. *Texture:* Thick and dense guard coat, not long nor soft. Coat is shorter when the winter coat is shed.

▲ American Cocker Spaniel

American Cocker Spaniel

Origins. A distinctive and glamorous gundog developed in America from Cocker Spaniels imported from England. It has now achieved a

▲ Alaskan Malamute

▲ American Foxhound

▲ **American Staffordshire Terrier**

considerable degree of popularity on both sides of the Atlantic, both as a companion and as a show dog.

Characteristics. The breed is the smallest member of the gundog group. It is sturdy and compact with a refined head. The eyes are round, full and look directly forward, the ears long and well feathered. The body is short and compact, the back strong, the chest deep and the quarters wide and well muscled. The tail is docked short. The dog makes a loyal and affectionate pet.

Group. Gundog. Sporting (AKC).

Size. Small.

Coat. *Colour:* Various. *Texture:* Silky, flat or slightly wavy and profuse.

American Foxhound

Origins. Fox-hunting in America is very different from fox-hunting in Britain and it follows that the hounds used will also be very different. The American breed, however, is to a large extent the product of a pack of hounds imported into the country in 1650 by Robert Brooke and of later imports, such as those in 1742 made by Thomas Walker. In the USA, Foxhounds are run in field trials, used for hunting a fox with a gun or raced along a predetermined trail.

Characteristics. The skull is fairly long and domed, the ears set moderately low, fine in texture, broad, long and pendulous. The eyes are large with a soft expression, the muzzle is fairly long. The chest is deep and narrower than in the English Foxhound, the hindquarters strong and well muscled. The tail is carried gaily with a slight brush. The American Foxhound is quite popular as a show dog in the USA but does not make a suitable pet.

Group. Hound (AKC).

Size. Large.

Coat. *Colour:* Any colour. *Texture:* Close, hard, medium length.

American Staffordshire Terrier

Origins. The American Staffordshire Terrier is one of a handful of breeds which has developed in the USA into a breed with very different characteristics from the British version. The Stafford was registered in the USA in 1935, but it was only in 1972 that the changes which had taken place were officially recognized by a change of name to American Staffordshire Terrier. However, since the nineteenth century, a distinctive breed has been developing under the various names of Pit Dog, Pit Bull Terrier, Yankee Terrier or American Bull Terrier. The first two names give a clue to the breed's use: they were and are used for organized fights against each other in the 'pit'. The breed, though a terror with other dogs, is gentle with people, impressive in appearance and, in the right hands, tractable.

Characteristics. The breed gives an impression of great strength, muscularity, agility and considerable courage. The shoulders are wide and slope into a fairly short back. The chest is broad, the front legs are straight, the hindquarters well-muscled.

Group. Terrier.

Size. Medium.

Coat. *Colour:* Various. *Texture:* Short, glossy, close and stiff to the touch.

Anatolian Karabash Dog (Anatolian Shepherd Dog)

Origins. The Karabash is a herding and guard dog much valued by Anatolian shepherds who developed the breed over very many centuries from the

▲ **Anatolian Karabash Dog**

mastiff dogs which existed in the Babylonian Empire over 3000 years ago. The breed retains a considerable likeness to these ancient mastiffs.

Characteristics. The head is large and broad, the ears V-shaped and pendant. The back is long, and the powerful loins slightly arched. The tail is long and carried low.

Group. Working.

Size. Large.

Coat. *Colour:* Cream, fawn or brindle with black points. *Texture:* Short and dense.

Australian Cattle Dog

Origins. From imported stock Australia has produced two distinctive and impressive working breeds, the Australian Kelpie and the Cattle Dog. The Cattle Dog has been known as the Australian, Blue or Queensland Heeler, Heeler being an old British word applied to cattle dogs. In its veins runs the blood of several working breeds which have combined to produce this superlative cattle dog.

Characteristics. The head is broad and wedge-shaped, the ears pricked, and the eyes dark. The chest is broad, the hindquarters are powerful. The tail is long, carried and furnished like a fox's.

Group. Working. Herding (AKC).

Size. Medium.

Coat. *Colour:* Usually blue, blue mottled with or without black markings, with some tan on legs and feet. It may also be red speckled. *Texture:* Short.

Australian Kelpie

Origins. The Australian Kelpie appears to have emerged, from crosses between imported herding dogs, as a distinct breed in the 1870s. Nowadays the Australian Kelpie works side by side with the ubiquitous Border Collie on the huge sheep farms of Australia where its keen sight, scenting powers and acute hearing make it highly valued.

Characteristics. The Australian Kelpie is a tough and muscular dog, rather fox-like in appearance with a strong, arched neck, moderately long back, and bushy tail carried low.

Group. Working.

Size. Medium.

Coat. *Colour:* Black, black and tan, red, red and tan, fawn, chocolate or smoke-blue. *Texture:* Short, straight, thick and harsh.

▼ **Australian Cattle Dog**

▲ **Australian Kelpie**

Australian Terrier

Origins. One of very few terrier breeds which originated outside the British Isles, though undoubtedly bred from old British breeds. The Australian's slightly old-fashioned appearance is probably closer to some of these old breeds than are their modern counterparts. Recognition of the breed came in 1892 and they were first registered by the AKC in 1960.

Characteristics. The Australian Terrier is a rather low-set dog, compact and active with a long head, a soft topknot and a low powerful jaw. The eyes are small, keen and dark in colour; the ears are small, set high on the skull, pricked or dropped towards the front and fringed with long hair. The neck is inclined to be long in proportion to the body, with a frill of hair. The forelegs are perfectly straight; the body is long in proportion to its height and the tail is docked. This little dog is spirited and affectionate.

Group. Terrier.

Size. Small.

Coat. *Colour:* Blue or silver-grey body with tan colour on legs and face, and the topknot blue or silver. Alternatively clear sandy or red. *Texture:* Straight hair 5–6 cm (2–2½ in) long, of hard texture.

▲ **Australian Terrier**

Australian Silky Terrier (Silky Terrier)

Origins. The Silky Terrier may be regarded as a second generation Australian since it is said to have originated from a cross between the Australian Terrier and imported Yorkshire Terriers. It is just as likely to be a smaller, silkier-coated variation of the Australian, retained and bred for its attractive appearance. In its homeland it has been recognized as a distinct breed since the early years of the century. It was first exhibited in 1907, had its original standard drawn up in 1909 and was recognized in the USA in 1959.

Characteristics. The Silky is a lightly built, moderately low-set toy dog of pronounced terrier character and spirited action. The head is strong, wedge-shaped and moderately long. The ears, V-shaped and pricked, are set high and carried erect; the eyes are small and dark, with a piercingly keen expression. The body is low set and fairly long, and the tail is set high and carried erect. This happy little dog makes an affectionate pet.

Group. Toy.

Size. Small.

Coat. *Colour:* Blue and tan, the topknot silver or fawn. *Texture:* Flat, fine in texture, glossy and silky.

▲ **Australian Silky Terrier**

B

BASENJI

Origins. This breed originated in Zaire. It is unique as a non-barking dog though it is an accomplished yodeller, and as a Spitz breed from Africa, still very close to its wild ancestors. Known as a guard, hunter and companion in Western Africa for centuries, it was not known in the Western world until two were brought to Britain in 1895; unfortunately both died shortly afterwards. It was not until 1937 in Britain and 1941 in America that imports became more successful and breeding stock became established.

Characteristics. The breed is remarkable for its great cleanliness, produced not only by its short coat but by its personal habits. Basenjis are lightly built, finely-boned aristocratic animals, tall, poised, alert and intelligent. The wrinkled head, with pricked ears, is carried proudly on a well-arched neck.

Group. Hound.

Size. Medium.

Coat. *Colour:* Pure bright red, or pure black, black and tan, all with white feet, chest and tail tip. *Texture:* Short, sleek and close, very fine.

BASSET GRIFFON VENDÉEN

Origins. A descendant of the white variety of the ancient St Hubert hound. As a hunting hound the breed is said to lack stamina.

Characteristics. The Basset Griffon Vendéen is an intelligent dog, sure of itself, distinguished in physique and gait. The head is well-rounded, not too broad. The eyes are large, dark and vivacious and the pendulous ears soft and narrow. The overall build is that of a Basset; its temperament is cheery, friendly and inquisitive.

Group. Hound.

Size. Small/Medium.

▲ Basset Hound

▲ Basset Griffon Vendéen

◀ Basenji

Coat. *Colour:* Fawn, white and orange, white and grey, tricolour. *Texture:* Long, bushy and heavy.

BASSET HOUND

Origins. This breed originated with the old French hounds, which were crossed with Bloodhounds to produce the dog which Shakespeare compared with Thessalian bulls. The breed was developed in Britain from a litter imported in 1872. Bassets are slow-moving, ponderous, deep-voiced pack hounds used for hunting the hare. Hounds bred for work and those bred for the show ring may nowadays be very different animals.

Characteristics. A somewhat hefty dog with very short legs, capable of moving smoothly. The head is big, domed and heavy, owing a lot in appearance to the Bloodhound; the ears are long and pendulous. It is a gentle, affectionate, good-mannered dog.

Group. Hound.

Size. Medium: a heavy body set on short legs.

Coat. *Colour:* Generally black and white and tan or lemon and white. *Texture:* Smooth, short and close without being too fine.

BEAGLE

Origins. This English breed is the smallest of the pack hounds and is used for hunting the hare with followers on foot. By the time Thomas Bewick was writing his *History of Quadrupeds* in 1790, he was able to speak of these small hounds which had already been known for over 300 years.

► **Beagle**

▲ **Bearded Collie**

Characteristics. Certainly one of the most popular hounds and one that makes a cheerful companion. The Beagle is compactly built giving the impression of great stamina and activity. It has a short body and very muscular hindquarters.

Group. Hound.

Size. Small/Medium.

Coat. *Colour:* Any recognized hound colours. *Texture:* Close, hard and of medium length.

BEARDED COLLIE

Origins. This Collie is one of the oldest of Scottish herding dogs though it is probably of central European origin. The breed was recognized in Britain in 1944 and admitted to the AKC stud book in 1976.

Characteristics. Should be alert, lively and self-confident, the body strong without giving a heavy appearance. The Beardie's face has a quizzical expression. The dog has a good temperament as well as plenty of energy and high spirits.

Group. Working. Herding (AKC).

Size. Medium.

Coat. *Colour:* Slate grey or reddish fawn, black, all shades of grey, brown and sandy, with or without white markings. *Texture:* The undercoat is soft, furry and close, the outercoat hair strong and flat. A long beard is a characteristic of the breed.

Bedlington Terrier

Origins. This is one of the sporting terriers which have their origins among the valleys of north-east England. As a breed it owes much to the old rough-coated breeds kept as vermin killers by the sporting farmers and shepherds of Northumbria. The first Bedlington club was formed in 1877, since which time the breed's original hardness and fighting qualities have been overlaid with a quiet gentle disposition.

Characteristics. A graceful, lithe, muscular dog. The head is pear or wedge-shaped and the expression in repose mild and gentle, though not shy or nervous. When roused, the eyes sparkle and the dog looks full of temper and courage. Bedlingtons are capable of galloping at great speed. Movement is distinctive: rather mincing, light and springy in the slower paces, and may have a slight roll when in full stride.

Group. Terrier.

Size. Small/Medium.

Coat. *Colour:* Blue, blue and tan, liver or sandy. *Texture:* Very distinctive, thick and soft, standing out well from the body.

Belgian Shepherd Dog (Groenendael)

Origins. The herding dogs of mainland Europe are all closely related and share several strong family characteristics. However it was not until Professor Reul at the end of the nineteenth century embarked on a study of these dogs, then generally simply referred to as Chien de Berger, that the various local breeds were accorded separate recognition. Among the three basic types recognized by Professor Reul was one with rather long black hair. The principal breeder of this type was Monsieur Rose of Groenendael.

Characteristics. The breed is intelligent, courageous, alert and faithful, protective of the person and property of its owners. It responds well to training and has been widely used as a working dog by the Belgian police force. The Belgian Shepherd Dog is a well balanced, square dog, elegant in appearance with a pronounced proud carriage of the head and neck. The head is strong, the ears stiffly erect, the chest deep. Forelegs are straight and strong, hindquarters are broad and heavily muscled. The tail is long and undocked.

Group. Working. Herding (AKC).

Size. Large.

Coat. *Colour:* Black. *Texture:* The outer coat is long, straight and abundant, of medium harshness. The undercoat is very dense.

► **Belgian Shepherd Dog (Malinois)**

▲ **Bedlington Terrier**

► **Belgian Shepherd Dog (Groenendael)**

BELGIAN SHEPHERD DOG (MALINOIS)

Origins. One of the three breeds of Belgian herding dogs now growing in popularity throughout the world.

Characteristics. As for the Belgian Shepherd Dog (Groenendael).

Group. Working. Herding (AKC).

Size. Large.

Coat. *Colour:* Rich fawn to mahogany with black overlay, black face and ears. *Texture:* Comparatively short, straight with dense undercoat.

BELGIAN SHEPHERD DOG (TERVUEREN)

Origins. One of the Belgian sheepdog breeds.

Characteristics. This breed differs from the Groenendael in little other than colour.

Group. Working. Herding (AKC).

Size. Large.

Coat. *Colour:* Fawn with black tips to the hairs. *Texture:* Long and fairly harsh.

▲ **Belgian Shepherd Dog (Tervueren)**

◀ **Bernese Mountain Dog**

▲ **Bichon Frise**

Bernese Mountain Dog

Origins. This is one of the European herding dogs developed from dogs left behind by Roman legions. Switzerland is home to four varieties of mountain dogs but it is the breed developed in the canton of Berne which, because of its rich black and tan silky coat, is the most distinctive.

Characteristics. The Bernese Mountain Dog is well balanced, active and alert. The eyes are dark, hazel-brown and full of fire, and the ears are V-shaped, set on high and in repose hang close to the head. The body is rather short, compact and strong.

Group. Working.

Size. Large.

Coat. *Colour:* Jet black with tan and white markings. *Texture:* Soft and silky with bright, natural sheen, long and wavy.

Bichon Frise

Origins. Italian traders returning from the Canary Islands in the fourteenth century brought with them some of the attractive little dogs which they had found in the islands. The dogs probably were descended from the Old Barbet or Water Spaniels from which the original name of Barbichon was derived. Later the name was contracted to 'Bichon' or changed to 'Teneriffe' and the breed began to gain favour in the Royal Courts of Europe.

Characteristics. The breed is sturdy and lively with a stable temper, has a stylish gait and an air of dignity and intelligence. The skull is broad and somewhat round with a dense topknot. The ears hang down and are covered with long flowing hair; the large, round eyes are dark and expressive. The neck is long and the head carriage is high. The tail is covered with long flowing hair, carried gaily and curved to lie on the back.

Group. Toy. Non-sporting (AKC).

Size. Small.

Coat. *Colour:* Solid white, or white with cream, apricot or grey on the ears and body. *Texture:* Profuse, silky and loosely curled.

Black and Tan Coonhound

Origins. This is the only recognized breed of half a dozen Coonhounds which include the very impressive Redbone Coonhound and the surprisingly named English Coonhound. These hounds hunt by night as the raccoon is a nocturnal animal. The Black and Tan Coonhound is only recognized in the USA and was admitted to registry by the AKC in 1945.

Characteristics. Slightly resembles a lightly built Bloodhound, essentially a working dog, powerful, agile and alert. Its expression is friendly, eager and aggressive and its movement is easy, powerful and rhythmic.

Group. Hound (AKC).

Size. Large.

Coat. *Colour:* Coal black, rich tan markings. *Texture:* Short and dense.

BLOODHOUND

Origins. In 1553, the physician and dog expert Dr Caius was able to describe the Bloodhound very much in terms which are applicable today, and was perhaps one of the first to mistakenly attribute the source of the breed's name to their ability to follow a blood trail. In fact the word is used in the same sense as in 'blood stock' as a reference to aristocratic breeding. Even so the breed's reputation as a formidable tracking dog had obviously already been established and has survived up to the present day. The breed is yet another of the English hound breeds originally derived from French stock.

▼ Bloodhound **► Black and Tan Coonhound**

◀ Border Collie

▼ Border Terrier

Characteristics. The Bloodhound is a powerful animal, larger than most hound breeds. It is characterized by a thin loose skin which hangs in deep folds, especially about the head, and gives the well-known lugubrious expression. The Bloodhound is a reserved dog, good-tempered and gentle with children.

Group. Hound.

Size. Large.

Coat. *Colour:* Black and tan, red and tan, red, called fawny in the USA. *Texture:* Smooth, short and glossy.

Border Collie

Origins. Arguably the world's finest sheepdog and now found wherever sheep are kept in appreciable numbers, often in environments very different from those in which the breed originated, in the hills of Scotland. By the mid-nineteenth century the breed was already well established but it was only recognized by the British Kennel Club in 1976.

Characteristics. A well-proportioned dog with a smooth outline which shows quality, grace and balance while giving the impression that the dog is capable of enduring long periods of active duty. The breed is very intelligent and loyal to its master but can become neurotic if not given enough to do.

Group. Working.

Size. Medium/Large.

Coat. *Colour:* Black and white, black, white and tan. *Texture:* Double, dense, moderately long, with a medium textured top-coat and short dense undercoat.

Border Terrier

Origins. The Border Terrier was developed to run with hounds, and to be able to eject a fox from its earth, and so was an essential part of the system of fox control in the hilly sheep country of Northumbria in northern Britain.

Characteristics. The Border Terrier is essentially a working terrier able to follow a horse and must combine activity with gameness. The head is a distinctive feature of the breed, resembling that of an otter, moderately broad in skull, with a short strong muzzle. The eyes are dark with a keen expression, the ears V-shaped and dropping for-

▲ Borzoi

ward close to the cheek. The body is deep, narrow and fairly long, the hindquarters strong. The tail is undocked, moderately short, and thick at the base. It is a good-natured, affectionate little dog.

Group. Terrier.

Size. Small.

Coat. *Colour:* Red, wheaten, grizzle and tan or blue and tan. *Texture:* Harsh and dense and not overlong with a close undercoat.

BORZOI

Origins. Until comparatively recently, when the Borzoi's name was changed from Russian Wolfhound, its origins were obvious. Before the Revolution every Russian nobleman maintained a pack of these hounds which were used in pairs for coursing wolves.

Characteristics. A very graceful, aristocratic and elegant dog possessing courage, muscular power and great speed. The head is long and lean, the neck is slightly arched and powerful, the back rising in a graceful curve, more marked in dogs than bitches.

► Boston Terrier

The legs are long, the feet hare-like and the tail long and well-feathered.

Group. Hound.

Size. Large: 73 cm (29 in) upwards.

Coat. *Colour:* Various. *Texture:* Long and silky, flat, wavy or rather curly.

Boston Terrier

Origins. An American breed, the Boston Terrier was the result of crosses between imported English Bulldogs and terriers bred in Boston in the 1870s. They were first exhibited as Round Heads or Bull Terriers, but as a distinct and stable type developed the name was changed to Boston Terrier. In 1891 the first breed club was formed in the USA and in 1893 the breed was recognized by the AKC.

Characteristics. The breed has a characteristi-

◀ **Bouvier des Flandres**

▲ **Boxer**

cally gentle disposition and is eminently suitable as a companion and as a house pet as it is both affectionate and protective. The Boston is smooth-coated, short-headed, compactly built and well balanced. The head is square, the muzzle short and the eyes large and round. The ears are carried erect and may be cropped. The shoulders are sloping, the back is short, the loins short and muscular. The tail is short, fine or tapering and may be straight or screw.

Group. Utility. Non-sporting (AKC).

Size. Small.

Coat. *Colour:* Brindle with white markings. *Texture:* Short, smooth, bright and fine.

Bouvier des Flandres

Origins. This dog is one of a small group of Flemish drovers' dogs used partly for herding cattle and partly as guards. Bouviers are now used as police and army dogs.

Characteristics. A compactly-bodied, powerfully-built dog of upstanding carriage and alert, intelligent expression.

Group. Working. Herding (AKC).

Size. Large.

Coat. *Colour:* Fawn to black. Pepper and salt, grey and brindle. *Texture:* Rough, tousled and unkempt in appearance. Topcoat harsh, rough and wiry, undercoat fine and soft.

Boxer

Origins. A German breed, this is one of several European breeds which have their origins in the mastiffs of Southern Europe, and which in the Middle Ages were developed as hunting dogs. Nowadays working Boxers are mainly used as police dogs and guard dogs.

Characteristics. A medium-sized sturdy dog of square build with a short back, strong limbs and short, tight-fitting coat. It is clean and hard in appearance and has a firm, springy stride. The head is square and short, with skin forming deep wrinkles. In the USA the ears may be cropped, but in Britain the ears lie flat and close to the cheeks. The mouth is normally undershot.

Group. Working. Non-Sporting (ANKC).

Size. Large.

Coat. *Colour:* Fawn, brindle and fawn in various shades from light yellow to dark deer red. *Texture:* Short, shiny, lying smooth and tight to the body.

Briard

Origins. The Briard comes from one of several ancient sheepdog breeds which probably came to Europe with the Mongol invaders and developed into different and localized breeds. This one is from France. A club was formed in France in 1900 to protect the breed and by 1930 an agreed standard had finally been adopted. The breed came to Britain after the First World War and to the USA in 1922.

Characteristics. A strong and substantially built dog, fitted for field work, lithe, muscular, well proportioned, alert and active. It is an intelligent dog, good-natured and tractable.

Group. Working. Herding (AKC).

Size. Large.

Coat. *Colour:* Various. *Texture:* Long, slightly wavy, stiff and strong.

Brittany

Origins. Oppian in AD 150 wrote of the uncivilized people of Britain and of their dogs. He, like other contemporary writers, used Bretagne to refer to Britain, whereas in a later period the word was used

▲ **Briard**

▲ **Brittany**

to refer to Brittany in France. The breed shares many characteristics with the Setter.

Characteristics. In appearance the breed has some resemblance to a very lightly built Springer: a compact, closely knit dog of medium size, with the agility and stamina to cover a lot of ground. The ears are dark, lying flat and close to the head. The body is square in outline, the shoulders sloping and muscular, the back short and straight, the chest deep. Hindquarters are broad, strong and muscular with powerful thighs. Some puppies are born without tails, others are docked short.

Group. Gundog. Sporting (AKC).

Size. Medium.

Coat. *Colour:* Dark orange and white or liver and white. *Texture:* Dense, flat or wavy.

BULLDOG

Origins. The Bulldog was originally used for bull-baiting, a sport which began in the early 13th century and continued until it was made illegal in 1835. The Bulldog as a distinct breed had evolved by the mid-17th century from crosses between mastiffs and more active terriers, and was then more like a Boxer or an old-type Staffordshire Bull Terrier. After bull-baiting became illegal the breed evolved to its present exaggerated form.

Characteristics. The general appearance is of a thickset dog, rather low in stature but broad, powerful and compact. The head is strikingly massive and large in proportion to the dog's size. The face is extremely short, flattened and wrinkled, which can lead to health problems. The tail is short and screwed, the forelegs are bowed. The formidable looks of the Bulldog hide a kindly and rather 'soft' nature.

Group. Utility. Non-sporting (AKC).

Size. Medium; weighing about 25 kg (55 lb).

Coat. *Colour:* Various, either whole or with a black mask round eyes and muzzle. *Texture:* Fine in texture, short, close and smooth.

BULLMASTIFF

Origins. Shakespeare commended the British mastiffs as being very valiant creatures of unmatchable courage. The Bullmastiff is a nineteenth-century development of these ancient mastiff breeds, the product of a cross with terriers to produce a smaller, more active dog.

Characteristics. The dog's temperament combines high spirits, reliability, activity, endurance and alertness. It is powerfully built, showing great strength but not cumbersome. The head is large and square, and the skin wrinkles when the dog becomes interested in something. The neck is well arched and very muscular, the chest broad and deep, the back short and straight. It is loyal and patient with children, but needs firm handling.

Group. Working. Non-sporting (ANKC).

Size. Large and heavy: average 54.3 kg (120 lb).

Coat. *Colour:* Any shade of brindle, fawn or red with a dark muzzle. *Texture:* Short and hard, lying flat to the body.

BULL TERRIER

Origins. The USA differentiates between white and coloured Bull Terriers, but in Britain no such

▲ Bulldog

► Bullmastiff

difference exists and they remain, white or coloured, the same breed. The breed is not of ancient origin, but was produced by crosses of the now extinct English White Terrier with the type of Bulldog which existed in the early nineteenth century to produce a 'gladiator' for dog fighting.

Characteristics. The Bull Terrier is strongly built, muscular, symmetrical and active, with a keen, determined and intelligent expression. It should be full of fire and courage, but amenable to discipline. The head is a characteristic of the breed being long, egg-shaped and free from hollows or indentations. The eyes are narrow, triangular and black or dark brown; the ears are small, thin and erect. The neck is long, arched and very muscular, fitting into strong and muscular shoulders. The body is well rounded, the back short and strong, the hindquarters powerfully muscled. It is good with children but may be less friendly towards other pets.

Group. Terrier.

Size. Medium, but varies considerably. There is a miniature version, with a height of 35.5 cm (14 in) or less.

Coat. *Colour:* White or coloured. *Texture:* Short, flat, even and harsh to the touch with a fine gloss. The skin should fit the dog tightly.

▲ **Bull Terrier**

C

CAIRN TERRIER

Origins. A descendant of the working terriers used in Scotland and the Isle of Skye and, though no longer in demand as a working terrier, the breed retains much of the appearance and some of the characteristics of the older breeds. Authorities in the past often saw the Cairn as a short-haired Skye Terrier, but after a protest by Skye Terrier breeders the name was changed to Cairn Terrier at the beginning of this century.

Characteristics. This terrier is an active, game and shaggy little dog, strong though compactly built, very free in movement. The hindquarters are very strong, the tail short with plenty of hair. It is a cheeky, courageous little dog; good company as a pet.

Group. Terrier.

Size. Small.

Coat. *Colour:* Red, sandy, grey, brindled or nearly black with dark points. *Texture:* Profuse, hard but not coarse outer coat, and a short, soft, close undercoat.

CAVALIER KING CHARLES SPANIEL

Origins. The Cavalier King Charles Spaniel is a recreation of the toy dog favoured by King Charles II and which bears his name, but which over the years had departed from its original form. Impetus to recreate this attractive toy Spaniel in its original form was given by a Mr Eldridge, an American, who, in 1920, offered prizes of £25 for Blenheim Spaniels possessing 'long faces, flat skulls, no inclination to be domes, no stop and a beauty spot in the centre of the forehead'. By 1928, a Club had formed and the breed was established.

Characteristics. The breed is active and graceful. The head is flat, the muzzle tapered. The eyes are large, dark and set well apart, the ears are long and set high. It is a good-natured, docile and very clean little dog.

Group. Toy.

Size. Small.

Coat. *Colour:* Black and tan, rich red, chestnut and white, tri-colour. *Texture:* Long, silky and free from curl, with ample featherings.

CHESAPEAKE BAY RETRIEVER

Origins. In the early part of the nineteenth century the nondescript indigenous Retrievers used in Maryland, USA, received an unexpected influx of new blood as a result of two dogs having been rescued from a wrecked English brig. The new blood so improved the native stock that other crosses were used and by the end of the century a distinct breed of Retriever had emerged. This dog was expected to work in the icy waters of Chesapeake Bay retrieving fallen duck.

Characteristics. The head and body, to some degree, resemble the Labrador Retriever. The skull is broad and round, the muzzle short, the ears small and pendulous and the eyes fairly large, clear and yellow or amber in colour. The chest is barrel round and deep, the body of medium length. Hindquarters are especially powerful to supply driving power for swimming. The Chesapeake Bay is a rugged individualist, full of courage, and needs firm handling.

Group. Sporting (AKC).

Size. Large.

Coat. *Colour:* Any colour varying from dark brown to a faded tan. *Texture.* The coat is thick and short with a dense fine woolly undercoat. The outer coat is harsh and oily and resists water.

▲ **Cairn Terrier**

► **Cavalier King Charles Spaniel**

▲ **Chesapeake Bay Retriever**

CHIEN FRANÇAIS

Origins. The French hound derives from the Billy and the Poitevin and in 1957 was divided into three varieties, by size and colour. The Blanc et Noir is the largest of the three and, apart from having a more domed skull, longer and narrower head, and thinner stern, is similar in appearance to the Foxhound. The Blanc et Orange and the Tricolore are similar in appearance, smaller than the Blanc et Noir; the Tricolore may have light coloured eyes.

Group. Hounds for big game. (FCI).

Size. Large.

Coat. *Colour:* White and black, tricolour or white and orange depending on the variety. *Texture:* Short, dense and rugged.

▲ **Chien Francais**

▶ **Long Coat Chihuahua**

▶ **Smooth Coat Chihuahua**

▼ **Chinese Crested Dog**

CHIHUAHUA

Origins. The immediate origin of the world's smallest breed of dog was the Mexican state after which the breed is now named, but whether it arrived there via trade routes to China or Japan or whether the breed was developed by the native Aztecs or Toltecs it is not possible to say. The first Chihuahua to be registered by the AKC was Midget registered in 1904.

Characteristics. The most obvious characteristic is its extremely small size. The head too is very distinctive, being round with an 'apple dome' skull, a characteristic also sometimes found in toy Japanese breeds. The eyes are full and round, though not protruding, and the ears large, set at an angle of about 45°. The dog is alert and swift with a saucy expression, it is small with a dainty compact appearance which is coupled with a brisk and forceful personality. There are two types, the Long Coat and the Smooth Coat; the Smooth Coat is the more popular in the USA.

Group. Toy.

Size. Small; weight of 0.9–2.7 kg (2–6 lb).

Coat. *Colour:* Various. *Texture:* In the Long Coat, the coat is soft, and either flat or slightly waved. Feathering on feet, legs, pants and ruff. The tail should be long and full as a plume. The Smooth Coat has a soft, close and glossy coat.

CHINESE CRESTED DOG

Origins. This is a breed from China. Hairless dogs exist in many parts of the world, such as Africa, Turkey, China and Mexico. Whether each shares a common origin or whether each is a mutant produced from a local breed it is not possible to say.

Characteristics. A small, active and graceful dog, medium to fine boned with a smooth hairless body, with hair on feet, head and tail only. The skull is slightly rounded with a fairly long muzzle, the eyes round and set wide apart, the ears large and upstanding. The tail is carried over the back or looped. The dog is very affectionate and becomes devoted to its owner.

Group. Toy.

Size. Small.

Coat. *Colour:* The skin can be any colour, plain or spotted. *Texture:* The crest on the head is flat, either high or long-flowing. The tail should carry a plume on the last two-thirds of its length.

CHOW CHOW

Origins. It is popularly and erroneously accepted that the Chow Chow was produced as a source of food in China. In fact the Chow as we know it today is very much a product of Western breeding from Chows coming from China in the late eighteenth century, which showed the unique blue-black

▲ **Chow Chow**

tongue and fearsome scowling expression.

Characteristics. A powerfully built dog, leonine in appearance with a proud dignified bearing, loyal yet aloof and with a stilted gait. The head is large and broad, the ears small, thick and rounded, the eyes small and dark. The body is short, compact and strong. The tail is carried well over the back. It has a reputation as a one-person dog.

Group. Utility. Non-sporting (AKC).

Size. Large.

Coat. *Colour:* Solid coloured black, red, blue, fawn, cream and white. *Texture:* Abundant, dense, straight and stand-off. Outer coat rather coarse with a soft woolly undercoat.

Clumber Spaniel

Origins. The Clumber is a very different animal from other spaniels – heavier, longer and lower to the ground – indicating that we should look for different origins. The body shape suggests some Basset Hound blood, while the heavy head is suggestive of the old Alpine Spaniel. By 1859 this breed was being shown and had achieved considerable popularity as a gundog particularly well adapted to a country with abundant game.

Characteristics. The Clumber is nothing if not distinctive: it is a dog with a thoughtful expression, very massively built but active, and moves with a rolling gait which is characteristic of the breed. The head is large, square, and massive with heavy brows. The eyes are dark amber, the ears large and vine-leaf shaped, well covered with straight hair. The body is long and heavy, close to the ground; the back is straight, broad and long. The hindquarters are very powerful and well developed. The Clumber is an intelligent dog with a calm, reliable temperament.

Group. Gundog. Sporting (AKC).

Size. Large; heavy body on short legs.

Coat. *Colour:* Plain white with lemon markings. *Texture:* Abundant, close, silky and straight. The legs are well feathered.

COCKER SPANIEL (ENGLISH)

Origins. The Cocker Spaniel, like other spaniels, is a descendant of the dogs which, in Spain, were used to drive birds into nets. It is referred to in the prologue to Chaucer's *Wife of Bath's Tale* showing that 'Spaynels', even as early as the fourteenth century, had attained some popularity in England. However, at this time the distinctions between spaniels of different types had not been drawn. By the eighteenth century, the breed was called the cocking-spaniel and used to flush out woodcock. Thus it came by its present name.

Characteristics. The general appearance of the Cocker is of a merry sporting dog, well balanced and compact. The head is well developed and cleanly chiselled, neither too fine nor too coarse. The eyes are full with an expression of intelligence and gentleness; the ears are long and set low, well clothed with long silky straight hair. The body is immensely strong and compact for the size and weight of the dog. The tail is usually docked. The Cocker makes a happy, friendly and gentle companion.

Group. Gundog. Sporting (AKC).

Size. Small/Medium.

Coat. *Colour:* Various. *Texture:* Flat, silky in texture.

▲ **Clumber Spaniel**

COLLIE, ROUGH

Origins. This breed originated, like the other three Collie breeds, Smooth, Border and Bearded, in the dark-coloured herding dogs of Scotland, from which the name is derived. 'Col' is Anglo-Saxon for black. For centuries they carried out their arduous work herding sheep on the northern hills, with only local recognition. In 1860, however, Queen Victoria visited Balmoral for the first time, saw the breed, fell in love with it and so assured its future popularity.

Characteristics. This is a strong and active dog, free from coarseness. The head is tapering, the expression alert, intelligent and inquisitive. It makes an excellent, loyal pet, responding well to training.

Group. Working. Herding (AKC).

Size. Large.

Coat. *Colour:* Sable and white, tricolour, and blue merle, each with white markings. *Texture:* Very dense, the outer coat straight and harsh, the undercoat soft, furry and very close. Mane and frill very abundant, legs well feathered.

▼ **Cocker Spaniel (English)**

COLLIE, SMOOTH

Characteristics. The Smooth Collie is similar in temperament and characteristics to the Rough Collie. As it lacks the glamour of a long coat, this dog looks rather angular.

Coat. *Texture:* Hard, dense and smooth.

◀ Smooth Collie

▼ Rough Collie

► Long-haired Dachshund

▼ Curly-coated Retriever

Curly-coated Retriever

Origins. The breed was produced as a gundog superbly adapted to working in water, on a basis of the Old English Water Spaniel, with the judicious introduction of Irish and English Water Spaniels, Newfoundland and Poodle.

Characteristics. A smart upstanding dog showing activity, endurance and intelligence. The head is long and well proportioned, with black or brown eyes, and rather small, low-set ears lying close to the head. The neck is moderately long and the body strong and muscular. The tail is shortish, carried straight and covered with curls.

Group. Gundog. Sporting (AKC).

Size. Large.

Coat. *Colour:* Black or liver. *Texture:* The main characteristic of the breed is a mass of small, crisp curls all over the body.

▲ Smooth-haired Dachshund

D

Dachshund

Origins. Dachshunds represent a small and distinctive subgroup within the hound group, differentiated from other hounds by their small size, the work for which they were intended and to some extent by the quarry they used to hunt. 'Dachshund' simply means 'badger dog', but must not be taken to mean that these diminutive hounds, whose history dates back to the fifteenth century, were used exclusively for that quarry. Larger hounds, weighing 13.6 kg (30 lb) or 15.8 kg (35 lb) were used for badger, while smaller ones were kept for stoat and weasel.

Characteristics. First and foremost a sporting dog, but is equally adaptable as a house pet. The general appearance is long and low, but with a compact and well-muscled body, with a bold defiant head carriage. The head is long, the eyes are of medium size, oval and dark in colour. The body is long and muscular, the chest very oval. The tail is high set, strong and tapering. There are two sizes, Standard and Miniature, and three coat varieties: Smooth-haired, Long-haired and Wire-haired.

Group. Hound.

Size. Small. The Standard Dachshund has a heavy body on very short legs; the Miniature version weighs up to 4.9 kg (11 lb).

Coat. *Colour:* Various. *Texture:* Short, dense and smooth for the Smooth-haired, soft and straight or slightly waved for the Long-haired and short, thick, hard and rough for the Wire-haired.

▲ Wire-haired Dachshund

▲ **Dalmatian**

DALMATIAN

Origins. The breed is said to have originated in Dalmatia on the Adriatic coast, though spotted dogs are found in many parts of the world. However, the breed has been established for so long in Britain, where it was used as a carriage dog, that it can perhaps be recognized as a British breed. In America its affinity with horses and carriages earned it a place with the horsedrawn fire engines and it became the Firehouse Dog.

Characteristics. Dalmatians should be strong, muscular and active. They are graceful in outline, elegant and capable of great endurance. The most obvious characteristic is the spotted coat. Dalmatians have great freedom of movement, a smooth powerful rhythmic action with a long stride. They are good-tempered dogs, intelligent and easily trained.

Group. Utility. Non-sporting (AKC).

Size. Large.

Coat. *Colour:* The ground colour is pure white, evenly covered with well-defined black or liver spots. *Texture:* Short, hard and dense, sleek and glossy in appearance.

▼ **Dandie Dinmont Terrier**

Dandie Dinmont Terrier

Origins. A breed which owes its present name to the character in Walter Scott's *Guy Mannering*, but which was certainly in existence in the Cheviot Hills long before the book was written. The Dandie is a close relation of both the Border and Bedlington Terriers.

Characteristics. The Dandie is a very distinctive breed with a strong and rather large head. The dark eyes, set wide apart, are full and round, the ears pendulous, falling close to the cheek. The forelegs are short with immense muscular development and bone, set wide apart. The body is long, strong and flexible, the hindquarters are set wide apart. The tail is rather short, carried a little above the level of the body. The loyal little Dandie makes a useful watchdog.

Group. Terrier.

Size. Small.

Coat. *Colour:* Pepper or mustard. *Texture:* A mixture of hardish and soft hair, giving a coat that feels crisp to the touch.

Deerhound

Origins. The Deerhound of today is just as it has always been when, having been produced out of the hounds used by Pictish hunters, the breed was used to bring deer to bay and were the prized possessions and constant companions of their masters.

Characteristics. The general conformation is similar to that of a Greyhound, but of larger size. The head is long, the eyes are dark and moderately full, the ears set on high and folded back. The neck is long and strong. The shoulders are well sloped and the forelegs are straight. The tail is long, thick at the root and reaches almost to the ground. The Deerhound makes a delightful pet; gentle, calm and affectionate.

Group. Hound.

Size. Large: 76 cm (30 in) or more.

Coat. *Colour:* Usually grey. *Texture:* Harsh and wiry on body, neck and shoulders and about 7.6–10 cm (3–4 in) long. It should be thick, close-lying, ragged and harsh or crisp to the touch.

Doberman(n) Pinscher

Origins. This breed is of such recent origin that it can be traced to the person who first produced it, Louis Dobermann, a German tax collector. Between 1865–70 he set about producing a first-class guard dog based on the concept of a giant terrier, combining agility with strength, speed and great intelligence. So well did he succeed that the

◀ **Deerhound**

Dobermann Pinscher demands the highest standards of its handlers.

Characteristics. A medium-sized dog with a well-set body, muscular and elegant, proud carriage and bold alert temperament. The breed is compact and tough with light, elastic movement. The head is long and clean, the eyes deep and almond-shaped. Ears may be erect or dropped, cropped in countries where the operation is permitted. The body is square, the back short and firm.

Group. Working. Non-sporting (ANKC).

Size. Large.

Coat. *Colour:* Black, red, brown or blue with rust-red markings. *Texture:* Smooth-haired, short, hard, thick and close lying.

▲ **Doberman Pinscher**

▲ **Dogue de Bordeaux**

DOGUE DE BORDEAUX

Origins. The Dogue de Bordeaux may lay claim to being the national dog of France.

Characteristics. In appearance the breed is very similar to the English Mastiff and is descended from the Roman mastiffs originally imported from the East. In France, the breed was developed as a fighting dog and was used as such until the beginning of the twentieth century. Nowadays, the breed makes an excellent watchdog as it is vigilant, faithful and has great strength.

Group. Working (FCI).

Size. Large.

Coat. *Colour:* Apricot, silver, fawn or dark fawn-brindle with black points. *Texture:* Smooth and short.

E

ELKHOUND (NORWEGIAN ELKHOUND)

Origins. The Elkhound is another of the Scandinavian Spitz breeds. It has arrived at its present distinctive appearance as a result of selection based on its ability to hunt the elk, bringing the animal to bay while summoning the hunters with its shrill barking.

Characteristics. The Elkhound is friendly and intelligent, with great energy and independence of character. However, it requires firm handling from its owner. In general appearance it is compactly built with a short body, thick, abundant coat, pricked ears and a tail curled tightly over the back. The head is broad, the eyes dark with a fearless and friendly expression.

Group. Hound.

Size. Large.

Coat. *Colour:* Grey of various shades with black tips on the long outer coat. *Texture:* Thick and abundant, coarse and weather resistant with a longish, coarse top coat and a light coloured, soft woolly undercoat.

ENGLISH SETTER

Origins. Although it is likely that the setters originally sprang from imported spaniel stock, there is evidence that by the late sixteenth century

▲ Elkhound

the two groups of bird dogs were distinctly differentiated. The Setter, with its long head, curly coat and well-developed ability to find and point game, showed evidence of crosses with Pointers, the large Water Spaniel and the Springer Spaniel. The modern breed was developed by intensely selective breeding in the mid-nineteenth century.

Characteristics. The English Setter is an intensely friendly and quiet-natured dog with a keen game sense. It is clean in outline, and elegant both in appearance and movement. The head is long and rather lean, the eyes are bright, mild and intelligent and of a dark hazel colour. The ears are set low and hanging close to the cheek; the tips are velvety, the upper parts clothed in fine silky hair. The tail is set almost in line with the back, the feather long, soft and silky.

Group. Gundog. Sporting (AKC).

Size. Large.

Coat. *Colour:* Black and white, lemon and white, liver and white or tricolour. *Texture:* Slightly wavy, long and silky, the breeches and forelegs well feathered.

English Springer Spaniel

Origins. In the early seventeenth century there was a tendency to refer to the larger spaniels, which were

▼ English Setter

▲ English Springer Spaniel

▲ **English Toy Terrier**

▲ **Estrela Mountain Dog**

used to startle game so that it sprang into the air, as Starter or Springer Spaniels. With the advent of quick-firing guns which increased their popularity, these early Springers were divided into the lighter Welsh Springers and the heavier English.

Characteristics. The general appearance of the modern Springer is that of a compact, strong, upstanding, merry and active dog, built for endurance and activity. The skull is fairly broad, the eyes dark hazel and the ears are lobular in shape, set close to the head. The neck is long and muscular, the body strong and the chest deep with well-sprung ribs. The tail is set low, well feathered and has a lively action.

Group. Gundog. Sporting (AKC).

Size. Large.

Coat. *Colour:* Usually liver and white or black and white. *Texture:* Close, straight and weather-resistant, without being coarse.

English Toy Terrier

Origins. The English Toy Terriers, formally called Toy Black and Tan Terriers or Toy Manchester Terriers, made their reputation in the rat pit in the nineteenth century. Often weighing no more than 2.7 kg (6 lb), they were matched either to kill a certain number of rats against the clock, or in competition with another dog.

Characteristics. A well-balanced, elegant and compact toy dog with a terrier temperament and characteristics. The head is long and narrow, the ears 'candle flame' shaped, thin and erect, and the eyes very dark, small and almond-shaped. The neck is long and graceful and slightly arched, the chest narrow and deep. Front movement is akin to the 'extended trot'; a hackney action is undesirable. This dog makes an affectionate pet and attaches itself to one person.

▲ Finnish Spitz

◀ Field Spaniel

Group. Toy.
Size. Small.
Coat. *Colour:* Black and tan. *Texture:* Thick, close, smooth and glossy.

Estrela Mountain Dog

Origins. The Estrela Mountain Dog from Portugal, like so many of the European dual-purpose herding and guard breeds, is a large and very powerful dog with great courage and stamina. It is independent by nature and needs careful training.

Characteristics. The head is massive, broad and moderately long. The skull is slightly domed with a strong muzzle. The eyes are almond-shaped, dark and wide-set. The ears are small and carried folded back. The body is rather longer than it is tall with a broad, muscular back and deep chest. The tail is long and carried low.

Group. Working.
Size. Large.
Coat. *Colour:* Grey, tawny and red, red or light tan. *Texture:* Short, thick and rather coarse, smooth and very slightly wavy.

F

Field Spaniel

Origins. During its early career in the show ring the Field Spaniel was classified with Cocker Spaniels and the breeds were only separated in 1892.

Characteristics. A well-balanced dog, noble, upstanding and sporting, built for activity and endurance and combining beauty with utility and unusual docility. The muzzle is long and lean, the eyes dark hazel in colour with a grave expression. The neck is long, strong and muscular set into long and sloping shoulders which give great activity and speed. The body is of moderate length, the chest deep, the back and loins strong and muscular. The tail is carried level with the back or below it.

Group. Gundog. Sporting (AKC).
Size. Medium.
Coat. *Colour:* Black, liver, golden liver, mahogany red, roan, or any of these colours with tan over eyes, on feet. *Texture:* Flat or slightly waved, silky and appears glossy and refined.

Finnish Spitz

Origins. In its own country this breed is very popular indeed. Originally these dogs were used to track down and mark with their piercing bark the position of a variety of game in the Finnish woodland; now they are principally regarded as bird dogs. In 1927, the breed was introduced into Britain where it is admired by a few enthusiasts.

Characteristics. The general outline is square, the head – with its keen eyes, erect pointed ears and pointed muzzle is distinctly fox-like. The back is short and straight, the chest deep. Forelegs are straight, hindquarters strong, and the bushy tail, in the typical Spitz manner, is carried over the back. The breed is loyal and useful as a watchdog but needs firm, gentle training.

Group. Hound.
Size. Medium.
Coat. *Colour:* Reddish brown or yellowish red. *Texture:* Short and close on the head and legs, longer on the body, with a mane of coarser hair.

Flat-coated Retriever

Origins. The breed is a subtle mixture of the St John's Newfoundland (a smaller version of the Newfoundland) with setters, sheepdogs and spaniels, and is a first-class retriever of water fowl. The breed was first shown in Britain in 1859 under a

► **Flat-coated Retriever**

classification which included curly coats, wavy or smooth-coated Retrievers, but had to wait until 1873 when Mr E. Shirley, founder of the Kennel Club, took an interest in it and stabilized type.

Characteristics. A bright, active dog of large size with an intelligent expression, showing power and raciness. The head is long and nicely moulded, the jaw long and strong. The eyes are dark brown or hazel of medium size and the ears small and fitting close to the side of the head. The neck is long, the chest deep and fairly broad, the back short. The tail is short, straight and carried gaily. The dog is intelligent and trainable.

Group. Gundog. Sporting (AKC).

Size. Large.

Coat. *Colour:* Black or liver. *Texture:* Dense, of fine quality and texture, and as flat as possible.

Foxhound

Origins. A breed which has been developed exclusively for a single purpose and which in Britain has not been diverted from its original purpose by popularity either as a pet or as a show dog, for in neither role has it achieved a place.

Characteristics. The skull is broad, the neck long and not thick, the body has plenty of heart room. The hindquarters are full and muscular. The Foxhound is bred as a pack animal and is unsuitable as a pet.

Group. Hound.

Size. Large.

Coat. *Colour:* A good 'hound colour' – black, tan, white in any combination. *Texture:* Weather-resistant, short, dense, hard and glossy.

Fox Terrier, Smooth

Origins. The Smooth Fox Terrier is undoubtedly the aristocrat of the terrier group, able to look back over a long history of work with hounds. At the beginning of the century, it was among the most popular of companions and show dogs. This early popularity has left a considerable literature devoted to the breed and a mass of carefully drawn illustrations which demonstrate that the breed has changed very little since, for example, the publication of Daniel's *Rural Sports* in 1801.

Characteristics. The dog must present a gay and active appearance and is compactly built. It has a short back but stands like a Foxhound, covering a lot of ground. It is intelligent and trainable but needs firm handling.

► **Foxhound**

▲ **French Bulldog**

◀ Smooth Fox Terrier

◀ Wire Fox Terrier

Group. Terrier.
Size. Small/Medium.
Coat. *Colour:* White predominates. *Texture:* Straight, flat, smooth, hard, dense and abundant.

Fox Terrier, Wire

Origins. The early Fox Terrier breeders did not differentiate between smooth and broken-coated dogs. Both coats appeared in the same litter but for companions and show dogs the smarter smooth coats were at first preferred. The wire coats followed them into the show ring about twenty-five years after their debut. Nowadays, with better skills in trimming and presentation, it is the Wire which takes the high prizes.

Characteristics. Similar to the Smooth in temperament and conformation, except for the coat. The texture is dense and wiry, like coconut matting and the face has plenty of whiskers.

French Bulldog

Origins. This breed has descended from Bulldogs introduced from Britain into France, probably at the end of the nineteenth century. Whatever its origins, this stylish miniature Bulldog speedily swept to popularity among the French, who called them the Boule-Dog Français even though the breed's British ancestry was obvious.

Characteristics. A French Bulldog should be sound, active and intelligent, of compact build. The head is massive, square and broad, with a domed forehead and loose skin forming symmetrical wrinkles. The bat ears are distinctively different from the ears of other Bulldog breeds. It is a very affectionate dog and a bit of a clown.

Group. Utility. Non-sporting (AKC).
Size. Small.
Coat. *Colour:* Brindle, pied and fawn. *Texture:* Fine, smooth, lustrous, short and close.

▲ German Shepherd Dog

▲ German Shorthaired Pointer

G

GERMAN SHEPHERD DOG (ALSATIAN)

Origins. A breed with origins and uses as indicated by its name. The first breed club was formed in 1899. By 1926 it was the most popular dog in Britain, where it was called the Alsatian Wolf Dog. Thoughtless breeding and ignorant handling gave the breed a dubious reputation which only the worst deserve. The best are intelligent, resourceful and eager to please but all these virtues must be in the hands of an owner able to develop them.

Characteristics. The characteristic expression of the German Shepherd Dog gives the impression of perpetual vigilance, fidelity, liveliness and watchfulness; fearless, but with a decided suspiciousness of strangers. It is a well-proportioned dog, with a long strongly boned body, obviously capable of endurance and speed and of quick, sudden movement.

Group. Working. Herding (AKC).

Size. Large.

Coat. *Colour:* Usually black and a sandy tan. *Texture:* Smooth and double texture with a thick, close, woolly undercoat and a close, hard, straight, weather-resistant outercoat.

GERMAN SHORTHAIRED POINTER

Origins. There are few records of the breed before the Klub Kurzhaar stud book was started in the 1870s, but it had long been established among those who appreciated its working qualities. The breed probably has its origins in the dogs introduced by homecoming crusaders, intermingled with indigenous bird dogs and the Spanish Pointer, with style and elegance being largely dependent on the blood of the English Pointer. Nowadays the breed has a high reputation as a general purpose gundog.

Characteristics. An aristocratic, well-balanced, symmetrical animal displaying power, endurance and agility. Its expression shows enthusiasm for work. The head is clean cut, the shoulders sloping, the chest deep and the back short and powerful. This is an obedient dog with a good temperament.

Group. Gundog. Sporting (AKC).

Size. Large.

Coat. *Colour:* Solid liver or any combination of liver and white. *Texture:* The skin is close and tight, the hair short and thick.

GERMAN WIREHAIRED POINTER

Origins. This dog was developed by selectively crossing several indigenous gundog breeds – the wirehaired Pointing Griffon, the Stichelhaar, the Puderpointer and the German Shorthair which, apart from the coat, it very closely resembles. The breed has been slow to gain recognition outside Germany, but now has a growing band of enthusiastic followers who appreciate the breed's outstanding abilities as an all-purpose gundog.

Characteristics. Essentially a dog of the Pointer type, of sturdy build, lively manner and with an intelligent, determined expression. In disposition the breed has been described as energetic, rather aloof, but not unfriendly. The head is moderately long with a broad skull, the ears are rounded but not too broad and hang close to the sides of the head. The body is a little longer than it is high, the back short, straight and strong.

Group. Gundogs. Sporting (AKC).

Size. Large.

Coat. *Colour:* Liver and white. *Texture:* Weather-resistant and to some extent water-repellant. Outer coat straight, harsh, wiry, lying flat, 2.5–5 cm (1–2 in) in length; the undercoat is dense in winter, thinner in summer.

GLEN OF IMAAL TERRIER

Origins. Very few of this breed are seen in the show ring or as companions outside their native Wicklow Mountains where their qualities as badger and fox hunters are highly prized among a select band of enthusiasts. The breed first appeared in the show ring in 1934, but has not taken to its new career with enthusiasm.

Characteristics. The Glen of Imaal Terrier is gentle with children and a lovable pet which usually abstains from fighting. Like all terriers of Ireland it loves water, it is silent in its work and about the house. The skull is strong, the ears pendulous, the eyes brown and placed well apart. The forelegs are short and bowed, the chest is wide and strong.

Group. Terrier.

Size. Small.

Coat. *Colour:* Blue and tan, wheaten. *Texture:* Long and coarse.

GOLDEN RETRIEVER

Origins. This breed originated when, in 1865, Lord Tweedmouth mated a yellow wavy-coated

◄ **Glen of Imaal Terrier**

▲ **German Wirehaired Pointer**

► **Golden Retriever**

▼ **Gordon Setter**

Retriever to a Tweed Water Spaniel, a breed from Scotland, and then bred on to further crosses with Tweed Water Spaniels, black Retrievers, an Irish Setter and a Bloodhound, so that by 1913 the Kennel Club was able to recognize the result as a separate breed.

Characteristics. The Golden Retriever is well-proportioned, active and powerful. The head is broad, the expression kindly, the eyes dark. The neck is muscular, the body well balanced. Feet are round and cat-like and the tail is well-feathered.

Group. Gundog. Sporting (AKC).

Size. Large.

Coat. *Colour:* Any shade of gold or cream. *Texture:* Flat or wavy with good feathering and dense, with a water-resistant undercoat.

Gordon Setter

Origins. As early as 1620 Markham, a contemporary writer, was able to remark that the 'black and fallow setting dog' was the 'hardest to endure labour'. But it was not until the end of the eighteenth century, when the fourth Duke of Gordon's kennel of Setters had made the breed famous, that the Gordon Castle Setters began to achieve fame outside Scotland. The Gordon Setter has never achieved the popularity of the Irish or English Setters and so has avoided some of the worst effects of popular demand and remains an honest, basically sensible gundog.

Characteristics. The breed is stylish, built on galloping lines, with a thoroughbred appearance. The back is strong, fairly short and level, the tail shortish and the head fairly long, with an intelligent expression. Eyes are of a fair size, dark brown and bright; ears are medium-sized and rather thin, set low and hanging close to the head. This stylish dog has a happy disposition and a strong will.

Group. Gundog. Sporting (AKC).

◄ Great Dane

◄ Greyhound

Size. Large.

Coat. *Colour:* Deep shining coal-black with tan markings of a rich chestnut red. *Texture:* Soft and shining, straight or slightly waved. Long hair on ears, under stomach and on chest, back of fore and hind-legs and under the tail.

GREAT DANE

Origins. In spite of its name the breed has no close association with Denmark. Indeed because drawings of very similar dogs were found on Fourth Dynasty tomb walls, some people might put its origins in Egypt, but it was in Germany that the breed was developed and achieved popularity. The breed was the one favoured by Bismarck and used to hunt wild boar.

Characteristics. Great Danes should be very large, very muscular, strongly though elegantly built. Their heads are carried high and they have a clean-cut, impressive look. They are loyal, easily-trained dogs that make good pets.

Group. Working. Non-sporting (ANKC).

Size. Large: 76.2 cm (30 in) upwards.

Coat. *Colour:* Brindle, fawn, steel blue, black or white patched with black or blue. *Texture:* Very short and thick, smooth and glossy.

GREYHOUND

Origins. There can be no doubt that Greyhounds are of very ancient origin. As early as 1016 Canute's law forbade 'mean persons' from keeping Greyhounds and, in 1408, Dame Juliana Berners used an older description of the breed in her Book of St Albans.

Characteristics. The Greyhound possesses remarkable stamina and its long-reaching movement enables it to move at great speed; indeed the Greyhound over a measured sprint is probably the fastest of all dogs. The head is long and elegant, the eyes bright and intelligent, the neck long and muscular. The chest is deep, the legs are strong, well boned and powerfully muscled. Though Greyhounds are usually kept for racing, they also make clean, affectionate companions.

Group. Hound.

Size. Large: average 74 cm (29 in).

Coat. *Colour:* Black, white, red, blue, fawn, fallow, brindle or any of the colours broken with white. *Texture:* Fine and close.

► Griffon Bruxellois

GRIFFON BRUXELLOIS (BRUSSELS GRIFFON)

Origins. Originally the Griffon was a humble adjunct of stables, used to keep down vermin and as an effective early warning system of unauthorized intrusion. Probably the breed has origins in the more ancient Affenpinscher.

Characteristics. The Griffon is a smart little dog with a pert monkey-like expression. It is well balanced, square in outline, lively and alert. The head is large and rounded, the eyes also large and round. Ears are small, semi-erect and high set. The chest is wide and deep, the back short, the hindquarters are well muscled. The tail is short, docked and carried high.

Group. Toy.

Size. Small.

Coat. *Colour:* Red, black or black and rich tan. *Texture:* Harsh and wiry.

GRIFFON VENDÉEN, GRAND

Origins. This dog is a descendant of the white variety of the ancient St Hubert hound of France.

Characteristics. The Griffon Vendéen is an intelligent dog, sure of itself and distinguished in physique and gait. The head is well rounded, not too broad, and the eyebrows bushy. The eyes are large, dark and vivacious, and the pendulous ears are soft, fine, narrow and covered with long hair.

Group. Hounds for big game (FCI).

Size. Large.

Coat. *Colour:* Fawn, white and orange; white and grey; tricolour. *Texture:* Long, bushy, heavy and hard.

H

HAMILTONSTÖVARE

Origins. The Hamiltonstövare is a breed produced by crosses between the Holstein, Hanover and Kurland Beagles and the Foxhound made by Adolf Patrick Hamilton, hence the breed's name.

Characteristics. The appearance is very much that of a small and lightly built Foxhound. It is a strong and willing hunter but does not make a

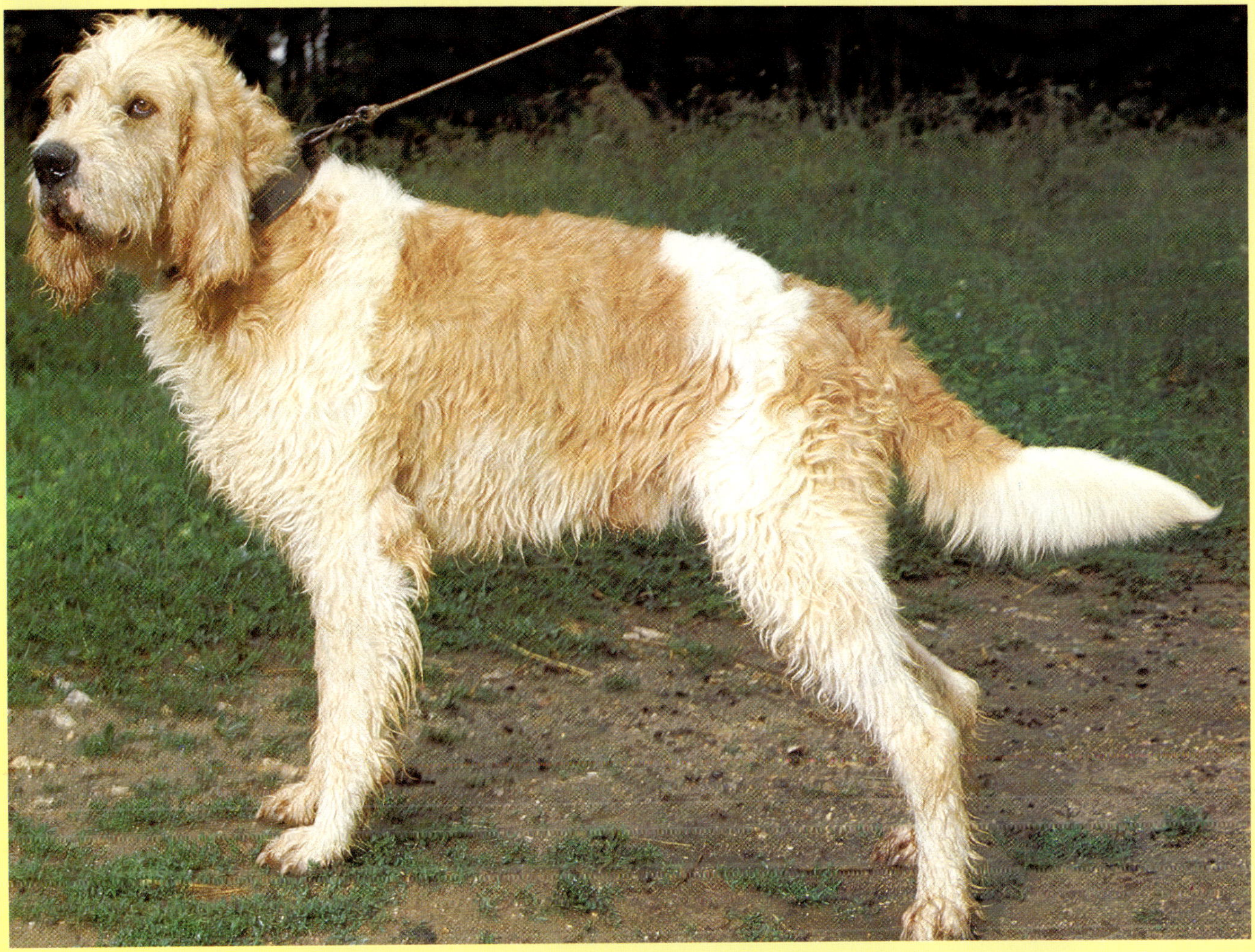

▲ Grand Griffon Vendéen

► Hamiltonstövare

▲ Harrier

▼ Short-haired Hungarian Vizsla

suitable pet.

Group. Hound.

Size. Medium.

Coat. *Colour:* The back black, shading to brown on the head and legs, with white on the muzzle, chest and legs. *Texture:* Short and dense.

HARRIER

Origins. In 400 BC Xenophon was able to describe two types of hounds, the Castorean and the fox-breed, said to be the product of a fox-dog cross. Xenophon listed the qualities necessary in hare hounds, qualities which were still relevant when Sir Elias de Midhope of Penistone gathered the first pack of Harriers together in 1260.

Characteristics. In every respect a small Foxhound. This is a hunting dog, not a domestic pet.

Group. Hound.

Size. Medium.

Coat. *Colour:* Any hound colour. *Texture:* Short, smooth and dense.

HUNGARIAN VIZSLA

Origins. The breed is sometimes called the Hungarian Pointer, which gives clues to its origins. Drawings dating from the Magyar invasions 1000 years ago show Vizsla-like dogs being used in conjunction with falcons.

Characteristics. The breed is robust yet lightly built, showing power and drive in the field, but with a tractable and affectionate nature in the home. The head is lean and muscular, moderately wide between the ears, which are thin and silky, hanging close to the cheeks. The neck is strong, smooth and muscular, the back is short and the chest moderately broad and deep. The tail is docked and set just below the level of the back. The gait is light-footed, graceful and smooth. There is a Short-haired and a Wire-haired version of the Vizsla; both are intelligent, loyal dogs.

Group. Gundog. Sporting (AKC).

Size. Large.

Coat. *Colour:* Solid, rusty gold or dark sandy yellow in different shades. *Texture:* Short, smooth, dense and close-lying, without evidence of a woolly undercoat. The wire-haired version has a wiry coat.

I

IBIZAN HOUND

Origins. One of the ancient sight hound breeds with origins in the lands around the Mediterranean and with a history which reaches back into ancient Egypt and the courts of the Pharaohs. In the tomb of Hemako a carved dish was found which carries the image of an Ibizan Hound; this dish was made during the 1st Dynasty between 3100 and 2700 BC. The tombs of Tutankhamen and the Ptolemies also provide evidence of the breed's ancient origin. Probably the hounds were first taken to Ibiza by Phoenician traders, where selection based on survival of the fittest produced a breed capable of hunting with skill, endurance and tenacity and with an exceptional jumping ability.

Characteristics. The head is long and narrow, the eyes small and ranging in colour from amber to caramel. The neck is long, slender and slightly arched and the dog has an elegant look. It has a friendly disposition but is only obedient when it feels so inclined.

Group. Hound.

Size. Large.

Coat. *Colour:* Red and white, or solid red. *Texture:* Short-coated hounds have a short hard coat; wire-haired hounds have a hard coat from 2.5–7.6 cm (1–3 in) in length.

IRISH SETTER

Origins. Ireland is the home of two breeds of setter, the Red and White and the Red. The former never achieved popular recognition and now survives only in the kennels of a few enthusiasts. The Red Setter, however, has achieved a degree of popularity which may not always have been to its benefit as it has led to the breed being carelessly bred.

Characteristics. Irish Setters are attractive, lively dogs with a kindly expression. The head is long and lean, the eyes are dark hazel or dark brown; the ears are of moderate size and fine texture and hang close to the head. The neck is moderately long, very muscular and slightly arched. The shoulders are deep and sloping, the chest is rather narrow in front and fairly deep. This is a loyal, affectionate dog with plenty of energy.

Group. Gundog. Sporting (AKC).

Size. Large.

Coat. *Colour:* Rich chestnut. *Texture:* Flat and sleek; long and silky on the ears, legs and tail.

▲ **Ibizan Hound**

▼ **Irish Setter**

Irish Water Spaniel

Origins. The Irish Water Spaniel represents a very old type of dog whose remains have been found in archaeological sites throughout Europe and which had emerged in Ireland as a distinct breed probably as early as the twelfth century. Nowadays, the Irish Water Spaniel is a gundog bred to work in shooting.

Characteristics. This is an intelligent dog, easily trained and very loyal to its owner. Its head is of good size, the muzzle long, strong and somewhat square, the face covered with characteristic curls and the topknot formed of longer curls. The eyes are small and dark, the ears very long and lobular, again covered with long curls. The neck is powerful, long and arched, set into sloping and powerful shoulders. The tail is distinctive, short and straight, set low and partly covered with curls, partly with straight hair.

Group. Gundog. Sporting (AKC).

Size. Large.

Coat. *Colour:* A rich dark liver. *Texture:* Dense, tight, crisp ringlets with a natural oiliness.

▲ **Irish Water Spaniel**

Irish Terrier

Origins. The Irish Terrier shares much the same origins as the Kerry Blue and made its debut in the show ring in 1879. The breed is hardy and adaptable like so many of the terriers: it is loyal, and makes an excellent guard.

Characteristics. The Irish Terrier is even-tempered especially with people, though sometimes fiery with other dogs. The dog is active, lively, lithe and wiry in appearance. The head is long, the skull flat, the eyes dark, the ears small and V-shaped. The neck of fair length, the shoulders fine, long and sloping, the body moderately long. The tail is generally docked.

Group. Terrier.

Size. Medium.

Coat. *Colour:* Various shades of red. *Texture:* Hard and wiry.

◀ **Irish Terrier**

Irish Wolfhound

Origins. In AD 391 Consul Quintus Aurelius recorded that a gift of seven wolfhounds had filled 'all Rome with wonder'. The breed was obviously already well established, but the extinction of the wolf led to the breed's decline, so that by the mid-nineteenth century the breed was almost extinct. However, in the 1860s the breed was recreated by Captain George Graham, a Scot living in Gloucestershire.

Characteristics. The breed's most obvious characteristics are its commanding appearance and the impression of considerable strength it conveys. The head is long, the skull not too broad, the ears small and Greyhound-like in carriage. The neck is rather long, and very strong and muscular. The chest is very deep, the back rather long, and the hindquarters long and strong as in the Greyhound. It has large, round feet. This gentle, dignified dog needs sympathetic training.

Group. Hound.

Size. Large and heavy: 78.7 cm (31 in) and 54.5 kg (120 lb).

Coat. *Colour:* Grey, brindle, red, black, white or fawn. *Texture:* Rough and hard on the body, wiry and long over eyes and underjaw.

▲ Irish Wolfhound

ITALIAN GREYHOUND

Origins. A breed of ancient origin which was certainly widely known and admired among the civilizations around the Mediterranean 2000 years ago, but which probably achieved its peak of popularity in sixteenth century Italy and in the courts of James I, Frederick the Great and Catherine the Great. The Italian Greyhound is prized today as it always has been for its elegance, its sweet nature and its beauty.

Characteristics. A miniature Greyhound, slender and elegant, with a high-stepping and free action. The skull is long, flat and narrow, the muzzle very fine, the eyes rather large, bright and full of expression and the ears are petal-shaped, soft and delicate. The neck is long, gracefully arched and set into long, sloping shoulders.

Group. Toy.

Size. Small.

Coat. *Colour:* All shades of fawn, white, cream, blue. *Texture:* Thin and glossy, like satin.

▼ Italian Greyhound

▲ Jack Russell Terrier

▲ Japanese Chin

▲ Japanese Spitz

J

Jack Russell Terrier

Origins. These terriers were originally bred in the nineteenth century by a sporting parson from Devon, and his pack of working terriers became known as 'Parson Jack Russells'. They are not recognized by the Kennel Club but are very popular in Britain, especially among owners who feel that some other terriers have been over-bred and lost their working character.

Characteristics. These tough, sporty little dogs are full of confidence and enthusiasm. As there is no breed standard, looks vary considerably and Jack Russells can be long or short-legged, prick or drop-eared. Their ears are dark brown and almond-shaped and the tail, usually docked, is carried high.

Size. Small.

Coat. *Colour:* Usually white with tan or black markings. *Texture:* May be short and smooth or longer and rougher.

Japanese Chin

Origins. Like so many of the toy breeds which originated in the Orient, the Japanese Chin, sometimes called the Japanese Spaniel, has long been associated with the Royal courts. The breed's ancestors probably arrived in Japan as gifts from the Chinese Emperor to his Japanese counterpart. The breed makes an excellent companion, but one with a mind of its own.

Characteristics. The Japanese Chin is a lively little dog of dainty appearance, smart compact carriage and with a profuse coat. It is stylish in movement, lifting the feet high, and carries its plumed tail over the back. The head is large in proportion to the size of the dog, with a broad and rounded skull, and the muzzle very short. The dark eyes are large and set wide apart, the ears small, V-shaped and carried slightly forward. The body is squarely and compactly built, and cobby in shape.

Group. Toy.

Size. Small.

Coat. *Colour:* Black and white or red and white. *Texture:* Profuse, long, soft and straight, and silky.

Japanese Spitz

Origins. This dog was bred from Spitz breeds taken to Japan which were used to form a breed with similarities to the Pomeranian.

Characteristics. The muzzle is pointed, the ears are erect and pointed. The tail, richly fringed, falls

▲ Keeshond

K

KEESHOND

Origins. For centuries this breed was used as a watchdog on the barges of Holland, but it has its origins among other more northerly Spitz breeds. Since its rise to popular recognition some two centuries ago, the breed has changed little.

Characteristics. The Keeshond has a short, compact body, alert carriage and fox-like head. It carries its well-feathered tail curled over its back in the typical Spitz manner. It is a vigilant watchdog with a sturdy, independent character.

Group. Utility. Non-sporting (AKC).

Size. Medium.

Coat. *Colour:* Wolf or ash grey. *Texture:* Dense and harsh, standing away from the body with a thick soft undercoat.

KERRY BLUE TERRIER

Origins. The Kerry Blue shares a common ancestry with the Soft-Coated Wheaten Terrier and shares, too, a common birthplace among the mountains of Kerry, where it was developed to provide sport, security and companionship for the sporting farmers of that area. Nowadays, by careful breeding, skilful trimming and painstaking presentation, it has been transformed into a very successful show dog, to a far greater degree than other Irish Terriers.

Characteristics. The Kerry Blue is a compact, powerful terrier with an attitude of alert determination. It is well proportioned, with a well-developed and muscular body. The head is long and lean, the jaw strong and deep, the eyes dark and the ears small and V-shaped. The tail is set high and carried erect. The Kerry Blue makes an excellent watchdog

► **Kerry Blue Terrier**

on the back. The body is compact and the general appearance handsome. The Japanese Spitz is characterized by great courage and its intelligent and cheerful disposition.

Group. Utility (KC).

Size. Medium.

Coat. *Colour:* Pure white. *Texture:* Straight and standing away from the body. The undercoat is short, soft and abundant.

► King Charles Spaniel

but is over-keen to fight with other dogs.

Group. Terrier.

Size. Medium.

Coat. *Colour:* Shades of blue. *Texture:* Soft, silky, plentiful and wavy.

King Charles Spaniel

Origins. A toy spaniel which derives its name from its popularity in the court of King Charles II, which was so great that few portraits of the period seem to be without the customary King Charles Spaniel reclining on milady's lap, or peeping from behind a chair. Though it was Charles II who gave his name to the breed, toy spaniels had been popular for some time before. Mary, Queen of Scots was fond of them and one even accompanied her to her death.

Characteristics. The King Charles has a massive head with large dark eyes full of expression, a short snub muzzle and long, pendulous, well-feathered ears, set low and lying close to the cheeks. The body proportions should be those of a miniature spaniel. It is a quiet, friendly little dog, very good with children.

Group. Toy.

Size. Small.

Coat. *Colour:* Black and tan, white and chestnut, chestnut red, and tricolour. *Texture:* Long, silky and straight.

▼ Komondor

Komondor

Origins. The herding breeds of Hungary and Russia form a loose family group; many are probably descended from the Aftschowka, an ancient breed from Eastern Europe. The Komondor probably has retained the closest resemblance to this breed which the Magyars have bred for more than a thousand years as guards to the flocks of sheep which graze the Puszta.

Characteristics. The Komondor is characterized by imposing strength and courageous demeanour. In general it is a big muscular dog with an unusual heavy white coat. The breed make excellent guards, being wary of strangers, earnest, courageous and loyal. The head is short and wide with a powerful muzzle, the ears are pendulous, the neck of moderate length and arched. The powerful deep chest is wide and muscular. Feet are strong and rather large with close arched toes.

Group. Working.

Size. Large and heavy: average 54.5 kg (120 lb).

Coat. *Colour:* White. *Texture:* Dense, weather-resisting and very soft in the puppy, but growing into heavy tassel-like cords in the mature dog; these cords form naturally.

Kuvasz

Origins. The breed is said to have been introduced into Hungary in the twelfth century by the Kurds, its name being a corruption of the Turkish 'Kawasz', meaning 'the protector'. Originally it was used to protect farm stock from marauding wolves and bears, but was also used, though purely as a side line, as a hunting dog.

Characteristics. A strongly boned dog, big and powerfully built, the head is noble with an intelligent expression, the chest deep and powerful. Forelegs are straight and well boned, hindquarters powerful. The Kuvasz makes an affectionate pet but is suspicious of strangers, so it makes a good watchdog.

Group. Working (AKC).

Size. Large and heavy: 73.5 cm (29 in) and 50 kg (110 lb).

Coat. *Colour:* Pure white. *Texture:* Long, straight or slightly wavy.

▲ **Kuvasz**

L

Labrador Retriever

Origins. In 1822 reports of 'small water dogs . . . admirably trained as retrievers in fowling and are

▼ **Labrador Retriever**

▲ **Lakeland Terrier**

▼ **Large Munsterlander**

otherwise useful' indicated that there existed in Newfoundland a breed of gundog which British sportsmen were quick to recognize as being first class and imported into Britain. Today Labradors make excellent pets; they have a reliable temperament and get on well with children.

Characteristics. The general appearance is that of a strongly built, very active dog, with a broad skull, broad and deep through the chest and ribs, with powerful hindquarters. The tail is a distinctive feature of the breed and is very thick at the base gradually tapering towards the tip and giving that peculiar rounded appearance which has been described as the 'otter' tail.

Group. Gundog. Sporting (AKC).

Size. Large.

Coat. *Colour:* Generally black or yellow, sometimes chocolate. *Texture:* The coat is short and dense and without wave, with a weather-resistant undercoat, and should be fairly hard.

LAKELAND TERRIER

Origins. The Lakeland was developed as a working terrier with the packs of hounds which hunt the rugged country in England's Lake District. Nowadays the breed has split to produce two distinct types: those which are still used for work and a refined type seen at shows.

Characteristics. The breed has a smart, workmanlike appearance with a gay, fearless demeanour. The skull is flat and refined, the eyes dark and the ears moderately small, V-shaped, and carried alertly. The chest is narrow, the back strong and fairly short. The hindquarters are strong and muscular. The Lakeland Terrier is active, exuberant and fearless, but needs firm handling.

Group. Terrier.

Size. Small.

Coat. *Colour:* Usually black and tan or red. *Texture:* Dense and weather-resisting, harsh with good undercoat.

LARGE MUNSTERLANDER

Origins. Known as a good working dog in Germany for centuries, this breed was originally classed as a German Longhaired Pointer.

Characteristics. The Munsterlander is a working gundog with sharp intelligence, vigour and fidelity, able to adapt quickly to any type of terrain or quarry. At home it is an excellent guard and a good-natured companion. The head is lean and distinguished, the nose brown, the muzzle is long. The eyes are dark, the ears light and pointed with good feathering. The neck is slightly arched and very muscular, the chest deep and broad. The tail is carried straight out.

Group. Gundog (KC).

Size. Large.

Coat. *Colour:* Usually black and white. *Texture:* Smooth and slightly wavy.

Lhasa Apso

Origins. In Tibet, the Lhaso Apso's homeland, the breed is known as Abso Seng Kye, the Bark Lion Sentinel Dog, a name which sums up its function. The Apso is one of four breeds now justly popular in the West which for very many years acted as guards within the precincts of the lamaseries in and around the sacred city of Lhasa.

Characteristics. The Apso is a solid dog with a gay and assertive character, yet chary of strangers. The head is narrow, with hair completely covering the face. The ears are pendant and heavily feathered. The tail is high-set and carried over the back. The Apso carries a considerable abundance of coat. It is an affectionate dog that needs plenty of company.

Group. Utility. Non-sporting (AKC).

Size. Small.

Coat. *Colour:* Golden honey, also various other colours. *Texture:* Straight and hard, long and with dense undercoat.

▲ **Lhasa Apso**

Löwchen

Origins. From the Middle Ages, dogs very like the modern breed of Löwchen appeared in paintings, and Lion Dogs are described by Bewick. Whether the modern Löwchen is the same as these dogs is a matter for conjecture, since it seems unlikely that these dogs had to be clipped in order to produce their lion-like appearance.

Characteristics. A small intelligent dog with an affectionate and lively disposition combining all the good qualities of a companion dog. The body is clipped in the traditional lion clip.

Group. Toy.

Size. Small.

Coat. *Colour:* Various. *Texture:* Fairly long and wavy.

▲ **Löwchen**

M

Maltese

Origins. This breed has been known in the Mediterranean islands probably since the time of the Phoenicians. Certainly the breed existed very much in its present form since, at the time of the Apostle Paul, Publius, the Roman Governor of Malta, owned a Maltese.

Characteristics. The breed is sweet tempered and very intelligent, smart, lively and alert. The

▲ **Maltese**

profuse white coat covers a well-made little dog with dark brown eyes and long pendant ears. The body is short and cobby and the tail is well arched over the back and feathered.

Group. Toy.

Size. Small.

Coat. *Colour:* Pure white, sometimes with slight lemon markings. *Texture:* Straight and silky.

Manchester Terrier

Origins. Old prints show that a great many of the old terriers of different types were black and tan. The Manchester Terrier was developed for sport by the working people of Lancashire, people who looked to a day's ratting or rabbiting with their terriers to provide recreation. The Manchester Terrier makes an ideal house dog, being clean, and a good guard.

Characteristics. The dog is compact, with a long head, narrow in skull, with small, dark, sparkling eyes, and small V-shaped ears carried above the top line of the head. The neck is fairly long and the forelegs quite straight and set well under the short body. The tail is naturally short.

Group. Terrier.

Size. Small.

Coat. *Colour:* Black with rich tan markings. *Texture:* Close, smooth, short and glossy; of a firm texture.

Maremma

Origins. The Maremma is a large, heavy-coated herding dog from Italy, very much in the pattern of other European herding breeds to which it is undoubtedly closely related. It was first imported and recognized in England in 1935.

Characteristics. The breed is large and strongly built, majestic in appearance, distinguished, robust and courageous. In general appearance the breed much resembles the Pyrenean Mountain Dog, with a strong build and large head.

Group. Working.

Size. Large.

Coat. *Colour:* Usually solid white. *Texture:* Very abundant, long and rather harsh with a soft undercoat.

Mastiff

Origins. One of the ancient mastiff breeds of Europe with origins in the war dogs of Europe, which fought alongside their masters to repel the invasion of Britain by the Roman legions in 55 BC. The Romans recognized their great courage and imported them to Rome to take part in gladiatorial contests against bulls, bears, lions and tigers. The breed was so greatly admired that mastiff-like dogs, generally called 'dogues', eventually were to give

▲ **Maremma**

▼ **Manchester Terrier**

their particular name to all domestic dogs.

Characteristics. A massive and powerful dog, combining grandeur with good nature and courage with docility. The head is square in appearance, the muzzle short and broad. The eyes are small, dark, and set wide apart. The ears are small and thin, lying flat and close to the cheek. The neck is very muscular, set into heavy, slightly sloping shoulders. The forelegs are heavily boned, straight and strong, the hindquarters broad, wide and muscular.

Group. Working. Non-sporting (ANKC).

Size. Large: 76 cm (30 in) upwards.

Coat. *Colour:* Apricot or silver, fawn or dark fawn, brindle with black on the muzzle, ears and nose and between the eyes. *Texture:* Short and close-lying.

Miniature Pinscher

Origins. Contrary to popular misconception the Miniature Pinscher is not a small Dobermann; its original name 'Reh Pinscher' referred to the breed's resemblance to small forest deer. It has existed for several centuries in Germany and Scandinavia, where it is valued as a very alert watchdog.

Characteristics. The Miniature Pinscher is structurally a sturdy, compact toy dog, naturally well groomed, proud, vigorous and alert. Its natural high-stepping gait, complete self-possession and its spirited presence differentiate the breed from other toy dogs. The head is narrow, the ears upstanding, cropped in countries where the operation is still allowed. The body is compact and muscular, the tail set high and docked short.

Group. Toy.

Size. Small.

Coat. *Colour:* Red or black with tan markings, solid brown or chocolate. *Texture:* Smooth, hard and short, straight and lustrous.

▲ **Miniature Pinscher**

◄ **Mastiff**

▲ **Neapolitan Mastiff**

N

Neapolitan Mastiff

Origins. Many of the European Mastiff breeds are of ancient origin and the Neapolitan Mastiff is no exception for, although it made its appearance in the show ring only after World War II, it is descended from the Roman fighting dogs.

Characteristics. The Neapolitan Mastiff is a first-rate guard dog but can make a docile and friendly pet. Its head is massive, its body deep and powerful. Its eyes are dark, its nostrils wide and its nose broad.

Group. Working.

Size. Large.

Coat. *Colour:* Black, or lead or mouse grey. *Texture:* Dense and smooth.

▲ **Newfoundland**

Newfoundland

Origins. The Newfoundland breed was primarily developed not, as is often suggested, as a canine lifeguard, but as a draught dog, big and strong enough to pull carts or carry heavy loads. However, its affinity with the fishermen of Newfoundland made it a superb water dog. Early prints suggest that the breed has its origins among the Huskies of Northern Canada.

Characteristics. The Newfoundland has an exceptionally gentle and docile nature and should be strong and active. The head is broad and massive, the eyes small and dark, the ears small, set well back and falling close to the head. The chest is deep and fairly broad, the forelegs are straight and well feathered, the hindquarters very strong. It becomes devoted to its owner.

Group. Working. Non-sporting (ANKC).

Size. Large and heavy: average 59 kg (130 lb).

Coat. *Colour:* Dull jet black, black with white markings, and solid bronze. *Texture:* Flat and dense, with a fairly coarse texture and oily nature, and water-resistant.

Norfolk Terrier

Origins. One of the smallest of the terriers, but one which retains all its sporting instincts. Until 1964, the breed could have either drop or prick ears, but at that time the two types were separated and the prick-eared variety became Norwich Terriers. (Both types are known as Norwich Terriers in the USA.)

Characteristics. The Norfolk Terrier has a lovable disposition, is not quarrelsome, has a hardy constitution and is alert and fearless. It is a small, low, keen dog, compact and strong with a short back. The skull is wide and slightly rounded, the muzzle wedge-shaped and strong, the eyes oval, deep set and dark, giving an alert, keen and intelligent expression. The ears are V-shaped and drop forward, close to the cheek. The tail is docked.

Group. Terrier.

Size. Small.

Coat. *Colour:* Usually red. *Texture:* Hard, wiry and straight, lying close to the body.

Norwegian Buhund

Origins. A typical Spitz breed, used as a general farm dog and guard. The breed formed the basis for the Icelandic Dog which was bred from stock taken to Iceland in AD 874. The ancient origin of the breed is thus established.

Characteristics. The breed is fearless, brave and

▲ Norfolk Terrier

◀ Norwegian Buhund

► **Norwich Terrier**

energetic, of medium size, lightly built with a short compact body. It is adaptable and makes a good watchdog.

Group. Working.

Size. Medium.

Coat. *Colour:* Biscuit, ripe wheat, light red, sable, black. *Texture:* Close and harsh with soft undercoat.

Norwich Terrier

Origins. The breed dates from the early years of the century when it was known as the Jones Terrier and shares its short history up to 1964 with the Norfolk Terrier.

Characteristics. Similar to those of the Norfolk Terrier, except for its pricked ears.

Group. Terrier.

O

Old English Sheepdog

Origins. The breed was probably developed, if it did not originate, in the West of England. The Old English Sheepdog was a drover's dog used for driving sheep and cattle to market. Drover's dogs were exempt from taxes if they were docked, hence the tailless outline of the Old English Sheepdog; hence also its popular nickname of 'Bobtail'.

Characteristics. A strong compact-looking dog, profusely coated all over, very elastic in a gallop, but

► **Old English Sheepdog**

◀ Otter Hound

▲ Papillon

when walking or trotting has a characteristic ambling movement. The bark is loud with a 'bell-like' ring to it. The head is large and rather squarely formed, the jaw fairly long and strong; the ears are small and carried close to the head. The body is short and very compact. The tail in puppies born with tails is docked short. The 'Bobtail' has a good temperament and gets on very well with children and other pets.

Group. Working. Herding (AKC).

Size. Large.

Coat. *Colour:* Any shade of grey, with or without white markings. *Texture:* Profuse and of good hard texture, shaggy and free from curl.

Otter Hound

Origins. Although otter hunting in England dates back to the early twelfth century, it was not until the reign of Edward II (1307–27) that a description of hounds which fits the modern breed was set down. Otter Hounds have been shown in the USA since 1907; in England only since 1977.

Characteristics. The Otter Hound is a large, rough-coated, squarely built hound, with an exceptionally good nose and deep musical voice. The head is large and narrow, the chest deep, the legs are heavy-boned. The feet are large, broad, compact and webbed. Movement is smooth and effortless, with the feet only just coming off the ground, and the dog has great strength and stamina. The Otter Hound is basically a pack animal, rather than a pet, but is friendly and good with children.

Group. Hound.

Size. Large.

Coat. *Colour:* Various. *Texture:* The rough outer coat is hard and 7.6–15 cm (3–6 in) long; the weather-resistant inner coat is short and woolly.

P

Papillon

Origins. Arguably Papillons or their Miniature Spaniel progenitors appear in more paintings by artists, such as Rubens, Watteau, Boucher and Fragonard, than any other breed of dog. As companions to the ladies of the courts of Europe, these elegant little creatures led a noble existence.

▲ **Pekingese**

Today they have lost none of their elegance or their great charm and vivacity. They have also to a large degree retained much of the toughness inherited from gundog ancestors.

Characteristics. A dainty, balanced toy dog with an attractive, slightly rounded head with finely pointed muzzle and round, dark eyes showing an alert, lively expression. The bearing is alert, movement sound, light and free. The ears are large, rounded at the tips, heavily fringed and carried like the spread wings of a butterfly, hence the name Papillon. It is very affectionate towards its owners and can become possessive.

Group. Toy.

Size. Small.

Coat. *Colour:* White with coloured patches. *Texture:* Abundant and flowing, long, fine and silky, with a profuse frill on the chest.

Pekingese

Origins. In ancient times the Pekingese was the sacred dog of China. Certainly during the Tang Dynasty in the eighth century these dogs were already highly prized, carefully bred and jealously guarded. Their introduction into the West came after the Imperial Palace in Peking had been looted, part of this loot was a fawn and white Pekingese which was given to Queen Victoria.

Characteristics. This is a well-balanced, thick-set dog with great dignity, a fearless carriage and an alert, intelligent expression. The head is massive, the skull broad, wide and flat between the ears and eyes. The nose is very short and broad, well wrinkled with a firm underjaw, giving a flat profile. The eyes are large, clear, dark and lustrous, the ears heart-shaped and carried close to the head, with long profuse feathering. The body is short with a broad chest, the forelegs are short, thick and bowed. The Pekingese is a determined, independent little dog.

Group. Toy.

Size. Small; heavy for its size.

Coat. *Colour:* Various. *Texture:* Long and straight with a profuse mane forming a frill round the neck, and profuse feathering on ears, legs, thighs, toes and tail, which is carried over the back. The top coat is rather coarse with a thick undercoat.

Pharaoh Hound

Origins. This dog originated in Egypt and North Africa. The Pharaoh Hound or Balearic Greyhound was much admired by Phoenician traders who introduced the breed throughout the Mediterranean countries.

Characteristics. Much the same in type as the Greyhound, but distinguished from it by its triangular head and large erect ears, unique among gaze hounds. The eyes are quite small and deep set, amber or light brown, the neck slender. The ears are large and erect. The Pharoah is a fast, agile and playful dog.

Group. Hound.

Size. Large.

Coat. *Colour:* White with chestnut or rich tan or yellow tan markings. *Texture:* Short, fine and glossy, with a soft skin.

◀ **Pharaoh Hound**

◄ ▲ Pointer

POINTER

Origins. Pointers have been used in Britain since the mid-seventeenth century to indicate by pointing just where game was hidden. Early in the eighteenth century, when guns came into use, the Pointer began to function as a gundog. The breed's distinctive appearance owes something to the Foxhound and something to the Greyhound; other ancestors include the Bloodhound and, of course, the 'setting' spaniel.

Characteristics. The Pointer is bred for work in the field and gives an impression of compact power and agile grace allied to intelligence and alertness. The head is aristocratic with an unusual dish-shaped muzzle, the ears pendulous, the eyes rounded and dark. The neck is long, clean, muscular, and slightly arched, the shoulders long and sloping. Forelegs are straight, hindquarters muscular and powerful with great propelling leverage. The gait is smooth and powerful with the head carried high. The Pointer is an obedient and devoted pet.

Group. Gundog. Sporting (AKC).

Size. Large.

Coat. *Colour:* Liver, lemon, black, orange; either a solid colour or with white. *Texture:* Short, dense, smooth with a sheen.

POMERANIAN

Origins. Originally sled dogs from Iceland and Lapland, the Pomeranian is possibly the smallest of the Spitz breeds, but one which retains all the courage and character of its larger cousins. During the last century the Pomeranian has been reduced in size and it is no longer used to herd sheep, but it remains an alert housedog, capable of giving warning of intruders with a surprisingly deep bark.

Characteristics. The Pomeranian is a compact dog with a head fox-like in shape and expression, eyes bright and dark in colour, ears small and erect.

► Pomeranian

► Standard Poodle, unclipped

▼ Standard Poodle, with lion clip

The neck is rather short, a shortness which is accentuated by the characteristic Spitz ruff. The tail is curled back over the body, nearly reaching the head.

Group. Toy.

Size. Small.

Coat. *Colour:* Usually orange. *Texture:* Double-coated: a short, soft thick undercoat with a longer, coarse, harsh-textured outer coat.

Poodle

Origins. Originating in France, the poodle was used as a gundog over a wide area, including France, Germany and Russia. Its adaptability, intelligence and unusual appearance soon led to its use for a wide variety of purposes, as well as in the production of other gundog breeds.

Characteristics. A very active and elegant dog, carrying itself proudly. The head is long and fine with almond-shaped eyes, the chest deep and moderately wide, the back is short and strong. The tail is docked. The Miniature and Toy versions have overtaken the Standard Poodle in popularity.

Group. Utility. Non-sporting (AKC). Miniature version: Toy (AKC).

Size. Medium (Standard) or Small (Miniature and Toy).

Coat. *Colour:* All solid colours, clear colours preferred. *Texture:* Very profuse and dense and of harsh texture. The coat has the advantage that it does not shed like most other breeds and lacks the distinctive and sometimes objectionable doggy smell. The distinctive appearance is achieved by careful and laborious clipping and grooming.

Pug

Origins. The Pug is another of the toy breeds with roots in ancient China, where it has flourished for the past 2000 years. Although very much a toy dog, the Pug has all the characteristics of some of the Eastern mastiff breeds which it so closely resembles.

▲ Pug

▲ Puli

Characteristics. The Pug is a square and cobby little dog, giving an impression of considerable substance packed into small size. The head is round, massive, and deeply wrinkled. The muzzle short and blunt, the eyes very large, bold and dark. The body is short and wide in the chest. The forelegs are strong and straight, the hindquarters muscular. The tail is curled tightly. Pugs are affectionate dogs with charming dispositions.

Group. Toy.

Size. Small.

Coat. *Colour:* Usually black or fawn with a black mask and black ears. *Texture:* Fine, smooth, soft, short and glossy.

Puli

Origins. This breed is a working partner of the Komondor and the Kuvasz and shares the same origins among the herding dogs which invading Magyars brought into Hungary. The Puli was used to herd and drive sheep.

Characteristics. A vigorous, alert and extremely active breed. By nature Pulis are affectionate and loyal, but being excellent guards are suspicious of strangers. The construction of the Puli is not exaggerated in any way, the head is of medium size, the neck strong and muscular. The chest is deep and fairly broad and the body of medium length, straight and level. The tail is never docked and is carried over the back.

Group. Working. Herding (AKC).

Size. Medium.

Coat. *Colour:* Usually rusty black. *Texture:* The coat hangs in tight, even cords.

▲ Pyrenean Mountain Dog

▲ Rhodesian Ridgeback

▲ Rottweiler

Pyrenean Mountain Dog (Great Pyrenees)

Origins. This dog is a descendant of the South European herding and guard breeds, originating in the mountains on the borders of France and Spain. It was the guard dog of the region.

Characteristics. The dog is serious in play and at work, gentle and docile to the point of self-sacrifice. A dog of great majesty, keen intelligence and kindly expression. The head is large, the neck short and muscular. The dog's protective instincts need careful training.

Group. Working. Non-sporting (ANKC).

Size. Large and heavy: 71 cm (28 in) upwards, 54.5 kg (120 lb).

Coat. *Colour:* All white or principally white, with markings of badger, grey or shades of tan. *Texture:* Fine undercoat and thick overcoat of coarser hair.

R

Rhodesian Ridgeback

Origins. The European farmers, who in the sixteenth and seventeenth centuries settled in South Africa, developed a hound suitable for the conditions and game encountered in South Africa, and which was also willing to act as a guard. They did this by crossing their dogs with a native hunting dog which had a ridge on its back. The dog had to be tough to withstand hard work in extremes of temperature, sufficiently versatile to either retrieve a partridge or put down a wounded buck, had to be easily kept and fit well into the family. The breed, which was developed by the Boer farmers, was introduced into Rhodesia in 1877.

Characteristics. The peculiarity of the breed is the ridge on the back formed by hair growing against the nap of the rest of the coat. The Ridgeback is a strong, muscular and active dog. The head is of fair length, flat and broad between the ears. The eyes are bright and coloured to harmonize with the colour of the dog. The chest is deep and capacious, the back powerful. The tail is carried with a slight upward curve.

Group. Hound.

Size. Large.

Coat. *Colour:* Light wheaten to red wheaten, with a little white on the chest and toes. *Texture:* Short and dense with a sleek, glossy appearance.

Rottweiler

Origins. Yet another of the European mastiff breeds which probably have their origins among the dogs which guarded and helped drive the herds of cattle which accompanied the Roman armies. The breed's courage, strength and forbidding aspect make it a marvellous guard for those able to control it. Good training is essential.

Characteristics. The Rottweiler is a compact dog, well proportioned and powerfully built to permit great strength, manoeuvrability and endurance. The bearing displays boldness and courage. The head is distinctive, broad, of medium length, with well-muscled cheeks. The neck is strong, round and very muscular, set into long and sloping shoulders. The body is broad and deep, the back straight and strong.

Group. Working. Non-sporting (ANKC).

Size. Large.

Coat. *Colour:* Black with clearly defined tan markings on cheeks, muzzle, chest and legs, as well as over the eyes and under the tail. *Texture:* Coarse and flat, with a medium-length topcoat.

S

St Bernard

Origins. The St Bernard's ancestors were probably brought to Switzerland by invading Roman armies. These dogs were crossed with native dogs to produce the Talhund and Bauernhund which, by the eleventh century, were in common use on Swiss

▼ **St Bernard**

◀ **Saluki**

▲ **Samoyed**

farms. In the seventeenth century they became known for their rescue work in the Alps.

Characteristics. The head of the St Bernard is massive and round with an expression of benevolence, dignity and intelligence. The neck is long, thick and muscular, and slightly arched. Forelegs are perfectly straight, shoulders are broad and sloping. The back is broad and straight, the chest wide and deep. Hindquarters should be heavy in bone with well-bent hocks. As a pet, this huge dog is gentle, docile and easily trained.

Group. Working. Non-sporting (ANKC).

Size. Large.

Coat. *Colour:* Orange, mahogany-brindle, red-brindle, white with patches on body of these colours. *Texture:* Long, dense and flat; there is a smooth-haired variety.

SALUKI

Origins. The breed existed when Alexander the Great invaded India, four centuries before the birth of Christ, and carvings on Sumerian and Egyptian tombs dating from 7000 BC are recognizable as Salukis.

Characteristics. The appearance of the breed is one of grace together with speed and endurance. The head is long and narrow, the eyes dark to hazel and bright. The ears are long and mobile and covered with long silky hair. The neck too is long, supple and well muscled, set into sloping shoulders. The chest is deep and moderately narrow, the back is muscular and slightly arched. The tail is long, low set and carried in a graceful curve, well feathered with long silky hair. The Saluki has an independent and sensitive nature.

Group. Hound.

Size. Large.

Coat. *Colour:* White, cream, fawn, golden red and other colours. *Texture:* Smooth and silky, with elegant silky feathering on ears, legs and tail, except in the breed's smooth variety.

SAMOYED

Origins. Just as the Saluki may lay claim to being the oldest of the Mediterranean sight hounds, so the Samoyed may claim to be the oldest of the Northern Spitz breeds. Originally bred as a guard for herds of reindeer, the breed also acted as companion, guard and sledge dog, in which capacity it accompanied Polar expeditions. The breed's strength, stamina and hardiness are belied by its childlike good nature and fairy-tale and soft appearance.

Characteristics. The Samoyed is intelligent, alert and full of action. The breed should be strong, active and graceful, with a muscular back of medium length allowing liberty of movement. The head is powerful and wedge-shaped, the eyes almond-shaped with an intelligent expression. The ears are erect and thick, covered inside with hair. The tail is long and profusely coated, carried over the back when alert.

Group. Working. Non-sporting. (ANKC).

Size. Large.

Coat. *Colour:* Pure white, white and biscuit, cream. *Texture:* A thick, close, soft and short undercoat, covered with an outer coat of straight harsh hair, which grows straight away from the body providing protection against extreme cold.

SCHIPPERKE

Origins. The Schipperke is descended from the same herding dogs which produced the Belgian Shepherd Dog (Groenendael), the latter remaining as herders and Schipperkes becoming smaller watchdogs. It was not until 1888 that their name was changed to Schipperke, which in Flemish means 'little captain', a reference as much to the breed's air of self-importance as to their association with the barges of the Flemish canals.

Characteristics. The general appearance is of a small, cobby animal with a sharp expression, intensely lively and alert. The head is distinctly foxy with small, rather oval, dark brown eyes and sharply pointed, stiffly erect ears. The neck is strong and rather short, the shoulders muscular and sloping. The rump is tailless and rounded; the feet small and cat-like. Apart from making a useful watchdog, the Schipperke is a perky, affectionate pet.

Group. Utility. Non-sporting (AKC).

Size. Small/Medium.

Coat. *Colour:* Black. *Texture:* Abundant, dense and harsh, smooth on the head, ears and legs, but erect and thick round the neck, forming a mane and frill, and with a good culotte on the back of the thighs.

SCHNAUZER

Origins. The Standard Schnauzer may be regarded as the forerunner of the three Schnauzer breeds: Miniature, Standard and Giant. The Schnauzer is a German breed with a long history dating back to the fifteenth and sixteenth centuries. It has been used in its various sizes as a vermin killer, a yard dog and a most effective guard.

Characteristics. The Schnauzer is a robust, sinewy, nearly square dog with a temperament that combines high spirits, reliability, strength, endurance and vigour. The head is strong, the eyes dark

◀ **Schipperke**

◀ **Standard Schnauzer**

▼ **Giant Schnauzer**

▲ Scottish Terrier

▲ Sealyham Terrier

▲ Shetland Sheepdog

and oval, the ears V-shaped, neat and dropping forward or cropped in countries where the operation is permitted. The tail is carried high and docked to three joints. The Schnauzers are loyal, stubborn and responsive to training.

Group. Utility. Working (AKC). Non-sporting (ANKC). Miniature Schnauzer: Terrier (AKC).

Size. Large (Giant Schnauzer) Medium (Standard Schnauzer) and Small (Miniature Schnauzer).

Coat. *Colour:* Pure black or pepper and salt. *Texture:* Hard and wiry, with a good undercoat.

SCOTTISH TERRIER

Origins. It is difficult to be precise about the history of the Scottish Terrier because the name has long and variously been used to describe any one of several terrier breeds which originate in Scotland. Certainly the terriers of Scotland have a long history dating back to the fourteenth century. Rawdon Lee writing at the end of the nineteenth century claimed that the Scottish Terrier was the original Skye Terrier.

Characteristics. The Scottish Terrier is a sturdy thick-set dog set on short legs, alert in carriage. The head gives the impression of being long for the size of dog, the almond-shaped eyes are dark brown, the ears neat, pointed and erect. The muscular neck is of moderate length set into long sloping shoulders. The back is short and very muscular, the hindquarters are remarkably powerful with big and wide buttocks. This dog is a stubborn individualist.

Group. Terrier.

Size. Small.

Coat. *Colour:* Black, wheaten or brindle of any colour. *Texture:* The undercoat is short, dense and soft, the outer coat harsh, dense and wiry.

SEALYHAM TERRIER

Origins. This is one of the very few breeds which owe their development to the work and inspiration of one man. Between 1850 and 1891 Captain John Edwardes of Sealyham in Haverfordwest, Wales, set out to develop a strain of terrier which would be able to hunt fox, otter or even badger. By 1910 the breed was appearing in the show ring.

Characteristics. The general appearance should be of a free-moving sturdy little dog. The eyes are dark and round, and the ears falling at the side of the cheeks are rounded. The neck is fairly long, thick and muscular, the forelegs short, strong and straight. The body is of medium length, the hindquarters are powerful, and the tail is carried erect. The Sealyham can be devoted to its owner but has an obstinate streak.

Group. Terrier.

Size. Small.

Coat. *Colour:* Usually white. *Texture:* Long, hard and wiry.

▲ Shih Tzu

▲ Siberian Husky

SHETLAND SHEEPDOG

Origins. The Shetland Sheepdog is a distinctive breed produced in response to the peculiar demands made by the hard climate and terrain of the isolated northerly islands of Scotland. The breed is undoubtedly of ancient origin but, due to lack of records, we know little of its history before it achieved the distinction of being recognized as a breed by the Kennel Club in 1914.

Characterstics. The Shetland is a dog of great beauty, intelligence and alertness. It should be affectionate and responsive towards its owner, but may be reserved towards strangers. The head is refined, a long blunt wedge tapering from ear to nose; the eyes dark brown and almond-shaped. The ears are small and carried semi-erect with the tips dropping forward. The neck is muscular, the chest is deep, the hindquarters broad.

Group. Working. Herding (AKC).

Size. Small.

Coat. *Colour:* Tricolour, sable, silvery blue-grey, black and white or black and tan. *Texture:* The outer coat is long, harsh and straight, the undercoat short and close. The mane and frill should be abundant.

SHIH TZU

Origins. Records dating from AD 624 show that dogs were given as tribute to the Tang Emperor by K'iu T'ai; paintings and carvings show these dogs and others offered in later tributes to have been very like the modern Shih Tzu. Whether these dogs originated in Tibet or in some part of the Byzantine Empire is not known, but the centuries of careful breeding which the Chinese have devoted to the breed must be regarded as sufficient to regard the breed as Chinese.

Characteristics. The Shih Tzu is a very active, lively and alert dog with a distinctly arrogant carriage. The head is broad and round, wide between the eyes with a short square muzzle. The eyes are large, dark and round and the ears are pendulous. The tail is heavily plumed and carried well over the back. The Shih Tzu makes a busily important housedog, friendly and affectionate.

Group. Utility (KC). Toy (AKC). Non-sporting (ANKC).

Size. Small.

Coat. *Colour:* Various. *Texture:* Long and dense but not curly, with a good undercoat.

SIBERIAN HUSKY

Origins. This is a breed forged in the hardest imaginable environment among the Chukchi people who inhabited the frozen wastelands of north-eastern Asia. The Chukchi were nomadic hunters who depended for their survival on the strength, speed, courage, intelligence and toughness of the breed they had developed by rigorous selection.

Characteristics. The general appearance is of a medium-sized working dog, quick and light on its feet and graceful in action. The moderately compact and well-furred body, erect ears and brash tail suggest its northern heritage. Its characteristic gait is smooth and seemingly effortless. The dog adapts well as a pet and companion.

Group. Working. Non-Sporting (ANKC)

Size. Large.

Coat. *Colour:* All colours, from black to pure white. *Texture:* Double, of medium length; the undercoat dense and soft, the overcoat straight and smooth-lying.

Skye Terrier

Origins. Some authorities argue that the Skye Terrier and the present Scottish Terrier share common origins and that the modern Skye, with its extraordinary appearance, is a fairly recent development.

Characteristics. The Skye Terrier is a one man dog, distrustful of strangers, but not vicious. The head is long with powerful jaws, the dark eyes are close set and full of expression. Ears may be prick or drop and should be fringed with hair. The neck is long and slightly crested, the shoulders are broad, the chest deep and the forelegs short and muscular. The body is long and low to the ground, the hindquarters well developed and muscular.

Group. Terrier.

Size. Small.

Coat. *Colour:* Dark or light grey, fawn, cream, black, all with black points. *Texture:* A soft, short, woolly, close undercoat is hidden by the long, hard, straight, flat topcoat which is such a characteristic feature of the breed.

► **Skye Terrier**

Sloughi

Origins. Although the Arab races are not particularly fond of dogs, they treat the Sloughi as if it were one of the family. The nomadic tribes of North Africa value the Sloughi as a hunter and as a guard. Much of their hunting takes place at night to avoid the heat of the sun and when the quarry is active. As a consequence of this the breed has itself a tendency to be nocturnal in its habits.

▼ **Sloughi**

▲ Soft-coated Wheaten Terrier

▲ Staffordshire Bull Terrier

Characteristics. The general appearance of the Sloughi is of a very racy dog, with a frame impressive for its muscular leanness and delicacy. In outline the breed closely resembles a racing Greyhound. This dog makes a good reliable pet.

Group. Hound (KC).

Size. Large.

Coat. *Colour:* Sable or all shades of fawn with or without a black mask. *Texture:* Smooth and close.

SOFT-COATED WHEATEN TERRIER

Origins. The breed shares much the same origins and original purpose in life as the Kerry Blue Terrier; indeed it could almost be argued that the two are but colour varieties of the same breed, their different appearance owing more to the hair-dresser's art than to any basic differences. Legend has it that terriers the colour of ripe wheat existed in Ireland before dogs from the wrecked ships of the Armada introduced the colour which produced the Kerry Blue.

Characteristics. The soft wheaten-coloured coat is the most obvious characteristic of the breed. In Ireland and in America the coat is trimmed, in Britain trimming is objected to by many breeders. The breed should be good tempered, spirited and game, full of confidence and humour; they make delightful, affectionate companions. Wheatens are of medium size, compact, strong and well built, standing foursquare with head and tail up. A good Wheaten makes a very attractive sight

Group. Terrier.

Size. Medium.

Coat. *Colour:* Wheaten. *Texture:* Soft and silky, loosely waved or curled.

STAFFORDSHIRE BULL TERRIER

Origins. One of the two gladiatorial members of the terrier group evolved to fight with other dogs or to bait bull, bear or badger. The old breeds used for these savage sports were mastiffs or Bulldogs and a dash of terrier blood was introduced to give speed and agility and so laid the foundations of the 'Bull and Terrier' breed. The breed still enjoys a good fight, but with people, particularly children, it is a most faithful companion and an excellent and fearless guard.

Characteristics. The Staffordshire has great strength for its size and, although very muscular, should be active and agile. The head is short, the skull broad, the fore-face short and powerful. The eyes are round and look straight ahead. The neck is short and muscular, set into wide, strong shoulders. The tail is low set and carried like an old-fashioned pump handle. This dog needs firm training.

Group. Terrier.

Size. Medium.

Coat. *Colour:* Red, fawn, white, black or blue, or

any of these colours with white. Brindle or brindle and white. *Texture*: Smooth, short and close to the skin.

SUSSEX SPANIEL

Origins. This distinctive spaniel has been bred since the eighteenth century, when breeding was organized in a very different way, utilizing large numbers of sturdy well-trained dogs. Conditions have now changed and spaniels with a greater turn of speed and able to cover more ground have become more popular.

Characteristics. The Sussex Spaniel is massive and strongly built, with a characteristic rolling movement quite unlike that of any other spaniel. The skull is broad, the eyes are fairly large, hazel coloured with a soft expression. Ears are thick, fairly large and lobular. The neck is long, strong and slightly arched, not carrying the head much above the level of the back. The shoulders are sloping, the chest is deep and wide, the back wide and fairly long. Hindquarters are strongly developed. This dog is very loyal and may attach itself to one person.

Group. Gundog. Sporting (AKC).

Size. Medium.

Coat. *Colour:* Rich golden liver. *Texture:* Abundant and flat, with ample undercoat.

▲ **Sussex Spaniel**

SWEDISH VALLHUND

Origins. Both the resemblance and the similar function in life argue some shared ancestor between the Väsgötaspitz and the Corgi. The fact that both have distinct Spitz characteristics seems to indicate origins in Scandinavia. This Swedish breed has only recently been recognized, in 1948.

Characteristics. The breed is low slung, long in the body, small and muscular. The carriage and expression indicate vigilance, courage and energy. The tail is naturally short, not docked. The Vallhund is an intelligent, loyal dog.

Group. Working (KC).

Size. Small.

Coat. *Colour:* Grey. *Texture:* Of fair length, hard and dense, the undercoat fine and tight.

T

TIBETAN SPANIEL

Origins. Throughout ancient history the rulers of China, Tibet and neighbouring countries showed

► **Swedish Vallhund**

great interest in the small breeds of dogs which they kept at their courts and which were their constant companions. These dogs were exchanged between the courts, dogs from Tibet moving to China with possibly the Happa becoming the ancestor of the Pekingese and the Carla becoming the ancestor of the Tibetan Spaniel.

Characteristics. The breed is gay, intelligent and aloof with strangers. The head is small in proportion to the body and proudly carried. The ears are of medium size and pendulous. The neck is moderately short, the body fairly long. The forelegs are slightly bowed, the feet small and neat. The tail is set high, richly plumed and carried in a gay curl over the back when moving.

Group. Utility. Non-sporting (AKC).

Size. Small.

Coat. *Colour:* Various. *Texture:* Double coat, silky in texture.

TIBETAN TERRIER

Origins. Legend places the Tibetan Terrier's origins in the Lost Valley of Tibet and, with a breed whose history stretches back 2000 years, legend may be as reliable as supposed fact. In Tibet they are called 'Luck Bringers' or 'Holy Dogs' and were kept purely as companions and symbols of status. The breed is healthy, tough and affectionate, an ideal companion.

Characteristics. The general appearance is rather like that of an Old English Sheepdog in miniature. The head is of medium length and slightly domed, the eyes are large and dark, the ears V-shaped and pendant. The forelegs are straight, the hind legs slightly longer. The body is compact and powerful for its size. The tail is of medium length, set fairly high and carried in a gay curl over the back; it is very well feathered and often has a kink near the end.

Group. Utility. Non-sporting (AKC).

Size. Small.

Coat. *Colour:* Any colour except chocolate or liver. *Texture:* Double-coated, the undercoat of fine wool and the top coat profuse, long and either straight or waved.

W

WEIMARANER

Origins. The breed has a history which only goes back to the beginning of the nineteenth century when it was produced by crossing Bloodhounds

◀ Tibetan Spaniel

▼ Weimaraner

◀ Tibetan Terrier

with native German hunting breeds, such as the Red Schweisshund, and became known simply as the Weimar Pointer. In its early days the Weimaraner was used to hunt Europe's larger game, boar and deer, but is now very much at home fulfilling the duties of a gundog accompanying modern sportsmen. The Weimaraner is not a kennel dog, being happier and working better when living as part of the family. The breed's distinctive grey colour, silent and effortless movement have earned it the popular name of 'Grey Ghost'.

Characteristics. The Weimaraner is fearless, friendly, protective and obedient. It is a large grey dog with considerable presence. Its head is moderately long and aristocratic; the eyes are unusually light, amber or blue-grey, and the ears long and lobular. The forelegs are straight and strong, the hindquarters powerful. The body is square in outline and the tail is docked.

Group. Gundog. Sporting (AKC).

Size. Large.

Coat. *Colour:* Silver grey or shades of mouse. *Texture:* Short, smooth and sleek. In the long-haired Weimaraner the coat is 2.5–5.8 cm (1–2 in) long on the body and the limbs are feathered.

Welsh Corgi (Cardigan)

Origins. The breed shares a common heritage with its more popular cousin from Pembrokeshire. (See below).

Characteristics. Apart from the fact that Pembrokes are without tails and Cardigans have good full ones, the two share considerable and obvious similarities. The tail in the Cardigan is moderately long and set in line with the body, closely resembling the brush of a fox. The Cardigan is also slightly larger, with not such a sharp head, and larger ears.

Group. Working. Herding (AKC).

Size. Small.

Coat. *Colour:* Any colour except white. Blue merles may be wall-eyed. *Texture:* Short or medium, and of hard texture.

◄ Welsh Corgi, Cardigan

Welsh Corgi (Pembroke)

Origins. The two breeds of Corgi, the Pembroke and the Cardigan, and the as yet unrecognized Lancashire Heeler, were developed as specialist cattle dogs sometime during the twelfth century. The Corgi is said to have been brought over from Holland by Flemish weavers who settled around Haverfordwest in west Wales. Certainly such a history would do much to explain the distinct Spitz characteristics carried by the Corgi and which may have produced, crossed with the Old Black and Tan Terriers, the lighter built Black and Tan Heelers.

Characteristics. The Corgi is low set, strong, sturdily built and active, giving an impression of substance and stamina in small space. The head in all respects is foxy, the neck and body fairly long. The legs are short, the tail is docked as short as possible, though some puppies are born without a tail.

Group. Working. Herding (AKC).

Size. Small.

Coat. *Colour:* Red, sable, fawn, black and tan or with white markings on legs, chest and neck. *Texture:* Short or medium length and of hard texture.

Welsh Springer Spaniel

Origins. History does not record the advent of the Welsh Springer Spaniel as a distinctive breed, though it is certain that red and white spaniels very similar to the modern Welsh have existed for very many years since they are to be seen in many old sporting drawings and paintings. The Welsh Springer is a first-class gundog and makes a good companion as well as an eye-catching show dog.

Characterstics. The head is of moderate length

▲ Welsh Corgi, Pembroke

and slightly domed. The eyes are hazel or dark, the ears set moderately low and comparatively small. The neck is long and muscular, neatly set into long, sloping shoulders. Forelegs are of medium length, straight, and moderately feathered; quarters are strong and muscular. The Welsh Springer is a happy, active and willing dog.

Group. Gundog. Sporting (AKC).

Size. Medium.

Coat. *Colour:* Dark rich red and white. *Texture:* Straight and thick and silky.

▲ **Welsh Springer Spaniel**

Welsh Terrier

Origins. The Welsh Terrier is the counterpart of the Lakeland which in some ways it resembles. It was used to accompany the hunts in Wales in order to drive fox or otter from places of refuge. Until the turn of the century there appears to have been little distinction made between the Welsh and the Old English Black and Tan Terrier.

Characteristics. The Welsh Terrier has a gay, volatile disposition and is only rarely shy. It is affectionate, obedient and biddable. The head is flat and rather wider between the ears than a Fox Terrier, the jaw is powerful. The eyes are small and dark, the ears are V-shaped and carried forward and close to the cheek. The neck is slightly arched and slopes gracefully into long shoulders. The body is short, the forelegs straight and muscular, the hindquarters strong with muscular thighs.

Group. Terrier.

Size. Small.

Coat. *Colour:* Black and tan. *Texture:* Wiry, hard, very close and abundant.

West Highland White Terrier

Origins. According to the Malcolm family, the breed has its origins in Poltalloch, Scotland, where for three generations the family bred these white terriers. Certainly the breed was called the Poltalloch Terrier and the Roseneath Terrier, but it is likely that these places only concentrated on devel-

◀ **Welsh Terrier**

▲ **Whippet**

▲ **West Highland White Terrier**

▲ **Yorkshire Terrier**

oping and refining a white strain of the old Scottish Terriers. In so doing, they produced a smart, courageous and hardy little sporting dog, which is now much valued as a companion and has achieved considerable success in the show ring.

Characteristics. The general appearance is that of a small, game and hardy terrier, with plenty of self-esteem. The breed is strongly built, deep in the chest and back ribs, the back level and the quarters powerful. The head is slightly domed, the eyes are set wide apart and are dark in colour giving a sharp and intelligent look. The ears are small and carried erect. The tail is 12.7–15 cm (5–6 in) long, not docked and is carried jauntily.

Group. Terrier.

Size. Small.

Coat. *Colour:* Pure white. *Texture:* Outer coat hard and free from curl, undercoat short, soft and close.

WHIPPET

Origins. The Whippet is not, in spite of obvious similarities, a miniature Greyhound. It is the working man's sight hound, intended for coursing small ground game and for racing against its fellows. The breed came into existence in the early nineteenth century and the breed's speed over a furlong made exciting racing, a sport which predates the more commercially organized Greyhound races which still flourish in England.

Characteristics. Whippets convey an impression of balanced muscular power and strength allied to elegance; the dog is built for speed. The skull is long and lean, the expression bright and alert, the ears fine and rose-shaped. The neck is long, muscular and slightly arched, the chest is very deep, the back broad. The tail is long and tapering. The breed is gentle and affectionate.

Group. Hound.

Size. Medium.

Coat. *Colour:* Various. *Texture:* Fine, short, as close as possible.

Y

YORKSHIRE TERRIER

Origins. Although by Victoria's reign the Yorkshire Terrier, because of its diminutive size and glamorous coat, had been taken up as a fashionable pet, its origins are much more humble. Originating among the Scottish Terriers, the breed was taken up in the 1840s by Yorkshire weavers who wanted a sporting little terrier for ratting expeditions or for competition in the rat pits. The breed in those days weighed anything up to to 9 kg (20 lb) with 4.5 kg (10 lb) being regarded as an ideal but, when killing rats ceased to be part of the breed's purpose in life, the size was even further reduced.

Characteristics. The Yorkshire Terrier is very compact and neat, its carriage conveying an air of importance. It is a brave, intelligent and affectionate little dog. The head is rather small and flat, the eyes dark and sparkling and the ears small, V-shaped and carried erect or semi-erect. The forelegs are straight, the body very compact with a good loin and level topline. The colour and length of the coat is very important for a show dog.

Group. Toy.

Size. Small.

Coat. *Colour:* A dark steel blue, with rich bright tan markings. *Texture:* Long and perfectly straight, glossy and of a fine silky texture.

▶ Yorkshire Terrier

THE NEW PUPPY

A new puppy is a delight but it needs special care to ensure that it grows into a healthy, well-adjusted dog. As a responsible owner, you will want to smooth its first days with its new family and make sure that it has a comfortable place to sleep, a suitable diet and plenty of love and attention. The puppy will need to be house-trained, to get used to a collar and lead and to learn the rules it is expected to live by. The way that you handle these early lessons can make all the difference to your dog's behaviour in the future.

You will probably be collecting your puppy at about seven weeks old, when it is fully weaned and at an age when it should adapt well to a change of ownership. Remember that going to its new home is one of the most unsettling and frightening experiences of its life. Its family and safe, familiar surroundings are left behind and it is being subjected to a bewildering variety of new scents, sights and sounds. A young puppy is still a baby and, like a baby, needs a great deal of affection. A bitch constantly licks, caresses and pushes her puppies about in play and 'talks' to them in soft tones, usually inaudible to humans. You will find that a tense or worried puppy will relax at the touch of a sensitive and sympathetic hand and a quiet, reassuring tone of voice.

Every dog should be trained in basic obedience and a well-behaved pet will fit better into your family life, to the benefit of everyone concerned. However, your new puppy will have no notion of the way it is expected to behave. You can indicate what you consider acceptable house manners from the beginning by making sure that the puppy knows which parts of the house and which items of furniture are out of bounds, that slippers are not for chewing and that begging at the table is not allowed. However, these early lessons must be taught with gentleness and patience. If you shout or smack, the puppy is more likely to associate the punishment with its new owner and the new home in general rather than with the 'wrongdoing'. This kind of treatment can turn a bold, friendly puppy into a timid, nervous creature within a matter of days, leaving the puzzled owners wondering what has gone wrong.

Dogproofing Your Home

A young puppy will chew everything within reach so you will need to keep slippers, gloves, children's toys and houseplants well out of reach and loop up any trailing electrical flex. Think how you would behave with an active toddler in the house and follow the same regime: make sure that the puppy cannot get into your stores of household disinfectant, dry cleaning fluid, pesticides, anti-freeze or even mothballs. You may need to fix a wire netting guard on the underside of an open tread staircase or over a stairwell, to prevent any damaging fall. One way of keeping the puppy out of trouble is to partition the area around the puppy's bed. You can use a pen with wire mesh panels and wooden frames, specially made for the job and obtainable through pet shops or improvize with a fireguard or a baby's discarded playpen, with wire mesh attached to the sides to prevent a tiny puppy from squeezing through the bars.

You will also need to guard against hazards out in the garden or yard; cover swimming pools and ponds until the puppy has been taught to keep away

A child's cot, lined with a washable blanket, can make a useful bed for puppies in the early weeks, keeping them out of danger and mischief when you are not there to supervise.

from them. Although most dogs can swim naturally, they cannot clamber out up steep sides and might drown through panic or exhaustion. You will need to fence off an area of the garden for your puppy's use or make sure that fences and gates are escape-proof.

Equipment

The puppy will need its own bed, set in a draught-free area. Initially, a sturdy grocery carton with a piece cut out of the front to allow easy access, lined with an old sweater or blanket, is ideal. It should be just large enough for the puppy to lie on its side; this size will give enough room for comfort but will convey a feeling of security. As the box becomes chewed and soiled, it can be replaced by another. It is pointless to provide young puppies with smart wicker baskets as these are almost made to be chewed and in any case, this type of bed is hard to keep clean and lets in draughts. Beds made of heavy plastic are fairly resistant to chewing, light in weight and easy to wash and disinfect. Another hygienic type of bed is the one filled with polystyrene beads that take on the shape of the dog, making a warm nest; these have removable, washable covers.

Your dog must have its own bowls and dishes of a design suitable for its breed so that it can eat and drink comfortably without getting its nose or ears submerged; these should be kept separate from the crockery used by the rest of the family. Plastic and aluminium dishes are too light and will frequently be upended, so a heavy pottery bowl may be more suitable.

Make sure that your puppy's toys are specially made for dogs. It will enjoy rawhide chews, a hard rubber ball too large to be swallowed and a substantial toy with an exciting squeaker inside. Make sure that none of the toys is made from soft rubber, that they have no sharp edges and no bits that can be bitten off and swallowed.

Collecting Your Puppy

Try to bring home your puppy at a time when the house is peaceful, without too much coming or going and when you will have plenty of time to spend with the little dog. Morning is the best time for collection, so that your new pet will have time to get used to its surroundings before you leave it alone for the night. If possible, take someone with you when you collect the puppy by car, so that one of you can wrap it in a warm towel or blanket and hold it on your lap. If you have to collect the puppy alone, it is wise to buy a cardboard box from the pet shop. Have plenty of newspaper and a roll of kitchen paper with you in case the puppy is sick.

If you are buying a purebred dog, the breeder will provide you with a copy of its pedigree, the record of its ancestry going back some four or five

Some breeds, such as the Spaniel, need feeding bowls designed to keep their ears out of their food.

Toys will give your puppy a great deal of pleasure but they should be carefully chosen so that they cannot be swallowed or chewed into pieces.

Puppies are always curious and love to explore, so make sure that they are in no danger, either indoors or outdoors.

A child and a puppy can spend long hours together but children must be taught that the little animal is not a toy and must be treated properly.

generations. If the puppy has been registered with the Kennel Club, you will also have a certificate to enable its particulars to be officially transferred to your ownership. You should check when the puppy was last wormed and when worming will be due again and whether any vaccinations have been given. Many breeders will give a detailed diet sheet but if not, find out what the puppy has been eating and follow the same diet, at least at the beginning, making any changes gradually.

Get home as quickly and smoothly as possible, holding the puppy close for comfort and talking to it in a soothing voice. At the end of the journey, the first thing the puppy will need to do is to relieve itself, so take it outside first and give it plenty of praise when it performs. After that, take it indoors and offer a small milk and cereal feed. It may accept the food or it may be too nervous to eat. If it refuses the meal and whines, wrap it in its blanket and put it in its prepared bed for a nap. Puppies spend a lot of time sleeping and this is necessary for their well-being, so leave it in peace and make sure that other members of the family are not constantly petting and cuddling it. On the other hand, it should not be left completely alone for long at first. At this stage, the puppy's play periods are about half an hour long, interspersed with long sleep sessions.

At night, play with the puppy until it is sleepy, then take it outside for a final elimination. As this is the first night it has spent alone, the puppy is likely to cry and whine. A well-wrapped stone hot water bottle will give it something comforting to snuggle up to and a ticking clock in a corner of the bed, simulating the mother's heartbeat, can help. Some owners decide that ignoring any sounds of distress is the most sensible course, as the puppy will quickly adapt and realize that there is no reason for fright; others go down a couple of times during the night to soothe the new pet. If you do this, it is important to maintain a matter-of-fact approach as you do not want the puppy to learn that it only has to make a noise to bring a sympathetic person running. You may get round the problem by putting a pen in a corner of your bedroom as this will give the new arrival a much greater sense of security. You can then accustom the puppy to spending short periods shut up alone during the day before you leave it alone for a whole night.

Children and Puppies

A healthy puppy is naturally playful and full of fun, so it is bound to enjoy playing with children. However, they should understand that the puppy is not a toy; they must never be allowed to smack it, pull it around on a lead or overdo the playing so that the puppy becomes too excited or exhausted. Any teasing at this stage may lead to aggressive behaviour that will be difficult to cure later. They should not feed sweets and tidbits to the puppy or throw small toys for it to chase, as it may swallow them and choke.

Encourage the children to keep the puppy's bedding tidy, change the water in its bowl and help prepare its meals. They can help to groom the little dog and get it used to having its ears, mouth, paws and tail examined without fuss. They need to know that they should never pick up a puppy by the forelimbs or by the scruff of the neck. Teach them to hold it carefully with two arms encompassing both fore and hindlimbs to give control and support.

Make sure that children do not play in any area where dogs urinate or defecate, teach them that they must discourage the puppy from licking their faces and that they should wash after playing with the dog.

Introduction to Other Pets

When introducing a new puppy to established pets, you need to ensure that the older animal has no cause for jealousy. Arrange the meeting between a puppy and an older dog in the garden. Hold the older dog on its lead, giving it plenty of attention and fuss as you bring the new puppy forward. They will probably sniff one another thoroughly then may begin some excited form of play but do not let the games get out of hand; the older dog may become exhausted or it may hurt the puppy unintentionally. If they get along reasonably well, then let the older dog loose and encourage them both to follow you into the house. In this way, the dog will feel that it has made the decision to bring the puppy into the family. Feed the dogs separately at first and keep the puppy in a pen whenever you leave the two alone together. So long as the older dog is given no cause for resentment, the two should become inseparable pals.

If the ruse does not work, you will have to spend a good deal of time with the dogs while they get used to one another. Do not allow growling and praise any sign of friendly behaviour. Do not leave them alone together but have them in the same room as often as possible when you are there to supervise. It is rare for two dogs to be completely incompatible and they will usually make friends eventually.

Before introducing a puppy to the family cat, trim the cat's front claws. The dog's first instinct is to rush forward and try to sniff the cat all over; the cat will resent this and try to claw the dog's nose and if the claws are sharp, the puppy will be hurt and upset. Most cats know exactly how to put a cheeky puppy in its place but it is important that they have a high shelf as a safe haven. The cat may spend a good deal of time away from home over the first few days, or even weeks, but it is important to give it a good welcome every time it comes in and show it that its place has not been usurped. Some cats end up sharing the dog's basket; others remain aloof.

Diet

From weaning until four months, a puppy needs four meals daily, two of meat and biscuit and two of milk and cereal. The biscuit should be good quality wheatmeal; the meat can be fresh meat, cooked and minced, or a canned meat specially prepared for puppies. If you use fresh meat, add a little bone meal for extra calcium. Cow's milk or diluted evaporated milk can be thickened by adding fine cereal of the sort made for human babies. Give a milky meal first thing in the morning and at teatime and meat meals at midday and dinner time.

When the puppy reaches four months, discontinue the first of the milk meals and bring the times of the other meals forward slightly, increasing the amounts as necessary. Observation will tell you if

The new puppy should be carefully introduced to other pets, though the family cat will soon put the newcomer in its place if it becomes over-familiar. It is a good idea to trim the cat's claws in advance.

your puppy is getting the right amount of food. If you are overfeeding, the puppy will be lethargic, with thickening around the waist and neck. If your puppy's ribs are showing through its skin, you are not giving enough food. At six months, feed two meals a day, both meat and meal; from nine months, you can feed one meal a day. This is sufficient for most dogs but you can split this into two meals a day if you prefer. Very small dogs, giant breeds and old dogs will probably benefit from two meals a day; this ensures that the stomach is not overloaded and makes digestion easier.

Puppy Health

Vaccination. Your dog needs vaccination to protect against the major canine diseases. An unvaccinated dog can easily become infected when playing in parks or sniffing round lampposts, staying in boarding kennels, taking part in dog shows or anywhere that it mixes with other dogs. Puppies are particularly susceptible to infection and should not be taken out of their home and garden until their vaccination programme is complete. They should receive a combined first vaccination against distemper, hepatitis and the two forms of leptospirosis at 6–8 weeks of age, with the second half of the course at about 12 weeks. Vaccination against canine parvovirus, a comparatively new disease, can be given on the same schedule. Booster injections should be given regularly throughout the dog's life.

Rabies vaccine, given at 9 weeks with a second dose a year later, is essential in countries where the disease is present. Subsequent vaccinations will be at one or three year intervals, depending on the vaccine used.

Worming. Most vets will advise routine fortnightly worming of puppies up to the age of three months. A well-reared puppy will have been wormed by the breeder as a matter of course. Your vet will prescribe a suitable product; proprietary medicines bought from a pet shop may not be suitable.

Teething. At about four months old, the puppy teeth are pushed out by the growth of the adult set. Most puppies teethe without any trouble, though occasionally sore gums will put them off their food for a day or two. If a puppy does go off its food, keep a sharp eye on it to make sure that teething is the cause and that it is not sickening for something.

Learning Its Name

One of the first things a puppy needs to know is its own name. Choose a name as soon as you acquire your pet and stick to it; changing names after the first couple of weeks because you think of something better or using 'Pup' some of the time, will leave the animal thoroughly confused and basic

A puppy that chews its owner's shoes must learn the meaning of the word 'No!', reinforced with a reproving index finger. Always give the puppy a suitable chewy toy as a substitute.

training will be more difficult. A short one-syllable or a simple, flowing two-syllable name is best and it should not sound too much like the command words used in training; 'No', 'Come', 'Sit', 'Stay', 'Wait', 'Down', 'Leave' and 'Heel'. You could hardly blame a dog called Kit for bounding towards you every time you told it to 'Sit' and if you call your dog Joe you may have to invent a different word for forbidding bad behaviour.

The puppy should associate its name with pleasure, so that it will always answer to it willingly. Call it by name when giving food, offering a tidbit, a game or plenty of fuss. Do not use its name when you are scolding. Call your puppy in a coaxing tone of voice. Attract its attention by clapping your hands, slapping your leg or something else that indicates that a game is possible. If your puppy ignores you, wait until it has finished what it is doing and try again when it is more likely to respond. Giving a command when it is unlikely to be obeyed only reinforces disobedience at this stage. Wait until the puppy looks as though it might come to you, then call it and when it comes, make a big fuss of it. If your pup is wilful and still fails to come, try turning and walking away slowly. This will often bring it bounding to your side, then you can pet and praise it.

Early Lessons

You will need to lay down rules for your puppy from the beginning and keep them. It is important to be consistent and every member of the family should help in teaching early lessons. No puppy will understand if it is allowed to snuggle into the best armchair one day and is shooed out of it the next. If you can prevent bad habits from forming in the first place – for instance, by making sure the puppy is always supervised when in the living room and not allowed to climb into the forbidden chair in the first place – you will find the whole training process much easier. Puppies are naturally lively and mischievous but you can often distract them from behaviour you consider unacceptable by giving them something else to do.

The puppy must learn the meaning of 'No', which should be said firmly, perhaps in a gruff voice like a growl, but not shouted. Dogs are very sensitive to nuances of tone and you can make use of this by the amount of enthusiasm or displeasure you show in

Play is very important in a puppy's life and this litter of Rhodesian Ridgebacks is learning the rough and tumble of family life. When you take a puppy into your home, you should continue the games it has learned to enjoy.

your voice. 'No' can be reinforced by a raised, reproving finger and if the puppy ignores this command, repeat it and physically stop the dog from its misdeed, perhaps emphasising your displeasure with a little shake. Never accept behaviour from your puppy that will be unacceptable in a full-grown dog. Make it clear that growling, for instance, is not allowed; give a little shake, hold the puppy up level with your eyes and rebuke it, even showing your teeth a little.

You will need to give plenty of praise and encouragement to compensate for the many times that you need to say 'No' and even the most wilful pet prefers petting to the stern chastisement of 'No'. Puppies vary in their need for encouragement; some are delighted with just a pat and a word of praise but others need a great deal of fuss to encourage good behaviour. Some dog-trainers suggest using a rolled-up newspaper as a training aid and with some dogs this may help but it is a risky tool. Extrovert dogs sometimes look on the waving newspaper as an invitation to a game rather than a mild punishment. The use of a newspaper may upset a nervous or introvert puppy and could engender resentment or aggressiveness.

Once the vaccination programme is complete, the puppy should be encouraged to mix with plenty of people outside the family circle and to become used to crowded situations and strange noises. If for instance, there is no man in the house, enlist the help of neighbours and friends to make sure that the dog does not build up a fear of men. It should also get used to children, even if there are none in your household, so that it will not behave unpredictably when confronted by children at some time in the future.

Play

The importance of play cannot be overemphasized. It is vital in preparing the young puppy both physically and mentally for adult life. When a puppy is taken from its canine family and made a part of your own, you will need to continue some of the games the young dog has come to enjoy. The commonest form of puppy play is the mock fight in which puppies in a litter engage in rough-and-tumble battles with each other. You can play such a game with your puppy. Taking care not to be too rough, push and roll it around on the floor, grasping the loose skin of the neck from time to time and giving it a little shake. The puppy will back off, then growl and pounce on your hand and arm and thoroughly enjoy the game. Never pull your hand sharply back, however, or the pup's sharp teeth could snag your skin. The puppy will snap, chew, and gnaw at your hand, but it will never close its jaws because the threats are all bluff. This form of play is designed to build up muscles and develop the reflexes. Another puppy game is 'tag', when young dogs take turns to chase one another. Here again you, as owner, can take the place of a litter mate and establish an excellent relationship with your dog.

It is imperative that your dog should both respect and really love you if you are to achieve good results from later training. The close relationship that develops from the early sharing of games gives an excellent start. When playing doggy games try to think and act like a dog yourself. Do not let the puppy become over-excited. The 'No!' command can be given to restrain its exuberance followed by praise and reward when the little dog relaxes.

Collars and Leads

A puppy can be taught to wear a collar from a very early age. The first collar can be of a cheap quality and must be very light in weight. It should be buckled around the neck, tight enough to stay on when the puppy lowers its head but loose enough for you to be able to insert two fingers between collar and neck. The collar must be checked at least every week; it is surprising how quickly puppies grow, and a tight collar can be dangerous. The puppy will soon accept its collar, and it may be left on all day if you wish. It is best to take it off at night, however, to prevent the puppy's neck from becoming marked.

Every dog should bear its owner's name and address on an engraved disc attached to the collar by means of a small split ring; it can then be transferred to each successive collar as the pup grows. Never add the dog's own name to the disc, as this could help anyone who tried to entice your dog away.

Your dog should not be allowed to mix with animals outside the family until its vaccination programme is complete and even then, it should never be allowed to roam unsupervised.

It is not necessary to lead-walk a young puppy, which gets all the exercise it needs by romping and playing in the house and garden. Indeed, long tiring walks can cause physical damage in the young dog. Nevertheless, you may begin lead training the puppy if you wish. Clip a light lead to the collar and allow the puppy to pull it around. After a few days hold the end of the lead and encourage the puppy to follow you. Always keep the puppy on your left-hand side; this will help with heel-work training later on. Praise the little dog when it walks eagerly alongside you. Never drag the puppy along by its lead, nor use it to tie him up or to smack him. The sight of the lead should fill a dog with excitement and anticipation of a training session or a walk; it should not be regarded as an instrument of punishment.

Never put a check chain or slip collar on a very young puppy. Such a collar could choke the little animal and the terrifying experience could make the puppy head-shy for many months afterwards.

When the puppy approaches six months serious training can begin. It is important to select the correct collars, leads, and other equipment according to the dog's size and breed. Short-necked and toy breeds often feel more comfortable wearing harnesses rather than collars, but harnesses are not recommended for a boisterous young puppy because continued pulling and romping could damage the animal's shoulders and forelegs. Rolled leather collars are comfortable to wear and are easy to keep in good condition. They need a weekly wash followed by an application of saddle soap, worked well in and then polished off and allowed to dry before the collar is put back on the dog.

Small dogs need long, light leads; short but strong dogs need long, tough leads and large dogs need short but strong leads. Avoid all leads with spring-clip attachments which can get caught in the fur, or snap shut on lips, ear flaps, and paws, causing pain and distress; sometimes they have to be removed by the veterinary surgeon. The best leads have clips which open and close with a sliding metal button. These are completely safe in use and are kept in good working order by applying one drop of fine machine oil to the sliding part whenever the lead is washed and cleaned.

Some owners delight in dressing-up their dogs and there are many designs available in both collars and leads. Heavily studded collars are quite unsuitable for a young dog. Others, in brightly coloured leather, are inclined to shed their dye if they get wet, tinting the dog's neck and sometimes giving rise to allergic reactions that cause irritation and distress. By visiting dog shows and training classes you will soon discover the sort of equipment knowledgeable dog handlers prefer to use.

GROOMING

If you establish a regular grooming routine from the earliest days with your puppy, it will grow up to enjoy the experience and the act of grooming will reinforce your dog's affection and trust. Grooming removes old dead hair and prevents the formation of felting or matting in long-coated breeds. It stimulates the blood supply to the skin, and this in turn improves the condition of the coat, giving the dog a healthier appearance. Correct grooming can also improve muscle tone in the dog's back and limbs and leads to a general sense of well-being.

Each type of coat requires its own set of grooming equipment. It is best to seek advice from the breeder at the outset in order to avoid buying expensive brushes and combs that turn out to be unsuitable.

Pure-bristle hairbrushes are needed for toy dogs and some of the smooth-coated breeds. Most types of dog require a good quality steel comb. Cheap combs are a false economy as the nickel plating soon wears through and peels off. Good combs have teeth with rounded ends so that they are not sharp enough to scratch the dog's skin. Choose a comb with correctly spaced teeth for your dog's coat type. Remember that the longer and thicker the coat, the wider the teeth should be spaced. Short satin-like coats are best rubbed down with a grooming mitten, and for short hard coats you can buy an excellent glove.

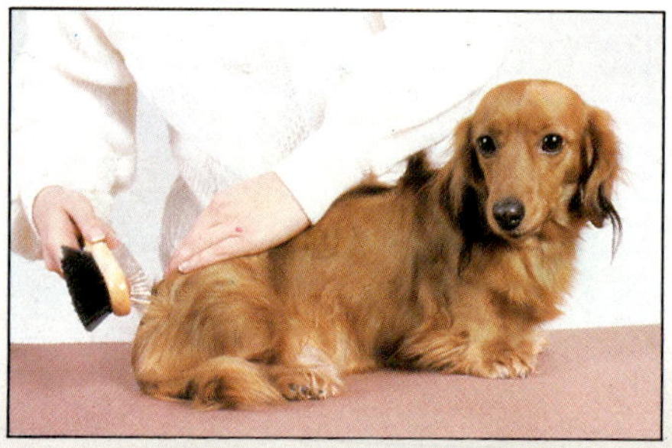

1 The top coat is lifted forward so that the undercoat may be thoroughly brushed.

2 The hind legs are dealt with first of all and groomed down to the pads.

3 The dog may be sensitive in this area and any knots should be teased out.

4 The tail must be treated gently, paying extra attention to the fine feathering.

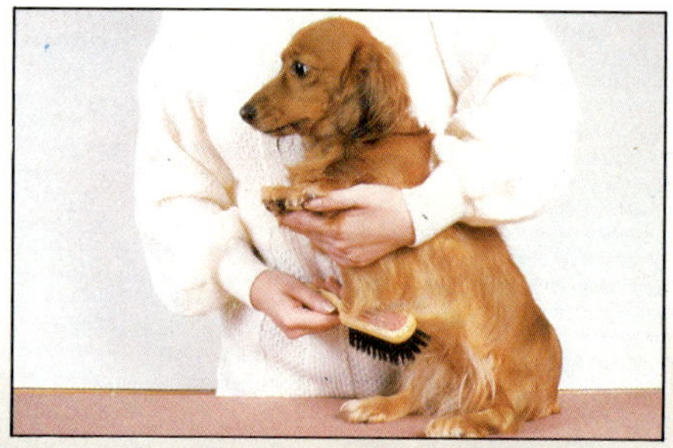

5 In using the wire brush, care must be taken to avoid scratching the dog's skin.

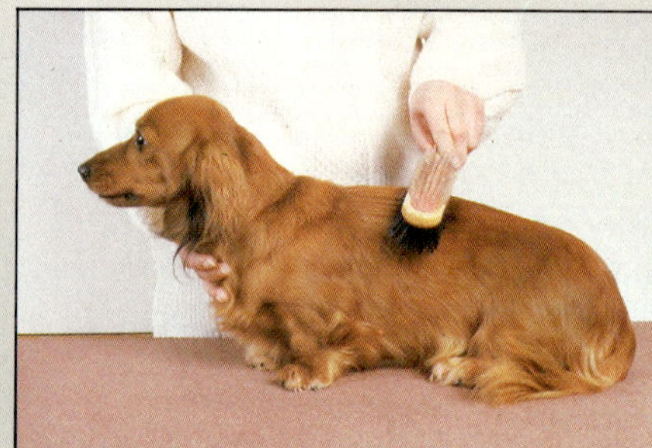

6 After dealing with the undercoat, each layer of top coat is smoothed into place.

7 The brush is then used down the throat and between the forelegs.

8 The bristle brush is used to groom the long, fine hair behind the dog's ears.

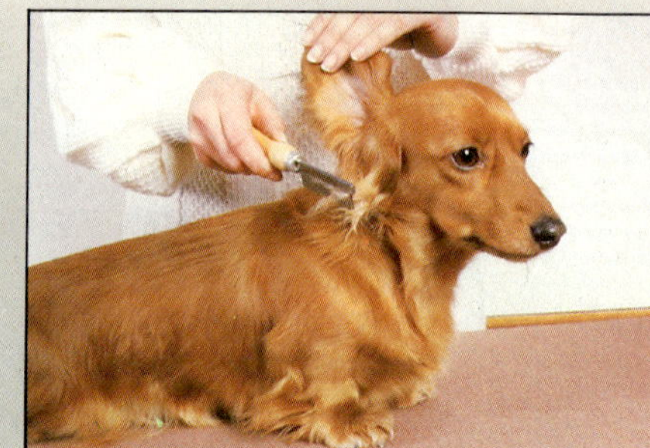

9 Careful combings of all soft areas can help to prevent the formation of matts.

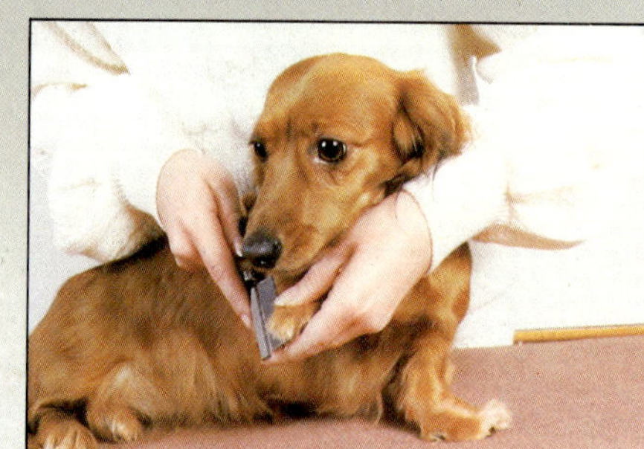

10 A fine-toothed comb removes grit, dirt and dust from the hair between the toes.

The coat. Generally speaking, the long-coated dogs need the most attention. A good wire brush is the best tool for separating the hairs. It should be of very good quality and have wire teeth that are neither too harsh nor too soft and are firmly set into a wooden base with a comfortable handle. The wire brush must always be used gently and with care, so that the teeth do not scratch the animal's skin.

When brushing out the long-coated varieties it is best to have the dog standing comfortably and relaxed on a bench or table. This is for your benefit rather than the dog's, for it will take some time to go right through the coat, and it can be a backbreaking job if you have to bend down to do it. If the dog is inclined to be restless, tie it up with a fairly short chain on its collar and talk soothingly to it throughout the grooming. Learning to stand still for grooming is an important feature of the dog's training and should be taught as thoroughly as any other part of the training programme.

Start at the rear end with one of the hind legs. Lift

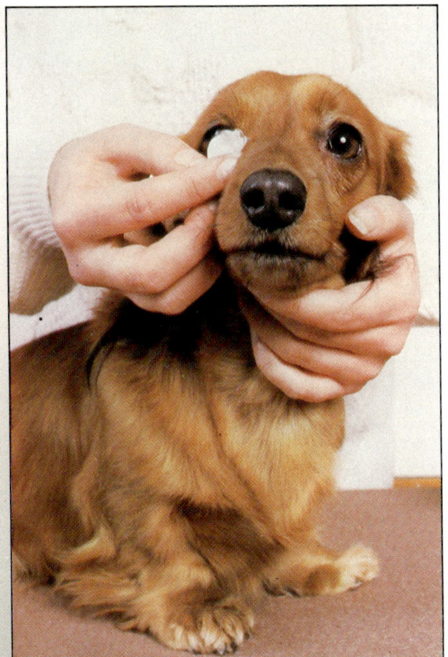

11 A fresh pad of dampened cotton wool is used carefully to clean each eye.

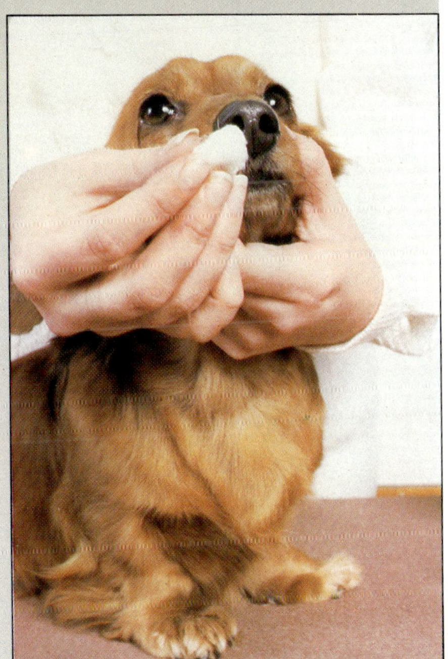

12 Another dampened pad is used to remove any discharge from the nostrils.

up the long outer hair and use the wire brush to go through all the undercoat of the thigh and down the lower leg. Brush carefully down the inner side of the thigh where the skin may be sensitive, then groom the top coat smoothly back into place. Repeat this procedure for the other hind leg, then thoroughly groom the rump and down the entire length of the tail. Brush out the front legs next, again lifting the top coat and grooming the undercoat first.

Grooming equipment

Pay particular care to the area between the forelimbs and along the belly; bear in mind that these parts can be ticklish and tender, and it will be necessary to tease out any small tangles or knots. In this area the hair can be extremely soft and fine, and easily mats together. Grass seeds and prickles get caught up in this soft hair and cause tangles which may have to be clipped out with blunt-nosed scissors if they are not promptly removed by brushing.

Groom the body hair from the shoulders back over the ribs to the hips. Brush down the neck and chest, then deal with any long hair on the face and the ears if they have long furnishings. After you have gone all over the dog with the wire brush and are certain that no areas have been missed, use a metal comb to deal with any feathering or extra long hair around the head, ears, legs or tail.

Follow the same general pattern for grooming short-coated breeds, starting at the hind legs, progressing to the body and finishing with the head. Most dogs benefit from a final polish with a soft, clean chamois leather or a silk or velvet pad to bring up a gloss on the coat. White legs and feet can be rubbed with powdered chalk to remove any trace of discoloration, and grooming powder will help to keep the hair from matting too quickly in fine, soft coats.

The feet. The dog's feet need careful attention, especially if there is long hair between the toes. All sorts of things can get caught here, like small stones or seeds which embed themselves into the soft skin and cause intense irritation. Feel between the toes with your fingers, then use a small comb to separate the hairs. The pads can receive a lot of punishment, especially when the animal takes a type of exercise outside the normal pattern. A dog which normally exercises on grass but has a day out involving lots of roads may damage its pads quite severely. A day at the beach may be an unusual and enjoyable experience for the dog but could possibly harm its feet. Take time during the daily grooming to examine the pads. Apply a little vegetable oil and work it well into the skin if they look dry or cracked, and pack in some antiseptic ointment if they are bruised or lacerated.

The face. Finish the grooming procedure by cleaning the dog's eyes and nostrils. Use a fresh piece of damp cotton wool to wipe out each eye and another piece for the nostrils. If the nose is inclined to dry up or become caked with dirt, try softening it with petroleum jelly rubbed well into the skin. The ears must be kept clean at all times. Use dry cotton buds to wipe away accumulated dust and wax from the complicated folds inside the ear flaps. Never use

Dalmatians should have a glossy look to their coats and this can be achieved by a daily rubbing down with a grooming glove to remove dead hairs and the dust collected from outdoor romping, and an occasional shampoo.

these buds to poke around within the ear, however. If you do so you may easily damage the ear's delicate structures.

HOUSE-TRAINING

House-training a puppy takes care, understanding and patience and you should use the puppy's built-in behaviour patterns as an aid to training. If you watch your puppy carefully you will see that after it wakes from a deep sleep it will start to play, then after 5 or 10 minutes it circles backwards before defecating. Play resumes for 15 or 20 minutes more, and is followed by an hour's sleep before the cycle starts again. Defecation also occurs about five minutes after each meal. It is not difficult, therefore, to guess when the puppy needs to be taken into the garden.

Prepare a section of the garden, preferably screened, for use by the dog. It is unsatisfactory to allow your dog to soil random areas of the lawn and flowerbeds; furthermore, the urine of the female dog soon patterns grassed areas with round brown patches. The chosen area of garden should be well drained and spread with a fairly thick layer of coarse sand ballast, gravel, or ashes topped by dry garden peat. Urine will filter through the top layers and droppings will soon dry out, when they can be removed and disposed of. A supply of fresh peat is useful for raking over the area from time to time.

During house-training the young puppy must be lifted and put on this chosen spot whenever you think it is likely to produce results. Remember to choose the most favourable times, five minutes after feeding or after the start of play. Say 'Be good!' or 'Hurry up!' and repeat it in a friendly but brisk tone. When your timing produces a successful result, be lavish in your praise of the puppy and rub its ears or pat its chest. Suitable praise words include 'Very good!', 'Good boy!' or 'Good girl!', as the case may be, with the emphasis always given to the first word. Only after several successes should you begin to punish errors; even then you must be satisfied that they are the fault of the puppy and not the consequence of your lack of attention.

On no account must you slap or smack a puppy at this stage; neither must you indulge in the old-fashioned and barbaric practice of rubbing the pup's nose in its puddles or messes. Any punishment must be given within 30 seconds of the misdeed, otherwise the puppy will not relate the action to the deed. The most effective punishment that you can give closely resembles the sort that would be given by the puppy's mother. A gruff 'No!' sounds very like a bitch's remonstrative growl and is quickly understood. Taking hold of the loose skin at the scruff of the puppy's neck and giving it a shake also works well and simulates canine behaviour, for a bitch will often shake her puppies in this way if they misbehave.

Always ensure that your puppy has a chance to relieve itself last thing at night and first thing in the morning as this will help to reinforce a good training regime.

Early failures in house-training are generally due to lack of surveillance. Dogs rarely bark to ask to go out but they do indicate their needs in many ways. During house-training you must be constantly attentive to the pup's needs.

Bladder control at night is slow to develop, so you should make sure that the puppy has the chance to relieve itself before settling down for the night, then get up early in the morning and take it outside at the first opportunity. The little dog will urinate as soon as it wakens, a routine that is quickly established. It will help to reinforce a successful training pattern. If your puppy persistently defecates at night, alter the feeding time by providing the last meal much earlier. This will give the puppy a chance to empty itself before bedtime. Replacing a milk and cereal feed with a smaller meat feed, or vice versa, sometimes helps, but as each puppy is different it is really a matter of trial and error with your own dog.

The kitchen with its washable floor is generally chosen as a young dog's first base. Any accidents should be wiped away with absorbent kitchen paper, the area washed with a mild solution of domestic bleach, then dried with more kitchen paper to prevent the puppy's pads from coming in contact with the chemical. Strong-smelling disinfectants could contain ingredients that are harmful to the young dog's health, but bleach is non-toxic and effectively kills all germs.

If you keep a small dog in an apartment, you may prefer paper-training, which involves spreading several thicknesses of newspaper on a washable floor and putting the puppy on this, instead of outside, for the purposes of elimination. The great disadvantage of this method of training is that the puppy may come to regard any newspaper as an invitation.

Keeping your dog on a lead at all times when out in the street is safer for the dog and for other people; these Chinese Crested Dogs look happy enough under restraint.

Car Travel

The sooner your puppy gets used to car travel, the better. The animal's first trip in a car has probably taken it away from familiar surroundings to a new home; all too often the next trip is to the vet for injections. If you allow the dog to associate car travel with frightening or unpleasant experiences, the journeys will always be a problem. Instead, take the puppy along when you take the children to school, so that they can play with it on the way, then feed it when you get home. Once the vaccinations are complete, take the puppy a short distance in the car, then take it out for a romp, so that it will associate the car with enjoyable events. If the puppy is obviously nervous of riding in the car, try feeding it inside when the vehicle is stationary and see that it has its own blanket and a favourite toy to play with.

Your dog must never be allowed to ride along with its head hanging out of the window, as this can cause serious inflammation of the eyes. You will need to train it to sit quietly on the lead and wait patiently until told to get into the car. It is even more important to train the dog to keep sitting quietly inside the car when the door is opened and to wait calmly until it is allowed to get out. It is very dangerous indeed if a boisterous dog leaps out in an uncontrolled way every time the car door opens.

Many puppies are carsick to begin with, so cover the seats with newspapers or old towels at first. Always allow at least three hours to elapse after the last meal before setting out on a journey and give the puppy a chance to exercise and empty itself before departure. Most dogs will grow out of travel sickness and the best way to cure them is to take them for frequent short runs so that they become accustomed to the car's motion.

If you leave a dog in the car at any time, make sure that it has adequate ventilation and that the car is parked in the shade on hot days. You should always see that the dog has a bowl of water on the floor.

Dogs and the Law

Every country has its own laws governing dogs and in countries like Australia or the United States, these can vary from state to state, so owners should check carefully on the regulations in their own area. In most parts of the United States dogs must be licensed once they reach four months of age and the licence is conditional on proof of vaccination against rabies. Some states have reduced licence fees for spayed or neutered dogs. 'Leash laws' and the strictness with which they are enforced, vary widely. In one city dogs may have to be muzzled on the streets or on the lead at all times when away from home; in others, they merely need a collar with a licence attached to be within the law.

In Britain, dog licences have been abolished but the law requires that every dog in a public place must wear a collar with an identity disc giving the owner's name and address. Owners can find themselves subject to heavy penalties if they allow their dogs to chase farm animals and farmers are within their rights to shoot a dog found worrying sheep. You are likely to be held responsible if your dog causes injury or damage to property or person and there are a number of insurance schemes covering this eventuality.

Responsible Dog Ownership

It is up to you, as an owner, to ensure that your dog does not cause annoyance to other people. First and foremost, you should train it to eliminate in the correct place, preferably in a suitably prepared corner of your own garden. Some parks have specially created 'dog lavatories' but dogs should never be allowed to use areas where children may play as toilets. If a city street is the only place where your pet can defecate, use a disposable scoop and bag to remove the mess immediately. Dogs get a bad name through fouling pavements but the owners, not the pets, are to blame.

When out in the street dogs should be on the lead at all times and your dog should never be allowed out alone. A loose dog may chase a cat across a road, causing an accident; it may be teased by children and react by biting; it may find and eat some poisonous substance. It is far safer, both for your dog and society at large, if you keep your pet at home except for its supervised exercise.

Gnawing at a large bone will keep a puppy happy for long periods and is good for its teeth but be sure that you never give the type of bone that will splinter.

TRAINING AND OBEDIENCE

Firm and sensitive training will turn a boisterous and uncontrolled animal into a tractable and obedient pet. A good grounding in obedience work means that you can control your dog under all circumstances so that you can keep it out of trouble and protect it from danger. Even if your dog already has a collection of bad habits – chewing your slippers, attacking your visitors, stealing food from the table or barking incessantly whenever you leave it alone – a suitable training regime, plus the right attitude and tone of voice, can achieve a transformation.

Training a dog in obedience takes a great deal of time and patience and the will to succeed but the results are well worth it. A spoiled dog easily becomes a neurotic dog; it will be happier and more settled if it leads the secure, structured life of a well-trained pet. Any dog can be trained and a mongrel may prove just as responsive as a pedigree animal. Some breeds do learn more easily than others but it is a mistake to think that the most intelligent dog will be the most trainable. A highly intelligent dog may be more resentful of new exercises, needing to be convinced that there is some point in performing them before it will respond to commands. A bold dog with an equable temperament is the best subject for training and may achieve high standards in obedience work while a shy, nervous dog may be able to master only basic exercises.

Joining a Class

Many owners feel that they need help in training their dogs and there are dog training classes and courses in most areas. Most people enrol dogs from the age of six months onwards but do not be discouraged if your dog is well beyond puppyhood and disobeys your every command. The old saying that 'you can't teach an old dog new tricks' is untrue; good training can do a great deal to remedy the situation. Training classes will teach you how to train your own dog and give the animal the chance to socialize with other dogs in a controlled setting. If possible, arrange to go along to a session as an observer before you enrol. You will then know what to expect and you will be able to see how other owners behave, so that you can avoid the more

Training classes can be useful in educating both dogs and owners; after initial training indoors, the class takes to the street, where obedience and good behaviour is essential.

Check chains can be invaluable in training but must be correctly fitted, as shown here, otherwise they can cause great discomfort.

obvious mistakes when you arrive with your own dog. Remember that not all teachers running classes are equally able; note how the teacher handles both dogs and owners and watch the dogs which have been coming to the class for some time. If they behave in the way you wish your dog to behave, then that is the class for you.

Preliminary classes cover all the basic commands; the more advanced classes are for those who wish to progress to the higher levels of obedience work required at competition standard. The classes can teach you valuable lessons but the success of training is up to you. You may need to modify the knowledge you receive to suit your dog's temperament and you will certainly need to reinforce the message of the lessons with daily practice. Many owners claim that the classes have failed, when the fault lies with them because they have not bothered to carry on with the necessary 'homework' between sessions.

Check Chains

A check chain collar is a very useful training aid. This is a chain with an equal-sized ring at either end; the lead is attached to one ring and the chain slips through the other ring to form a loop. Fitted correctly, the loop will hang loose round the dog's neck but a slight tug on the lead will tighten it so that you can attract the dog's attention or check undesirable behaviour. Remember when choosing a check collar that large curb links that twist to lie flat are the most comfortable. Narrow chains look very elegant but hurt the dog unduly, cutting into the neck whenever a corrective jerk is given on the lead. To find the correct length of chain collar for your dog, measure around the neck midway between the head and shoulders and add 50 mm (2 in) to the measurement; this is the length of chain your dog will need.

Use the check collar only during training sessions and remember to remove the dog's normal collar beforehand. You will not be able to use the check collar correctly if it is impeded by the normal one. Always remove it after training as a check collar can be dangerous if left on an unsupervised dog; the ring may catch on something and strangle the animal. Your pet will soon understand that the training collar means lesson time and if the sessions are as enjoyable as they should be, it will show keen excitement when the check collar is produced.

Training Sessions

Proper training should begin when your puppy is between six and eight months old. By this time it should know its name and it should be used to going out wearing a collar and lead, even if it does leap about and tug you along. Fit a good quality check collar of the right size and put this on just before you start the daily lesson. All early training should be carried out on the lead, so that you can reinforce any command you give to the puppy.

Whether the lesson is at home or at training class, make sure that your dog has a good romp beforehand to get rid of excess energy and has every opportunity to relieve itself. Three or four hours should elapse between the dog's last meal and the lesson. Never begin a training session if you are short of time or feeling tired or tense; if you end up snapping at your dog or jerking at its collar impatiently, you may undo a great deal of good work. Lessons need only be about 20 minutes long and shorter lessons of five minutes or so can be worked in with other things, such as playtime.

You must be calm and consistent at all times. A firm, authoritative tone will indicate to your dog that you mean business. Once you have given a command, you must be prepared to persevere until your dog has obeyed. Never shout or attempt to bribe an unwilling dog with tidbits and never, never allow yourself to lose your temper; your dog will only become worried and confused and do even worse. It is a good idea to begin each lesson by repeating exercises that the dog has learned already, so that you can give plenty of praise and the lesson begins on a happy note. You can use the same ploy at the end of the session and at any time during the lesson if things are not going well. The dog should never be allowed to feel a failure; repetition and praise are the keys to training success.

'Come!'

This simple exercise, to teach your puppy to come when called, can be used at the start of each lesson. Have your dog at your left-hand side. Walk smartly forward and allow the dog to walk or trot ahead of you. Call its name and say 'Come!' invitingly, at the same time walking backwards and pulling the slack lead towards you. The first two or three times you do this, you may need to give the lead a smart jerk to attract the dog's attention and to encourage it to follow you; but very soon the dog will come to enjoy this almost as a game, and will bound towards you with pleasure. Give it lots of praise.

The Release Word

Before you continue with true training, you need to decide on a 'release' word or phrase which you can use every time you wish to release your dog from the position in which you have left it. Some trainers say 'Okay!', some prefer 'Paid For!' or 'Free Now!'; but whatever you choose, make sure that it cannot be confused with any of the command words that you intend to use during training. The release word may be accompanied by a physical release gesture, and the well-trained adult dog can be taught to respond to either the word, the gesture, or a combination of the two. The release word is used when you feel that the dog has performed well during training and you have praised or rewarded it. When it is praised or rewarded the dog must not relax its position; but the release word indicates that it may now romp or play.

It is now time to teach the basic 'Sit!', 'Stay!', 'Down!', and 'Wait!' commands as well as correct walking at heel. Keep the lessons short and well structured. Make all the lessons enjoyable; never continue with an exercise when your dog is tired, bored, or distracted by circumstances beyond your control. Try to use the same training lead for every lesson. Your dog should enjoy learning and show signs of excitement when the training equipment is produced.

'HEEL!' AND 'SIT!'

In teaching your dog to walk at heel you want it to stride eagerly along on your left-hand side with its right shoulder about even with your left knee. Fit the check collar correctly so that it can be tightened or slackened at will. Attach it to the training lead. Hold the spare length of lead in your right hand and level with your waist. It should have a slight loop in it so that no tension is exerted on the check collar. To start the exercise, give the command 'Heel!' in a firm and business-like manner, jerk the lead very slightly and move off with the left foot. Your stride should be short and bouncy and the pace fairly brisk. Keep your left hand free of the lead and use it to encourage the dog to keep close by tapping your left thigh or clicking your fingers. You may find it helpful to carry a small article in your left hand to keep your dog interested – one of its favourite squeaky toys, perhaps, or a biscuit. Avoid grabbing at your dog as this could make it hand-shy, which is difficult to cure.

Start by walking in straight lines. If your dog is inclined to pull to the left, walk close to a fence or wall. Repeat the command 'Heel!' from time to time, using a pleasant tone and chat to your dog while it walks along. Keep the dog constantly alert and do not let its attention wander from the lesson. If it drags behind, give the lead a short sharp jerk to bring the dog forward, repeat 'Heel!' and keep on walking. You may need to repeat this once or twice. When the dog comes forward to the correct position, give it verbal praise.

Some dogs persistently pull forward on the lead during heel-work training but it is a great mistake to try to counteract this by pulling on the lead. If you

It is essential to teach a young dog to come to you whenever you call. This exercise is taught by having the dog on a long training lead and encouraging it to come forward eagerly when it is asked to do so.

When the dog is walking to heel (below left) it should follow the handler's changes of direction while maintaining its position, with the shoulder alongside the handler's left knee.

When teaching the 'Sit!' command (below right), hold the dog's head in position with the lead, and at the same time press down on the hindquarters. The dog will soon get the idea.

do this, the walk will become a trial of strength with you and the dog pulling against each other. When the dog is walking correctly, the lead will be slightly slack; as soon as the dog pulls forward, give a reminder on the check collar by taking the slack of the lead in the left hand and jerking it sharply backwards. Your dog will soon learn that it is most comfortable to trot along at your side, and that pulling forward or hanging back results in an unpleasant jerk on its neck.

Every time you decide to stop, put your dog into a sitting position on your left side, facing forward, and with its right shoulder still near your left knee. To encourage it to sit from the walk, give the 'Sit!' command, raise your right hand to keep the dog's head high and lean over and use your left hand to push down on the dog's rump. The 'Sit!' command should be given in a firm voice and slightly drawn out, emphasising the 't'. Insist on instant reaction from your dog in this exercise. Do not accept sloppy results with the dog swivelling around to sit sideways, half sitting, going right down or rolling over. Repeat the 'Heel!' and walk for a few paces, then repeat the 'Sit!'. Try to avoid giving the commands at the same points in the garden as it is important to prevent your dog from connecting landmarks with commands.

When the dog sits correctly and you have praised it, wait a moment, and then give your release word in a pleased voice along with your chosen release gesture, best given with a gentle tap of the foot to a small dog or a nudge with the knee. Using hand gestures for release is not a good idea, as you use your hands for praise and reward and the dog could misunderstand your wishes. Most dogs enjoy being released and leap around excitedly like small boys let out of school.

When your dog walks well to heel on straight lines, start teaching it right-hand and left-hand circles. Begin by walking in a fairly large circle to the right. Encourage the dog to keep close to your left knee by giving slight jerks with the lead in your right hand, slapping your thigh with your left as an encouragement, and continually repeating the 'Heel!' command. Continue to reinforce the 'Sit' exercise while working on the circle, give lots of praise when the work goes well, but stop and start again if it seems to be going badly.

Try not to scold for poor results at first. It is better to ignore bad work and immediately praise the dog when it gets something right. Never let the lesson go on until the dog becomes bored. If things have gone badly, go back to an earlier exercise such as walk to heel on a straight line, put the dog in the sit position, give it praise, and release it for the day.

Walking in a left-hand circle is more difficult, and it is all too easy to fall over your dog until it understands just what is required. It helps if there is some sort of guiding line around which you can steer the dog; your parked car would do, or some

chairs arranged in a circle. Start with the dog sitting at your side in the usual manner. Give the 'Heel!' command and move off with your left foot. Raise the lead slightly with your left hand to guide the dog over to the left if necessary; take longer strides than normal and use your left leg to ease the dog's head and neck into the left-handed circle you require. As soon as you achieve a satisfactory result, praise the dog and end the lesson. Repeat it at the start of the next day's session. Be sure to add lots of sit exercises on these circles, and remember to give the commands at different places each time.

At about this stage in the training, your dog may be getting lax about its sitting position and slow in assuming it. It is important to expect accurate and instant responses at all times, and if you praise the dog for a movement that it has not performed well you will have reinforced the error. Once made and allowed to pass, mistakes are hard to erase; if they are also rewarded with a pat, they may never be erased. If your dog does get lazy about the 'Sit!' command, some stern effort is required to put it right. Walk briskly forward with the dog at heel, give it the order to 'Sit!', jerk up the head slightly with the check collar and press down the dog's rump; ensure that the dog is pressed well up against your left leg. Walk on and repeat this several times, giving praise when the exercise is well performed. The first time it is done perfectly, praise the dog and release it.

Practise heel-work daily, and prevent boredom by varying your pace, walking in zig-zags, serpentines and figures-of-eight as well as in straight lines, squares with sharp corners, and alternate circles. It might seem difficult at first, but with correctly given praise words and the proper use of the check collar, both you and your dog will become extremely proficient.

'Sit and Stay'

When your dog sits well on a verbal command and no longer needs the additional aids of lead and hands, proceed to the 'Sit and Stay' exercise. Tell the dog to 'Sit!' in the normal way, then let the slack of the lead loop down to the ground and change the end of the lead from your right to your left hand. Show the dog the palm of your right hand: hold it near its face and give a firm and slightly drawn-out command 'Stay!'. Repeat the word, hold the hand towards the dog and take a long slow step to your right. Extend the left arm so that the lead does not pull the dog towards you. The dog should remain sitting and watching you. Repeat the word 'Stay!' and reverse your step until you are next to your dog once more. If the dog does not move, praise it and repeat the exercise once or twice more, but keep this first lesson quite short. If the dog does move, either to lie down or to follow you to the right, put it back in position and try again. Punish movement with a stern 'No!' before re-positioning the dog with the 'Sit!' command. Repeat this exercise daily; when the dog seems really steady, develop the movement.

This is done in stages. The first progression is carried out by looping the end of the long training lead onto the thumb of your left hand. Sit the dog in the usual position, give the 'Stay!' command and take the long step to your right. Fully extend your left arm so that your hand is virtually over the dog's head. Using your left thumb as a pivot point, slowly walk anti-clockwise right around your dog until you are back in the normal training position once more. The dog must not move. If it does, start again from the beginning and revert to the original Sit and Stay exercise if necessary until you achieve a positive result, then praise profusely and release the dog. Work the Sit and Stay exercise in with daily heel-work and random sits so that the dog has variety in its exercises.

When you are confident that the dog will stay in the Sit position while you circle round, try the Stay without the lead. Practise first of all by putting the end of the lead on the ground while you ask for the 'Stay!' and take your long step to the right. If this is successful, walk in a circle around your dog and return to the training position. If your work is progressing satisfactorily the dog will remain motionless; if you are rushing things or have a slow or wilful dog, go back to a previous stage and work up to the 'Stay!' once more.

The next stage is to remove the lead while the dog is at Sit and Stay and to walk away. Always take the side step first before moving forward so your dog does not think it should go forward at heel. Your dog should, by now, connect your sideways step with remaining motionless, and your left-foot-forward step with going to heel.

Walk only a few paces away from your dog at first and keep repeating the 'Stay!' command in a calm and steadying manner. Always return to the training position before praising the dog, then either continue with a new exercise or give the release. Vary your procedure so that the dog never anticipates the release and waits for your next instruction at all times. When you and your pet have mastered this exercise, you will have reached an important stage in training, and your dog will realise that 'Stay!' always means that you are going to return to its side.

'Wait!' and 'Come!'

When you want the dog to remain in its position initially and then to come to you when you call, you must teach a different word to avoid confusion in the animal's mind. 'Wait!' is a very important command, and must be thoroughly and correctly taught from the outset. The easiest way to start this exercise is to sit the dog in the normal way, praise it a little, then move quietly round in front of it. Place your right hand in front of the dog's nose, showing the palm, and say 'Wait!' in a low and drawn-out way. Holding the end of the slackened training lead in your left hand, take small steps backwards away from your dog, repeating the command, until you get to the end of the lead. If the dog remains motionless, call its name and say 'Come!' in a pleased and welcoming way. Give a little pull on the lead if it seems reluctant to obey. When the dog reaches you, praise it and try to get it to sit facing you.

If all goes well, the 'Wait!' command can be given again while you move back once more to reinforce the lesson. If the dog moves forward as you start to reverse, you must begin again, taking one small step at a time. This exercise must be taken very slowly

and built-in to the previous programme without letting your dog get bored. Only when it is completely mastered should you go on to the next stage.

Replace the training lead with a long thin cord so that you can extend your distance from your dog while remaining in control if it moves away from its sitting position. Always make your 'Come!' command as welcoming as possible, and fuss your dog in its favourite way whenever it responds correctly. A tidbit encourages some dogs, especially those of wilful or scatterbrained breeds which are easily distracted. Keep a favourite biscuit or liver treat in the palm of your hand and make sure your dog knows that it is there. In the 'Come!' exercise, recall your dog and add an arm gesture by holding your hand up to your chest or by extending your arms. If the hand with the tidbit is held up to your chest, the dog is likely to race towards you and sit immediately, looking up at your face expectantly, hoping for the tidbit. Do not give a tidbit every time; vary the reward so that your dog does not require constant food bribes in order to perform correctly.

When you are certain that the dog will come to you from the Wait position when you recall it, remove the cord. If you have some failures and your dog runs off or will not come right up to you, revert to more controlled methods for a while.

At this stage, your young dog should be giving you a great deal of satisfaction, walking to heel at all paces, sitting when told and staying on command until your return.

'Down and Stay'

Once your dog reaches this point in training, you are ready to teach the 'Down!' command. If your dog was apt to collapse in a heap every time you wanted it to sit, you may find that it is slightly bewildered to find that you now want it to take up that previously unacceptable position. Teach your dog to lie down on command by pulling the lead forward, giving the command 'Down!' in a low voice and, if necessary, getting down on the ground with the dog. With a large dog you may gently pull its forelegs forward and press down on its shoulder blades until it is in the desired position. Praise the dog when it is down correctly. If it persists in getting up, persevere until you are successful. Take several days perfecting this exercise. Only when your dog goes into the down position promptly and without any fuss should you progress to the 'Down and Stay' exercise.

This is taught in exactly the same way as the Sit and Stay. Use a loosely looped lead and step away to the dog's right then walk slowly around in a circle. Praise the dog only when it remains in the down position; if it deviates from this, start from the beginning again. End the lesson as soon as you achieve the desired result. Never recall your dog

1 Having given the command and shown the dog the flat of her hand, the handler takes a side step to the right before moving smoothly and slowly away.

2 The stay command is constantly repeated and reinforced by the hand signal until the handler has reached the limit of the training lead's length.

from the Down position. It should be fixed in its mind as a stationary posture, so that it always remains in position until you return and give the release signal.

If your dog has successfully performed all these exercises it will have reached an acceptable level for a family dog. Try and perfect these simple exercises until your dog happily responds both on and off the lead. The Down exercise should be practised frequently and at length, until your dog immediately drops down at your command, no matter what it is doing. This training can save a dog's life, as you can control it from a distance, even in a hazardous situation.

'Leave!'

The command 'Leave!' can be a life-saver. The aim of the exercise is to teach your dog to leave an object alone until you free it with a simple command.

A good way of teaching the lesson is to show the dog a favourite treat, like a tasty biscuit, but make the animal leave it alone until you give permission. Put the dog on its check collar and lead, and hold it in check with your left hand. Start at the Sit position, as this makes control easier. Show the dog the biscuit and say 'Leave!' in a very commanding voice. Put the treat on the ground just out of the animal's reach. The dog will naturally go to take the biscuit but you must pull it back with a short jerk, repeating the 'Leave!' command. When you wish the dog to take the biscuit use a different release word. If 'Okay!' is your normal release, use 'Paid For!' or 'Fetch it!'. Dogs quickly learn this exercise and before long you will be able to add refinements such as rolling the biscuit past your dog, or even throwing it, and the dog will not pounce on it until you indicate that it is allowed to do so.

The exercise can be expanded to include all sorts of things. Dogs can be prevented from being destructive by learning this command. You can shout 'Leave!' from your bedroom window when you notice your pet digging up a rose bush or about to chase the neighbour's cat. It can prevent the inquisitive dog from being stung by bees or wasps and stealing cake from the tea table. As usual, it is important that your dog obeys the command instantly and without question, knowing that it will eventually receive a reward.

The Retrieve

Many dogs have a natural instinct to retrieve objects. It presumably dates back to their ancestors' wild state when food was carried to the den. Some gundogs are bred for their propensity to retrieve, and such breeds can be trained very easily. A young puppy should be encouraged to carry its toys around in its mouth; if it has been scolded for doing so, it will be more difficult to teach this exercise.

Train the retrieve by having your dog on a long line or cord and sitting at your left-hand side. Throw a suitable article, either a proper training dumbbell or a piece of wood of similar size, and give the 'Fetch!' command in an encouraging manner. The dog should run and pick up the article. Once this has occurred, gently pull the line and give the 'Come!' command. When the dog responds, ask it to sit in front of you and praise it for holding the article well. Take the dumbbell or wood in both hands, give a command such as 'Drop it!', and gently remove the article from the dog's jaws. Take care not to hurt your pet's mouth in removing the object, and praise it profusely for a job well done. It is a short progression to working off the lead, and then to training the dog to fetch any article you point to. If a young dog races about excitedly with the object retrieved, you must go back to an earlier stage of the exercise.

Tricks

If your dog proved to be a good learner you might like to try teaching it a few party tricks. This should only be attempted after your dog has completely

3 After a successful retrieve, the dumbbell should be taken gently from the dog's mouth, with plenty of praise for a job well done.

This little Cairn Terrier cheerfully begs for a tidbit but this trick should not be taught too early as the puppy's back may not be strong enough.

mastered its basic training and can be relied upon to be obedient and well-behaved in all situations. It would be unfair to encourage your pet to perform in a way that makes it appear foolish or to let the dog feel a failure if it does not master a particular trick. Tricks are taught by encouraging the desired behaviour in easy stages and giving rewards when they are properly performed. Though in basic training the rewards may be a pat and verbal praise, tricks are usually rewarded with a tidbit.

One of the favourite tricks is having the dog sit up and beg. It is only suitable for small to medium-sized dogs of the right conformation. Dogs with very long backs or long legs find it virtually impossible to balance while sitting up on their haunches and it is unkind to try to teach them to do so. Short-legged, stocky dogs like Pugs or Sealyhams find this trick very easy and hardly need any teaching. Wait until your puppy is at least six months old, then start by holding a tempting tidbit just out of reach over its head. Say 'Beg!' or 'Up!' in a pleasant but firm manner and gently lift up the front end of the pup. Find the point of balance and repeat the command, simultaneously giving the reward. Repeat the process, encouraging the dog to balance itself. Take plenty of time or it may panic, and be ready with a steadying hand at the first sign of a wobble. If the dog is very unsteady, try practising in a corner, so that the walls give support and a feeling of security. A perceptive puppy grasps this trick very quickly and soon your puppy will be sitting up appealingly at every opportunity. Never reward this behaviour when the family is eating or your dog will become a mealtime pest that has to be banished from the room. Reward sitting up only after you have given the command and not when the dog does it voluntarily, trying to scrounge an extra tidbit.

As your dog grows up, you may notice little habits which can be developed naturally into its own particular tricks. Some dogs are able to throw objects; some, particularly the retrieving breeds, enjoy carrying articles in their mouths; others learn to lift a rug and hide an article underneath. These actions are variations of normal canine behaviour and can be expanded by encouragement and reward, as well as a command or signal to indicate when they should be carried out.

One of these tricks is 'shaking hands'. Tiny puppies instinctively knead at the bitch to stimulate the milk supply, so kneading becomes an action associated with pleasure. As they grow up, the puppies often feed off the bitch as she is standing up and as they would topple over if they tried to knead, they sit down and reach up with one paw. This is why so many dogs seem to teach themselves to 'shake hands'. To teach a dog to shake hands on command, sit or kneel and have the dog sitting in front of you. Give the command 'Shake hands!' and

Some dogs love to carry things in their mouths (right) but it may mean that your newspaper arrives slightly damp.

It is part of the dog's hunting instinct to chase and carry a ball, so this is a very easy form of behaviour to teach; some dogs find it just as easy to catch a ball thrown by the owner.

at the same time press against its right shoulder with your left hand. This will make the dog move its paw off the ground, so take the paw in your other hand and praise the dog well. Gradually ease the left hand pressure, simply giving the command and holding out your other hand. Once the dog has grasped the idea, repeat the process with the other paw, saying 'Now the other one'.

To play 'dead' or 'die for your country' is a little more difficult. Assuming that you have taught your dog to lie down on command, the next step is to teach it to lie on one side: give a command such as 'On your side!', gently push the dog into position and hold it there. Once the dog will do this on its own and remain steady, give the command 'Dead!' in a harsh tone of voice that will tend to make it 'freeze'. Try to keep your dog quite still even for a few seconds at the beginning. Once the dog understands the command and responds, encourage it to go straight into the 'dead dog' position from standing, pushing it down gently with your hand. Do not praise or reward too soon or the dog will not stay in position long enough.

It can be useful, as well as entertaining, if a dog can bark on command. To begin with, give the command 'Speak!' every time the dog barks of its own accord. As it begins associating the word with the action, offer a tidbit and say 'Speak!'. When the dog gets the idea and barks, give the tidbit and plenty of praise. Practise often enough and the dog will soon be barking each time you give the command.

Some dogs are naturals at learning to catch on command but others seem to miss every time at first. Put your dog on the lead and have it sitting or standing in front of you. Have a pocketful of small biscuits and show it the food in your hand. When it is watching, give the command 'Catch!'. At first, throw the biscuit towards the dog from a very short distance. If it misses, check it with the lead, pick up the biscuit yourself and try again. If you are lucky and the dog catches a piece fairly soon, praise it and finish the training for the day. If the dog does not seem to be making any progress, finish for the day by dropping a piece of biscuit into its mouth and praising it well. Each lesson must finish with a success, no matter how small it may be, so that the dog feels happy and will be pleased when the next session starts.

Curing Bad Habits

Many dogs grow up with bad habits – leaping uncontrollably at every visitor who steps into the house, barking when left alone, growling when you try to push them off your best bedspread and so on. If your dog exhibits bad behaviour, it may be due to nervousness, insecurity, loneliness or over-excitement but whatever the cause, bad habits can be cured if you adopt the right strategy and persevere until you are successful.

The overall rules are much the same as those used in initial training but there are several important 'don't's' for owners of problem dogs:

- Don't take the easy way out. If you give a command, work to see that it is obeyed; otherwise your dog will not see any reason to change its ways.
- Don't threaten your dog. You may frighten it into obedience in the short term, but it will learn nothing – except, perhaps, to keep out of your way at the crucial time.
- Don't punish bad behaviour unless you catch the dog in the act. Any punishment or reprimand must be given within 30 seconds of the offence, otherwise the animal will not link the two events.
- Don't rush. Bad habits will not be cured overnight. You will need to consolidate each small advance before going on to the next lesson.
- Don't give a dog that is apt to misbehave when you are out of the house a stiff lecture just before you leave. It will not understand and you may leave it so anxious or excited that its bad behaviour becomes even worse.

Aggression

Never allow your dog to growl, snap or show its teeth at you. When a dog shows aggression within the home, it may be trying to dominate the family members and needs to be shown its proper place in the hierarchy. Increasing the standard exercises of obedience training to several short sessions a day will help to establish your place as pack leader. Make sure that you are in control at all times. If your dog gives out any aggressive signals, ignore it completely; when it comes to you for a pat, brings its ball for a game or puts its head on your lap, simply walk away without speaking. Then when you are ready, give it the command 'Down!' and when it obeys, give it the petting or the game it was seeking. If your dog only growls when it is in a particular position, such as under the table, on the bed or in a favourite chair, then wrap heavy plastic

This American dog-walker has her hands full, coping with a bunch of dogs that have not been well-trained in walking to heel and obeying commands.

round the table legs to block off the area, close the bedroom door to keep the dog out or remove the chair altogether. If this is impractical because your dog has so many little 'territories' that it guards aggressively then keep it on the lead while in the house and use the lead to move it from place to place, so that you can be dominant without putting your hand near the bared teeth. If the dog is only aggressive towards one particular member of the family, then that person should practise obedience training with the dog, when it is restrained on its check chain and lead. Otherwise you might try putting that person in charge of feeding the dog; if it is very aggressive, you might need to keep it on the lead during feeding times at first, punishing any show of aggression with a sharp jerk, so that the dog learns that this behaviour will not be tolerated.

Climbing on Furniture

Most dogs have an unerring instinct for finding the most comfortable piece of furniture in the living room and, if allowed, will monopolize the best armchair or spread themselves over the sofa. If you do not want your dog to sit on the furniture, you should train it from its first days in your household. Alternatively, you might allow it to sit on one chair but not another; with attentive training, the dog will quickly grasp the difference. If you find that the dog sneaks onto the forbidden furniture when there is no one to see, then either exclude it from the room altogether when there is nobody to supervise or stand the seat cushions on end when you are out of the room for a time. If you allow your pet to sit on a particular chair, it is wise to train the dog to vacate it instantly when ordered to do so. Make sure that the command you use will not be confused with 'Down!' or any other command used in basic training. 'Off' or 'Go' might be suitable, if you do not use them for different activities.

Pulling on the Lead

Never allow yourself to be hauled along by a dog that pulls on the lead or the dog will take a delight in pulling you faster and faster.

If your dog pulls on the lead, the worst thing you can do is to let yourself be pulled along faster and faster. This simply tells the dog that this is a delightful pastime. Sufficient attention to heel-work should cure the problem but if a normally obedient dog is a habitual puller, try giving the 'Heel' command as soon as the dog starts pulling, then to turn smartly and walk in the opposite direction, so that the dog follows you, not the other way around. It may be difficult to make these methods work with large, strong dogs capable of pulling their owners off their feet. This is one of the few occasions when a rolled-up newspaper may come into its own. Begin walking with your dog at your side and every time it tries to pass you to pull ahead, tap its nose with the newspaper. The dog will try to avoid this, so practise alongside a fence or wall. Many large dogs get very excited when they know that they will soon be going for a walk. A quick run around the garden off the lead helps to take the edge off this excitement.

WANDERING

If your dog persistently jumps over the garden fence and runs away for the day you must take action. No dog should be allowed to roam free, for no matter how well-behaved it may be at home, you have no means of knowing what it would do in an unusual situation, and it could cause injury to itself or others. Make the fence higher if your dog is able to jump over it, or keep your pet on an extendable running line when it is left alone in the garden. Such lines can easily be fastened onto a hook on an outside wall, or looped around a gatepost. The end is clipped onto the dog's collar and the line pulls out of the holder as the dog runs around. Any slack is drawn back in, so that there is no chance of the animal becoming entangled. However, keeping a dog on a running line should not be used as a substitute for proper exercise and playtimes, and it should not be left alone out of doors for long periods, as loneliness and boredom will only encourage other bad behaviour, such as barking.

MOUNTING

Owners become very worried when their young dogs begin mounting table legs, or other male dogs, convinced that their pet is over-sexed. Though many dogs do stop this behaviour when they become adult, it is better to put a stop to it as early as possible, before it becomes a habit – a dog that is continually trying to mount a visitor's leg is an embarrassment. If the object of unwanted affection is always the same, such as a cushion or a child's cuddly toy, the answer may be as simple as shutting it away where the dog cannot find it. Otherwise, watch the dog closely and, the moment the mounting begins, issue a firm 'No!'. If necessary, take the dog by the scruff of the neck and give a little shake. Then ignore it completely for a few minutes. If there are particular occasions when this behaviour happens, such as the exciting few moments when a visitor arrives, then pre-empt it by calling the dog to 'Sit!' before the visitor enters. Of course, this will only work if your dog is trained in basic obedience already. If your dog is mounting anything and everything and nothing that you do has any effect, consult your vet. A short course of hormone injections may improve matters; otherwise castration may be the answer.

PHOBIAS

Some dogs become terrified of certain noises: fireworks send many pets into a panic but everyday noises like the vacuum cleaner or the ringing of the phone can have the same effect on some animals and others cower in terror whenever a visitor arrives at the door. This behaviour will not cure itself and will probably get worse if neglected. It may be worth asking the vet to prescribe tranquillizers for a scheduled firework party and tranquillizers may also be useful for calming the dog while you retrain it, but they are not a long-term solution. Instead you will need to spend time 'desensitizing' the dog, in a process similar to that used for human phobia sufferers. If, for instance, your pet cowers shivering in a corner or runs in frenzied circles every time the phone rings, enlist the aid of a friend who will make a series of calls on schedule. Muffle the phone with a blanket and take your dog to the part of the house furthest from the instrument. At first your friend should let the phone ring four or five times; while it is ringing, stay with the dog, talk soothingly and feed it tidbits. Once your dog can remain calm under these circumstances, progress in easy stages until the phone is in the same room. Organize two or three rings on a muffled phone to begin with, still petting and soothing your dog, then progress to longer calls, then remove the blanket from the phone. Follow the same pattern if, for instance, your dog is afraid of visitors. First ask someone to walk up the path without coming to the door, then to walk up the path and stand on the step, then to ring the doorbell without coming in, and so on. Never try to speed up the process or you will undo all your good work. The more patient you can be, the better the final results.

DESTRUCTIVE DOGS

The puppy naturally chews things to help in the cutting of its second teeth, and because of this, it may well cause damage in the home. A young dog should never be left alone where it can spoil valuable property or furnishings. It should be confined within a playpen while you are out of the house and given its own toys and rawhide chews to play with. Some adult dogs resent being left alone and become distressed, scratching at doors and carpet. Unless checked, this behaviour may develop into determined tearing and chewing. It is pointless to punish such misdeeds as soon as you arrive home, because the dog will be so pleased to see you that the punishment will seem to the dog to be linked with the exuberance of its greeting. If you expect to leave your dog alone for long periods, you should prevent the onset of destructive behaviour by early training.

If the problem has become ingrained you have several alternative solutions. The first and most obvious is never to leave your dog alone. You may have the sort of job which enables you to take your pet to work. Other dogs give up destructive behaviour if they are allowed the complete run of the house, but it may be impracticable to try this out

Most owners find it useful to have a dog that will bark to warn of approaching strangers, but if it barks at every sound, or goes on barking for long periods, it becomes a nuisance to the whole neighbourhood.

for the first few days, especially if you have valuable belongings. The third alternative is to buy a second dog. When the two animals become friends you will probably find that all destructive behaviour ceases completely.

Positive action is needed to retrain a destructive dog. Start by leaving the room and closing the door. Return a minute later and check for damage; if there is none, praise the dog. If some damage has been caused, make a point of examining it but totally ignore your dog. Do not punish the dog as that will not help matters. Sooner or later – and you may need a lot of patience – the dog will be left for a short period without doing any damage. This is the breakthrough point. Take care to extend the periods of isolation very, very gradually until the dog is retrained and may confidently be left alone. Some dogs are less troublesome if the television is left on for company.

Barking

A dog that barks incessantly for no apparent reason is a nuisance to owners and neighbours and such behaviour must be stopped at once. Young puppies are unable to bark at all, and when they first learn to do so they often look surprised at the noise they manage to produce. Although it can be tempting to encourage the puppy to bark it is a mistake to do so and is difficult to correct later on. A dog will learn to bark aggressively when it feels that either itself or its property is being threatened. If the dog learns this naturally, barking will likely be kept to the minimum and you will know that a bark from your dog really does mean that a stranger is around and not that the animal is merely feeling a bit bored and wants some action. While you must accept the fact that your dog will bark when visitors arrive at your door, the animal must be trained to stop barking when you have let them into the house. The best way to do this is to slip the check collar and lead onto your dog while it is barking and the doorbell is ringing. Praise the dog, take it to the door and tell it to 'Sit!'. Open the door and invite your guests in while restraining the dog in the Sit position. Punish further barks with a stern 'No!', then allow your dog to meet and greet the visitors.

A dog that persistently barks when left alone in a

Some dogs cannot resist stealing food at any opportunity. This is unhygienic, as well as annoying, and should be stopped by use of aversion therapy.

room can be difficult to retrain. You must shut it in the room then creep away. Immediately it starts to bark, scold it with a series of severe 'No!' commands. This can be reinforced by clapping your hands as you give the commands. If it still has no effect you may have to punish the dog physically by shaking the scruff of its neck or even giving the animal a short sharp slap. Only do this while the dog is still barking, not after the barking has ceased.

JUMPING UP

An exuberant dog will often run up to visitors and friends and jump up against them, trying to get its mouth as close as possible to the visitor's face. While this is natural behaviour for the dog, it is usually unacceptable to people, particularly if the dog has been romping in the garden and has muddy paws. Jumping up is easily corrected in any dog, but the sooner it is done the better. Have the dog on a check collar and a long training lead or length of line and set up the situation beforehand with an assistant. The assistant should walk naturally in through the front gate, for example, or through a door. The dog will run forward as usual in greeting. Just as the dog starts to jump up, jerk the lead hard and command a very stern 'No!' Give the 'Sit!' command, and if it is obeyed the assistant can make a fuss of the dog. This may have to be repeated a few times, but in most cases the dog will quickly learn acceptable manners.

If your dog runs up to you and jumps up, the check collar will be of little use. The easiest way to stop this behaviour is to bring your knee up into the dog's chest at the moment it jumps forward. While it is still bewildered by this unkindness, give the 'Sit!' command, then praise the dog. Here again the younger dog should learn very quickly. The lesson, once learned, should never be relaxed, and no one should be allowed to encourage your dog to go onto its hind legs.

STEALING FOOD

It is asking rather a lot of the dog to expect it to sit patiently alone in a room where lots of tempting food is set out and not to steal any. It is a different matter, however, when your dog habitually takes tidbits from your kitchen work-surface or dining table when your attention is elsewhere for a moment or two. Teach your dog the 'Leave!' command and get it used to staying away from items of food when you have told it to do so. This behaviour can be reinforced by aversion therapy. Fill a soft chocolate or similar delicacy with a teaspoon of mustard and put it on the table. Give the 'Leave!' command then go out of the room for a moment. If the dog has left the decoy well alone, praise it profusely upon your return. If it has eaten the bait it will have had punishment enough. Some dogs swallow tidbits so fast that they might not taste the mustard, in which case you should offer larger baits that need to be chewed. Repeat this process until your dog is convinced that all stolen food tastes awful. The mustard should deter your dog from stealing, but is not harmful when swallowed.

CHASING CATS

Curing a dog of cat-chasing can be quite difficult. The best way undoubtedly is to have a dog-proof cat – a really tough and fearless animal which, instead of running away from the dog, fluffs up and gives it a good scratch across the sensitive end of its nose. If your dog chases your own cat you will need to work hard at trying to make them friends. Have your dog on the check collar and lead; every time the cat makes off and the dog leaps up in pursuit, jerk the lead and give a stern 'No!' command. Never encourage your dog to chase anything except a ball or one of its toys that you have thrown, and scold it whenever it shows signs of running after birds in the garden.

CHASING VEHICLES

Chasing cars and bicycles is a bad habit which should be stopped promptly before a serious accident occurs. Dogs should never be allowed to

Plenty of petting and handling from puppyhood is the best way to ensure that a dog will allow examination of any part of its head and body.

roam the streets freely, and it is also dangerous if a dog on its lead tries to leap at passing vehicles. To break this aggressive habit, attach a training collar and lead and take the dog to a stretch of road where the traffic is fairly heavy, where there are few pedestrians and the pavement is reasonably wide. Make your dog sit correctly on your left side and wait quietly for the first car to pass. As the dog starts to leap forward or bark, jerk it back on the check collar and give a severe 'No!' command. When this has had some effect, try walking with the dog at heel with traffic coming from behind. Correct impulsive forward moves by the dog until success is achieved. Finish the lesson on a positive note and take the dog home. Repeated and regular lessons are required until your dog is calm with all traffic. It is useful to have a friend ride past you on a bicycle each day while you train the dog to accept this experience in a similar way.

Chasing Sheep

Sheep have an excitable effect on most dogs. They look vulnerable and run away in an inviting sort of way, often turning to look back at the dog. A great deal of harm can be done to such valuable livestock when they are chased around: pregnant ewes drop premature lambs, for example, and other sheep become so distressed that they may die of heart failure. Dogs sometimes gang up and methodically hunt down a sheep before savaging it to death – an example of ancient instincts coming to the fore despite centuries of domestication. It is virtually impossible to teach an ordinary family dog not to chase farm animals so you must therefore ensure that your dog always remains under your control. Keep it on a lead during country walks, and if it likes to lope around and explore, use a long cord or line in place of the normal lead.

Digging Holes

All dogs love to dig. This innate behaviour dates back to the days when dogs buried the uneaten portion of their kill to hide it from other predators. Nowadays, bitches dig burrows in which to whelp, and overheated dogs dig earthy pits in which to cool off from the sun. As digging is a natural part of canine behaviour, it is very difficult to stop when it is done in an unacceptable place, like the middle of the lawn or around the prize rose bushes. Try to distract the digging dog and give it some other exhausting exercise for a while. Give a firm 'No!' command every time it looks as if it is going to start on another excavation. If these ruses are not effective, you will have to confine your dog to unimportant areas of the garden or buy a running chain or portable run.

Resentment of Handling

Your dog may show resentment or even aggression when you attempt to touch a particular part of its body. If it has a coat that demands a lot of grooming and it has suffered at your hands through tugging at knots and tangles, this is quite understandable. It is up to you to undo the harm by gentle and careful retraining. It is extremely important for an owner to be able to handle his or her dog under any circumstances and at any time. At the scene of an accident, for example, ease of handling could mean the difference between life and death for your pet. If a puppy shows any resentment when a certain area is touched you will need to begin a familiarization programme. Stroke or groom the sensitive part, talk soothingly to the puppy and praise it the moment it ceases to resist. Older dogs take a little longer to retrain, but with plenty of patience success can be achieved.

If a dog tends to snap during this type of training you may have to use a muzzle at first. Properly-made leather muzzles are available in all sizes and the one you choose should fit snugly. If it is too large the muzzle may slip off at the crucial moment; if it is too small it will hurt the dog and cause more resentment. If a muzzle is used, put it on the dog from time to time during normal playtime and exercise. Never let the dog connect the fitting of the muzzle with an unpleasant aspect of training.

A dog-guard fitted behind the back seats of his estate car ensures that the dogs cannot jump over the seats and distract the driver.

URINATING INDOORS

If your pet urinates indoors, it may be an extension of the territorial marking that normally goes on outside. This may happen when another dog or a human visitor arrives in the house and the visit stimulates it to mark out its ownership. Your best defence is vigilance: noticing the danger times and moving quickly to prevent the behaviour. Dogs usually have favourite spots for territorial marking and you may be able to rearrange furniture or close doors to make the spot unavailable. Clean up the spots very thoroughly with bleach or biological stain remover.

Some dogs urinate when they are over-excited and an owner who then gets angry and shouts or smacks the dog is only raising the excitement level and compounding the problem. Instead, you should ignore the dog if it wets the floor and concentrate on keeping its life as calm as possible. If your dog is so excited about your return home that it loses control of its bladder, stop greeting it with enthusiasm and open arms; instead greet it coolly without looking at it and save the petting until later when the dog is calmer. If it tends to urinate when it gets over-excited while playing, try to make sure that you only initiate games where urinating will not cause a problem.

Submissive urination happens when a dog, particularly a puppy, feels insecure or intimidated. If you find that your dog tends to urinate a little when you greet it, then try not to tower over the dog; squat down for your greeting, don't look the dog straight in the eye and speak softly. Make sure that visitors do not swoop on the dog but wait until they are sitting down before they take any notice of it.

COPROPHAGIA
(eating faeces)

For wild dogs, the eating of the droppings of large herbivores probably provides essential roughage and minerals, as well as quantities of the B group of vitamins, so what seems to us a revolting habit has its roots in natural behaviour. Members of a dog pack often eat part of each others faeces and also wash one another's anal regions. This may help to ensure that all the pack members have the same micro-organisms living within their intestines, so lessening the likelihood of outbreaks of disease within the group. Most dogs grow out of coprophagia, especially when they find that it displeases their owners. You can help to break the habit by disposing of faeces promptly and by distracting your dog by some other activity if it is tempted while you are out walking. The family cat's litter tray may be a problem area; if your dog is large, then a covered tray with a small entrance for the cat may be the answer, otherwise you may need to put the litter tray out of the dog's reach. The cat will adapt easily to a tray on a high surface and will probably welcome the peace and privacy.

CAR TRAVEL PROBLEMS

If your dog refuses to stay still when travelling in the car, you may be a danger to other road users; if you are distracted at a crucial moment, a serious accident could result. If you travel regularly, it is a good idea to fit a dog-grille, so that the dog is confined to its own area of the car and cannot jump over the seats. Alternatively, you will need to work at extending obedience training to the car. Work on the basic 'Down!' and 'Stay!' commands until your dog will lie down when told and stay there until released. Then have your dog maintain this position in a stationary car with the doors open. Make sure that you always practise with the dog lying where you want it to travel, whether this is on the seat or the floor. Once this is accomplished satisfactorily, ask a friend to drive so that you can make sure that the dog stays in position then begin by making very short journeys, then lengthening them.

DOG FIGHTS

Play fighting is first seen in young puppies of four to five weeks of age and it is these competitive trials of strength that lead to the formation of a social hierarchy. Most adult dogs avoid actual fights: males establish their territorial rights by urine-marking whenever possible and simply threaten other dogs by assuming various body postures like walking stiff-legged, holding the tail rigid, and perhaps giving a few warning growls.

When a serious fight breaks out between two dogs, most owners dive into the midst of the battle and try to separate their pets. This is foolish in the extreme and usually results in injuries to all those involved. Each owner should simultaneously pull his dog away by gripping it at the root of its tail. This must not be done however, if one dog has a firm grip with its teeth or else the other dog could suffer extensive damage. To make a dog release its hold, insert a forefinger into its rectum. The dog will react immediately to this and relax its grip. It should then be smartly pulled away from its adversary and prevented from returning to the attack. A bucket of cold water poured over two fighting dogs might force them apart, but they need to be quickly caught and controlled before they fall upon each other once more.

When two neighbouring dogs constantly threaten one another and are always spoiling for a fight, it is sometimes thought wise to let them sort out their battle for dominance once and for all. This was the practice on farms in the past when it was considered preferable to allowing feuds to continue. Once two dogs have settled the matter they need never fight again.

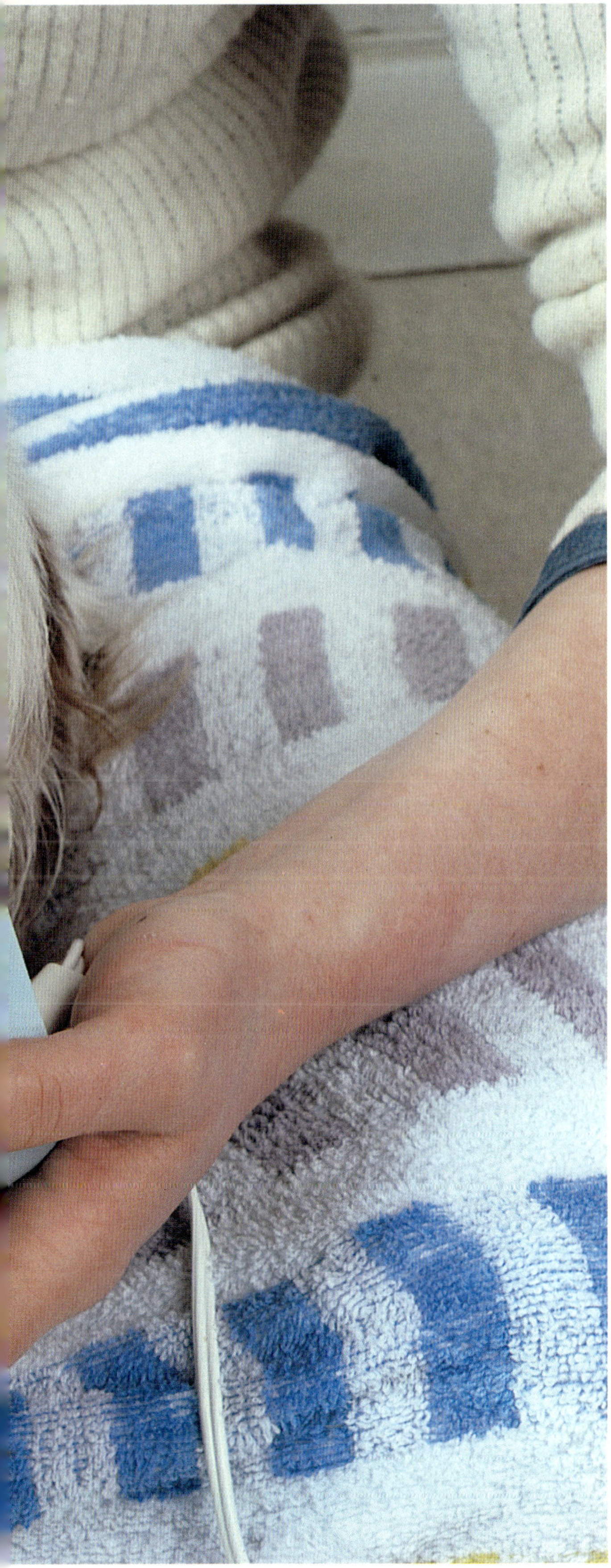

CARE OF THE DOG

From youth to old age, your dog will be dependent on you for loving care, and its health and wellbeing will show in its bright eyes, its shining coat and alert reactions. As it grows old, it will need and deserve special consideration. Your dog may go through its whole life without accident or illness but it is very important to know how to administer first aid and how to detect the first signs and symptoms of disease. There are times when recognizing a developing problem and taking veterinary advice quickly can make all the difference between a quick recovery and a serious illness.

The amount of food needed by individual dogs varies considerably; a gundog like this Welsh Springer Spaniel needs much more than a pet leading a sedentary life.

Many breeders maintain that 'half the pedigree goes in at the mouth'; in other words, correct feeding from the beginning will make a great difference to the dog's future condition and wellbeing. Though adult dogs are adaptable and will eat a wide variety of foods with enjoyment, any dog will be healthier and happier if fed a well-balanced diet. In past generations, pet dogs were fed on table scraps and leftovers but today so much of our food is processed, pasteurized, dehydrated, preserved and so on, that a diet of scraps would probably be lacking in some essential ingredients.

In the wild, dogs would eat other animals and consume the whole carcase, which would provide them with proteins, carbohydrates, fats, minerals and vitamins. Breeding and domestication do not seem to have had any marked effect on the dog's digestive functions so domestic dogs should be fed on meat and plenty of roughage.

Food and Feeding Habits

There are three main types of prepared proprietary dog food:

Canned food is usually cooked meat in various forms. Better quality products have more meat than gravy and as meat is 75 per cent water, make sure that you buy this type, otherwise your dog may end up with a meaty drink rather than a filling meal. It makes very little difference what meat is in the cans so if you find that your dog prefers liver, chicken, rabbit or beef, serve what it likes best. Most of these foods are supplemented with vitamins and minerals and they may or may not have cereal added. It is important to check whether the canned food you buy is intended as a complete diet or whether you must also buy biscuit to supply carbohydrate.

Dried food may take the form of flakes or pellets and is specially formulated to give all the necessary nutrients, so long as it is given with plenty of water. The flaked type of food has the advantage that it can be fed moist if the dog prefers, though some manufacturers claim that the pellet form is more easily digested. It is important to remember that dried foods have only a water content of 8 per cent, as against the high water content of meat, so that the success of the diet depends on fresh water being available to the dog at all times.

Semi-moist foods are popular with many dogs. They are softer in texture than dried foods and may be more convenient to store than cans. The product keeps well until opened but must then be used up fairly quickly.

Foods produced by reputable firms will contain all the essentials but dogs, like people, are individuals and what suits one may not suit another. If your dog is not enjoying its dried food, try canned and so on. When switching to another food, make the change gradually or gastric upsets may result.

It is almost impossible to give advice on the amount of food to give an individual dog. Like people, some dogs are good food convertors, some are not. Some of the very lively toy breeds and the small energetic terriers will need more food in proportion to their body weight than larger, slow-moving dogs. The amount of food required also varies widely according to the dog's lifestyle. For example, a German Shepherd working as a police dog may need 750 g ($1\frac{1}{2}$ lbs) of meat and the same quantity of biscuit daily. A similar animal leading a sedentary life as a pet would probably need only half this quantity, while a bitch of a similar size nursing three-to-four-week old puppies will need at least three times as much. An adequate diet is one that leaves the dog looking neither fat nor thin, lively and alert, with its coat in good condition. In our society, there are probably more overfed than underfed dogs and overweight owners tend to have overweight dogs. Overfeeding a dog is no kindness as it will become lazy and lethargic, its coat will shed constantly and its life may be shortened.

Food should be served at room temperature; if it is given straight from the refrigerator it can cause gastric upsets. Always put the food in a clean bowl of the right size and shape for the breed. A healthy dog fed a suitable amount will eat its food very quickly and lick the bowl clean. Never leave a dish of uneaten food on the floor; it will only attract flies and can lead to infection and disease. Feed your dog at regular times but do not give it a heavy meal just before taking it for a run. Make sure it has access to clean water, always keep the water bowl in the same place and wash it every morning before refilling it.

Avoid giving your dog tidbits at the table; it encourages begging and greed. Special chocolate drops or other candy do no harm if they are given in moderation, as an aid to training or for some special reward. Give your young dog an extra biscuit at bedtime. Chewing the biscuit prevents the boredom that often leads to destructive behaviour at night and the biscuit also helps to remove tartar from the teeth. A large raw marrowbone is excellent for your dog but cooked bones, especially poultry or chop bones, are very dangerous. Cooking makes them brittle and they can splinter and pierce the dog's intestines with disastrous results.

If your dog has a well-balanced diet it will not need extra vitamins or tonics. You may find, however, that a little margarine or vegetable oil added to the food will help to counteract a dull or scurfy coat at moulting time and the occasional egg or dish of liver or fish will benefit the dog's general health.

Special Grooming

Some breeds require specialist trimming or clipping to keep their coats in order and you should make sure that you know what is necessary for your particular breed. It is only possible here to give a general idea of the grooming needed by some popular breeds:

Yorkshire Terrier. Brush with, then against and finally with the growth of hair. The coat parts in the middle of the back and falls straight to the ground. After grooming, trim the coat in a straight line to prevent it from trailing along the floor. Many pets have their coat trimmed to 10 cm (4 ins) above the ground so that it is easier to look after. Trim around the feet in the shape of the paw and trim the hair between the toes. Gather up the topknot and fasten with wool or ribbon; take care never to tug as this can break the hair. In a pet, the topknot can be trimmed into a fringe. Trim the hair from the top of the ears, scissoring from the tips to where the ears widen out.

Shih Tzu. It is important to brush the coat regularly to remove matts and give a glossy sheen. Again, make a central parting and tie up the hair on the head. Keep the body hair underneath scissored in a straight line and clean the hair between the pads of the feet.

Poodle. The adult Poodle will need its coat clipping and bathing every six to eight weeks, and it is usual for the dog to go to a beauty parlour for this to be done. Puppies need to have only their feet and tail trimmed and this should be done at about four months. There are a multitude of different pet trims or clips for you to choose from, all aimed at keeping the coat within manageable proportions. Show dogs are kept in the puppy clip up to the age of one year and then have to be shown in either lion or continental clip. In the lion clip, the face and body

Each breed has its special grooming needs: this Dandie Dinmont has its topknot combed upwards to give it a 'woolly' appearance.

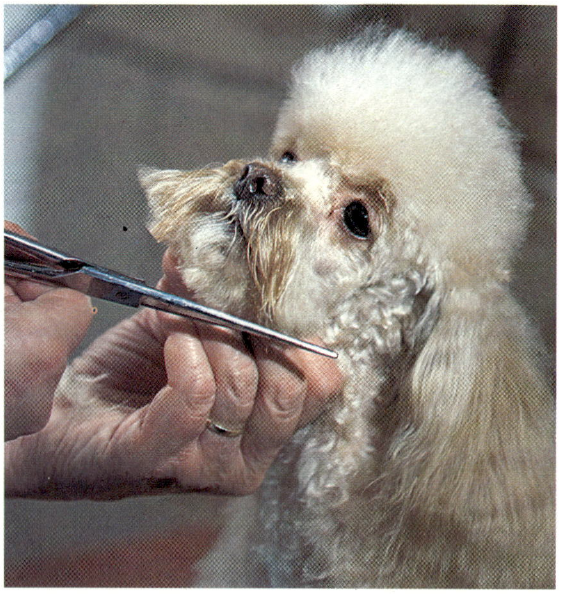

This Poodle is obviously accustomed to having its beard trimmed and waits patiently for the job to be completed.

of the dog are shaved, leaving a luxurious mane of hair over the shoulders and part of the rib cage. The hair is shaved off the front legs leaving two bracelets of hair on each leg. A pom-pom of hair is left on the end of the tail. The continental clip is similar, but leaves patterns of hair on the hindquarters.

Good diet, a healthy lifestyle and regular grooming all show in the general appearance of the dog; these Irish Setters are obviously fit, happy and in the peak of condition.

Cocker Spaniel. It is important to brush vigorously and particularly important to get out the dead hair so that the coat looks flat and gleaming. The feet should be neatened by trimming round them with blunt-ended scissors and the hair should also be snipped from between the toes. This helps to keep the foot compact and prevents the dog from bringing too much mud indoors. Thinning scissors should be used on the feathering down the back of the legs and on the tops of the ears to prevent it from becoming too profuse. The show presentation of a Cocker Spaniel is a job for the specialists.

Pekingese. The Pekingese needs a great deal of brushing with a good quality bristle brush. The hair should be brushed out from the sides of the body and the brush then taken upwards in a lifting motion; this gives the impression of fullness. Ears are groomed towards the face and the coat between the ears is brushed outwards to give a ruff-like effect. The tail is parted down the middle and the hair brushed to fall either side of the body in a fan shape. Combing should be done sparingly as in time it will reduce the density of the coat by taking out too much hair. Some Pekingese grow a great deal of hair on their feet and this should be trimmed for their own comfort. Great care must be taken when grooming round the eyes as even a slight knock or scratch on the eye can lead to ulceration.

Afghan. When grooming an Afghan as a family pet, your main concern will be keeping the long flowing coat free from tangles. You can help this by scissoring between the pads of the feet, being careful not to nick the skin. Trim round the feet to give a club-like appearance. Taper the tail feathering carefully. The Afghan's coat is parted from head to tail and the hair must be brushed downwards from the parting. The long, lean face should be kept free from straggling hairs by carefully plucking them out with the fingers; the same technique should be used with odd hairs appearing along the centre parting. Stripping combs or knives should never be used on Afghans.

Old English Sheepdog. Trimming establishments do not have time to cope with the great thick coat so they usually run clippers down the body from head to toe. The typical look of the Old English Sheepdog should be preserved by regular brushing and careful removal of matts. Hair round the eyes should be trimmed into a squarish shape to reveal the eyes. Scissor round the paws and clean hair from between the pads of the feet. When brushing, work in layers. Begin at ankle level, part the hair a few inches up and across the leg, brush the lower hair down then comb. Take a section above and repeat the procedure. With the dog lying on its side, part the hair on the body from neck to tail and proceed as for the legs.

Nails

If your dog is regularly exercised on hard surfaces its nails are unlikely to need any attention as they will naturally wear down to the correct length. The nails of dogs confined to grassy areas, or walked only in the park, can grow excessively long, however, and must be clipped back to enable the animal to walk properly. Always use guillotine-type nail clippers to cut your dog's nails, and ask your veterinary surgeon to show you how to use them correctly. Dogs dislike having their nails cut at any time so it is doubly important for you to know the correct point at which the nail should be shortened to avoid cutting the sensitive quick. If you cut too close to the quick you will hurt your dog; and if the nail is cut too short it will bleed profusely.

Anal Sacs and Glands

The dog has a pair of sacs lying inside the body cavity just below and on either side of its anus. These sacs store a distinctively and powerfully pungent grey-brown fluid produced by the anal glands. A small duct leads from each sac to the opening of the anus. Each time the dog defecates, a little of the fluid passes up the tube and is smeared on the stool, giving it its characteristic doggy odour. This scent is important in the wild dog, acting as a territorial marking agent.

The anal sacs sometimes present problems in the domestic dog, becoming impacted and failing to drain adequately. An affected dog may drag its seat across the ground in an attempt to relieve the irritation, or it will try to bite the area. If neglected the anal sacs will become infected and antibiotic treatment will be required. The veterinary surgeon can empty the sacs manually whenever necessary and will show you how to do this yourself if you wish.

To empty the sacs, put on rubber gloves and take a large piece of cotton wool in one hand. Hold the dog by the root of its tail with the other hand, place the cotton wool over the region of the anal sacs and press inwards and upwards with your thumb and forefinger. This action does not hurt the dog and the offensive matter will pass out into the cotton pad.

Fed a good diet and given adequate exercise, some dogs never have any trouble with their anal sacs while others seem to spend a good part of their lives going to and from the surgery. If the problem is persistent it is advisable to have the sacs and glands removed surgically, which does not seem to affect the dog adversely.

Bathing Your Dog

It is not necessary to bathe your dog as long as it is kept clean and sweet-smelling with normal grooming. Bathing removes the coat's natural oils which act as weather-proofing agents, so that a dog living in the open could be detrimentally affected by too-frequent tubbings. Pet dogs living in centrally heated homes often shed a lot of hair and may need fairly frequent baths to keep fresh, clean and tidy. Apart from removing the coat's oils, bathing is not otherwise detrimental to the dog's health so long as it is carried out correctly and the animal is thoroughly dried before it can catch a chill.

Some short-coated dogs may go their entire lives without ever needing a bath. Others which need regular stripping, clipping or trimming are often bathed at these times as the freshly washed coat is then easier to handle. Long-coated breeds, and those which are regularly shown, may have quite frequent bathing sessions. Bathing a smallish, short-coated dog is comparatively easy, but bathing a large, long-coated dog may take time and a great deal of patience especially if the animal is unco-operative.

Small breeds can be bathed in an old baby-bath, or a large bowl; larger breeds will need the family bath tub or may be placed near a drain outlet, preferably on concrete, and have warm water poured over them from a bucket or tub. If it is necessary to bath a dog outdoors, it must be done on a warm day. If the bath or sink is used, place a small rubber mat at the bottom to help the animal feel more secure. Every dog must be thoroughly

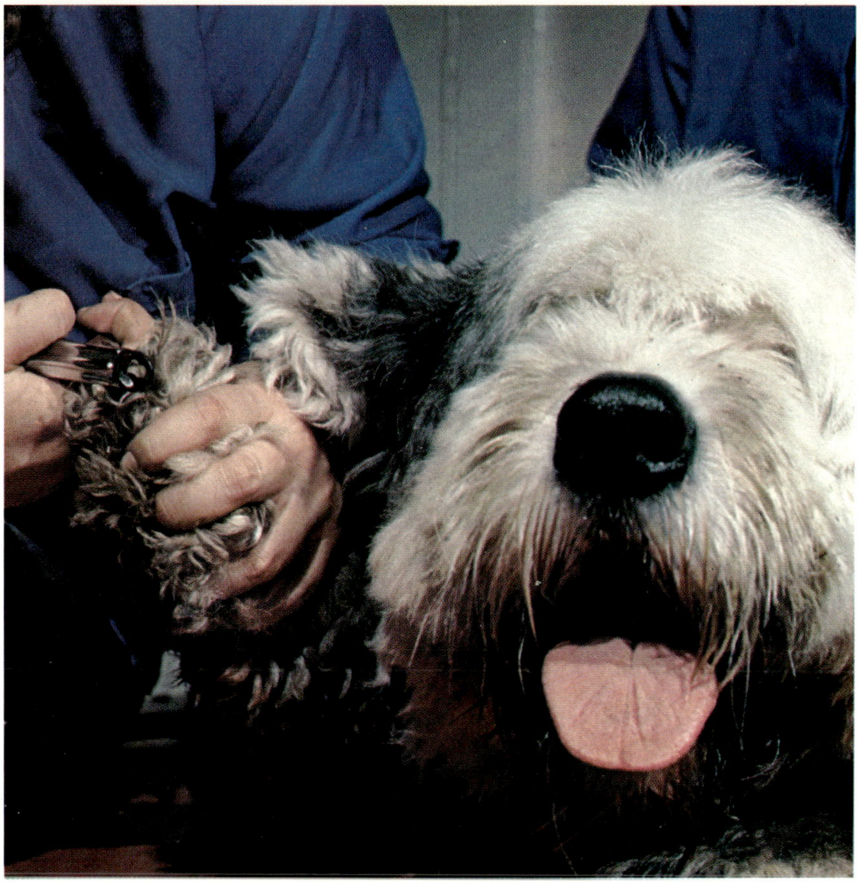

When nail clipping is needed, it must be carefully done with special clippers but it should seldom be necessary for a dog taking plenty of exercise on hard surfaces.

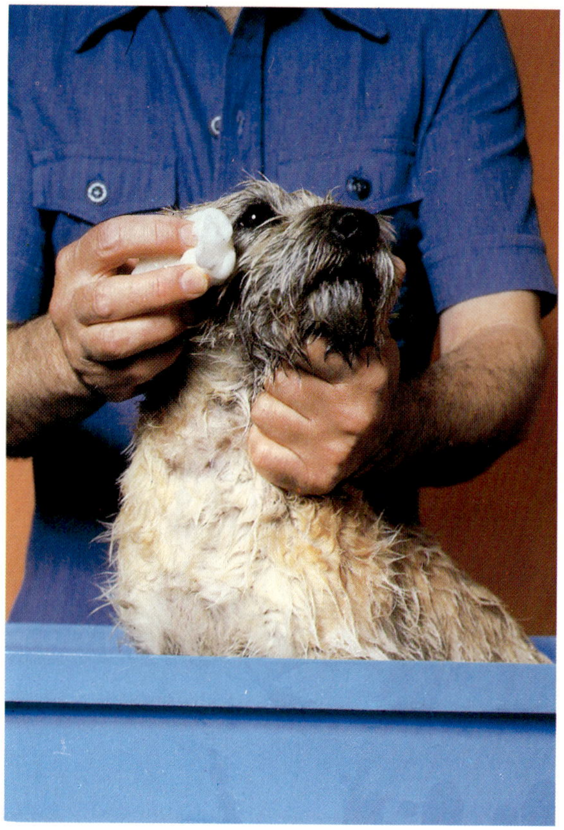

1. When bathing a dog, wash the face first, using clean water to wipe the eyes and nostrils and to wash any soiled areas around the mouth.

2. When the entire coat is thoroughly wet, apply a special dog shampoo, rubbing it well into the coat, following the manufacturer's instructions.

groomed before bathing, with any matted hair being teased or clipped out. Make sure the dog has a chance to relieve itself before you begin.

A hand spray is useful for wetting the coat and giving the final rinse; alternatively, you can use a jug or large sponge for the purpose. A large plastic apron or a plastic raincoat worn back to front will help to keep you dry. Remove everything from the bathing area before you begin in case the dog slips through your wet hands, and firmly shut the door.

Take off the dog's collar and sit the animal in the bowl or tub. Wash its face carefully and wipe out the ears; put a smear of Vaseline along the eyelids and plug the ears with non-absorbent cotton wool, also smeared with Vaseline. Thoroughly wet the coat from the neck downwards then apply the dog shampoo, following the manufacturer's directions, and work up a lather. Wash the dog's coat thoroughly and pay particular attention to the underparts, around the tail and between the toes. Use fresh water to rinse every trace of shampoo from the coat. Take care to keep the shampoo and rinsing water out of the dog's eyes, nose and ears and use tepid water only throughout the bathing process.

When you rinse the dog, squeeze as much of the surplus water as possible out of the coat and down the legs, envelop it in a large towel and place on the floor. Encourage it to give a really good shake. Towel as much moisture as you can from the coat, then use a drier or another dry towel to finish the job. If you have a breed that needs regular bathing, it would be wise to invest in a drier specially made for dogs. Long straight coats should be groomed into place during drying. You will need one hand for the brush and one hand for the drier, so tie the dog up or have it held throughout this rather long and tedious process. If you do have to tie up your dog, be sure to use a metal check chain or similar collar because a leather collar may shed dye onto the coat around the dog's neck when it gets wet.

Health and Sickness

Many owners can tell almost instinctively when something is not quite right with their dogs but many illnesses are not detected quickly enough. Disease may be acute or chronic: acute disease develops rapidly and the signs of illness will be obvious but chronic disease is insidious and may remain unnoticed until the illness is far advanced. The ability to tell whether or not a dog is healthy comes from a combination of observation and experience and a concerned owner takes notice of

3. Rinse all traces of shampoo from the dog's coat, using tepid water and taking care that the water does not get into the ears or eyes.

4. Finally, dry the dog thoroughly using a rough towel. Some dogs will allow you to finish off the drying process with a hair dryer, set at cool.

any change in normal behaviour as this may be the sign of a developing problem. Knowing the normal signs of health in a dog is the first essential and a methodical check of your dog's body and assessment of any change in behaviour patterns will often help to confirm the suspicion that the dog is not well and can be a great help in describing the problem to your veterinary surgeon.

Signs of a Healthy Dog

Appetite. Healthy dogs usually have a good appetite but a sick dog may eat less than usual. Acute disease is often accompanied by a complete refusal to eat but even a slight loss of appetite may indicate chronic illness. Never ignore excessive thirst as this may be the first sign of certain diseases. Make sure that you know the normal weight for the age and breed of your dog and never neglect any gradual, prolonged loss of weight.

Sleep and waking. All dogs sleep a good deal but should be alert and lively when they are awake. Sluggishness may result from a variety of causes, from old age or obesity to a serious disease like acute anaemia. If a dog becomes slow and lethargic, it should be a cause for concern.

Show dogs need bathing far more often than pets and may be dried with a hot air blower.

Healthy dogs sleep a lot but when awake should be alert and lively.

A dog's temperature should be taken with a snub-nosed rectal thermometer.

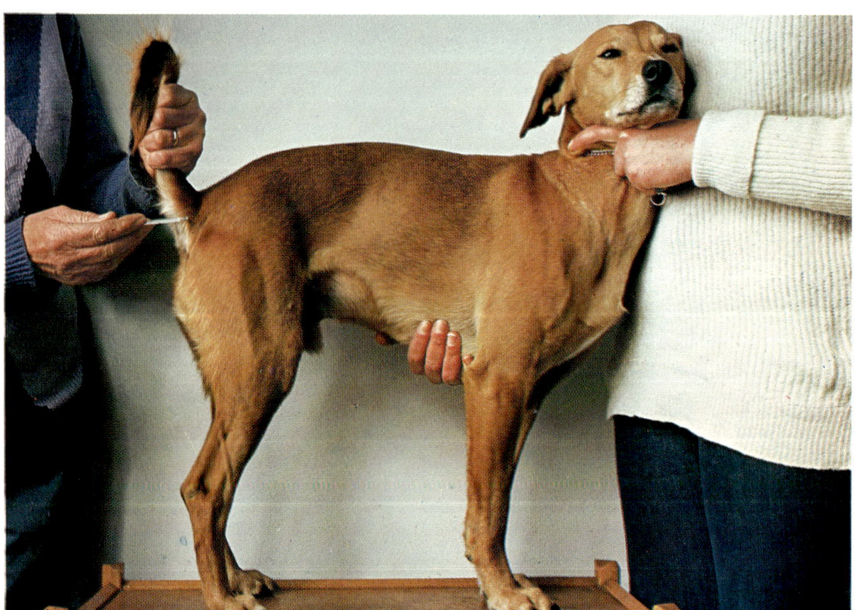

Eyes. The eyes should be bright, the whites clear looking, with no sign of swollen veins or discharge, but not excessively pale. The lower part of the eyeball should be bright pink.

Ears. The inside of healthy ears look clean and pink. They should be smooth, with no signs of wax, no black or grey deposits and no unpleasant smell. Matted hair in the ears is often a problem with Poodles as this can lead to a more serious ear infection.

Nose. This should be smooth and free from any discharge or encrusted material. If a normally cold, moist nose feels hot and dry, it may be wise to check the dog's temperature.

Skin. This should be elastic and spring back into place rapidly after it is lifted away from the animal's body. The feel of the skin may vary from breed to breed. A Labrador puppy's skin, for instance, always feels several sizes too large but it still has that healthy elasticity.

Body. Careful owners will make a regular check of head, limbs and trunk for unusual swellings or skin wounds, any sign of hair loss or sore inflamed patches. Standing or moving, the dog should appear comfortable: a haunched stance or lameness always indicates that something is wrong.

Temperature. The most popular guide to determining health is the dog's temperature, which is normally between 38° and 39°C (100.5° and 101.5°F). Excited or nervous dogs may run temperatures up to two degrees higher and a bitch's temperature may fall two or three degrees before whelping.

There is no reason why a careful owner should not take a dog's temperature. Use a snub-nosed rectal thermometer and grease the end. Shake down the mercury, then hold the dog in a standing position, talking soothingly, while you insert and hold it in the dog's rectum for approximately half the thermometer length, applying slight sideways pressure to hold the bulb against the wall of the rectum. Hold it in place for a full minute. Wipe it before reading and wash it afterwards in cold water and disinfectant.

Giving Medication

Medication prescribed for your dog should never be mixed with food. The correct dosage is important and your dog may detect the substance in the food and spit out half of it, or may leave the food untouched. It might be too ill to eat its food or only take a mouthful before walking away. With all but the fiercest dogs, however, giving liquid medication or pills is a fairly simple matter.

Liquid medication. Liquid medication is usually in 5 ml (one teaspoon) doses. You can give them by means of a plastic measuring spoon, which may be provided with the medication, or with a plastic syringe obtained from your vet. Have the dog sitting comfortably by your side and measure the dose. Hold the dog's jaws closed, tilt the head well back, then pull out the flap of the lip on one side of the mouth. This forms a natural funnel down which the liquid can be poured. Keep holding the dog's head and do not release it until you have seen it swallow. Rub its throat gently to help the process along.

Powdered medication. Medication supplied in powder form should never be poured into the dog's mouth because the fine particles can cause choking. Instead, mix powders with honey or margarine and smear the resulting paste on the dog's tongue with the handle of a spoon. Dogs usually enjoy the taste and look forward to the next dose.

Pills. The technique for giving tablets, pills and capsules requires a little practice. Sit your dog in front of you so that it looks towards your right. Place your left hand over its muzzle, just in front of the eyes, and gently press its lips inwards onto the teeth. With your right hand, open the mouth by pressing the front of the lower jaw downwards. At the same time, close your left hand slightly so that the dog's lips cover its teeth. This effectively prevents the dog from closing its mouth, but make sure that you do not hold the mouth so tightly that your pet is hurt, struggles or whines. Take the pill or tablet in your right hand and place it at the back of the dog's tongue. Allow its mouth to shut, hold the jaws closed and the nose pointing upwards and use the right hand to rub the dog's throat until you see it swallow. Once the pill is swallowed, pet and praise your dog. These instructions are for the right-handed owner, so left-handed owners should reverse them.

Ear drops. The dog's ear is a delicate organ and you should never put anything into the ear canal unless advised by your vet. Owners often puff or pour patent canker powders into a dog's ears with all the best intentions but they only clog the ear and cause the dog a great deal of irritation and discomfort, only relieved by syringing by the vet. Veterinary ear drops, however, are specially formulated and individually prescribed and your vet will show you how to administer them.

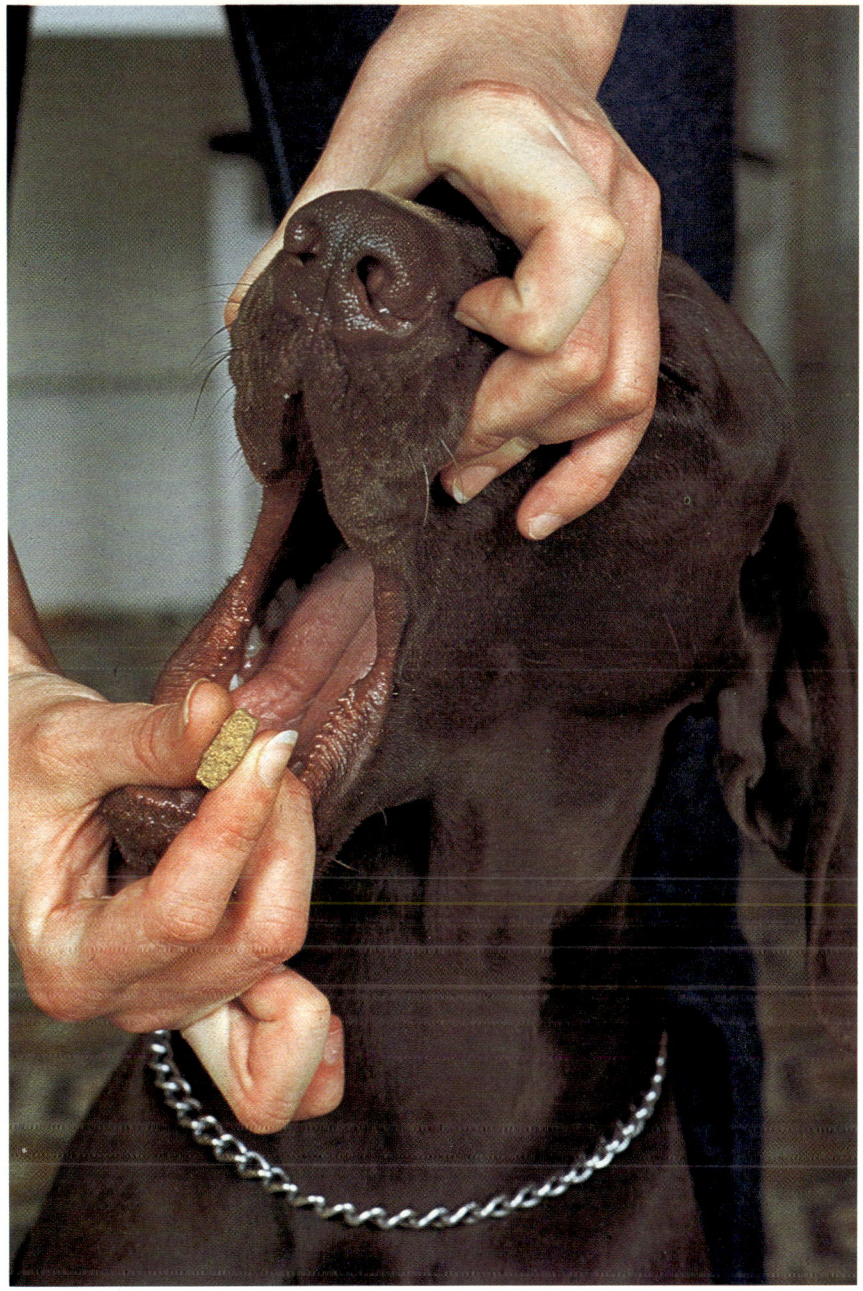

When giving a dog a pill, hold the mouth open gently while you put the pill on the back of the tongue, then close the mouth and stroke the throat to encourage swallowing.

Though an injured dog should be moved as little as possible, a dog hurt in a road accident can be lifted gently onto a blanket and taken immediately to the veterinary surgery.

Eye ointments. Dogs suffer from inflamed and sore eyes for a variety of reasons but two main causes are dusty bedding and travelling by car with the head sticking out of the window. The dog's eyes are very delicate and must be handled carefully. If the whites of the eye look bloodshot or there is a discharge, clean each eye with a separate piece of cotton wool dipped in saline solution or a mild eyewash made for human use. Saline solution is made by dissolving one level tablespoonful of common salt in one pint of boiling water, allowing it to cool, and storing it in a spotlessly clean, sealed bottle.

Persistent eye trouble must receive veterinary attention. If you are given ointment to apply at home, it is very important to apply it exactly as shown by your vet and to continue using it for the full length of time. Even if the eyes appear better, always continue the treatment until it is completed: the trouble may only be masked and could return.

First Aid

Road accidents. Move a dog injured in a road accident as little as possible, as it is likely to be suffering from shock and may have internal injuries. Try to stop any excessive bleeding straight away. First check that there is nothing in the wound, then apply a pad of gauze if any is available (if not, use a clean handkerchief, torn sheet or the most suitable clean covering you can find). Then bandage firmly over the pad. If blood seeps through, rebandage on top and take the dog to the vet immediately. To move a large injured dog with the least possible disturbance, use a blanket and enlist a helper. Slide the blanket gently under the dog and, with one person at each end holding two corners, gently lift the dog into a car.

If the dog is suffering from internal bleeding, its breathing will be rapid and shallow, its skin will feel clammy, its pulse will be rapid and it may be unconscious. If this is the case, simply get the animal to the vet as fast as you can.

Burns. Extensive burns are very dangerous. The only recommended first aid is to immerse the burned area in cold water and get professional help immediately.

Heat stroke. In very hot weather, or when shut in a closed car on a sunny day, dogs can suffer badly from heat stroke. The dog will probably be panting, weak and near to collapse. It might be vomiting and its temperature will be very high. Lower the temperature as soon as you can – if you are indoors, immerse the dog in a cold bath; outdoors you may be able to find a hose or fill a bucket with water to pour over it. Once the dog shows signs of recovery, towel it dry, keep it in a cool place and encourage it to drink.

Drowning. Not all dogs are able to swim and even a normally good swimmer may fall into water and injure itself or get trapped in a steep-sided pond. Once you have pulled the dog out, place its head lower than its body, pull out its tongue, try to drain out any excess water from its mouth and apply artificial respiration. Place the dog on its right side, tongue out and head forward, put your hand over its ribs behind the shoulder blade, press down on its ribs and release the pressure immediately. Repeat at intervals of about five seconds with short, sharp movements until the dog starts breathing normally.

Bites. If your dog has been involved in a fight, it is wise to examine it for wounds. These may be very minor but frequently become infected so that an abscess forms. Bathe any wound with cotton wool and warm water immediately to clean the area, then take the dog to the vet who will decide if antibiotic treatment is necessary.

Choking. Small rubber balls are the most usual cause of choking in dogs. The dog will be in great distress and, although able to breathe, will be unable to swallow and will salivate profusely. You will probably be able to feel the ball in its throat. The dog should be seen as soon as possible by a vet, who may have to anaesthetize it before removing the object.

Dogs sometimes get a rubber ball stuck behind their molar teeth, causing an obstruction. If possible try to remove the ball but be careful not to push it further down. Bones, pieces of stick and even stones can become lodged in the back of the mouth and cause a nasty wound. A dog with something wedged in its mouth usually paws frantically at its mouth or rubs it along the ground, slobbering profusely. Open its mouth carefully, taking care not to get bitten, and try to pull out the offending object. If you cannot get hold of it, take the dog to the vet, who will give it an anaesthetic before removing the object and treating the wound.

Prevention is better than cure so try to keep your dog safe from accidental injury by observing commonsense precautions. Never let it run loose on the streets and never leave it shut in a closed car. Keep your dog away from toxic substances, cooking stoves, needles and sharp bones. If, in spite of your precautions, your dog does suffer an accident, you may need to apply suitable first aid, then get veterinary treatment as soon as possible.

Remember that any dog in pain after an accident is likely to bite in fear and it is only commonsense to protect yourself by putting an emergency muzzle on your pet. You can use a large handkerchief, soft belt, panty hose, tie or scarf. Make a loop, slip it over the dog's nose and pull the knot tight under its chin; take both ends back and tie them firmly behind its ears. You should then be able to handle the dog safely.

Consulting a Veterinary Surgeon

All pet-owners should be familiar with the consulting hours of their vet and keep the phone number and out-of-hours emergency number along with the number of the family physician. Some vets hold open surgeries where you simply go along with your pet and wait your turn, though you should phone in advance if the case is likely to take longer than normal to deal with or if you suspect that your pet may be suffering from an infectious disease. Other practices run an appointment system where you will need to make a booking. The receptionist will normally want your name and address, the dog's name and the reason for the visit, given as briefly as possible.

The decision to hospitalize a dog for treatment is primarily one for the vet but it will be influenced strongly by the owner's attitude and circumstances. Whenever possible, it will be better for both of you if you take the dog home again after treatment or routine operations, as care and love are very important in the recovery process. In familiar surroundings, secure with its family, the dog will be more relaxed and will get better faster. However, there may be cases where a dog which has not fully recovered from an anaesthetic or is in need of specialized care, will be kept in the animal hospital for a time. For instance, if an intravenous drip is needed, the equipment must be set up by trained staff and continuously monitored and adjusted. In addition, the patient needs to be restrained and every veterinary nurse knows how to cope with a

When an emergency muzzle is necessary, use a length of bandage or material; this owner has used the belt of a dressing gown.

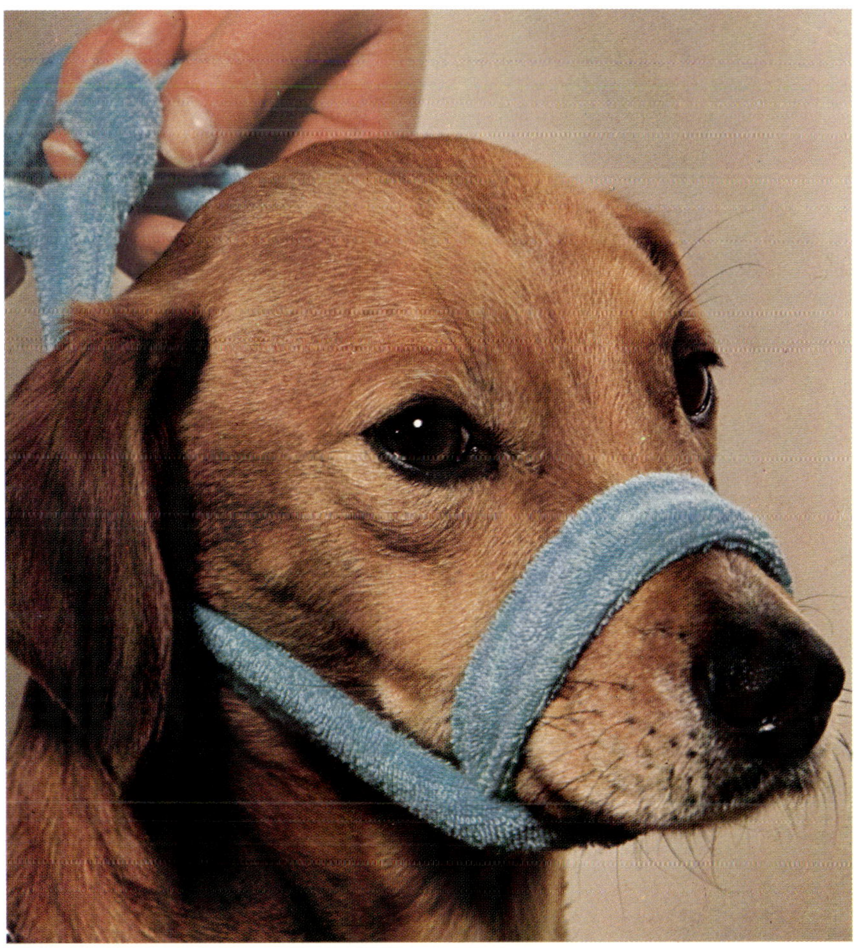

All dogs will need an occasional visit to the veterinary surgery to ensure that they keep in good health.

dog that suddenly decides to get up.

It may be necessary to hospitalize a recovering dog if the owner is out at work all day and unable to provide the constant observation and attention necessary, so it is important to discuss the question of care with the vet.

A to Z of Canine Ailments

Allergy. Dogs can suffer from allergies, like their owners. The most usual symptom is an itchy skin (*see also* **Eczema**); less common is a runny nose, sneezing and watering eyes. The cause may be dusty bedding, fleas, household products such as aerosol sprays or detergent used to wash bedding, particular materials like wool or nylon, or food. It is worth experimenting to find the cause as if this can be identified and eliminated, the problems will disappear; otherwise desensitizing injections may be necessary.

Arthritis. Inflammatory disorders of the joints are common in dogs, particularly in the heavier breeds. Although usually associated with older animals, this disease may occur in dogs less than one year old when they are afflicted with such problems as hip dysplasia and Legge-Perthe's disease (a disorder of the hip bone). The cause of arthritis is not completely understood, but it frequently follows physical injury. Obesity tends to aggravate the condition. Signs are usually insidious, with slowly developing pain and lameness, often noticeable as stiffness in the morning which wears off with exercise. Diagnosis may require X-ray examination. Treatment is palliative, but weight reduction of obese dogs should be attempted, and the dog's bed should be warm and dry.

Bad breath. An offensive smell from a dog's mouth may result from infection in the mouth itself, either a specific bacterial infection or ulcers, from decaying teeth and associated gum disease, or from generalized disease such as chronic nephritis (See below). It may also occur when the dog appears to be in perfect health otherwise. There is no first aid treatment for bad breath caused by disease; it will be necessary to have the dog seen by a veterinary surgeon. Foul stomach smells, if temporary, may respond to a dose of milk of magnesia. The dog with chronic bad breath, which is not caused by apparent disease, will probably respond only temporarily to veterinary treatment but a complete change of diet may succeed. This change may need to be drastic, such as a diet of rice and rabbit instead of beef and biscuits.

Canker see **Ear diseases.**

Cannibalism. Bitches at whelping, even normally placid ones, may become sufficiently psychologically disturbed to attack, kill and even occasionally eat their offspring. There is no treatment, but it is essential to have as undisturbed and peaceful a situation as possible at whelping time, and to allow the bitch to whelp in surroundings with which she has become familiar, preferably over weeks rather than days. Quiet vigilance is needed rather than over-anxious 'help.'

Car sickness. Some dogs have this trouble and others don't. There is no certain way of preventing it, but if a dog starts to be travel sick it is important to treat it before it becomes a habit. Depending on the puppy's size, up to half an anti-travel sickness tablet may be effective, otherwise a veterinary surgeon can prescribe something. Tablets may take a long time to work, so the dose should be given about an hour before the journey. Much of the sickness suffered by older puppies and grown dogs is due to nervousness from remembered previous occasions. A few trips protected by tablets may overcome the problem.

Constipation. Simple constipation occurs fairly often as a result of eating bones or indigestible matter. It may also arise from the dog's refusal to defecate because of pain from infected anal glands, or even matted hair around the anus. There are other, more fundamental causes and chronic constipation, particularly if it is associated with alternating bouts of diarrhoea, needs veterinary attention. Constipation is accompanied by frequent attempts to defecate. A dog which makes no attempt to pass faeces for several days is not necessarily constipated. The best first aid is probably liquid paraffin by mouth, about a dessertspoonful for small dogs and four or five times that amount for larger dogs.

Cough. Coughing is simply a sign of irritation in the dog's throat or bronchial tubes. It must be considered with other symptoms in determining the cause. Only rarely is a foreign body such as a bone involved, but an apparent attempt to clear the throat of something is often a sign of tonsilitis or kennel cough, a highly infectious although usually not serious disease. There is now a vaccination against kennel cough. It can be given as part of the standard distemper, hepatitis and leptospirosis shot. Any persistent cough requires veterinary attention. If the cough is accompanied by distress, or refusal of food, the attention should be prompt.

Cystitis. This is an inflammation of the bladder, more common in females than males. The animal will be in pain, straining to pass small amounts of urine frequently and the urine may be blood-stained. The vet will treat cystitis with antibiotics but in some dogs the problem does tend to recur.

Deafness. This is not common in dogs, but it can occur as a congenital condition and be noticed by an observant owner while puppies are still very young. A simple hand-clap will usually show whether or not the puppy is reacting to noise, but hearing which is simply less acute than normal may be extremely difficult to determine. Deafness frequently accompanies old age. There is usually no treatment available. Cleansing the ears of wax is unlikely to be of more than marginal benefit.

Diabetes mellitus. Diabetes is caused when the pancreas produces insufficient insulin so that the sugar level in the body builds up and spills over into the kidneys. It occurs most in overweight bitches, rather than males or spayed females. Particularly susceptible breeds include Dachshunds and Poodles. In spite of eating more than normal, the dog loses weight and it is constantly thirsty. A diabetic dog may require daily insulin injections and a strictly regulated diet. Once the condition is controlled, the dog may be able to live out its normal life. The vet may recommend that diabetic bitches should be spayed.

Diarrhoea. Although most attacks of simple diarrhoea probably have a nutritional cause, specific diagnosis and treatment is necessary if an attack progresses to enteritis, or persists for longer than 48 hours or if any other symptoms such as vomiting or blood in the stools are present. First-aid treatment for simple diarrhoea consists of removing all sources of food and drink and giving the dog a little plain boiled rice (possibly flavoured with chicken stock or something similar). Allow small amounts of glucose and water, given frequently. If the dog refuses rice, give it no food for 24 hours.

Distemper and Hard pad. Both terms refer to a disease caused by a single virus that may show some variation in symptoms. The first sign of either form of the disease is a high body temperature, about 39°C (120°F). The dog refuses food and may have a cough or diarrhoea; the whites of the eyes are usually inflamed. If infection progresses it will eventually affect the nervous system leading to intractable fits. The hard pad symptom occurs when the virus affects the horny layers of the pads, causing enlargement and leathery feel to the feet. Modern veterinary treatment, through the use of antibiotics, has tended to obscure the classic signs of pneumonia and enteritis in distemper. Little progress has been made in controlling the nervous involvement from which a high proportion of affected dogs die.
NB Vaccination is highly effective in preventing the disease.

Ear diseases. Head shaking, ear scratching and an unpleasant smell are usually the first signs of ear

Dogs with floppy ears need their ears cleaned regularly but never probe into the inner recesses of the ear.

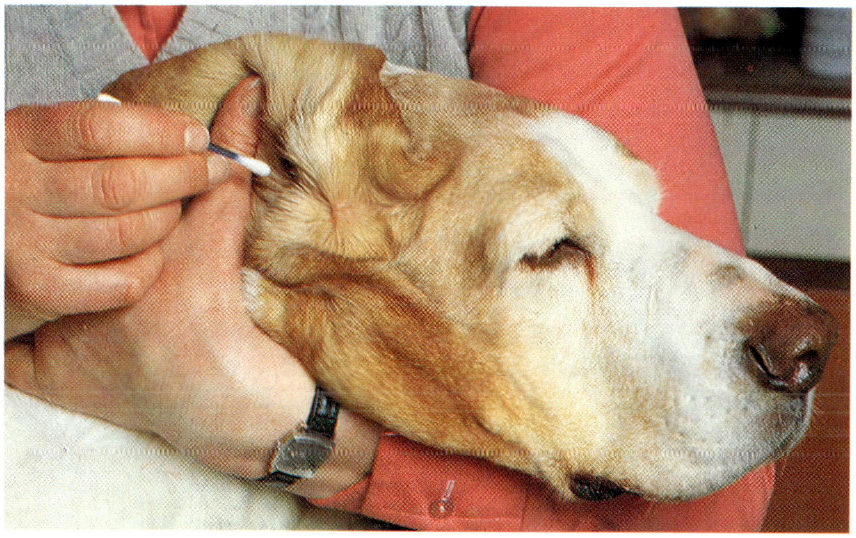

disease, and when this is noticed the ears should be examined. If the ear looks sore the dog needs veterinary attention. If the ears are simply dirty or contain a little clean-looking wax, clean them with liquid paraffin. Pour a small amount into the ear, work it gently from the outside and mop it with cotton wool. It is not safe to push pads of cotton wool into the ear unless you know there is nothing further down causing trouble. Acute inflammation, particularly in Spaniels, is often caused by a grass seed. More chronic infections frequently start off with ear mite infestations. Veterinary treatment depends on the cause, and in some cases may even require surgery to expose the inflamed area. Diseases of the ear are sometimes loosely referred to as 'canker' although it is a term that veterinary surgeons rarely use.

Eczema. Most skin conditions in the dog have a considerable element of self-infliction, and a dog can turn an itchy spot into a large patch of severe moist eczema in less than an hour. The first step in preventing eczema is to stop the animal scratching or biting itself. Then try to find out what is causing the irritation. In more than 7 cases out of 10 the cause will be parasitic, probably fleas. Most other cases will be diagnosed as allergic. Treatment of parasitic skin disease, while usually straightforward, demands far longer and more determined attention than it frequently receives.

Eye troubles. Eye infections are common in the dog, usually as conjunctivitis, and prompt treatment with antibiotics usually effects a cure. Ulcerated corneas may be more serious and any indication of blueing, or damage to the surface of the eye, should be attended to without delay. An acute eye problem is usually signalled by watering of the eye and closing, partially or completely, of the eyelids. Gentle examination may reveal the cause. If it is a foreign body, such as a piece of grass and it can be removed by the fingers or the corner of a handkerchief, do so. But do not attempt greater interference than that.

Fits. The presence of intestinal worms may occasionally cause fits in young puppies. The remedy is to give a regular worm dose to puppies under six months old. Epilepsy is a common cause of repeated fits in adult dogs, often starting when the dog is between 12 months and three years old, but loss of consciousness (usually without the typical nervous spasms of a fit) also occurs during the course of a heart attack. The best treatment is to remove any object that might injure the dog; do not attempt to put anything into the animal's mouth 'to stop it choking.' This won't help and you may get bitten. Then take the dog to a vet.

Fleas see **Parasites.**

Fractures. Suspected broken bones can only be confirmed and treated at a veterinary surgery. Despite a widespread belief to the contrary, sensible movement of the dog is unlikely to make the injury worse. The animal should be carried, if necessary on a blanket, and taken as soon as possible for treatment (See page 156).

Gastric distension. Bloat, gastric torsion, or gastric distension, is a well-recognized problem in larger breeds of dog. Two to four hours after feeding the dog may show signs of obvious distress and pain. The abdomen will be distended and hard. This is a surgical emergency and must be treated immediately by a veterinary surgeon.

Gastritis. Vomiting is the most likely indication that a dog has an inflamed stomach, or gastritis, but grass-eating without vomiting may occasionally be a sign (See below). Gastritis is often associated with simple diarrhoea, as in 'diarrhoea and vomiting' and in the more serious disease of gastro-enteritis. Both of these may have mechanical origins, possibly a swallowed rubber band or undigested bone, or be caused by bacterial or virus infection. *See also* **Diarrhoea.**

Grass-eating. This may be a simple habit of no significance whatsoever, or it may indicate irritation in the stomach (*see* **Gastritis**). It is generally believed that a dog instinctively takes grass to induce vomiting. Grass is most effective in wrapping itself around jagged foreign bodies in the stomach, so helping to prevent damage to the bowel.

Hair loss. Shedding of hair in a seasonal pattern is normal in most breeds, other than those with a Poodle-like coat, but central heating seems to have interfered grossly with the pattern in many dogs. Hair loss occurs after whelping or regularly in an unbred bitch's cycle, again normally as part of her annual cycle. No treatment can reduce or avoid coat-shedding; but regular grooming is essential at these times to prevent matting and itchiness from the dead coat. On occasions the loss may be so heavy that skin irritation becomes sufficiently severe to require veterinary treatment.

Hard pad *see* **Distemper and Hard pad.**

Heart disease. Heart disease is almost as common in dogs as it is in humans, and often has similar causes. The obese Labrador, for instance, is particularly at risk. Congenital heart conditions can receive effective attention. The canine 'blue baby' syndrome is recognized and can be treated by surgery, but most cases of myocardial or valvular disease are treated by drugs rather than surgery. Proper management of cardiac patients is important. Weight loss is frequently required and moderate but not excessive exercise usually desirable. Many dogs will indicate their own exercise tolerance limits quite obviously.

Hepatitis. Viral hepatitis is infectious among dogs. Adult animals may develop fever, with temperatures of up to 41°C (105°F), lose appetite and show blood-stained diarrhoea and vomit. Intensive veterinary care is required, but death can result. Vaccination is a preventive measure against hepatitis, and is 99 per cent effective.

Hernia. Externally noticeable hernias in the dog are almost always congenital, and may occur at the umbilicas or in the scrotal or inguinal areas. Small hernias are not significant and are composed of fat trapped in a sac of tissue. If the bulge varies in size veterinary attention is necessary to advise on possible surgery. The rare, serious sequel to a hernia is 'strangulation' when intestines or some other vital organs become trapped in the sac. Prompt surgical treatment is required.

Hip dysplasia. This is a deformity of the hip joint caused when the joint is too shallow and the head of the femur is malformed. It occurs more often than usual in some breeds, such as St Bernards and German Shepherds. It manifests itself by pain in the area of the hip and by a swinging gait and a 'hopping' run. X-ray is needed for accurate diagnosis although there is no cure. Pain can be alleviated by drugs or through surgery. This deformity is generally considered to be hereditary, although the extent of this is unknown; in any case, no dysplastic dog should be allowed to breed.

Jaundice. Obvious jaundice with yellowing of the skin and membranes is comparatively uncommon in dogs, but the underlying causes – blood breakdown or liver disease – are regularly seen. The jaundice itself is a minor symptom but should never be ignored. Leptospirosis and viral hepatitis may both cause jaundicing of the tissues. These diseases are extremely serious. Effective vaccines are available for both and are usually included in the routine vaccinations administered to puppies.

Kidney diseases. Nephritis, inflammation of the kidneys, results from infections, including leptospirosis in particular (See below). Chronic nephritis may progress over a long period and the dog will drink more fluid and urinate more often than normal, as well as losing weight. Acute nephritis usually involves a sudden rise in temperature, pain in the abdomen and constant vomiting. The dog will be thirsty and may urinate more often, or not at all. Treatment will probably include a special diet.

Lameness. The precise location can be extremely difficult to pinpoint; it is hard to tell sometimes which leg is affected. It is useful to remember that the dog nods its head downwards as the sound leg touches the ground; similarly its rump will drop as the sound hind leg is put to the ground. It will help diagnosis at the veterinary surgeon's if you notice whether, for instance, the lameness is worse first thing in the morning, or if it is intermittent. Careful observation will help. Pain on slight pressure, indicated by tensing of muscles and withdrawal of the leg, may guide you to the site of the lameness. Any lameness that is not obviously improving in 24 hours needs veterinary attention, but young puppies will often be crippled with lameness at one moment and virtually sound in half an hour.

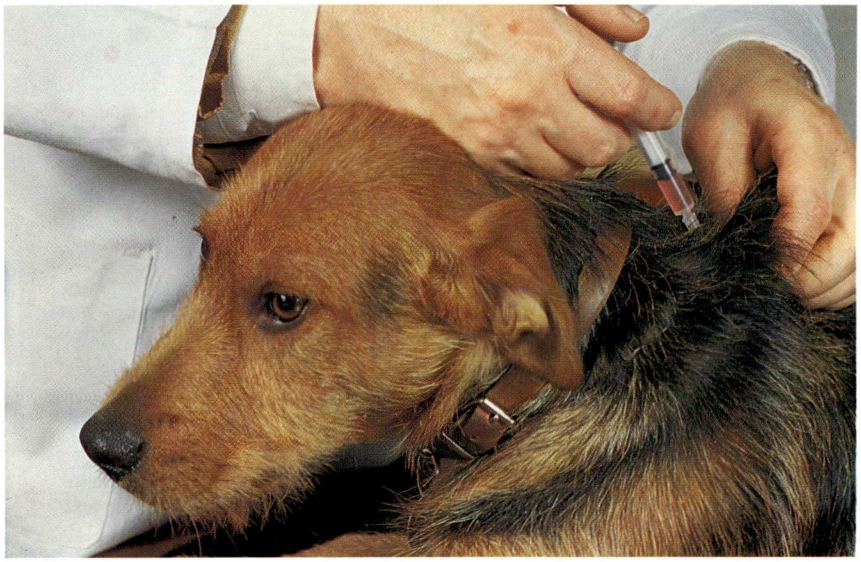

The veterinary surgeon will give injections in the loose skin at the back of the dog's neck, where they will not cause pain.

Leptospirosis. This is a common but serious bacterial infection of dogs. Although one type of the infection can be caused by contact with rats, the most frequent transmission is by carrier dogs' urine. For this reason the infection is considered to be more common in male dogs as they are more prone to lamp-post sniffing than bitches and consequently more likely to be contaminated by infected urine. In country districts carrier foxes may transmit the disease. It causes fever, marked depression, sometimes diarrhoea with yellow faeces, and often bright yellow urine. Visible jaundice is rarer, but both liver and kidneys are affected. Treatment is by antibiotics and effective nursing care. The disease can be prevented by annual re-vaccination.

Lice *see* **Parasites.**

Mites *see* **Parasites.**

Nephritis *see* **Kidney diseases.**

Paralysis. Hind-limb paralysis is frequently seen in the long-backed breeds of dog because of pressure on spinal nerves including injury caused by the protrusion of intervertebral discs. Treatment may be prolonged, but should be continued while the dog has muscular tone in its hind limbs. Conscientious breeders have managed to control hind-limb paralysis in the most affected breeds such as the Dachshund. Weight control and exercise also help to prevent spinal and associated problems. Generalized muscular paralysis is sometimes a sequel to distemper, but is otherwise uncommon in dogs. Sudden paralysis of the back legs occasionally occurs through pressure caused by simple constipation. It will disappear when the constipation is treated.

Parasites. Common external parasites include fleas, which are light or dark brown, very mobile and readily visible when numerous. They are often passed back and forth between dogs and cats. Lice are also quite common. The lice or their egg cases are quite firmly attached, often around the ears; they are white in colour and can be mistaken for skin scales or dandruff if not examined closely.

Sarcoptic mange is very serious and is caused by a smaller parasite that is not easily seen. It causes intense itching and skin sores.

Harvest mites are visible on careful examination. They occur usually in comparatively small numbers on the legs and lower parts of the body. They are not mobile, and cause intense local irritation.

Ticks are rarely important in Europe although they are carriers of serious diseases in Africa and parts of the United States. The sheep tick, *Ixodes*, is the common one to affect dogs in temperate climates. It looks like a small grey bladder when mature and is very firmly attached. It should either be left to fall off itself after a few days, or be removed very carefully by hand after anaesthetization with spirit. The sheep tick has long mouth-parts that are difficult to remove from the skin and cause localized infection if left in place.

Tropical ticks are easily removed, but may carry the blood parasite *Babesia*, which causes tick fever.

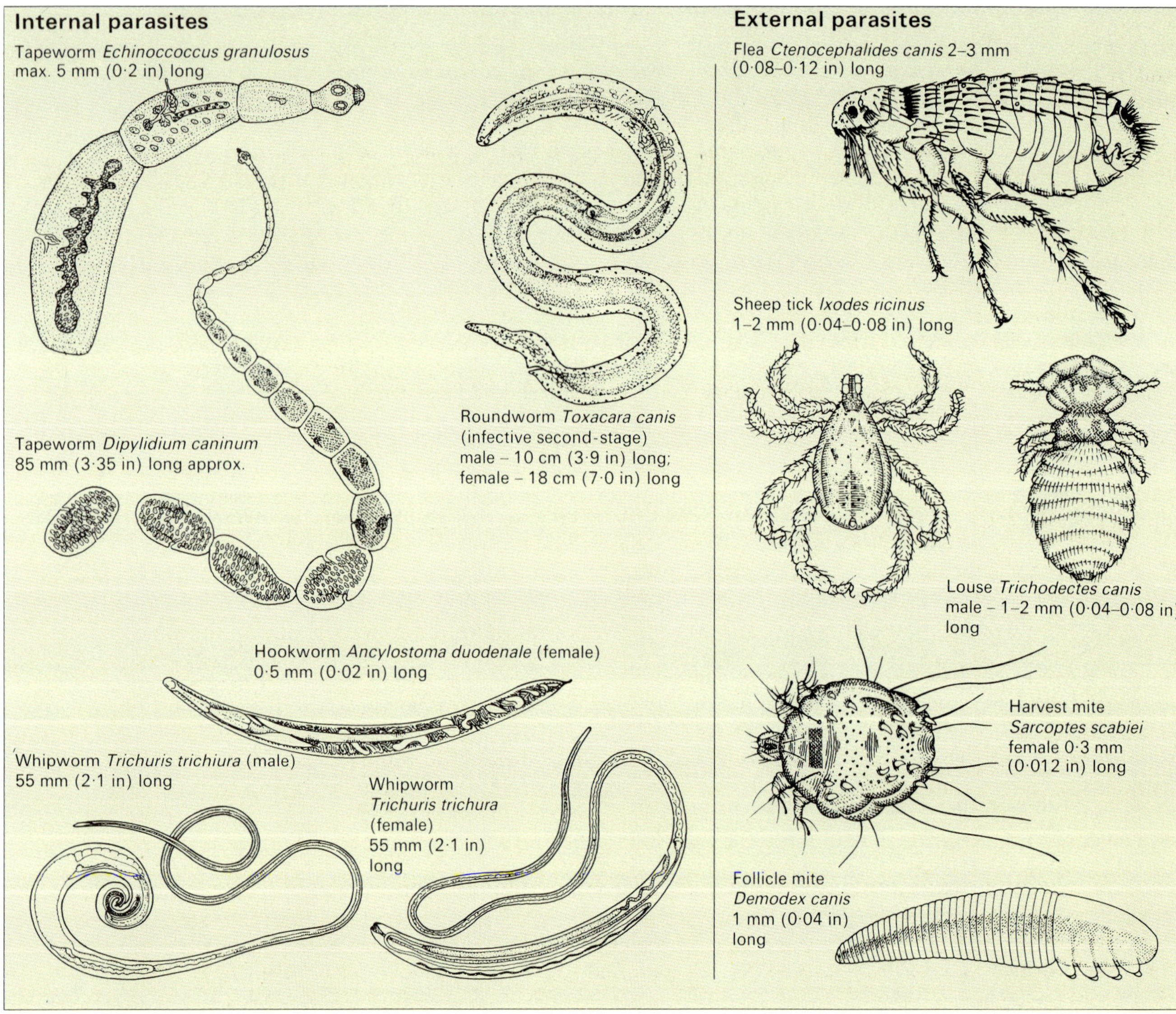

All these parasites may be controlled by baths, powder or spray insecticides. Determined application over weeks or months may be necessary to eliminate them altogether.

'Fly Strike' occurs in untreated wounds of dogs. Certain flies lay their eggs in the dog's coat, attracted by the decaying flesh, and small white larvae hatch in a day or two. Treatment of the wound and insecticidal attack on the larvae is essential. Fly egg deposits in faecal matter caught around the anus of hairy breeds such as Old English Sheepdogs can be a serious problem also.

Internal parasites include the common intestinal worms. Round worms infest almost all young puppies and are passed on from the dam and all puppies should be dosed from about three weeks of age. The eggs of the roundworm pass from an infected dog into its faeces and develop into the infectious larval stage. If faecal material is left lying about, in parks or in the garden, where children may come into contact with it and then lick dirty fingers, the larvae may pass into the child's bloodstream. Some children have lost the sight of an eye because of the infection so it is very important that dogs are regularly wormed and that dogs are not allowed to defecate in places where children may play.

Tapeworms are common. All have a life cycle that includes a secondary host. The commonest dog tapeworm is one that has the dog flea as its secondary host. Other tapeworms have a life cycle involving sheep and are a great nuisance in sheep-farming countries. New Zealand, for example, has a compulsory treatment programme for dogs.

Hookworms and whipworms are less common, but they both cause intermittent diarrhoea and other symptoms.

Different drugs are effective individually against each of these worms. Some newer ones are able to combat most worms. It is worth discussing a routine with your veterinary surgeon.

Parvovirus. This serious virus disease swept through North America, Britain and Australia in 1978. It is spread by contact with infected dogs or their faeces, so it can be contracted direct or brought in on shoes or clothing. It can spread very quickly and needs immediate treatment if it is not to be fatal. The symptoms are vomiting, diarrhoea (often bloodstained), depression, loss of appetite and high temperature. Every puppy should be protected by vaccination which should be renewed annually.

Peritonitis. Acute peritonitis is uncommon in dogs despite the variety of apparently dangerous objects many of them swallow. Signs include high temperature and a tense, painful abdomen. More chronic inflammation can occur with remarkably few symptoms. Take the dog to a veterinary surgeon if you suspect peritonitis.

Pneumonia. Although bacterial pneumonia is no longer the scourge it once was it is still a serious disease. If suspected it needs prompt attention. The signs include difficult or distressed breathing and general malaise. A deep cough is usually apparent and the dog's temperature is raised. Virus infections are also involved. Apart from conventional treatment with antibiotics and nursing, the use of oxygen may be helpful.

Poisons. Poisoning in dogs is uncommon. Signs fall into two general groups. There is nervous involvement with either heightened reactions ranging from muscular twitching to convulsions, or reduced reactions leading to coma. Modern insecticides are prominent in the poisons involving the nervous system. There is also the 'eutectic' group causing acute symptoms of gastro-enteritis, with vomiting and diarrhoea. Caustic poisons result in an inflamed ulcerated mouth and tongue, and the 'Warfarin' (Coumarin) type of rat poison may cause severe blood disorders in dogs. In cases of suspected poisoning do not treat the dog without reference to a veterinary surgeon. Take any suspected container or material with you when the dog goes for treatment.

Prolapse. Rectal prolapse can sometimes occur through straining during defecation, more especially in old dogs with weak muscles. Vaginal prolapse is an even less common sequel to whelping, but prolapse of vaginal polyps, giving the appearance at first sight of vaginal tissue itself, is more often encountered. The prolapsed tissue should be kept as clean as possible and the dog prevented from licking or biting the lesion. Veterinary attention should be sought.

Rabies. All warmblooded animals can spread rabies, a disease which has horrible consequences, and once it has taken hold it is invariably fatal. In countries where rabies is present, it is frequently carried by raccoons, bats, skunks and foxes. Bites from these creatures can infect a pet dog which may then pass the infection to humans. For this reason, it is important to check your dog regularly for bites or puncture marks and if you find evidence of a bite, take the dog to the vet immediately. A person who is bitten by an animal should consult a physician as speedily as possible, as effective vaccine can be administered if action is taken in time.

If a dog has been infected with rabies it can take months for the symptoms to appear. The first sign may be a personality change with a normally gregarious dog avoiding company, a gentle dog becoming aggressive or a placid dog becoming restless. Its bark may become high pitched and it may find bright light irritating. One frequently reported symptom is a sudden and inexplicable fear of its owner. After that the dog may progress to

When a sick dog finds it difficult to eat or drink, it can be fed glucose through the side of its mouth with a syringe-like applicator.

'dumb' or paralytic rabies, so that paralysis sets in and it is unable to eat or drink. Some dogs may go through a 'furious' stage where they become angry and snappy, likely to bite anything that gets in their way and liable to wander off, spreading the disease over a wide area.

Quarantine regulations in a country like Britain, where rabies is not present, are aimed at preventing rabies from entering and should be strictly observed. It is highly irresponsible to try to smuggle animals into the country, however good your intentions may be. Any animal suspected of entering a rabies-free country illegally should be reported to the authorities. In countries where rabies is present, like the United States, it is essential to vaccinate pets regularly.

Rheumatism. Muscular rheumatism is common in dogs, occuring generally but not invariably, after they are six or seven years old. The signs include intermittent pain, which may be localized or in various limbs. The condition is not usually serious but demands treatment nevertheless. Drugs are usually successful in alleviating the pain. A warm and comfortable bed may help.

Rickets. Rickets is a disease of growing animals, caused by an imbalance of Vitamin D, or calcium or phosphorous. There may be lameness, but the most obvious signs are enlarged limb joints, even enlarged bone-cartilage junctions down the length of the ribs. Giant breeds are particularly prone to the disease. A well-balanced diet is the best means of prevention.

Sex play. Male or female puppies will mount each other, or humans, in apparent sex play (see page 140). In the young this is considered more as 'dominance play' than an act of overt sexual implication and should be regarded in that light. The sometimes aggressive sexual behaviour of mature male dogs to their owner may have the same origins, but it becomes actively sexual and anti-social if not curbed. It can sometimes be cured only by castration.

Shock. Shock occurs readily in dogs exposed to typical situations involving trauma, such as road accidents. The symptoms may include apparent fright or dullness, rapid shallow breathing and pale gums. Shock, rather than injury, is often the cause of death after an accident. The dog should be kept quiet and calmed until veterinary assistance is obtained.

Ticks *see* **Parasites.**

Tumours. Both benign and malignant tumours can affect dogs and you should report any lump or bump that appears on your pet's body to the vet promptly. In cases of cancerous tumours, early detection can mean a complete cure. Any moles that spread or bleed should also be reported immediately.

Vomiting. The usual cause of vomiting is some degree of gastritis but other causes include digestive upsets, bacterial infection and the presence of foreign bodies or indigestible bones. Vomiting is a symptom, not an illness in itself. Dogs can voluntarily vomit. If your dog does vomit, and this happens more than a few times in a short period, if blood is present or the dog appears to be in pain, seek veterinary help. *See also* **Gastritis.**

Warts. Older dogs of most breeds suffer from warts, but they are particularly common in Spaniels and Poodles. Surgical removal may be necessary, particularly if the warts become infected, as often happens. A vaccine may be effective in preventing their reappearance. Young puppies occasionally suffer from a crop of warts, but treatment to prevent soreness until they disappear is usually all that is necessary.

Worms *see* **Parasites.**

The Older Dog

The first sign of ageing in a dog is usually greying of the muzzle. The coat may become duller and coarser and the dog may slow down in its movements. It is usually the eyes that begin to fail first, then the hearing. A dog will normally adapt quite well as its eyesight deteriorates, as scent will have played a much larger part in its life than sight, but you should make sure that its bed, food and waterbowls are always in the same place. Regular routine is important and any children in the family should be taught to approach gently, giving good warning of their presence. A dog that no longer sees or hears well may get an unpleasant shock if someone pounces suddenly, flinging loving arms round its neck and even a placid pet may react angrily. However, it should be shown plenty of gentle affection and not ignored if it spends more time sitting in its basket and fails to run to greet you.

Old dogs need quiet and warmth – though in very hot weather they should have a cool, shaded spot – and a bed large enough to allow them to stretch out, as their joints may be too stiff to allow them to curl up comfortably. The diet should be good quality, with less carbohydrates than when the dog was younger, and perhaps two smaller meals a day rather than one large one. If the dog seems to be less interested in food, it may be that its sense of smell is poor and serving liver, pilchards or perhaps a good quality cat food may help to reawaken its appetite; you might also try warming the food so that it smells more appetizing. If the dog seems to have difficulty eating, have its teeth checked for problems. In cases of constipation, add a little bran to each meal but do not serve very dry food – mixing in a little warm gravy can be a good idea.

Always let an elderly dog take life at its own pace. If it still enjoys a long walk, then there is no reason to cut down its exercise but never force it to walk further than is comfortable. If it slows down or seems to be panting, carry it home or, if this is not possible, let it lie down and rest until it feels like carrying on.

Any persistent weight loss, coughing, excessive urination or thirst should be reported to your vet without delay and in any case, six-monthly veterinary checks are advisable once a dog reaches 10 years. Diagnosis of a serious ailment does not necessarily mean that euthanasia is the only answer. With careful treatment, many dogs with kidney or heart problems can live a reasonably good life. Deciding whether or not a sick pet should be put down always causes a great deal of heartache but if you are hesitating over the decision, ask yourself one important question: is the dog still enjoying life? Your vet will advise on the likely progression of any disease and if you watch your pet dog carefully, you will be able to tell if it is feeling pain.

Some families, looking ahead to the time when their pet dies and leaves an empty basket, bring in a new puppy. Though some dogs take kindly to the new arrival, which may even give them a new lease of life, it is not usually a wise course. It is natural for a puppy to get a great deal of attention and the old dog can become jealous and unhappy. This can rebound on the puppy, which finds itself snapped and snarled at so often that it becomes uncertain and shrinking.

TRAVELLING

Transporting dogs abroad if, for instance, the owner is emigrating or is posted abroad for a long period is a business for the experts. It will be necessary to contact one of the agencies specializing in handling animals in transit; they will provide a travelling crate which will conform to the regulations and make sure that the dog travels comfortably. Each country has its own regulations for health tests and vaccinations and it is essential to ensure that all the documentation is correct, otherwise the dog may not be admitted on arrival.

You should accustom your dog to its travelling quarters a week or so before the journey by feeding it inside the crate, then confining it inside for a short time. Gradually increase the time until the dog will happily spend the night inside. This will lessen any anxiety the dog feels during the journey.

Most dogs will adapt well to air travel and arrive in excellent condition but a sea passage may be overlong. Special kennels are often provided but the lack of exercise and temperature changes can mean that the journey has a debilitating effect on the dog. Several countries have quarantine regulations to prevent rabies being brought into the country by an infected animal. In Britain every dog arriving from abroad, even from a rabies-free country, must spend six months in a government-approved quarantine kennels and during this period it does not come into contact with any other animal. If the dog does not develop any symptoms during this period, it is released to its owners.

BOARDING

If your dog cannot go with you on holiday and there is no one to look after it at home, you will need to leave it at a reputable boarding kennels. Anywhere with good facilities and caring staff will be booked months ahead, so be sure to make arrangements in good time. Your vet or the local canine society may be able to recommend a suitable kennels; otherwise you will have to rely on the telephone directory and personal inspection. Arrange to visit the kennels to talk to the staff. Look for spotlessly clean premises with no unpleasant smells, where the dogs are housed singly in sleeping compartments with an adjacent run. You will be able to see if the dogs look happy and come readily towards the staff when they approach.

Any responsible kennel operators will require each owner to produce a current vaccination certificate for a boarder. If they do not, then do not leave your dog there. Make sure that the kennel staff have details of your dog's normal diet, to avoid any upsets caused by changing food. Ask if you can take your dog's bed and blanket, to help it to settle into the new environment but do not take along the dog's feeding dishes unless you are asked to do so. Often the staff will expect you to leave your dog in reception and to collect it from the same place. This is to prevent upset and over-excitement among the other boarders.

BREEDING

The process of breeding from domestic dogs needs careful management if you are to ensure a litter of good quality, healthy puppies. The stud dog, the time of mating and the whelping area must all be chosen with care. Understanding the changes in the behaviour of the bitch when she is about to whelp and her instincts after the birth of the puppies will help you to take the correct action; it is also essential to watch for any signs of problems after the birth and be ready to help any puppy that is not feeding properly. Occasionally, you may even have to rear a puppy by hand.

The gains you will make from breeding dogs come mainly in the pleasure of handling and raising the pups, the close relationship you will develop with your breeding bitch and the contacts and friends you will make among your customers. Dog breeding is unlikely to make money unless it is done on a large scale, in conjunction with exhibiting and perhaps a boarding kennels, so that each facet of the business feeds the others. For small-scale breeders the cost of stud fees, food, vet's bills and advertising will soon swallow up any profits from the sale of the pups.

Preparations

Your schedule should be planned so that you are available when the bitch starts whelping, and then for several days afterwards you should be on hand to resolve any problems which the dam or litter may have. After three weeks the pups will need to socialize, they must be weaned and shown to prospective owners. The next six weeks or so, before they leave for new homes, are very busy for an owner.

You will need to set aside suitable accommodation for the whelping, secluded from too much household bustle. A spare bedroom is often a good choice though many breeders like to set aside a corner of their own bedroom, so that they are on hand to attend to the pups by night as well as by day. A garage or shed is only suitable if it is warm, dry and light and if the bitch has settled in well before the event. At 21 days the pups will need to move downstairs, or indoors, so that they can get used to the sight and sound of people and you may need to fence off a corner of the kitchen or hall. An enclosed porch may be suitable, provided it is neither too hot nor too cold and the pups can be shielded from draughts. The pups may outgrow this accommodation by the time they are six weeks old and by then they will be active and lively, though not housetrained. A shed or kennel, for daytime use at least, is the best answer; in good weather an enclosure in the garden may be suitable, providing it has some form of shelter. Puppies at this age can be very destructive if left loose in either house or garden.

Mating

Your bitch should be at the peak of condition when she is mated. Have her checked over well in advance by the veterinary surgeon to make sure that she is in good physical condition and does not have any defects that might give problems during gestation, whelping or lactation. She should have her annual booster shots so that, being fully protected herself, she can pass on the maximum amount of antibodies against disease to her pups in the colostrum, or first milk. This protection will last the pups for about eight weeks and then they will be able to start their own vaccination programme.

The breeder of your bitch may be able to advise on the choice of a stud dog. A local dog is preferable to one that lives a long distance away. A bitch in season is naturally stressed and a long, tiring journey may upset her so much that she rejects the dog's advances on arrival. For a bitch's first mating it is important to use an experienced stud. Temperament is of prime importance in choosing the sire for a litter of pet puppies: a good-tempered, cheerful dog is more likely to produce offspring with equable temperaments, who will settle well into family life with their new owners. If you are aiming to produce a litter of quality show puppies, then you may want to choose an outstanding champion as the sire. In that case, you can find advertisements in the specialist press or you can go to championship dog shows, taking your bitch's pedigree, and discuss mating with the owners of the winning dogs.

Bitches come into oestrus (season or heat) for the

For the first five or six weeks after the birth of her puppies, this Great Dane bitch will be a devoted mother; after that she is less closely involved.

A stud dog is specially trained from a young age and his lifestyle is quite different from that of a pet.

first time at about 8 months old, though this can vary from 6 to 15 months. It is not usually wise to mate a bitch at her first season as she is not yet fully mature and may make a poor mother, so most breeders will wait until the second or third season.

The usual time for mating is between the 10th and 12th day after the beginning of the red discharge. At the optimum time, the bitch will be taken to the dog. If the stud owner has the necessary facilities, it may be better to board the bitch for two or three days, so that she becomes used to the dog and they can mate at will. Otherwise two visits, not more than 48 hours apart, may be necessary, as one mating will not always do the job. The mating fee, negotiated with the stud owner, does not guarantee pregnancy but most owners will allow a free mating at the next season if no litter results.

Mating may be a brief encounter lasting 10 minutes or so, or a protracted affair of an hour or more. If the bitch is at the suitable stage in her heat, she will stand patiently while the dog mounts her and mating takes place. The anatomy of the dog is such that the mated pair are unable to separate immediately after mating. The dog gets down from the mating position and turns so that the pair stand back to back in the attitude known as the tie. Both dogs must be kept relaxed and calm at this time and under no circumstances should anyone try to separate them. After a while, the dogs will part naturally and both will clean themselves.

GESTATION

The gestation period is nine weeks, but the puppies may appear a few days earlier or later than this. During those 63 days the pups slowly develop and the bitch's abdomen increases in size in order to accommodate them. There is very little change in appearance and behaviour in the first four weeks; by the fifth week, however, the mammary glands show signs of enlargement and the bitch may have slight morning sickness. By the sixth week the abdomen is definitely larger. You should now start to give an extra meal in the middle of the day.

The pregnant bitch should have high-quality and well-balanced meals throughout the gestation period. She must be kept fit and not allowed to get fat. Your veterinary surgeon will tell you whether you should give any extra vitamin or mineral supplements. Tell him of the expected birth date in case you need to call him out. Towards the end of the pregnancy, the bitch's shape may change dramatically as the development of the puppies speeds up, and her breasts might secrete a milk-like substance.

WHELPING

Loss of appetite is one of the first signs that whelping is imminent, and the bitch may go without food for 24 hours. She will also appear very restless and may repeatedly go to the whelping box and tear at the newspaper placed there. This tearing of paper harks back to the behaviour of the wild dog, which would start to dig a deep burrow at this time in preparation for the birth. Just before the actual birth begins, the bitch's temperature will drop from 38.5°C to 38°C (101.3°F to 100.4°F).

Although whelping is a natural process, you may wish to call your veterinary surgeon so that he is ready to come out to help if necessary. Most whelpings are quite normal and even the maiden bitch copes beautifully. Many novice owners are distressed by the frantic panting that the bitch often makes in the first stages of labour, but the panting subsides when whelping gets under way. Regular contractions usually produce the first puppy about an hour or so after straining begins, and the rest of the litter arrive at about 30-minute intervals. With very large litters, the bitch may tire and the last puppies will be spaced further apart.

Each puppy is born enclosed in its foetal sac, which the bitch removes by vigorous licking. This frees the youngster's head and enables it to breathe. The bitch usually cleans away the membranes and, in doing so, severs the umbilical cord. It is quite usual for her to lick up and swallow all the debris of birth, including the placentae. (In the wild, these provide the bitch with valuable nourishment while she rests and recovers from the birth of her litter.) If the bitch is unable to clean and stimulate her puppies, you must do it for her. The most important thing to remember is to quickly clear the puppies' mouths and nostrils so that they can breathe. Dry the puppies with clean, rough towel-

This white Standard Poodle has produced a fine litter of puppies.

Puppies still enjoy feeding on their mother's milk, even after they have begun eating solid food.

ling. You do not have to be in too much of a hurry to cut or break the umbilical cord.

After giving birth the bitch's instincts are to hide and protect her babies. She does not like an audience at the birth or during the first days with her litter. Take care to see that nothing happens which will cause her to be distressed or unduly disturbed.

When your bitch has produced her last puppy, she will settle down and gather them all to her. You should remove some of the soiled wet bedding and replace it with paper towelling or a blanket of the special polyester fur material made expressly for such occasions. It is important that the puppies all suckle and receive the special first-milk, or colostrum, which contains the precious maternal antibodies that protect the puppies from possible disease during the first weeks of life.

The Litter

Puppies are born blind and deaf but with a keen sense of smell that enables them to find the bitch's teats.

If the bitch has had a lengthy whelping or is ill, or if for some reason her milk has not developed well, you may need to give some supplementary bottle feeds to the pups; sometimes it is also necessary to do this for early arrivals during a lengthy whelping. Any pup looking thin and empty may be fed by a premature baby bottle several times a day. Give each pup as much as it will take eagerly. It is always better to bottle-feed as a supplement to the mother's milk, rather than to take some pups away from her entirely. (For more details *see* Hand-rearing puppies, page 175) The pups should make no more than a warm humming noise, and any wailing cry or restless crawling about the box means that something is wrong.

Very few puppies are born looking like the breed standard; Dalmatians are born all white; some grey dogs are born black; brindle markings are not easily distinguishable; dogs known as 'red' look a mousy colour; in all cases the proper coat colour develops later. When the eyes open they are blue and this colour, too, will alter later.

After the first few days following the whelping, the bitch will begin to want extra food in order to produce enough milk for her pups. This should be well balanced, served at four meals a day and generous in amount. At maximum milk production time, when the pups are three weeks old, the bitch will require three to four times as much food as normal, with vitamin and mineral supplements in proportion. By now you will find you are spending a great deal of money on your litter, but this is essential in order to rear strong and healthy puppies and to avoid the bitch 'feeding the puppies off her back' so that she becomes pitiably thin and loses all her coat.

If the puppies' tails need to be docked, this should be done when the pups are 3–4 days old, and ear cropping, in countries where this is permitted, comes at about 12 weeks of age. Toe-nails should be clipped soon after birth and a tiny amount taken off twice weekly thereafter in order to stop the pups scratching the bitch's teats. Navels should be inspected daily, and when the eyes open on the eighth to tenth day they should do so in a clean manner, without pus at the corners or lids.

Above left: both yellow and black Labrador Retrievers may occur in the same litter.

In some breeds, the coat will change colour as the dog matures; for instance, this Old English Sheepdog pup will be grey and white as an adult.

Although the ears are only just developing and hearing does not come until later, you should talk to the pups every time you see them, to accustom them to the human voice and to give them confidence. Until the pups are 20 days old, they and the bitch should remain in seclusion and not have visitors, not should the bitch go into the street for exercise. The noses of the pups will remain bright pink in most breeds. Black pigmentation begins as little dots which later fuse together to give the jet black nose desirable in all but the grey and liver breeds and the yellow Labrador Retriever.

The health of the bitch must be watched all the time she is feeding the pups as any poor appetite or refusal of food is a danger sign at this time. She should also be groomed and kept free of fleas and lice, but any powder or substance which the pups may lick must not be used. The great calamity which may overtake the bitch is eclampsia, a failure of her body to mobilize calcium which can, if neglected, lead to her death in a few hours. The symptoms are best described as 'odd behaviour' – hiding under furniture, eating plaster off the walls, continually glancing at walls and ceiling, paralysis of hind-quarters, or any deranged and unnatural demon-strations. The next stage will be convulsions,

Each puppy should have its own feeding bowl but it can be difficult to make sure that each gets its fair share.

prostration and death. Immediate veterinary help, day or night is essential from any vet if your own is not available. The reversal of the condition is quite dramatic and the bitch will be perfectly all right if you get help in time. This condition occurs most frequently when the pups are around three to four weeks old but it may come at any time, even just before the birth.

WEANING

Changing the puppy's diet from its mother's milk to a more solid diet can begin at three weeks of age or a little later. In the wild, the mother would regurgitate her own partly digested food as her milk began to dry up and breeders imitate this diet by soaking baby cereals in warm milk. You can begin by teaching the puppies to lap warm milk from a saucer. Introduce it to the puppies by wetting your finger in the milk and smearing it on their muzzles. Offer a fresh saucer of milk three times a day; first thing in the morning, at midday and in the early evening. As the puppies begin to lap, start reducing the mother's food and keep her away from the litter for periods of two or three hours.

Once the puppies are lapping freely you can introduce solid food. Soak a little baby cereal or specially prepared puppy meal in an equal volume of hot milk and allow the mixture to cool to blood heat. Offer this food two or three times a day at what you intend to be regular mealtimes. It is a good idea to feed puppies on a flat tray, large enough for all the heads to go round it, as this encourages competition. At first the pups will try to suck out the milk but in about a week they should be eating solid food. The texture should not be sticky but consist of separate, soft, moist pieces. Continue to reduce the bitch's food and remove her from the pups except at night and for one or two brief periods during the day.

After about six weeks the puppies should be fully weaned and it is now important to increase the quantity of food rapidly to keep pace with growth. Keep the midday meal small while increasing the quantity of solid food, but not of milk, at the morning and evening meals. Water must now be freely available and a little warm milk can also be offered in the late evening. The total amount of milk each day should range from about 0.15 litres (¼ pt, ⅝ cup) for very small breeds to 0.5 litres (1 pt, 2½ cups) for giants. At this stage, the puppies should be fed in individual bowls so that each gets its share.

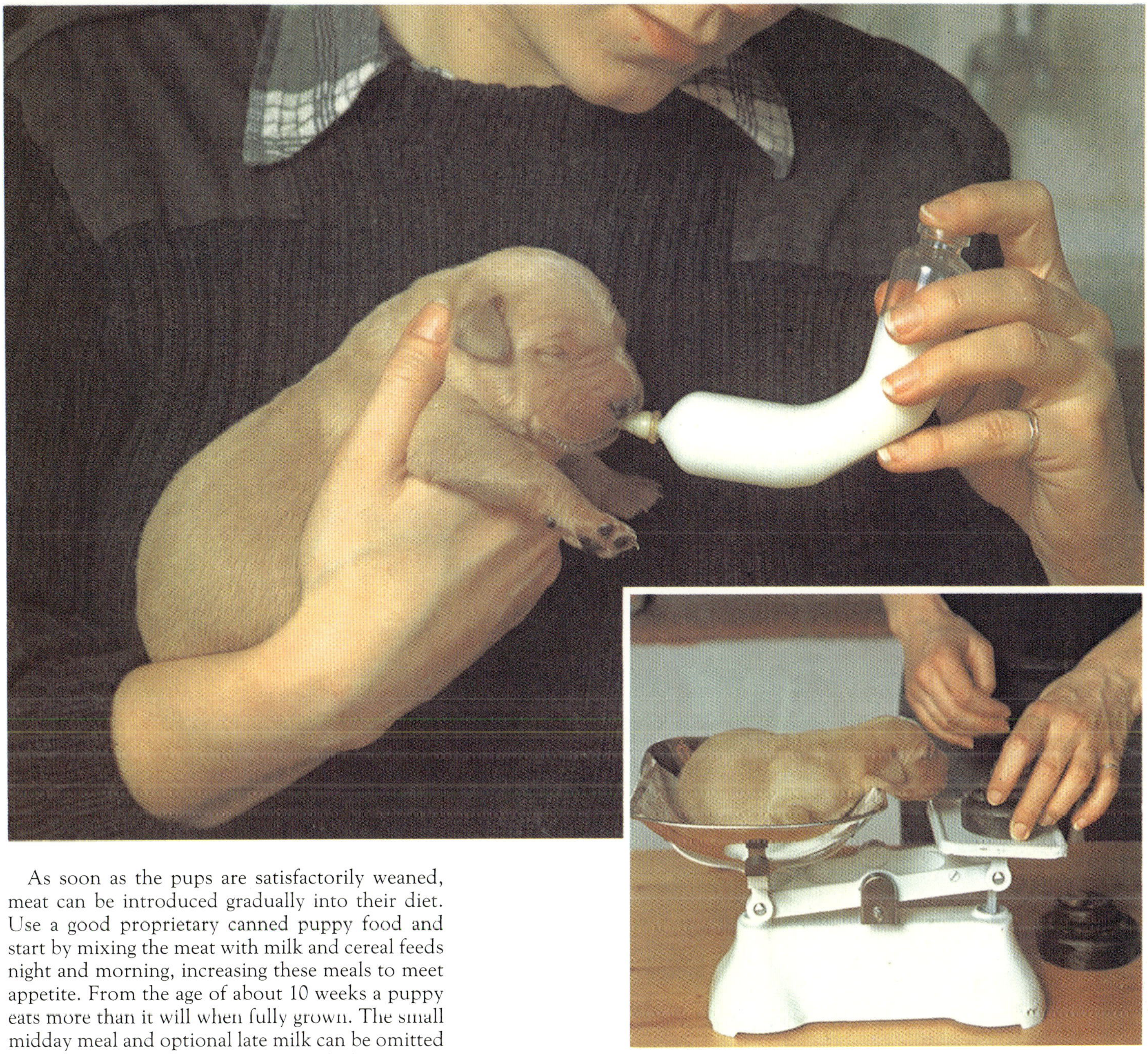

As soon as the pups are satisfactorily weaned, meat can be introduced gradually into their diet. Use a good proprietary canned puppy food and start by mixing the meat with milk and cereal feeds night and morning, increasing these meals to meet appetite. From the age of about 10 weeks a puppy eats more than it will when fully grown. The small midday meal and optional late milk can be omitted from the age of three months, if not before.

Hand-rearing Puppies

It is sometimes necessary to hand-rear puppies if, for instance, they are orphaned at birth, they are rejected by the mother or she is unable to feed them. If the puppies are weak and sickly, your vet will advise on how they should be fed. If they are normally healthy, they can be fed with a proprietary canine milk substitute, mixed fresh every day and fed lukewarm. Do not feed puppies on human baby milk, as this is not rich enough for them. Use a premature baby's feeding bottle or a special animal nursing bottle; either will prevent the puppy taking in too much air. Feed at two-hourly intervals at first, lengthening to three-hourly after a couple of days, then six feeds a day within a week. After that, four feeds a day should be sufficient until weaning. Do not hold a puppy on its back while feeding, like a baby. Instead, support the puppy from underneath, with your hand under its chest, leaving its legs to move freely, as they would when feeding from its mother.

Newborn orphans must be kept warm and you will need to stimulate them to empty their bladder and bowels. You can do this by gently massaging the abdominal and anal area after each feed, using a tissue moistened with warm water or baby oil.

A puppy can be hand-reared, using a special feeding bottle and a canine milk substitute. It is advisable to keep a regular check on the puppy's weight, to ensure that it is making progress.

These two Golden Retriever puppies are at a most appealing stage.

SHOWING

Every year thousands of dog shows are held all over the world, from informal local events to prestigious championship shows with only the best eligible to compete. Some shows concentrate on conformation, others include obedience trials. Apart from the opportunity to have your dog compared and assessed against others, these are social events where dog lovers can meet and share their enthusiasm, and showing can become a year-round hobby for the whole family. However, presenting your dog to its best advantage is an art and you need to be prepared to spend time on preparing your dog's appearance and behaviour for the show ring.

The Irish Wolfhound is one of the breeds that might have died out, but for breeding by enthusiasts for showing purposes.

In the days when dog fighting, bull- and bear-baiting were popular activities, dogs were bred for their speed, stamina and ferocity but when these cruel sports were banned, owners began matching their dogs with one another for appearance only. The first record of an organized dog show was in Newcastle-upon-Tyne in England in June 1859, with one class for Setters and one for Pointers, and the following year the first 'exhibition' for all breeds was held in Birmingham. The British Kennel Club was founded in 1873 and the American Kennel Club in 1884. These Kennel Clubs are still recognized as the ruling bodies in their respective countries. The clubs lay down standards for the breeds, and these are the 'blueprints' against which individual dogs are judged. The breed standard covers conformation, colour and type of coat, colour and shape of eyes, gait and temperament. Some breeds are not universally recognized; for instance the Löwchen and the Swedish Vallhund are recognized by the Kennel Club in Britain but not by the American Kennel Club. Dogs such as the Border Collie, the Australian Kelpie and the Chinese Crested Dog, all recognised in Britain, are placed in a 'Miscellaneous' class in the United States. This means that they can compete in obedience trials or Miscellaneous classes at conformation shows but they are not eligible for championship points. Dogs in the Miscellaneous class will only be fully recognized if the Kennel Club is convinced that there is a genuine nationwide interest in the breed.

The merits of dog shows are frequently criticized, with opposing factions maintaining that certain breeds have been either improved or ruined as a result of showing. The supporters claim that some breeds, such as the Irish Wolfhound and the Old English Mastiff, would be extinct if it were not for dog shows and that the breeding of an animal to certain standards of perfection is a never-ending source of pleasure and satisfaction. The detractors claim that breeding to supposedly desirable standards has meant that the appearance of some dogs has been exaggerated to the point where it affects their health: the Bulldog's nose is so snubbed that it has breathing problems, Basset Hounds are

so long and heavy that they are vulnerable to back trouble and the miniaturizing of the Poodle has led to weak hip joints and slipping kneecaps.

Show Organisation

Dog shows fall into two main categories: those confined to a particular breed and those covering many varieties of the breeds registered with the governing Kennel Club. The more serious shows are run under strict rules but there are informal shows where beginners, both competitors and judges, can gain experience. In Britain these are called 'exemption' shows, because they are exempt from Kennel Club rules, and they have classes for both pedigree dogs and pets. In the United States, informal events are 'dog matches', usually with both conformation and obedience classes.

Shows in each country have separate classes for dogs and bitches and the classes for each sex are subdivided, so that numbers do not become unwieldy.

Regular classes at an American dog show are as follows:

Puppy. This may be divided into puppies from 6 to 9 months and puppies from 9 to 12 months.

Novice. Dogs at least 6 months old which have not won other adult classes and have not won Novice more than 3 times.

At a show, dogs are judged on how well they measure up to an ideal standard for the breed. Top dog handler Mr P. Green shows a Wire Fox Terrier at the Montgomery Dog Show, USA (left), while an Afghan Hound is given a final grooming before a show at Bull Run, Virginia, USA (right).

Bred by exhibitor. Dogs aged 6 months or more, bred and shown by the same person or the co-breeder.

American bred. Dogs 6 months and over, bred in the USA.

Open. Dogs 6 months and over, including imported dogs.

The divisions in Britain, where dog shows are some of the largest in the world, are far more complicated and details can be obtained from the Kennel Club.

For many, the highlight of a dog show is the

This long-coated Chihuahua has been a top winner at Crufts, Britain's most prestigious dog show.

selection of Best in Show. First, the best dog and the best bitch in each breed are chosen from the individual class winners. The dog and bitch then meet and one is chosen as Best of Breed. The Best of Breeds are then judged in their relevant groups (Hound, Gundog, Working Dog, Toy, etc) and one is chosen as Best of Group. The group winners then appear again in the ring so that the judge can choose the Best in Show.

Show Judging

Different countries use different procedures for awarding the title of champion in dog shows. The United States uses a points system. To become a champion a dog must accumulate 15 points. Points are awarded to the best of each sex in accordance with the number of dogs of the breed competing at each show. The numbers governing the points value of a show vary in different parts of the country, in an attempt to give more equal chances to the less popular breeds, or the more sparsely populated areas. The lowest rating is 1 and the highest 5. Two of the shows at which a champion has succeeded must be major shows carrying, 3, 4 or 5 points. The Canadian Kennel Club runs a similar system to the American one, though at least 10 points must be awarded by at least three different judges.

In Britain, dogs become champions when they have been awarded three Challenge Certificates by three different judges, at least one after the dog is 12 months old. Judges at Championship shows may award Challenge Certificates to the best of each sex in a breed but the award is not automatic and the judge must consider that the animal is worthy of the title of champion. These certificates are much prized because it is considered more difficult to achieve champion status under the British system than under others. A modified form of the British system is used in Commonwealth countries, except for Canada.

The Scandinavian and west European kennel clubs, as well as some in South America and eastern Europe, operate under the auspices of the Fédération Cynologique Internationale (FCI). This body was founded in 1911 by the French, German, Belgian, Dutch and Austrian kennel clubs to organize and control dog shows. The FCI creates champions by awarding Certificates of Aptitude, Championship International, Beauty (CACIB). The dog must win at least four of these in at least three different countries under three different judges.

The routine of judging is broadly similar in each country, though it varies slightly from one individual to another. The combination of hand and eye tells a good judge all he or she needs to know about a dog. The assessment involves looking, feeling and the study of the dog's movement. Movement is often the most searching assessment, as many blemishes can be concealed when the dog is posed by a clever handler. Toes with a tendency to turn out can be placed in the correct position and a dog with hindlegs tucked underneath can be trained to stand with them placed well out behind. Loose elbows, a badly carried head or cow hocks may not be detected when the dog is standing still but once it moves, all is revealed. The judge can assess the dog's gait, the carriage of the tail and head.

Judges measure each dog against their idea of the ideal dog in a particular breed. Judging dogs according to group involves comparing entries with the standards for each breed. A Pekingese is not compared to a Great Dane as such but the winner will be the dog which comes nearer to the judge's picture of the ideal for its breed. For instance, if the Great Dane was a fine, elegant specimen, sound in movement, with a good head and well-arched neck, while the Pekingese had a 'weak' head and protruding nose, as well as a long and oversized body, it would be easy to judge the Great Dane the winner. Working on the same principles, a skilled judge can rank 20 dogs in order.

Preparing for Showing

Owners who are interested in showing their dogs should spend time at shows, both small local events and championship shows, observing the routine and talking to breeders and professional handlers. Watch how the experts handle their dogs and display them to the best advantage. You may hear stories about judges who 'judge the other end of the leash' from owners who have shown a dog unsuccessfully for a long time, then sold it to another

The Yorkshire Terrier's long, silky tresses are rolled in tissue paper and secured by rubber bands to prevent them breaking or becoming matted before the show (top right).

German Shepherds are often successful in obedience trials, which include retrieving a dumbbell (below right).

owner who immediately starts winning classes. The truth is probably that the new owner has managed to present the dog to perfection, instead of dragging it round the show ring like the first owner. Presentation and showmanship may not be able to turn a bad dog into a good one but it can improve its appearance considerably.

Breeds vary so much that preparation for a show varies just as much. A book devoted to your particular breed of dog will give detailed advice on preparing the animal for the show ring and you can pick up plenty of tips by talking to experienced exhibitors. However, several general points apply to any show dog. Good condition 'goes in at the mouth' and no amount of grooming and training can make up for an incorrect diet. Adequate exercise is also essential, though 'adequate' is the key word. A showdog does not need to be as fit as a racing Greyhound; in fact, it should carry more flesh to give a more rounded appearance.

Handling

To win in the show ring the dog must walk well on the lead, stand to be handled by the judge and have a general air of self-possession. Training your dog to walk on the lead, adjusting to your pace and stopping when you stop, is very important; it should also be accustomed to trotting on the lead without breaking stride, holding up its head. Your pet should be used to other dogs, to noise and bustle, so training classes can be very useful and some canine societies run handling classes for 'beauty' dogs, as opposed to 'obedience' dogs.

Practice posing your dog in the correct position – head up, feet well-placed – from puppyhood. Ask friends to help by examining teeth and, on a male dog, the testicles, so that your dog is used to being handled and examined. Judges have a very short time available in which to assess a dog and the best of specimens can miss out on prizes if the animal is fidgeting and fighting the judge's hands instead of standing quietly and calmly.

Nerves will soon communicate themselves to your dog and a nervous owner will not inspire confidence in an animal. This is one of the reasons that some owners put their dog in the hands of a professional handler, who prepares and shows the dog. Professional handling is very common in America and for some breeds in Britain, with most Wire Fox Terriers and several other terriers being handled by professionals. Professional handlers often start as breeders who find that they have the knack of presenting dogs to the best advantage. Some 1000 handlers are licensed by the American Kennel Club. Some take dogs for specific shows, grooming and preparing them, then showing them in the ring; others take a number of dogs on a 'circuit', such as the Florida Circuit or the Deep South Circuit, showing them at a series of shows in

Show dogs become used to parading in the ring and usually enjoy the outing. The Mixed Terrier class at the Montgomery Dog Show in the USA waits patiently for the judge's decision.

a particular area. It may be more difficult for a novice handler to win against the professional but, given a good dog and a confident owner, it does happen and the satisfaction of beating the 'experts' is enormous.

THE SHOW DAY

Necessary equipment for a day at a show includes:
* Collar and bench chain
* Show lead
* Dog food and feeding dish
* Water from the dog's usual supply and a water bowl
* Dog blanket
* Grooming equipment
* Pencil and paper to take notes
* Sensible non-fussy clothes (large pockets are useful) with nothing that jangles or flaps to distract dog or judges

Plan to arrive at the show in plenty of time so that you can exercise and play with your dog, making the outing more relaxing and enjoyable for both of you. If you arrive at the last minute, in a whirl of fuss and bother, your tension will communicate itself to your dog and it is unlikely to show at its best. Keep grooming to a minimum and allow your dog to eat and relieve itself according to its normal schedule as far as possible, though it is unwise to feed a dog just before judging as this may leave your pet sleepy and unresponsive.

Novices are often confused to find that the judge at one show will often reverse the placings of a judge at another. Though judging is according to the standard laid down for each breed, different judges may interpret the standard in different ways. One

judge's idea of 'moderately wide between the ears' will differ from another's. Probably this is just as well, because if everyone could agree on the perfect dog, then that dog would win all the prizes and there would be no point in anyone else showing. Experienced exhibitors learn which judges prefer their type of dog and try to show under those judges.

Obedience Competitions

Obedience classes and competitions are often held at general dog shows, in a ring similar to that used for breed classes. However, the look of a dog and the lack of conformity with the breed standard counts for nothing in obedience competitions; what matters is the precision with which the dog carries out a series of standard exercises. Competition rules vary from country to country but novice classes include basic obedience exercises such as heel, left and right turns, sit and stay and recall. Of course, any well-trained pet can perform these exercises but this does not mean that it could hold its own in competition, where the standards will be very high and any hesitation or inexact positioning is penalized. A slight movement by the dog can make all the difference between success and failure.

In obedience competitions the aim is for the dog to work in a happy, natural manner. Although the performance of both dog and handler is judged in relation to closely defined criteria, great emphasis is placed on the dog's willingness and enjoyment of its work and on the smoothness and naturalness of the handler's control. It is very much a team effort and a nervous or over-managing handler can cause a good dog to fail.

Long hours of work are required from both dog and handler and it is essential to enlist in a good obedience class as part of the training schedule, so that the instructor can observe your work from a distance and draw attention to any faults. Remember, however, that a class is only as good as the teacher, so it is worth making enquiries among competitors and show organizers over as wide an area as possible before enrolling.

When you feel that your dog is ready for competition, obtain a copy of the rules and regulations from your Kennel Club and make sure that you read them carefully; there is no point in arriving at a show to find that you have neglected one of the required exercises. Beware of overtraining your dog so that it is bored with the whole procedure. Some strong, energetic dogs may need practice on the day of the show to calm their high spirits; others will lose interest if they have to keep repeating the same exercises over and over again. Once in the show ring, listen carefully to what the judge says and

In obedience trials penalty points will be incurred by any dog breaking the line, like this Pointer.

Beagle trials, where the dogs pursue cottontail rabbits or hare, are very popular in the United States.

follow it exactly. Move only when you are asked to move and do not stop until you are told to stop; a near-perfect performance can be spoiled if you anticipate instructions.

Field Trials

Field trials for gundog breeds are held in both the United States and Britain. All field trials are held in conditions as near as possible to those of an ordinary day's shooting, so anyone with an obedient, tender-mouthed, sensible dog has a chance of competing successfully. However, skilled handling is essential; many a good dog has its chances spoilt by bad handling – too much whistling, or too many confusing commands.

In Retriever trials the dog must walk to heel and wait with its handler, remaining quiet at all times.

When a bird is shot it must go out on command and retrieve it, either from land or water. Dogs are assessed for their steadiness, ability to mark the fall of game, their drive and style while retrieving and their nose work. The degree of control required by the handler is also noted.

In Spaniel trials the dogs are assessed for their questing and quartering, game finding and flushing as well as for their ability to retrieve and deliver.

The dog must stay within gunshot range as it hunts for game, respond to directions and enter any cover, whether gorse, bramble or thorn bushes. The Spaniel's training should be geared to having the dog completely under control while still keeping it working stylishly and enthusiastically.

The task of the Pointers is to quarter the ground ahead of the guns and when game is found to come to a 'point' to indicate its whereabouts. After coming to a point the dog is usually sent ahead to flush the birds for the following guns and it must drop immediately the birds rise and remain steady until receiving further commands.

The United States also has trials for hounds – Beagles, Dachshunds and Bassets – which compete by trailing cottontail rabbits. The hounds must be fast and tough, neither running mute, nor behaving as 'babblers' (giving tongue for no good reason). A good nose is, of course, essential. Beagle trials are particularly popular with hounds run as a brace on rabbit, as small packs on rabbit and hare and as large packs on hare. American Foxhounds also have their own trials, usually run at night. These Foxhounds need tremendous stamina and excellent noses as they may have to trail a fox for as long as 12 hours. Coonhound trials are mostly run at night with the hounds working in swampy country where they have to find and 'tree' a raccoon. Judges take a lot of notice of their 'voices' and owners identify their own hound by its individual voice. There are also Coonhound races in the daytime, when hounds have to swim across wide, fast rivers and 'tree' a raccoon on the other side.

This Pointer, on an American hunt, is alert and ready for a day's hard work.

INDEX

Page numbers in *italic* refer to the illustrations

accidents, first aid, 156–7
Affenpinscher, *34*, 35
Afghan Hound, 12, 25, 26, 27, *34*, 35, 150, *181*
ageing, 164–5
aggression, *19*, 22, 137–9, 143
ailments, 158–64
Airedale Terrier, 28, 35–6, *35*
Alaskan Malamute, 36, *36*
allergies, 158
Alsatian, 68, *68*
American Foxhound, *36*, 37, 187
American Kennel Club, 34, 180, 183–4
American Staffordshire Terrier, 37, *37*
anal sacs and glands, 14, 151
Anatolian Karabash Dog, 37–8, *37*
anatomy, 14–18
appetite, healthy dogs, 153
arthritis, 158
artificial respiration, 156–7
Assyria, 12
Australia, 125
Australian Cattle Dog, 38, *38*
Australian Kelpie, 38, *38*, 180
Australian National Kennel Club, 34
Australian Silky Terrier, 39, *39*
Australian Terrier, 39, *39*

Babesia, 162
bad breath, 158
bad habits, 137–45
barking, 14, 137, 140, 141–2, *141*
Basenji, 26, 28, 40, *40*
baskets, 113
Basset Griffon Vendéen, 40–1, *40*
Basset Hound, 16, 25, 26, 27, 28, *40*, 41, 180–1, 187
bathing, 151–2, *152–3*
Bayeux Tapestry, *13*
Beagle, 25, 26, 27, 41, *41*, 187
Bearded Collie, 41–2, *41*
Bedlington Terrier 27, 42, *42*
beds, puppies, *112*, 113
begging, 136, *136*
behaviour, 18–19
  bad habits, 137–45
Belgian Shepherd Dog: Groenendael, 42, *42*
  Malinois, 43, *43*
  Tervueren, 43, *43*
Bernese Mountain Dog, 44, 44
Bichon Frise, 44, *44*
bicycles, chasing, 142–3
biscuits, 115, 149
bitches: cannibalism, 158
  choosing a dog, 22
  eclampsia, 173–4
  feeding after whelping, 172
  mating, 169–71
  pregnancy, 171
  season, 18, 22
  spaying, 22
  weaning puppies, 174–5
  whelping, 171–2
bites, 19, 157, 163
Black and Tan Coonhound, 44–5, *44*, 187
bladder control, 123
bleach, 123
bloat, 160
Bloodhound, 26, 45–6, *45*
boarding kennels, 165
body, healthy dogs, 154
body signals, 13
bone meal, 115
bones, 14–16, *15*
  broken, 160
  gnawing, *125*, 149
Border Collie, 19, 27, 28, 46, *46*, 180
Border Terrier, *26*, 27, 46–7, *46*
boredom, 140, 149
Borzoi, 47–8, *47*
Boston Terrier, 26, *47*, 48–9
bottle feeding, 172, 175
Bouvier des Flandres, 48, *49*
bowls, 113, *113*
Boxer, 26, 28, 48, *49*
brain, 16
breathing, 16
breed standard, 180
breeding, 167–75
  development of, 12
  hand-rearing puppies, 175
  the litter, 172–4
  mating, 169–71
  preparations for, 169
  weaning, 174–5
  whelping, 171–2
breeds: buying, 29
  choosing a dog, 25–8
  descriptions, 33–108
  drawbacks, 28
Briard, 49, *49*
Brittany, 49–50, *49*
brushes, 119, *120*
Brussels Griffon, 72, *72*
Bull Terrier, 26, 50–1, *51*
Bulldog, 15, *25*, 26, 50, *50*, 180
Bullmastiff, 50, *50*
burns, first aid, 156
buying a dog, 29

Cairn Terrier, 52, *52*, *136*
calcium, 115, 173
Canadian Kennel Club, 182
canidae, 10
canine parvovirus, vaccination, 116
canis familiaris, 10
canker *see* ear diseases
canned food, 148
cannibalism, 158
car sickness, 158–9
Cardigan Corgi, 106, *106*
care of the dog, 147-65
cars: chasing, 142–3
  travel in, 124–5, 145
castration, 22
catching, 137, *137*
cats: chasing, 142
  introducing puppies to, 115, *116*
  litter trays, 145
Cavalier King Charles Spaniel, 27, 52, *52*
cereal, 148, 174
cervix, 18
chalk, grooming with, 122
check chains, 119, 129, *129*, 131
Chesapeake Bay Retriever, 52, *52*
chewing, 140–1
Chien Français, 53, *53*
Chihuahua, 14, 27, 28, 54, *54*, *182*
children: dog bites, 19
  family dogs, 27
  and puppies, 114
China, 12
Chinese Crested Dog, 28, 54, *54*, *124*, 180
choking, 157
choosing a dog, 21–31
Chow Chow, 54–5, *55*
circles, walking in, 132–3
classes, obedience, 128–9, *128*
clippers, nail, 151
clipping, Poodles, 149–50, *150*
Clumber Spaniel, 55–6, *56*
coat: ageing dogs, 164
  choosing a dog, 26–7
  diet and, 149
  grooming, 26, 119–23, *120–2*, 143
  hair loss, 160
  moulting, 27, 149
  puppies, 172
Cocker Spaniel, 27, 150
  English, *31*, 56, *56*
  American, 36–7, *36*
collars, 118–19, 125
  check chains, 129, *129*, 131
Collie: Rough, *26*, 28, 56, *57*
  Smooth, 56–9, *57*
colostrum, 172
colour-blindness, 13
combs, 119, *122*
'come!', training, 129–30, *131*, 133-4
communication, 13–14
constipation, 159, 165
coprophagia, 145
Corgi, 26, 106, *106*
coughs, 159
coyotes, 10
Curly-coated Retriever, *58*, 59
Cynodictus, 10
cystitis, 159

Dachshund, 16, 26, *58*, 59, *59*, 187
Dalmatian, 26, 28, 60, *60*, *122*, 172
Dandie Dinmont Terrier, *60*, 61, *149*
Darwin, Charles, 10
'dead', playing, 137
deafness, 159
dealers, 29
Deerhound, *16*, 61, *61*
defecation, 123, 151
destructive dogs, 140–1

diabetes mellitus, 159
diarrhoea, 31, 159
'die for your country', 137
diet *see* feeding
digestive system, 16–18
digging holes, 143
discipline, house-training puppies, 123
diseases, 152, 158–64
disinfectants, 123
distemper, 159
  vaccination, 116
Doberman Pinscher, 26, 27–8, 61–2, *62*
dogproofing the home, 112–13
Dogue de Bordeaux, 62, *62*
domestication, 11–12
'down and stay', training, 134–5
dried food, 148
drops, ear, 155
drowning, 156–7
drying dogs, 152

ears: care of, 122–3, *159*
  cropping, 172
  diseases, 159–60
  drops, 155
  healthy dogs, 154
  puppies, 173
eclampsia, 173–4
eczema, 160
Egypt, *11*, 12
Elkhound, 62, *63*
English Setter, 27, 62–3, *63*
English Springer Spaniel, *26*, 63–4, *63*
English Toy Terrier, 64–5, *64*
epilepsy, 160
equipment, for puppies, 113
Estrela Mountain Dog, 64, *65*
evolution, 10
exercise, 28, *28*
eyes, 13
  ageing 164–5
  ailments, 160
  cleaning, *121*, 122
  healthy dogs, 154
  ointments, 156
  puppies, 172

face, grooming, 122–3
faeces, 17, 145
family dogs, 27
farm animals, 125, 143
fear, 19, 140
Fédération Cynologique Internationale (FCI), 34, 182
feeding, 148–9
  diet sheets, 114
  lactating bitches, 172
  older dogs, 165
  pregnant bitches, 171
  puppies, 114, 115–6, 172, *174*
  weaning puppies, 171–5
feet, grooming, 122
'fetch!', training, 135
Field Spaniel, 65, *65*
field trials, 186–7
fighting, 145
Finnish Spitz, 27, 65, *65*
first aid, 156–7
fits, 160
Flat-coated Retriever, 65–6, *66*
fleas, 31, 162, *162*, 173
'fly strike', 163
follicle mites, *162*
food, stealing, 142, *142*
foreign bodies, in the mouth, 157
fossils, 11
Fox Terrier, 28
  Smooth, 66–7, *67*
  Wire, 67, *67*, *181*, 183
Foxhound, 66, *66*
fractures, 160
French Bulldog, 66, *67*
furniture, bad habits, 139

gastric distension, 160
gastritis, 160
genitals, 18, *18*
German Shepherd Dog, *14*, 27–8, 68, *68*, 148, *148*, *182*
German Shorthaired Pointer, 68, *68*
German Wirehaired Pointer, 68–9, *69*
gestation, 171
gestures, release, 130, 132
Glen of Imaal Terrier, 69, *69*
gloves, grooming, 119, *122*
gnawing bones, *125*, 149
Golden Retriever, *19*, 22, 27, 69–70, *69*, *177*
Gordon Setter, 70–1, *70*
grass-eating, 160
Great Dane, 22, 28, 71, *71*, *169*, 182
Greece, 12
Greyhound, 12, 15, *16*, 25, 71, *71*
Griffon, 28
Griffon Bruxellois, 72, *72*
Griffon Vendéen, Grand, 72, *73*
Groenendael, 42, *42*
grooming, 26, 143
  bathing, 151–2, *152–3*
  nails, 151, *151*
  puppies, 119–23, *120–2*
  special grooming, 149–50, *149*
grooming powder, 122
growling, 137
guard dogs, 11–12, 19, 27–8
gundogs, 12, 25, 135, 186–7

hair *see* coat
hairbrushes, 119
Hamiltonstövare, 72–4, *73*
hand-rearing puppies, 175, *175*
handling, show dogs, 183–4
hard pad, 159
harnesses, 119
Harrier, 74, *74*
harvest mites, 162, *162*
health, 26
  puppies, 116
  signs of, 152–4
hearing, 13
  ageing, 164–5
  puppies, 173
heart disease, 160–1
heat, 18, 22, 169–71
heat stroke, 156
'heel!', training, 131–3, *132*
hepatitis, 161
  vaccination, 116
herding instinct, 19
hernias, 31, 161
hip dysplasia, 161
holes, digging, 143
hookworms, *162*, 163
house-training puppies, 123, *123*
howling, 14
Hungarian Vizsla, 74, *74*
hunting instinct, 19
Husky, Siberian, 101, *101*

Ibizan Hound, 12, 74–5, *75*
identity discs, 118, 125
illness, 152, 158–64
injections, *161*
instincts, 18–19, *19*
insurance, 125
intestines, 17
Irish Setter, 75, *75*, *150*
Irish Terrier, 28, 76, *76*
Irish Water Spaniel, 76, *76*
Irish Wolfhound, 28, 76, *77*, 180, *180*
Italian Greyhound, 77, *77*
Ixodes, 162, *162*

Jack Russell Terrier, 78, *78*
jackals, 10
Japanese Chin, 78, *78*
Japanese Spitz, 78–9, *78*
jaundice, 161
jaws, 14–15
judging, shows, 182
jumping up, 142

Keeshond, *78*, 79
Kennel Club, 17, 29, 34, 114, 180, 181
kennels, boarding, 165
Kerry Blue Terrier, 27, 28, 79–80, *79*
kidneys, 18
  diseases, 161
King Charles Spaniel, 28, 80, *80*
Komondor, *80*, 81
Kuvasz, 81, *81*

Labrador Retriever, 26, 27, 28, *29*, 81–2, *81*, *172*, 173
Lakeland Terrier, 28, 82, *82*
lameness, 161
Large Munsterlander, 82–3, *82*
laws, 125
leads: lead-training, 119
  pulling on, 139–40, *139*
  walking at heel, 131

'leave!', training, 135
legs, 15–16
  lameness, 161
leptospirosis, 161
  vaccination, 116
Lhasa Apso, 28, 83, *83*
lice, 162, *162*, 173
licences, dog, 125
liquid medication, 155
liver, 17-18
longhaired dogs: bathing, 151
  breeds, 26–7
  grooming, 120–1
Löwchen, 83, *83*, 180

male dogs: choosing, 22–4
  stud dogs, 22, 169–71, *169*
Malinois, 43, *43*
Maltese, 12, 28, 83–4, *83*
Manchester Terrier, 84, *84*
mange, 162
Maremma, 84, *84*
marking, territorial, 145
marrowbones, 149
Mastiff, 12, 84–5, *85*
mating, 18, 22, 169–71
meat, 115
medication, 155–6
Miacis, 10
Middle East, 12
milk, 115, 174
milk teeth, 16
minerals, 148
Miniature Pinscher, 26, 28, 85, *85*
mites, 162, *162*
mittens, grooming, 119
Molussus dog, 12
mongrels, 25, 128
moulting, 27, 149
mounting, 140, 164
muscles, 16, *16*
muzzles, 143, 157, *157*

nails, care of, 151, *151*, 172
names, learning, 116–7
Neapolitan Mastiff, 86, *86*
neck, vertebrae, 15
nerves, 16
nervousness, 19
Newfoundland, *86*, 87
Norfolk Terrier, 26, 87, *87*
Norwegian Buhund, 87–88, *87*
Norwegian Elkhound, 62
Norwich Terrier, 88, *88*
nose: care of, *121*, 122
  healthy dogs, 154
  puppies, 173
novice shows, 181

obedience: competitions, 185–6, *185*
  training, 127–37
oestrus *see* season
ointments, eye, 156

Old English Mastiff, 180
Old English Sheepdog, 26, 88–9, *88*, 150, 163, *173*
older dogs, 164–5
Otter Hound, 89, *89*
ovaries, 18
overfeeding, 149
overseas travel, 165

pack instinct, 18–19
pads, care of, 122
panting, 16, *16*
paper-training, puppies, 123
Papillon, 26, 28, 89–90, *89*
paralysis, 161–2
parasites, 162, *162*
parvovirus, 163
pedigree dogs, buying, 25
pedigrees, 113–14
Pekingese, 12, 22, 27, 28, 90–1, *90*, 150, 182
Pembroke Corgi, 106, *106*
penis, 18
peritonitis, 163
pet shops, 29
Pharaoh Hound, 91, *91*
pheromones, 14
phobias, 140
Phoenicians, 12
pills, giving, 155, *155*
play, 19, 114, 118, *118*
pneumonia, 163
Pointer, 27, 93, *93*, *185*, 187, *187*
poisons, 163
Pomeranian, 28, 93–5, *93*
Poodle, 27, *94*, 95, 149–50, *150*, 164, *171*, 181
pounds, choosing dogs from, 24–5
powdered medication, 155
pregnancy, 171
prolapse, 163
Pug, 12, 26, 28, 95, *95*, 136
Puli, 95, *95*
pulling on the lead, 131–2, 139–40, *139*
punishment: bad behaviour, 137
  house-training puppies, 123
puppies, 111–25
  buying, 29
  car travel, 124–5
  chewing, 140
  and children, 27, 114
  choosing, 24–8, 30–1
  collars and leads, 118–19
  collecting, 113–14
  diet, 114, 115–16
  docking tails, 172
  equipment, 113
  feeding, 172, *174*
  grooming, 119–23, *120–2*
  hand-rearing, 175, *175*
  health, 116
  house-training, 123, *123*
  introduction to other pets, 115
  learning its name, 116–17
  obedience training, 129–37
  and older dogs, 165
  play, 118, *118*
  safety in the home, 112–13
  shows, 181
  sleep, 114
  teething, 116
  training, 112, 117–18, 119
  vaccinations, 124
  weaning, 174–5
  whelping, 171–2
  worms, 116, 163
Pyrenean Mountain Dog, *96*, 97

quarantine, 164, 165

rabies, 163–4, 165
  vaccination, 116, 125
Rameses VI, tomb of, *11*
rectal prolapse, 163
rectal thermometers, *154*, 155
release word, training, 130
reproduction, 18, *18*
resentment of handling, 143
respiration, 16
Retriever trials, 186–7
retrieving, training, 135, *135*
rheumatism, 164
Rhodesian Ridgeback, *96*, 97, *118*
rib-cage, 15
rickets, 164
road accidents, 156, *156*
roaming dogs, 140
Romans, 12
Rottweiler, 27–8, *96*, 97
round worms, *162*, 163
running lines, 140

safety, 112–13, 157
St Bernard, 14, 22, 97–8, *97*
Saluki, 12, 98, *98*
Samoyed, 98–9, *98*
sarcoptic mange, 162
scent: anal glands, 151
  marking, 14
scent hounds, 25
Schipperke, 27, 28, 99, *99*
Schnauzer, 28, 99–100, *99*
Scottish Terrier, 27, 28, 100, *100*
scurf, 149
Sealyham Terrier, 28, 100, *100*, 136
season, 18, 22, 169–71
semi-moist foods, 148
senses, 13
sex play, 164
shaking hands, 136–7
shampoo, bathing dogs, 152
sheep, chasing, 125, 143
sheep ticks, 162, *162*
shelters, choosing dogs from, 24–5
Shetland Sheepdog, 28, *100*, 101
Shih Tzu, 27, 28, 101, *101*, 149
shock, 164
shorthaired breeds, 26–7
  grooming, 122

shoulders, 15–16
showing, 12, 179–85, *181–4*
choosing puppies for, 31
handling, 183–4
preparation for, 182–3
Siberian Husky, 101, *101*
sickness, 152, 158–64
sight hounds, 25
Silky Terrier, 39, *39*
'sit!', training, 131, 132, *132*, 133
'sit and stay', training, 133
skeleton, 14–16, *15*
skin: eczema, 160
healthy dogs, 154
puppies, 30–1
skulls, 14–15
Skye Terrier, 102, *102*
sleep, 114, 153
slip collars *see* check chains
Sloughi, 102–3, *102*
smell, sense of, 13–14, *13*
snapping, 143
Soft-coated Wheaten Terrier, 103, *103*
Spaniel trials, 187
Spaniels, 12, *113*, 164
spaying, 22
sperm, 18
spine, 15
Spitz breeds, 26
Staffordshire Bull Terrier, 26, 103–4, *103*
'stay!', training, 133–5
stealing food, 142, *142*
stomach, 17
stud dogs, 22, 169–71, *169*
Sussex Spaniel, 104, *104*
Swedish Vallhund, 104, *104*, 180

tails, docking, 172
tapeworms, *162*, 163
tartar, 149
teeth, 16–17, *17*, 149
teething, puppies, 116
temperament: breeding dogs, 169
and obedience training, 128
temperature: healthy dogs, 154–5, *154*
panting to control, 16, *16*
terriers, 15–16, 26, 148, 183, *184*
territories, 22, 145
Tervueren, 43, *43*
testicles, 18
thermometers, *154*, 155
threat signals, 13
Tibetan Spaniel, 104–5, *105*
Tibetan Terrier, 105, *105*
ticks, 162, *162*
tidbits, 149
tie, 171
Tomarctus, 10
toy dogs, 12, 26, 119, 148
toys, 113, *113*, 140
training: curing bad habits, 137–45
house-training, 123, *123*
lead-training, 119
obedience, 127–37
preparation for shows, 183
puppies, 117–18, 119
tricks, 135–7, *136*
tranquillizers, 140
travel, 165
car, 124–5, 145
travel sickness, 125, 158–9
tricks, training, 135–7, *136*
tumours, 164

umbilical hernia, 31, 161
undershot jaws, 15
United States of America, 125, 164, 180, 181, 182, 183–4, 187
urine, 18, 123
urinating indoors, 145
uterus, 18, *18*

vaccinations, 114, 116, 124, 169
vagina, 18
prolapse, 163
vertebrae, 15
veterinary surgeons, 157–8, *158*
vision, 13
vitamins, 148, 149
vomiting, 160, 164
vulva, 18

'wait!', training, 133–4, *134*
walking at heel, 131–3, *132*
wandering dogs, 140
warts, 164
watchdogs, 27–8
water, drinking, 148, 149
weaning, 174–5
Weimaraner, 26, 28, 105–6, *105*
Welsh Corgi, 28
Cardigan, 106, *106*
Pembroke, 106, *106*
Welsh Springer Spaniel, 106–7, *107*
Welsh Terrier, 107, *107*
West Highland White Terrier, 27, 107–8, *108*
whelping, 171–2
whining, 14
Whippet, 26, 108, *108*
whipworms, *162*, 163
wire brushes, 120–2
wolves, 10, 11–12
worming, 114, 116
worms, 30, 160, *162*, 163
wounds, 'fly strike', 163

Yorkshire Terrier, 28, 108, *108*, *109*, 149, *182*

Reader's Digest

DRAWING & PAINTING TECHNIQUES

A READER'S DIGEST BOOK

Published by The Reader's Digest Association Limited
11 Westferry Circus
Canary Wharf
London
E14 4HE

www.readersdigest.co.uk

We are committed to both the quality of our products and the services we provide to our customers. We value your comments, so please feel free to contact us on 08705 113366, or via our website at www.readersdigest.co.uk
If you have any comments about the content of our books, you can contact us at gbeditorial@readersdigest.co.uk

ISBN 0-276-42935-4

A CIP data record for this book is available from the British Library

This book is based on the partwork *The Step-by-Step Art Course,* designed and edited by De Agostini UK Ltd.

Produced by Amber Books Ltd
Bradley's Close
74–77 White Lion Street
London N1 9PF
www.amberbooks.co.uk

Printed in Singapore

Contributing Artists:
Alistair Adams: 142, 143, Chris Bramley: 113, 144, 145, 146, 147, Xiaopeng Huang: 172, 173, 174, 175, 176, 177, 178, 179, Dave Jordan: 76, 87, 88, 89, 98, 99, 144, 145, 146, 147, 148, 149, 150, 154, 155, 156, 157, Claire Martin: 66, 67, 68, 69, 70, Ian McCaughrean, 196, 197, 198, 199, 200, 201, Melvyn Petterson: 60-63, Matthew Rake: 188, 189, Tom Robb: 81, 82, 83, 94, 95, 96, 97, 196, 197, 198, 200, 201, Jenny Rodwell: 192, 193, Michael Sanders: 180, 181, Ian Sidaway: 8-9, 31, 32, 33, 34, 84b, 85, 86, 102, 103, 104, 105, 118, 119, 120, 121, 122, 123, 235, Adrian Smith: 188, 189, 240, 241, Adrian Taylor: 16-17, 255, 256, George Taylor: 13, 14, 15, 18, 19, 20, 21, 23, 28, 29, 30, 32, 33, 34, 35, 36, 37, 44, 45, 60-63, 46-47, 56, 64, 65, 66, 67, 68, 69, 70, 78, 79, 80, 81, 82, 83, 84-86, 90, 91, 93, 94, 95, 96, 97, 100, 101, 102, 103, 104, 118, 119, 120, 121, 122, 123, 125, 142, 143, 151, 152, 153, 158, 159, 160, 161, 168, 169, 170, 171, 172, 173, 174, 175, 176, 177, 178, 179, 180, 181, 182, 183, 184, 185, 186, 190, 191, 192, 193, 194, 195, 196, 197, 198, 199, 200, 201, 203, 204, 205, 206, 225, 249, 251, 252, 253, 254, Michael Warr: 154, 155, 156, 157, Albany Wiseman: 23-27, 48, 49, 50, 51, 52, 53, 54, 55, 56, 57, 58, 59, 127, 128, 129, 130, 131, 158, 159, 160, 161, 161, 168, 169, 170, 171, 182, 183, 184, 185, 186, 203, 204, 205, 206, Shona Wood : 7, 8, 10, 11, 12, 105, 106, 107

Picture Credits:
Elda Abramson: 84(t), **AKG/Solomon R. Guggenheim Museum, New York**: 112, **Archivio IGDA**: (G.Dagli Orti) 134, 214-5, **Brenda Holton**: (© Brenda Holton) 190, **Bridgeman Art Library**: (Gemaldegalerie, Dresden) 38, (Louvre, Paris) 39, (Ca'Rezzonico, Museo del Settecento, Venice) 40, (© ARS, NY and DACS, London 2004) 43, (Musée D'Orsay, Paris) 92, (Caves of Lascaux, Dordogne, France) 109(tl), (Villeneuve-les-Avignon Hospice, Anjou, France) 110(b), (National Gallery, London) 111(t), (Musee d'Unterlinden, Colmar, France) 111(br), (Private Collection, Peter Willi) 113, (Galleria Nazionale delle Marche, Urbino) 114(br), (Pinacotecca, Sansepolcro: 114(tr), (Galerie Daniel Malingue, Paris © ADAGP, Paris and DACS, London 2004) 115(tr), (Museum of Fine Arts, Budapest © ADAGP, Paris and DACS, London 2004) 115(tl), (Courtauld Gallery, London) 116, (National Gallery, London) 117 (tl), (Christie's Images) 121(br), (National Gallery of Scotland) 132, (Fitzwilliam Museum, (Courtauld Gallery, London) 135, (University of Cambridge) 136, (Victoria & Albert Museum, London) 137, (The Fleming-Wyfold Art Foundation, every attempt has been made to identify the copyright holder of this image)138(t), (National Gallery, London) 138-9, (Pushkin Museum, Moscow) 139(t), (Sheffield Galleries and Museums Trust © Courtesy of Artist's family) 141, 151, (Musée D'Orsay, Paris)180-181, (Musée Marmottan, Paris) 187(cr), (Pushkin Museum, Moscow) 187(cl), (Hermitage, St Petersburg, Russia) 200(b), (Chatsworth House, Derbyshire) 207, (Roy Miles Fine Paintings) 208, (Galleria Nazionale d'Arte Moderna, Rome) 209, (Galleria Degli Uffizi, Florence) 210(t), (Kunsthistorisches Museum, Vienna) 210(b), (Private Collection © ARS, NY and DACS, London 2004) 211, © 1998 Kate Rothko Prizel and Christopher Rothko/DACS 2004) 212, (Courtauld Gallery, London) 213, (Musée D'Orsay, Paris) 216, (Christie's Images, London © ADAGP, Paris and DACS, London 2004) 217, (Private Collection, France/Peter Willi © ADAGP, Paris and DACS, London 2004) 218, (National Gallery, London) 221, (Burrell Collection, Glasgow) 222(tr), (National Gallery of Scotland) 222(b), (Musée D'Orsay, Paris) 223(b), (Lauros, Giraudon) 224, (Musée D'Art, et d'Industrie, St. Etienne © ARS, NY and DACS, London 2004) 227(b), (Metropolitan Museum of Art, New York) 229, (Civica Galleria d'Arte Moderna, Milan © DACS 2004) 230, (Victoria & Albert Museum, London) 231, (Louvre, Paris) 234, (Musée Fabre, Montpellier, France) 236, (Harold Samuel Collection, Corporation of London) 237, (Christie's Images, London) 238, (Louvre, Paris) 243, (Musée des Beaux-Arts, Rouen) 244, (Musée D'Orsay, Paris) 245, 246, 247, **Collection of the Modern Art Museum of Fort Worth**, (Museum purchase made possible by a grant from The Burnett Foundation): 41, **Corbis**: (Francis G. Mayer) 124, (Bettmann) 125t, (© DACS 2004) 126, (Bettmann © ADAGP, Paris and DACS, London 2004) 228, **David Hockney**: (© David Hockney) 42, **Ken Howard**: 239, Hayward Gallery, London: 226(tl), **Mary Evans Picture Library**: 77, **National Gallery, London**: 75, 104, 215, 219, 242, Private Collection: 132-3, **Rijksmuseum, Amsterdam**: 232, **Jenny Rodwell**: 71, 72, 73, **The Roland P. Murdoch Collection, Wichita Art Museum, Wichita, Kansas**: 233, **Tony Stone Images/Deborah Davies**: 148-9

Reader's Digest

DRAWING & PAINTING TECHNIQUES

82 practical, problem-solving lessons, expert hints and tips

Published by the Reader's Digest Association Limited
London New York Sydney Montreal

CONTENTS

Before you begin	*6*
SETTING UP A WORK SPACE	7
ORGANISING YOUR WORK SPACE	10
KEEPING A SKETCH BOOK	13
PORTABLE ART MATERIALS	16
CHOOSING THE BEST PALETTE	18
CHOOSING THE BEST EASEL	20
From bamboo to ballpoint	*22*
USING A BAMBOO PEN	23
USING CONTÉ CRAYONS	28
INTRODUCING MARKER PENS	30
SOFT PASTELS	32
OIL PASTELS	34
PASTELS FOR PORTRAITS	38
THE ART OF ACRYLICS	41
USING ACRYLIC MEDIUMS	44
USING OIL MEDIUMS	46
'PAINTING' WITH GRAPHITE	48
DRAWING WITH FIBRE-TIPPED PENS	52
USING GRAPHITE STICKS	56
DRAWING WITH BALLPOINTS	60
WATERCOLOUR MEDIUMS	64
USING MIXED MEDIA	66
PENS FOR DRAWING	71
Papers, panels and brushes	*74*
THE VERSATILE PAINTBRUSH	75
BRUSHES	78
USING COLOURED PAPER	81
SPECIALIST PAPERS	84
EXPERIMENTING WITH TEXTURED PAPERS	87
TINTED PAPERS	90
THINNING OIL PAINTS	92
WASH-OFF TECHNIQUES	94
WASHING ONTO WATERCOLOUR PAPER	98
WORKING ON CANVAS	100
PREPARING PANELS	102
TRICKS OF THE TRADE	105
Creating colour	*108*
PIGMENTS AND PAINTS	109
THE POWER OF COLOUR	112
KEEPING YOUR BALANCE	114
PICK AND MIX	116
MIXING ORANGE	118
MIXING GREEN	120
MIXING PURPLE	122

MIXING GREYS 124
WHITE ON WHITE 127
COLOUR IN SHADOWS 132
COLOUR FOR SKIES 134
A COLOUR FOR ALL SEASONS 137

Tried and tested techniques *140*

DRAWING ELLIPSES 141
DRAWING WITH A GRID 144
APPLYING PAINT WITHOUT A BRUSH 148
PAINTING WITH A KNIFE 151
USING PATTERNED BACKGROUNDS 154
LETTERING ON CURVED SURFACES 158
PAINTING GLASS 162
FABRIC TEXTURES IN CHARCOAL 168
DETAILS AND TEXTURES IN WATERCOLOUR 172
IMPASTO 180
ADDING COLOUR TO SCRAPBOARD 182
PAINTING IN CHANGING LIGHT 187
SCUMBLING TECHNIQUES 190
SPATTERING EFFECTS 192
USING ADHESIVES 194
USING RESISTS 196

Further techniques *202*

CHOOSING THE BEST FORMAT 203
CREATING EMOTIONAL IMPACT 207
BLUEPRINT FOR A PAINTING 209
ABSTRACT PAINTING 211
POINTILLISM 213
COLOUR FOR COLOUR'S SAKE 216
A SENSE OF PERSPECTIVE 219
BREAKING THE RULES 222
OUTDOOR COMPOSITION 224
OPTICAL EFFECTS 226
CAPTURING MOVEMENT 228
FRAME WITHIN A FRAME 231
BROADENING YOUR HORIZONS 234
UNDERSTANDING TONE 237
SKETCHING LANDSCAPES 240
FROM DARKNESS INTO LIGHT 242
PAINTING REFLECTED LIGHT 245

And finally… *248*

WORKING WITH FIXITIVES 249
USING VARNISHES 251
PHOTOGRAPHING YOUR ARTWORK 253
CARRYING AND STORING YOUR ARTWORKS 255

BEFORE YOU BEGIN

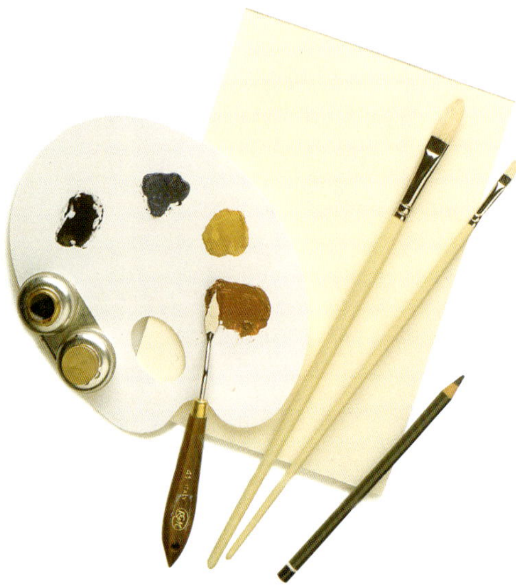

While nothing should stop you simply picking up a paintbrush if the inspiration takes you, a little bit of preparation can help you get much more out of your art. This chapter explains how to set up and organise your work space, what sort of art materials you may need and how to choose the best easel and palette for your work.

Setting up a work space

You are more likely to pick up a pencil or brush if you have somewhere specific to work – even if it is only the corner of a living room.

Few amateur artists have the luxury of a large, dedicated studio space. The lucky ones can convert a spare room, garden shed, conservatory or garage. Most have to make do with a corner of a dining room or part of the living area.

Space and light

Whatever your situation, the basic requirements are enough space and light to work comfortably. You also need somewhere accessible to store your kit and a place to keep finished works safe, clean and dry.

A dedicated studio space would be ideal. You can close the door on work in progress and return to it whenever you like, without tidying up at the end of a session or spending time setting up at the start of the next one. You can also guarantee privacy. Consider your home carefully – is there any unused space, in an attic perhaps, or a garden shed?

An alternative is to exploit a little-used space such as a guest bedroom, dining or breakfast room. You can leave your work out most of the time, but will need storage spaces where things can be packed away neatly when the room reverts to its primary function. (The set-ups below will give you an idea of the space you need for oil, acrylic and watercolour painting.)

Screening it off

Screens are useful if you have to work in a living or study area – they can be pulled around to mask the clutter.

SET-UP FOR OILS AND ACRYLICS

Oils and acrylics are usually painted on a vertical surface, so you will need an easel. The size will depend on the scale you work at – and your budget. A good studio easel is a costly item, but reasonably-priced models are available, especially if you buy mail order. A sketching easel is suitable for small-scale works, and the metal versions are remarkably sturdy. Your paints and mediums should be within easy reach, on either a table or a trolley – some artists have a palette fixed to the top surface, while others work from a hand-held one. You may need a stool or chair to sit on, though many artists prefer to work standing up.

▶ A studio easel and a trolley provide a compact and flexible work area. Make sure that there is enough room to step back and assess your progress.

SET-UP FOR WATERCOLOURS

Watercolours are usually painted on a nearly horizontal surface so the washes do not run. Things happen fast so you must have everything to hand. You need a sturdy work surface, large enough to hold the work and all your equipment easily. A cramped surface impedes the painting process and results in accidents. If you don't want to buy a table easel, you can prop up your drawing board on a book or piece of wood. Paint, palettes and jars of water should be close to hand on your favoured side. Spare brushes can be placed bristle-end up in a jar on the far side of the work surface. Always have plenty of clean rags or kitchen paper for mopping up spills and runs.

◀ For watercolours you can work on one surface – but make sure it is large enough for your painting, paints, palettes and water.

Avoid working in a sleeping area if you intend to use oil paint or pastels – sleeping in a room with solvents and dust in the air is not good for your health.

The mobile studio

If you are really pushed for space you can make do with a combination of portable equipment and good storage. Table, portable and box easels fold away and can be quickly and easily set up. A box easel has integral storage compartments and is compact when folded. Table easels can be adjusted to various angles and are excellent for watercolour painting, drawing and small-scale work in other media (see Choosing the best easel, pages 20-21).

You will need one or more boxes for your drawing and painting tools. A plastic toolbox with inset or cantilevered storage compartments is a versatile and inexpensive choice. They come in a range of sizes to suit your requirements. In art-supply shops and catalogues, they are sometimes called 'art bins'. A portfolio to protect supports and finished works completes your 'mobile studio'. Your easel, toolbox and portfolio can be stashed away in a cupboard, attic or under the bed when not required.

A studio in a shed

Quiet and private, a garden shed can provide the ideal studio space. One drawback is the lack of running water – a nearby garden tap is useful, especially if you work mainly in water-based mediums.

Also, think about heating and lighting. You can run electricity from your house, but this is a major job involving laying armoured cabling underground. Instead, for heating, try using calor gas or paraffin heaters. For lighting, it might pay to replace an existing wooden door with a glass one or, if possible, add windows.

The garden studio above is made from a prefabricated horse loose box. Large French windows were added so that the entire front of the studio opens out into the garden. This greatly increases not only the light but also the space available.

In the right light

You also need good lighting, so that you can judge colours and save your eyes from strain. Ever since Leonardo da Vinci (1452-1519) recommended them in *Treatise on Painting*, artists have preferred north-facing windows. This is because north light comes reflected from the sky (not directly from the sun) and is, therefore, fairly consistent throughout the day. It doesn't have the yellow cast of direct sunlight, so it is easier to assess colours and their relationships accurately.

Remember, though, that your painting might be viewed in artificial light which will modify the colours. However, artists rarely have any control over the conditions in which a work will be seen, so they still try to 'key' their colours to look right in natural light.

Controlling the light

Leonardo recommended that the artist's north-facing windows should look out on to an external courtyard that could then be covered by a linen tent to control the amount of light. Today it is more convenient to control natural light with blinds and curtains. Translucent roller blinds can be used to soften bright light – or you can tape tracing paper or tissue paper over the glass.

Restricting yourself to natural light limits the hours you can paint, especially in winter. If you can work only in the evenings – or are a night owl by nature – you will need to rely on artificial light. Try using daylight bulbs, available from good electrical stores and art-supply shops. The bulbs are coloured blue to compensate for the warmish cast of artificial light. This produces a fairly neutral, consistent light, which is easy on the eyes and excellent for assessing colours and tones. Fluorescent tube lighting gives a similar effect.

THE IDEAL STUDIO

Few artists have an ideal work space, but most of the ideas in this studio can be adapted for less perfect spaces. You could have different aspects of the studio in different parts of your house – a work space in a well-lit room, storage in a darker one. Remember if you use solvents, keep the room well ventilated by opening the window.

WALLS
These should be plain white or a neutral colour. Use them to display finished works, works in progress, sketches and inspirational photos and images from magazines.

STACKING CANVASES
Stack stretched canvases against a wall.

PLAN CHEST
This allows you to store works on paper flat and to keep them away from the light.

HARD FLOORING
Tiles, laminates, vinyl and lino are non-absorbent and easy to clean.

Setting up portraits and still lifes

If you work directly from life, you will also need to light your subject. Effective lighting can be supplied by

TASK AND SPOTLIGHTS
An adjustable lamp provides ideal task lighting in a work area. Spotlights can also be set up for task lighting or to provide mood lighting on a subject.

NATURAL LIGHT
A north-facing window is ideal, as the light is consistent and even. If your windows face other directions, use translucent fabric or papers to soften the sunlight.

EASEL
A solid studio easel is best for large canvases. Castors ensure that it can be moved easily.

SHELVING
You can never have enough shelving – for materials, reference books and still-life material that you might want to paint. Adjustable brackets provide the most flexible system.

WORK SURFACE
A board on trestles is a cheap and flexible alternative to a table. You can then have boards of different sizes for different projects. Make sure there is enough space for the artwork and your materials. A drawing board can be propped up on a table easel or on a book.

MATERIALS TROLLEY
Store your paints and mediums on a small shelved unit. It should have castors for mobility. Adapt an existing cabinet or look for suitable trolleys or units in kitchen supply stores.

spotlights, table lamps and long-necked work lights. Experiment, too, with sheets of white card or polyboard to bounce light back on to the subject.

Light or white walls are probably best for your work space as they reflect and enhance the light and are not distracting. However, when very pale colours are used as the background for a still life, they can be a bit stark. Watercolours might work well with a light background; oils, however, often call for a darker one. If you paint many still lifes, it pays to build up a good selection of paper and fabric in different colours and tones to use as backgrounds.

Castors and cups

When space is restricted, mobile units come into their own, allowing you to shift the contents of your studio around to accommodate the requirements of different projects and media. A drinks trolley or a kitchen one makes a handy mobile work station.

Most large easels and some small plan chests are supplied with castors, but otherwise it is relatively easy to attach them. Alternatively, stand the legs of studio furniture in plastic 'cups' that will slide over hard floors – they are available in furniture and DIY stores.

Spills are inevitable in a studio space. A carpet is less forgiving to water, inks, oil paints, acrylics, turpentine and pastel dust than are vinyl, timber, tiles or laminated flooring. If you have to work in a carpeted area, protect the floor with a dust sheet, an old rug or plastic matting.

Organising your work space

You'll save yourself both time and money if you keep your art materials readily to hand and in good condition. So get organised!

A place for everything and everything in its place is the golden rule for the artist, especially when space is limited. Spend some time finding a home for your equipment and you'll be able to work more comfortably and effectively. You will also save money. Remember, art materials are costly, so it is worth making them last. On the following pages, various storage methods are described to help you keep your materials and artworks in perfect condition.

Looking after your brushes

Store brushes bristle-end up in a jar or tin, but make sure they are dry first. Dry brushes flat – if they are dried upright, water runs down under the ferrule, loosening the hairs.

If you have a large collection of brushes, group those of a similar size together so that you can find what you want when you want it. You should always separate brushes used for oil painting from those used for water-based media, as traces of oil on a brush can ruin a water-based mix or wash. For long-term storage, put brushes away in a box or tin, but make sure they are thoroughly dry first. Lay them flat and add a few mothballs to ward off insect attacks.

A temporary home

You also need somewhere to put your brushes while you are working on a painting. Acrylic brushes should be rinsed out as soon as you stop using them, because the paint is almost impossible to remove once it has dried. If you have to leave the painting for a short time, plunge the bristles into the water jar – resting a brush on its bristle end won't do it any harm for a few moments.

Other media are more forgiving, so you can leave brushes loaded with paint during a short break. Simply put the brushes on a ridged brush rest or in a piece of florist's oasis, as shown right.

SORTING OUT YOUR ART TOOLS

Keep frequently used pencils, brushes and pens upright in a jar or pot, where they are easily accessible. Alternatively, store coloured and pastel pencils in shallow tins, organising them by colour – warm to cool, for example. A piece of foam cut to size and laid on top will keep them in place. If you work with a range of media, store them in separate boxes or a set of labelled, small plastic drawers. A plastic toolbox or fishing-tackle box with cantilevered trays is ideal for items such as pencils, erasers, brushes, palettes and nibs. These are sold in art-supply shops as 'art bins', but often at a higher price. When you are actually painting, use a ridged rest or piece of oasis to hold your brushes.

▲ **Put brushes, pens and pencils upright in pots, tins or jam jars.**

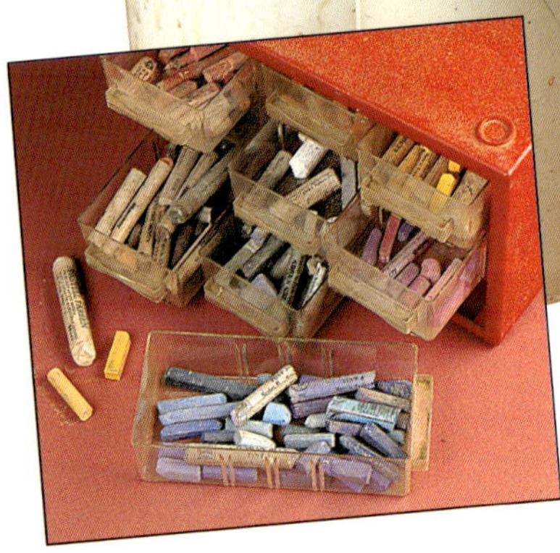

▲ **Store pastels by colour in a transparent plastic drawer unit – you can then put your hand on the right stick straight away.**

▶ **A slab of florist's oasis is a useful temporary resting place for oil paint brushes. Simply stab the brushes, bristle-end up, into the oasis.**

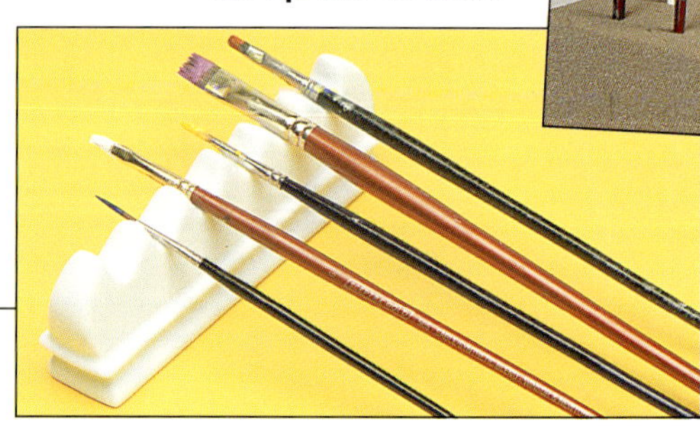

▶ **A brush rest is a cheap and useful piece of equipment when painting. The ridges prevent the brushes from rolling off.**

STORING PAPER AND ARTWORKS

The best form of storage for plain paper, or drawings and paintings on paper, is a plan chest. These substantial items of furniture have shallow drawers designed for storing artwork. They are available in a range of sizes and materials. Wooden plan chests are cumbersome and heavy, but lighter and cheaper styles in tubular metal and plastic are available from specialist suppliers, often by mail order. The size you choose will be dictated by the scale you work at.

Interleave your drawings and paintings with sheets of acid-free tissue paper or tracing paper. Pastel and charcoal drawings need to be handled with special care. Fix them using an aerosol fixative, or fixative and a diffuser.

Always spray your work in a well-ventilated place away from other surfaces, ideally out of doors. Prop the drawing so that it is vertical and spray lightly, keeping the spray moving over the surface to get an even coverage.

If you don't have the funds or the space for a plan chest, a portfolio is a good alternative. Consider investing in two, one for finished works and one for pristine paper. They should be stored somewhere dry – in a cupboard, in the loft or under a bed, for example.

Paper should be handled as little as possible, as the edges become grubby and tattered with constant handling and fingers leave greasy marks that can disrupt a watercolour wash. For easy identification of each weight and type of paper, place sheets of coloured paper or sticky notes between different batches, then write a description on each one.

▲ Use sticky notes to label different types and weights of paper. This avoids having to rifle through the plan chest or portfolio and possibly damaging or marking the papers. And keep sample packs of papers, as they are useful for practising on.

▼ Charcoal and pastel drawings are easily smudged, so fix them (see right) before storing them. Interleave drawings with tissue or tracing paper to protect them.

▲ The most convenient way of fixing a powdery medium is with an aerosol fixative, but a diffuser is the traditional method. Bend the diffuser to create a right-angle, immerse one end in the fixative, then blow briskly through the mouthpiece to create a fine spray. Practise on scrap paper first until you can achieve an even coverage.

STORING CANVASES

Spare canvases can simply be leant against a convenient wall. Place the largest canvas facing the wall with smaller ones stacked against it. For long-term storage, cover the stack with a dust cloth or plastic, or wrap individual paintings in plastic. Protect the corners with corrugated card or buy special corner protectors from art suppliers.

If space isn't a problem, you can construct a simple rack from 50 x 50mm (2 x 2in) timber. Fix some lengths of timber to the floor, so that the canvases rest on them to provide ventilation around the paintings. Canvas boards can be stored against a wall, in a rack or in a plan chest or portfolio.

▲ Remove paintings on canvas from the stretchers to transport or store them. Roll the canvas with the paint on the outside to prevent the paint film from cracking.

▲ Stack canvases with the largest one next to the wall. Lean stretchers against other stretchers or cross pieces, so that the canvas does not get dented.

If you are intending to work away from home, on location or on holiday, you need to think about how you will transport your brushes. The most important thing is to protect the bristles. A brush roll is a cheap, light and compact way of transporting your brushes. It consists of a rectangle of fabric with pockets into which brushes can be slotted – it is then rolled up and tied with ribbons. You can make one by stitching elastic on to a piece of sturdy fabric, or threading loops of elastic through a split-cane or raffia mat. Brushes can also be carried in plastic brush tubes.

Pin up images

A useful addition to your work space is a pinboard, on which you can keep track of all art-related matters: important exhibitions, and the phone numbers of art suppliers, models or the local adult education centre. You can also display inspirational photographs and images torn from magazines and newspapers – the more you look at them, the more likely they are to trigger an idea for one of your next paintings.

A few shelves for holding reference and sketch books are also useful additions to your working area. Items that are awkward to store, such as a hairdryer, kidney-shaped palettes and viewfinders, can be hung on hooks underneath the shelves.

Rags and bins

A painter can never have too many rags. They have all kinds of uses: applying paint and blotting it off, wiping up spills and cleaning brushes and palettes. Never throw away waste cotton fabric, such as old sheets or tea towels. Instead, cut or tear it into useable pieces and stash them in an accessible box or bin.

Old paint tubes and rags are messy if left lying around, especially if you work in oils. A pedal bin with a plastic binliner is an ideal solution. Paint rags are flammable – empty the bin regularly so that they are out of your house as soon as possible.

Mobile storage

If you have to move your painting materials around – to put them away at the end of every working session, perhaps – a small shelved unit with castors is invaluable. Look for trolleys or similar units in kitchen supply stores.

Keeping a sketch book

Whether you use it to make preparatory drawings, to try out different mediums or to create a visual diary, the sketch book is an invaluable tool for the artist.

Artists have been known to make sketches on old envelopes, shopping lists – and even on the back of the hand! But it is much simpler if you carry a sketch book at all times. In this way you can make on-the-spot drawings and jot down visual ideas whenever and wherever you like – and you always know where to find them when you need them.

The sketch book habit

For most artists, carrying a sketch book is more effective than carrying a camera. True, you can take a photograph in a fraction of a second and it will give you a detailed rendition of a particular scene. However, unless you are a skilled photographer, you cannot use the camera as creatively, as it tends to render everything in the same way.

A sketch book, on the other hand, provides a personal record. In it, you can record not only what you see, but also what you feel. You can emphasise certain elements, and leave out others. If you are struck by a particular facial expression, for example, you can make a quick sketch, capturing the essence of that expression without worrying about detail, colour, texture and so on.

It is a good idea to buy a small sketch book – one which fits into your pocket or a bag that you always carry – and to use it whenever the opportunity arises. Record people and places, and sketch details of what is happening around you. Above all, jot down any ideas you might have for future paintings. Your sketch book – unlike your memory – won't let you down. Once you have made a drawing, it is there forever to provide inspiration.

The quality of the paper in sketch books varies enormously. You can, for example, buy books of handmade paper, often bound with elaborately marbled or fabric covers. These sketch books are beautiful objects in their own right.

The right paper

However, a very expensive sketch book can be quite daunting for the amateur artist who might be afraid to ruin it with poor sketches. Remember also that a sketch book with a delicate, ornate cover will get damaged easily if you intend to carry it around with you.

It is probably better to begin by using an inexpensive book – but avoid very cheap pads that contain thin, shiny paper. These are generally bought from stationers rather than art shops. Usually, the paper is too hard to use with anything except a ball-point or fountain pen.

Most art shops stock sketch books in a range of cartridge and drawing papers, from 95gsm (45lb) sketching paper to the heavier 290gsm (140lb). Also available are pads of assorted coloured and tinted

▲ **Large or small, spiral-bound or case-bound, landscape or portrait, there is a sketch book to meet the needs of every artist.**

papers, ideal for pastel and coloured pencil work. However, these are not usually made in pocket sizes, A5 generally being the smallest.

Choosing a sketch book

To a large extent your choice of sketch book will depend on what drawing materials you use. Cartridge paper is a good all-rounder, suitable for most drawing tools. However, pen and ink and technical pens are best used on very smooth papers; coarse surfaces are good for chunky mediums such as soft pencil, pastel and charcoal.

▶ **In upright sketchbooks, you can attain landscape-format drawings simply by working over the spine.**

▼ **A sketch book can also be used to keep dried flowers, commercial packaging or anything that stimulates you visually.**

Watercolour pads

Like sketch books, watercolour pads come in a range of sizes starting from around 180 x 130mm (7 x 5in). They are made with proper watercolour paper and have a strong backing board for rigidity and stability. The papers range from very rough to smooth hot-pressed. They are available either spiral-bound or as a block which is gummed on all four edges to reduce the need for stretching.

Sketch books come in various shapes and sizes. Some are rectangular and upright ('portrait' format), others are rectangular and horizontal ('landscape' format). The portrait format is perhaps the most versatile, because you can always work across two pages, taking your drawing over the spine for a landscape subject.

Spiral- or case-bound?

The spine of a sketch book can be either case-bound (that is, stitched or gummed) or spiral-bound. The spiral-bound ones don't allow you to sketch across two pages, but they do let you remove pages without ruining the book. This means you can discard sub-standard sketches and mount and frame exceptional ones.

What's more, the spiral-bound books can easily accommodate mounted materials. To make your book really attractive, feel free to include visually interesting items such as pressed flowers and leaves, postcards, tickets, invitations and scraps of fabric – anything, in fact, that may prove useful as a reference, inspiration or as a memory-jogger. Your sketch book is, in effect, a visual diary.

You can also use your sketch book for painting outdoors. Most heavier sketch book papers of around 290gsm (140lb) are fine for light watercolour washes. However, for very wet colour, you should always use a watercolour pad (see above right).

▲ **Carefully worked watercolours that run right up to the edge of the page can look stunning in your sketchbook.**

For sketching with acrylic paints, you can buy pads of canvas-textured paper. Oil paints are not really a suitable sketching medium, since they take so long to dry.

Colour notes

Painting out-of-doors can be a delight, but you often find yourself running out of time or stopped in your tracks by a change in the weather. It is difficult to finish the painting at home, because you cannot remember the colours.

The answer is to make colour notes in your sketch book before you start work on the painting. Make a very rough line drawing of the subject in your sketch book. Then you can write the names of the colours on the sketch or, even better, paint an actual blob of colour in the relevant area. These approximate colour guides will provide the reference you need to complete the painting at home.

ONE SKETCH BOOK, MANY STYLES

Use your sketch book to experiment with different drawing styles and mediums. The sketches below – all by the same artist – give some indication of the styles you might like to include in your book. The top picture is a line drawing in pencil, but has blocks of tone dotted across the composition to add variety. The middle picture is also in pencil – but colour has been added with washes of coffee!

The bottom sketch was done in watercolours. Paints might not seem the ideal sketching medium – but you can easily carry around a small watercolour set that contains all you need (see Portable art materials, pages 16-17).

Portable art materials

At some stage, every artist will want the challenge of painting outdoors, but you need to make sure you take the right equipment.

Practical considerations play an important part when it comes to deciding what to take when painting away from your home or studio. You must plan in advance – taking enough materials to meet your needs, while avoiding unnecessary weight or bulk.

First and foremost, comfort is crucial. There is nothing more miserable than trying to work in extreme weather conditions without the right sort of clothing. Depending on your chosen destination, pack a wide-brimmed hat to protect against the sun, or fingerless gloves to help keep you warm.

Are you sitting comfortably?

When using oils or acrylics, working with your painting on your lap or propped up against a handy tree trunk might be okay in emergencies, but the frustration and discomfort involved will eventually make a proper easel essential.

For the travelling artist, a box easel is the ideal choice. This combines a materials container and an easel in a compact, portable case with a handle for carrying. The legs are adjustable, so you can choose to stand or sit as you paint.

Sketching easels

Alternatively, a folding sketching easel is lightweight and usually suitable for all but very large or heavy paintings. On soft ground, you can make the easel more stable by tethering the legs with string and metal skewers (just as you would stabilise a tent). If you prefer to work sitting down, a good-quality, modern folding stool or chair is a worthwhile investment.

Whatever medium you're working in, limit yourself to a few colours. This is not simply convenient, it is also a good discipline – colour mixing becomes easier and more automatic, leaving you free to observe and appreciate the subject.

Carry only as much paint as you will need. Even oils and acrylics are available in small (20ml) sizes. It is a

◄ Handy equipment for the travelling artist includes a backpack (A), a foldaway stool (B) and a light folding sketching easel (C). (The backpack shown here converts into a stool.)

To paint in watercolours outdoors, you need a sketch pad (D), a pencil (E) for preliminary drawings, brushes (F) and a watercolour set containing pans of paint and a palette area (G). You also need water – why not keep it in a couple of mineral water bottles? For oils and acrylics, you need a palette and paints, clip-on dippers (H) to hold thinners and mediums, perhaps a palette knife (I), and a selection of brushes (J). Canvas paper (K) is a portable, lightweight surface to paint on, and a charcoal pencil (L) can be used for an underdrawing.

good idea to keep the large economy tubes for the studio, and to invest in a few less bulky tubes for painting trips.

Paints of all types can be bought in handy sets – some come in lightweight, attaché-style carrying cases, complete with accessories such as palette, brushes and mediums. The initial choice of colours is that of the manufacturer, but, as you use the set, you can gradually substitute your favourite colours for the ones supplied.

Customised painting sets

Better still, why not make your own customised, portable painting set? This can be a wooden box, designed to carry your usual colours and mediums as well as your favourite palette and brushes.

Watercolourists will find that pads of paper are easier to carry than individual sheets. As the pads have a stiff card backing, there is no need for a board or other rigid surface to work on. Special blocks of paper, which are glued on three sides and do not need to be stretched, are particularly useful if you intend to work with watery washes.

For oils and acrylics, the cardboard-backed pads of canvas-textured paper are ideal for on-the-spot painting. These come with sheets of primed paper in a choice of sizes and grades – fine, medium and coarse. Alternatively, use prepared and ready-primed stretched canvases or canvas boards.

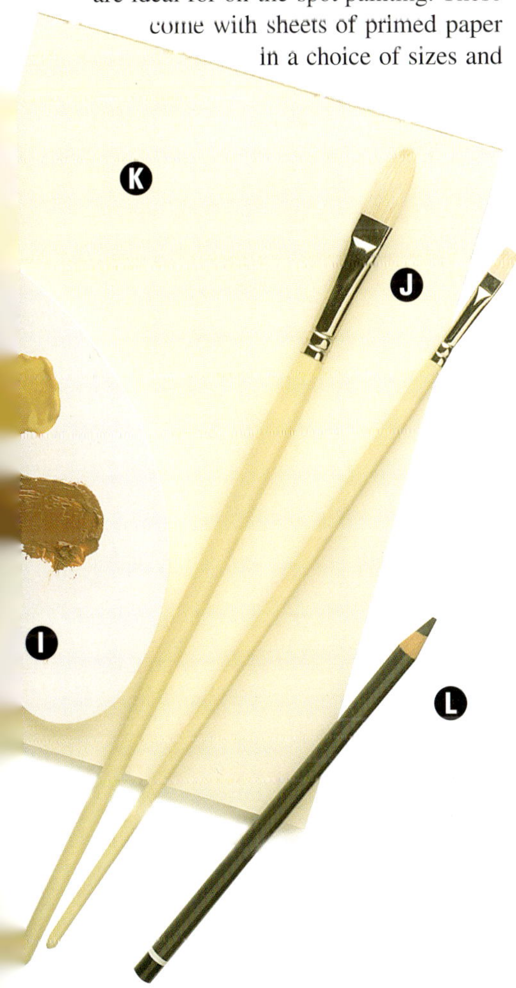

THE COMPLETE WATERCOLOUR SET

As you need only a few lightweight materials, watercolours are particularly well suited to painting outside. You can buy compact, all-in-one sets that fit into virtually any bag and contain everything you need.

As well as a water container, palette, sketching pad and brushes, these sets have pans of colour, which are more practical than tubes because you can see and mix the colours instantly, without having to squeeze out paint and replace caps. Always carry a second bottle of water so that you have one for mixing colours and one for cleaning brushes.

For very small paintings, you can buy tiny watercolour sets – some of which will slip into your pocket.

Avoid travelling with a traditional wooden drawing board, which is heavy and cumbersome to carry. If you really need a board, try a sheet of lightweight plywood or hardboard instead.

Bottles, boxes and containers

Pliable plastic food containers – the type used for freezer storage – come in a wide range of shapes and sizes and are invaluable to the artist. Use the lightweight lidded boxes for carrying paints, crayons, pastels and other materials.

Pourers and bottles with plastic lids are excellent for holding water, turpentine and liquid mediums. You need one source of clean water or turps for diluting the colours and another for cleaning brushes. If you are travelling by air, remember that it is illegal to take flammable substances, which include turpentine and white spirit, on the plane. In some countries, real turpentine is difficult to come by, so it is worth making a few enquiries before you go.

On any painting trip, you need plenty of clean rags or kitchen paper for cleaning palettes and brushes. Also take clingfilm or plastic bags, so you can carry a dirty palette home without getting paint everywhere. Alternatively, use disposable paper palettes.

For transporting canvases with wet oils and acrylics, carry paintings face-in, as shown below. To transport drawings and watercolours, cover the surface with a sheet of clean paper, or roll them into a cardboard tube. Remember, soft pencil, pastel, chalk and charcoal smudge easily so drawings should be sprayed with fixative as soon as you have finished.

▼ The trouble with oil paints is that they take time to dry, so it is easy to smudge the colours. A convenient solution is to push panel pins through corks so that both ends of the pins protude. Then cut the blunt ends off the pins with pliers, and use these to attach two paintings, facing inwards, together. You can then carry the canvases around without touching the paint.

Choosing the best palette

Essential to creating good paintings is colour mixing – and to do this successfully, you first need to have the right palette.

Artists' palettes are made from a variety of materials and come in an enormous range of shapes and sizes. Your choice depends largely on the paints you are intending to use. For example, you will need a flat palette for oils and acrylics, and deeper mixing dishes for watercolours.

It is important to work with a palette that is big enough to accommodate all the colours you are likely to need. There is nothing more frustrating than trying to mix on a cramped surface – either you tend not to use enough of each colour or the mixes overlap, creating muddy colours.

Oil paints

The kidney-shaped wooden palette with a hole for the thumb is traditionally used for oil paints. This design has been in use since the advent of the medium in the early fifteenth century. The best wooden palettes are made from mahogany or mahogany veneer, but there are now cheaper options, including plywood and other wood composites.

When choosing a wooden palette, try it out for size, weight and comfort. The ideal palette can easily be held in a horizontal position – usually by using the forearm as support. A badly designed one will be difficult to hold up and will soon make your thumb and wrist ache.

Before using your palette for the first time, seal the wood by rubbing it with linseed oil. This helps prevent the palette from absorbing oil from the paint, causing the colours to dry out. After one or two painting sessions, the palette ceases to be as absorbent and provides an excellent paint-mixing surface. Cared for properly, a good wooden palette will last a lifetime.

Acrylic paints

For acrylics, use a plastic or plastic-laminate palette – one is given away free with this issue. Acrylic paint dries quickly and, if left for several hours or overnight, the paint turns first rubbery, then hard. On a wooden palette the colours will stick fast to the slightly irregular, pitted surface and will be difficult to remove. However, the smooth surface of a plastic palette provides no key for the paint, which can be removed easily by soaking, then peeling it off.

A special 'wet' palette is also available for use with acrylics and is designed to keep the colours moist for as long as possible. The palette works on the principle of osmosis. It consists of a shallow plastic tray with a sheet of absorbent wet tissue placed in the bottom under a thin membrane paper. When the acrylic paint colours are laid out on the membrane, the moisture from the wet tissue is drawn through, so preventing the paints from drying out.

Alternatively, you can make your own wet palette from a plastic or foil dish and some sheets of wetted kitchen paper, with a sheet of greaseproof paper for the membrane.

Watercolour and gouache

Palettes for mixing watercolour or gouache must be deep enough to hold watery mixtures without the colours running together. They are available in a range of shapes and sizes from small round dishes, known as tinting saucers, to much larger, more complex palette trays which have 24 or more recesses for mixing colour.

Watercolour palettes are usually made of ceramic, plastic or enamelled metal. Plastic palettes are light, tough and inexpensive – excellent for painting expeditions and for working outdoors. However, the plastic surface has a slightly repellent effect on water and the paint tends to break

INTEGRAL PALETTES

Most enamelled watercolour boxes have lids that open out to form a small palette. They are often divided into two or more recesses and sometimes unfold to provide a larger mixing area. These boxes are particularly handy for outdoor work and sketching.

up into globules rather than forming even pools. Although this makes no difference to the colours, it can be irritating and makes it difficult to judge how much colour you have mixed. In addition, some plastics stain easily and soon lose their whiteness. For these reasons, many artists prefer to use ceramic palettes.

Improvised palettes

Lack of a proper palette need not prevent you from painting. For oils and acrylics, you could always improvise with a sheet of plastic, perspex, laminate or glass. The latter can be made safe by binding the sharp edges with tape. One great advantage of a homemade palette is that you can choose a size and shape to suit your needs. It can be as large as you like, perhaps even cut to fit a particular table top.

Other alternative palettes for oils and acrylics are greaseproof paper, old plates and other discarded kitchenware. You can also buy disposable paper palettes in tear-off pads. For watercolour, use old dishes and saucers.

Consider the colour

Be aware that the colour or tone of your palette affects the appearance of the colours you mix. For example, on a white palette all your colours will look comparatively dark, whereas on a dark palette, they will appear paler.

Cleaning an oil palette

To clean your oil palette, you need a knife and some diluent – for example, white spirit or turpentine left over in a dipper after a painting.

1 ▲ **Remove excess paint** Scrape off left-over colours with a knife while the paint is still wet.

2 ▲ **Wipe the palette** Dip a rag in diluent and wipe the remaining paint off the palette.

Watercolour palettes are always white, so that they will give an accurate idea of how the colours will appear on white paper. Most oil paintings, on the other hand, are executed in a darker tonal range, and the artist often blocks out the bright white canvas in the early stages of a painting. For the oil painter, therefore, a wooden palette provides a better idea of how the mixed colours will look in the finished painting.

Some artists like to use a sheet of clear plastic or glass as a palette. They can then put a sheet of coloured paper underneath, matching the paper they are using as a support.

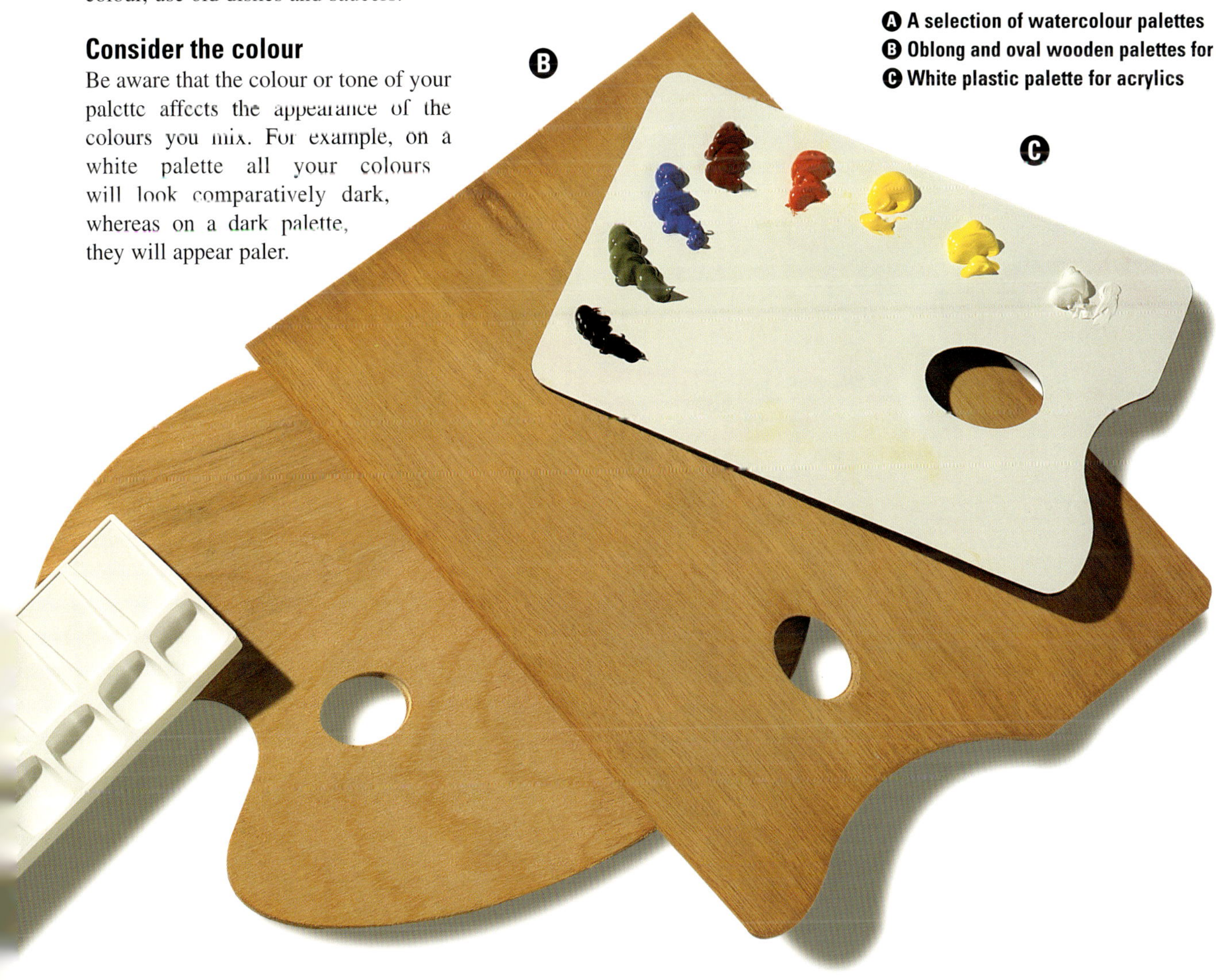

A A selection of watercolour palettes
B Oblong and oval wooden palettes for oils
C White plastic palette for acrylics

Choosing the best easel

A stable easel, which holds your work rigidly in one position, will avoid the frustration of trying to work with your picture precariously propped up on a table or on your lap. You'll soon find it's a necessity rather than a luxury.

A good easel is an artist's best friend. It will last a lifetime and is one of the most important and permanent pieces of studio equipment, so take time to look around and buy a model that meets all your requirements. Your choice of easel depends on various factors – the available space in your working area, whether you like to work standing up or sitting down, and whether you tend to work mostly indoors or outdoors. It also depends on the medium you generally use and on the scale of your work. For example, watercolours are much easier to use with an easel that can be tilted to the horizontal, so your washes won't run down the paper.

Outdoor easels

Lugging a heavy easel on painting expeditions is no fun at all, so choose a compact, portable model for outdoor work. A sketching easel (see easels E-H opposite) could be the answer, being both lightweight and foldable. These are made in wood or aluminium, are fully adjustable and can usually be positioned for both watercolour and vertical painting.

Sketching easels can accommodate surprisingly large boards and canvases, but this depends on the make and type. Check the distance between the top and bottom easel grips to make sure that the easel will take the size of support you prefer.

A box easel (see right, below and easel N) is more stable, though slightly heavier than an ordinary sketching easel. However, it is easy to fold up and carry, and also incorporates a box or drawer for holding paints, brushes and other materials.

Easels for indoor work

For large or heavy canvases, a traditional upright studio easel (easels I-L opposite) is probably your best bet. These can be bulky – some even have castors, so that they can be moved around more easily – but they are reassuringly solid.

If your work space is limited, a radial easel (J) is a versatile alternative. This consists of an upright spine with tripod-type legs. The whole easel can be adjusted, so you can angle your work to suit the light, though not to the horizontal position necessary for watercolour painting. When it is not in use, the radial easel can be folded for easy storage.

A tilting radial easel is also known as a 'combination' easel (K), because it brings together features of both the radial and the sketching easel. It has a central joint, so

◄ The versatile box easel is ideal for the artist who likes to work both in the studio and out-of-doors. For storage and carrying, the easel folds down to a box shape with a handle for easy carrying (right).

that it can be adjusted to any position from upright to completely horizontal, and it is therefore an ideal choice for the artist who works in a variety of media.

If your studio space or work area is limited, a sketching easel or a box easel will be just as versatile indoors as outdoors. Alternatively, if you work on a fairly small scale, a table-top easel in wood or aluminium (see easels A-D) might be all you need.

Looking after your easel

Apart from the lightweight sketching easels made from aluminium, most artists' easels are robustly constructed from hardwood, traditionally beechwood. They require little regular maintenance, although the wood benefits from an occasional coat of wax polish, especially when an easel is used outside or in damp conditions. Also, the metal adjusting nuts can get stiff and should be kept lubricated with oil.

THE RIGHT EASEL FOR THE JOB

TABLE EASELS

A Sturdy wooden easel with an 'H' frame, which can be tilted to provide the ideal working angle.

B Light, portable tripod-type wooden easel with rubber-tipped non-slip feet.

C Extremely light aluminium easel with adjustable telescopic back leg and rubber-tipped feet.

D Wooden easel, which can be set at four different angles and folds flat when not in use.

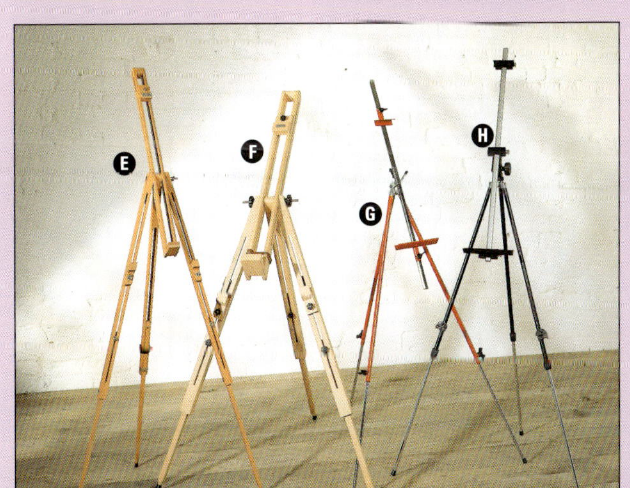

SKETCHING EASELS

E Lightweight easel with an adjustable tilting facility, making it suitable for all media, including watercolour.

F Substantial tilting, sketching easel appropriate for all media.

G Folding, tilting metal easel with telescopic legs and adjustable canvas grip.

H Fully adjustable metal easel with a camera mount fixing, so that it can be used as a photographic tripod.

STUDIO EASELS

I Sturdy studio easel with an adjustable lower shelf for the canvas or board, allowing simple adjustment of the working height.

J Rigid, adjustable radial easel, which can be tilted backwards and forwards, but not horizontally for watercolour work.

K Combination easel, which can be secured in any position and is suitable for use with all media.

L Artist's 'donkey' or platform easel – a comfortable sitting easel which takes up very little space when folded.

M Simple, popular 'A' frame easel with a metal ratchet on the lower support for adjusting the working height.

N Box easel with a container for paints, brushes and other art materials. Ideal for studio or outdoor work.

FROM BAMBOO TO BALLPOINT

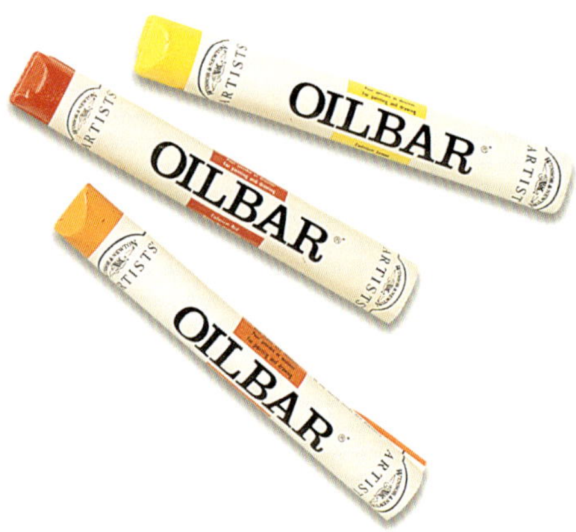

This chapter explores the myriad of different media available to the artist, from conté crayons and pastels to the humble ballpoint pen. It looks at the some of the effects you can achieve using different types of paint and drawing implements and contains practical advice to help you use them most effectively.

Using a bamboo pen

Cut your own bamboo pen and make a lively ink drawing. The spontaneous marks capture the rustic feel of fresh vegetables in a trug.

In spite of the extensive array of art equipment available these days, some of the liveliest pictures are those drawn with the simplest tools. This still life of vegetables was drawn in pen and ink, using both a bamboo pen that you can make for yourself (see overleaf for instructions) and an ordinary dip pen.

Fluid lines

With a bamboo pen, you can create wonderfully fluid and expressive lines. The nib has a softer feel than a metal nib and moves smoothly over the paper. You can make both heavy and fine lines, depending on the pressure you use. If a few blots and irregular marks appear here and there, these simply add to the excitement of the drawing. After using the pen for a while, you can resharpen the nib with a craft knife to keep it firm.

For a spontaneous effect in your drawing, try working in ink right away, without an initial pencil sketch. Alternatively, you can plot the outlines in pencil first, then work over the top in pen.

▼ To convey the variety of wonderful textures in this still life, the artist used both a metal-nibbed pen as well as a bamboo one.

CUT A BAMBOO PEN

Making your own bamboo pen is simple, inexpensive and fun. All you need is a length of bamboo, readily available from garden centres, and a few basic tools. For safety when using a craft knife, make sure you direct the blade away from your body.

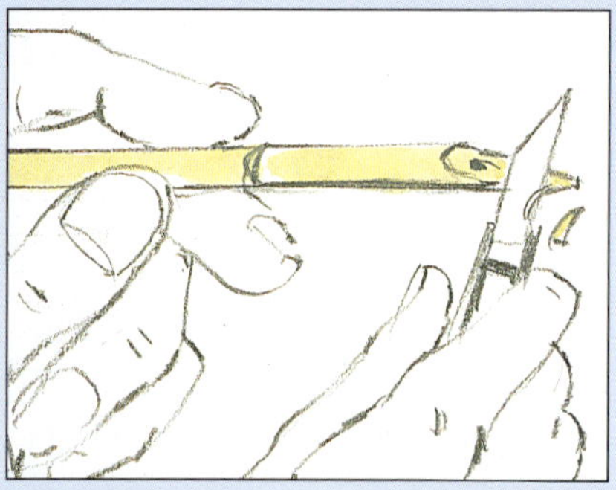

1 ▲ Shape a nib Cut a 20cm (8in) length of bamboo with a junior hack-saw. Trim one end at a 45° angle. With a craft knife, flatten the angle of the tip and carve away the sides until the nib is the thickness and width you want.

2 ▲ Cut a slit Rest the nib on a cutting board and, using the craft knife, cut a slit along the centre. The ink is held in this slit and will be slowly released as you draw with the pen.

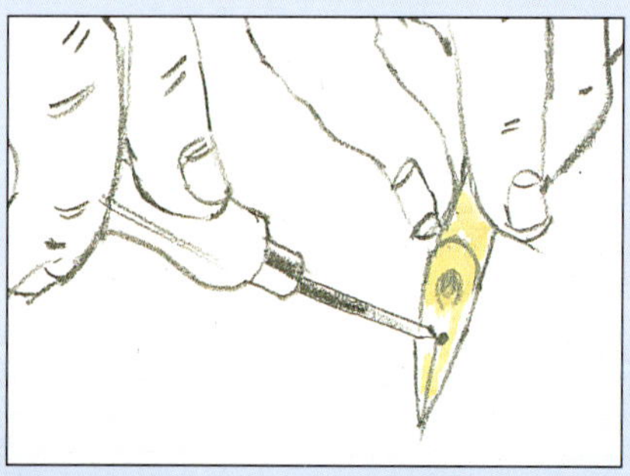

3 ▲ Make a reservoir Using a bradawl, bore a small hole at the base of the slit. This creates a reservoir so that the pen can hold a little more ink. To make the pen more versatile, cut a second nib of a different width at the other end of the bamboo.

YOU WILL NEED

- Piece of white Bristol board
- Handmade bamboo pen
- Black Indian ink
- Bleedproof white gouache
- Dip pen with fine nib
- No.4 soft round brush

FIRST STEPS

1 ▲ Make an ink sketch Dip a bamboo pen into black Indian ink and draw the outline of the trug and the vegetables. Don't worry if you make errors – you can rectify these by painting them out with bleedproof white gouache.

2 ► Put in the cast shadows Develop the shape of the broccoli by drawing its florets in more detail, then begin putting in the gills of the mushroom. Look at the shapes of the shadows cast on to the white surface and hatch these in lightly with fine lines.

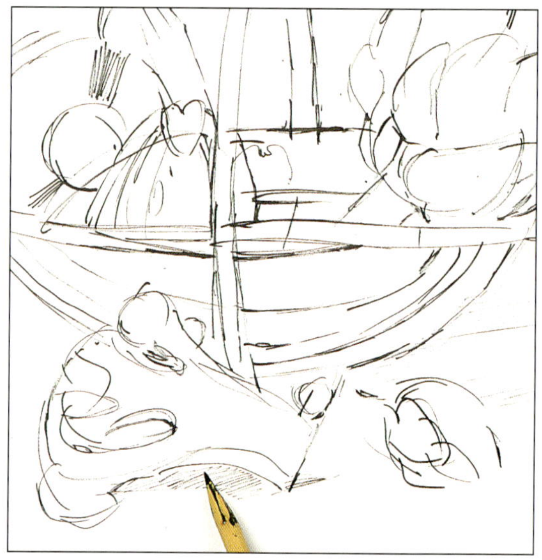

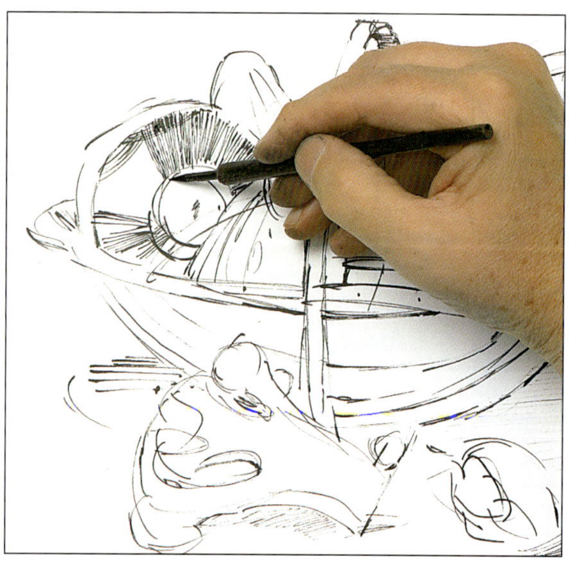

3 ◄ Change to a metal nib With the bamboo pen, draw the cast shadow of the trug on the left with a few lines. Now change to a dip pen with a fine metal nib and draw more mushroom gills, making the lines slightly irregular for a natural look. Use cross-hatching to darken the shadow at the top of the mushroom.

MAKING MARKS IN PEN AND INK

The type of mark you make in pen and ink depends on the nib you are using and how much pressure you apply to it as you move it over the paper. Some metal nibs are more flexible than others and give a greater range of strokes. Bamboo pens give characterful, slightly irregular marks.

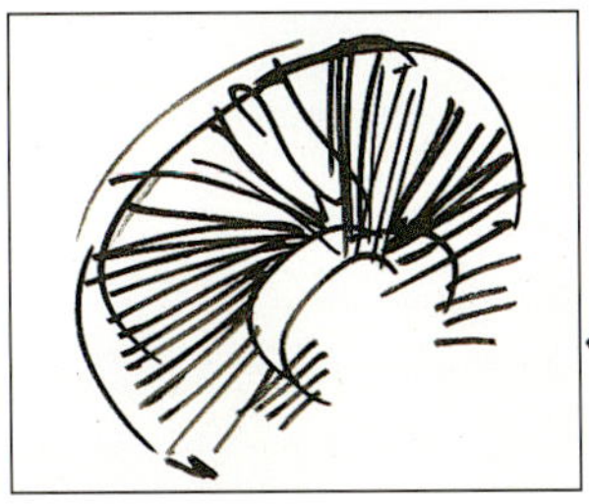

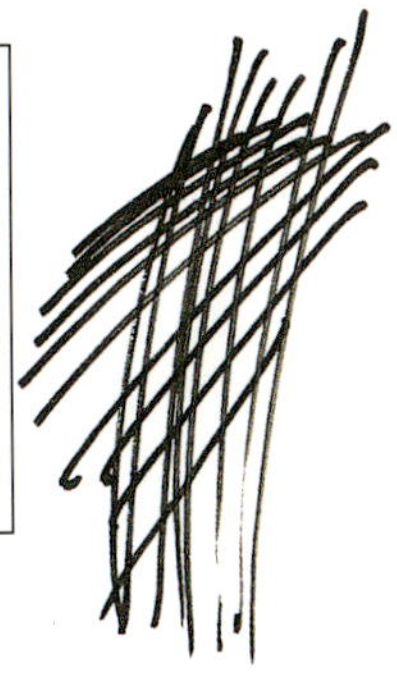

▲ **These bold, decisive lines and dark hatching were made with the tip of a bamboo pen.**

▲ **A fine metal nib was used to create delicate lines, dotted textures and light hatching.**

CONTINUE WITH THE DETAILS

Carry on working with the dip pen with the fine metal nib to develop fine detail on the vegetables. Darker outlines and tones can be filled in later with the bamboo pen.

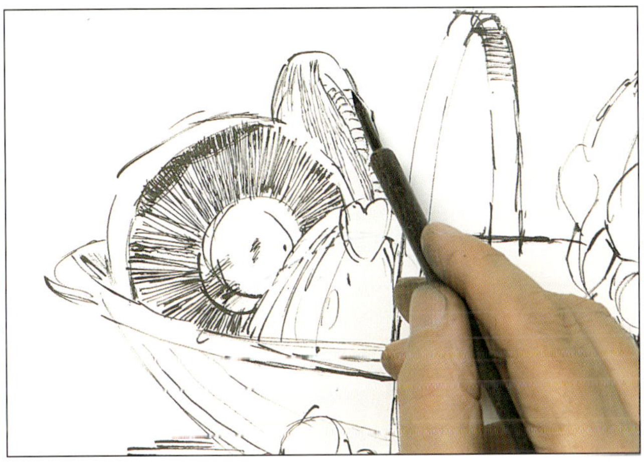

4 ▲ **Put in the corn kernels** Hatch tone under the trug handle. Complete the mushroom gills and make the shadow at the top even darker with closely worked lines. Draw the papery texture of the corn-on-the-cob leaves with loose hatched lines and the neat rows of kernels with small semicircular lines.

5 ▲ **Show more textures** Begin work on the red cabbage in the trug, alternating the straight spines of the leaves with the crinkly texture in between. Turning to the artichoke, show the fibrous texture of the leaves with thin ink lines. Make the lines irregular so that the effect is not too rigid, using the same technique as for the mushroom. Render some dark tone to show the shadows between the leaves.

6 ◂ **Develop the drawing overall** Continue working texture into the artichoke leaves, then move to the small artichoke in front of the trug and roughly hatch in texture on this too. Use hatched lines to indicate shadows on the top rim of the mushroom. Then strengthen the outline of the broccoli florets. Make long, irregular horizontal strokes to show the wooden texture inside the trug.

7 ▼ Work on the trug Darken the shaded area under the front rim of the trug. Using loose, sweeping lines, shade the front of the trug – these lines also help to build up the trug's curved form. Complete the shadow cast by the trug with a series of bold, well-spaced straight lines.

8 ▶ Add texture to the broccoli Create texture on the broccoli head with tiny circles, blotting some of them with your finger to achieve a variety of tones. Shade the hollows between the stalks, using close marks for the dark tone and lighter hatching for the mid tone.

9 ▼ Return to the bamboo pen Using the thicker nib of the bamboo pen, mark a dark outline around the mushroom gills. With the same pen, put in some darker lines and dotted texture on the red cabbage.

TROUBLE SHOOTER

CORRECTING MISTAKES

The joy of working with pen and ink is the spontaneity of the technique. Occasionally, however, you might misjudge a proportion or overdo a flourish. Small errors are simple to rectify by painting over them with opaque, bleedproof white gouache. Alternatively, on hard, smooth papers, you can first scrape away most of the ink marks with the blade of a craft knife without damaging the paper surface.

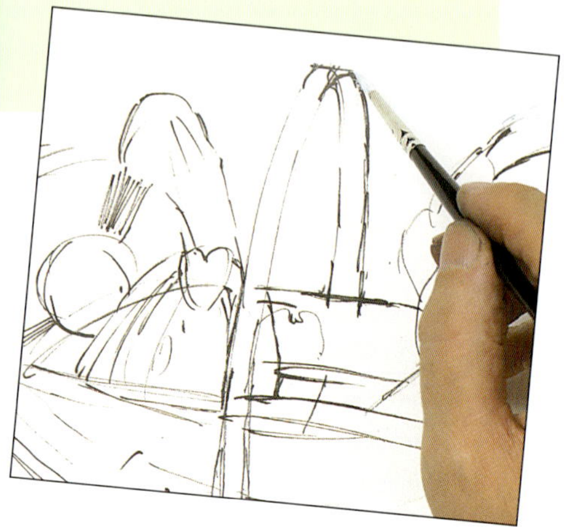

10 ▲ Improve the textures Change back to the metal nib to complete the lines inside the trug. Then return to the bamboo pen to darken the tone on the small artichoke and cross-hatch its shadow. Suggest the texture of its leaf tips with small circles. Clean up any errors with bleedproof white gouache and a No.4 round brush (see Trouble Shooter above).

A FEW STEPS FURTHER

If you want to work on the drawing a little more, you could heighten the tonal contrast by darkening the shadow areas. Extra details will sharpen up the picture.

11 ◄ Increase the contrast Use the bamboo pen to hatch more horizontal lines along the trug handle. Render darker tone on the side of the large artichoke. Darken the hollows in the broccoli and dot more texture on to the florets.

12 ▲ Put in the final details With the metal nib, add detail to the mushroom stalk. Draw fine fibres and more corn kernels on the cob. Use the bamboo pen to mark nails on the rim of the trug and dark lines between the segments of the trug's base.

THE FINISHED PICTURE

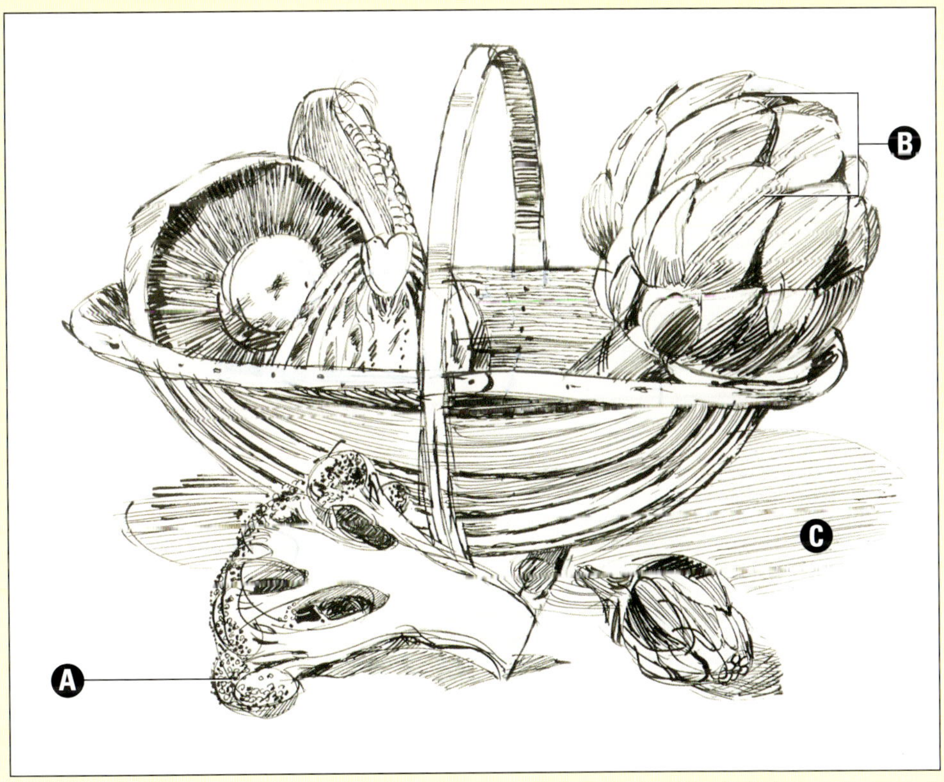

A Textural effects
The texture of the broccoli florets was created by working tiny circles and dots close together. Both bamboo and metal nibs were used for a range of effects.

B Contrasting line widths
The fine lines on the artichoke leaves were made with a metal nib, while the thicker marks were made with the broader nib of a bamboo pen.

C Tonal shadows
The cast shadows are varied in tone – mid tones were rendered with well-spaced hatching lines, while a dark effect was created by much closer hatching.

Using Conté crayons

Less messy to handle than charcoal or chalk, Conté crayons are versatile drawing tools that make attractive marks. They are ideal for sketching as well as for more finished work.

Nicholas-Jacques Conté (1755-1805), the French artist who invented the modern graphite pencil, also gave the world another popular drawing material – Conté crayons. These distinctive, square-sectioned drawing sticks were patented in Paris by Conté more than 200 years ago.

The square ends of the crayons enable you to use them to produce both broad and fine lines. You can even draw with the side of the stick to fill in large areas of colour quickly and easily. This versatility has been appreciated and exploited by many – not only by famous artists such as Hilaire Germain Degas (1834-1917) and Henri de Toulouse-Lautrec (1864-1901), but also by generations of art students who have been encouraged to use Conté as a clean and manageable alternative to charcoal and chalk.

Conté crayons look rather like pastels but, unlike most pastels, they do not crumble or create powdery deposits. Although some very hard pastels are similar, Conté crayons are generally waxier and harder than most other products on the market. They are also available in pencil form.

An array of colours

The original Conté crayons were made from a few earth pigments, clay, graphite, wax and a little grease. These ingredients produced a limited range of colours: black, white, sanguine, sepia and bistre.

Today, the Conté palette includes not only the original earth pigments, but also a huge array of other colours, giving a selection that compares favourably with the ranges available in paints, pastels and other artists' materials. In addition, there is a tonal set of crayons.

The tonal range

Conté's selection of shades matches the tonal scale, which runs from black to white with a range of greys in between.

▶ Earth colours: Traditional earth colours are made from clay and other mineral deposits. Chalk is added for paler tones.

▶ Tonal selection: For monochrome drawings and tonal sketches, Conté crayons are available in a range of greys as well as in black and white.

▶ Coloured selection: Conté crayons also come in a wide range of colours, which can be bought either individually or in sets.

▶ Hard pastels: Some hard pastels have a high wax content and are used in a similar way to Conté crayons.

▼ Conté is available in pencil form. The pencils can be sharpened using a craft knife or scalpel.

▲ Reddish-brown sanguine pigment comes from red clay, the colouring being caused by ferric oxide. This and other earth pigments are used to make Conté crayons.

▲ For an even, graded effect, overlap two or more colours. A third colour is created where the two colours overlap.

With this selection of crayons, you can depict any subject by building up gradations of tones instead of blocks of colour.

The best way of judging tones is to try to see your subject as it would look in a black-and-white photograph. Obviously, you can use white and black Contés for the whites and blacks in the subject. Between these two extremes, choose pale greys for light colours, such as yellow, and dark greys for the deeper colours. If you can visualise what kind of grey each colour would be in a black-and-white photograph, you have also understood its tonal value.

Use a mid-toned paper rather than pure white for this exercise. In this way, you can relate the light and dark tones to the medium background tone and both will show up clearly.

Earth colours

The original earth colours, including warm sanguine red and cool brown bistre, are still the most popular in the Conté range. These same earthy pigments have been used for thousands of years. Stone Age cave painters worked with them, as have many artists since then, including Leonardo da Vinci (1452-1519) and Michelangelo (1475-1564). No wonder that works executed with this handful of colours have such an evocative, antique appearance.

Whatever your subject, provided that you restrict yourself to the earth selection and choose a suitable paper, the colour scheme of your Conté drawing will appear harmonious and considered. Earth colours work especially well on tinted papers, particularly those in neutral browns and muted greens and blues.

Making marks with Conté

Unlike traditional crayons, Conté crayons have a sharply squared-off end, which means that you can make a variety of marks simply by turning the crayon round and using a different part of the stick. In this respect, they are very similar to charcoal. And like charcoal, you can achieve different depths of colour and texture effects by using more or less pressure on the crayon as you work.

Fine lines Although they appear quite chunky, Conté crayons can be used for delicate work, too. To make a fine line, draw with the sharp edge of the squared end.

Undulating lines Hold the crayon firmly and use the broad end and sharp edge alternately to get an undulating line of varying widths and textures.

Blocks of colour To block in an area of colour, work with the entire length of the stick. You may find this easier if you break the crayon into shorter, more manageable lengths.

Wide lines Use the broad end of the crayon to draw a wide, regular line with parallel sides. Thick lines like this are well suited to large-scale work.

Introducing marker pens

Whether you're sketching outdoors or working on a finished drawing indoors, marker pens provide a colourful and convenient medium.

If you thought marker pens belonged in the office or the children's playroom – think again! Vigorous, brilliantly coloured drawings can be made with this modern medium, which is especially convenient for outdoor sketching. A set of marker pens is light, compact and clean, allowing you to make full-colour sketches without the need for cumbersome paints, palettes and jars of water.

The only drawback with markers is that they contain dyes rather than pigments, so the colours tend to fade in time when exposed to strong sunlight. You can, however, minimise the risk of fading by keeping your drawings in a portfolio or hanging them well away from direct sunlight.

Types of marker

There is an enormous range of markers to choose from, in literally hundreds of colours and with various sizes and shapes of tip. Art and graphic suppliers sell the best-quality pens, but the ones sold in stationers and supermarkets are cheaper and perfectly adequate for sketching and practice work.

- **Fibre tips** have tips made from nylon or fibre-glass. They are hard-wearing and smooth-flowing.
- **Felt tips** have thicker, slightly more flexible tips made from wool or a synthetic substitute. They flow smoothly and make soft, dense marks.
- **Fine-liners** have tips made from plastic or a similar synthetic material. They are hard and durable and produce thin, spidery lines.

Tip shapes

As well as being made from a variety of materials, felt and fibre tips have a range of tip shapes, varying from fine points to broad, chisel-shaped wedges.

- **Wedge-shaped tips** are the most versatile. By turning the marker as you draw, you can use the edge and the different sides of the tip to make broad, medium and thin lines. You can also fill in areas of flat colour by working quickly in broad, horizontal lines, taking each line over the previous one before it has time to dry.
- **Bullet-shaped tips** produce medium and bold marks, and the rounded tip can be used for stippling effects.

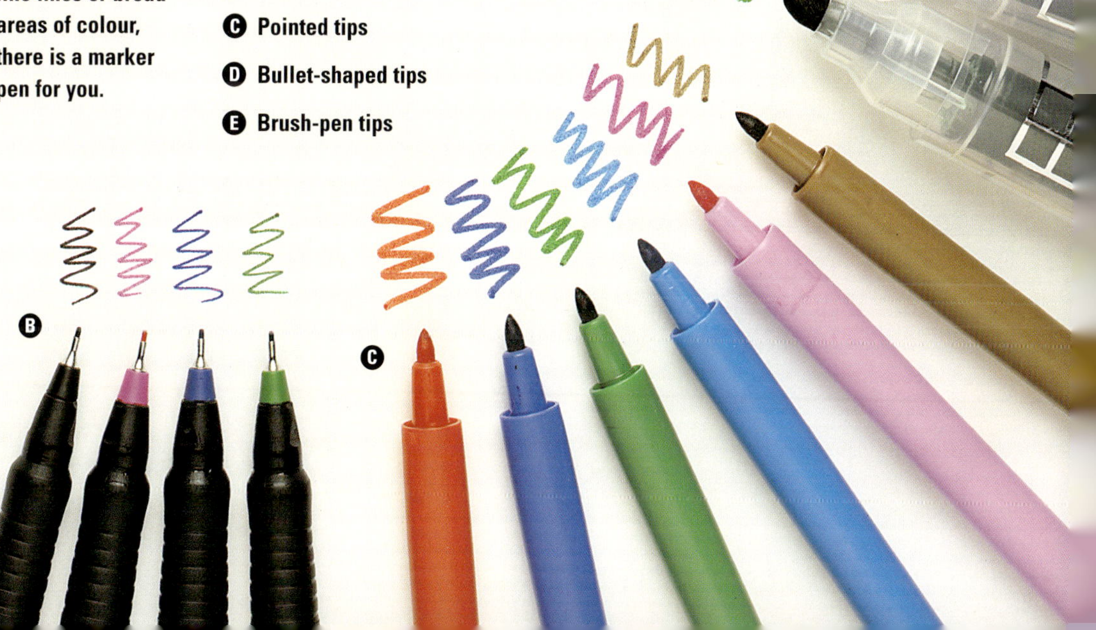

▼ **Whether you want to work with fine lines or broad areas of colour, there is a marker pen for you.**

A Wedge-shaped tips
B Fine-liners
C Pointed tips
D Bullet-shaped tips
E Brush-pen tips

● **Pointed tips** produce thin lines of uniform thickness. They are good for defining outlines and for rendering fine details.

● **Brush-pen tips** are made of elongated, flexible fibres that come to a point, and create a variety of marks that look similar to those made with a watercolour brush.

Two types of ink

Another important consideration with marker pens is whether they contain water-based or spirit-based inks. The water-based inks tend to lie on the paper surface for longer, making it easier to blend colours. Interesting soft, feather-like effects can be achieved by drawing on dampened paper.

The spirit-based colours, by contrast, are readily absorbed into the paper, permanent and waterproof. They tend to 'bleed' beyond the shape drawn by the nib, though for fine-art purposes this doesn't usually matter. They also tend to bleed right through the paper, so when working on a sketch pad, place a sheet of scrap paper beneath the drawing surface.

Spirit-based pens that are drying out can be rejuvenated by tipping a few drops of lighter fuel into the cap before putting it back on the pen. After a few hours, the nib should have absorbed the fuel and, although the colour will be lighter, the pen will last longer.

Papers

It is fun to experiment with different drawing surfaces as each influences the character of the drawn lines, depending on how readily they absorb the marker dyes. You can buy special marker paper which resists colour bleeding. This paper has a hard, non-absorbent surface and is ideal when you want to produce crisp, clear marks and fine details. Alternatively, try drawing on smooth white card or even white scraperboard.

Delicate effects

If you want a more delicate effect, try drawing on ordinary cartridge paper or watercolour paper. The marks produced will be softer and fatter as the colour sinks into the surface and spreads slightly. On the highly absorbent Japanese rice papers, the marker dye spreads rapidly, like ink on blotting paper, producing effects similar to watercolour painting.

Practice is the key to successful marker work. Bear in mind that markers are not a subtle medium, and they do have certain limitations. The colours are bright and brash – they cannot be lightened with water or white paint and mistakes cannot be rectified. Also, the marks cannot be blended on the paper as easily as, say, watercolour or pastel.

On the plus side, a single marker can produce a whole range of lines, tones and textural effects according to how you hold it and the pressure you apply. So buy a selection of pens with different nib shapes and experiment by making marks on sheets of scrap paper.

Different strokes

Marker pens lend themselves to a surprisingly wide range of drawing techniques. Fine-liners are ideal for stippling or cross-hatching (see top row of apples below). By cross-hatching in colour, you can create great optical mixing effects by overlaying different hues. On the bottom-left apple, look at the way red has been hatched over green to create a brown suitable for the shadowed side. With chisel- and bullet-shaped pens, try making use of the transparency of the inks by laying flat areas of colour over each other (see bottom-right apple). To avoid getting muddy tones, limit the colours you overlay to three or four.

Stippling in monochrome

Cross-hatching in monochrome

Cross-hatching in colour

Building up layers of colour

Soft pastels

Working with pastels is highly rewarding – they are extremely versatile and produce a rich depth of colour not found in other media.

◄ **Pastels can be divided into two main groups – hard and soft. But within each group there are degrees of hardness and softness. Pastels also come in pencil form.**

Soft pastels produce matt, velvety colours that range from the intensely brilliant to the palest of pale pastel shades. The most vibrantly coloured sticks are made from pure pigment; lighter tones are made by adding chalk or white pigment to the main colour. But whether you choose pale lemon or deep, resonant gold, the powdery pastel pigments will give you a richly dense colour that cannot be matched by any other medium.

Because they come in stick form, soft pastels are generally thought of as drawing materials. But they are far more than simply coloured drawing sticks. Pastels are also a versatile and effective 'colouring' medium – excellent for laying down areas of colour, tone and texture as well as for drawing lines. Used in this way, soft pastels are more like paints than pencils, and this is why pastel pictures are often referred to as paintings rather than drawings.

Soft pastels also have one very important advantage over paints: when working with pastels, you do not have to wait for one colour to dry before applying the next. The powdery colours cannot run, so you can apply each pastel colour when and where you want it, even overlapping or directly adjacent to another colour.

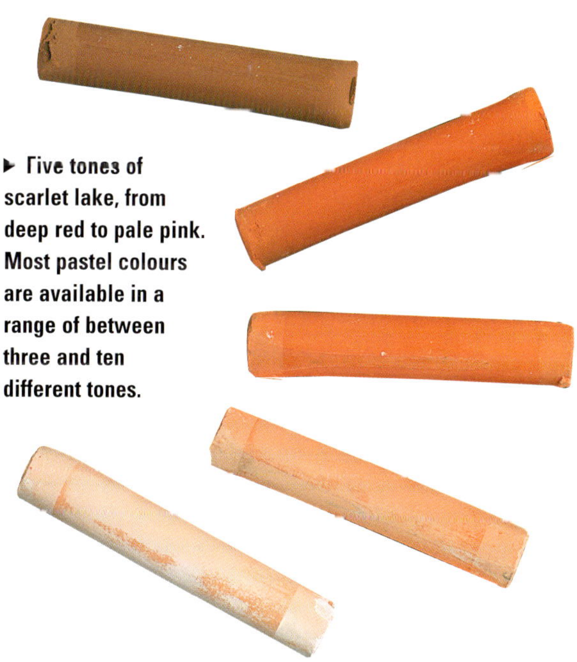

► **Five tones of scarlet lake, from deep red to pale pink. Most pastel colours are available in a range of between three and ten different tones.**

▲ **The more chalk that is added to the pure pigment, the lighter the tone of the soft pastel. A huge variety of shades of the same colour can be achieved in this way.**

Making pastels

Soft pastels have been in use since the early eighteenth century. Until that time their nearest equivalents were hard crayons, usually bound with wax and available in only a few muted colours such as earthy reds, browns and blacks.

Although soft pastels contain exactly the same pigments as paints and other artists' materials, they are a dry medium, requiring no water or any other liquid. Soft pastels are made by mixing the powdered ingredients with enough binder to hold them together. The mixture is then rolled or moulded into sticks and left to dry.

The most usual binders are gum, resin or starch. However, some pigments need a more powerful binding agent than others. For instance, chalky pale shades may be held together with nothing stronger than skimmed milk, whereas others such as cadmium red require a stronger binder. It is the strength and quality of the binding agent that determines how soft or hard a pastel will be.

Hard, soft and very soft

For the sake of simplicity, all artists' pastels can be divided into two main groups – hard and soft. Soft pastels are characteristically chunky and crumbly and are the most popular of the various types of pastel. However, it is worth

BLENDING SOFT PASTELS

You can use a paint brush to blend two pastel colours together. Brush gently, as a harsh movement will remove the pigment altogether.

For large areas of colour, a soft tissue or paper kitchen towel blends different shades of pastel quickly and effectively.

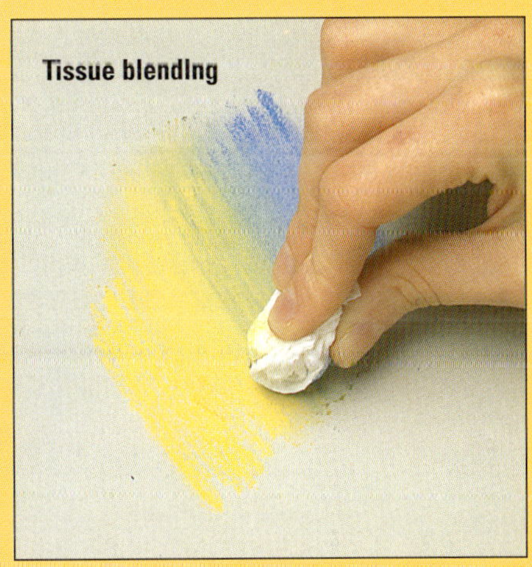

The quickest and easiest way to blend two areas of pastel colour is simply to rub them together with a clean fingertip.

The pointed end of a torchon, a stump of tightly rolled white paper available from art shops, is ideal for blending small, precise areas of pastel colour.

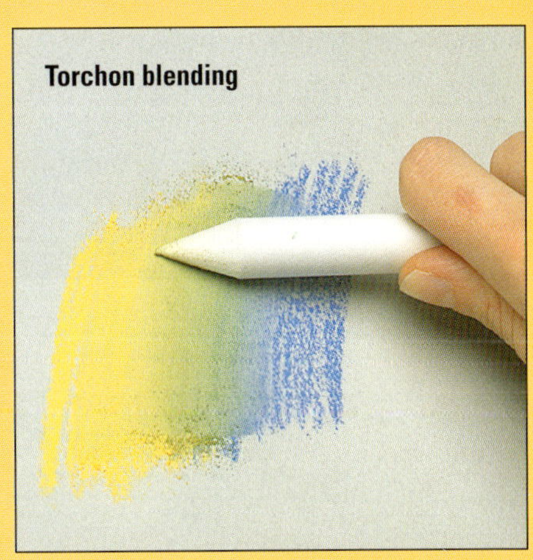

▲ **Keep your pastels clean by storing them in a box of dry rice. The dirt and loose pigment particles on the pastels will rub off on the grains of rice instead of on each other.**

remembering that even within the category of 'soft' pastels, there are varying degrees of softness. Very soft pastels include those made by Unison, Sennelier and Schminke, the latter being the softest of all. Winsor & Newton's soft pastels and the Talens' Rembrandt range are slightly harder.

Hard pastels come in the form of compressed sticks, often rectangular in shape. The best known of these is the Conté range, although most manufacturers now have their own product. Hard pastels contain more gum than soft pastels and the colours are usually less intense. Hard pastels will be covered in more detail in a later issue.

Colour mixing

Unlike paints, soft pastel colours cannot be easily mixed. You will need a different pastel not only for every colour you wish to use in a painting, but for every shade of that particular colour. This is why most pastel ranges are so extensive. Some manufacturers offer as many as 500 different pastels, including several versions of each colour.

Depending on the make, a range of soft pastels can include up to ten versions of any one colour, from very light to very dark. The tonal range is often indicated by a number, although the system varies from one manufacturer to another. For example, in the Winsor & Newton range, Scarlet Lake 1 is very pale pink and Scarlet Lake 5 is a much deeper, richer colour.

Although soft pastels are used by many professional artists, their enormous colour range makes them an excellent medium for the beginner. Freed from the worry of mixing colours, the artist is at liberty to concentrate on other aspects of the work. In other words, when you use soft pastels, the manufacturer does most of the colour mixing, not you!

Surfaces

The right surface is important. Papers and boards made specifically for soft pastel work have a definite texture, sometimes referred to as the 'tooth', which may be either coarse or velvety.

On a smooth paper, which has no tooth, soft pastels will simply slide around and produce unsatisfactory, weak patches of colour. However, on the correct surface with the right amount of tooth, the pastel dust will fill the holes gradually, enabling you to build up several layers of matt, impastoed colour. You will know when your paper has reached its limit, because it becomes difficult to make the colours adhere and the loose pigment stays on the surface of the paper.

Fixing

Soft pastels smudge very easily and your finished picture will be vulnerable until it has been sprayed with fixative. Fixative may slightly darken the colours, so use the spray sparingly. Hold the can about a foot away from the vertical painting and spray slowly and evenly from side to side until the whole surface has been treated.

Care of pastels

Soft pastels are extremely fragile and will easily become damaged if they are not properly cared for. If you drop pastel sticks on the floor or press too hard with them on the paper, they may break, and you can end up with short stubs that are difficult to hold and fiddly to use.

Piles of much-used pastels get very grubby because they pick up pigments from your hands and from each other. Before long, it can become difficult to see which colour is which. An excellent way of avoiding this is to put the pastels into a tray of dry rice when not in immediate use. In this way, the grains of rice get dirty and the pastels stay clean.

When you have finished a session, put the pastels back in their box. If this is not possible, store the sticks between sheets of corrugated cardboard.

▶ **Keep a sheet of sandpaper to hand for maintaining a point on soft pastels. To achieve an even point, apply a little pressure as you turn the pastel slowly.**

Oil pastels

If you like drawing with bold, vigorous strokes, you will enjoy the effects you can achieve with the lively medium of oil pastels, which are available in a range of bright rainbow colours.

Oil pastels are tough, bright and bold – altogether different from the crumbling sticks of chalky pigment that we know as traditional pastels. Pure pastels are chosen for their soft, velvety colours, whereas oil pastels are much harder and produce thick, waxy lines. In fact, their very name is misleading because oil pastels are not actually pastels at all, having far more in common with oil paints and wax crayons than with pure pastels.

A perfect sketching medium

Oil pastels call for a bold, confident approach. They are excellent for quick colour sketches and drawings in which movement and expressive strokes are more important than a very realistic finish. In fact, because of their chunky nature, oil pastels are not particularly well suited to fine, detailed work. Artists who work on a small scale or with subtle colours are likely to find oil pastels too bright and broad for their purpose, although the pastels can be sharpened with a knife to achieve a finer line.

However, for an immediate effect and for lively, on-the-spot colour sketching, oil pastels are second to none. Unlike most drawing materials, they enable you to work quickly on a large scale in colours that are both bright and strong. In this respect, oil pastels have all the

▶ Oil pastels produce dense, waxy marks and come in a range of intense colours. Unlike soft pastels, they contain wax and oil and do not break easily or crumble.

▶ Oil pastel proved to be the perfect medium for this bold, colourful still-life sketch. These pastels are at their best when applied in strong, loose strokes.

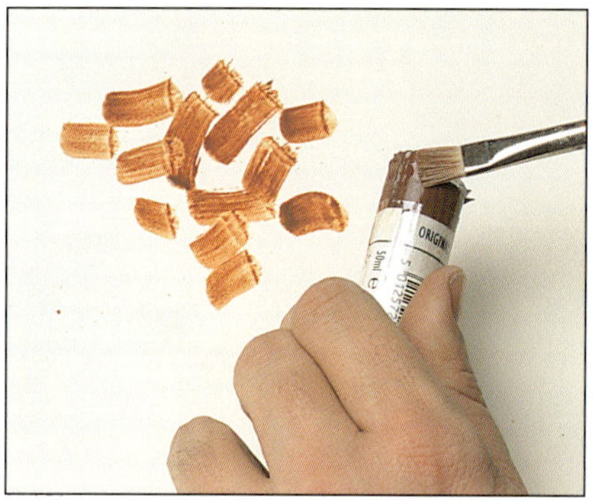

▲ **Oil sticks can be used for painting as well as for drawing. This is done by dissolving the colour with turpentine and applying it to the support with a brush.**

advantages of oil paint, but with the added bonus that they are more portable and more convenient.

For working outdoors, simply slip a sketch book and a few oil pastels into your pocket and you are equipped and ready to go. The pastels can be used without any liquid medium and may be applied directly to sturdy paper, oil paper or primed canvas.

Colour blending

Because of their hard, waxy nature, oil pastel colours are not easy to blend unless dissolved with a thinner such as white spirit or turpentine. This is normally done on the drawing, so you must first apply the oil pastels to the support. You can then blend the colours with a brush, tissue or finger dipped in the thinner.

An alternative method is to dampen the support with thinner before applying the pastel to it, as shown below left. Note that when blending with thinner, you should work on oil paper or primed canvas; other papers are too absorbent.

As a general rule, blending is more effective when used on a few selected areas of a drawing, or when combined with vigorous, textural strokes. Too

BLENDING OIL PASTELS

Dampening with thinner

Instead of blending oil pastels once they are on the paper, you can wet the support with turpentine or white spirit first and then apply the pastel to the dampened area.

Tissue blending

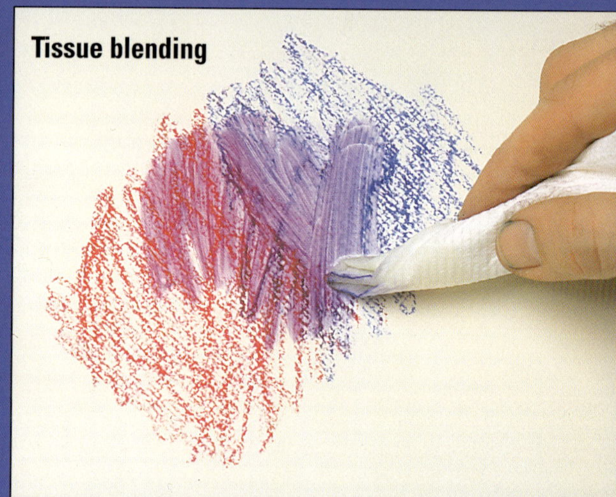

Roughly apply two colours so that they overlap, then blend these together with a rolled-up piece of tissue or kitchen towel dipped in turpentine or white spirit.

Brush blending

Use a brush dipped in solvent for blending two or more colours together. An oil-painting brush is stiffer and blends more effectively than a soft brush.

Finger blending

Many artists instinctively use a finger to blend dissolved colours quickly. If you like working in this way, make sure you wash your hands immediately afterwards, as some pigments are toxic.

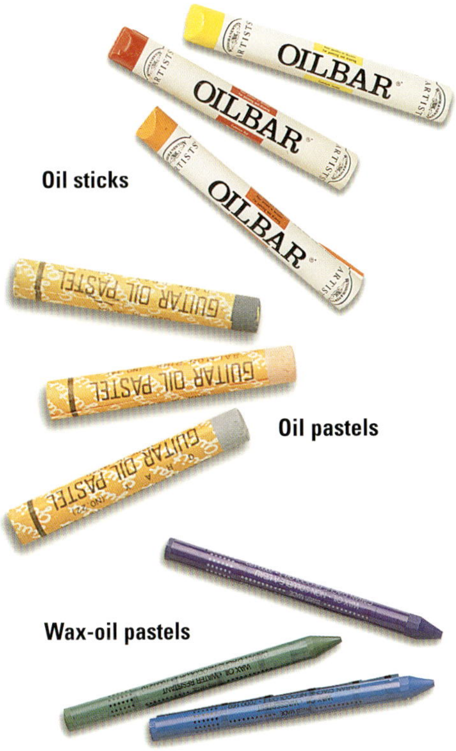

Oil sticks

Oil pastels

Wax-oil pastels

▲ Depending on the brand, pastels contain varying amounts of wax and oil. The higher the wax content, the harder the pastel.

much blending can destroy the direct, spontaneous quality of the medium and your picture might start to look smooth and rubbery. An alternative approach is to wait until the blended colours have dried, then to apply bold textural strokes on top of the blended areas.

Overlaid colour

As with all pastels, oil pastel colours can be mixed on the paper by overlaying two or more colours. For example, if you apply yellow over blue, you will get the impression of green. Even though the colours are not actually mixed, they appear to be. Remember, the top colour is the dominant one, so blue on top of yellow produces a bluer green than the other way round.

Oil pastel with oil paint

Oil pastels are compatible with oil paints. Not only can they be used for the initial drawing prior to starting an oil painting, but they are also effective for adding texture and linear detail to the finished painting.

For a softer effect than that given by oil pastels, try oil sticks. The consistency of the fat sticks of colour comes between oil pastels and oil paint – harder than paint but more malleable than pastels. Oil sticks (sometimes called oil bars) are quite a new invention and, like oil pastels, are excellent for making broad, chunky drawings. Alternatively, you can use oil sticks as a painting medium by dipping a brush in turpentine or white spirit and taking the dissolved colour from the top of the stick.

Oil and water do not mix

An opposite approach to that of using oil pastels with oil paint is to actively exploit the incompatibility of oil and water. First the oil pastel is laid down, then a water-soluble colour such as watercolour, gouache, coloured ink or even thin acrylic is painted over it. The oily marks repel the water-soluble colour, leaving the coloured pastel marks showing through.

This technique, known as resist, can be used to create a variety of marks and textures. It is an exciting way of using oil pastels because the results are sometimes unexpected.

Building up texture

Oil pastels are essentially a drawing material, good for making lively line drawings, with the bold strokes providing texture and colour. However, if you build them up thickly, oil pastels create a dense layer of solid colour and the result is rather like an oil painting.

Once this solid colour has been established, you can then scratch into the waxy surface. Use a scalpel blade or any other sharp instrument to make textures and patterns by revealing the white paper underneath. Another variation of the same technique, known as sgraffito, is to apply one colour over another. By scratching the top layer, you will reveal the colour underneath.

Although they can be used alongside so many other materials, oil pastels are very much a medium in their own right. They provide a powerful means of expression and encourage a bold, overall approach, which is excellent for the less experienced artist who wishes to branch out and experiment. With oil pastels, there can be little subtlety, but you will be pleasantly surprised at the results you will be able to achieve.

MORE TECHNIQUES

Resist Try painting watercolour or other water-soluble colour over an area of oil pastel. The waxy marks repel the paint and show through the painted colour.

Added texture Small strokes of oil pastel applied on top of a blended area of colour can lend contrasting texture to a smooth, flat surface.

Sgraffito Use a painting knife, scalpel or other sharp implement to scratch pattern and texture into layers of thick colour.

Masking Apply colour roughly over the torn or cut edge of a piece of sturdy paper or thin card to give a crisply defined edge to an area of oil pastel strokes.

Pastels for portraits

Pastel sticks were first used in the sixteenth century – but they really came of age as a medium for portraiture two hundred years later.

Pastel is sometimes unfairly dismissed as a lightweight medium, inferior to oils and associated with over-sentimental portraits of children. Yet pastel has a long and distinguished history, particularly in the field of portraiture.

As a portrait medium, pastel has the advantage over paints of greater speed and directness. Applied with only crayons and fingers, there is nothing to get in the way of the artist's direct response to his subject, enabling him to capture the sort of fleeting gesture or expression that reveals more about the sitter than merely outward appearance.

A 'dry colouring method'

Pastel sticks – simply pure pigment bound with gum – first came into use in the sixteenth century. They were invented by Jean Perréal (*c.*1455-*c.*1530), a minor French artist, who used them to enhance his chalk drawings. Leonardo da Vinci said that he learned the 'dry colouring method' from Perréal, who travelled to Italy several times at the turn of the sixteenth century.

Initially, pastel was used merely to heighten charcoal and chalk drawings with touches of colour. But eventually artists began to paint portraits entirely in pastel, recognising the realism that was possible using pastel on tinted papers.

Carriera's society portraits

Pastels were taken up in eighteenth-century France by the Venetian artist Rosalba Carriera (1675-1757). A popular painter of snuff-boxes and miniatures,

◄ Pastels are often associated with a loose, impressionist style, but in *The Chocolate Girl* (*c.*1744-45) Jean-Etienne Liotard shows the remarkable precision and detail that can be attained with the medium. Look, in particular, at the glass.

CHARDIN'S REVOLUTIONARY TECHNIQUE

Jean-Baptiste-Siméon Chardin is primarily known for his oil painting of everyday middle-class life – but he was equally adept at portraits in pastels. He introduced methods of building form and suggesting light with parallel hatchings of pure colour. This is particularly evident in his *Self Portrait with Spectacles* (1771) below. In using broken colour and visible strokes that emphasise the texture of the medium itself, Chardin anticipated the style of the French Impressionist master of pastels Edgar Degas (1834-1917). Chardin was an artist who was truly ahead of his time.

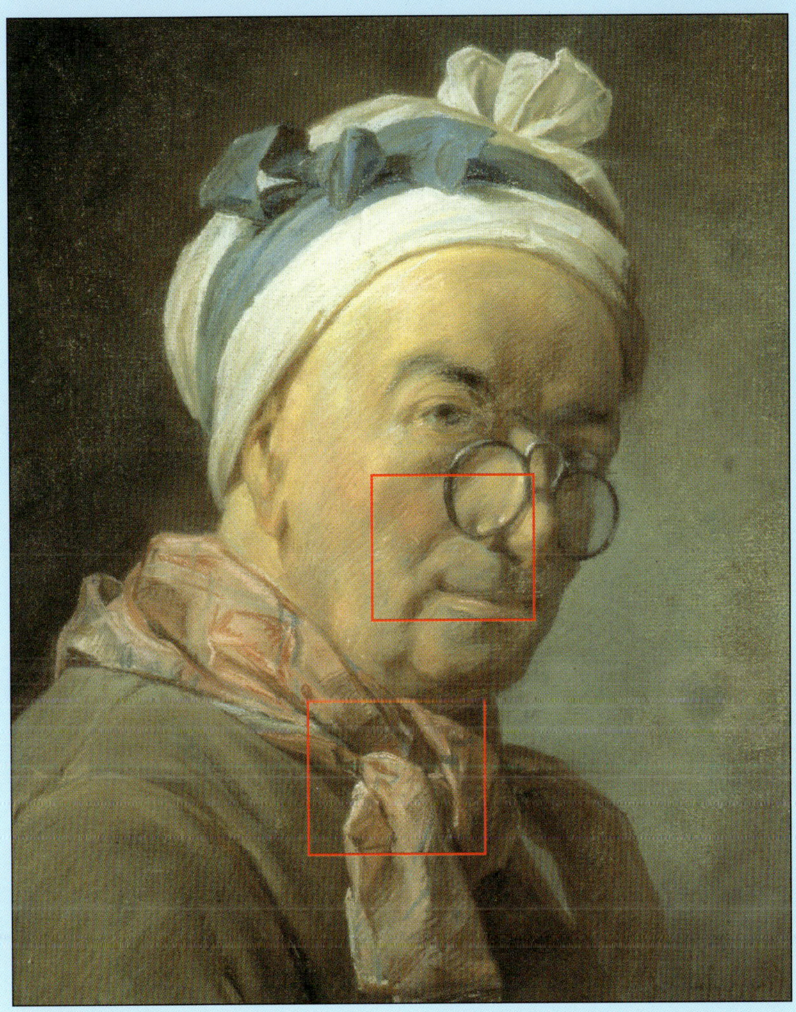

▲ In close-up, you can see the individual strokes of pure pigment which, from farther away, merge together and create new colours.

she took up pastels in her middle age and her portraits of society figures were in great demand throughout Italy.

In 1720 she travelled to Paris, where she enjoyed huge acclaim. Female portraits were very popular in the eighteenth century (often their purpose was to make young ladies known to prospective husbands), and during her one-year stay in France she painted countless portraits of nobility.

Harmonious palette

Carriera was gifted with a glowing sense of colour and a superb mastery of pastel technique. She used a softly harmonious palette of pinks, blues and whites and applied her colours in broad, flat strokes, often blending them with a stump to create velvety, vaporous textures. She also knew how to flatter her sitters, portraying them in low-necked dresses and with flowers in their hair.

Carriera's influence resulted in a lighter, more playful style of portrait than had gone before. Sitters were shown in bust-length (head and shoulders), often with one hand visible, with the shoulders in front view and the head turned. Portraits by François Boucher (1703-70) and Jean-Baptiste Perroneau (1715-83), who worked both in oils and pastels, depicted the frivolous life of the court of Louis XV, a world of sumptuous silks and satins, powdered wigs, scented fans and powder-puffs.

Latour's speed and vivacity

The success of Carriera prompted Maurice Quentin de Latour (1704-88) to take up pastels and he became the most celebrated pastellist of the eighteenth century. Latour handled his 'coloured dust' with great speed and vivacity, aiming to convey the personalities of his sitters by recording their fleeting expressions and emotions. 'Unknown to them,' he said, 'I descend into the depths of my sitters and bring back the whole man.'

'Miraculous work'

Latour painted two huge, ambitious portraits in order to prove that pastel could hold its own with oil painting. His consummate technical skill is evident in his portrait of Gabriel-Bernard de Rieux, in which he contrasts the weight of the sitter's linen robe, the delicacy of his lace ruffles and the lightness of his hair. One admirer declared, 'It is a miraculous work, it is like a piece of Dresden china, it cannot possibly be a mere pastel.'

Latour's other masterpiece is a full-length portrait of Madame de Pompadour, the king's adviser and mistress. She is depicted surrounded by objects symbolising literature, music, astronomy and engraving. As with all royal portraits, only the head was painted from life, using a round piece of paper which was later pasted in position on a larger sheet; the portrait was completed using a stand-in wearing the royal robes.

Chardin's close-up studies

During the latter half of the century, some artists began to move towards greater realism and naturalness in painting. The greatest of these was Jean-Baptiste-Siméon Chardin (1699-1779). He did not take up pastel until the age of 72, when failing eyesight forced him to abandon painting in oils.

At the same time he began to tackle a subject he had hitherto avoided – studies of the human face. His portraits and self-portraits focus on the face in close-up. The extreme simplicity of their composition and the lack of any background trappings allows the inner, private self of the sitter to become the focus.

While most of his contemporaries produced dazzling but somewhat superficial portraits, Chardin's portraits are intensely alive – he was able to get 'beneath the skin' of his sitter and reveal the inner person. Furthermore, he developed a new and distinctive way of applying the pastels – see Chardin's revolutionary technique, page 39.

The flamboyance of Liotard

One of the most accomplished pastellists was the Swiss painter Jean-Etienne Liotard (1702-89). He was capable of creating highly finished works and rendering detail with an astonishing accuracy. Having spent four years in Constantinople, he completed many portraits of people in Turkish dress. These included self-portraits – he himself adopted Turkish dress and a beard. His exotic work and flamboyant personality brought him success in Paris, the Netherlands and Britain.

With the outbreak of the French Revolution in 1789, pastel fell out of favour for a time because it was associated with the frivolity and excesses of the *ancien régime*. It would be another 30 years before pastel enjoyed a revival, in the hands of the great Romanticist, Eugène Delacroix (1798-1863).

▶ For the most part, Rosalba Carriera uses blended pastel strokes in her portrait, *Sister Maria Caterina* (1732). But notice how she captures the texture of the fabric around the neck, using individual strokes of a blunt white pastel.

The art of acrylics

Within a few years of their invention, acrylic paints had attracted some of the most renowned artists in Europe and, in particular, the United States.

Modern Art Museum of Fort Worth, purchase made possible by grant from The Burnett Foundation © 1969 Morris Louis

▲ **The excitement in Morris Louis' *Dalet Kaf* (1969) arises from his beautiful handling of thin acrylic paint – the colours drift into each other, creating new, unexpected hues. The triangles of dark paint at the sides help to guide the eye into the centre of the painting.**

For more than 500 years, artists had been working with the same basic painting media – egg tempera, oils and watercolours. Then, in the 1950s, a new type of paint arrived in the United States that was to revolutionise art. And, by a happy coincidence, acrylic paints emerged just at the moment when young abstract artists were seeking new ways to express themselves.

One advantage of acrylics over oils is that they can be used directly on raw canvas without the risk of harming the fabric. This was a technique employed by the American painters Helen Frankenthaler (b.1928) and Morris Louis (1912-62), who were leading figures in the Colour Stain movement of the 1950s. They poured and squeegeed dilute colour directly on to the absorbent surface of unprimed canvas to achieve translucent, overlapping 'stains' of colour that allowed the canvas weave to show through.

Meditative mood

The Colour Stain painters were contemporaries of the Abstract Expressionists and Action Painters and, as they were also creating non-figurative art, their work is often grouped with these schools. However, most Abstract Expressionists, such as Jackson Pollock (1912-56), Franz Kline (1910-62) and Robert Motherwell (1915-91), generally worked in oils, building up thick impasto layers of paint. This gave a rather agitated and even tortured feel to their paintings. However, Frankenthaler and, in particular, Louis, created a much more meditative mood in their art. In a Louis painting, you can relax and enjoy the waves of colour that seem to drift across the support.

Acrylics remained popular even when the loose, expressive approach to art in the 1950s gave way to a more considered, restrained one in the 1960s. Frank Stella (b.1936), a leading Hard Edge painter, used acrylics to create rigid compositions of straight bands of intense colour separated by fine lines of unprimed canvas (see right). He used masking tape to achieve his razor-sharp edges, brushing the paint on to the masked areas. Acrylics were ideal for this approach, as the paint dried quickly to form a flat, opaque surface without visible brushmarks.

Acrylics finally reached Britain in the 1960s. Bridget Riley (b.1931), a leading Op artist, had begun her career using ordinary household emulsion paints, but picked up on acrylics as soon as they became available. She combined the medium with masking tape to create optical illusions, with rigidly formed stripes and geometric patterns. On both sides of the Atlantic, Pop artists – including Andy Warhol (1928-87), Roy Lichtenstein (b.1923) and Peter Blake (b.1932) – used the flat, bright, instant acrylic colours to make an ironic comment on the popular culture and consumerism of the time.

It was David Hockney (b.1937), however, who – perhaps more than any other artist – popularised acrylics. The British-born Hockney was converted to acrylics when he moved to California in 1964, finding their intense colours and smooth opacity ideal for the vivid light

▼ In *Portrait of Nick Wilder*, Hockney's characteristic use of flat areas of colour are in evidence in the sky, the building and even in the swimming pool.

David Hockney "Portrait of Nick Wilder" 1966 Acrylic on canvas 72x72" © David Hockney

© ARS, NY and DACS, London 2004

▲ ***River of Ponds*** **(1968), with its brilliantly coloured, flat shapes and precise edges, is an example of Frank Stella's Hard Edge style of painting.**

of the West Coast. His famous 1960s paintings such as *Portrait of Nick Wilder* (1966, left) or *A Bigger Splash* (1967) – were characterised by flat, unmodelled areas of paint. These images, with their almost abstract arrangement of colour and shape, had echoes of the Hard Edge paintings.

In the early 1970s, Hockney's style began to loosen and he began also to exploit the versatility of acrylics. In *Beach Umbrella* (1971), for instance, the umbrella is rendered by just staining the canvas with paint. This allows the weave of the canvas to show through, giving an uncanny resemblance to the texture of the umbrella fabric. Hockney also mixed acrylics with detergents to capture the elusive quality of sunlight playing on the water of his beloved swimming pools.

Eventually, his experiments led him back to oil paints again. In the mid-1970s, he wrote, 'When you use simple and bold colours, acrylic is a fine medium: the colours are very intense and they stay intense… But because I'm using oil paint again, I'm getting interested in texture. You can manipulate oil paint on the canvas, but you can't do that much with acrylics.'

California dreaming

Hockney has since used a variety of media, but he will perhaps be best remembered for his early acrylic work. In it, he seemed to create the definitive picture of West Coast America – this, ironically, from an Englishman. The images have a carefree optimism that seems peculiarly Californian and the use of bright acrylic paint is totally suited to the brash world of Los Angeles.

Working with acrylics

Acrylic paint is much more versatile than any other medium. Used straight from the tube, it handles like oil paint; when diluted, it handles more like watercolour. Here is just a sample of the techniques and effects you can achieve. You can take these further by adding mediums to the paints (see Using acrylic mediums, pages 44-45).

Glazing

Acrylic paints are ideal for applying successive layers of transparent colour. Because they dry so rapidly, and are waterproof once dry, you can paint one transparent colour over another in quick succession. The addition of gloss medium increases the transparency of the paint and enriches the colours.

Impasto

Paint applied straight from the tube or thickened with gel medium can be applied with a brush or painting knife to build up a thick, textured surface. Note acrylic paints dry fast, so you might want to add retarder in order to have more time to manipulate the paint.

Flat colour

Fluid acrylics have a high degree of opacity and can be easily brushed out to give flat, even areas of colour. This property is ideal for abstract techniques such as Hard Edge painting and Op art, which feature flat areas of pure colour with crisp, precise edges.

Staining

Here, fluid acrylic colour is poured and manipulated on unprimed canvas. The colours sink into this porous surface to give an even, matt stain of colour. The paint is controlled by tilting the canvas or using sponges, squeegees and brushes.

Collage

Acrylic paint is an excellent adhesive and can be used to bind papers, fabrics, sand and other materials to the support. Acrylic gel medium or texture paste can be used to stick larger objects.

Using acrylic mediums

Adding mediums to your acrylic colours can completely change the look of your pictures. You can make your paints glossy or transparent – or even create textured and sculptural effects.

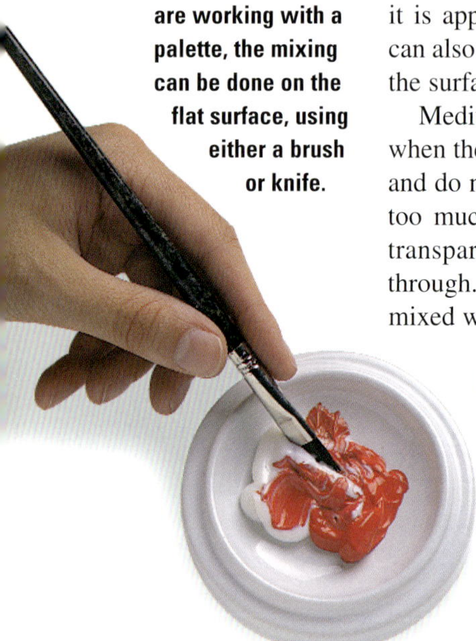

▼ **Thoroughly mix the medium and paint using a clean, stiff brush. If you are working with a palette, the mixing can be done on the flat surface, using either a brush or knife.**

Used on their own, acrylics are opaque and can dry with a rather dull finish. However, there are a number of mediums that will alter the appearance and character of the paint, making it glossy, matt, transparent, textural or flat. These mediums are usually added to the wet colour before it is applied to the painting, although one or two can also be used to prime the support and to protect the surface of the finished picture.

Mediums appear cloudy in the pot or tube, but when they dry they become completely transparent and do not therefore affect your colours. However, too much of any medium will make a colour so transparent that the colour underneath shows through. On white paper, for example, a colour mixed with a lot of medium will appear paler.

Retarder and flow improver

If you find the quick-drying nature of acrylics difficult to handle, the answer could well be a retarder, which slows down the drying time of the colours by several hours. Remember, this medium is only effective if you paint fairly thickly – very diluted colours will dry quickly however much retarder you add to them. Use flow improver to help the paint spread more evenly and smoothly. This is particularly good for hard-edge painting when you are using masking tape, as the flowing colour remains thick enough not to run under the edge of the tape.

Gloss and matt

Gloss medium gives colours a shiny finish; matt medium produces a flat, unreflective surface. You can buy both in either fluid or gel form – the fluids improve the flow and make the paint easier to apply, the gels create slightly thicker colour. Both fluid and gel mediums increase the paint's transparency without making it thin and watery.

Fluid-type mediums are excellent for mixing glazes – for applying a layer of transparent colour over another colour so that the undercolour shows through. Depending on the effect you want, mix the gloss or matt medium with the glazing colour in a ratio of up to 10:1. Gloss medium is the general favourite for glazing because it produces particularly luminous, brilliant colours.

An alternative to varnishing

Fluid mediums can also be used to seal the canvas or paper prior to painting and used instead of a varnish to protect the surface of a completed painting. In both cases, apply the medium carefully with a

Making paint

Mixing your own acrylic paint is straightforward and should be done just before you start work. If you end up with more paint than you need, you can keep the mixture for a short time in a plastic airtight container.

1 ▸ **Mix with powder** Using a palette knife, mix dry powder pigment well with either gloss or matt medium to create your own painting colours.

2 ▸ **Use it or lose it** The mixed colours are ready to use immediately. Like manufactured paints, these colours dry fairly quickly – so mix only as much as you need for one painting session.

ADDING TEXTURES

Here are some of the textures you can make by adding various grains and particles to acrylic medium. The adhesive medium binds the texture-making substances, which can either be left in their natural state or painted.

Dry sand Scatter this on modelling paste for a medium-textured effect.

Sawdust and wood shavings Mix with gel medium for a soft, complex texture.

Fired clay Mix this with gel medium for a fine-textured result.

Grit and gravel Gel medium mixed with these will create a really rough effect.

large brush, using smooth parallel strokes. Take care not to do too much brushing, as you'll produce tiny air bubbles that affect the dried surface.

Impasto effects

Although paint thickened with gel medium will to some extent retain the shape of the brush marks, this will produce only a moderately textured surface. For a more dramatic textured effect you will need to mix the colour with acrylic impasto medium – especially good for knife painting and for covering areas with thick colour quickly.

For a really pronounced impasto, try using modelling, or texture, paste. This can be applied to build almost sculptural swathes of colour, which can be sanded or even carved when dry. Mix the paste with colour prior to painting or, alternatively, apply the paste on its own and then paint it when dry. Unlike other mediums, modelling paste is white and opaque and might slightly lighten the colour, so you should make allowances for this.

A word of warning: thickly applied modelling paste is not wholly flexible and can crack if used on a non-rigid surface such as canvas. Counteract this risk by mixing the paste with equal parts of gel medium. Also, the risk of cracking is reduced if you build up the paste in layers, allowing each layer to dry before applying the next, instead of working in thick wedges.

Making textures

Some mediums contain tiny particles of various inert substances to create specific instant textures. These include sand, flint, pumice and even tiny glass beads. The glass beads are often used for creating the effect of frothy air bubbles in water or adding decorative touches to the image.

Special effects

You can easily make your own special-effect mediums by adding gritty or granular materials to any one of the standard mediums (see Adding textures, left). All acrylic mediums are adhesive, so choose one to give the effect you want – gloss medium for a shiny texture, impasto medium or modelling paste for a thickly applied effect.

For example, to capture the effect of a sandy beach in a seascape, you might mix real sand with a little matt medium. You could then go on to experiment with sawdust, particles of clay and dust, or any other materials you can think of. You will be amazed at the difference a few creative textures will make to your pictures.

Make your own paints

Some acrylic artists never use manufactured paint, preferring instead the more direct approach of mixing powdered pigment with gloss or matt medium. As the mediums have no colour of their own, the pigment retains its full strength and intensity in the painting. The mediums are also flexible when dry, so your home-made paints can be used on canvas or paper.

▲ **GLOSS AND MATT**

For a shiny paint surface, add a little gloss medium to your acrylic colour (top). Matt medium mixed with the paint (bottom) will produce a more non-reflective surface.

Using oil mediums

For centuries, artists have used traditional natural materials to dilute their oil paints, and these are just as popular today. In addition, there are now other mediums that make painting in oils easier and more versatile.

Oil paint is wonderfully stiff and buttery when you squeeze it from the tube – perfect for textured effects but too thick for most other purposes. Fortunately, oils are easily diluted. The traditional method is to use a combination of oil and turpentine. You can also try oil mediums, which can be added to the paints to alter their consistency and give exciting effects.

Oil and turpentine

Real turpentine comes from pine trees and is one of the oldest solvents for diluting oil paints. Because the solvent thins the oil in the paint, the colours dry with a matt finish and, if a lot of solvent is used, it tends to dull the colours. For this reason, turpentine is usually used in conjunction with an oil to replace the lost sheen. Linseed oil is the most popular, although there are alternatives to both linseed oil and traditional turpentine.

Ideally, use a double dipper like the one below for the oil and turpentine. This small container clips on to the edge of the palette and is designed to minimise the risk of spills. Mix the colour on the palette, adding turpentine and oil with a brush until you have the consistency you want. If you need a large amount of diluted colour, mix it separately in a jar rather than on the palette. Note: avoid using a turpentine substitute or white spirit as an inexpensive alternative to real turpentine for thinning paint. Both these solvents tend to deaden the colours and produce a cloudy patina on the paint surface.

Painting 'fat over lean'

Oils should be applied 'fat over lean'. In other words, start by blocking in the subject with very thin colour diluted with turpentine. Gradually add more oil colour and less turpentine to the paint as the picture progresses.

▶ **A palette laid out with oil colours, oil mediums, turpentine and linseed oil.**

A Turpentine
B Linseed oil
C Oil colours
D Gel medium
E Liquid medium

MIXING OIL MEDIUMS WITH PAINT

TURPENTINE AND LINSEED OIL

Use a double clip-on dipper for the oil and turpentine. Dilute the colour by loading the brush from the dipper and adding to the paint.

GEL MEDIUM

Squeeze gel mediums directly on to the palette. Mix in the colour using a knife or a stiff brush. The mixture generally becomes stiffer if left to stand.

LIQUID MEDIUM

Pour the liquid medium on to the palette or into a container. Many mediums dry quickly, so don't use too much. Add to the colour, mixing with a knife or brush.

Using this method, the underpainting dries quickly without holding up the rest of the work, and the finished surface has a rich, glossy colour.

Other mediums

There are various specialist mediums designed to alter the paint for specific purposes. Depending on the product, a medium can make oil colours thicker or thinner, improve the flow, create a matt finish, or speed up the drying time of the paint. Some mediums are simply ready-mixed versions of traditional ingredients; others contain synthetic materials.

Colour thickeners

Thick mediums come in tubes, in gel or paste form. They can be squeezed on to the palette alongside the colours and added to the paint as required. For a very thick consistency, use a paste, but gels are best used where expressive brushwork is required. Mix the paint with the gel or paste and leave to stiffen before use. These mediums can also be mixed with a solvent to make the paint flow more easily.

Liquid mediums

Oil paint diluted with turpentine alone dries with a dull, matt finish, but if you add a little liquid medium, the paint will dry with a smooth, shiny surface. Most liquid mediums are also suitable for glazing – they dilute the colour to make it more transparent without affecting the glossy nature of the paint. Alternatively, buy a glazing medium made specifically for the purpose.

Despite their name, 'liquid' mediums are not necessarily completely liquid in consistency. Although some are quite runny, others are more like jelly. Small amounts of the latter can be poured directly on to the painting palette, but very liquid mediums are best kept in a separate container.

Trying out the mediums

If too much of any medium is added to an oil colour, it will inevitably alter the opacity and strength of the colour. Only by trial and error with a particular product will you find out exactly how much of the medium you can introduce without spoiling the particular result you are aiming to achieve.

Also, it is important to bear in mind that mediums are essentially additives which change the nature and chemistry of the paint. If you overdo them, you might reduce the durability of the completed painting.

▶ GLAZING
Mix the paint and glazing medium to the consistency of single cream and apply this to a dry undercolour. Some colours, such as lemon yellow, are naturally transparent and work particularly well in glaze mixtures.

‘Painting’ with graphite

With water-soluble graphite, you can combine the fluid finish of watercolour with controlled line work, as well as developing a range of tones.

◄ **Just a small amount of water will transform a graphite drawing into a monochrome painting with a watercolour look.**

Water-soluble graphite pencils, are very versatile drawing tools. When used dry for sketching and drawing, they behave exactly like ordinary graphite pencils. However, water-soluble pencils are capable of more than just straightforward mark-making on paper. If you brush a little water over an area shaded with soluble graphite, it dissolves to create a grey wash. Depending on the wash strength of the pencil (they are available in various grades), or on how much graphite was laid down in the first place, the wash can be very pale or velvety black. You'll find that your brush picks up a lot of graphite as you work, so keep rinsing it in water and wiping it clean.

Dark and light

Another way in which you can use a water-soluble pencil is to dip the lead into water and then draw with it. This makes very dark marks, ideal for emphasising details or filling in deep shadows. Hold the pencil almost upright so that the water can flow down more easily.

As with all watercolour painting, you should work from the light areas of the picture to the dark ones. If the brush picks up too much graphite and gives too dark a tone on the paper, you can rescue this by going over the same area with clear water to lift off excess graphite.

It is best to use watercolour paper with water-soluble pencils. Stretch the paper first to prevent it from cockling (blistering or puckering), or, if you don't intend to use lots of water, simply fix the paper to the drawing board with masking tape to keep it flat and smooth.

FIRST STEPS

1 ▶ Make an initial sketch Using a medium water-soluble pencil, draw in the line where the worksurface meets the tongue-and-groove background. You can then use the vertical boards as a measuring guide when you draw the folds of the soft tool bag and the angles and smooth curves of the tools.

2 ▼ Fill in tone on the bag Begin adding medium tone with hatched lines to define the folds of the bag. In the recesses of the folds, where the shadow is deepest, press harder with the pencil to give a darker tone.

YOU WILL NEED

Piece of 190gsm (90lb) NOT watercolour paper

3 water-soluble graphite pencils: medium; soft; very soft

Medium-sized soft round brush

Jar of water

4 ▲ Concentrate on details Complete the surface of the file with lines of cross-hatching. Shade in some very dark tone where the bag handle folds over. Define the zip and tag on the bag with hard, fine lines.

3 ▼ Develop the tools Darken the shaded surfaces of the tools, such as the inside of the plane handle. Indicate the pattern on the hammer handle and begin to show the rough surface of the file with diagonal hatched lines.

5 ▲ Tidy up the drawing Shade light tone over the saw and indicate some of the teeth. Follow the form of the hammer handle with curved lines and show its cast shadow. To complete the shading on the bag, hatch in medium tone and then change to a soft pencil to strengthen the darkest shadows. Firm up the hard lines of the tools.

ADDING WATER TO THE DRAWING

Once you feel that the overall tone of the drawing is correct, you have reached the exciting stage where you can begin to 'paint' with the graphite.

6 ▲ **Begin using water** Load a little water on to a soft round brush and use the side of the brush to wash over the bag, working from light areas to darker ones. The water smooths out the graphite shading to create a more uniform tone.

7 ▲ **Shade the background boards** Using the paper palette method described in Expert Advice below, brush a very pale wash of graphite over the tongue-and-groove boards behind the tool bag.

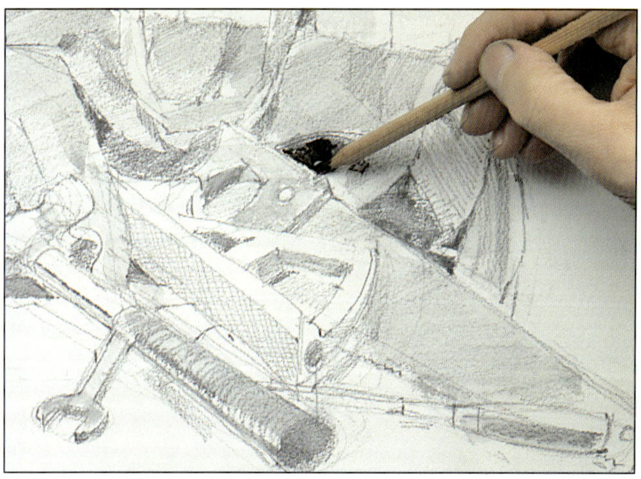

8 ◀ **Develop the tone further** Brush water over the saw and the hammer handle. Using the tip of the brush, paint water over the folds of the bag to give a dark watercolour effect. For the black interior of the bag, dip the lead of a very soft water-soluble pencil into water and shade with this.

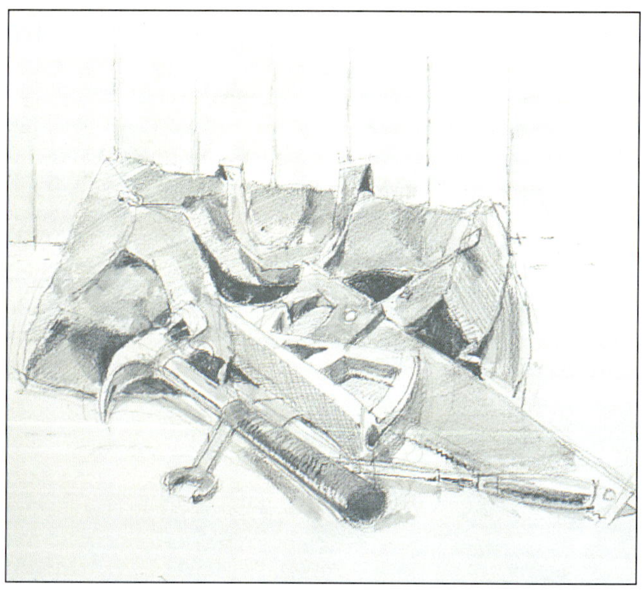

9 ▲ **Continue with the wet pencil lead** Emphasise all the darkest folds of the bag with the wetted tip of the very soft pencil. Returning to the brush, stroke water lightly over the rough surface of the file. Picking up graphite from a paper palette, develop the medium-toned shadows on the bag, and paint cast shadows under the chisel and hammer.

EXPERT ADVICE
Using paper as a palette

Instead of brushing water directly over your drawing, you can pick up pigment from a patch of graphite shaded on to a spare piece of paper. In this way, you can control the depth of colour more easily, especially if you want a very pale wash.

A FEW STEPS FURTHER

The drawing now shows various levels of tone, some achieved with a pencil used dry, some with a wash of water and the darkest with a wet pencil lead. You can add interest to the picture with some extra detail drawn with a wet pencil and brush.

10 ▶ Draw the fine lines Using the medium pencil dipped in water, draw fine, dark lines to strengthen the stitching on the bag, the edges of the zip and the edges of the handles. Accentuate the rivet on the saw handle and the pattern on the hammer handle.

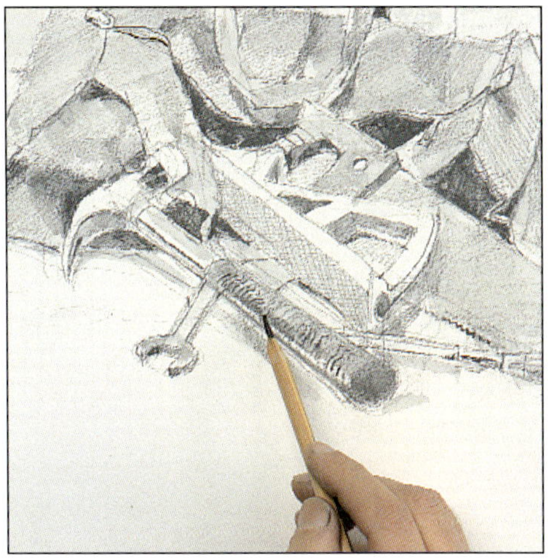

11 ▲ Add finishing touches Using a wet brush and a little graphite, very lightly show the knots in the wooden worksurface. Firm any edges, if necessary, with a wet pencil – for example, the top of the saw blade, the plane handle or the zip.

THE FINISHED PICTURE

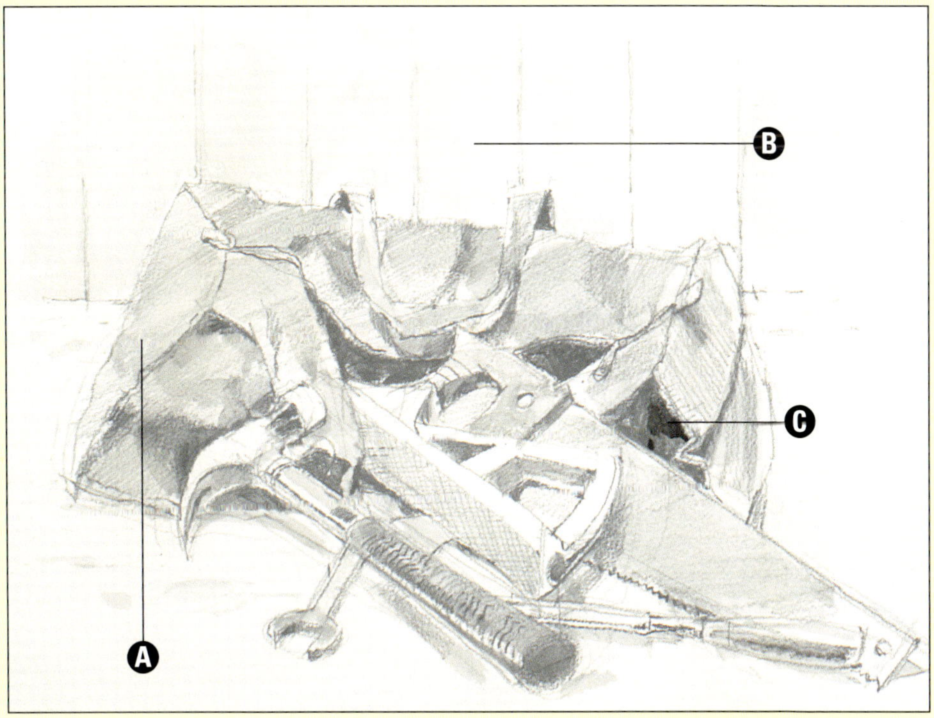

A Mid tones
The areas of medium tone, such as on the tool bag, were created by brushing water over dry graphite shading.

B Palest tone
The light wash on the tongue-and-groove background was achieved by using a wet brush tip to pick up graphite rubbed on to a piece of paper.

C Dark tone
Very black shadows in the creases of the bag were drawn in with the tip of a very soft water-soluble pencil dipped in water.

Drawing with fibre-tipped pens

Interpret the fascinating geometric pattern and sharp, spiky leaves of a pineapple with the crisp, decisive lines produced by a fibre-tipped pen.

Drawing with a pen requires a different technique from drawing with a pencil, charcoal, pastel or other softer medium. A pen gives a well-defined line that cannot easily be erased or altered, so you need to be decisive in your approach from the beginning.

There are many different types of pen available to the artist, ranging from drawing pens with fine tips for graphic designers to dip pens hand-made from goose quills and bamboo. Each has its own character and its own advantages and disadvantages to the artist, some pens being more suitable for precision work and others for freer interpretations of a subject.

The pineapple in this project was drawn with a fibre-tipped pen rather than a dip pen and ink. You'll find a wide range of fibre-tipped pens to choose from at any art shop. Ideal for line illustrations, cartoons and quick sketches, as well as finished drawings, these pens come in a variety of tip sizes, graded in numbers from the very fine 005 and 01 to the thicker 08 and 10. Versatile brush pens are also available if you want more flexibility. When working with a fibre-tipped pen, remember to replace the cap each time you finish using it, or it will dry out.

Use cartridge paper when drawing with a pen – you'll find the nib moves easily over its smooth surface.

Showing tone in pen

While you can show tone with a soft pencil or a stick of charcoal simply by shading with the edge or pressing hard, you'll need a different approach with a fibre-tipped pen as it creates lines which are all of a uniform thickness. One way to convey gradations of tone is to draw hatched lines either close together (for dark areas) or further apart (for paler areas). To create an even darker tone, add lines of cross-hatching as well. Alternatively, change to a pen with a thicker tip for areas of deep shadow.

◄ This pen drawing of a pineapple combines well-defined outlines with subtly drawn areas of tone to give a highly realistic finished image.

YOU WILL NEED

Large sheet of cartridge paper

3 fibre-tipped pens: 01, 07, 05

Bleedproof Designer's White

No.5 round brush

FIRST STEPS

1 ▶ **Make a sketch** Holding one of the pens vertically, compare the height of the pineapple to the height of its leaves – the proportion is about half and half. Using an 01 pen, begin to sketch the pineapple, some of its leaves and the paper bag underneath it. Draw the body of the pineapple as a smooth oval, marking diagonal lines across it to help you interpret the regular growth pattern on the skin.

2 ◀ **Map out the pattern** Notice how the pattern on the pineapple forms a diagonal grid. Sketch in the crossing diagonals, curving the lines slightly to show the pineapple's rounded shape.

3 ▲ **Develop the leaves and pattern** Draw more leaves, checking that they emerge symmetrically from the top of the pineapple by lightly marking a centre line through the fruit. Hatch in a little dark tone where the leaves are in shadow. Begin to draw some of the distinctive segments inside each diamond shape on the pineapple.

EXPERT ADVICE
Trying out the pattern

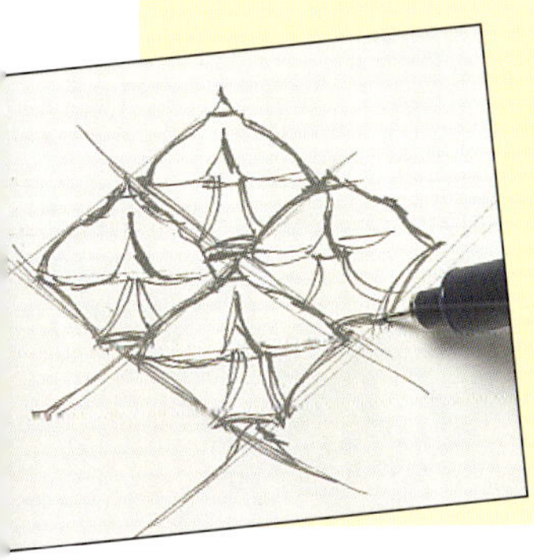

Practise sketching a small section of the pineapple's pattern before you begin the drawing. Each segment is based on a simple diamond shape. Build it up with a short, flat base, a point at the top and curves at the sides. Draw a horizontal line across the shape – the small spike sticks up from this with two lines below it.

HOW TO DEVELOP TONE

As the pineapple is in shadow on the right, you will need to develop darker tones on this side of the fruit. With fibre-tipped pens, the most effective way to achieve gradations of tone is with hatching and cross-hatching.

4 ► Shade with a thicker pen Change to an 07 pen and fill in the darkest areas of shade on the leaves and where they cast shadows on the pineapple. Return to the 01 pen to hatch in light tone across the shaded right-hand side of the fruit. Create texture with cross-hatching and add the spikes visible along the right-hand edge.

5 ◄ Define the segments further Use an 05 pen to work on each segment individually, emphasising its features. Then change back to the 01 pen to hatch in a little light shading on the left side of the pineapple.

6 ► Work on the shadows Show the creases on the paper bag with directional lines and, changing to the 07 pen, fill in the dark tone with firm hatching lines. To depict the dark shadow under the bag, make long, feathered strokes with the 05 pen. Use the finest pen to build up the shadow of the pineapple with light, well-spaced hatching.

7 ▲ Return to the leaves Render areas of tone on the leaves with parallel marks made with the 05 pen, keeping the look crisp and well-defined. Work the lines close together for dark tones and further apart for medium tones. Add the softest tones to the leaves with the 01 pen. These hatched lines also suggest the fibrous nature of the leaves.

A FEW STEPS FURTHER

Apart from a few minor tonal adjustments, the illustration of the pineapple is finished. In spite of being built up entirely with line work and cross-hatching without any really solid shading, it is a very realistic image.

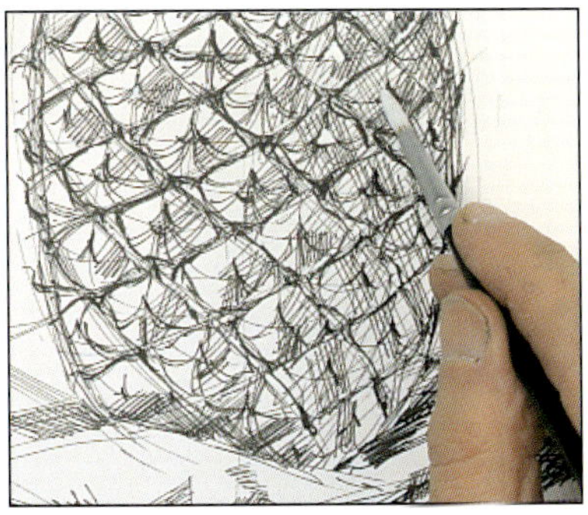

8 ▲ Add highlights If you want to add a few highlights to the drawing, you can blank out some of the pen lines with an opaque white liquid called Bleedproof Designer's White. Pick up a small amount on a No.5 round brush and dab it on to the tips of the spikes to make them catch the eye. You can also remove the early construction lines around the pineapple by painting over them with this liquid.

9 ▲ Darken the overall tone Outline the segments on the pineapple's skin with the 07 pen. Changing back to the 01 pen, darken the pineapple's right side, especially at the upper and lower edges, with more cross-hatching.

THE FINISHED PICTURE

A Regular pattern
The distinctive pattern on the skin of the pineapple was built up gradually, using a diamond-shaped grid as a guide.

B Graded tone
Variations in tone on the surface of the pineapple were achieved with hatched and cross-hatched lines drawn either very close together or further apart.

C Light shadow
Long, fine lines made with a sweep of the wrist created a patch of light tone to represent the shadow cast by the pineapple on to the horizontal surface.

Using graphite sticks

The bold, expressive marks of chunky graphite sticks are perfect for capturing the hustle and bustle of this quayside fish market.

Markets are always full of life, with interesting characters manning the stalls and a variety of produce on display, making them an inspiring subject for a drawing. As there is constant movement in a market, make a few sketches on the spot first or take some photographs to capture the scene, then work from these later at home.

A broad medium

Graphite sticks are useful drawing tools for this type of subject, in which an overall impression of the hustle and bustle is more important than fine detail. These chunky sticks are made of compressed and bonded graphite and produce broad lines and bold shading, ideal for sketching the shapes of figures in a crowd or suggesting the features of distant buildings. If they are well-sharpened, they can also be used to add the odd detail.

▶ **Lively marks and loose blocks of tone made with graphite sticks give this drawing a spontaneous, sketchy quality.**

USING THE PUSH-DOWN LEAD PENCIL

Graphite sticks can be rather messy to take with you when you are sketching outdoors. For preliminary sketches, try using the push-down lead pencil (right) given away with this issue. The lead can be retracted when not in use and the clip allows you to simply pop it into your pocket. Try to get into the habit of carrying it around so you can practise your drawing in free moments.

YOU WILL NEED

- Piece of cartridge paper
- 2 graphite sticks: 9B and 4B
- Pencil sharpener
- Glasspaper
- Putty rubber

▶ **Graphite sticks come in various grades and shapes. Some have a casing to protect your hands. They can be sharpened with a pencil sharpener or by rubbing the tip on glasspaper.**

FIRST STEPS

1 ▶ Set the scene Using a 9B graphite stick, draw the verticals of the buildings in the background and the tall lamp-post in front of them. Then put in the roof-line. Sketch in the main activity in the mid and foreground – the woman and her stall, some of the passers-by and the parasols. Outline the boxes of fish on the road.

2 ▲ Fill in some tone Change to a 4B graphite stick and block in some medium tone on the stallholder's jacket. Very loosely, scribble in a little tone to indicate the dark clothing of the passers-by. Use long, light strokes to shade the walls of the buildings.

3 ▲ Continue shading Block in the shadows cast on the road by the stall and by the figures on the left. With the 9B graphite stick, work across all the figures, shading in dark tones on their clothing and hair. Use heavy strokes to draw the legs of the stall, then rough in the lettering on the side.

4 ◀ Work across the picture Using the tip of the 4B graphite stick side-on, block in the dark area of road on the right (see Expert Advice). Begin shading some of the roofs and windows of the buildings, and suggest the windows on the left with a grid of lines. Fill in light tone on either side of the lettering on the stall, then shade in the dark stripes on the parasol.

GIVING THE SCENE CHARACTER

Once the main outlines and tonal areas have been established, start adding character to the scene. Develop the people and the buildings with loose strokes, keeping any slightly more detailed work for the fish stall and traders in the foreground.

5 ▶ Put in some detail Build up tone on the hair and clothing of the figures in the middle ground. Darken the stallholder's boots and jacket with heavy black tone. Suggest the fish on the stall and in the box with dashes of the 4B graphite stick – this is a shorthand way of describing the pattern they form.

6 ▲ Develop the buildings Pick out the architectural features of the buildings in slightly more detail, but keep the overall effect simple so that you don't detract from the action in the foreground. Outline more windows with simple crossing lines and shade in the dark areas on the roofs. Draw the canopies over the windows of the hotel in the centre.

7 ◀ Work on the lettering Change to the narrow 9B graphite stick for this detailed work. Fill in around the outlines of the letters, so that they show up as white against a dark background – press hard with the stick to make a good, dense black.

8 ▲ Add overall definition Sharpen the profile of the stallholder by darkening the clothing of the woman behind her, then add some linear details to her jacket. Dash in short vertical lines for the windows on the distant buildings, then indicate some of the balconies. Check the tones of the buildings, darkening them where necessary. Add more fish to the left-hand box and draw the plastic sheet in the box on the right.

EXPERT ADVICE
Blocking in large areas

The chunky tip of a graphite stick used side-on is ideal for filling in large areas of tone quickly. Each sweep of the stick will make a broad rectangular mark, and you can layer these to build up texture and tone in the drawing.

A FEW STEPS FURTHER

There is always room for a little more detail in a busy scene such as this – the thinner graphite stick will produce quite fine lines.

9 ▶ Refine the details Give more character to the two figures in the foreground by outlining their profiles with a well-sharpened 9B graphite stick. Darken a few of the windows with heavy strokes.

10 ▲ Lift out tone Check the tones over the whole drawing. If you want to lighten any previously shaded areas – for example, the white coat – you can lift off the graphite by using a putty rubber.

THE FINISHED PICTURE

A Groups of people
The clusters of figures in the middle ground were suggested with simple, sketchy marks that indicated just the rough shapes of the bodies.

B Facial detail
Although basically a broad medium, a graphite stick was sharpened finely enough here to give a precise outline to the woman's profile.

C Quick shading
Large areas of tone, such as the dark road in the foreground, were quickly and easily rendered with a graphite stick by using the tip on its side.

Drawing with ballpoints

The everyday ballpoint pen, or Biro, is not usually considered an artist's medium, but this humble writing tool has much to recommend it.

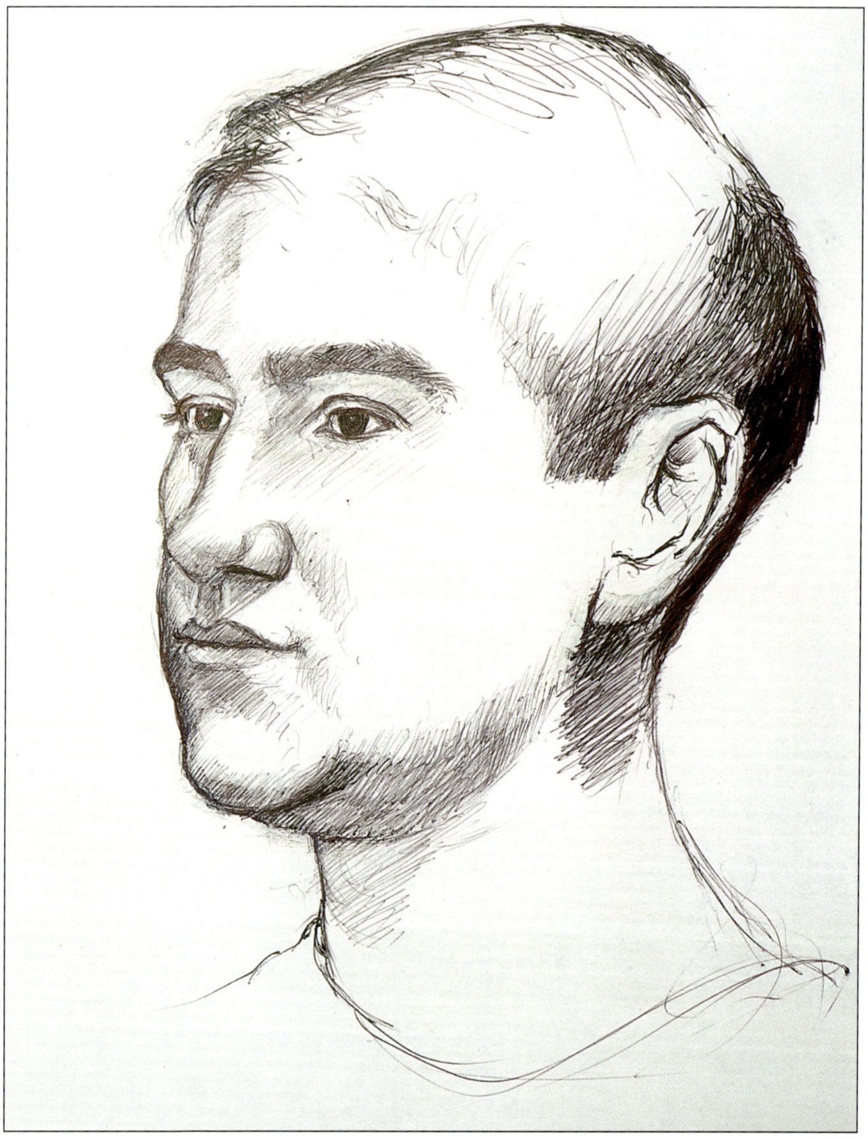

▲ **A combination of ballpoint, rollerball and fibre-tip pens was used for this portrait.**

Ballpoint pens, invented in the 1930s by Hungarian journalist Lazlo Biro (1899-1985), make interesting, if slightly unconventional, drawing tools. They have many advantages, as they are cheap, easily portable, and can be used on most types of paper.

Black and blue

For the artist, black is probably the most useful ballpoint shade. It gives a strong, positive image, as you can see from this portrait. And it is also the least likely to fade.

Blue, although not quite as lightfast, makes a useful alternative colour for the artist, creating a brighter and perhaps more unusual effect. Experiment by trying a little sketching and drawing with both colours to see which you prefer.

Fine lines

Ballpoints produce fine lines of consistent width – you can't vary the character much by applying more or less pressure to the pen. The line has a wiry, mechanical quality and is ideal for hatching, cross-hatching, scribbled hatching and stippling. Even the broken line of a pen that is about to run out can be exploited.

In the portrait, the darker areas of shadow were applied with black rollerball and fibre-tip pens. These produce marks that are significantly bolder than the ballpoint lines, and so create a strong contrast of tone.

YOU WILL NEED

Piece of cartridge paper 35.5 x 25.5cm (14 x 10in)

3 black pens: Ballpoint; Fibre-tip; Rollerball

Bleedproof white gouache paint

No.4 round brush

FIRST STEPS

1 ▶ **Establish the left eye** Using the fine black ballpoint pen, locate the sitter's nearer (left) eye – this is the pivot for the entire portrait. Draw the edges of the lids and the line of the eye socket. Outline the iris and hatch shadows under the eye and beside the bridge of the nose. Sketch in the curve of the eyebrow.

TROUBLE SHOOTER

WHITE IT OUT

Ink from a ballpoint pen can't usually be erased, so check proportions and angles before you put pen to paper. If you do need to hide a mistake, you can cover lines with some bleedproof white gouache. Here, it is applied with a No.4 round brush.

2 ▼ **Develop the eye** Darken the iris, leaving a highlight to give sparkle to the eye. Develop the eyebrow and indicate the lower lashes. Start to build up the tone, using loose hatching.

3 ▼ **Position the second eye** Measure with your pen to locate the position of the right eye, which is partially hidden behind the bridge of the nose. Establish the upper and lower lids, the pupil, the iris and the curve of the eyebrow.

4 ▼ **Draw the nose** Use your pen to measure the length and width of the nose. In this view, the base of the nose looks broader than the eye. Add dark tone under the nose to make the tip advance and the underside recede.

DEVELOPING THE FEATURES

Continue working up the features to complete the face, then start to work outwards to establish the shape of the whole head.

5 ▶ **Add the mouth** Lightly sketch the edge of the right cheek, using short pen strokes – these are easier to correct and look more natural than a single hard line. Draw the outline of the lips and the indentation between the nose and top lip.

6 ▶ **Work on the face** Finish drawing the mouth and plot the line of the chin. Add shadows on and around the lips and on the tip of the chin. Work across the drawing, developing the graduations of tone. The sitter has dark, well-defined eyebrows, so use small strokes of the ballpoint pen to add more texture and tone to these.

8 ▲ **Develop the skull** Continue working on the head, adding the dark shadow at the back of the skull that helps to convey the volume and roundness of the form. Use regular hatched strokes for this.

9 ▶ **Define the left eyebrow** Use bleedproof white gouache applied with a No.4 round brush to tidy up the outline of the left eyebrow. Apply the white paint above and below the brow. Leave to dry.

7 ▼ **Plot the skull** Add shadow under the right eye. Now outline the skull and ear. Notice how the skull is an egg shape, broader at the top. Note, too, how the top of the ear lines up with the eyebrow while the bottom aligns with the area under the nose.

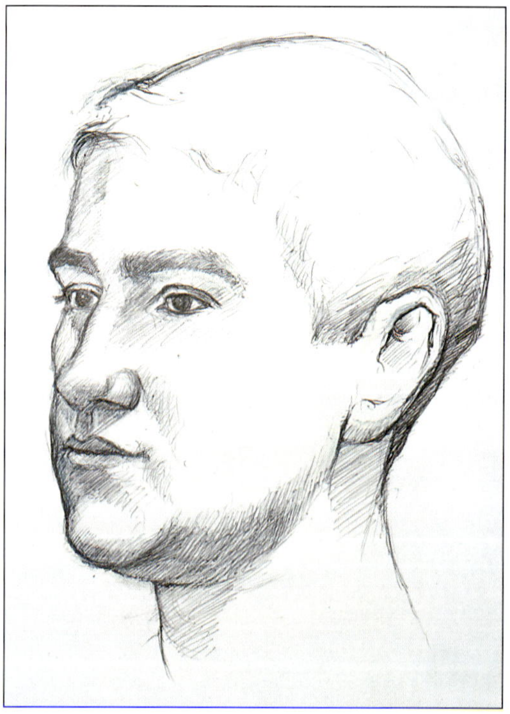

10 ▲ **Add more tone** Using regular hatched strokes, apply the shadow cast by the ear on to the neck, and the shadow within the whorl of the ear. Use a curving stroke for the shadow under the jaw to suggest the softness of the flesh. Add light shading across the forehead.

A FEW STEPS FURTHER

Stand back and review your progress. The likeness is excellent, and the head has a sense of solidity and volume. Study the way the light falls across the sitter's head and consider developing the tonal contrasts in the finishing stages.

11 ▸ Add more tone and texture A black fibre-tip pen gives a darker, more emphatic mark. Use it to add definition to the shadow at the back of the head.

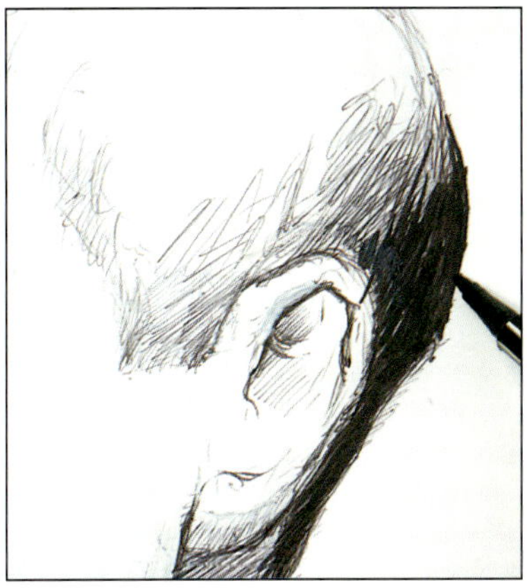

12 ▴ Suggest the hair Using a black rollerball pen, make loose, scribbled marks to indicate the hair on the top of the head. It isn't necessary to work up the hair over the entire head – simply indicate its texture at key points, such as the crown and around the ears, and the viewer's eye will fill in the areas between.

THE FINISHED PICTURE

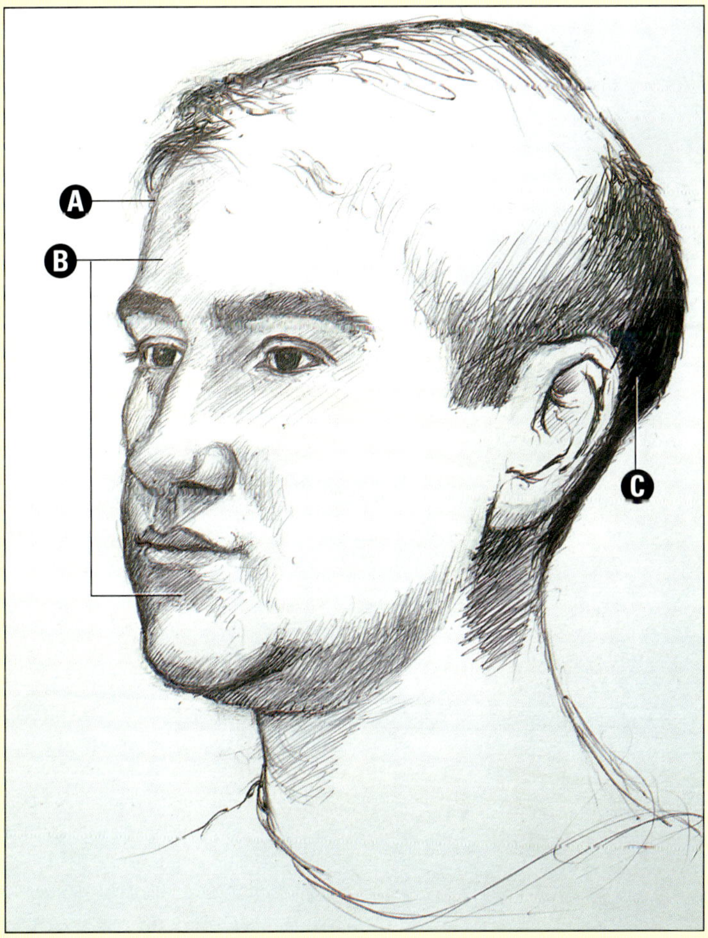

A Broken line
The outline was built up from an overlapping series of short lines applied with the fine tip of a ballpoint pen.

B Hatched tones
Mid and dark tones were created with closely laid hatched strokes – straight and regular on flat planes such as the forehead, and curving around more rounded surfaces such as the jaw.

C Fibre-tip for emphasis
The darkest darks – at the back of the head – were applied with a fibre-tip pen. This has a blacker line that is more fluid and less wiry than the marks of the ballpoint.

Watercolour mediums

If you would like to experiment with watercolour, try mixing it with some of the special additives that change the character of the paint.

The fluid nature of watercolour means that it is ideal for creating washes of translucent colour and delicate tones. However, this is by no means the end of the story. You can actually change the consistency of watercolour by adding one of several mediums to the paint. In this way, your colours become more versatile and you will be able to invent many different textures and surfaces. For example, watercolour mixed with the appropriate medium can be used with masking tape, painted in stiff peaks and even applied with a knife.

Gum water and gum arabic

Gum water and gum arabic are useful additives that enhance both the colour and texture of watercolour. A little of either medium mixed with the paint will give a rich gloss to the picture

WATERCOLOUR MEDIUMS

Choose a watercolour medium to make the colour thicker or thinner; to improve the flow; to slow down or speed up the drying time; to get a glossy finish; or to paint impasto textures.

A Thickening paste
B Gum water
C Gum arabic
D Glycerine
E Ox gall liquid
F Drying medium

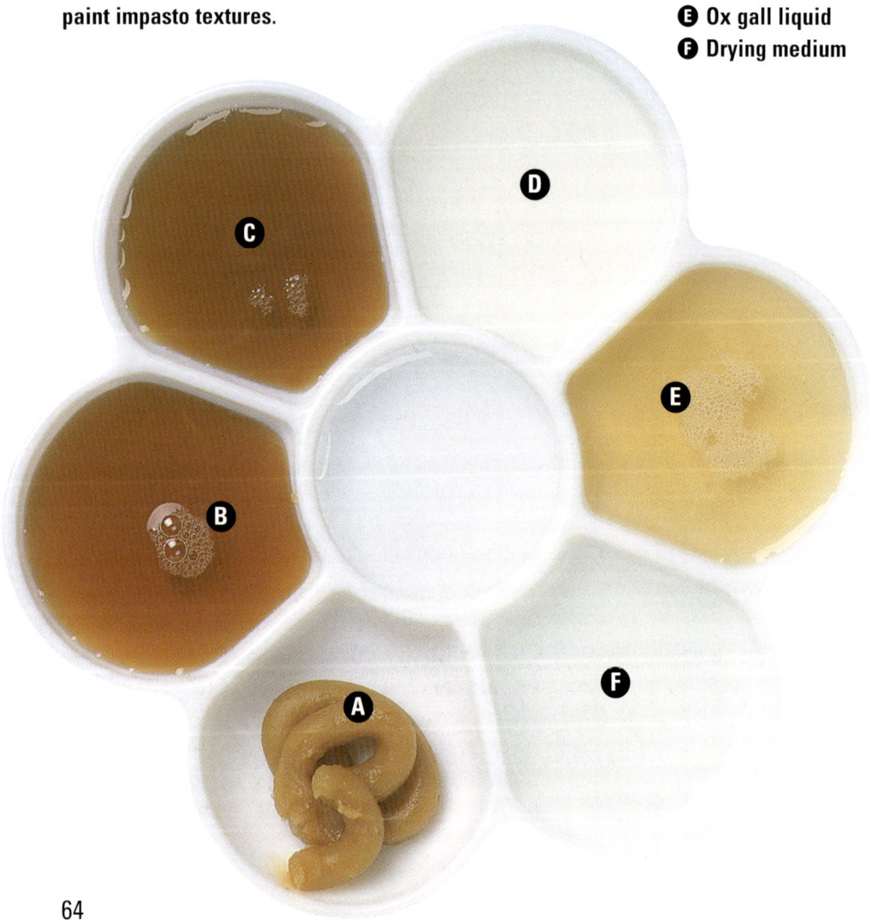

USING GUM ARABIC

To achieve a glossy sheen, add a little gum arabic to the diluted watercolour with a brush, then try the following experiments.

MOTTLED PATTERN
Drops of water applied with a small brush will dissolve dry, thickened colour and disperse the pigment particles to create this attractive mottled texture.

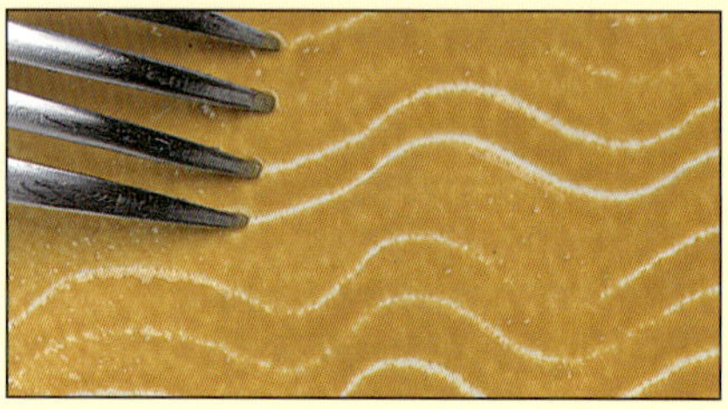

SGRAFFITO
Use a fork or other sharp tool to scratch patterns into wet, thickened colour. The white paper or underlying colour will show through the paint.

SPATTERING
Using a toothbrush, flick clean water on to dry, thickened colour. Wait for a few seconds until the water has had time to dissolve the colour, then blot the excess.

MASKING TAPE
Press strips of tape firmly down on the paper and apply the thickened colour. When the colour is dry, carefully peel back the tape to reveal the crisply painted stripes.

THICKENING PASTE

Stiffer than gum arabic, thickening paste is particularly suitable for impasto watercolour and other highly textured effects. As it is often translucent rather than transparent, too much of the paste can affect the colour of the paint and produce a cloudy effect. Once watercolour paint has been thickened with this medium, it can then be applied with a painting knife as well as with a brush.

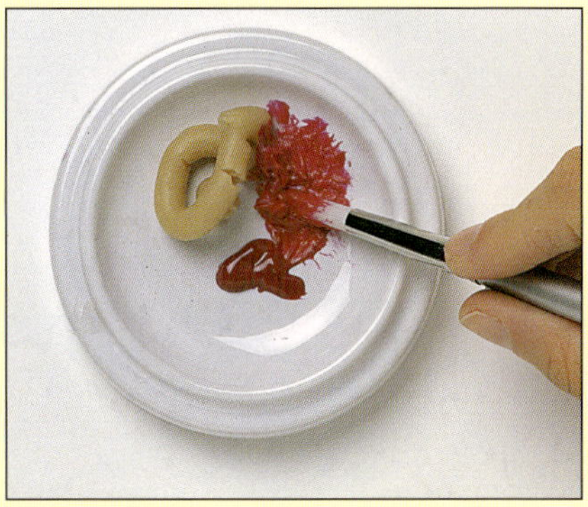

MIXING
Blend the paste and colour together well using a stiff brush. If the mixture is too firm for your purpose, add a little water.

IMPASTO
Use the flat blade of a painting knife to apply thick layers of colour and to create wedges of overlapping paint.

SGRAFITTO
Pronounced ridges and other scratched patterns can be made using a fork, comb or other implement on the wet colour.

BRUSH MARKS
Thick colour retains the marks of a stiff brush so experiment with different types of brush stroke – dabs, swirls, and so on.

STIPPLING
Pat the wet colour with the flat blade of a painting knife to create raised peaks of colour in a coarse, stippled effect.

surface. Both mediums can be spattered or sprayed on to an area of dry colour to create a speckled or mottled texture.

Gum arabic is less fluid and more viscous (sticky) than gum water. When watercolour paint is mixed with gum arabic, it can become stiff enough to hold the shape of brush marks. The thickened colour allows you to create other surface textures such as combing or stippling. However, too much gum arabic will make the paint jelly-like and too slippery to be workable.

Thickening paste

For a heavy impasto effect, try adding thickening paste to your watercolours. The resulting mixture can be so stiff that it looks quite unlike traditional watercolour paint – in fact, many purists disapprove of the additive for this reason. However, it is always fun to experiment, and watercolour applied with a painting knife is certainly an intriguing idea. Also, if used discerningly on selected areas of a painting, thickening paste can add textural interest and enhance the surface of the paint without detracting from its more classical qualities.

Thickening paste comes in tubes and looks similar to equivalent mediums made for oil and acrylics. Take care, when purchasing the medium, to buy a product that is made specifically for watercolour.

Flow improvers

Ox gall medium is the best known of the 'flow improvers', which are used to disperse colour evenly, particularly in washes and wet-in-wet techniques. It is a brownish-yellow liquid originally made from the gall bladders of cows and is normally added to the water rather than to the paint. Although still available, real ox gall has generally been replaced by synthetic alternatives.

In addition to ox gall, a number of other proprietary mediums are available to improve the flow of watercolour and to disperse the pigment evenly.

Drying mediums and retarders

If you have ever tried painting wet-in-wet on a very hot day, when the colour dries as soon as it touches the paper, you will appreciate the value of glycerine. A few drops of this heavy, honey-like liquid added to the watercolour will keep your painting moist and workable for considerably longer by delaying the natural drying time of the paint.

Conversely, watercolour paint dries surprisingly slowly in damp and humid conditions. This can be frustrating, especially if you are waiting to apply colour to a dry surface. Happily, you can speed up the drying time by using a proprietary drying medium. Alternatively, a few drops of alcohol added to the paint will also have the same effect.

Using mixed media

Once you feel confident using a range of drawing and painting materials, try combining two or more of them in a single image.

YOU WILL NEED

- Short lengths of tree branch with interesting patterns
- Sheet of rough-textured paper
- 6B pencil
- 5 oil pastels: Cadmium yellow; White; Flesh tint; Light brown; Black
- 2 watercolour paints: Sepia; Ivory black
- Brush: No.3 round

Certain media, such as pastels and watercolour, or charcoal and chalk, work well together because their different qualities enhance or complement one another. By using a combination of different media and techniques, it is possible to create optical and textural effects that will broaden the range of your work. It is exciting to experiment to see the results that can be achieved and to decide which suit your style.

In the three projects that follow, the aim is not to create finished pictures but to make a series of quick studies from nature by experimenting with mixed media. You can combine different drawing media, a mixture of painting media, or even a combination of both. The idea is to use your creative imagination to interpret patterns and textures with a range of materials that you feel are compatible with the subject.

PROJECT 1

Making studies of found objects is an absorbing exercise that will develop your powers of observation and your ability to draw well.

These tree branches have interesting surface patterns that lend themselves well to a mixed media approach. Try homing in on a small area of the subject and enlarging it on the page.

1 ► **Draw the outlines** Decide which parts of the branches you are going to concentrate on and lightly sketch their outlines using a 6B pencil. Map in the 'snake-skin' pattern on the right-hand branch.

▼ **Isolated areas of bark pattern can have a fascinating abstract quality.**

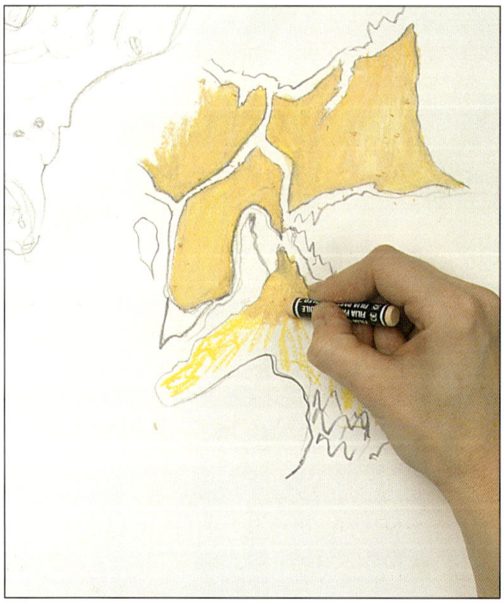

2 ◄ **Work on the right-hand branch** The base colour of the right-hand branch is a bleached yellowish-white. Recreate this using pastels, applying strokes of cadmium yellow, white and flesh tint on top of each other, and then blending them together with your finger to create a thick, even layer of colour. Leave the dark patterns untouched for the moment.

3 ▲ Work on the left-hand branch Add colour to the left-hand branch, using overlaid strokes of flesh tint, cadmium yellow and light brown. Mix light brown with black for the dark areas, and with white for the light areas. Blend white pastel into the pencil outlines to soften them.

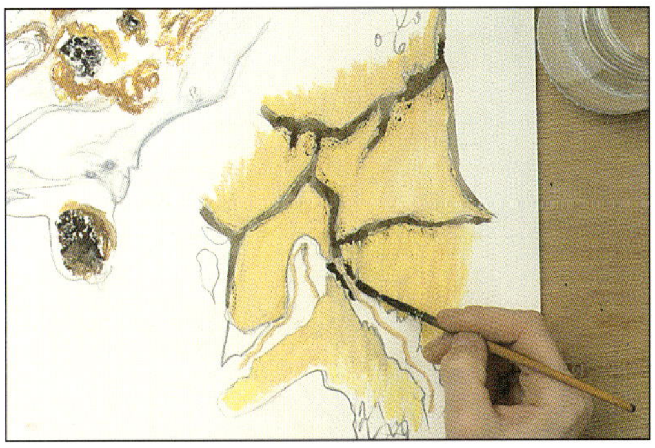

4 ▲ Add lines with watercolour Returning to the right-hand branch, fill in the dark lines with sepia watercolour, using a No.3 round brush. Go over the edges of the drawn lines slightly – the surrounding pastel resists the paint, which dries in feathery streaks. Use the same method to add small, random marks to the pastel areas between the dark lines. Leave to dry.

5 ▲ Complete the left-hand branch Return to working on the left-hand branch. Mix a dilute wash of sepia and ivory black and brush this over parts of the branch, leaving some areas of bare paper to indicate bleached wood. While the paint is still wet, draw lines and whorls with the 6B pencil, pressing quite hard so that the paper is slightly indented.

6 ◄ Complete the right-hand branch Close observation of the branch on the right shows long, vertical, slightly wavering lines over the pale areas of bark. Finish off the sketch by drawing these lines over the blended pastel areas with the 6B pencil. This extra definition gives a subtle indication of texture and detail to the bark, and makes the study more realistic.

7 ▲ The finished study Although this mixed media exercise is a study rather than a finished image, it conveys a strong sense of form and pattern, based on direct observation from nature. The use of watercolour with pastels conveys the natural, organic appearance of the bark.

PROJECT 2

An irregular fragment of tree bark with a rough, peeling surface is the inspiration for this study. To create a realistic image, a sheet of paper is first placed over the bark and rubbed gently with a soft graphite stick so that the texture comes through – a technique known as 'frottage'. The image is then built up in colour, using watercolour, soft pastels and coloured and graphite pencils.

▲ **The intricate texture of this bark is recreated using four different media.**

YOU WILL NEED

- Piece of bark
- Sheet of cartridge paper
- 6B graphite stick
- Putty rubber
- 3 watercolour paints: Sepia; Ivory black; Chinese white
- Brush: No.12 round
- 2 soft pastels: Burnt umber; Sap green
- 5 coloured pencils: Vandyke brown; Golden brown; Copper beech; Scarlet lake; Cedar green
- 6B pencil

1 ▶ **Use the frottage technique** Lay a sheet of paper over the tree bark and gently shade with a 6B graphite stick until the texture of the bark is revealed. Use small, localised movements with the stick rather than long sweeping ones, and don't press too hard.

2 ▶ **Soften the marks** Use the corner of a putty rubber to soften the textural marks made in step 1 and lift off some of the graphite so that it doesn't mix with the watercolour wash that is to be applied at the next stage. Do this very gently, with short dabbing motions, so that the texture of the bark is still visible – if you pull the eraser right across the paper, the marks will disappear.

3 ▲ **Add a watercolour wash** Apply a thinly diluted wash of sepia and ivory black watercolour paints over the bark, using a No.12 round watercolour brush. The bark has a silvery sheen in places – suggest this by applying thin washes of Chinese white to these areas while the previous wash is still slightly damp.

4 ▲ **Start to suggest texture** Define the rough surface of the bark and the warmer brown tones using a pastel stick in burnt umber. Use the tip of the pastel to make short vertical lines and the side of the pastel to make broader, horizontal blocks. Then do the same with a sap green pastel.

5 ▼ **Continue building up the texture** Work on top of the pastel marks, using coloured pencils to add small lines and marks that suggest the cracked and peeling texture of the bark. Here, coloured pencils in Vandyke brown, golden brown and copper beech (which provide dark, light and medium shades) are being used, along with touches of scarlet lake and cedar green.

6 ▲ **The finished study** The study is completed by using graphite once again, this time in the form of a 6B pencil. Press hard with the pencil to suggest the edges of the flaking pieces of bark.

PROJECT 3

Using a piece of tree bark once more, this three-dimensional interpretation involves working over a thick layer of PVA glue with pastels and acrylic paint. These bond with the dried surface of the glue to create random, mottled patterns that magically suggest the rough texture of the bark. The final details are added using graphite and coloured pencils.

▶ **This chunky piece of bark has a tactile, sculptural quality that offers a special challenge.**

YOU WILL NEED

- Piece of bark with interesting texture
- Sheet of thick cartridge paper
- 6B pencil
- 6B graphite stick
- PVA glue
- Large flat hog's hair brush
- 2 soft pastels: Burnt umber; Raw umber
- 2 coloured pencils: Vandyke brown; Golden brown
- 1 acrylic paint: Burnt umber

1 ▲ **Draw the bark and apply the glue** Use a 6B pencil to draw the bark, varying the pressure to create light and heavy lines. Observe which areas have the heaviest texture and pour PVA glue over these parts of your drawing, using the bottle as though it were a drawing tool. Let the glue form ridges that stand proud of the surface.

2 ▲ **Create a 3-D surface** Recreate the bark's gnarled texture by using a flat hog's hair brush to move the glue around on the paper. Make stabbing marks in the surface of the glue or dab the brush with a stippling motion, leaving some areas raised. Allow to dry overnight.

3 ▶ Apply pastel colours Check that the glue is completely dry. Using burnt umber for the dark areas and raw umber for the light areas, apply pastel to the patches of bare paper between the glued areas. Then rub with your fingers to spread the colour over the surface of the glue. The pastel blends into the glue to create mottled patterns.

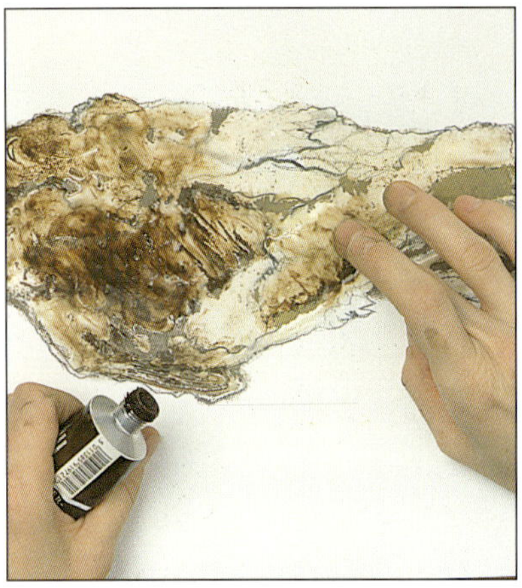

4 ◀ Add acrylic colour Squeeze a small amount of burnt umber acrylic paint from the tube, pick it up on the tip of your finger and then rub it gently over the areas where the bark is dark in tone. Apply the paint thickly for the darkest parts and skim lightly over the surface where the colour is lighter. The paint settles into the indentations on the glued surface, once again creating interesting mottled patterns.

5 ▶ Add linear details Finish off by working over the surface with a 6B pencil and a 6B graphite stick, making random lines and hatchings that suggest the cracks and fissures in the bark. Add coloured lines too, using coloured pencils in Vandyke brown (dark) and golden brown (light). Apply the dark brown to light areas of the bark and vice versa.

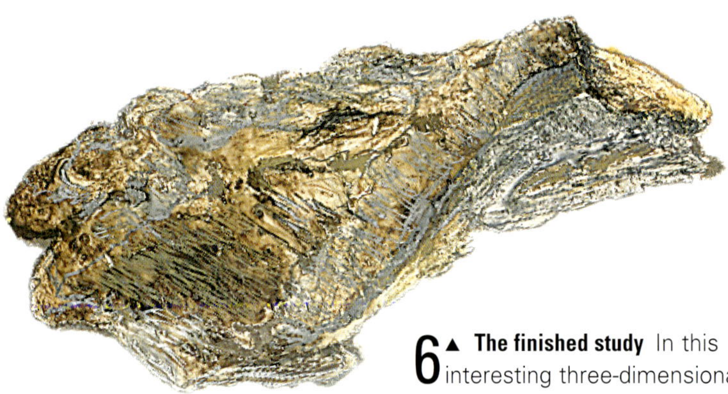

6 ▲ The finished study In this interesting three-dimensional study, the richly worked surface not only describes the form of the subject but also gives it life and character.

Master Strokes

John Constable (1776-1837)
Tree Trunk

Constable's love of nature shows in this masterly painting of a tree trunk, which is so realistic that it has a photographic quality. His rendition of the bark is done in the single medium of oils, with which he skilfully interprets every fissure on the surface.

The interpretation of the tree trunk shows beautifully observed detail on the bark.

The less detailed background helps the viewer to focus on the subject of the painting.

Pens for drawing

The range of pens available to the artist is vast and inspiring, ranging from traditional dip pens made from quill, bamboo or reed to fibre-tipped pens in many shapes, sizes and colours. Here we review the choices available.

Your choice of pen is very personal and most artists have a favourite. However, it is worth knowing what is on the market because you might have special requirements from time to time.

Dip pens are the most basic type. As their name suggests, they are loaded by being dipped into ink and have to be recharged at intervals. At the other end of the scale is an ever-expanding range of innovative markers and brush pens which come in a vast array of colours.

Traditional dip pens

These are made from quills, bamboo and reed. Quill pens are cut from the flight feathers of birds such as swans, ravens, ducks or geese, and usually produce a slightly scratchy line. They are particularly popular with calligraphers. Bamboo pens are very tough and vary in size depending on the piece of bamboo used. Reed pens are more flexible than bamboo pens, but tend to chip easily. Both reed and bamboo pens are still used in Japanese and Chinese art today.

Metal dip pens

The metal pen has been traced back as far as Roman times, but it wasn't widely used until the nineteenth century, when technical innovations made it possible to mass-produce steel nibs. From this time, steel nibs became more popular than quill, bamboo and reed. Most metal dip pens consist of a shaft or handle into which a separate metal nib is slotted. It is worth experimenting with some of the many different nibs available to discover the marks they are capable of producing and to find out which suits your needs and your style of drawing.

Script pens Old-fashioned script nibs consist of a shaped piece of metal with a slit cut in it down which the ink can flow. Some have fine or rounded points, while others are chiselled for italic lettering. They are ideal for sketching.

Mapping pens These have slender, straight nibs with very fine drawing points. They are specially designed for detailed work such as technical drawing and map-making.

Lettering pens The nibs used for lettering pens are available in various shapes, which are designed to produce the special serifs, flourishes and ribbon shapes used

VARYING THE LINE WIDTH

Technical pen
The fine lines produced by a technical pen are ideal for delicate drawings with a lot of detail. Use hatching for darker areas.

Brush pen
With the flexible tip of a brush pen, you can adopt a more fluid approach, using both thick and thin lines in a sketch.

Marker
A marker with a chisel tip makes thick, bold lines that can fill shapes such as the flowers' stalks with a single stroke.

DIP PENS AND THEIR MARKS

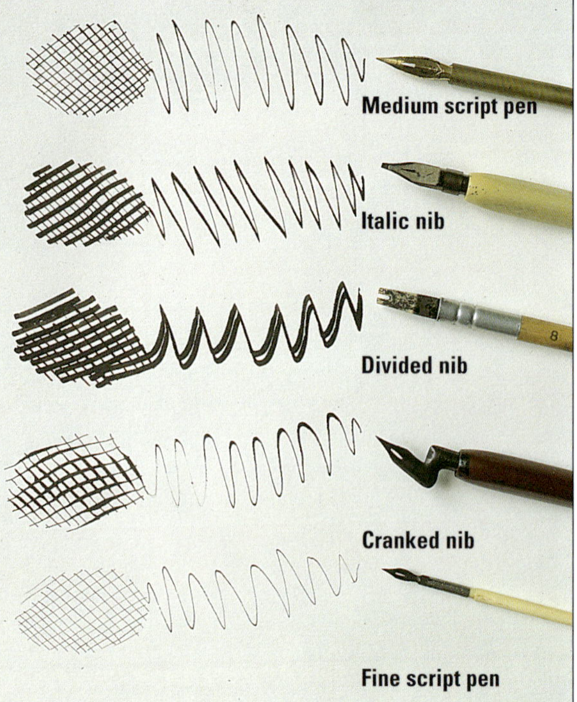

TYPES OF DRAWING PEN

- **A** Ballpoint
- **B** Fineline ballpoint
- **C** Chisel-tipped marker
- **D** Brush pen
- **E** Fibre-tipped pen
- **F** Three chisel-tipped markers
- **G** BiC ballpoint pen
- **H** Technical pen with nib units

in calligraphy. Nibs consisting of two pieces of metal are designed to hold more ink. Some lettering pens have broad nibs with two or three splits in them, making it possible to produce a wide line. Others are divided, giving parallel lines for calligraphy. Pens for musical notation are cranked (bent at an angle so that the tip of the nib is not in line with the pen shaft), which makes them more springy.

Reservoir pens

These pens contain their own store of ink and are ideal for use on location, as you don't have to carry a bottle of ink with you.

Fountain pens The ink for these pens is carried either in a replaceable cartridge or a refillable, pump-action reservoir. Most are designed for writing, but others are for sketching.

Technical pens Originally designed for illustrators and draughtsmen, these pens produce consistent lines in specific widths. The nib units fit into a holder and can be changed when you require a different line width. Use technical pens with the correct ink, never leave the nib exposed and wash out the units from time to time.

Ruling pens These are also specialist drawing tools. The reservoir is filled using a brush or dropper, and the size of the tip can be adjusted by turning a screw. They give a consistent line and don't have to be recharged as often as dip pens.

Markers and fibre-tipped pens

This category includes a wide and colourful range of pens, some of which are designed for professional applications, while others are intended for everyday use.

Markers Chisel-tipped felt pens, or markers, leave a broad, transparent line and can be used to build up layers of vibrant washes. Most manufacturers also produce markers with bullet (rounded) tips in the same colours. Some ranges include double-ended markers, with a chisel tip at one end and a bullet tip at the other. They dry quickly and can be blended if you work fast, or you can use a special blender to slow down drying. There is also a huge range of general-purpose markers with medium to fine tips, ideal for adding colour to sketches.

Most markers are fugitive – they fade over time if exposed to the light – so they are best kept for sketches rather than for

images that will be displayed. Solvent-based markers should always be used in a well-ventilated space.

Fineliners These allow you to work with more precision, although the tip will eventually become blunt. Some fineliners are available in specific line widths.

Brush pens The tip on a brush pen is longer and more pliable than on other markers, and some ranges have a huge choice of colours. By varying the pressure, you can produce fine, medium or bold strokes. Some double-ended pens have a brush pen on one end and a fine fibre tip on the other.

Ballpoint pens

The first ballpoint pen was invented in 1938 by a Hungarian journalist called Laszlo Biro, who was inspired by the quick-drying, smudge-proof ink used for commercial printing presses. The thicker ink would not flow from an ordinary nib, so he devised a pen with a tiny ball-bearing in its tip. Biro is often used as a generic term to describe ballpoint pens. One of the most popular ballpoint pens today is the BiC, launched by the French Baron Bich in 1950. Ballpoint pens are cheap and convenient, and can be a useful addition to your sketching kit.

Rollerballs These pens work on the same principle as ballpoints, but the ink in them is more like that used in cartridge pens or fibre-tipped pens. It dries quickly by evaporation and does not create blotches as ballpoints sometimes do.

Inks

The main distinction between inks is whether they are waterproof or water-soluble. Waterproof ink allows you to lay a wash over a line without dissolving it, whereas a water-soluble ink will spread and run. Indian ink is the best-known drawing ink – it is black, permanent and waterproof. Coloured waterproof drawing inks are dye-based and not lightfast, so are best used in sketchbooks where they won't be exposed to light for long periods. Waterproof inks should not be used in fountain pens, as they will clog the mechanism.

Liquid watercolours and acrylics Like coloured inks, these can be used with dip pens and are available in a wide array of shades. Liquid watercolours are soluble once dry, while liquid acrylics are not.

- **I** Selection of nibs for a dip pen
- **J** Divided nib for parallel lines
- **K** Mapping pen
- **L** Cranked nib for music notation
- **M** Script pen
- **N** Ruling pen
- **O** Sketching fountain pen
- **P** Selection of coloured fibre-tipped pens
- **Q** Bullet-tipped pen
- **R** 3mm ($\frac{1}{8}$in) chisel-tipped pen
- **S** Fineliner

PAPERS, PANELS AND BRUSHES

This chapters takes you though the different surfaces available to draw on, from handmade papers to more conventional panels and canvasses, and explains how to prepare your surface for painting and choose the best brush or other tool for the job.

The versatile paint brush

Using a brush is the simplest and most conventional method of applying paint. It is also the most versatile, as you'll see from the effects shown in this chapter.

A single brush has many uses. With this one tool you can fill in large areas of colour, or you can paint delicate lines. You can create a whole range of exciting marks, textures and patterns on any surface you choose.

Artists' brushes come in a variety of shapes, each designed for a specific purpose. For example, brushes with square-cut bristles are often used for painting areas of flat colour, while brushes with fine points are good for detail and for painting tapering lines. A brush with a full head of bristles generally holds more paint than a flattened or fine brush, which means that you don't need to dip it in the paint quite so often.

◀ **The flat, square cut broad brush (top) is ideal for backgrounds and areas of flat colour; the finer, tapered brushes are better for detail work and highlighting.**

▲ **Strong, swirling brush strokes are used to astonishing effect in Van Gogh's immortal *Sunflowers*.**

A variety of effects

Any paint brush can be used in a variety of ways to create many different marks. The marks you make depend upon whether you use the side of the brush or the tip, how much pressure you apply and the sort of movement you make as you paint. Many artists use one type of brush for everything and even create beautiful paintings using the same brush – sometimes until it wears out!

Experiment with whatever brushes you have to see what effects you can create. Discover, too, how many different marks you can make with a single brush. Your confidence will soon increase and you'll begin to develop your own painting style, which is as unique to you as your handwriting.

▶ **This detail from *Sunflowers* reveals the thick, juicy texture of the oil paint, a technique known as *impasto*.**

PLAYING WITH TEXTURES

Invent your own textures, using the brush and paint in as many different ways as you can. Try painting with a dry brush, dipping only the tips of the bristles into the paint, so that patches of the paper show through the colour. Instead of laying conventional horizontal brushstrokes, why not try stippling the colour using a vertical stabbing motion to create a stubbly paint surface? The possibilities for making textures with paint and a brush are almost endless.

Paper and canvas have textures of their own and it is worth experimenting with both thick and thin colour on a variety of painting surfaces. Many artists like to see the weave of canvas or the texture of rough paper through the brushstrokes and deliberately use thin or sparse colour to create this effect.

Dry brush

Stippling

Paint dabs

Horizontal dashes

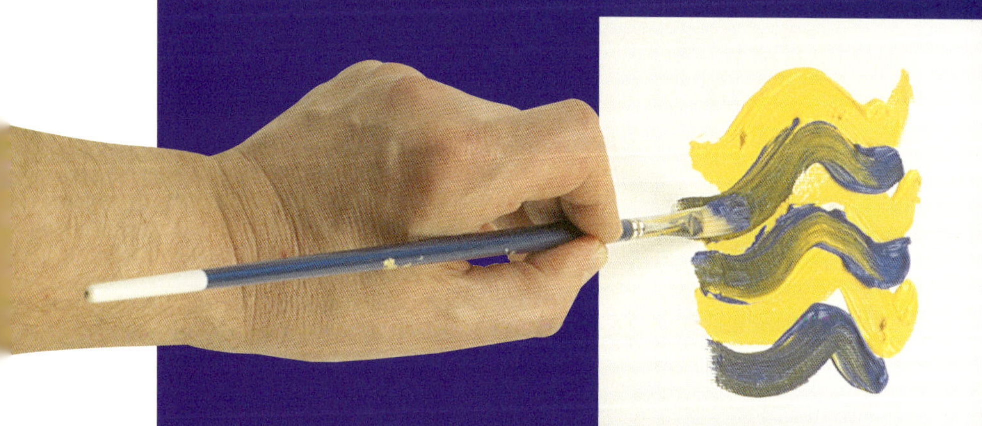

Swirling lines

Magic brushmarks

If you lack confidence in your brushwork, why not start by making the brush do the painting for you? You can simply use the shape of the brush bristles to create a shape on the paper. For example, take a round brush, dip all the bristles in the paint, lay the side of the bristle head on the paper and you have a perfect petal shape. Paint these in a circle and you have a daisy.

The same shape can also be used to paint buds and leaves. Add a few stems and stalks using the point or thin side of the bristles and you have a complete plant. Carry on painting flowers and leaves in this way and before long you will have created an effective and colourful garden landscape, without either drawing the shapes or filling them in. It's easy!

Swirling brushwork

Oil and acrylic paints can be used undiluted, straight from the tube. The buttery, succulent colour holds the shape of the brush strokes and you can build up beautiful textures and patterns in your pictures.

For inspiration, look at the famous paintings of sunflowers by Vincent van Gogh, or the lovely waterlilies and flowers in the giant garden paintings of French Impressionist Claude Monet. Van Gogh often used thick, unmixed colours, following the shapes of the flowers with his expressive brushstrokes. Monet frequently painted flowers and leaves with single brush strokes of pure colour, building these up to create an impression of a garden more real and convincing than any amount of detail could have produced.

▶ This Japanese print, entitled *Winter Landscape with Countryfolk*, shows how both lines and washes can be made with a well-pointed brush to create images of great charm.

▲ **Letting the brush do the painting: striking effects with the simplest of strokes.**

Dots and dabs

A spontaneous and fun way of painting is to apply colour in tiny dabs or dots, especially if you use two or more colours. For example, paint an area of yellow and red dots, then stand back to look at the effect. You will discover that the reds and yellows appear to merge together to give the impression of orange. Try 'mixing' other colours in this way: blue and yellow to create an impression of green; blue and green to make turquoise and so on.

▲ **Small, separate dots and dabs of colour appear to merge in the viewer's eye and create exciting and vibrant effects.**

Painting lines

The type of line you produce depends very much on how you hold the brush and how hard you press down as you paint. A lot of pressure causes the bristles to splay out to give you a fat line. To paint a fine line, hold the brush lightly, so that just the tips of the bristles touch the paper. If your brush has square-cut bristles, turn it so that you are working with the narrow side of the bristles.

For a tapering effect, start lightly, then gradually thicken the line by applying more pressure. For undulating lines, vary the pressure, or try twisting and turning the brush as you paint. A single stroke can convey a surprising sense of movement and rhythm.

Going oriental

In China and Japan, the same brushes and brushstrokes are used for lettering as for painting. This is why the term 'calligraphic' is often used to describe the decisive, flowing lines found in much oriental art. This deft brushwork, often painted over delicate washes, enables artists to capture an entire landscape with just a few strokes of paint or ink. Blossoms and bamboo leaves look so lifelike that they appear to sway in the breeze.

Traditionally, Chinese and Japanese artists used oriental brushes with bamboo handles, designed originally as writing tools. However, any pointed soft-bristled brush - the type normally used with watercolour - works well with this technique.

Brushes

It's worth building up a collection of different brushes as they will help you achieve a wide range of exciting paint effects.

▲ **Brushes are available in many sizes. These sable rounds range in size from the finest No.0000 to the much larger No.20.**

Artists' brushes come in an enormous range of shapes and sizes, corresponding to the various purposes they are intended for. They may be made from several different kinds of natural bristles or from synthetic fibre, and the difference in price between the different types of bristle can be considerable. The choice is wide, but in the end the decision as to which to buy and use is a personal one, often depending on trial and error. Initially, it is a good idea to experiment with one or two brushes at a time to see how you get on.

WHAT TO LOOK FOR

Small and large

Most artists' brushes are available in a range of sizes, usually numbered. For example, a standard watercolour brush range can start with a tiny No.0000, used only for the very finest work, going up to No.20 and even larger. However, it is worth remembering that each brush manufacturer has a slightly different system. Hence a No.2 brush made by one manufacturer is not necessarily exactly the same size as a No.2 brush produced by another. The size of some flat brushes may be expressed in terms of total bristle width instead of numbers – 25mm (1in), 51mm (2in) and so on.

Types of brush

Each type of brush is designed to make a specific kind of mark. Choosing a brush depends very much on the effect you want to achieve, but if you have one or two of the following basic brush types they will be all you need to begin with.

Round This is a brush with a rounded ferrule. It is a popular, general-purpose brush with a full bristle head that holds a lot of paint. Large rounds are useful for laying washes and wide expanses of colour. The point can be used for painting lines and detail.

Flat or chisel headed This brush has a flattened ferrule with a square-cut bristle head. The wide bristles are good for applying paint in short dabs and for laying flat areas of colour, while the narrow edge of the bristles is useful for making thinner lines. A flat with very short bristles is sometimes referred to as a 'bright'.

Filbert Somewhere between a flat and a round, a filbert has a flattened ferrule but with tapered bristles. It is a popular and versatile brush, combining the functions of other brush types.

Fan The attractively shaped fan brush, or blender, as it is also sometimes known, has widely splayed-out bristles and is used primarily for blending colours together smoothly.

Fan

Round

Filbert

Fla

Watercolour brushes

Watercolour brushes are usually softer than those used with oil and acrylics. The very best-quality watercolour brushes available are sable brushes. These are made only from the tail-end hairs of the sable, a small, fur-bearing animal that is found in certain regions in Siberia. This is why pure sable brushes are so expensive. To reduce the cost, manufacturers sometimes mix sable with other natural hair. This is usually ox or squirrel hair, but occasionally goat, camel or even mongoose hair is used.

Why are sable brushes so good to work with? For a start, they combine strength with suppleness, and this allows you to paint in a lively yet controlled way. They also wear well, and will keep their shape. If properly cared for, a sable brush can last a lifetime.

However, manufactured bristles have improved enormously in quality in recent years. They fall into two main categories. Soft brushes are made especially for watercolour paints and have a texture and pliancy which aims to match the qualities of natural hair. Stiffer, general-purpose nylon brushes are made mainly for use with oil and acrylics, but are occasionally used by watercolourists to give a textured surface.

Caring for watercolour brushes

Each time you use a brush, rinse it in water. Either hold your brushes in your free hand while you work, or lay them down on a flat surface. Never leave them standing head down in water, because this will bend the bristles. Once this has happened, it can be difficult to restore a brush to its proper state.

At the end of a painting session, wash each brush thoroughly in warm soapy water, then rinse well under running water. Gently shake the bristle head back into its natural shape. If necessary, reshape the bristles with your thumb and index finger. Store brushes upright with the handle end downwards.

Special brushes

You may come across various eye-catching and exotic-looking brushes in the art shop. Though they may appear unusual and have intriguing names – rigger, oriental, mop and spotter – these brushes are very practical and invaluable for creating specific effects.

Rigger So-called because it was originally used to paint fine ship's rigging in marine paintings, the rigger has long, tapering bristles. Today it is used more generally for all linear work, but especially for lettering, poster writing and also calligraphy.

Oriental brushes Recognisable by their cane or bamboo handles, these brushes produce the characteristic, flowing lines which give Japanese and Chinese paintings their distinctive quality. The bristles taper to a fine point and the brushes can be used for painting fine lines as well as for creating broad strokes and laying washes.

Spotter Miniature paintings and all fine detail can be executed with a retouching brush, or spotter. This is a small round brush with short bristles, good for all precise work.

Wash brushes There are several large brushes that are designed specifically for laying flat washes. Most artists use a soft, flat brush; others prefer a large round, or a mop. The mop brush has a large, rounded head and is especially good for laying textured washes such as sea and sky.

Brushes for oil and acrylic

Brushes made for oil and acrylic paints are stiffer than those used for watercolour painting. However, watercolour

WATERCOLOUR BRUSH MARKS

Rigger

The long bristles of a rigger are designed for linear work.

Flat or chisel headed

A flat brush can give broad or narrow lines of paint.

Round

Use the whole brush for painting large areas, and the tip for details.

ACRYLIC BRUSHMARKS

Round

The oval marks made by a round brush echo the shape of the bristle head.

Flat or chisel headed

The rectangular profile of a flat brush produces regular dabs of acrylic colour.

Filbert

Filbert bristles curve gently to a point and give strong, tapering strokes.

Fan

Use a fan-shaped brush for delicate blending effects with acrylics.

brushes can also be used with oils and acrylics, especially if you are painting areas of thin colour or painting detail.

Oil painting brushes are traditionally made from a natural bristle, usually hog's hair. There are also excellent synthetic brushes now available and some artists actually prefer these, finding them easier to clean and harder-wearing.

Certain synthetic brushes have been specially developed for use with acrylic paints, but as a general rule, both natural bristle and synthetic brushes can be used with either oil or acrylic paints. One word of warning, however: oil and water do not mix. Brushes which you have already used with oil paints should be carefully cleaned before you go on to use them with acrylics, which are water soluble.

Care and cleaning

Whether you are using oils or acrylics, paint should never be allowed to dry on the brush. At the end of every painting session, clean your brushes carefully by first wiping off excess paint with paper or kitchen roll. Brushes used with oil paint should then be rinsed in turpentine or white spirit, wiped clean and washed in warm water and household soap. Rub the soapy brush in the palm of your hand to loosen the paint that has accumulated round the ferrule. Rinse the brush well, then shake it to remove the water. If necessary, carefully reshape the bristles then leave the brush to dry in a jar, with the bristle end up.

Acrylic brushes should only be cleaned in warm water and soap. Because acrylic paint dries so quickly, it is a good idea to keep brushes moist during the painting session when you are not using them. Do this by laying brushes in a dish of water with the handles resting on the side of the dish.

If you let acrylic paint dry on the brush accidentally, you can rescue it by soaking the bristles overnight in methylated spirits. This will soften the paint, which can then usually be washed off with soap and warm water.

Other handy brushes

Once you have experimented with the range of recognised artists' brushes, you might like to try other kinds. Small house decorating brushes are excellent for painting flat areas of colour and can save time if you like working on a large scale. Avoid very cheap ones – they tend to moult and you may waste any time you would have saved picking loose bristles off your painting. The very best decorating brush is still much cheaper than the equivalent artists' brush. Other useful brushes include a stencilling brush with a flat end to create stippled colour; a sash brush for painting large areas; and an old toothbrush for spattered effects. A fitch is a cheaper alternative to a sash brush.

Synthet

Hog's h

Sa

Stencilling

Decorating

Fitch

Using coloured paper

Applying watercolour to toned paper breaks with tradition but, as these quick sketches show, the results can be both striking and instructive.

A watercolour painted on coloured paper is quite different from a classical watercolour picture on white or pale cream paper. White paper intensifies the transparent colours without changing them. On coloured paper, the underlying support shows through the paint and can alter the colours.

Underlying colour

The colour of the support will modify the painted colours in precisely the same way as if that colour had been added to the paint on the palette. Yellow paper, for instance, will push red towards orange and blue towards green.

One useful characteristic of tinted paper is the unifying effect it can have on the finished painting. While some artists create harmony in a painting by including a little of one particular colour in every mixture on the palette, others find that they can achieve a similar effect simply by painting on coloured paper. This is because the underlying paper colour effectively mixes with each of the painted colours to create a general, unified colour theme.

Testing colours

It is helpful to make a colour test to find out how the painted colours will appear when applied to a particular paper. You can do this by cutting a small strip from the paper you intend to use for your painting. On this test strip, try out the colours from your usual palette, as well as any of your favourite mixtures, before introducing them into the paintings.

Colour and tone

It is easier and quicker to establish light and shade on toned paper than it is when working on white paper. For example, the seated figure in the watercolour painting below is lit by an overhead window, which creates strong highlights and dark shadows. To bring out these contrasting tones, the artist chose medium-grey paper – a tone that is approximately halfway between the dark shadows and white highlights.

Having established this paper as the mid-toned colour, it was then a

WORKING ON MID-TONED PAPER

To discover the benefits of using tinted paper in a tonal study, try making a quick monochrome watercolour sketch of a figure on a sheet of medium-grey paper. Treat the paper tone as the mid tone in the picture – this stands for the limbs, the face and the clothing. Then add the background and shadows with washes of darker grey, and put in highlights with simple strokes of opaque Chinese white. Use broad brush strokes to avoid detail, relying on the tonal contrasts to build up the form.

1 ▲ **Block in the background** Using a No.4 sable brush, wash Payne's grey over the background. Paint around the figure, and dot in one or two of the darkest shadows.

2 ▲ **Add dark tones** Change to a 25mm (1in) flat brush. Establish shadows on the chair and figure in a dilute Payne's grey that is slightly darker than the background wash.

▼ **Highlights have been picked out in Chinese white watercolour, which shines out against the grey paper.**

relatively simple matter to add the shadows and a few highlights that show up clearly against the medium grey of the paper. To accentuate the tonal contrast, the artist simplified the tones, using Payne's grey for the shadows and Chinese white for the highlights.

Tinting your own paper

What happens if you cannot find paper in the colour of your choice? You can make your own tinted paper quite easily by applying a watercolour wash to a sheet of white paper or even over another colour. This will allow you to choose exactly the right tone and colour for the purpose.

The paintings opposite are both made on paper that has been tinted by the artist. An evening landscape (top) is painted over a multicoloured wash. In the second watercolour (below), a washy blue makes an attractive background for the darker blue of the painting.

▼ These strips of coloured paper, each painted with the same colours, show the considerable effect that background colour can have on the appearance of watercolour paint. Grey paper, for example, tends to mute the colours. On red paper, the yellow and orange almost disappear.

LOCAL COLOUR

Brightly coloured paper can give dramatic results, but it is important to choose the right colour for the subject. The main colours in this still-life arrangement of a basket of fruit are yellow, orange and brown. By selecting a bright yellow support, the artist was able to leave patches of unpainted paper to represent the local colour of the yellow fruit as well as to show the highlights. So, by choosing an appropriate colour, you will find the paper does most of the work!

Keep the painted colour to a minimum, using thin mixes that allow the yellow paper to glow through the transparent paints. Add just a few deeper patches for the shadow areas. This way of working creates an overall warmth and harmony in the finished painting.

1 ▲ **Paint outlines** Using a No.4 round sable brush, outline the fruit and basket in dilute orange mixed from cadmium red and cadmium yellow.

2 ▲ **Deepen the tone** Paint the shadow on the basket and the dark areas on the fruit, using a 25mm (1in) flat brush. Add burnt sienna to the mixture and block in the background.

3 ▲ **Put in the dark tone** Paint the pattern on the cloth in dilute burnt sienna. Mix a wash of raw umber and burnt sienna to complete the shadows on the fruit and basket. Suggest the basket texture with the brush's narrow edge.

▼ The bright yellow support complements the paint colours and gives an overall golden glow to the finished picture.

TINTING PAPER WITH A MULTICOLOURED WASH

An interesting way of tinting paper is to use more than one colour. Choose colours that will become an integral part of the painting. Here, four bands of colour are washed across the paper to represent a sky tinged with pink, and a line of foliage reflected in water. A simple landscape is added, but this method would work equally well for a more complex scene.

1 ▲ **Lay the background** Working on a slightly tilted board and using a large, flat brush, paint the background in broad overlapping stripes of dilute cadmium yellow, ultramarine, cadmium red and sap green.

2 ▲ **Add grey** Allow the background to dry. Using dilute Payne's grey and a 25mm (1in) flat brush, paint ripples on the water and dab in clouds. Suggest trees and reflections with short vertical strokes.

▲ **All that is needed to finish off this simple impression of a landscape are minimal horizontal and vertical brush strokes, using Payne's grey over the sap green band.**

TINTING PAPER WITH A SINGLE WASH

If you think pure white paper will look too stark, a solution is to tint it with a toning pale colour before beginning to paint. In this watercolour sketch, the artist decided to tint the paper with a dilute blue wash, which provides a harmonious background for the buildings and figures all of which are overpainted in a darker tone of the same colour.

1 ▶ **Tint the paper** Using a large, flat brush and starting at the top of the paper, apply a dilute wash of ultramarine in broad, overlapping strokes. Work on a slightly tilted board.

2 ▶ **Paint the buildings** Allow the wash to dry. Using a No.4 round brush, paint the buildings in a stronger wash of ultramarine. Use the tip of the brush for the fine lines.

3 ◀ **Fill in the foreground** Finally, use the same colour to paint the fountain in the foreground and to add the figures as solid strokes of colour.

▼ **The pale blue tint harmonises with the painted linework and, at the same time, adds substance to the background.**

Specialist papers

Bored with the same old cartridge and watercolour papers? Take your pick from a variety of surfaces from around the world.

Papers made from banana skins, rice and even tea leaves might sound unlikely supports for the artist. But these and many other exotic papers from countries all over the world can be used with almost any medium to give unusual and beautiful results.

There is a fascinating range of textures and surface patterns – from gossamer-like tissue made in Japan to the thick, chunky papers of India and Nepal. Many papers are still made by hand using traditional techniques.

▲ **Coloured inks work particularly well on khadi paper, as Elda Abramson's *Tulips* shows. The rough texture of the paper is visible through the transparent washes and seems to add vigour to the painting.**

Choosing a paper

Unlike conventional artists' supports, these papers are not necessarily made specifically for painting or drawing. They are also used by bookbinders and other craft workers. It is therefore important to make sure that a particular paper is suitable for your needs.

For example, some papers are very porous and need sealing with size so that the paint does not soak in. Size is available at good art stores and is simply brushed on to the paper and left to dry. Other papers, such as many Japanese ones and the Thai tissue paper overleaf, are quite fragile and will not withstand robust drawing, wet washes or thick colour. It is often obvious by simply looking at and feeling the paper whether it will be up to the job. If you are not sure, do a test on a small sample of the paper.

There are also important aesthetic considerations. Some of the most striking papers are those in which real flowers, leaves and other recognisable objects are clearly visible. While these are often very beautiful in themselves,

▼ **There is a huge range of papers on the market, including khadi papers from India, Lotka papers from Nepal and Thailand, and Kozo papers from Japan.**

KHADI AND TISSUE PAPERS

Among the best-known imported papers are the khadi papers from India. They are made from khadi, the handspun cotton yarn that has been produced in rural India for thousands of years. They are generally robust and take most media. Some of the best tissue papers come from Japan and Thailand (see bottom). These are often too fragile for drawing media and need to be handled with care.

PASTEL ON KHADI PAPER
This cold-pressed paper from Northern India is ideal for soft pastel. The paper is thick and card-like and the rough surface holds the pastel pigments well.

WATERCOLOUR ON THAILAND TISSUE
This flimsy, off-white paper is made from the lokta plant and is photographed here on a dark surface in order to show the fibres and mottled pattern. The surface is very absorbent and the watercolour washes bleed slightly, giving a soft edge and a blurred image.

they are not necessarily suitable for artists because the decoration may be too dominant and can interfere with the drawn or painted image.

Hand-made papers

The character of a paper is determined by the manufacturing process and by the kind of fibrous plant material used to make the pulp. Additional materials are often introduced to add colour, texture and surface pattern.

The first manufactured paper was papyrus, made from the fibres of the papyrus reed that grew abundantly in Ancient Egypt. Papyrus is still produced and it is one paper that is guaranteed to last for centuries – papyrus scrolls have been found in Egyptian tombs dating from 2700BC! Today, however, it is expensive and difficult to source.

Other handmade papers are made from cotton or linen rag (literally off-cuts and seconds from the clothing industry) as well as various wood barks, mulberry wood, hemp and any other suitable fibres that can be pulped and pressed or moulded into sheets.

Delicate papers

The indigenous crops and trees determine the sort of papers made in each region. So papers from a particular country tend to be made from the same basic materials. For example, the delicate lokta papers from Nepal and Thailand are made from the bark of the lokta shrub which grows abundantly in the Himalayas and other regions, and Japanese kozo papers come from the inner fibres of the native kozo, a type of mulberry tree.

Added materials

In papers made from traditional cotton rag and natural fibre, the colour and texture comes from various materials added during the manufacturing process. These include banana leaf, recycled jute sacking, sugar cane and algae. The black specks found in some paper may well be recycled tea leaves, added after the workers' tea break! Brighter coloured papers are made by adding dyes to the paper pulp during manufacture.

Japanese papers

The range of Japanese papers is enormous. Many are made especially for painting, drawing and printmaking. Others are too fragile to be used in this way, but are wonderful for collage.

Decorative papers include the translucent ginwashi, which has delicate strands of short fibres embedded in each sheet; crumpled momi papers, which may be pearlised or flecked with real gold and silver; and the see-through lace papers, made by the falling-water process, which involves vigorously spraying each freshly made sheet of paper to create a distinctive lacy pattern.

Handmade paper from overseas is a comparatively recent arrival on the art scene. This is partly because a lot of imported paper comes from remote areas, and this used to make quality control and regular delivery difficult. Availability and uniformity could not be relied on and, with some exceptions, artists generally preferred machine-made products that were consistent, affordable and easy to obtain. During the last few decades, however, the picture has changed dramatically. Handmade paper from all over the world is now readily available and appreciated by artists for exactly those qualities that once made it unpopular – its distinctiveness and irregularity.

Swatches and sizes

Some imported papers can be found in general art shops; the more unusual ones are only available from specialist suppliers. The latter sometimes provide specimen swatches and offer a mail delivery service.

As they are often made especially for the international market, many papers are available in standard sizes from A2 to A5 as well as in several traditional paper sizes. Indian atlas, a khadi paper measuring approximately a metre by a metre and a half, is probably the largest available handmade paper in the world.

COTTON PAPERS

There are many papers made with cotton yarn and rag – what you see here is the tip of the iceberg! Seek out your own exotic papers and experiment to discover the exciting effects that can be achieved using your favourite colours and drawing tools. These papers can be used with most media – although many are not strong enough to support thickly applied oils or acrylics.

PEN AND WASH ON PAPER WITH HUSKS
Surprisingly, the pen nib rides smoothly over this irregular, textured paper – probably because the paper is very compact and the surface has a slight sheen.

GOUACHE ON BANANA FIBRE PAPER
Apply the gouache thickly to cover the slightly porous, rough surface of the paper. The paper takes the paint well and the natural beige colour enhances the bright pinks and reds of the painting.

ACRYLIC ON COTTON RAG PAPER
This off-white paper has an attractive, woven look and a rough surface. Acrylic can be applied directly on to the paper – however, for a large painting, it's best to seal the surface with size first.

COLOURED PENCILS ON ALGAE PAPER
It is hard to believe that the green, hair-like lines in this paper are actually algae. However, they complement the coloured pencil lines beautifully and the paper is easy to work on.

Experimenting with textured papers

The paper you use will have a huge effect on your finished work. Try drawing on a whole range of textured surfaces to see which ones you like best.

Paper surfaces come in a wide range of interesting textures from coarse and craggy to slippery and smooth. Paper can be hard and gritty or, at the other extreme, it can feel velvety soft to the touch. When you are planning a piece of work, you might choose a handmade paper with an irregular texture, or you may prefer the even, mechanical surface of one of the many machine-made papers – it depends on the medium you are using and the final effect you wish to achieve.

Get to know your surfaces

Whether you are using pencil, pastel, ink, or any other drawing medium, the texture of the paper makes an enormous difference to the work. You can have great fun experimenting to discover which effects you like best.

Textured papers have tiny indents on the surface known as the 'tooth' and the bigger the indents, the rougher and more pitted the paper will feel. The colour of a textured paper is important since drawn or painted marks tend to sit on the paper surface, leaving the little indents visible as paper-coloured flecks.

This flecked appearance is especially pronounced on very coarse papers and the colour of these tiny flecks directly affects the colours you work with. For instance, when drawing or painting in blue on a textured yellow paper, the yellow flecks will make the blue appear green. Similarly, red over yellow will produce orange, and so on.

The 'wet and dry' rule

As an initial guide, drawing materials can be divided into two very broad categories – 'wet' and 'dry'. The 'dry' drawing materials, including pastel, charcoal and coloured pencils, are not very effective on an extremely smooth surface because they simply slide around and leave a rather feeble mark

◀ Pastels require a textured surface so that the crumbly grains of colour have something to cling and adhere to.

Conversely, most 'wet' drawing materials, such as pen and ink and felt-tips, are excellent on smooth surfaces. In fact, 'wet' drawing materials can be quite difficult to use on a very toothy surface because the texture of the paper interferes with the

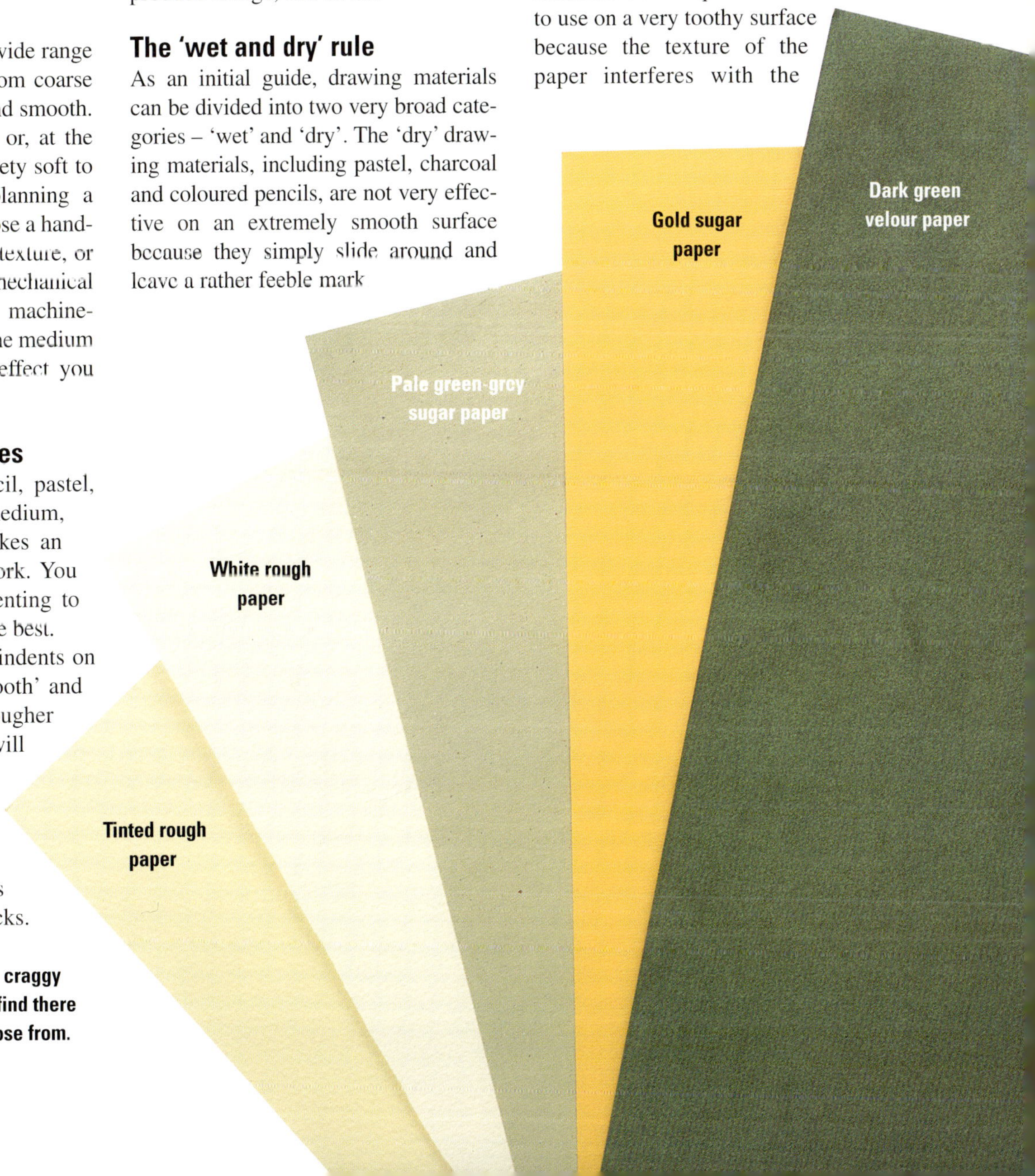

▶ From smooth velour paper, to craggy and toothed rough paper, you'll find there are a wealth of surfaces to choose from.

flowing lines. This is especially true of fine-nibbed pens, which tend to catch on the toothy surface.

Most papers are targeted at a single market – watercolour papers for use with watercolour paints, pastel papers for pastel work, and so on. But you should never feel restricted by this. For example, watercolour papers are excellent for pastel, pencil and coloured pencil work, while pastel papers are good with drawing pencils and coloured pencils.

Improvised surfaces

Although watercolour paints require a heavy or stretched paper to prevent cockling most drawing materials are far less exacting. It is useful to practise drawing on any number of inexpensive papers to see what results you can get. A roll of lining paper is good value for large sketches in chunky charcoal or pastel, and dressmakers' stiffening paper can be used effectively with pastels and paints.

Watercolour papers

Choose watercolour papers for drawing according to the type of effect you want to create. Hot-pressed (HP) papers are smooth and work well with pen and ink and hard pencils. Not ('not' hot-pressed) paper is good used with most drawing materials and lends a slightly granular feel to the work. Rough paper is excellent for bold drawings and sketches, but the effect is definitely rugged, and you will not be able to draw detail.

▶ This thick application of green and blue soft pastels shows how they break down into tiny crumbs. Only textured papers provide a sufficiently rugged surface to allow the colour to be built up in layers.

Pastel papers

Pastels are soft and crumbly to use and the right sort of paper is crucial. There are lots to choose from, but initially it is a good idea to buy papers specially made for pastel work. These have a definite tooth which holds the crumbs of pastel dust and allows you to build up colours.

When the pastel is drawn lightly over the surface, the coloured paper underneath shows through to give characteristic flecks of broken colour. If, however, you work on a smooth paper, the pastel will slide around and you will get skid marks instead of the beautiful matt colours which can be achieved on the right paper. See the box, right, for more information on pastel papers.

Exotic papers

There are literally hundreds of different kinds of handmade oriental papers, made from bamboo, rice, straw and many other plants and fibres. Some of these will not stand up to vigorous handling, but others make beautiful and unusual drawing papers, so experiment to find out which you like.

Japanese papers are too delicate for robust drawing and rubbing out. However, the intricate surface textures look stunning under soft pastel or deli-

◀ Expensive papers are not a prerequisite for good drawing. Look around your home – you will probably be able to find brown parcel paper and rough-surfaced card, or other similar recycled materials, to experiment with.

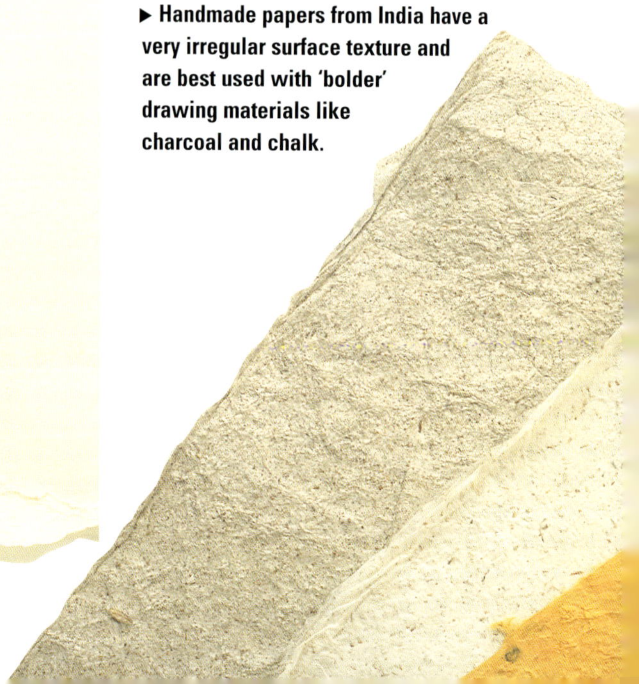

▶ Handmade papers from India have a very irregular surface texture and are best used with 'bolder' drawing materials like charcoal and chalk.

CHOOSING THE RIGHT BACKGROUND

White chalk on black
Chalk isn't only used by teachers on a blackboard – artists also use it to create bold drawings. White chalk glides easily onto black velour paper and makes an obvious impact.

Charcoal stick on gold
Fragile charcoal sticks crumble easily and make a rich dark mark. They look particularly good against the lighter range of backgrounds, such as this gold-coloured sugar paper.

Charcoal pencil on grey
Charcoal pencil also works well on sugar paper. Since the charcoal is compressed, marks made with pencils appear harder, cleaner and less crumbly. This is good for more detailed drawing work.

cate watercolour washes. Why not try painting on them with a soft brush, or even a bamboo brush? Don't forget to leave plenty of empty spaces in the painting so you can see the paper in between the painted colours.

Indian papers

Indian papers are generally tougher than Japanese ones – more like rough watercolour paper or papier maché. Most have a coarse, irregular texture and you can buy them in a range of tones. They are great for pastel, charcoal and chalk, and also for bold watercolour painting. So go ahead and experiment!

▶ There are all sorts of plain or tinted papers available for pastel work. Pastels used lightly will allow the paper surface to show through, giving a broken-colour effect. Pastel pressed firmly into the tooth of the paper will give solid patches of colour.

PASTEL PAPERS

Ingres and Canson Mi-Teintes	These are traditional pastel papers, made in a wide range of colours with just the right surfaces for pastel work. The surfaces are similar, allowing flecks of the paper to show through when colour is applied, but try them both to see which you like best. Both also work well with chalk and charcoal.
Velour papers	A velvety surface is the main attraction of these papers. Pastel colours adhere beautifully, allowing you to create such rich, dense areas of colour that little of the velour paper shows through. Try them also with other drawing materials for a soft, broad effect.
Sansfix papers	These have a fine, slightly gritty finish which holds a lot of colour and allows you to build up quite thick layers of pastel. Experiment using them with other drawing materials too.
Sandpapers	Cabinet paper, flour paper and artists' sand-grain paper are all included in this category. They have a definite gritty tooth which gives a bold, rugged effect to the work. However, these coarse surfaces wear away pastels, chalks, charcoal and pencils surprisingly quickly.

Tinted papers

If you have used only white paper in your work up to now, why not try some of the temptingly coloured papers available in art shops and see how they can change the character of a drawing or painting?

If you use yellow paint or coloured pencil on a red paper, you are likely to end up with orange or with a yellow that has a distinctly orange tinge. Similarly, if you use blue on yellow paper, the result will be green.

In other words, the colour of the paper you are using will show through and directly affect the marks you make. This is why watercolours and other transparent materials are traditionally painted on white paper; the bright whiteness shows through, making the transparent colours clear and vivid.

Only with very opaque materials, such as undiluted gouache or acrylic, will the colour be thick enough to obliterate the effect of the underlying paper.

Mix and match

A huge selection of coloured papers is available, ranging from the lurid and luminous to the sombre and muted. The only way to discover the effect of each type of paper on the various media and different colours is by trial and error. Have a look at some of the pastel papers, including the popular Canson Ingres, Mi-Teintes and Fabriano Ingres. These papers are just as good for coloured pencil and mixed media work as they are for pastels. Also consider sugar paper, which, although fairly flimsy, is good for charcoal or chalk drawings. Coloured tissue paper, while not suitable for drawing and painting on, is excellent for collages and mixed media.

Bear in mind that watercolour and other wet media require sturdy papers, and that pencils and pastels tend not to work as well on very smooth papers as

▼ Different coloured papers can subtly alter the colours of the marks you make on them. The illustration below shows how a yellow shade in various media changes character depending on the paper used.

Coloured pencil

Soft pastel

Watercolour

Gouache

CHOOSING A PAPER COLOUR

Landscape

▶ A warm, pinkish paper contrasts effectively with the blue sky and green grass of this landscape.

▶ The same landscape on a cool, blue paper is less dramatic. Instead, the mood is more tranquil.

Still life

▶ Flecks of a mid brown paper show through the pastel marks in this drawing of an orange. The effect is to enhance the overall warm tones of the picture.

▶ Blue paper gives the subject a different, though equally effective character. It cools the warm orange shades, at the same time toning with the dark shadow and foreground.

they do on those with some texture. But apart from these practical considerations, the best idea is to buy a few samples of different types of coloured paper and have fun experimenting!

Choosing a coloured paper

Whichever medium you are using, the colour of the paper you choose should play a positive role in the picture, complementing the subject. If you have only white paper, you can easily tint it before beginning your painting with a wash of watercolour or gouache, or by lightly applying a layer of pastel colour with the broad edge of the stick. However, a pastel tint is not ideal for detailed work.

A landscape worked mainly in cool shades of green can look good on a cool paper such as blue or grey. However, exactly the same subject will often work equally successfully on a warm orange or brown paper, though the resulting picture will be very different in mood. As you can see from the group of illustrations on this page, the character of a subject is fundamentally affected by your choice of background colour.

Lights and darks

Light colours show up well on dark paper, whereas darker colours are accentuated by a lighter paper. If your subject is mainly dark, with just a few pale areas or highlights, then it makes sense to start off with a dark-toned paper. A moonlit landscape, for example, looks wonderfully dramatic on black or dark blue.

Most of us are familiar with grey sugar paper, which is still standard issue for art classes in many schools and colleges because it is inexpensive. It may have seemed dull at the time, but this shade of paper provides an excellent medium-toned background colour for many drawing and painting materials.

Grey sugar paper is particularly effective for drawings made in chalk and charcoal used together. By starting with a mid-toned background, you can immediately begin work on the tonal aspects of the drawing by establishing the extreme lights and darks, relating each of these to the tone of the grey paper. Use black charcoal for the shadow areas and white chalk for the highlights and other paler areas.

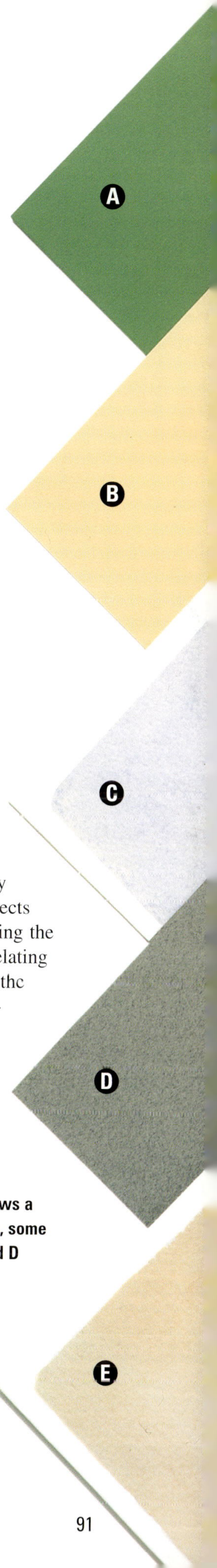

▶ This selection of papers shows a range of light and dark colours, some warm and others cool. A, B and D are examples of Fabriano Ingres paper; C is a white watercolour paper that has been tinted with a layer of pastel, while E is the same paper colour-washed to give an interesting tone.

Thinning oil paints

If used straight from the tube, oil paint is generally too thick. By simply adding solvents – or thinners – to the colours, you can manipulate them more easily.

◄ **Henri Toulouse-Lautrec's works in oil are characterised by the use of very thin paint. In *Woman at her Toilet* (1896), this has allowed him to create subtle glazes, where one thin, transparent mix is laid over another to create wonderful new colours.**

When oil paint is squeezed from the tube, its consistency is thick and buttery. It is too slippery to use unless you are deliberately seeking a chunky, impasto effect or want to apply the colour with a knife.

For most painting purposes, you need to dilute your oil colours, especially if you want to paint details or areas of flat colour. Unlike most other paints, however, oil colours cannot be diluted with water. They must be thinned with a solvent – often called a thinner or a diluent. By far the most popular of all artists' solvents is spirit of turpentine.

Turpentine

Turpentine is obtained from the sap of pine trees, then distilled to form a pure, long-lasting solvent. It has been used for diluting oil paints since they were first developed some 500 years ago.

Always buy double-distilled, or rectified, turpentine, available in small quantities from art shops. The type used by decorators can be slow-drying and may turn yellow with age. Like all spirits, turpentine evaporates when exposed to the air, so pour out only a little at a time and make sure you screw the top back on the bottle properly.

Alternative solvents

If you dislike the smell of turpentine, try the fragrant oil of spike lavender, which is slightly slower-drying. Artists' white spirit, which has a far less pronounced smell than turpentine, is another alternative.

General-purpose white spirit – the sort that is available in hardware shops – is also occasionally used as an inexpensive solvent. However, it can leave a white residue on the dried colours, especially if the paint has been diluted a lot. So it is generally best to keep it only for cleaning brushes and palettes.

Adding oil

If you add solvent to an oil paint, the colours dry more quickly. Unfortunately, they also lose some of their oiliness and as a result the paint surface can look matt and a little dead. This effect is countered quite simply by adding a little extra oil to the paints when you dilute them with a solvent. This restores the gloss and gives the paints a succulent, shiny finish.

There are a number of artists' oils for you to choose from. Depending on the manufacturer, these vary slightly in thickness, colour and speed of drying. The classic purified linseed oil is a good starting point. You might also try bleached linseed oil, which is pale and fairly fast-drying, or poppy oil, which is pale and dries comparatively slowly. Alternatively, try standard linseed oil, which is altogether more viscous.

One of the most traditional oil-painting techniques is to apply the colours 'fat over lean'. In other words, the initial layers of paint should be thin, or lean, with little or no added oil; the final layers should be comparatively oily, or fatty (see below).

Reduce the risk of cracking

The layers can be built up over a number of hours, days or even weeks. When the painting is dry, the top layers of paint will be more flexible than the lower ones and the risk of cracking is reduced. However, if the colour becomes too thick as you build up the layers, the picture surface can become unworkable. In this case, blot off excess paint with newspaper at the end of your painting session. By the next day, the canvas should be dry enough to continue working.

Fat over lean

Try working 'fat over lean' by painting a simple cup and saucer. You will need only turpentine, linseed oil and a few oil colours. Remember, the term 'fat' describes paint that has been mixed with oil to create a shiny, lustrous surface. 'Lean' paint has been diluted with turpentine or another solvent to speed up the drying time. A primed white canvas is not usually the most suitable starting point for an oil painting, so a logical first step is to give the whole canvas a coat of very thin colour. As this is the first layer of colour – a 'lean' layer – dilute the paint with turpentine and add no linseed oil. Linseed oil is added gradually as you build up subsequent layers.

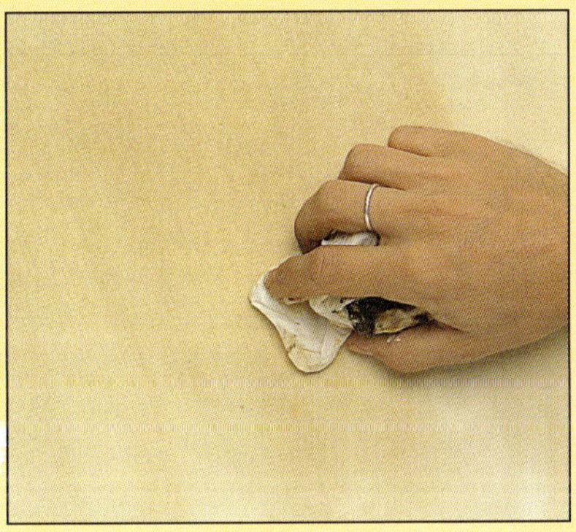

1 ▲ **Start with a wash** Mix up burnt umber with a lot of turpentine to create a very thin colour. Apply it across the whole canvas with a large brush, sponge or soft cloth.

2 ▲ **Introduce a darker wash** Add more burnt umber to your mix and use it to block in the initial dark tones, using a soft brush. No oil is used at this stage.

3 ▲ **Add a touch of oil** Continue to dilute the colour with turpentine, but now add a touch of linseed oil to the mix. The colours should start becoming slightly thicker.

4 ▲ **Gradually add more oil** For the highlights on the cup, increase the thickness and shininess of the paint by mixing the colour with approximately equal quantities of oil and turpentine.

5 ▲ **Use thick, textural paint** Complete the painting by using strokes of thick textural colour mixed with turpentine and oil in a ratio of approximately 3:2.

▲ **Built up layer upon layer, the finished painting has a rich, thick and glossy surface.**

Wash-off techniques

Watercolour or ink applied over white paint can be washed off to reveal striking areas of white in the finished picture.

Two wash-off techniques are shown here – the first suitable for misty and textural effects and the second that creates bold, graphic images similar to those produced by woodcuts.

For the seascape, the artist started by applying white gouache all over the support to prevent subsequent colour washes staining it. This allowed the colour to be lifted off with a brush dipped in water, producing soft areas of white suitable for clouds and mist.

In the boats picture shown here, certain areas are painted in white gouache, then the whole image is covered with black waterproof ink. When soaked with water, the gouache dissolves, taking with it the covering layer of ink. This leaves white areas with an attractive texture created by remaining ink marks.

Water-soluble white

Any thick, water-soluble white paint can be used for these wash-off techniques. Our artist chose gouache simply because that was the material closest to hand. Poster colour or Chinese white watercolour work equally well, although the latter may prove expensive for painting large areas. Acrylic white is not suitable because the paint dries with an impermeable surface that cannot be washed off.

White paint applied to an off-white support will probably show up sufficiently well for you to see what you are doing. However, when working on a pure white support, it is a good idea to tint the paint with a touch of yellow ochre or another colour with a similarly weak tinting strength. This makes the paint visible, but doesn't stain the support.

▼ You don't need specialist equipment to make wash-off paintings. A watercolour set (A), Chinese white or white gouache paint (B) and waterproof Indian ink (C) are all that is required for the initial painting. Water (D) and a sponge (E) or brush will enable you to wash the paint off. For the support, a piece of mountboard (F) will be strong enough to survive the most vigorous of wash-offs.

CLOUDS IN THE SKY, TEXTURE ON THE BEACH

Hazy, atmospheric effects can be created by covering the support with white gouache before applying watercolour. The colour can then be dabbed off in the final stages, as it has not had the chance to stain the support. This technique works best with a rapid, loose application of watercolour. On a highly worked painting, the watercolour might disturb the underlying white gouache, causing the colours to go cloudy. For this picture, you need: a piece of white mountboard, a 25mm (1in) decorator's brush, a 25mm (1in) soft flat brush, white gouache, paper tissue and four watercolours – Payne's grey, ultramarine, alizarin crimson and yellow ochre.

1 ▶ Apply white gouache Dilute white gouache to the consistency of single cream and apply all over the board, using a 25mm (1in) decorator's brush. Work in even, horizontal strokes, keeping the paint as flat as possible – ready for the watercolour to be applied in step 2. Allow to dry.

2 ▲ Paint the sky Change to a 25mm (1in) soft flat brush and wash over the sky with very dilute Payne's grey watercolour mixed with ultramarine. Strengthen the colour towards the horizon.

3 ▲ Brush colour over the beach Add a streak of dilute alizarin crimson to the horizon. Suggest the beach in dilute yellow ochre mixed with a little of the sky colour.

4 ▲ Wipe off paint Add the rocks as short strokes of Payne's grey watercolour. Use a paper tissue to wipe off some of the newly painted beach – this lighter tone gives an impression of wet sand.

5 ▼ Add clean water Wash the brush and apply dabs of clean water to the beach and sky. This dissolves the colour to create patchy white cloud and a pebbly texture.

▼ The wash-off technique used for this seascape has created a delicate effect with plenty of white to lighten the overall tone.

CREATING A WOODCUT EFFECT

For this painting, start with a broad outline drawing in waterproof Indian ink. Then block in cast shadows and other dark areas as solid shapes. When the ink is dry, apply thick white gouache to the exposed areas, deliberately leaving untidy edges along the black lines. These ragged lines help to create the woodcut effect in the finished picture.

Next paint the entire support with waterproof Indian ink. When it is dry, flood the picture with water. This washing off dissolves the white gouache, leaving areas of the support exposed. Elsewhere, the waterproof ink remains intact. Some flecks of black are left behind, even in the gouache areas, giving the image an attractive printed quality. You might feel that the work is complete at this stage. Otherwise, tint the white areas with watercolour as shown here. The result is rather like a stained-glass window.

For this painting, you need a piece of mountboard (or very heavy watercolour paper), two brushes – a No.4 round and a 25mm (1in) decorator's, black waterproof Indian ink, white gouache, a sponge, and ultramarine and yellow ochre watercolours. Note the washing-off process soaks the paper – if the support is too flimsy, it will simply disintegrate.

1 ▼ **Outline the main features** Start by painting a simple, bold outline of the subject, using black waterproof ink and a No.4 round brush. Paint in the shadows and buoys in solid black.

2 ▲ **Fill in with white gouache** Block in the spaces between the outlines with thick white gouache. Work with loose, bold strokes, taking the white sketchily up to the black lines to create untidy edges. Leave streaks of unpainted board (or paper) when blocking in the sky. This deliberate imprecision will produce an attractive textured effect in the finished picture.

3 ▲ **Paint on black ink** When the work is completely dry, start to paint over the entire picture area in waterproof Indian ink, using a 25mm (1in) decorator's brush.

4 ▲ **Cover the paper with the ink** Continue applying the Indian ink until the whole picture is covered in solid black. Allow to dry – this may take a few hours.

5▸ Wet and rub the paper Flood the whole picture with clean water, while at the same time gently rubbing with a brush or sponge to dissolve and remove the areas of white gouache and the black ink covering them.

6▾ Complete the rinsing process Rinse the painting once more to remove excess white gouache and black ink. Allow it to dry.

7▾ Colour the sky Mix a very dilute wash of ultramarine watercolour. Apply this to the sky with the decorator's brush, using broad horizontal strokes.

8▾ Fill in the beach With the same brush, loosely block in the sand with dilute yellow ochre watercolour, taking the colour around the boats.

9▾ Paint the sea Mix a wash of ultramarine darker than the one used for the sky. Brush in the strip of sea.

▾ The finished painting has an attractive grainy appearance where ink marks are left on the sky and beach.

Washing onto watercolour paper

Laying a flat wash onto paper is the first step that most artists take when working with watercolours. Here's how to do it.

Laying a wash onto paper is the starting point for most watercolour paintings. The wash can be flat or graduated (fading in colour towards the top or bottom of the picture) and then serves as the base colour onto which other colours can be applied.

Test the wash first

The wash technique is often used in landscape painting or for large areas of plain sky. Two good tips are to make sure that you mix enough paint to complete the wash, and to test its strength on a piece of scrap paper before you start painting. This is because watercolour dries lighter than it appears when initially applied.

The type of watercolour paper used is important as most lightweight papers require stretching to avoid cockling (see the 'Expert Advice' box, right). The stronger and heavier papers, however, will withstand the wettest of washes and still remain fairly flat. The texture of the paper will also affect the quality of the wash. So the best option for practising laying washes is to use a sheet of cold pressed (or Not) paper heavier than 140lb. See the box on 'Types of paper' below right, for more information on the three main types you can use.

Equipment

Any painting project will only benefit from good organisation, so the starting point will always be to lay out your equipment. For this exercise, make sure that you have a flat (or chisel ended) brush, a jar of clean water with a wide

Laying a flat wash

YOU WILL NEED

- Sheet of NOT 140lb+ paper
- Jar of water
- Mixing palette or dish
- Flat brush
- Watercolour: Cobalt blue

1 ▲ Lightly wet the paper Dip the brush into a jar of clean water and, holding it at arm's length, wet the paper using a series of horizontal and vertical brush strokes. Ensure that all the paper is covered. This allows the paint to flow freely when applied.

2 ► Drag the brush across the paper Leave a minute or two for the water to be absorbed. In the meantime, pour some water into a palette or white saucer and, using a wet brush, mix in some of the cobalt blue paint provided with this issue. Make sure you mix enough paint to complete the wash. Then drag the loaded brush over the top of the paper in a single, smooth, even stroke, applying even pressure all the way along.

3 ► Continue moving downwards At the end of the stroke, lift the brush and repeat the procedure directly underneath – reloading your brush with paint if required and making sure that you leave no gaps between the new brushstroke and the one above. Continue moving down the paper in the same way, maintaining even pressure throughout.

4 ► Leave to dry Despite its initial appearance, the paint will dry to a smooth, even finish. Resist the temptation to work on the wash further.

EXPERT ADVICE
Preventing cockling

Paper lighter than 140lb should generally be 'stretched' before a wash is laid onto it. Otherwise, the wetness on the paper will cause it to contract as it dries, leaving a buckled surface. When this happens, the paper is said to be 'cockled', like the painting shown right.

Full step-by-step instructions for stretching paper will appear in a later issue. Until then, use board or paper heavier than 140lb for your watercolour projects, since these are heavy enough not to need stretching, and will not cockle.

enough neck to accommodate the brush, and your paint all laid out together on one side of the paper. If they are on opposite sides, you will inevitably end up reaching across the paper with a water- or paint-laden brush, which may then drip onto your work. So being prepared pays dividends.

Washing
This wash technique is best practised at arm's length to achieve fluid movement and an even result. You can also use a block to ease the flow of the paint down the paper and to allow the wash to flow smoothly downward without dripping. The resulting wash will initially look rather patchy and untidy, but resist the temptation to fiddle with it, or attempt to re-work it. Just allow the paper to dry naturally and the result will be an even wash.

What next?
Having mastered the basic skills of laying a flat wash, you can try your hand at a graduated wash. This involves increasing or decreasing the intensity of colour towards the top or bottom of the wash, to give a fading effect.

This can be achieved either by adding more water to the paint mixture each time you drag the brush across the paper – or by starting off with a very watery mixture and then adding more paint with each successive application.

▲ A palette is the ideal tool for mixing washes. Clean water is placed in the round wells and colours are then mixed in the flat, slightly sloping sections below.

TYPES OF PAPER

Watercolour paper comes in three main types:

Hot-pressed or Smooth	A textureless paper which is good for pen and ink and for line work
Cold-pressed or Not	A slightly textured general purpose paper, ideal for beginners
Rough	A highly textured paper best suited to vigorous painting techniques

▼ A single streak of watercolour paint running through ten different weights and textures of paper shows clearly how the various paper types react with the paint, and how this affects its appearance.

Working on canvas

Canvas is one of the most satisfying surfaces for oil or acrylic painting because of the way in which it responds to the brush, and it is quite straightforward to prime and stretch it yourself.

Ever since artists first started using oil paints in the fifteenth century, canvas has been the most popular surface to paint on. There is something very special about the way stretched canvas responds to the brush; no other surface matches its springy spontaneity. Unlike rigid supports, the taut fabric 'gives' a little with each dab of colour, and the weave provides a key or 'tooth' to hold the paint. The result is a rich, resonant paint surface.

An added advantage is that canvas is light and easily portable. A finished painting can be removed from its stretcher (see overleaf), rolled up and stored without taking up much space.

Canvas types

Canvas is usually bought in lengths cut off a roll. There is a choice of fabrics, weights, widths and textures to suit your pocket. If you do a lot of painting, it might be worth investing in a whole roll and cutting it up yourself – this works out cheaper in the long run.

Flax canvas is made from raw flax, and is extremely strong and hard wearing. Artist's linen is similarly tough, but is finer and has a more even texture. Both flax canvas and linen canvas are made from the stalks of the flax plant and retain the brownish-grey colour of unbleached linen.

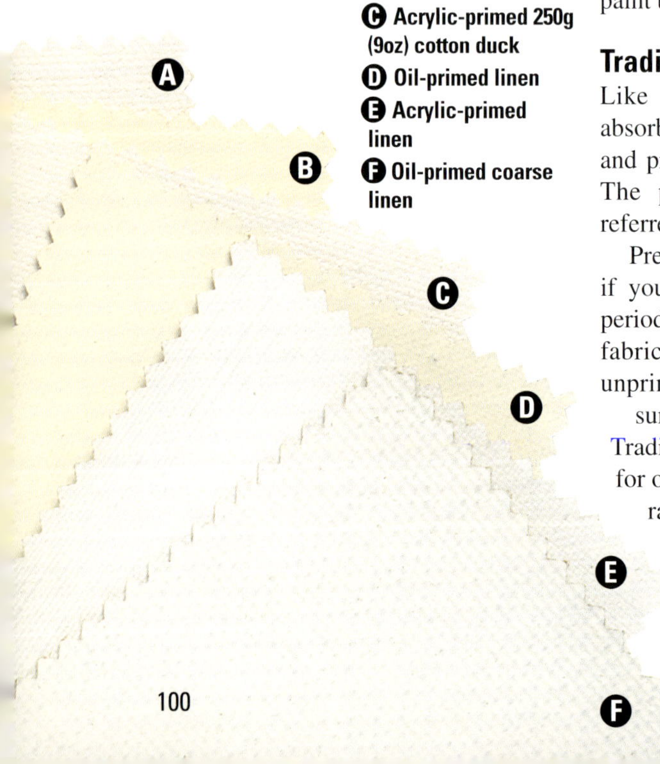

▼Pre-primed canvases are ready to stretch and use without further preparation.

A Acrylic-primed 350g (12oz) cotton duck
B Oil-primed cotton 250g (9oz) cotton duck
C Acrylic-primed 250g (9oz) cotton duck
D Oil-primed linen
E Acrylic-primed linen
F Oil-primed coarse linen

Alternatives to linen

Cotton canvas is a popular cheaper alternative to linen. It is densely woven and creamy-white in colour. Compared with linen, cotton is soft and floppy. It may stretch or shrink depending on the moisture in the atmosphere, so it does not remain taut on the stretcher. Wedges driven into the back of the stretcher will normally solve the problem.

Hessian makes a chunky, unusual painting surface. It is inexpensive, but its loose, open weave absorbs a lot of paint unless it is well sealed and primed.

Traditional priming

Like most fabrics, canvas is very absorbent and must normally be sealed and primed before you can paint on it. The prepared surface is sometimes referred to as a ground.

Preparation is particularly important if you are using oils because, over a period of time, the oil paint will rot the fabric. Acrylics can be used on unprimed canvas, but the absorbent surface will soak up a lot of paint. Traditionally, canvas that is to be used for oil painting is sealed with a coat of rabbit-skin size followed by two or more coats of oil-based white lead primer. More recently, household undercoat is sometimes used instead of lead primer. Rabbit-skin glue has a low adhesive power but it remains flexible when dry, so it will not crack when the canvas is rolled.

Although many artists still like to prepare their canvases in this way, the finished ground is suitable only for oils, not acrylics. Also, mixing the glue and waiting for the glue and primer to dry between coats is time-consuming.

Acrylic primer

This provides a speedy alternative to traditional oil priming. It is the ideal ground for acrylic paints and can also be used with oils. The primer is bright white and can be applied directly to the canvas – there's no need to seal it with rabbit-skin glue first.

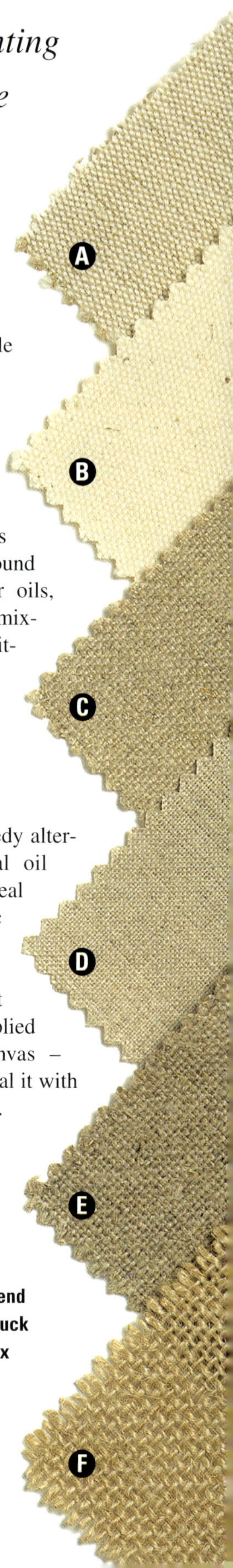

▶This selection of unprimed canvases shows some of the fabrics and weights available.

A Linen and cotton blend
B 500g (18oz) cotton duck
C 370g (13oz) superflax
D Superfine linen
E 350g (12oz) flax
F Fine hessian

Stretching a canvas

If you cannot find a ready-stretched canvas of the size you want, you can stretch and prime your own. You will need wooden stretcher pieces, available in pairs from art shops. Assemble the stretcher by slotting the four wooden stretcher pieces together. Then cut a piece of canvas about 5cm (2in) larger all round than the stretcher.

1 Staple the sides Starting at the centre of a long side, staple the canvas to the stretcher. Pull the canvas across the frame and staple the centre of the opposite side. Repeat on the other two sides. Now staple the canvas on each side of the central staple, working first on one side and then on the other. Repeat all the way round.

2 Staple the back Lay the stretcher face down and staple the canvas to the reverse side of the stretcher. Again, start at the centre of each side and work outwards towards the corners. This gives a neat finish and gives the stretched canvas extra strength.

YOU WILL NEED

- Assembled stretcher
- Piece of canvas to fit over it
- Scissors
- Stapler and staples
- Wooden wedges
- Hammer
- Acrylic gesso
- Small decorating brush

3 Staple the corners Fold the flap of canvas at the corner, making the fold as neat and flat as possible. Staple the canvas in position.

4 Tap in the wedges If there is any slack in the canvas, gently tap the wedges into the slots at the corners of the stretcher. However, do not make the canvas too tight at this stage – the tension can always be adjusted later.

5 Apply acrylic gesso Finally, use a small decorating brush to paint the canvas with two coats of acrylic gesso to prime it. Allow the gesso to dry in between coats.

For a particularly flexible, easy-to-apply ground, try mixing acrylic primer with an equal quantity of acrylic emulsion. Both materials are available from art stores. Acrylic primer is sometimes called acrylic gesso, but take care not to confuse this with real gesso, which is made from chalk and is very inflexible.

Prepared canvases

If you do not want to prepare your own canvas, you can buy a ready-primed length. This can be fixed to a wooden stretcher or taped to a drawing board to make an instant painting surface.

Alternatively, pre-primed canvases stretched over light wooden frames are available in a range of standard sizes. They can be made of linen or cotton duck, and may also contain a proportion of synthetic fibres. Make sure you choose the right texture. Some have a fine grain and are good for detailed work, while others are coarser so that the weave of the canvas may be visible through the paint to produce a more rugged effect on the final painting.

An inexpensive alternative to stretched canvases are canvas-covered boards. These have a good 'tooth' and are available with very fine or slightly coarser surfaces.

A word of warning. Most ready-made canvases and canvas-covered boards are primed with an acrylic ground, and therefore suitable for use with either acrylic or oil paints. Others are primed with an oil-based primer, and should be used only with oil paints. It is important not to use acrylics on an oil-primed canvas because the oily surface will eventually cause the paints to peel and flake. Always read the manufacturer's label to make sure you are getting the right surface.

Preparing panels

Rigid supports for oil and acrylic painting can be made from a range of readily available materials including wood, plywood and MDF (medium density fibreboard). The secret of success lies in the preparation.

Until the time of Giotto (*c.* 1267-1337), only wood was considered to be a suitable support for easel painting (that is, work intended to be framed and hung on a wall). However, as easel paintings increased in size, the limitations and technical complications of wood became increasingly obvious. Wood is heavy, and to make a large panel several planks have to be joined together and battened to prevent warping. The surface then has to be sized and given a finish that will accept the paint.

Painters began to use fabric stretched on to a framework, as this was lighter than wood. Although fabric widths were narrow, they could be joined together to make large supports. Today, artists can choose between a flexible, yielding canvas which is alive to the touch of the brush, or a rigid panel which is firm and can be given a smooth surface. Both types of support have their appeal and advantages; what you choose is entirely a matter of personal preference. Frans Hals (1582/3-1666), for example, sometimes chose canvas and sometimes wood, irrespective of the size of the painting.

Panels must be prepared before they can be painted on, and the nature of the preparation will depend on the medium. Paint bonds to a surface through a combination of its own adhesive qualities and the surface's absorbency and texture. A good oil support must have sufficient roughness or 'tooth' to hold the paint, but

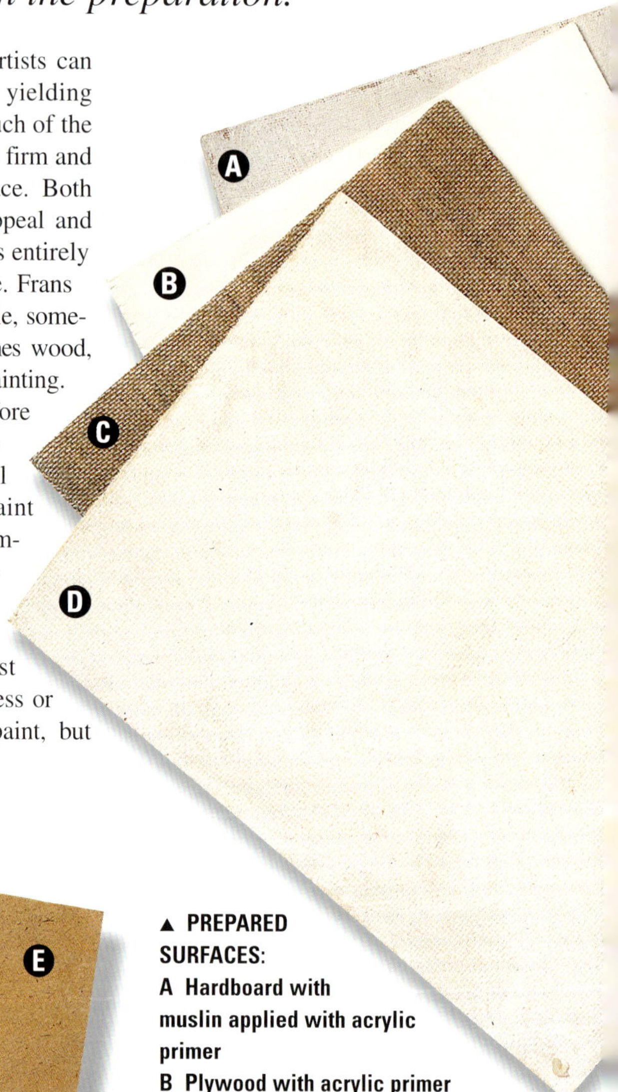

▲ **PREPARED SURFACES:**
A Hardboard with muslin applied with acrylic primer
B Plywood with acrylic primer
C Plywood with scrim applied with acrylic medium
D Hardboard, rough side, sealed with acrylic primer

◄ **UNTREATED SURFACES:**
A Hardboard, rough side
B Cardboard
C Medium density fibreboard
D Plywood
E Hardboard, smooth side

must not absorb the oil. If the oil is leached out, the pigment loses its bond and eventually the paint flakes off.

Acrylic differs from oil in that it is not necessary to treat the support before you paint on it. Acrylic can be used on a wider range of supports than any other medium. Nevertheless, it is advisable to have a painting surface that provides a key for the paint. Surfaces must be oil-free, as oil and water are incompatible.

Types of support

If you like painting on panels, you can easily prepare them yourself. Wood, especially poplar, is traditional, but the cheapest and most readily available materials are cardboard, plywood, hardboard and MDF.

Wood If you use wood, make sure it is well seasoned to minimise warping. Battening the back and sizing both sides will also help to stabilise it.

Card Available in different weights and colours, this is ideal for small to medium-sized paintings. It can be used untreated for acrylic paintings, but because it is very absorbent the image will have a chalky appearance that can be quite appealing. If you are using card for oils, it must be sealed with size, an acrylic medium or an acrylic primer. As some cards are an attractive warm mid-tone in colour, you might want to incorporate the colour of the card in your work. In that case, you should seal it with acrylic medium or with PVA.

Hardboard This is a popular support. It is relatively cheap and available in large sheets which can be cut down to the size you need – most timber merchants can be persuaded to supply it cut to your requirements. It has two different surfaces: one side is rough, resembling woven cloth, and the other is smooth. Hardboard is a tough material, but the edges are brittle and larger sizes may need protective battens at the back.

Applying fabric to a panel

YOU WILL NEED

- Wooden panel
- Scrim
- Scissors
- Acrylic medium
- Decorator's brush

Any panel can be given a woven textile finish by gluing a fabric such as muslin or scrim to the painting surface. This is a cheap and quick way of creating a very acceptable support, similar in texture to canvas.

1 ▲ **Cut the scrim** Lay the panel on the scrim and cut the fabric to size, allowing a 5cm (2in) overlap all round.

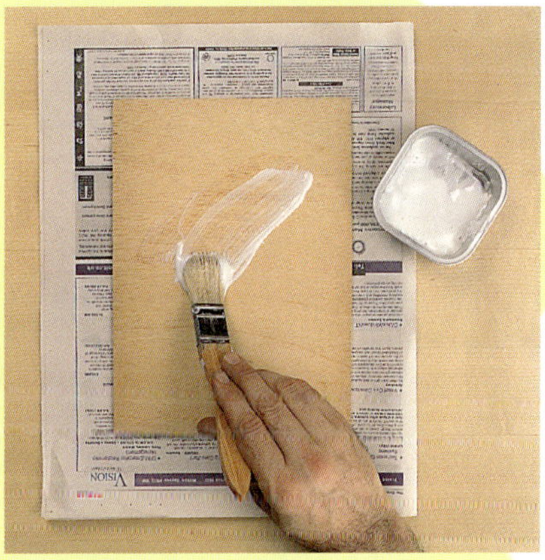

2 ▲ **Apply acrylic medium to the board** Cover the work surface with newspaper, lay the board on the paper and apply a coat of acrylic medium.

3 ▲ **Apply the scrim** While the acrylic medium is still damp, lay the fabric over the board. Smooth it out gently and then apply another coat of acrylic medium, brushing it into the fabric.

4 ▲ **Turn the board** Turn the board over and balance it on a container so that the wet surface is lifted clear of the work surface.

5 ▲ **Fold the fabric** Fold back the edges of the fabric and paste down with acrylic medium. Make neat folds at the corners. Seal the back of the panel with medium to prevent warping.

Using gesso

Gesso is a ground made of gypsum or chalk mixed with water or size to provide a dense, brilliantly white surface traditionally used for egg tempera or some types of oil painting. Now, acrylic gesso primer is widely available. It combines the matt white quality of a true gesso, but is less absorbent, and it comes ready-mixed so preparing a board is much simpler. It can also be used on canvas and paper.

YOU WILL NEED

- Panel
- Acrylic gesso primer
- Decorator's brush
- Sandpaper and block
- Acrylic medium

1 ▲ Applying the first coat Cover the work surface with newspaper, lay the board on top and apply a coat of acrylic gesso with the brush. Work across the board. Leave to dry.

2 ▲ Sand the board When the board is completely dry, lightly sand the gessoed surface with medium grade sandpaper wrapped around a block.

3 ▲ Apply a second coat of gesso Apply more gesso but work at right angles to the direction of the first application. Leave to dry and sand lightly. Two coats should be sufficient for most purposes. If you wish to build up a smooth, brilliant surface, apply more coats, sanding between each one and changing the direction of application each time.

▲ Hans Holbein the Younger painted *Lady with a Squirrel and a Starling* in oil on an oak panel nearly 500 years ago.

Like canvas, hardboard needs to be sealed. Start by roughening the surface of the smooth side to give it a key, then size both sides of the board – this prevents warping. When it is dry, apply primer (an oil primer for oils, or an acrylic primer for oil or acrylic) to the side you intend to use.

The rough side of hardboard is absorbent and difficult to work, and will wear out your brushes. Several coats of primer will create a good seal and will smooth the surface so that it is easier to work on and kinder to your brushes.

MDF In the lighter weights, MDF makes a good painting surface. It is very rigid and smooth and should be roughened with sandpaper to give it a key before a primer is applied.

Plywood Readily available in different thicknesses, its surface resembles wood, and it feels more natural than MDF or hardboard. Like the other panel materials, it should be sized so that the surface is sealed. It can then be used with or without a ground. Treat both sides to prevent warping and batten large sizes.

Sealing and preparing a ground

You can seal the support without obscuring the colour by covering the surface with glue size or one of the acrylic mediums, or alternatively PVA, which is sold in DIY shops as an adhesive and sealer. As these treatments are transparent, they will not obliterate the colour and will retain most of the texture of the surface.

If you prefer to start working on a crisp, white ground, you can apply a white primer over the top of the size. You can also apply several coats of acrylic primer directly to the support, or even use emulsion paint. A half-and-half mixture of emulsion paint and acrylic medium or PVA will also make a excellent primer.

Acrylic gesso produces a softer and chalkier surface, which is generally more absorbent than ordinary primers.

◀ Scrim (left) is a coarse, loosely woven fabric, dark in colour and made from linen or a cotton-linen mix. Muslin (near left) is a fine, loosely woven cotton fabric, creamy white in colour.

Tricks of the trade

Art materials are expensive – but with a little care you can extend the life of your equipment and even rescue materials that have seen better days.

To keep your costs as low as possible but maintain the quality of your painting, it really pays to look after and restore equipment – and, indeed, improvise tools if necessary. The handy tips that follow will help you extend the life of your materials.

IMPROVISED EASEL

If you enjoy working on big canvases but don't have the space or cash for a large easel, metal shelving with adjustable brackets provides a neat and flexible alternative.

Fix the metal uprights to the wall a suitable width apart, then insert the brackets at the required height. Alternatively, a pair of angled brackets screwed to the wall are fine if you tend to work on the same size of canvas and don't need to adjust the height.

New life for old brushes

Brushes last longer if you clean and dry them properly. However, you can often rescue neglected brushes with a little special treatment. A brush that has lost its condition can be washed in warm, soapy water and then treated with hair or fabric conditioner. Rinse off the product, reshape the brush with your fingers and leave it to dry.

If stray hairs are sticking out, or the fibres are misshapen, you can sometimes restore the shape by suspending the brush in a jar of water for a few days. Push the brush handle through thin card and rest this on the rim of the jar so that the brush hangs in the water without resting on its bristles.

If this process fails to restore the brush to its intended shape, take a little gum arabic between your fingertips and smooth the bristles into shape. Leave to dry. Hair gel can also be used to reshape an unruly brush. Whatever you use, rinse the brush carefully before you next use it.

Another good way to reshape a brush is to wrap toilet paper around the wet bristles. The paper contracts as it dries, pulling the bristles into shape.

Flattening dented canvases

Remove bulges from a canvas by dampening the back. As it dries, the cotton or linen fibres shrink to give a smooth surface. If this does not work, you might need to apply heat. Dampen the canvas, then steam off the water by holding a hot iron just above the surface (test first on a scrap snipped from the edge). Try not to put the iron directly on the canvas, as this will stretch it.

▲ **Dampen the canvas** Lay the canvas face down on a surface protected by a blanket. Dampen with a brush, cloth or sponge and leave to dry.

▲ **Heat the canvas** To eradicate serious dents, dampen the back then hold a hot iron over the area. The rapid drying will flatten the canvas.

Dried-on acrylics

Acrylic paint dries quickly and is then almost impossible to remove from a brush. It is a good idea to use two jars of water for acrylic painting – one for cleaning brushes, the other for diluting the paint. Add a drop of washing-up liquid to the cleaning water to prevent paint accumulating on the brush.

If you leave your brushes too long and the acrylic paint has dried on the bristles, soak them in methylated spirit for up to 12 hours, then wash them under running water.

Dealing with masking fluid

Masking fluid is particularly tough on brushes. Apply it with old brushes (kept in a separate jar) or use a dip pen or a stick. If you rub a brush on household soap before you dip it into masking fluid, it will be easier to clean.

Making your paints last

To prevent your paints from drying out, always replace the cap on the tube when you have finished with a colour. Wipe the threads at the top of the tube clean before replacing the cap – a little lubricating jelly or glycerine applied to the threads will prevent the cap from sticking. If a cap does stick, a brisk tap with a heavy object is sometimes all that is needed to loosen it. A strip of sandpaper wrapped around the cap will improve your grip.

To loosen caps on watercolour or gouache paint tubes, run hot water over the neck. If that fails to loosen them, soak the tube upside down in hot water overnight. For oil paint tubes, substitute turpentine or white spirit for hot water.

You can also use a pair of pliers or a jar opener to shift unyielding caps. Alternatively, wedge the cap between the edge of the door and the jamb – pull the door towards you so that it acts as a vice, then twist the paint tube.

Reviving dried-out paint

Always squeeze tubes of paint from the bottom upwards, as this keeps the paint together and prevents it drying out too quickly. Get the last drop of paint out of a tube by laying it on a flat surface and scraping a palette knife along its length from bottom to top. However, if a tube of paint has dried out, you can sometimes access usable paint at the base of the tube by piercing it with a pin. Stick masking tape over the hole to seal it.

For dried-out watercolour or gouache, cut the end off the tube and add a few drops of water through the newly made opening. Leave the water to work its way into the paint, then mix it into a paste. Alternatively, cut the tube open and use the paint as pan colour.

CLEANING AND CARING FOR BRUSHES

Get into the habit of cleaning your brushes after every session. Wipe excess paint on tissue, a rag or an old telephone directory – tear off the top page after you have wiped your brush on it, leaving a clean sheet ready for next time. Rinse the brush in the correct solvent – turpentine or white spirit for oils, water for watercolour, gouache and acrylic. Next, hold it under cold running water, rub it over a bar of plain household soap or solid brush cleaner, then work up a lather. Rinse under the tap until the water runs clear.

Flick your wrist to remove excess water. If necessary, shape the brush with your fingers, then leave to dry flat.

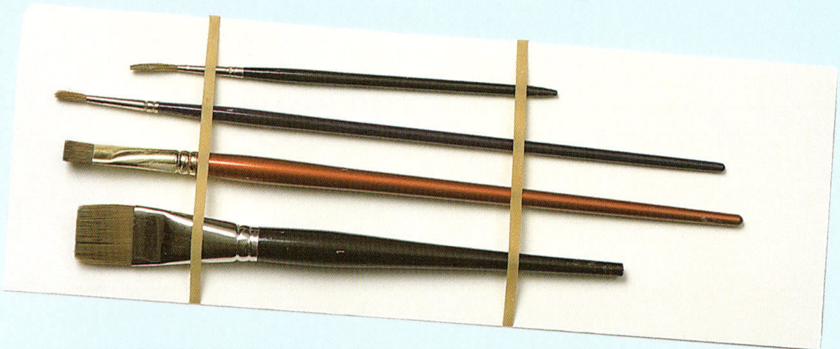

▲ TRANSPORTING BRUSHES
Make sure you protect your brushes when you're on the move. Cut a piece of stiff card wide enough to accommodate your collection of brushes side by side and longer than your biggest brush. Stretch two elastic bands around the card, one at the top and one at the bottom. Insert your brushes under the elastic bands.

◄ USING A BRUSH WASHER
A brush washer is a useful piece of equipment that allows brushes to be left in solvent without damaging their bristles. Slot the brushes into the coiled handle so that their bristles are suspended above the base. Fill the bottom of the container with enough solvent to cover the bristles. The dissolved pigment from the bristles settles at the bottom of the pot – some designs have a filter so that the pigment can be removed and the solvent re-used.

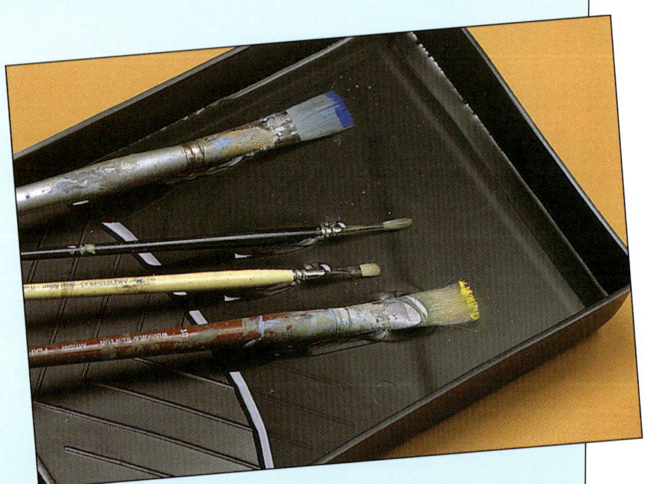

▲ KEEPING ACRYLIC BRUSHES WORKABLE
Acrylic paint dries quickly and, once dry, is almost impossible to remove. During a painting session, keep brushes workable by laying them in a shallow dish of water, such as a decorator's roller tray – rest the handles on the rim to avoid pressure on the bristles.

HOME-MADE PALETTES

Palettes can be improvised very easily. Use old white plates and saucers for watercolour and gouache. Mix larger washes in yoghurt pots.

You can make palettes for acrylics and oil paints from offcuts of wood, ply or laminates. Seal timber or ply with several layers of varnish or paint first. Glass makes an excellent mixing surface, too, as it is smooth and easy to clean.

Acrylic paint dries quickly on the palette and, once dry, cannot be re-wetted. You can make a moisture-retaining palette (see below) that works in the same way as those available from art suppliers.

If you are planning a long break from your painting, cover watercolours, acrylics or oils with cling film and put the palette in the freezer. Allow it to thaw for about an hour before you plan to use it.

▲ USING A GLASS PALETTE
A sheet of glass makes a good palette. Make sure the glass has a bevelled edge so that you don't cut yourself. Put a sheet of paper underneath, in a shade that matches your ground so you can judge how the mixes will appear when applied. Lay out the colours in an orderly way – here they are organised warm to cool, with white at the end.

▲ MOIST PALETTE FOR ACRYLICS
To keep acrylic paint workable for longer, make a moisture-retaining palette. Line the base of a shallow plastic tray with wet blotting paper. Lay a sheet of greaseproof paper on top to form the mixing surface.

▼ COVERING WITH CLING FILM
If you have unused acrylics left at the end of a session, cover the tray with cling film to keep the paints moist.

▲ SPRAYING YOUR PALETTE
Use a plant sprayer to mist the palette if watercolour or acrylic paints are drying out. You can also spray the support to keep the paint surface wet and workable, but don't overdo it or the paint will run.

PASTELS

When working in pastel, lay out your sticks on a sheet of corrugated card, arranged in colour groups. The hollows will prevent them rolling off the work surface.

If different coloured pastels are stored together, the colours rub off on each other and the sticks begin to look grubby. To remove surface dirt, put the pastels in a jar of rice and shake.

▲ ORGANISING PASTELS ON CARD
Corrugated card prevents the pastels you are using from getting mixed up – and they won't roll off the work surface.

▼ CLEANING PASTEL STICKS
Rice in a small jar will brighten dirty pastel sticks. Put the pastels in the jar and shake for about a minute or so.

CREATING COLOUR

Nothing brings a painting alive like a splash of bold colour and even the most subdued tones can lend depth and dimension to your work. This chapter begins with a description of the role of colour and the importance of balance, before going on to describe techniqes for mixing paints and using colour for painting complex subjects such as skies and skin.

Pigments and paints

We take our paints very much for granted these days. But not so long ago paint was a highly precious and sometimes significant material.

◀ The cave paintings at Lascaux, dating back to *c.* 14,000 BC, were created with just three basic colours – manganese (soot) plus red ochre and yellow ochre. The red and yellow ochre vary in hue and tone, as the earth was collected from different sources.

Today's artists have a fabulous selection of colours at their disposal in an ever-growing range of mediums. We are spoilt for choice and can select a colour for its exact hue, for its transparency or opacity and for its reliability or brilliance.

However, not so long ago, an artist's life was much more challenging. It was 1842 before the first paint was produced in a tube and indeed commercial manufacture of paints began only in the 1700s. Before then, the raw ingredients for making them were not only expensive but also often difficult to obtain.

Some of these ingredients might have graced any witch's book of spells: the root of the madder plant; the leaves of the plant *Indigofera tinctoria* from India; the crushed bodies of tiny beetles; ink sacs from cuttlefish or squid; arsenic; mercury; and even pieces of Egyptian mummies. Other ingredients are less surprising, including coloured earths and rocks, although in some cases the latter could be expensive.

The earliest paints we know of (which are still some of the most reliable around) are based on pigments found in the earth. At Lascaux in France, cave paintings made using earth colours have been found, which are thought to be over 15,000 years old. Some of these paintings are deep underground and difficult to reach, so it is clear that they were not simply 'domestic' decorations. It is likely that they had spiritual or magical importance, and it is possible that the colours chosen had special significance.

Certainly as civilisation evolved, the colours that became most prized were those not readily available as earth colours. For instance, the first true violet (that is, not made by mixing red and blue pigments together) was Tyrian purple, made from the murex – a Mediterranean whelk. It was so expensive and so prestigious that only the fabulously rich, such as Roman Emperors, could afford it or were permitted to wear clothes dyed in it.

Costly colours

Perhaps because of its immense value, purple was seen as an emblem of heaven in Classical times and this idea continued up to the early Middle Ages. Later, two other colours took over. These were the ones that came on either side of purple in colour-mixing terms – violet-blue ultramarine on the one hand,

▶ The first paintings were created with earth colours, pigments that occur naturally in soil and clay. They include (left to right) yellow ochre, raw umber and red ochre.

and scarlet on the other. These, too, were extremely costly.

Ultramarine was made from lapis lazuli, a mineral that could be obtained only from the East. To create pigment from this rock was both difficult and time-consuming. This meant that it carried a huge price tag. A lot of ultramarine in a painting indicated an extremely wealthy patron. (Until the 1800s, the patron usually provided the most expensive and brightest pigments.) Money was certainly no object, then, when it came to commissioning the *Wilton Diptych* (far right) by an unknown artist. In this painting, ultramarine was used lavishly on the Virgin and the angels – this would have cost more even than the textured gold that was used as the background colour. This panel would have been worth a fortune in terms of materials alone, not to mention the value of its superb workmanship.

If you look at Classical mosaics and medieval paintings, you will see that ultramarine and other blues weren't the only major colours. Blue's chief rival was red, associated with life-giving blood and vigour, and the sacrifice made by martyrs. To add to its importance, a

▶ Today, scarlet, ultramarine and purple are produced cheaply by artificial means – but in the past, they were prized pigments. Scarlet was made from the cochineal insect, purple from the murex (a Mediterranean whelk), and ultramarine from the mineral lapis lazuli.

▼ In Enguerrand Quarton's *The Coronation of the Virgin* (1453), the eye is drawn to the figures of Christ and God in brilliant scarlet and the Virgin with her ultramarine robes.

▲ The *Wilton Diptych* (1395-9) was an altarpiece commissioned by King Richard II (shown kneeling on the left panel). The lavish use of ultramarine was an indication of not only Richard's spiritual devotion but also his enormous wealth.

▶ On a wing panel of the *Isenheimer Altarpiece* (*c.* 1515), German painter Mathis Grünewald shows the Resurrection of Christ. He emerges from his tomb, robed in red and with a reddish halo, the colour suggesting martyrdom and the energy of life.

particular red, made from the shells of the cochineal insect, was fabulously expensive. Indeed, the Aztecs used the dried bodies of female cochineal insects as tribute money. In Europe, during the Middle Ages, cochineal was used to make an expensive woollen cloth called 'scarlet'. And in 1467 Pope Paul II decreed that cardinals' robes should be dyed cochineal red rather than purple.

Colour of Christ's robes

It wasn't just cardinals who appeared in red – artists began depicting the clothing of Christ (especially in Resurrection scenes) and the martyred saints in this colour. It represents not only the blood of their martyrdom but also, again, the wealth of the patron who commissioned the work. Once you start to look for these bright colours in medieval paintings, they seem to leap out at you everywhere, drawing your eyes to the important figures – just as they would have done to contemporary viewers.

So what of the other colours? Bright yellows (rather than yellow ochres) were prized by the artist, especially to show the effects of sunlight. Until the 1300s, the best yellow was made from orpiment, a rare and extremely volatile mineral. This was superseded by yellow made from tin. In the 1700s, Indian yellow was made from the urine of cows fed only on mango leaves. However, it was replaced by chrome yellow in the 1800s, as cows didn't take to the diet!

Green could be obtained from the earth colour terre verte, but in the Middle Ages artists began using a vivid green made from copper, turpentine and bitumen. Occasionally, green was mixed (at great expense) from lapis lazuli ultramarine and a tin-based yellow.

The power of colour

Colour is the painter's most versatile tool. It has the power to excite, control space, create atmosphere, express emotion and represent the illusion of reality.

▲ **Franz Marc's (1880-1916) *The Yellow Cow*, complete with blue patches and red foreground, makes the point that colour can be used to great effect expressively, as well as realistically.**

It was not until after the invention of the camera in the mid 19th century that artists recognised light as the prime factor in the way we see colour in the world around us. Before then, the 'local' colour was most often taken as the first consideration: sky is blue, grass is green – but is it that simple? If you look at the sky on a sunny day, it's much bluer overhead than it is on the horizon, where not only is it paler, it also has some yellow in it. Colour is dependent upon light, and we need to understand how it works.

The theory of colour

White light (sunlight), passing through a raindrop, splits into the colours of the rainbow spectrum. When these are fanned into a circle to make the colour wheel (see above, right), the principles of colour mixing can be seen. Red, yellow and blue are known as the primary colours: they are pure colours and cannot be mixed from any others. The other three (orange, green and violet), are called secondary colours because they are formed by an even mixture of their two immediate primary neighbours in the circle.

This can be extended to make tertiary colours by mixing any of the primaries with either of its secondary neighbours. For example, blue and green will produce a colour generally called turquoise. In fact mixed colours are often named

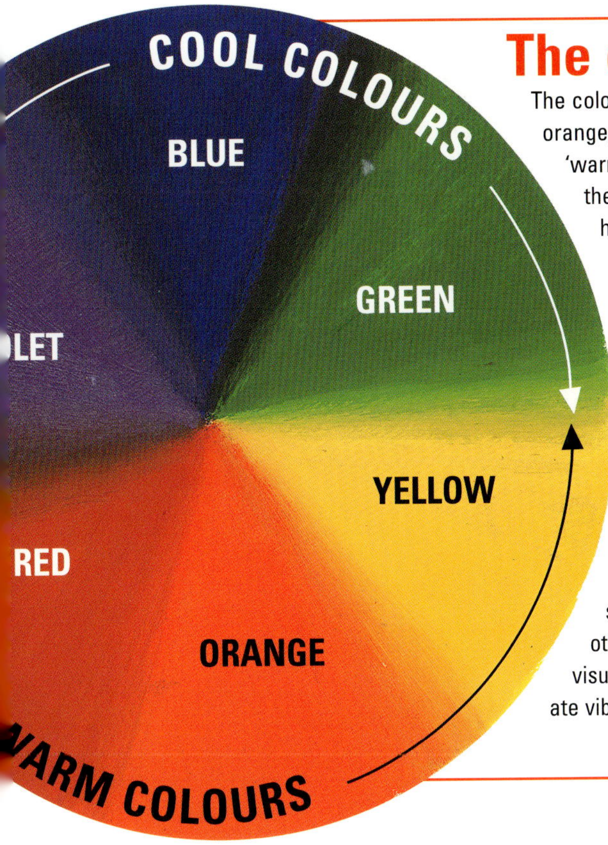

The colour wheel

The colours in one half of the wheel (red, orange, yellow) are specified as 'warm' and appear to advance from the page, while those in the other half (blue, violet and green) are 'cool' and seem to recede. This factor can be used in landscape painting for example, where trees in the distance can be made to recede by making them more blue-green than those in the foreground.

Colours opposite each other in the circle are described as complementary. Placed side by side they react against each other and fight to dominate the visual space. Artists use this to create vibrancy and contrast in pictures.

A BASIC PALETTE

There are certain colours which, when mixed together, can form the backbone of your art. The colours listed below are all good 'mixers' in any medium. If you have viridian, two blues and two yellows, you can mix most greens you are likely to need. Practise mixing pairs of all the colours without white.

Be careful when using black on its own, since it can 'deaden' a painting if overdone (remember, it is not really a colour!). Raw umber mixed with ultramarine is a good substitute.

after the gemstones or flowers which they resemble and these are the sort of labels you will see on tubes of paint in an art shop.

Black and white

You will notice that the circle does not contain either black or white. When light falls on an object, the object will absorb some of its wavelengths and bounce back others which make up the colour we see. Black soaks them all up and white bounces them all back, so black is the absence of any colour and white is all the colours rolled into one.

Brown

And what of brown? An object seen as brown is absorbing very few of the spectrum of light wavelengths (just those at each end of the rainbow) and bouncing all the others back. By mixing the three primaries together or the three secondaries in different proportions, a whole range of browns can be made.

Warm versus cool

Colour temperature is also part of the equation (see the colour wheel), while colour can also be said to be opaque or transparent, dark or light, translucent or impasto, flat or textured, matt or gloss, vibrant or dull.

▸ Claude Monet (1840-1926) used colour to convey passing impressions of light and atmosphere – in this case a group of waterlilies which seem to dissolve into the water around them.

Keeping your balance

Composition is a vitally important factor in picture making. Take a closer look here at both the traditional and a revolutionary approach.

One of the major difficulties with painting has always been how to make the flat surface look three-dimensional. After Albrecht Dürer had clarified the laws of perspective by constructing a simple machine to demonstrate them in about 1525, possibilities for artists to push deeper into the picture space opened up considerably.

Rectangular construction

Before then, it was generally accepted that a picture would be set in quite a shallow space, with the main characters in the story occupying the foreground as actors do on a stage. Paintings were constructed within a rectangle and were planned rather like an architectural design to give stability and a sense of order. Like architecture, painting was a 'high art' and in Renaissance times was also closely linked with science.

Leonardo da Vinci was probably the last great practitioner of both art and science, but all artists of that period applied some mathematical principles to their compositions. The one who best illustrates the artists' serious concern with geometric composition, was Piero della Francesca, who died in 1492.

Long and short division

When we come to explore the geometry of composition further, on page 209, we will see how symmetry can be avoided and a rectangle 'balanced' in a different way by applying the rules of the Golden Section. Piero's tempera painting of *The Flagellation of Christ* (right) has a very

▲ Renaissance artist, Piero della Francesca, used various geometric devices to construct his painting *The Flagellation of Christ*.

GEOMETRY

Piero della Francesca relied heavily on the triangle to keep the viewer's attention within the rectangle of the painting, pulling the eye in from the corners. If you look closely at *The Resurrection* (below right), you will see that he uses an equilateral triangle standing rigidly on its base at the bottom of the picture with its tip at Christ's chin, between his forked beard. He repeats the triangle shape several times to reinforce the structure. You can see a second triangle resting on the top of the tomb and slanting up through the outside of the arms, with its tip at the top of the head. A third triangle has the same base, but the right-hand diagonal starts at the back of the neck and through the ear of the soldier with the lance and follows the line of Christ's knee, inner arm and a point directly between the eyes, to peak at the tip of the flagpole.

In addition, if you imagine where Christ's standing foot would be behind the tomb, this spot is the tip of a number of upside-down triangles formed by the legs and arms of the soldiers. Can you see, too, another, 'suggested' triangle, the three points of which are all outside the painting itself? Starting from somewhere above the top of the flagpole, the right-hand side of the triangle can be followed down through the sky and the line of the trees; on the left, the edge of the little hill points the way down.

Stability is added to the whole piece by the strong verticals, like the tree trunks, and the horizontals. These give symmetry to the composition.

▲ **Marc Chagall's (1887–1985) *The Violet Cockerel* is a circular composition. People and animals float illogically around the focal point formed by the clown's bunch of flowers.**

◄ **Chagall's *Village in Blue* also has a basically circular structure, but the composition is balanced by two strong right-angled triangles, at top left and bottom right.**

unusual composition. By placing a strong vertical shape (the column) in the centre, Piero divides the painting into two separate pictures – the one on the right in close up and the one on the left in the middle distance. But notice how he positions the figure of Christ just over a third of the way in, following the rules of the Golden Section (page 209).

Slanting lines

In addition, Piero deploys his usual triangular construction (as shown on the previous page), using the slanting lines of the ceiling and roof to lead you into the action. The two halves of the picture are pulled together by the long horizontal divisions linking certain features, sometimes in a rather contrived way (look at the hems on the cloaks of the men on the right).

Contrast

This painting is also an excellent example of the use of 'contrast' as an important tool in composition, in this case using light and dark tones. These are not evenly distributed, but they balance each other overall.

Partly because of the influence of photography on art, the last hundred years have seen artists deliberately breaking the 'rules' of geometric composition. Marc Chagall, for example, painted fantasy pictures with no logical proportions or scale. Everything is topsy-turvy and people, animals and objects often swirl around a central focal point, as though the picture isn't big enough to contain them. In *Village In Blue* (above), they randomly collide with the edge of the canvas or extend beyond it.

Many of Chagall's paintings rely on the geometric structure of a circle. Notice, too, in *Village in Blue* the strong, balancing right-angled triangles at top left (along the line of the mule's neck) and bottom right (slanting down through the roof tops to the baby's groin).

Holding attention

Whereas Piero's compositions produced static images, Chagall was concerned with vitality. Although outrageous, his zany compositions hold your attention and that, remember, is the basic aim.

ADDING AND SUBTRACTING

Try your hand at 'live' composition. Collect together lots of different objects. Try to vary their shapes as much as possible – tall and short, thin and fat, regular (geometric) and irregular – to achieve good contrast.

YOU WILL NEED

- Large sheet of white cartridge paper
- Charcoal or a very soft pencil
- Putty rubber

1 **Arrange the still life** On a table top, arrange a still life of four or five of the objects. Start by trying to organise them into a triangular composition, using a tall object for the apex. Begin drawing, working quickly with long strokes of the arm to emphasise angles and directions, particularly following the lines of perspective.

2 **Change your composition** After about ten minutes, take one object away and add two more. By drawing over the top and rubbing out afterwards, you can watch and control your changing composition.

3 **Repeat the process** Repeat the changeover of objects every ten minutes or so to keep widening the possible options.

The process in this exercise is more important than the end product. Think about verticals, horizontals, diagonals and other geometric connections in the still life arrangements you put together. Try, also, to incorporate the rules of the Golden Section (page 209), and above all, keep your balance!

Pick and mix

▼ **Seurat's (1859-91) pointillist technique can be seen in his painting *Young Woman Powdering Herself*. Tiny dots of paint mingle to create myriad subtle colours.**

Developing skills in colour mixing takes practice and familiarity with your preferred medium, but it is vital if you want to interpret a subject effectively.

One of the most important concepts to grasp when learning to paint is that the tonal range of the paint palette is nowhere near as broad as that of natural light. The brightest and lightest colour you can put down on paper is pure white, but this can never match the intensity and brightness of white light. There is a similar challenge when trying to match the depth of dark tones and colours.

Working order

In practical terms, if you are painting in oils, it is best to start with the darker colours and gradually work up to the lighter ones. Keep in mind that the brightest object in the picture cannot be brighter than pure white.

If you are using watercolours, remember that the lightest areas are created by leaving the paper unpainted. In contrast to oils, you should put in the darkest tones and colours last.

Mix and match

Mixing colour to try and match what you see is a subtle process. You will need to observe your subject carefully and make small adjustments to represent the 'local' colour accurately. As you build up your picture, you might want to mix colours that are tonally lighter or darker, warmer or cooler, more intense or softer and 'muted'. You might also choose to make the colours more transparent or opaque.

Grass greens

Try mixing some colours to represent a stretch of grass. Mix a green using ultramarine and cadmium yellow as a base. For the shadowed areas, you could add more blue to lower the tone and make a cooler green. Or, for a warmer shade, you could add one of the umbers.

Where the grass is lighter, you might mix in some lemon yellow and perhaps a little white to raise the tone; but you may find that the colour has now lost its 'greenness'. In this case, it may be better to start again, using viridian mixed with cadmium yellow or lemon yellow as an alternative base.

With two yellows and two blues plus viridian, there are countless combinations that make a basic green. Even so, if you are working with a limited palette, it is not always possible to mix a perfect match. Even if you added another twenty colours, some shades might still not be achievable. The best you can aim for is what is called a 'visual equivalent' – a range of tones and shades of a given colour (sometimes described as colour 'values') that is broadly parallel to what you see in reality.

Optical mixing

There are further ways of creating different colours, other than adding extra shades to a basic colour. The most

▲ **Degas (1834-1917) relied on optical mixing in many of his pastels, particularly in his nude studies. In this painting, *After the Bath*, the pastel marks in different colours merge visually to produce the convincing flesh tones.**

FINDING THE PERFECT MATCH

YOU WILL NEED

- Piece of A3 cartridge paper
- Scraps of plain coloured papers including two white
- Glue
- 11 acrylic paints colours as suggested for basic palette (page 113)

This exercise suggests how you can practise mixing paints to match specific colours as exactly as possible. Use the range of eleven paints shown in the basic palette illustrated on page 113.

Collect together some scraps of different coloured papers, preferably plain rather than patterned. Make sure you include two or three scraps torn from printed paper such as wrapping paper, postcards or magazines. Other papers you could use include sugar paper, copying paper or letter paper. A couple of your pieces of paper should be in different shades of white. Acrylic paint is the best medium to use for this exercise. You can use oil paints, but the drying time will slow down your progress.

1 **Make a collage** Tear or cut some random shapes from your selection of papers and stick them down on the left-hand side of an A3 sheet to make a small, abstract collage. Overlap the shapes, but don't make the collage too complicated.

2 **Match the colours** Now paint a version of the collage on the right-hand side of the paper, trying to match the colours (and shapes) you see as exactly as you can. Notice that pastel shades are much easier to match than raw, pure colours, especially those produced by printing inks. Remember, too, that the appearance of colours can be changed by those placed next to them.

notable of these is to place small spots of different colours close together, so that when viewed from a distance they are seen by the eye as a single colour – an effect called 'optical mixing'.

This technique, generally known as 'pointillism', was developed by Georges Seurat, a nineteenth-century French painter. He and his followers used only the colours of the spectrum plus white. By carefully intermingling painted dots of these colours, they found that they could create innumerable colours and tones, provided that the viewer stood an appropriate distance away so that the optical mixing process could take place.

Limited technique

The pointillist technique has its limitations. If it is used for a small painting, the dots have to be very tiny so the desired effect is achieved when the painting is viewed close-up. Also, being a rather 'scientific' approach, it is not particularly expressive or personal.

Glazing and scumbling

Paint used thinly can be transparent, allowing the colours underneath to show through. This enables another type of optical mixing, called 'glazing', to take place. Dark colours are usually laid over lighter ones once they are dry (for example, blue can be laid over yellow to make green). The results are less easy to control than with direct mixing, but it is worth practising the technique to see the effects that can be achieved.

The opposite of glazing is 'scumbling'. Here, an opaque colour (usually containing some white) is put over a darker one in broken patches by rolling the brush. This allows the darker colour to show through and optically mix with the lighter one.

▼ **Camille Pissarro (1831-1903), like some of the other Impressionists, began using small brush strokes of various colours placed next to each other in an attempt to make them more vibrant. This is shown to great effect in his oil painting, *The Flood at Eragny*.**

Mixing orange

In the first of three sections covering the secondary colours, we look at the secrets behind rendering a variety of oranges.

The basic rules of colour mixing are taught in primary school. There, painstakingly scribbling one coloured pencil over another, we discovered that red and yellow make orange. Easy!

As orange is a secondary colour, it can be mixed very simply by combining the two primary colours next to it on the colour wheel – red and yellow. In terms of paint, the equivalents of these primaries are cadmium red and cadmium yellow.

The range of oranges

However, cadmium red and cadmium yellow alone will probably not provide you with all the oranges needed for painting a wide range of subjects. Instead, you should experiment with the many other reds and yellows available to the artist.

We tend to associate orange with the bright, acidic colour of the fruit – but think also of the variety of mellow tints in autumn leaves or the earthy colours of sand and brickwork. As this still life arrangement shows, 'orange' is a very general label used to describe a wide range of colours.

Experimental mixing

Depending on the brand and type of paint, there are up to 20 yellows on a manufacturer's colour chart. Counting the earth colours, the yellows include lemon, cadmium yellow, chrome yellow, aurora, aureolin, Naples yellow and Indian yellow, as well as yellow ochre and raw sienna. The range of reds is equally wide and includes cadmium red, vermilion, scarlet, rose madder, permanent rose, alizarin, Venetian red, Mars red and Indian red.

In theory, by combining every available yellow with every available red, you could have a palette of hundreds of

▶ The oranges in this watercolour came from cadmium yellow, yellow ochre, Naples yellow, cadmium red, cadmium scarlet and alizarin crimson plus two bought colours – chrome orange and cadmium orange. Sepia and burnt sienna helped darken the cast shadows and top.

Cadmium yellow + alizarin crimson

Cadmium orange + Naples yellow

Yellow ochre + burnt sienna

Cadmium orange + cadmium red

different oranges at your fingertips. In reality, many of these mixes are so similar that you can't differentiate between them. And as no artist is likely to need such a range of oranges, confine your mixing experiments to the yellows and reds normally on your palette.

Practical mixtures

On the working palette of almost any painter you will find at least two or three reds and two or three yellows. Typically, these will be: a bright yellow, usually cadmium; an earthy yellow such as yellow ochre or raw sienna; and a cooler colour, for instance lemon. In the painting on the left, the artist chose Naples as the cooler yellow because it is very effective at neutralising, or 'knocking back', a strong red or orange.

The same palette will probably also contain cadmium red and a cool red such as alizarin crimson. You might also add a third red that falls somewhere between them in colour temperature – for example, cadmium scarlet. A warm earth colour, such as Venetian red, Indian red or burnt sienna, is also useful.

Note that by varying the proportions of any mixture you will get a different result. For example, cadmium red and cadmium yellow will produce a range of results from yellowish-orange to deep reddish-orange.

Bought colours

In addition to those colours you can mix yourself, there are also a few manufactured oranges. The most common are cadmium and chrome orange, both of which are strong and bright. The former is slightly lighter but considered to be more permanent.

A bought orange is by no means essential. However, it can also provide a consistent starting point for certain standard mixtures. For example, portrait and figure painters commonly use orange mixed with white as a pale flesh tone.

Note that mixing bright yellow with bright red sometimes produces a slightly duller orange than you would expect. To avoid this, try to choose pigments with a degree of natural transparency. For example, yellow mixed with alizarin crimson will give you a brighter orange than when mixed with cadmium red, which is a more opaque pigment.

Mixing green

By mixing and modifying the manufacturers' greens it is possible to expand your palette well beyond the range available otherwise.

For many artists – especially those interested in the natural world – green is probably the most important colour on the palette. Rural landscapes, flowers and plants, as well as many still-life subjects, call for a variety of greens.

A common misconception

However, the great versatility of the colour green is often underestimated. Beginners sometimes believe that, because green is mixed from blue and yellow, all things green must therefore be painted from equal mixtures of these two colours.

Many first attempts at landscape painting are disappointing for this reason – simply because the artist has failed to distinguish between the different greens in the subject.

Experiment first

One way to overcome this difficulty is to experiment with green mixtures before starting to paint. Look at the subject and pick out as many different greens as you can. Where there are highlights and shadows on a green area, take note of the light and dark tones these create.

Try your hand at mixing the greens you have detected on a separate sheet of paper. The process will initially be one of trial and error, but you will be surprised at the extraordinary range that can be achieved by mixing and modifying the colours on a very limited palette.

Mixing greens

Start by exploring the possibilities of a pair of colours, and see how many different shades of green you can get. For instance, by varying the proportions of ultramarine and cadmium lemon, you can obtain colours ranging from lime green to deep blue-green. Repeat the experiment, substituting yellow ochre for lemon yellow, and you will create an equally varied range extending from golden green to deep olive.

Modifying a green

Bought greens are also useful – in this fruit-and-vegetable still life, the artist made full use of them. However, they can be very strident – so more often than not you'll need to modify them with other colours. Again, it is useful to experiment and to extend your repertoire before

▶ Although it's possible to obtain greens by mixing blues and yellows, it's often best to use bought greens and, where necessary, modify these with other colours.

Payne's grey + sap green

Payne's grey + terre verte

Emerald green

painting. Choose a strong shade, such as emerald, viridian or sap green, and make some test samples. Modify the tone by adding varying amounts of a neutral colour such as raw umber or Payne's grey. This will give you a choice of rich and interesting dark greens. Avoid using black as this can deaden the colour.

Alternatively, any green can be modified or toned down by adding a little of its complementary – red. Try using different reds in varying quantities to produce a range of muted greens and neutrals.

Bought greens

Five manufactured greens were used in this painting. If you have not used these pigments before, now is the opportunity to try out the new colours.

- **Emerald green** is more brilliant than any green you could mix yourself. It is useful for capturing man-made colours, such as the bright green band around the plate here. The clear emerald stands out beautifully from the natural greens of the fruits and vegetables.
- **Terre verte** is the oldest known green. Made from natural earth pigments, it works well when painting vegetation and other organic forms. Here, it is used with a little ultramarine for the blue-green broccoli. The table top and shadows are painted in a mixture of terre verte and Payne's grey to create a cool, neutral and unobtrusive background.
- **Olive green** varies depending on the manufacturer, but it is generally a muted natural green, good for foliage and vegetation. Here, it is used with plenty of water to put a glaze on the shadowed side of the rosy apple.
- **Viridian** is very powerful and needs careful handling. It can easily take over and dominate your picture. Used in small quantities and modified by other colours, it is a useful ingredient in mixtures. Otherwise, viridian is best restricted to specific areas. Here, it is mixed with varying amounts of water for the light, medium and dark tones of green on the leaves of the leek.
- **Sap green** is a warm, leafy green and is often used for painting grass and foliage, especially in spring. Here, it is mixed with cadmium lemon for the green apple and with Payne's grey for the dark green pepper.

Mixing purple

Discover how to create rich variations on a theme by mixing bought purples with blues, reds and neutrals.

Purple is rare in nature. The earliest purple pigment came from the shells of the 'purpura', a large whelk found on the shores of the Mediterranean. The Phoenicians are reputed to have ground several million purpura shells to make enough purple to dye their emperor's clothes. The colour they used was known as 'royal purple' and it is still produced today.

Nowadays, purple is a far more accessible colour, but even today real purple pigments are comparatively few in number. The majority of manufactured purples and violets are actually combinations of existing blues and reds.

Purple mixtures

Many artists find it unnecessary to buy ready-mixed purple. Instead, they prefer to make their own by mixing various blues and reds to get the colour they need. Fortunately, it is possible to mix a range of good purples yourself. The brightest of these are achieved by using a cool red, such as alizarin crimson, rose madder or magenta. The addition of white to these mixtures will give various shades of mauve and violet.

If you have ever tried to mix purple using cadmium red, you will know that the result is not a bright colour at all, but a muted brownish-purple. This is because cadmium red contains yellow, which gives the mixture a brown bias.

Mix your own

To discover the potential of the colours on your basic palette, try making some simple two-colour mixtures. Start with alizarin crimson and ultramarine, combining these colours in equal proportions. The result will be a strong, bright purple.

By varying the proportions of the ultramarine and alizarin crimson in the mixture, you can then go on to produce a range of purples with either a red or a blue bias.

Do some more tests, this time substituting cerulean blue for ultramarine. Because cerulean is a cool, pale blue, the resulting purple will be less bright and slightly more opaque.

It is worth repeating similar experiments, using a number of different blues and reds. The resulting mixtures will

▶ The purples in this still life include bought colours used alone and mixed with reds, blues and neutrals (such as Payne's grey or raw umber). Don't forget to try mixing red and blue as well – such as the alizarin crimson and Prussian blue used here.

Winsor violet + Payne's grey

Winsor violet + phthalo blue

Mauve

Winsor violet + raw umber

Winsor violet

Cadmium scarlet + violet carmine

Purple madder alizarin + Winsor violet

Alizarin crimson + Prussian blue

vary enormously and not all of them will be purple. Some will be brown or muddy grey. Only by trial and error is it possible to have control over your palette and the colours it can produce.

Shadow colours

Purple is frequently used for painting shadows. If you look carefully at those that initially appear to be grey or brown, you will notice that they often contain traces of purple and violet. In this watercolour still life, the thrown shadows are mixed from the purples and violets used on the fruit and vegetables, toned down with neutral colours, such as Payne's grey or raw umber.

You can try mixing your own shadow colours by adding raw umber, Payne's grey or another neutral to any of the purples and violets below. Adding a little of their complementary colour, yellow, can also tone down purple and violet.

Bought purples

Our artist chose four manufactured purples for this still life, modifying these to acquire all the colours needed for painting the fruit and vegetables:

- **Mauve** may have a red or blue bias, depending on the manufacturer. The mauve used for the plate in this painting has a definite red tinge and stands out distinctly from the other colours. It is used here as a dilute wash.
- **Winsor violet** is a transparent colour with a powerful staining capacity. A little goes a long way, so use it sparingly. It is shown here unmixed; modified with Payne's grey and phthalo blue to obtain cool purples; and mixed with raw umber to create the neutral tone of the table top.
- **Purple madder alizarin** is a rich natural colour somewhere between brown and purple. It is popular with landscape artists for painting the warm tones of foliage and trees. Purple madder alizarin is mixed with a little Winsor violet for the dark shadow on the persimmon fruit.
- **Violet carmine** is a clear, transparent purple, used here with cadmium scarlet to depict the cool orange-violet of the persimmon fruit.

Cobalt violet is another bought purple you could try. It is not used here but it provides an attractive warmish purple that cannot be mixed from other colours.

▲ **This 1871 painting by James Abbott McNeill Whistler (1834-1903) is often called *Portrait of the Artist's Mother*, but Whistler actually gave it the title *Arrangement in Grey and Black No.1*. He explores the many subtle shades within his chosen limited range, and at the same time produces an unusual but moving portrait.**

Mixing greys

You might think that grey is simply a mixture of black and white, but you'll find that greys are actually much more subtle than that.

Making grey is not just a matter of mixing black and white. A painting with this type of grey in it would become lifeless because the grey would really be a tone, not a colour. This is valid in a monochrome work where only black and white are used, but for colour painting you will be dealing with a more exciting range of greys.

So what exactly is grey? It is important to remember that black is not a colour, but the absence of colour – in other words, the absence of light. So a grey object should be described as 'dark white' rather than 'light black', because you can't actually see black.

This concept is easier to understand if you look at some white objects placed in strong natural light or against a white window frame. Away from the light, the shadowed areas could be described as grey, and on a curved form it is immediately noticeable that there is more than one shade of grey. In addition, because the white colours are likely to be

► In *Eleven a.m.* by Edward Hopper (1882-1967), dark and mid-toned greys on the walls and furnishings of this interior contrast with the pale grey shadows on the white skin of the naked woman. The overall greyness of the room contributes to the atmosphere of solitude in the painting.

slightly different, you will see that there is also more than one *colour* of grey. This variety of grey colours might be exaggerated by colours reflected from the surroundings and the colour of the light source. Grey shadows are similarly affected (see page 132-133). So, if you were trying to paint all these possible greys, you would struggle to be accurate using only black and white.

Mixing greys

Distinguishing subtle colour changes (hues) in greys takes practice, and a little colour theory might help here. Each of the primary colours (red, blue and yellow) is neutralised by its complementary colour (green, orange and violet). If you mix a primary colour with its complementary in varying quantities, shades of brown and grey will emerge.

Try the exercise on the right to experiment with mixing a range of greys using various combinations of warm and cool blues and reds. Once you have tried this, do the same exercise using blue and yellow pairs instead of blue and red pairs – this will provide a range of greens, the cool and warm primary mixes giving 'greyer' greens. Adding a

MIXING GREYS

Try the following experiment on a white painting surface, using oils or acrylic paint. Mix two small dabs of each pair of primary colours listed below, then mix in small touches of each of the grey-making yellows in the last column to make warm and cool greys.

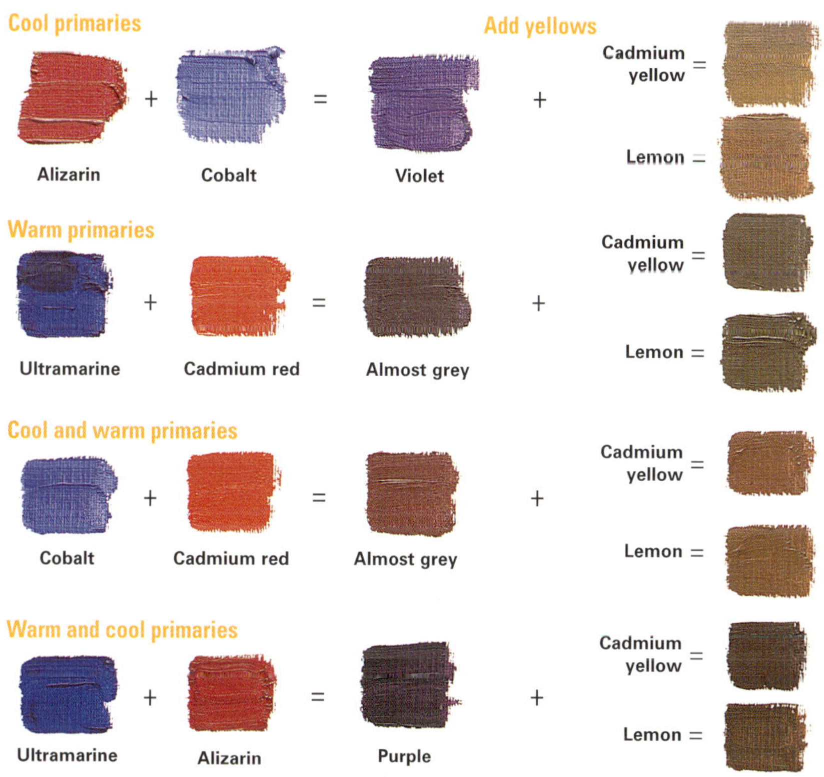

little extra of either of the two blues (warm or cold) to any of the above colour combinations will add to their 'greyness'. You should be able to make at least eight discernably different greys, from warm brownish greys through the more neutral green-greys to cool blue-violet greys.

Tones

The addition of white will, of course, give lighter shades of each of these greys. To darken them, you don't need to use black – try adding a mix of raw umber (and/or burnt umber) and ultramarine or viridian. This will affect the colour of the grey as well as the tone, but more greys will be discovered! Greys are very useful in painting landscapes, which often have more green-greys in them than actual greens. Notice, too, how often greys occur in interiors.

Exploring a range of greys

Gather together a range of white and perhaps a few grey objects. Choose some different whites – enamel, for example, is usually bluer than china, which tends to be more creamy in colour.

YOU WILL NEED

Canvas board at least 40 x 50cm (16 x 20in)

Medium-sized round brush

Oil or acrylic paints

1 **Set up a still life** Place the items on white, grey or even black paper against a white painted wall in a strong light by a window.

2 **Make a painting** Look hard at the objects to work out the colour bias of the different greys – are they greenish, blueish or pinkish? Start painting, using the pure colour greys you discovered in the mixing exercise opposite. Then add white or darker colours (no black) to adjust the tones.

3 **Discover the greys** When the painting is dry, take a strip of white paper and make half a dozen holes in it about 1cm (⅜in) across and 5cm (2in) apart. Move this around over the surface of the painting and you'll discover how many different colours of grey you have made.

▼ The Italian painter Georgio Morandi (1890-1964) exploits the variations of the colour grey in his series of mystical still life paintings – below is *Still Life* (1946). The soft neutral hues give a feeling of tranquillity.

White on white

Drawing white objects against a white background will help you to develop your skill in using shading to render shape and volume.

This all-white still life may seem a daunting prospect at first, but you will find it a worthwhile exercise in both observation and the use of tone. It is important that the objects you are painting are strongly lit from one side so that they cast dark shadows in a single direction only; this simplifies the composition and allows the white flowers and china objects to stand out against the background.

Softer, subtler shadows on the rounded objects themselves convey their shape and also differentiate them from the white fabric backdrop.

Grading shadows

You will discover how to give a sense of depth to your picture by grading the shadows from dark – in the folds of the cloth behind the vase and on the leaves of the tulips – to light in the foreground. Accurately judging the density of the shading will help your composition by making the china objects 'sit' realistically on the horizontal surface.

You will find darker shadows can be drawn most successfully with a soft 4B graphite pencil. You should switch to a B pencil for finer details, such as the tulip petals.

Negative shapes

By shading the background you create dark positive shapes, which form light negative ones in front of them. You will find the final effect is much more convincingly three-dimensional than if you give each object a hard black outline.

▲ In this white-on-white still life the artist has used graduated shading to render the curved surfaces of the china objects and the soft folds of the draped fabric. The dramatic side lighting casts strong shadows against which the white objects stand out well.

YOU WILL NEED

- Sheet of cartridge paper
- Graphite pencils: 4B and B
- Putty rubber

► It's worth making a couple of preliminary thumbnail sketches to decide on the best format for your picture. Here, the artist has chosen a landscape image to show more of the fabric folds, which help to balance the composition.

FIRST STEPS

1 ▲ **Sketch in the shapes** Lightly sketch in outlines of the teapot, vase and jug to establish their positions in relation to each other. Use light lines to indicate the edges of the shadow areas and the shapes of the tulips. Use the 4B pencil, which is easy to rub out, as these lines will be removed later.

2 ▲ **Start the shadows** Next look carefully at the objects to see where the strongest shadows fall. Start blocking these in, using the side of the 4B pencil lead to give a dark, soft effect. Begin with the area behind the teapot, then render the shadows cast by the flowers and the fabric folds.

3 ▶ **Fill in the shadows** Continue filling in the background shadows. Using the tip of the pencil, draw the shadow made by the teapot with soft, even hatching strokes, then fill in the dark area between the vase and jug. Hold your pencil well away from the lead tip so that you can move your hand freely.

EXPERT ADVICE
Sharpening your pencils

It is best to use a craft knife rather than a pencil sharpener to sharpen your drawing pencils. In this way not only will you make a sharp tip but you can bare a long expanse of lead and use the side of it for shading.

HOW TO DEVELOP THE DRAWING

Pause to look at your drawing so far: all the elements are in place and the relative areas of light and dark have been indicated. Notice how the background shadows have created the outlines of the china objects as negative shapes. Now you can go on to work on the details.

4 ▲ **Shade the objects** Start shading the objects themselves to render their rounded surfaces. Change to the B pencil, as you want this shading to be lighter and finer than the background shadows. To achieve a straight edge for the shadow on the vase, mask off the left edge with a piece of paper while shading. This will leave a narrow white strip of unmarked paper, representing the band of light (reflected from the white fabric) on the edge of the vase.

5 ▼ Strengthen the shadows Add shading to the teapot and jug, making this stronger on the left, furthest from the light source, to give the objects a realistically rounded appearance. Change back to the 4B pencil and continue defining the jug by strengthening the shadow around it.

6 ▶ Draw the leaves Now start working on the tulips. Begin with the leaves: parts of them are tonally darker than the background shadows, so shade these more heavily.

7 ▼ Adjust the balance of tones Strengthen the background shadow behind the teapot lid. Whenever you change one element in your picture, always stop to look at the whole composition, to make sure the relationship of tones and shapes is still harmonious.

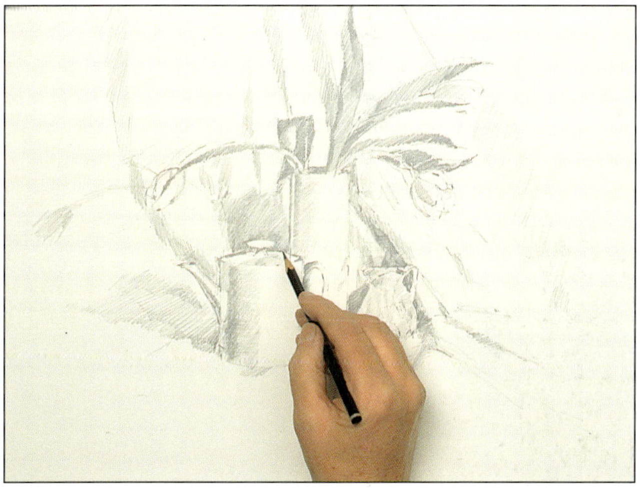

8 ▲ Draw the flowers Draw the flower heads with the B pencil to achieve more delicate shading. Remember to keep your pencil well sharpened so that you have a fine point to work with.

9 ▲ Shade in the folds Finally, add a little more shading to the shadows in the folds of the fabric to diffuse the edges and give them a gently rounded shape, remembering to use the edge of your pencil. This completes the picture, but if you feel you would like to develop it further, you could draw some more of the softly folded fabric.

A FEW STEPS FURTHER

You can extend your drawing by adding more folds to the foreground and to the right of the picture. This will help frame the objects and make a pleasing composition. It will also help to define the horizontal surface on which the china objects stand, locating them in space and giving them extra solidity.

10 ▲ Add more folds Add shading to represent the folds in the fabric in the foreground. Use the 4B pencil, but remember to keep the shading very light as the shadows are much paler in this area than in the background.

11 ▲ Enlarge the picture area Extend the picture to the right by adding shading to show where the folds of fabric 'break' from the vertical to the horizontal plane. This will help to develop the perspective of your picture.

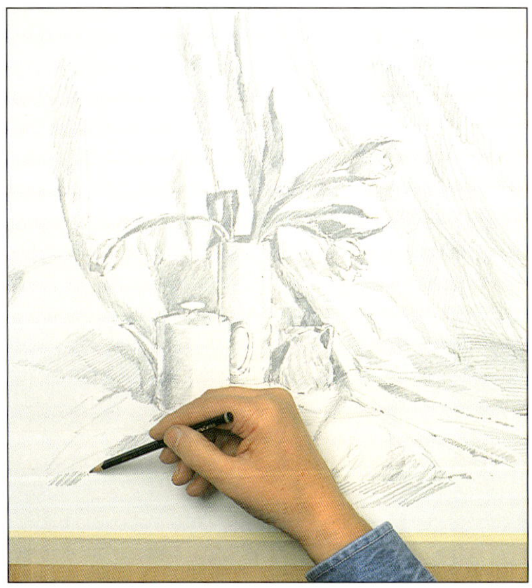

12 ▲ Indicate the table edge Continue to develop the folds to the right of the picture. Next add a line of shading along the bottom of the picture to indicate where the fabric falls over the edge of the table. This will help define the edge of the picture and enhance its three-dimensional effect.

TROUBLE SHOOTER

CORRECTING HIGHLIGHTS WITH A PUTTY RUBBER

The lightest tones in this drawing are created by letting the white paper show through. If you shade over an area and then decide it should have a highlight, use a putty rubber to erase the pencil marks. One of the advantages of this type of eraser is that it can be moulded to a fine point, enabling you to make adjustments very accurately.

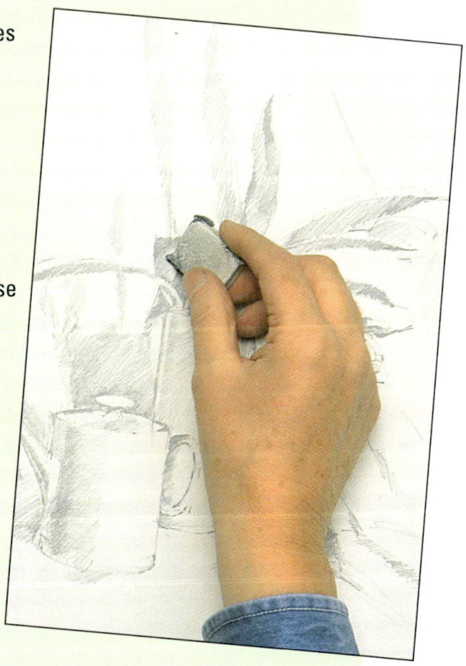

13 ◄ **'Frame' the picture** Use the putty rubber to remove any of the early construction lines that are still visible and clean up the paper. Now the picture is finished, you can 'frame' it by drawing a pencil line to confirm the composition and define the area you are including. This line would be the guide for a mount if you wanted to mount and frame your picture. Note that the artist has deliberately cut off the shadow of the flower-head on the left and some of the folds on the far right. You do not have to include every element of the picture; often you can improve the composition by cropping off details at the edges.

THE FINISHED PICTURE

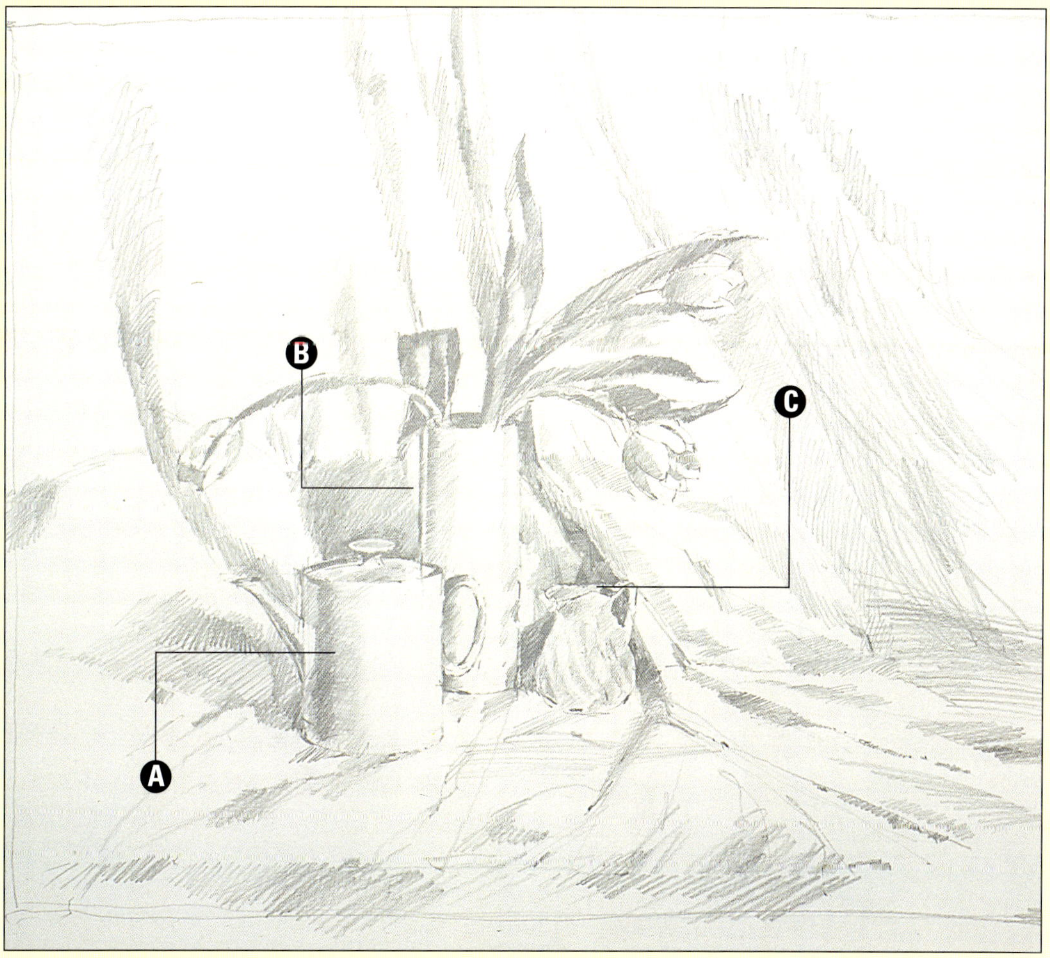

A Curved surface
Graduated shading was used on the side of the teapot furthest from the light source to convey the curved surface.

B Sharp shadows
Shading over a piece of paper has given a sharp, straight edge to the shadow on the left of the vase.

C Dense shading
The 4B pencil was used for the densest shading to indicate the darkest areas of shadow.

Colour in shadows

Shadows are rarely black or solid. They are full of complex colour and light reflected from surrounding surfaces.

When you look carefully at shadows, you will generally find that they are neither black nor opaque. Their tone and colour, and the quality of their edges, vary depending on the direction and intensity of the light source. The more you study shadows, the more varied, nebulous and complex they appear. While some are crisply defined and velvety dark, others are vibrant and suffused with luminous colour, or barely discernable at all.

In painting you will come across two types of shadow: cast shadow and shading. A cast shadow is the area of darkness projected by an object, either on to the surface it is sitting on, or on to the other objects and surfaces nearby. Shading is the area of darkness on an opaque object that you can see on the side facing away from the light source.

Graded shading

The gradations of shading around an object help us to understand and model its form, while cast shadows are useful in painting because they define the surface on which an object is placed. In landscape painting, shadows provide clues to the position of the sun, the time of day and even the season of the year.

In the nineteenth century, there was an awakening of interest in the theory of colour. The Director of Dyeing at the

Gobelins tapestry workshop near Paris, Michel-Eugène Chevreul (1786-1889), discovered two phenomena involving complementary colours – simultaneous contrast and successive contrast. These effects are concerned with the ways in which different colours affect each other when placed side by side.

Impressionist shadows

The Impressionists painted outdoors, working directly from the subject. They sought to create a spontaneous and authentic rendering of the world by carefully observing and replicating the effect of natural light on objects.

They noticed how colours appeared to 'dance' from one area to another as they were reflected from adjacent surfaces. With an understanding of Chevreul's theories, they were able to see that the

◄ Twelve of Monet's haystack studies show a winter setting. In *Haystacks: Snow Effect* (1891) he has painted cool blue shadows, creating a chilly scene in spite of the warmer tones of the sun-tinged snow.

▲ **In *Haystacks at Sunset, Frosty Weather* (1891) Monet has created a scene that is suffused with a rosy glow from the setting sun; the dappled shadows in the foreground are a soft grey.**

complementary colour of an object was present in its shadow, together with reflected colours. By including the complementary, the Impressionists were able to enliven their shadows so that they became as vibrant as other parts of the painting. Shadows in Impressionist paintings are complex areas of broken and layered colour. Their luminosity mirrors the complexity of natural light.

Snow scenes

Coloured shadows are a particularly important feature of Impressionist paintings of sunlit snow scenes. The colour in these shadows can be very complex indeed, including several different tones, reflections from nearby objects and the reflected blue of the sky. The German romantic poet, Johann Wolfgang Goethe (1749-1832) published a book entitled *The Theory of Colour*, in which he describes the ever-changing colours of shadows on snow: 'During the day, owing to the yellowish hue of snow, shadows tending to violet had already been observable; these might now be pronounced decidedly blue, as the illuminated parts exhibited a yellow deepening to orange. But as the sun was about to set, and the rays began to diffuse a most beautiful red colour over the scene around me, the shadow colour changed to a green, in lightness to be compared to a sea-green, in beauty to the green of the emerald.'

In summer landscapes, Impressionists used purplish-reds for the shadows of trees, and muted violets for the shadows of rocks or shadows falling across dusty roads. The artist Claude Monet (1840-1926) explored the colour of light and shadows in his series paintings. The first of these was the *Haystacks* or *Grain Stacks* series, which he began in 1890.

Monet would go out to paint in the early morning or just before sunset, taking paints, easels and several partially completed canvases, often carrying his equipment in a wheelbarrow. He would work first on one canvas, then on another as the light changed, finding the canvas that most resembled the scene in front of him. In this way, he was able to record precise shifts of light and tone, and subtle nuances of colour throughout the day and through the seasons. He was trying 'to convey the weather, the atmosphere and the general mood'.

You can use the discoveries of Monet and his fellow Impressionists in your own work. When painting a subject, study the shadows with care, looking for reflected colour and for the complementaries in them. Try exaggerating these phenomena to add vigour to your work.

Shadows in art

- There are no shadows or gradations of tone in ancient Egyptian wall paintings or on Greek vase painting.
- Leonardo da Vinci (1452-1519) disapproved of harsh shadows, exploiting a technique known as *sfumato* to achieve subtle transitions between one tone or colour and another. He made analytical drawings of light falling on objects to aid his understanding of shadows.
- In the seventeenth century, Caravaggio (1573-1610) and his followers favoured stark realism and the heightened drama of sharply defined shadows
- Cast shadows were often used by the Old Masters to create optical illusions. By carefully rendering the shadows on columns and niches, they were able to deceive the viewer into thinking that they were seeing a three-dimensional surface.
- In Japanese art, shadows were usually ignored because they interfered with the clarity of the image and the narrative.
- In the nineteenth century, the Fauves dispensed with shadow and shading in order to to focus on pure colour and decorative surface.
- The Cubists deliberately distorted and exaggerated shadows to create an ambiguous image.

Colours for skies

When you've perfected the sky, your whole landscape will come together – so it's well worth practising to get it right.

▲ **This atmospheric sketch in oils, *Sky Study, Clouds,* is the result of one of Constable's numerous 'skying' expeditions. He believed that skies were supremely important, painting them again and again.**

Trying to capture the ever-changing moods of the sky seems rather daunting at first – where do you start? The sky changes constantly, as the sun rises and sets and as atmospheric effects such as clouds, rain and mist move across it. But if you watch the sky regularly and make notes, practise using different media and familiarise yourself with colours and techniques, you'll soon have the confidence you need to render skies skilfully and convincingly.

Sky sketches

The great landscape painter John Constable (1776-1837) sketched the sky constantly, working in oils directly from the subject – a process he called 'skying'. On 23 October 1821, Constable wrote to his friend Archdeacon Fisher, emphasising the importance of the sky in landscape painting: 'That landscape painter who does not make his skies a very material part of his composition, neglects to avail himself of one of his greatest aids.... The sky is the source of light in nature, and governs everything.'

Follow Constable's example and study the sky as often as you can. Make notes about the location, time of day, season and weather conditions. This process will help you to understand what you are seeing when on location, and will enable you to reproduce sky effects in your work.

Sky relationships

The sky is the backcloth to the landscape and should relate logically to the rest of the painting. If the sky is bright blue, the landscape should be sunny. Think about where the sun is and create shadows that are appropriate: small or non-existent if the sun is overhead, long and clearly defined if the sun is lower in the sky. If the sky is overcast and leaden, the tones in the landscape will be muted and shadows absent or indistinct.

Linking sky to landscape

A toned ground laid over the entire support will subtly modify the sky and the landscape and pull the two areas together. If you add tiny dabs of sky

▲ **A range of greys mingle with browns in this Constable study; the paint was applied loosely and the ground shows through.**

colour to the landscape, as delicate touches or highlights, this will help to mirror the way in which light is constantly reflected from one area to another in nature.

The colour of the sky

The colour and brightness of the sky depends on factors such as the amount of cloud cover, the quantities of dust and water droplets in the air, and the position and strength of the sun. The sky is at its deepest blue between showers of rain, while on a beautiful summer's day it is often bright but not very blue because of the dust particles in the air.

To check the precise colour and tone of the sky, hold something blue or white up to it. You will find that generally the sky is brightest and whitest close to the sun, and that it often becomes paler again as it approaches the horizon.

The way you reproduce the sky will depend very much on the medium you are using and the style of your painting. In a cloudless sky, you need subtle gradations of colour and tone. You can achieve this in watercolour by laying a graduated wash, or in oil by working wet into wet to create subtle blendings. You can create skies of great depth and luminosity by applying layers of glazed and scumbled colour. You can even use a rich impasto, applying and smearing the paint with a knife – a painting such as *Starry Night* by Vincent Van Gogh (page 180) demonstrates the truly dramatic potential of impasto.

Special effects

Sunrise, sunset and special effects, such as rainbows, provide colourful spectacles – and each occasion is different. At sunrise and sunset, the sky is suffused with reds, oranges and yellows, which flow gradually into one another.

To describe these subtle transitions, use blending and wet-on-wet techniques. Clouds at sunset create emphatic shapes which are best painted wet-on-dry, or wet-on-damp in watercolour.

In the picture opposite, the artist Eugène Boudin (1824-98) has painted a sunny day on the beach at the seaside

KNOW YOUR SKY COLOURS

Cerulean blue
This warm blue has a slightly greenish tinge, useful near the horizon.

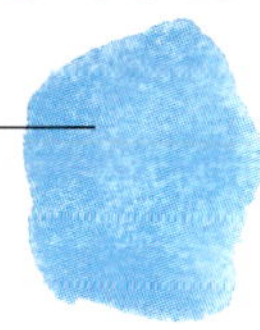

Prussian blue
A cold shade for rainy weather, Prussian blue also contains a hint of green.

French ultramarine
This deep shade is a warm violet-blue, perfect for sunny days.

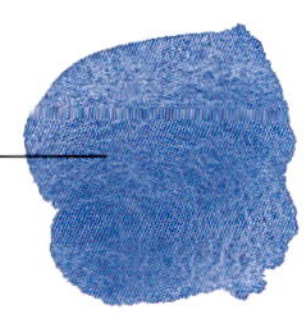

Cobalt blue
Cobalt blue provides a good balance between warm and cold.

Payne's grey
A blue-grey, ideal for moody skies and storm clouds.

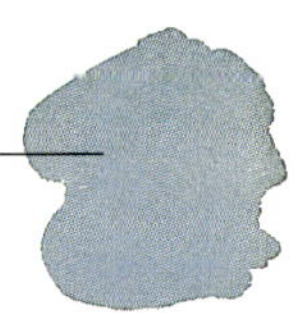

resort of Deauville in northern France. The clouds scudding across the sky give us a sense of the sea breeze.

The sky dominates the composition, occupying almost three-quarters of the canvas. The paint layer consists of thin veils of colour, which have been skimmed over the canvas so that the light itself seems trapped in a delicate web of atmospheric colours. The brushwork is soft, loose and informal, the most solid paint applications being reserved for the deep, intense blue of the sky at its highest point.

Sky moods

Despite the apparent simplicity of the subject, Boudin's painting is pervaded by a marvellous sense of space, light and airiness. If you visualise this sunny scene under a brooding, stormy sky, or gilded by the setting sun, you will see that by simply changing the sky you can create an entirely different picture.

MIXTURES AND DILUTIONS

The colours you choose depend on the key of your painting, the effect you are trying to create and the appearance of the sky itself. So, for an intensely blue sky, you could use French ultramarine at the highest point, graduating through pure cobalt blue to cobalt blue muted with vermilion at the horizon.

Mix...

A range of warm greys can be very useful when painting cloudscapes.

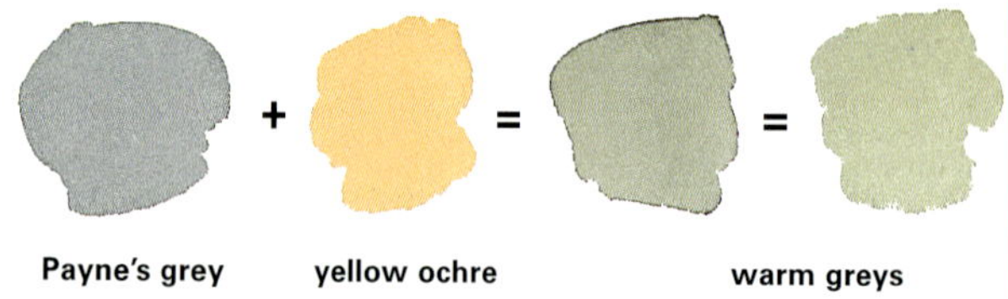

Add a little vermilion to cobalt blue to create atmospheric muted violets.

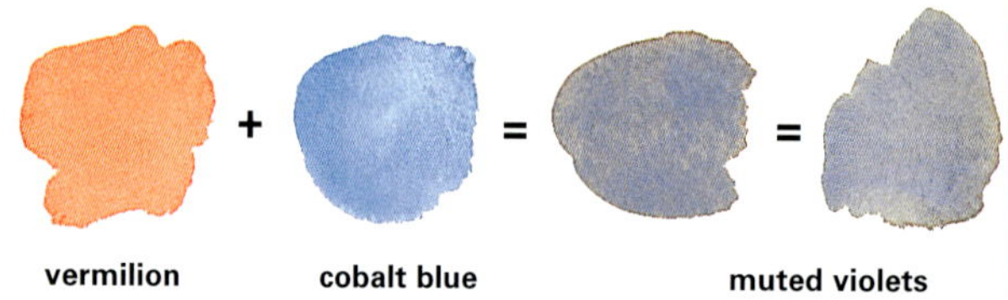

...and dilute

Cobalt blue is a very useful sky colour. In watercolour, it can be diluted to create a range of tints. With other media, you can achieve a similar effect by adding white.

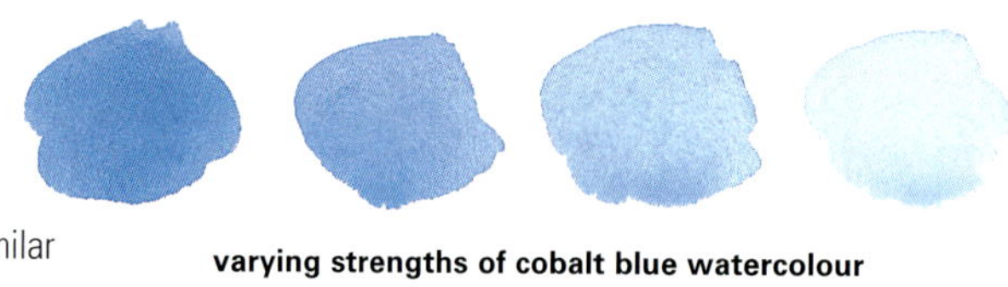

▼ One of Eugène Boudin's many beach paintings, *Deauville, 1893*. You can almost feel the blue sky and bracing air of a breezy day by the seaside.

A colour for all seasons

Nature's annual cycle has always provided inspiration for artists, challenging them to respond to its changing colours and moods.

In 1530, a German painter called Albrecht Altdorfer painted a picture of pine trees and rocky hillsides. It had no figures in it and told no story, thus beginning a long obsession that artists have had ever since with landscape and nature as subject matter for pictures.

Some of the early landscape painters, such as Claude Lorrain (1600-1682), idealised nature in a romantic way. J.M.W. Turner (1775-1851) created dramatic scenes of extreme weather conditions. Gradually, as painters tried to be more truthful, working directly from nature became more popular. John Constable (1776-1837) and later the Impressionists recognised that the way the light changes, both during the day and with the seasons, has a marked effect on the colours in a landscape.

Watching the changes

In order to observe and record the changing colours and tones of each season for yourself, it is useful to paint four different versions of the same scene at about three-monthly intervals. A garden is an obvious choice, because it shows distinct colour changes as flowers bloom, berries ripen and leaves fall.

A more subtle approach would be to select a view where the changes occur within the colours themselves as the light varies with each season. You might decide to observe some brightly painted buildings by the sea, for example, or in a wooded landscape.

To achieve the strongest contrast between the four versions of the scene, try to paint on days when the weather and atmosphere are most typical of the seasons. Work in the early morning in spring, when the light is crisply bright, or when it is hot and sunny in summer. Evening light is dramatic in autumn, while a frosty atmosphere sets the scene for a winter painting. Remember to

▲ In this watercolour painting, *In a Shoreham Garden* (*c.* 1829) by Samuel Palmer (1805-81), the white blossom tinged with pink typifies a spring scene. The deeper yellows and greens around the central tree act as a foil to the white, throwing it forwards in the picture.

◀ **The strong blues and warm greens and yellows in the foreground of this Scottish landscape, *The River Goil, Argyllshire, 1913*, by George Houston (1869-1947), conjure up a bright summer's day. The hills and sky behind fade to a soft, hazy colour in the distance.**

place yourself in exactly the same spot each time, whether you are painting directly from observation or taking photographs to use as reference.

Colours of the seasons

There are certain paint shades that will help you to portray the essence of each season when used with your basic palette (see page 113). A word of warning, however – too many colours in your palette can be a hindrance rather than a help. Be selective and try working with just one extra colour from those mentioned below for each season.

Spring This season brings crisp, clean yellows, greens and blues into a landscape. These shades suggest the use of pure colours directly, without too much mixing, and are particularly appealing to the watercolourist. Look out for long mauve and violet shadows cast when the sun is very yellow and low in the sky. Notice the fresh, light appearance of colours in sunlight at this time of the year, and try to paint them without using too much white.

Summer The heat-haze of summer will soften the colours in a distant landscape creating atmospheric blues, whilst reds, purples and violets really come into their own as rich, dominant hues in the foreground. The greens of the foliage and meadows become warmer – mix these shades using the deeper yellows, such as chrome yellow and transparent gold ochre, with either of the blues from your basic palette. Cerulean blue is a useful addition to widen the options for painting water and skies, and to mix the chalkier greens on the horizon.

Autumn We often think of autumn as being a 'golden' season and you should certainly explore the range of warm colours from the deep yellows (ochre, raw sienna and burnt sienna) and the coppery reds (Venetian red and Indian red), through to the rich browns (burnt umber). The 'season of mists and mellow fruitfulness' also provides soft shadows and a damp atmosphere, offering the artist a selection of subtle mauves and generally warmer blues and greens.

Winter In winter, sharp tonal colour contrasts are revealed, especially when snow has fallen. Greys, dark blues, greens and browns predominate, but these are often complemented by small patches of very bright colour such as red or orange berries. Winter encourages you

◄ **Steely grey and teal blue in the leaden wintry sky and the shadows on the icy ground cool down the warmer ochre shades in this Impressionist painting, *Frosty Morning in Louveciennes* (1873), by Alfred Sisley (1839-99).**

to practise mixing warm and cool greys without using black. Useful additions to a basic palette might be Payne's grey in watercolour or phthalo blue in oils.

The seasons indoors

Seasonal colour can also be explored in still life by bringing together natural forms and objects at different times of the year – for example, fruits of the harvest in late summer, or pine cones and the pale green Christmas rose in winter.

The seasonal theme has inspired some contemporary artists to make abstract compositions, reflecting moods and rhythms through shape and structure as well as through colour. Alan Davie's *Music of the Autumn Landscape* (1948) and Ivon Hitchens' *Autumn Composition* (1932) are paintings which use warm greens and browns in a still-life format.

◄ **The browns, russets and ochres of autumn are just starting to take over from summer's greens in *An Autumn Landscape with a View of Het Steen in the Early Morning* (*c.* 1636) by Peter Paul Rubens (1577-1640).**

TRIED AND TESTED TECHNIQUES

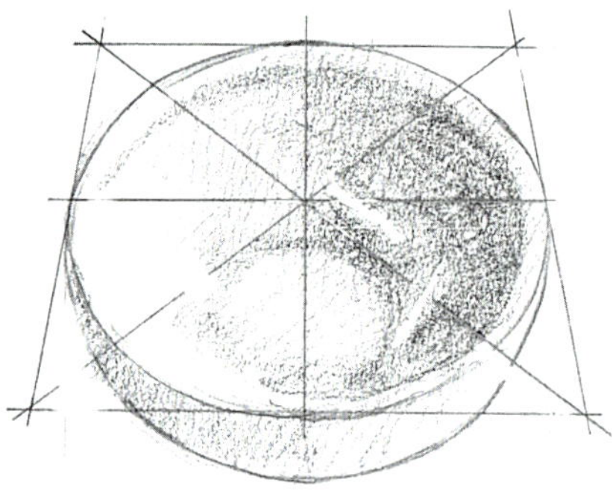

This chapter describes how to take a simple brush stroke or pencil line one step further. Among other techniques, the section explains how to use patterned backgrounds, draw ellipses, paint with a knife, use spattering effects and letter on curved surfaces. Once perfected, these skills will allow you much more freedom and expression when painting.

Drawing ellipses

Discover how to render circular shapes as accurate ellipses and you'll tackle any still life with a new-found confidence.

▲ **In *Still Life on a Table*, Anne Redpath accurately renders both the shallow ellipses of the jug and pot at the back, and the rounder ellipses of the bowls at the front.**

When viewed at an angle, any circular shape flattens out and becomes an ellipse. Elliptical shapes are used frequently in both drawing and painting: still-life groups, for example, often include plates, jugs, vases and bowls, as well as flowers with circular blooms.

Drawing circles and cylinders in perspective, though, is trickier than rendering squares and cubes in perspective. Indeed, many first attempts at drawing curves and rounded forms resemble the lop-sided rejects from a beginners' pottery class! However, once you understand that the rules governing the perspective of curved objects are the same as those for straight-sided objects, you will be able to tackle ellipses with confidence.

Just as you see less and less of the top of a box the lower your eye level is, so you will see less and less of the surface of a round object such as a plate. Try it for yourself: hold a dinner plate upright in front of you at eye level – it is perfectly circular. If you tilt the plate away from you the circle becomes an ellipse which gradually flattens as the angle of the plate is further inclined. This is because you are now seeing the plate from a foreshortened viewpoint.

SQUARING THE CIRCLE

First, try drawing three circles in perspective (marked A), which you can then use to create fully finished drawings of a bowl (marked B). Since circles fit into squares, it follows that drawing a square in perspective and fitting a circle into it will result in an accurate ellipse. Of course, this is a rather mechanical way of drawing but it will help you to begin with. Eventually you will be able to tackle ellipses freehand. Once you've mastered rendering a bowl from different angles move on to a cylinder.

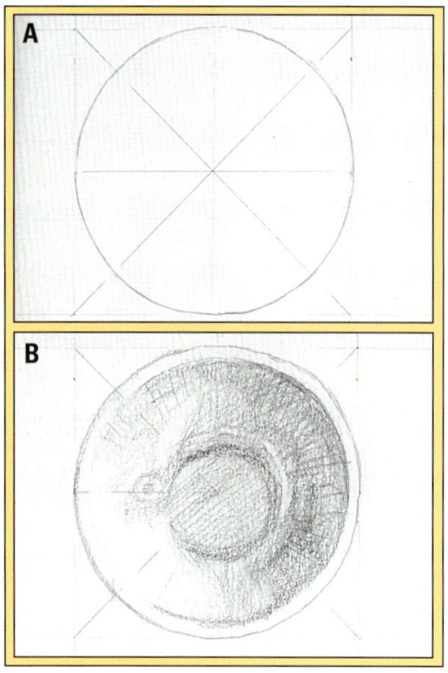

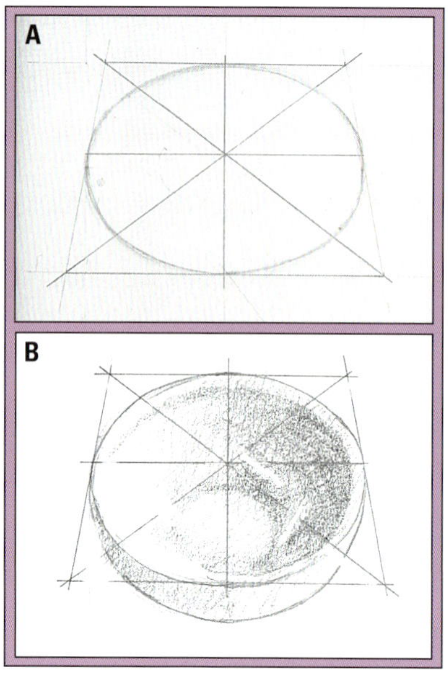

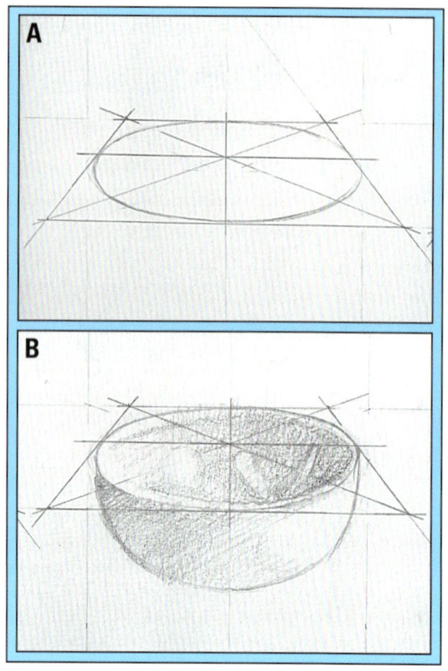

Start by drawing a bowl viewed from above (left). First draw a square and find its centre by drawing diagonals between the corners. Next, divide the square again, by drawing a horizontal and a vertical through the centre point. Use these guide lines to draw the curves of the circle. If you want to render a circle seen from an angle (middle), first you must draw a square in one-point perspective (see pages 219-221). The four near sections will be larger than the upper ones, helping you to create an ellipse. You can increase the foreshortening by drawing a square at an even more oblique angle (right).

DRAWING CYLINDERS

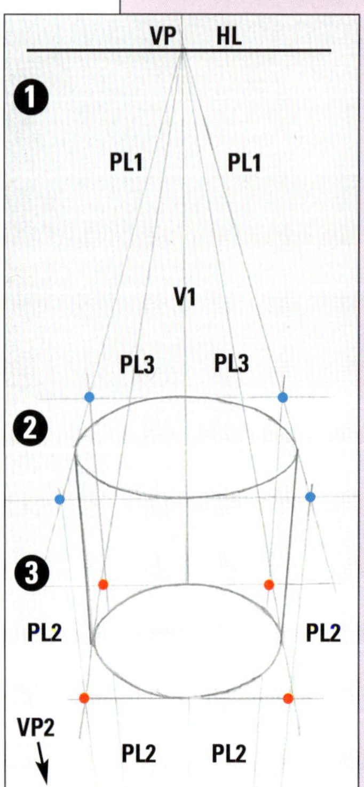

When drawing a cylindrical object, such as a vase, think of it as being transparent. You will now see two ellipses – the top and the base. The ellipses have different shapes because one lies closer to the horizon line. To draw a cylinder in perspective follow these steps:

❶ Draw in the horizon line (HL) at the top of the page and select a vanishing point (VP) in the middle of it. Then draw a vertical (V1) from the VP down to the bottom of the page.
❷ Draw the top square in one-point perspective by extending two perspective lines (PL1) from the VP down either side of V1. Put in two horizontal lines to complete the square. Draw an ellipse within it.
❸ Draw a perspective line (PL2) down from each corner of the square (blue) to another vanishing point (VP2) on V1 well below the page. Extend two more perspective lines (PL3) down either side of V1 but inside the two PL1s. Where this third set of perspective lines crosses the second gives you the four corners of the bottom square (red). Complete the square and draw the second ellipse. Join the edges of the ellipses with straight lines to form the cylinder.

COMMON ERRORS

▶ Try not to draw the ends of the ellipses with a definite point (left). Instead, make sure they curve all the way round (right).

▲ Do not draw a cylinder's base too flat (left) – instead make sure it is slightly more curved than the top (right). The further an ellipse is from the horizon or eye-level line, the more open the curve becomes.

WORKING UP WHEELS

Ellipses are also involved when drawing the wheels of cars, lorries, bicycles and so on, except that now they are placed on the vertical. (The same might apply in a still life if, for instance, you have a jar lying on its side and turned at an angle.) Once again, placing the circles inside squares will help to make sure you get the wheels accurately in perspective.

DRAWING A BICYCLE

❶ Determine the angle of the bicycle by sketching in the perspective lines (PL1 and PL2). These should meet at a vanishing point (which is off the page in this drawing).
❷ Establish where the wheels should be and draw verticals (V1, V2, V3, V4) to attain two squares in perspective. Draw in diagonals.
❸ With these segments as guides, draw circles inside the squares. The wheels will appear to lie in the same plane as the rectangle of the bicycle.

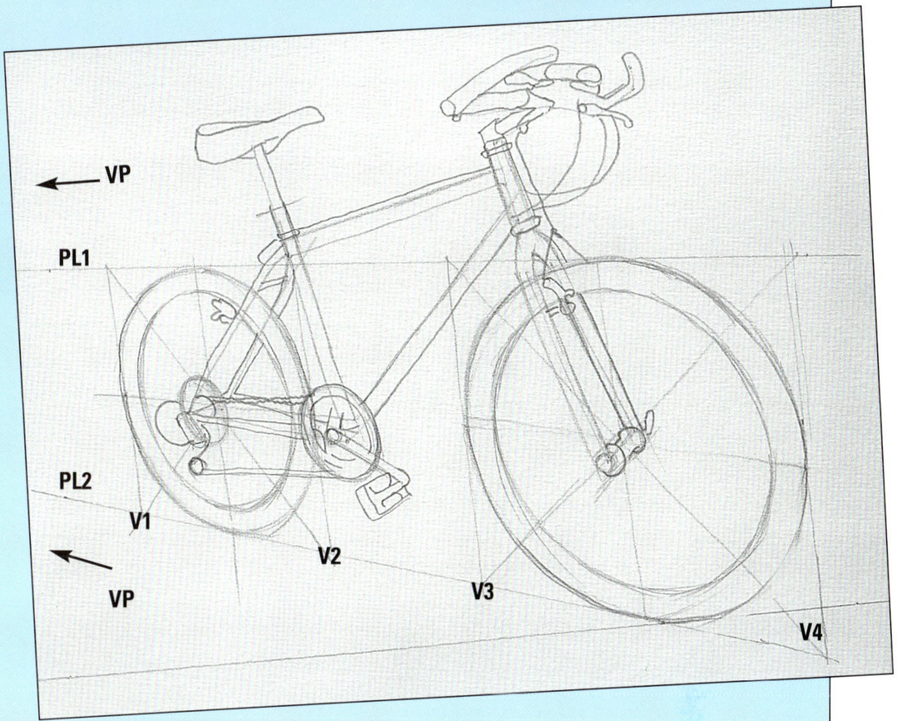

Putting it into practice

To practise drawing ellipses, make a sketch of a group of cylindrical objects of varying heights, such as the bowl, bottle and glasses here). Start by lightly establishing your eye-level line on the paper – which is just above the top of the wine bottle here. Remember that the depth of an ellipse changes according to your eye level, so take care to keep a consistent viewpoint as you work. And to help you achieve an accurate drawing follow these tips:

- Don't press too hard with your pencil or try to draw the ellipse in one single line, but hold the pencil lightly and 'feel out' the form as you draw.
- Even if the objects are not actually transparent, draw them as if they were. By drawing both what is seen and unseen, you go beyond just drawing the outer shape to capturing the underlying structure.
- Use light strokes and if necessary go over your lines again until you are satisfied that the shape is correct. Use construction lines as support if you wish.

Drawing with a grid

Make a grid to help you position objects on paper and create a balanced outline. Then shade in the composition using your free charcoal pencil for a bold effect.

There's no need to go anywhere special to find interesting subjects to draw. It is quite possible simply to stay at home and pick out some of the objects around you to create a worthwhile composition.

Mapping size and position

Even experienced artists can have difficulty in accurately mapping the size and proportion of objects. One solution is to stand a sheet of white card with squares drawn on it behind your still life, then to rule a corresponding grid onto your drawing paper. This makes it easier to plot the height and volume of different objects.

Another plus point is that the white backdrop encloses the objects, aiding concentration while making a clear surface for any shadows to fall on. In this project however, it is the outline of the objects, their place within the grid and their 3-D form that is important.

Using a charcoal pencil

The outline is drawn using a 2B pencil, which is easy to rub out in case of mistakes; but the shading is done with the charcoal pencil supplied free with this issue to create strong, dark lines. In fact, because charcoal handles so differently to the graphite pencil you used to shade an apple last time, it's a good idea to get a feel for it first.

On a scrap piece of paper, move the pencil freely from side to side. Press lightly at first, then harder, and note the difference in the strength of the impression. Then go over your initial strokes with further strokes in different directions and check the varied textures you create. You will soon become familiar with the way that charcoal pencils work.

▲ It is much easier to draw a still life if you plot the position of the objects in it against a grid.

YOU WILL NEED

- Piece of white card approx. 43cm (17in) high by 1m (40in) or more
- Masking tape
- Metal ruler
- Rubber
- Pencils: 2B; Charcoal
- Scalpel or pencil sharpener
- Large sheet of lightly textured drawing paper

HOW TO MAKE A GRID SCREEN

1 Mark a vertical line about 20cm (8in) from each end of the pliable white card. Cut along these lines, then tape the severed pieces of card back in place with masking tape. This creates the moveable side flaps that will allow the screen to stand upright. Then use a 2B pencil to mark out the limits of the grid, making sure its base is positioned as close as possible to the bottom of the card.

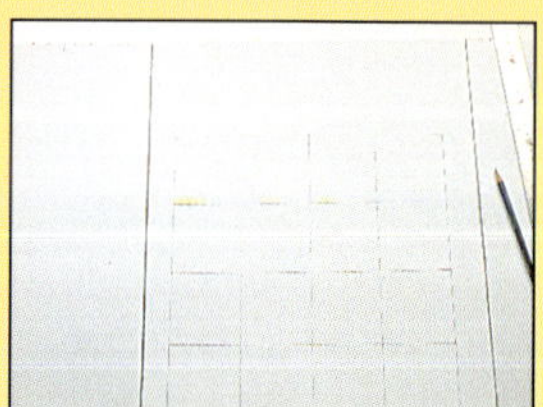

2 Continue ruling horizontal and vertical lines on the card to complete the grid. The version shown here has 16 squares, each 8 x 8cm (3 x 3in) in size. Then arrange your still life group at eye level and stand the grid screen behind it. You are now ready to start drawing.

HOW TO USE THE GRID METHOD

1 ▲ Draw a corresponding grid onto your paper Using the 2B pencil, draw another grid onto the drawing paper. You will need to divide it up into the same number of squares as appear on the card screen – although they do not have to be the same size as those you drew previously. The squares shown here measure 6 x 6cm (2.5 x 2.5in).

3 ▶ Check as you draw Continue drawing the bottle, including its stopper, referring frequently to the grid lines behind the object. Use a series of small strokes rather than a single line.

EXPERT ADVICE
Paper for charcoal

Charcoal, being a powdery substance, works best on slightly textured paper, which gives it something to 'grip' on to. If you use smooth or shiny paper, you will see the charcoal slide all over the place. Once you are familiar with how it handles, you can try using charcoal on paper with a highly textured surface. As the grain on this type of paper is prominent, it adds a distinctive character to the drawing.

2 ▲ Start drawing the bottle outline Start with the bottle because it is the tallest object in the group. Study where and how its outline crosses the squares on the grid behind it. Then start drawing in the bottle's outline using the 2B pencil. Make sure that you place each individual line in the corresponding grid square on your piece of paper as you draw.

ADD IN THE OTHER ITEMS IN THE GROUP

Once you have established the position of the first object in your still life – in this case, the bottle – you can add the other items around it. By continuing to follow the grid lines, you will ensure that the objects relate to each other as in the original.

4 ▲ Sketch the outline of the glass Again using the grid lines for reference, draw in the outline of the glass. The glass is positioned just in front of the bottle, so it appears slightly 'lower' in relation to the bottle's rounded base.

5 ▲ Draw the coffee pot Next, sketch the outline of the coffee pot, once again following the grid lines. Study the shape carefully and thicken up the lines slightly where the contours seem more intense – for example, on each side of the lid. If you use the rubber to correct any errors, you are likely to rub out the grid lines as well. Make sure to pencil these back in.

6 ▶ Complete the pencil sketch Add the details on the coffee pot. You have now achieved your initial sketch – a well-proportioned group of objects ready for developing with the charcoal pencil.

A FEW STEPS FURTHER

7 ▲ Shade the bottle Study how the light falls on the group of objects that you have just been drawing. Then use the sharp charcoal pencil and a combination of intense and lighter strokes to shade the bottle, building up areas of light and dark tones and leaving the highlights bare.

8 ▶ Give form to the glass Use the sharp point of the pencil to give form to the bottle's stopper. Then turn to the glass. Use heavy strokes to create the shaded areas along its right-hand edge and around the lower half; then medium strokes to give form to the other areas. Leave the highlights on the left and near the top of the glass untouched so that the white paper shows through.

9 ▶ Work on the coffee pot

Place a sheet of paper over the finished parts of the drawing to prevent them smudging as you work. Then start to shade the coffee pot, leaving the main highlights as wide, vertical strips.

10 ▶ Build up the tones on the coffee pot

Gradually work up and darken the shading on the coffee pot. Reduce the main highlights to a few narrow bands, where the light bounces most intensely off the shiny, curved surface of the object.

THE FINISHED PICTURE

A The grid
The way the objects in the picture relate to their surrounding grid lines should mirror the way in which the original still life is positioned against the grid on the card screen. You can rub out the grid on the paper to complete the picture.

B Use of charcoal
The lines made with the 2B pencil, which was used to create the initial sketch in case of error, are completely hidden by the subsequent shading with the charcoal pencil. The charcoal produces darker tones and gives a softer finish.

C 3-D form
Once the shapes and arrangement of the three objects in the still life had been established on the grid, the artist then created the 3-D quality of their curved surfaces. This was achieved by the use of shading, and by creating highlights.

USING WATER SOLUBLE COLOURED PENCILS

If you would like to introduce colour into your still life, you can achieve a very different effect from a charcoal drawing by using water soluble coloured pencils. These are extremely versatile, as you can first draw your subject with them and then add water with a brush to soften the outlines and blend the colours. The final result is similar to a watercolour painting. You can then add more pencil strokes over the top of the blended areas once the paper is completely dry. There will be more information about how to use and create pictures with this exciting medium in future issues. Coloured water soluble pencils also form part of your free art set.

Applying paint without a brush

A brush isn't the only way of applying paint. You can use all kinds of other tools and techniques, from stippling with a sponge, to spattering with a toothbrush.

Whereas a regular brush is the most conventional tool for transferring paint onto paper, contemporary artists have developed exciting alternative ways of applying colour. Paint can be sprayed or sponged, dribbled or dabbed. It can be wiped on with a cloth or spread with a knife. In fact, any method of getting colour onto the paper or canvas is valid so long as it produces an effect you like.

Painting with a knife

Specially made painting knives have very pliable blades, which are good for moving paint around on the canvas. But you will need to practise. Initially you may find yourself scraping off the paint as quickly as you are putting it on.

◄ All sorts of things that you wouldn't think of as typical painting tools can be used for applying colour or creating texture. From the left are: a decorator's brush; a painting knife; a fork; a scraper; bamboo skewers; and a natural sponge.

Try painting with different parts of the blade to see what effects you can achieve – use the tip of the knife to dab dots of colour, the edge of the knife to create lines, and so on.

Colour can be laid in thick, flat wedges rather as you would spread butter on a slice of bread. By using the knife in a circular motion you will get swirls and arcs of colour. Pat the paint with the flat side of the blade, and the result will be a stippled effect with the paint standing up in tiny peaks.

Obviously, for knife painting, the paint must be thick enough to hold its

▲ Two different colours of ink dropped onto wet paper will bleed into each other, forming a ragged edge and a new colour mix where the two inks meet.

▼ If paint dropped directly onto paper is sprayed with water using an atomizer, this creates interesting shapes and different consistencies of colour. Similar effects can be achieved by blowing the paint around with a straw.

◀ Spray cans are a good option if you want to cover a large area of paper or canvas quickly. They are also ideal for creating flat areas of even colour. Graffiti artists have been using this technique on walls for years.

shape, so it's best to use acrylics and oils. Acrylics are particularly effective, because they are fast-drying and layers of colour can be built up very quickly.

Adding texture to paint

Any flexible blade other than painting knives will produce exciting results. Try using a kitchen spatula, a paint scraper, or even one of the plastic spreaders that come with adhesives and tile grout. Some of the latter have serrated blades and will give a ridged texture.

The tip of a knife blade can be used to scratch textures and patterns into thick paint. Alternatively, experiment with combs, forks and any other objects. Keep your samples for reference in case you want to incorporate a similar texture into a painting at a later date.

Sponged texture

Natural and synthetic sponges are excellent for applying all types of paint quickly. A natural sponge gives a honeycomb appearance, and is especially effective when one colour is sponged over another that has been allowed to dry. Try using this technique to suggest a pebbled beach, distant trees or the craggy surface of rocks and stones.

A synthetic sponge has a more regular, even texture. Stippling with this can produce a finely granulated effect very similar to the gritty surface of cast concrete. Synthetic sponges are firm and can easily be trimmed into any shape you want. Alternatively, apply colour with the whole sponge scrunched up. This will quickly cover a wide area with bold, irregular texture.

Rivulets of colour

Liquid paint, dribbled randomly onto a sheet of paper, will spread to form rivulets and runs of colour. These can be encouraged and controlled to some extent by blowing gently across the paper. Experiment with inks, diluted watercolour, gouache or acrylic, dropping the colours with a brush, sponge or pipette. Provided you do not overdo the mixing, two or more colours will merge to form vivid, multi-coloured shapes.

Use a similar technique to paint flowers, leaves or any other simple subject. Do this by first painting the shape you want on paper with clean water. Then drop colours into the wet area. They will be contained by the shape of the water but will run together to give a brilliant, marbled effect. This works well with watercolours and coloured inks.

Spraying techniques

For a fine, controlled application of paint, try spraying. This technique is perfect when you want a completely flat area of colour, or a graded effect. If you use an airbrush, colour can be applied with great precision and for this reason, the airbrush is often used to produce works that are more like prints

▶ You can buy acrylic paints in bottles with a pipette attached to the lid for dropping colour directly onto a surface.

PLAYING WITH TEXTURES

Once paint has been applied to a surface, it can be manipulated in any number of ways to create different textures and add interest to a painting. In the examples shown below, a natural sponge, a knife and a fork were used with different hand motions to produce a variety of effects. Experiment yourself using not only the tools mentioned, but any other potential texture-making implements you may have to hand.

Sponge - twisting

Sponge - stippling

Sponge - stroking

Knife - using the edge

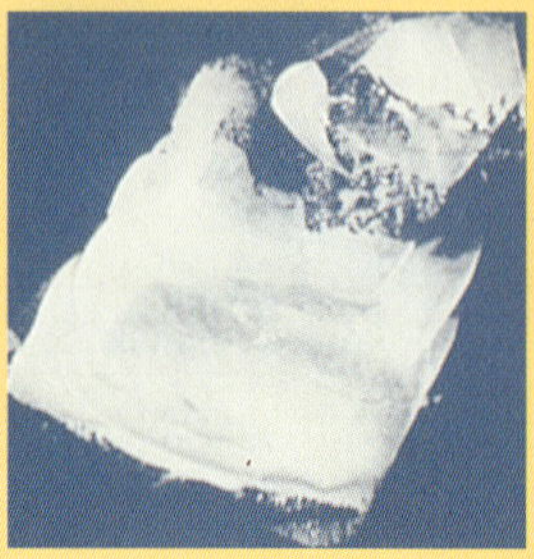
Knife - spreading

Fork - dragging

or photographs than paintings. Because of this, some artists find airbrushed colour very mechanical and prefer the more expressive quality of other textures.

Although airbrushing is the most common means of spraying colour, mouth atomizers can also be used. Colour from a jar or bottle is simply blown through a diffuser, generally giving a more speckled effect than airbrushed colour.

Rapid results

Sprayed colour can provide a useful starting point for a painting, perhaps for filling in a flat background or for painting a large expanse of sky in a landscape. The work can then be continued with a brush.

For an instant result, you can't beat spray paints. Graffiti artists have been using them for years! They come in a wide range of colours including fluorescent and metallic finishes, and are either enamel, cellulose or acrylic based. These paints are perfect for large-scale work, especially for covering large areas quickly. Read the manufacturer's instructions for safety precautions.

◀ If paper is first wetted and then paint dropped onto it, the colour will flood into the shape that has been created and be contained by it.

Whether you are using an airbrush, atomizer or a spray can, you will need to practise. The trick is to keep the sprayed colour moving slowly and evenly across the surface. Linger too long in one spot and the paint starts to drip and will dry unevenly.

Spattering

To achieve a spattering effect, take a small decorating brush, dip the bristles in paint, then flick the colour briskly on to a sheet of paper. For a finer texture, try the same technique using an old toothbrush. Dip the tips of the

▲ Create a ghostly tree by washing watercolour onto paper, then scraping out the shapes of the branches using the pointed tip of a painting knife.

bristles in colour, drag the bristles back with your finger, then let them go suddenly to flick the colour forward.

Spatter white and red onto a green background, and you have a meadow of poppies and daisies. Also, white paint spattered over blue, green or grey water gives a realistic impression of froth on breaking waves. Spattering can also be used effectively simply to break up an area of flat colour.

A vigorous spatter can cover a wide area, so if you want to aim at a specific spot, use a piece of newspaper to protect the areas you want to remain spatter-free.

Be selective

It is a good idea to experiment and to become familiar with as many approaches as possible before embarking on more ambitious paintings. Have fun and be as innovative and creative as you like at this stage. As a result you will have a mass of skills at your fingertips.

▲ Spray paints come in a wide variety of colours including fluorescent and metallic finishes.

Painting with a knife

Using painting knives encourages you to work quickly and directly. The result is loose, lively paintings, quite unlike anything achieved with a brush.

There is an immediacy and directness about painting with a knife. You can build the colours freely, applying them in swirling strokes or chunky wedges. And the knife marks remain visible and play an important part in the finished work.

Although paint thickness varies depending on how you work, it is a good idea to start by blocking in the initial colours in thin layers, using a long-bladed knife. Then it is a simple task to build up subsequent layers of thicker paint. If you feel the initial colour is too thick, scrape it back with the knife.

Knife marks tend to start with a thick ridge of colour which tapers off to a thin scrape, revealing the texture of the canvas or paper underneath. Fragments of colour are often retained in the grain of the support, creating an attractive speckled effect. You can exploit these contrasting textures to introduce different textures and tones into your subject.

Taking the direct route

Colours can be mixed quickly on the palette and applied equally rapidly and boldly to the picture, using broad strokes of the knife to cover large areas at a time. This direct approach will give you fresh colour and a lively picture surface. The bolder you are with your strokes the more emphatic these qualities will be.

Above all, knife painting is a 'one-hit' technique. Apply each stroke in a single movement, then leave it alone.

▲ In much of his early work, such as this still life of a leg of mutton and bread, from 1865, Paul Cezanne (1839-1906) made great use of palette knives to build up colour and scrape the paint into coarse, thickly textured, almost deformed shapes.

Let the knife marks show. By all means, scrape back colour and add texture to flat areas of paint – but do not be tempted to go back and tidy up the edges of a stroke or smooth the surface because you will inevitably destroy its freshness. If you are over-fussy or try to depict too much detail, the painting will lose its rugged, spontaneous qualities. You might as well work with brushes.

Traditionally, painting with a knife is an oil-painting technique, used for creating small areas of texture or for adding final touches such as highlights and reflections, usually using the tip of the knife. However, because oil colours are slow-drying and tend to crack if the colours are too thick, you should limit knife painting with oils to small areas of fairly shallow colour.

Working with acrylics

For more dramatic knife painting, acrylics are by far the best choice. Unlike oils, which can take weeks and even months to dry, the thickest acrylic paint will be ready to work on after a few hours. For even quicker drying, build up the acrylic paint gradually in several layers, allowing each one to dry before adding the next. (Use a hair-dryer to speed the process.)

For best results, use the paints undiluted. Some brands are thicker than others and these are usually ideal for knife painting. However, for a really built-up or sculpted effect, you can mix acrylic colours with modelling paste or textured medium to stiffen the paint. You can also buy textured mediums containing marble dust, sand and other inert materials to build up an impasto effect and create a variety of surface effects in your painting.

Knife shapes and sizes

Painting knives come in a range of shapes and sizes, making it possible to vary the scale of the marks and strokes according to the size of your painting.

In the landscape demonstration, our artist chose long-bladed knives for the initial expanses of sky and fields, then changed to a smaller diamond-shaped blade for the swirling white in the sky and for the trees. However, there are no hard-and-fast rules about which knife to use.

Marks and textures

The mark you make is determined by the shape and size of the blade and the way in which you hold the knife. Here, the two most common shapes of knife – long-bladed (top row) and diamond- or trowel-shaped (bottom row) – were used to create a variety of effects. A little practice will enable you to develop a large repertoire of marks, textures and patterns.

Laying flat colour Pick up a quantity of paint on the length of the blade and drag this evenly across the support in one motion. Keep the long edge of the blade parallel to the support.

Scraping back Use a clean, long-bladed knife to scrape back a wedge of colour to let the texture of the support show through. Work in smooth, unbroken movements to avoid creating ridges.

Texturing Manipulate thick paint by swirling, dabbing (shown above) or scratching back. You can create different textures by using diamond- or oval-shaped knives.

Stippling Using a broad-bladed knife, gently pat wet colour with the underside of the blade to create tiny peaks on the painted surface. Add modelling paste to your paint to really emphasise the texture.

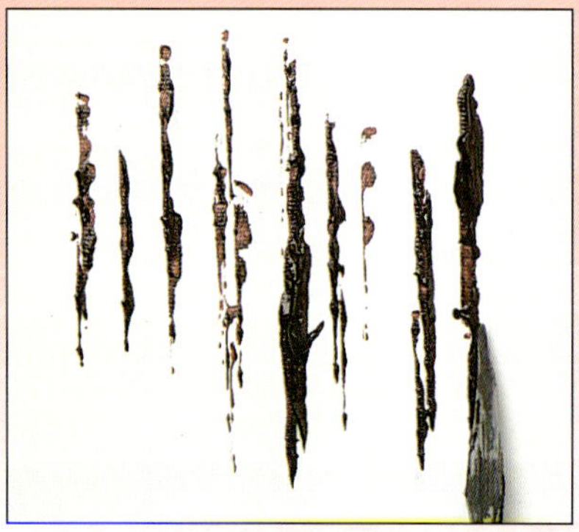

Fine lines Squeeze a length of colour on to the palette, dip the edge of the blade into the paint, then press the paint-loaded edge firmly down on the support. (The tree trunks opposite were done in this way.)

Broken colour Pick up a small amount of colour on the end of the pointed knife blade and spread this in thin, irregular strokes on to the support. The result is a subtly textured area of paint.

KNIFE EXERCISE

Try painting this simple landscape, using only knives – no brushes! The artist here used seven acrylic colours: cerulean, white, lemon yellow, oxide of chromium, cobalt blue, burnt umber and Payne's grey. However, as the palette is less important than the technique, you might prefer to work with colours that you already have. To apply the paint, he used two lengths of long-bladed knife as well as large and small diamond-shaped ones.

Any primed support can be used for knife painting, although a textured surface – such as the acrylic paper used here – produces the most interesting results.

1 ▲ **Establish the sky** Mix undiluted cerulean and white and spread this across the sky area, using a long diamond-shaped painting knife. Work quickly, leaving patches of white paper for the clouds.

2 ▶ **Begin on the fields** For the distant fields, mix oxide of chromium with a little white and lemon yellow and apply this with a long-bladed knife, using short downward strokes. The knife marks lend a grassy texture.

3 ▲ **Paint the foreground** Mix a darker green for the foreground from oxide of chromium with a little cobalt blue. Apply this in broad horizontal strokes, using a long-bladed knife.

4 ▲ **Paint the grass** Add white to the oxide of chromium and cobalt blue mix and apply this in thick diagonal strokes to create long, windswept grass in the foreground.

5 ▲ **Add fluffy clouds** Load a smaller knife with undiluted white and paint the clouds, using short, decisive strokes. Soften the edges by dragging some paint into the blue sky.

6 ◀ **Block in the trees** Mix dark green from oxide of chromium, cobalt blue and a little lemon yellow and paint a row of trees on the horizon. Do this with a small knife, painting each tree as a simple block of colour.

▶ **As a finishing touch, put the tree trunks in with a mix of burnt umber and Payne's grey, using the side of a small knife. You now have a wonderful textural landscape – with thick impasto marks for the clouds and trees as well as thinner, scraped areas in the grass and sky.**

Using patterned backgrounds

When you are faced with a blank sheet of paper, it is reassuring to have a reference point for your drawing.

In this exercise, you will find out how you can 'loosen up' your drawing. For the exercise on pages 144-147, you used a screen with a squared 'grid' to help you plot the positions of objects in a still life group very precisely. Here, we are going to look at an alternative way of using a visual reference when drawing a group of objects.

Instead of a specially drawn grid, some striped wallpaper provides a helpful background to set behind a few simple objects. The regular vertical and horizontal stripes act as an excellent, informal grid reference. Choose objects with plain colours for your still life, so that they stand out clearly against the patterned background.

Positioning the light source

As in some of the previous exercises shown in this book, a light source in the form of a lamp is used here. This time, however, because of the nature of the composition, the light comes from the left as the objects would be in the shade if lit from the right. When you are setting up a group of objects for yourself, do bear in mind where the shadows fall, so you ensure that each object is clearly illuminated.

Adding water

Water soluble pencils can add a new dimension to your drawing skills. But if the thought of using water scares you, don't worry. The pencils may be used dry – although in such a case it will not be possible to obtain the effects seen in the final stages of this drawing. Adding water is fun, so pluck up your courage and have a go!

YOU WILL NEED

- Piece of cartridge paper
- Water soluble graphite pencils: B and 2B
- Rubber
- Scalpel or pencil sharpener
- Round brush with a point

FIRST STEPS

1 ▸Draw the wallpaper 'grid'

With a water soluble B pencil, sketch in the vertical lines of the wallpaper. Add a few horizontals too. These lines will give you a reference point for drawing the top of the flower pot. Once this shape is established, it will help you determine the positions of some of the other lines and shapes. Remember to keep looking at the wallpaper 'grid' while creating your initial sketch.

2 ▲ **Begin sketching the mortar** Start drawing the mortar (bowl), using the flower pot and background grid pattern as a reference. Remember that at this stage you can still work in a light, sketchy manner. You will be defining the outlines with a softer pencil later on...so take your time!

3 ▶ **Draw the garlic** Complete the mortar and then add the large garlic bulb and and the two garlic cloves. The mortar and the flower pot act as a reference for the position of the garlic.

4 ▶ **Add the pestle** Now it's time to include the pestle (stick), erasing the lines of the mortar that cut through it. Determine the angle of the pestle by looking at the striped background and the flower pot. The pestle starts just to the right of a vertical line on the wallpaper and ends at a horizontal line just above the flower pot. Assessing the position in this way illustrates how the stripes on the wallpaper provide a constant useful background reference for your drawing.

5 ▲ **Draw the outlines of the shadows** There are some shadows on the flower pot and the mortar. Lightly draw in their outlines at this stage.

TROUBLE SHOOTER

REMOVING WATER SOLUBLE PENCIL

You can erase dry water soluble graphite pencil easily with a normal rubber, but be warned! When water is added to the drawing, this acts as a 'fixer' and it is no longer possible to rub out the pencil marks. If you need to remove part of the drawing at this later stage, add a little more water to the area and lift it off immediately using a tissue or absorbent kitchen towel.

HOW TO STRENGTHEN THE LINES AND TONES

Once your initial sketch is complete, change to a 2B water soluble pencil. This softer grade will strengthen the outlines and shaded areas, while its soluble nature will set you up for adding water, if you want to tackle the 'Few Steps Further'.

6 ▶ **Shade in the wallpaper** The background wallpaper needs some shading in order to explain its pattern more clearly. Still using the B pencil for this and holding it quite loosely, work hatching to show the darker areas of the background.

7 ▲ Begin to define the drawing Now change to the 2B pencil and draw over the existing lines if you are happy with their positions. Also at this stage, fill in the shadows that you outlined in step 5.

8 ▲ Give form to the objects Work shading on the objects, for example, along the pestle and on the right of the mortar, in order to give them some form. Light hatching will suffice for this, so that there will be a sufficient difference between shading and any shadows cast. The drawing could now be considered complete, but if you want to, you can add water to the drawing for a different effect.

EXPERT ADVICE
Adding water

When adding water to a drawing produced with water soluble graphite pencils, there is no need to flood the paper – a small amount of water will be sufficient. You need just enough to activate the pigment in the pencil. If you use too much, the drawn areas will become grey and will merge together, causing the finished work to look washed out and undefined.

A FEW STEPS FURTHER

Now that the still life group is complete, you can add some water and move the drawing on a stage. Rest your hand on a piece of kitchen towel as you work to prevent smudging; this can also be used for 'lifting off' if you apply too much water.

9 ▲ Hatch in more shadows Before you begin adding water to your drawing, you can give the composition greater depth by defining the shadows cast on the horizontal surface on which the still life is standing. Work these dark areas by hatching with a 2B pencil.

10 ▶ Brush water over the wallpaper pattern Now load a round, pointed brush with clear water and begin to brush the water on to the patterned wallpaper. Now it should become apparent why the shading was added here in step 6. It has provided pigment, which intensifies when water is applied, creating a stronger version of the background pattern.

11 ▲ Add water to the whole drawing Continue adding water to all parts of the drawing. A pointed brush will cope with fine lines as well as the broader areas such as the shadows and shading. Notice how the lines and shapes appear stronger as the water is added. After all the hard work of drawing, this is the fun part!

THE FINISHED PICTURE

A Wallpaper 'grid'
The distinctive pattern of horizontal and vertical lines on the wallpaper was used to determine the positions of the objects in front of it. Unlike a specially drawn grid, the pattern of lines forms an integral part of the finished still life picture.

B Strong outlines
The light pencil marks used for the initial sketch of the objects were later strengthened with a softer pencil to define them. The still life stands out crisply from the more muted lines of the wallpaper in the background.

C Dark tones
When water was brushed over the dark areas of shadow, the tones here were deepened even further to form a stark contrast with the white paper and the more lightly shaded areas of the still life.

Lettering on curved surfaces

A still life of bottles with interesting labels is ideal for improving your skills at drawing lettering and small graphic details.

Bottles make versatile subjects for a still life. Not only do they come in pleasing shapes and colours and have a surface that produces fascinating reflections, their labels also offer a wealth of detail that is fun to explore in a drawing.

Drawing lettering

It requires a fair degree of precision to draw printed letters that look convincing. Once you start observing drinks labels, you will be surprised at how many different styles of lettering, or typeface, they feature. Modern letters are bold and plain, such as in the words 'Pimm's' and 'Chardonnay' on the labels shown here, whereas the classical typefaces are more complex and have an elegant appearance. Other letters, such as those in signatures, have flowing curves. If you ignore these differences in style, your drawing will not look sharp and accurate.

Unlike the lettering on a flat object, such as a book, the letters on a bottle label will follow the curve of the bottle shape and therefore need to be drawn to show this. You will find it helpful to mark some faint, curved guide lines on your drawing first, into which you can then fit the letters.

If some of the letters on a label are very small, it might be impossible to render them accurately. In this case, replace them with little symbolic marks, which will represent them convincingly.

▶ **Reproduce the lettering and graphics on the bottle labels with great clarity using a set of sharpened coloured pencils.**

YOU WILL NEED

Piece of Hot Pressed water-colour paper

17 coloured pencils: Mid-grey; Black; Pale grey; Magenta; Scarlet; Yellow; Ochre; Dark brown; Dark green; Purple; Orange; Bright green; Olive green; Violet; Mid brown; Light green; Dark blue

Craft knife (for sharpening pencils)

FIRST STROKES

1 ▶ Sketch the bottles Using a mid-grey coloured pencil, outline the bottles, making sure that the sides are balanced. Indicate the labels – some show through from the back of the bottles. Put in a little shading on the right-hand side of the bottles and labels. Begin to sketch in some of the letters lightly.

2 ▼ Draw the reversed-out letters Change to the black pencil and work around the shapes of the white, 'reversed-out' letters at the top of the label on the olive green bottle. If you feel unsure about doing this just by eye, sketch in the outlines before filling in the background.

3 ▶ Continue the Chardonnay label Indicate the small circle, the crest and the tiny lettering on the label with the black pencil. Then put in curved guidelines and plot the outlines of the black capital letters. As the letters come towards you, the spacing between them appears to become slightly wider.

4 ▲ Work on the Pimm's label Deepen the shading on all the labels and bottle tops with pale grey and mid-grey pencils. Change to magenta and scarlet to fill in the letters on the Pimm's label. For the gold lettering and border, use a mixture of yellow and ochre, with a little dark brown and black.

EXPERT ADVICE
Creating classical letters

In a classical typeface, the letters are finished off with little triangular devices known as 'serifs'. Put these in with a sharp pencil once you have drawn each letter. Notice, too, how some of the letters are made up of a combination of narrow and wider strokes.

5 ◄ Develop the labels Draw mid grey and dark green letters on the Lambrusco label. Darken the Pimm's letters in the shadow area with purple, then put in the letters on the small label. On the Chardonnay label, sketch the illustration in orange, bright green and olive green.

6 ► Add more label details Draw the two small illustrations on the Lambrusco labels with violet, black, dark green, yellow and scarlet pencils. Going back to the Pimm's bottle, work the lettering on the cap in orange and black, and draw the red stripes.

HOW TO ADD COLOUR TO THE BOTTLES

When the labels are developed to your satisfaction, you can begin to fill the bottles with colour. Use several shades for each one to reproduce their rich, glowing tones, leaving the white paper for highlights.

7 ► Colour the dark green bottle With the dark green pencil, fill in the colour with long hatched lines. Make the tone darker on the left of the label. Use olive green at the base and go over some areas with bright green.

8 ▲ Fill in the Pimm's bottle To show the tawny colour of the Pimm's bottle, blend dark brown, orange, mid brown, scarlet and magenta. Add a little black for the tone around the label and down the left side, where the dark green bottle is reflected.

9 ► Complete the third bottle Hatch strokes of light green and ochre over the bottle, using olive green and dark brown to indicate the label and the edge of the Pimm's bottle showing through from the back. Suggest the tiny lettering on the lower Pimm's label with short lines in ochre.

A FEW STEPS FURTHER

The drawing is now almost complete, the glowing colours of the bottles setting off the intricate labels beautifully. Just a few shadows and reflections need to be added now.

10 ▲ Put in the cast shadows Use long, loose hatched strokes of mid grey to indicate the shadows thrown by the bottles on to the white surface. Darken the Lambrusco label on the shaded side in the same way. Use a little dark blue on the shaded letters here.

11 ▲ Show the bright reflections Look closely for the brightest greens – you'll see these at the bottom of the bottle where the light shines through the glass and on the white surface adjacent to this area. Indicate these reflections with the bright green pencil.

THE FINISHED PICTURE

A Glowing colours The jewel-like colours of the glass bottles were rendered by combining several different coloured pencils.

B Curved labels The lettering follows the curve of the labels around the bottles. Guidelines were drawn to help position the letters correctly.

C Simplified detailing Rather than try to depict the illustration on the label in detail, the artist simplified it into basic blocks of colour.

Painting glass

Pick up some useful tips for creating realistic-looking glass objects in this acrylic still-life project.

Many still lifes lend themselves to a dry-brush approach, but the shimmer and reflections of glass objects call out for loose paint handling. In this study of two wine bottles and a glass fishing float, the artist mixed the acrylic paints to the consistency of single cream – encouraging him to paint in a free and lively manner. Look, in particular, at the fluid rendering of the bottles and the 'dancing' brush strokes used for the cast shadows. Only later, when details were required, were drier mixes of paint applied.

Decide on the lighting

One of the advantages of painting a still life is the degree of control you have over what you want to include and how to light your subject. In this exercise, where the subject matter is glass and reflected light, the light source is all-important. Set up your bottles so that there are two sources of light – one directly overhead, illuminating the tops of the bottles and glass sphere, and another coming from the right-hand side, reflecting off the sides of the bottles and casting gentle shadows behind them. Positioning the reflections accurately will help to define the form of the shiny objects and make them appear more realistic when you paint them.

▶ In this acrylic still life, loose paint handling and strong, sparkling highlights capture the qualities of glass.

YOU WILL NEED

Piece of primed canvas panel 40 x 30cm (16 x 12in)

10 acrylic paints: Raw umber; Titanium white; Dioxazine purple; Cerulean blue; Mars black; Sap green; Cadmium yellow; Yellow ochre; Raw Sienna; Cadmium red

Brushes: No.0 soft round; Nos.3 and 1 rounds; 25mm (1in) flat

Mixing palette or dish

FIRST STEPS

1 ▼ Outline the main shapes Make a dilute pale grey mix of raw umber, titanium white and a touch of dioxazine purple. Using the tip of a No.0 soft round brush, establish the main shapes in the still life.

2 ▲ Start adding colour Complete the underdrawing by adding the net around the float and the folds in the background cloth. Change to a No.3 round brush and mix a watery blue from cerulean blue and white. Apply this carefully around the bottles and glass float.

3 ▼ Build up the background Notice how the cloth is not a uniform blue. It has areas of light and dark, depending on how the light strikes the folds in the fabric. Use a 25mm (1in) flat brush to block it in, varying the proportions of blue and white in the mix and working with broad, loose strokes in different directions.

DEVELOPING THE PICTURE

With the underdrawing and background completed, turn your attention to the bottles and float, building up their tone to bring out their curved forms and reflective surfaces.

4 ▲ Model the edges Use the No.3 round brush and a blue-grey mix of cerulean blue, white and purple to paint the float, leaving the central area clear. Change to the No.0 soft round. Add a touch of Mars black to the blue-grey mix and outline the clear bottle. Make a mix of sap green and cerulean blue and outline the green bottle.

5 ▲ Mould the contours of the float With the No.3 round brush and the dark blue-grey mix used to outline the clear bottle, strengthen the edges of the float. Suggest the roundness of the float by painting certain areas darker and leaving other areas light – for the darker areas, add more cerulean blue and a little purple to the original blue-grey mix from step 4.

6 ▲ Work on the bottles Apply vertical slashes of colour on the bodies of the bottles. For the clear bottle, use mixes of cerulean blue, white and purple, leaving strips of canvas unpainted. For the green bottle, use varying amounts of sap green, cerulean blue and white, but this time cover virtually all of the glass. Paint the neck with the dark blue-grey from step 5.

Express yourself

Glass in watercolour

Watercolour, being a naturally transparent medium, works well for painting glass. Here, the same items have been painted with dilute washes of colour, leaving plenty of white paper showing through. The green bottle, however, provides a strong dark tone at the centre of the composition.

7 ◄ Paint a cast shadow Add a little black to the green mix from step 6. With the resulting dark green, define the base of the green bottle seen through the glass. Add more cerulean blue, then paint a dark shadow along its right-hand side. Now mix a dark blue-grey from cerulean blue, black and white, and describe the web-like shadow cast by the netting on the float.

8 ▼ **Define the netting** Add more white to the dark blue-grey and paint the shadows cast by the bottles. Model the green bottle with bands and circles of shadow, using the dark green from step 7. Now paint the netting, using a No.1 round brush and combinations of cadmium yellow, yellow ochre, raw sienna and white. Add the gathers at the top with a thicker mix of yellow ochre and raw sienna.

9 ▲ **Paint reflections** With the No.0 soft round, paint a dark blue-grey circle inside the netting to show the plug of glass. Place dots of the string colour where the netting is knotted to make it appear more three-dimensional. With a similar colour, add detail to the gathers and start painting the reflections of the netting in the clear glass bottle.

10 ▼ **Continue modelling the bottles** Complete the reflections of the netting in the clear and green bottles, making your lines irregular to suggest distortions in the glass. Referring back to the photo, add mid and dark greens from the palette to the glass accordingly to where the shadows fall. The right-hand side of the green bottle is the darkest, so go over this with a dark mix of sap green, cerulean blue and black.

11 ▲ **Paint the clear bottle** Add highlights to the float and the green bottle with dabs of white. Now look at the clear glass bottle – it both reflects light and allows it through, so you need to convey a sense of transparency and reflection simultaneously. First, suggest its transparency by showing the blue cloth seen through two layers of clear glass. The cloth appears darker than it actually is, so mix shades of blue-grey from cerulean blue, white and a little black and apply them to the bottle with loose, vertical strokes.

12 ◀ **Add reflections** Because there are two light sources, dozens of reflections dance off the surfaces of the bottles. Add more dots of white to them. Now, encircle the dots on the clear bottle with halos of pale blue (see Expert Advice), and those on the green bottle with yellow-green halos mixed from sap green and cadmium yellow. Emphasise the dark neck with stripes of blue-black mixes, then add white highlights to the rim, following its contours.

EXPERT ADVICE
Tips for reflections

When painting reflections on rounded surfaces, make sure you position the highlights correctly as they help to define an object's form. Ensure that they are bright – titanium white is the brightest white, so apply it thickly. Surround each highlight with a second colour, in this case a pale blue.

Master Strokes

Willem Claesz. Heda (1594-1680)
Breakfast with a Crab

The Dutch artist Heda painted many still-life studies known as 'breakfast pieces' – arrangements of decorative tableware and delectable foodstuffs that might have been eaten for a morning meal by wealthier people of the time. In this still life, light is reflected off all kinds of shiny surfaces. Highlights glisten not only from the glassware and metal objects, but also from the items of food such as the olives and the crab shell. Note how the white cloth provides a broad expanse of light tone that balances the darker tone of the still-life objects.

The still life contains a series of ellipses viewed from a variety of angles. Our eye is encouraged to jump from ellipse to ellipse.

The draped tablecloth is an exercise in skilful handling of tone; it has a tactile, three-dimensional feel. Note how the colour as well as the tone varies – the paler areas have a warm yellow tinge while the shadow tones have a cooler green bias.

A FEW STEPS FURTHER

The still life works well – the composition is pleasing and the bottles and float, with their different degrees of transparency, seem totally believable. You could stop here, but there's still room for improvement.

13 ▲ Add weight to the netting Beef up the netting with touches of browny reds mixed from raw sienna and cadmium red. Apply the paint with the No.0 soft round, placing the colour alongside the lines of ochre to suggest shadows.

14 ▲ Add interest to the background The cloth seems a little flat, so accentuate the folds and shadows with slashes of greenish-blue mixed from cerulean blue and sap green. Accentuate the cast shadows with greenish-blue too.

THE FINISHED PICTURE

A Reflecting contours
The highlights help define the bottle's form. There are pale vertical bands that run almost the length of the cylindrical bodies and bright points where spots of light bounce off the shoulders.

B Dark edges
The edges of the glass objects were painted slightly darker than their main body. This is a good technique to use for rounded forms, suggesting the surface moving away from you into the shadow.

C Translucent paint
A translucent wash of acrylic was applied over the background, leaving the white of the canvas showing through in places. The loose brush strokes, worked in varying directions, are clearly visible.

Fabric textures in charcoal

The soft feel of fabric can be convincingly rendered by drawing in charcoal and blending tones with a stump.

When drawing fabric, you need to adopt a technique that will suggest its tactile surface and gentle folds convincingly. Charcoal or charcoal pencils are excellent to work with, as they create appropriate textures on the paper, yet can be sharpened to a fine point for drawing details.

An Ingres pastel paper, which has a textured surface, was used for this still life to provide a tooth for the charcoal. As you progress with the picture, it is a good idea to rest your hand on some spare paper to avoid smudging the lines you have already drawn.

Using a stump

If you use charcoal in conjunction with a stump, you can achieve an even more realistic fabric effect. Stumps, or tortillons, are small tubes of tightly rolled paper. They come in various thicknesses and can have either a pointed or flat end. By rubbing a stump over an area of charcoal, you can blend it to a smooth tone. With a pointed stump, you can work into small corners easily.

You can also use a stump to pick up charcoal pigment and transfer it to your drawing. Vary the tone by changing the pressure you apply.

▲ The softly blended look in the picture is achieved by rubbing a stump, or tortillon, over charcoal pencil shading.

FIRST STEPS

1 ▶ Make a charcoal sketch Using a hard charcoal pencil, sketch in the main lines of the still life, showing the curves and folds of the soft objects. Indicate the tartan pattern on the cushion.

YOU WILL NEED

Piece of buff Ingres paper

3 charcoal pencils: Hard; Medium; Soft

2 stumps: Medium with pointed end; Fine with flat end

Craft knife to sharpen charcoal pencils

Putty rubber

Fixative

2 ▼ Establish dark and medium tones Change to a medium charcoal pencil to put in the darkest tones in the folds of the cap. Block in the dark squares on the tartan cushion and shade in the medium tone on the glove.

3 ▲ Develop the tartan cushion Shade in the mid and light toned green bands on the tartan pattern, working carefully around the edge of the cap as you do so. Leave the lightest squares of the tartan unshaded for the moment.

HOW TO SHADE WITH A STUMP

Now that you have developed some of the dark and medium tones, you can begin using the stumps to blend and smudge the charcoal. This technique will give the shaded areas a soft appearance reminiscent of the surface of the fabrics you are portraying.

4 ▶ Blend the darkest tones With a soft charcoal pencil, suggest the very dark tone where the tartan cushion is in shadow. Then blend the charcoal by rubbing over it with the pointed medium-sized stump.

5 ▲ Smooth the tartan pattern Rub the medium stump over the dark squares and medium-toned bands of the tartan cushion, smudging the charcoal into an even tone. Build up the folds and shadows in the glove, using the charcoal and stump alternately to develop the form.

7 ▲ Work on the scarf With the medium charcoal pencil, begin to indicate the striped pattern on the scarf. The curves of these lines will help to show how the scarf is folded and draped. Rub over the shadow areas on the scarf with the fine stump.

EXPERT ADVICE
Applying charcoal with a stump

For subtle shading, apply charcoal to your drawing with a stump. To do this, scribble the soft charcoal pencil aggressively over a spare piece of paper so you create some charcoal powder. Then rub the tip of a stump in the powder and use this to render the light and mid tones in your picture.

6 ► Develop the cap Using the method described in Expert Advice above, suggest the drapes of fabric in the foreground with the medium stump. Draw the shadows on the cap with the medium and soft charcoals, then rub over them with a fine stump. Change to the hard charcoal to put in the stitching, strap and eyelets.

8 ▲ Adjust the tones Fill in the pale stripes on the scarf with charcoal applied with the medium stump. Use this method to also add light tone to the green tartan squares, then draw the fine lines with the medium charcoal pencil. Deepen and blend the tones of the glove, as well as the tip of the yellow cushion.

A FEW STEPS FURTHER

The surfaces in the still life now have a pleasing soft feel to them that suggests the texture of fabric. All that remains is to add a little contrast in the form of some sharp detail.

9 ▶ **Create a highlight** Put in a suggestion of the background by rubbing on charcoal with the medium stump. To emphasise the light falling on the glove, lift out a light patch along one side, using the tip of a putty rubber. Define the pattern on the scarf in more detail.

10 ▲ **Check the last details** Darken the shaded folds of the foreground fabric, leaving the buff paper to represent the ridges of fabric that are catching the light. Add any details that you might have missed, such as the pattern on the wrist of the glove and the tassels on the scarf. Spray the picture with fixative.

THE FINISHED PICTURE

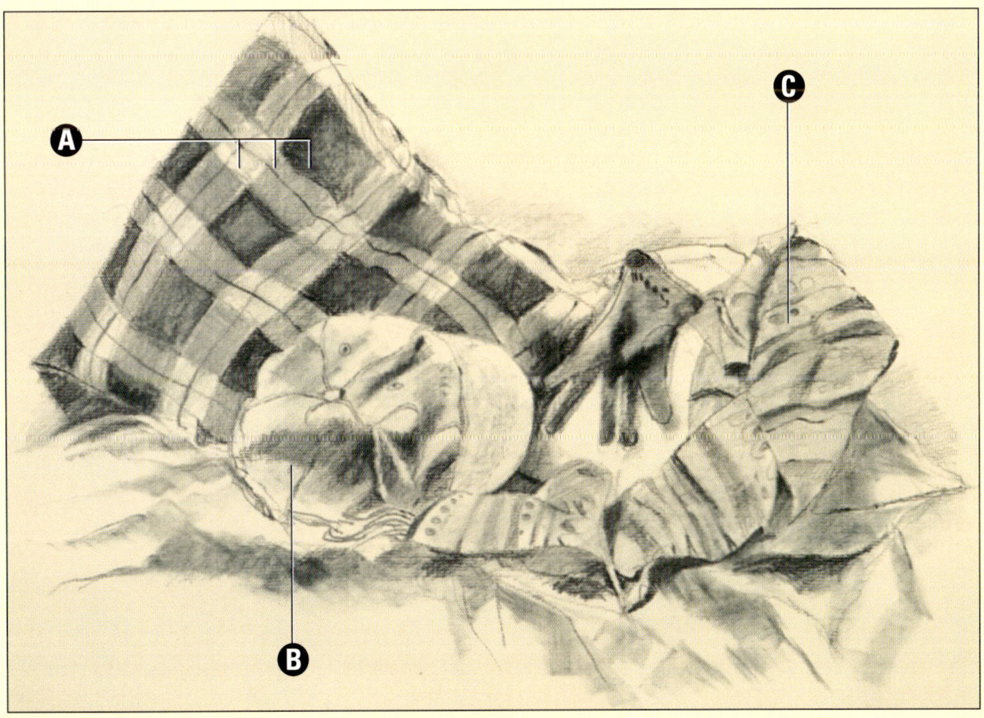

A Tonal contrast
By using a variety of hard, medium and soft charcoal pencils, a range of light, mid and dark tones is established in the drawing.

B Smudged effect
Blending shaded areas of charcoal with a stump gives a soft, hazy look that suggests the texture of woven or knitted fabric.

C Fine lines
To contrast with the softly blended tones in the drawing, the fine, distinct lines show pattern and details such as stitching.

Details and textures in watercolour

Although watercolours can be used in a free and loose manner, they can also be used to create intricate, highly finished paintings.

Using a simple pocket set of watercolour paints, the artist for this step-by-step created a sweeping rendition of a Scottish landscape – full of subtle variations of colour and texture.

In the foreground, features, such as the tree branches and intricate shadows, are brought into sharp focus using carefully controlled lines made with a fine brush. In contrast to these lines, lively elements have been created by applying the paint in unconventional ways.

Flicking paint

Sprays of seeded grasses, for example, were added in the foreground by gently flicking paint on to the paper. And outstretched, leafy branches have been implied by blowing small pools of wet paint across the paper. These details give the impression of wind blowing across the scene, playing on the grass and foliage as it passes.

In the background, however, little detail has been added. Instead, broad strokes have been used to create the smooth surface of the mountain in a harmonious range of greens, browns and blues. To create these colours, you need constantly to mix small amounts of different colours into your main washes.

It is, therefore, vital to wash your brush often to avoid muddy colours. Dry off the brush on a wad of tissues, or flick the spare water out on to a newspaper positioned on the floor.

▶ The artist has used aerial perspective to create a sense of depth. The distant mountain is rendered in cool blues and greens, while the grassy areas are painted in warm browns. Note also that the figure in the reference photo (top right) has been omitted to create an unsullied scene.

YOU WILL NEED

Piece of 300gsm (140lb) Not watercolour paper 40 x 60cm (16 x 24 in)

HB pencil

Brushes: Nos.8, 6 and 2 flats; Nos.4 and 00 rounds

Large jar of water

10 watercolours: Ultramarine; Cobalt blue; Crimson; Burnt umber; Emerald green; Ochre; Orange; Forest green; Cadmium yellow; Black

Large flat mixing dish

Paper tissues

FIRST STROKES

1 ▼ Sketch out the scene With an HB pencil, sketch out the main features of your scene. In the palest areas, press only lightly with the pencil, capturing the faintest impression of the ragged outlines of the foliage. In darker areas, you can block in the shadows with a firmer scribbling action. These pencil marks are an important foundation on which to build your detailed composition.

2 ▲ Prepare the sky Use a No.8 flat brush and clean water to wet the sky area, making a neat edge along the line of the mountain. Do not let the area get too wet, or the paper might become wrinkled – but put on enough water to make the paper surface glisten.

3 ▶ Wash in the sky colours Put touches of ultramarine and cobalt blue into a pool of clean water on your mixing dish. Working quickly on the wet paper, boldly mark in the blue sky above the mountain. The water on the paper will make the edges of the colour blend into the white areas. Clean the brush. With tiny spots of crimson and burnt umber, colour a second pool of water and wash in the undersides of the clouds.

DEVELOPING THE PICTURE

Now that you have established the basic outlines and washed in the sky, you can begin work on the landscape itself. To achieve a range of lively textural effects, use various methods of applying the paint, from dabbing and hatching to spattering.

4 ▶ Block in the foliage With clean water, wet the paper in the main areas of foliage. Mix a wash of emerald green with touches of burnt umber and ultramarine. With a No.4 round brush, block in the foliage, using a dabbing action. Let the patches of colour overlap and run into one another, leaving patches of plain white paper in between.

5 ◀ Establish the foreground Wash the paper in the foreground with clean water. Mix a wash of ochre and burnt umber with a touch of orange, then use the flattened tip of the No.8 flat brush to sketch in the grass. Create strong, textural strokes to make these foreground features stand out. As you work, pull touches of other colours into your wash – emerald green, forest green, burnt umber, ochre and cadmium yellow.

6 ▲ Work into the shadows With a strong wash of ultramarine, forest green and a tiny touch of black, use a No.8 flat brush to work in the deep shadows under the bushes. Visually, this makes a strong line to draw the eye across the painting. Use tight hatching marks along the edge of the grassy area to give the impression of grasses growing up across the shadows.

Master Strokes

Robert Adam (1728-92)

Landscape with Bridge over a Stream

In this landscape, Scottish artist and architect Robert Adam has used a palette of colours similar to that of the step-by-step project, combining warm browns and ochres with a range of subtle greens and cool blue-greys. As in the step-by-step, the textures are varied – dabs and washes of colour contrast with meticulously painted details, such as the tree branches and the bridge.

The warm-toned bush on the right catches the viewer's attention. It offers a strong contrast to the more muted greens in the other areas of the landscape.

Cutting diagonally across the picture, the bridge leads the eye into the middle distance of the painting.

7 ▼ **Establish the mountain** Wait until the sky area is dry so that the edge of the mountain will remain crisp. The mountain is worked on dry paper with a wash of burnt umber, plus touches of cobalt blue and ultramarine to give it a cold, distant appearance. Use long, flat strokes of the No.8 flat brush following the contours of the mountain. Draw a touch more ultramarine into the mix for the darker (right) side of the mountain.

8 ▲ **Develop the foliage** Using a No.6 flat brush, dab emerald green with a little ochre and burnt umber on to the leafy areas. For a lively effect, identify pools of green paint around the edge of the tree. With your face close to the paper, blow sharply across the surface to throw spurts of paint outwards from the tree. Remove unwanted spots of paint with a tissue.

9 ▶ Mark in the twigs Use a No.00 round brush and burnt umber paint to mark in the trunk and main branches of the tree. Some are visible between the green patchy areas. Others stretch out sideways to support external foliage. Refer back to your subject to ensure that your marks remain characteristic of the tree. To mark out the finest twigs, see Expert Advice on page 177.

10 ▲ Work a foreground tree To create a light area, draw a wet brush along the line of the trunk. Dry the brush on a tissue, then draw it down the same line to leach out the colour. Use a mix of forest green, ultramarine and a little black for the shadows around the tree. Develop the foliage of the large tree and bushes, using the same colours as in step 8. Add ochre to help the foreground tree stand out.

11 ▲ Enliven the foreground grass Add touches of orange and emerald green to ochre and use a No.6 flat brush to paint in coarse, grassy marks in the foreground of the composition. For a lively texture, make some flicking marks upwards from the base of the grass stems. To do this, load the brush with paint, then hold it in one hand close to the paper and pull the bristles back with the fingers of your other hand. Release with a flick upwards to spatter paint across the picture. Remove unwanted spots of paint quickly with a tissue.

TROUBLE SHOOTER

REMOVING PAINT SPOTS

If paint splashes on to a plain area such as the sky, it can be removed with some quick action. While the paint is still wet, press a clean paper tissue on top of the mark. Add a drop of clean water to the mark, blot with tissue and repeat until the mark disappears.

12▼ Develop the middle distance Using a No.6 flat brush, mix a wash of cadmium yellow with a tiny touch of burnt umber to block in the field in the middle distance, behind the bushes. Put more burnt umber and a touch of orange into the wash, then use a stiff-bristled toothbrush to scrub the colour across the middle range of the grassy area. Mimic the textural lines of the grasses with your strokes.

13▼ Deepen the tree shadows Add a touch of black to burnt umber and, using the tip of a No.4 round brush, work in the deepest shadows on the trunk and branches of the tree. Use the black paint very sparingly, saving it for really striking details such as these.

EXPERT ADVICE
Indenting fine marks

Before you paint the finest twig lines in the tree structure, use the pointed wooden end of a paint brush to press indentations into the surface of the watercolour paper. These will make tiny 'rivulets', which will hold the dark paint neatly in delicate twig shapes.

14▲ Strengthen the features Stand back from the picture and judge the tonal balance between the different areas. Using the No.8 flat brush, strengthen the main features. Use a wash of ultramarine with touches of black and crimson to deepen the shadow areas on the mountain. Draw more ultramarine into the mix to establish the deepest shadows. Add ochre to emerald green in varying proportions to enliven the upper parts of the bushes.

15▼ Add distance detail Use the technique from step 10 to leach out colour from under one of the bushes. With a No.00 round brush, wash in a mix of cadmium yellow with a touch of burnt umber. Once dry, paint black trunk details.

16▲ Finalise the balance Using the No.8 flat brush and a mix of cobalt blue, ultramarine and emerald green, wash in the lower area of the mountain behind the distant trees. Add trunks and branches to the small tree on the left using the techniques from step 13. With the No.6 flat brush and a mix of forest green and ultramarine, use a dabbing action to develop the leaf detail of both the small and large trees.

A FEW STEPS FURTHER

The composition is now complete, but you might wish to draw out some of the character of the scene with more work on fine detail, such as the grass and branches.

17▲ Develop the detail With a strong mix of burnt umber and black, and using a No.2 flat brush, paint in more branches and twigs on the largest tree. Strengthen existing branches to the front of the tree, but leave the ones nearer the back more washed out, to give a sense of three dimensions.

Express yourself

Focus on texture

The chosen scene is characterised by contrasting areas of smooth sky, sculpted mountain surface and detailed foliage areas. To focus on these textures rather than the colours, discard your paints and take up a piece of charcoal or, as here, a burnt umber soft pastel. Working with a loose style on Not watercolour paper, capture the textures with a variety of strokes. Use soft, scribbling motions for the shadows, flowing marks for the contours of the mountain, and a hatching action for the grass. Use the charcoal or pastel on its side to block in larger areas of smooth shadow.

18 ▸ Add sweeps of colour As a finishing touch, you could convey the impression of the sweeping movements of a strong wind. Make up a strong mix of burnt umber and ochre. With a No.4 round brush, make bold, slanting marks across the foreground area to suggest the blown and tumbled grasses.

THE FINISHED PICTURE

A Sense of distance
The cool blues and greens of the distant mountain recede, helping create a sense of depth. They contrast with the warmer ochres, oranges and browns in the foreground.

B Contrasting textures
Hatched brush strokes and spattered paint created a lively texture for the scrubby grassland. This contrasts with the smooth sky and sculpted surface of the mountain.

C Strong diagonal
The line of trees and the slope in the middle distance helps create dynamic diagonals that cut across the picture. They provide a pleasing echo of the sloped profile of the mountain.

Impasto

Painting 'impasto' is a good way to overcome inhibitions and achieve striking textured results quickly.

Vincent Van Gogh sometimes used his fingers to achieve the thick swirls of colour for which he is famous. He also took great delight in loading his brush or knife with paint and applying it directly to the canvas without diluting the colour at all. Whatever Van Gogh painted – rippling grass or stormy skies – lively paintwork is one of the most memorable aspects of his painting. He used thick colour to bring his subjects to life.

Textured surface

Some paints can be applied thickly enough to build up a beautifully textured surface in which the brush and knife marks are clearly visible. This technique, in which the colour is sometimes so stiff and paste-like that it stands out from the canvas in an almost sculptural way, is often referred to as 'impasto'. Painting in this way is not only great fun, but is also very satisfying. It is a spontaneous and extremely direct approach – a good way to achieve striking results quickly.

To understand impasto properly, take a look at Van Gogh's *Starry Night*. The richness of texture in this and many other of his paintings is the result of bold, gestural brush strokes and thick, impastoed paint. The surface of the painting is as important as the colour, composition or subject.

What sort of paint?

Acrylic is generally considered the best medium for impasto painting because the paints are flexible and can be used undiluted, directly from the tube. However, it is advisable to build up the colour gradually, layer by layer, because even acrylic paint can flake and crack if too much is applied in one go.

The consistency of acrylic colour varies depending on the manufacturer, but most types are thick enough to allow you to achieve satisfying impasto effects. The great advantage of acrylic paints is that they dry very quickly – even a thick layer will dry in a few hours. This means you can build up the colour to get an almost three-dimensional effect in a comparatively short time.

IMPASTO WITH A KNIFE

Try some of the impasto effects shown here using acrylics or oils and keep your samples for future reference.

Solid colour

Scoop up a good amount of undiluted colour on the underside of the blade and apply this in broad parallel strokes. Slightly overlap the stripes to create a solid area of colour.

Stippled texture

Pick up undiluted paint on the underside of the blade and apply it by gently patting the canvas with the knife. The result is a stippled texture with flat areas of colour alternating with tiny peaks of paint.

Linear marks

Dip the edge of the blade in thick paint and impress the colour onto the canvas. This produces sharp, well-defined lines that are useful for painting grasses, foliage and tree branches.

◀ **In *Starry Night* Vincent Van Gogh (1853-90) uses impasto to dramatic effect, with heavily encrusted paint strokes indicating the play of light.**

Impasto with oils

Oils are also suitable for painting impasto, and Van Gogh was not the only artist to have created lively, textural pictures using oil paints. Since the medium was first developed during the Renaissance period, many different painters have used encrusted colour and bold brush strokes to describe form, create depth and lend texture to their work.

However, in some ways oils are less versatile than acrylics and should be used with caution. As with acrylics, oil paint can be built up to form layers of heavy colour, but the slow-drying nature of the medium can make this a time-consuming process. Also, thick oil paint can take days or even weeks to dry and even then the colour may wrinkle and crack as it dries out. Oil paint should always be applied in layers and built up gradually. That being said, if they are applied carefully, oils can be used to create beautifully impastoed surfaces, which are not only lovely to look at, but will also stand the test of time.

Texture with a brush

Thick paint retains the shape of the brush strokes, especially if you load your brush with plenty of colour before applying it to the canvas. To make the most of this exciting technique, you will need to use bold marks. It is no good being tentative and dabbing away at the surface of the canvas – this will only flatten the paint and kill the effect. For the liveliest brushwork, use the paint undiluted, apply the colour to the picture in confident strokes – and then leave it alone!

The shape and size of the brush will affect the marks you make, as will the way you hold the brush. Use the tip of the bristles and work with short stabbing strokes to get dots and staccato marks; to paint swirling lines, move your whole arm. Try out different kinds of brushes and the marks they make.

Knife painting

The brush is the most usual tool for painting, but some effects cannot be achieved with a brush alone. A knife is particularly useful for building up solid areas of flat colour in a way not possible with a brush. In fact, many artists paint with just a knife and prefer never to use a brush. Ideally, choose a proper painting knife with a raised handle. This will allow you to spread the paint evenly without smudging the colour with your hand. Painting knives come in a range of sizes and shapes and can be used to create a wide variety of marks.

For an area of flat impastoed colour, scoop the thick paint from the palette and drag it across the canvas, keeping the knife parallel to the surface. This is rather like spreading butter, so if you do not have a painting knife try using any other knife with a straight, flexible blade. Alternatively, a piece of stiff card is a good substitute.

IMPASTO WITH A BRUSH

Brushes give different textures with thick paint, depending on the shape of the bristles and how you manipulate them.

For a dense, regular texture use a flat brush and paint with the flattened side of the bristles. Use undiluted paint and apply this in close, neat lines. This is a useful trick for creating the texture of grass.

Use a loaded flat brush to paint parallel, overlapping lines. Resist the temptation to flatten the resulting ridges – these lend freshness and spontaneity to the painting.

Do what Van Gogh did! Load a round brush with plenty of thick colour and paint in loose, swirling strokes. Leave the marks just as they appear without attempting to tidy them up.

Experimental effects

Above all, do not be frightened to experiment. It is possible to build up a whole vocabulary of paint marks, and it is worth while exploring the possibilities of different painting tools to do this. For example, you can create an unusual ridged texture with the plastic spreader sold with floor adhesives and tile grouts.

▶ **Experiment to discover new ways of applying thick colour. Here an adhesive spreader, available from hardware and decorating shops, is used to spread thick colour.**

Adding colour to scraperboard

Combine strong tonal contrasts and bright hues in a garden scene, using scraperboard with coloured inks.

This view across a beautifully tended garden calls out to be drawn on scraperboard. The photograph has strong tonal contrasts – for example, between the hedges and their sunlit tops, and between the dark, clipped conifers and the light lawn behind them. This dramatic lighting effect is ideal for scraperboard work, which is most effective when used for compositions that have black areas close to pale ones, without too many mid tones in between.

To create the type of scraperboard picture shown here, you can use a pointed tool to make the fine lines and a curved tool for the broad areas. In this project, an asymmetrical pointed tool is added – with this you can make fine lines and, by turning the blade on its side, wider ones, too, without needing to change from one blade to another.

A touch of colour

Scraperboard work does not have to be just black and white. It looks very effective with the addition of a little colour on the white areas. Here, a few touches of coloured ink enliven the view and give the garden a more summery feel.

Don't flood the board with ink – keep your brush fairly dry and work within the white areas you want to colour rather than brushing too much ink over the surrounding black.

▶ **Coloured inks enhance this country garden view with the tints of nature.**

YOU WILL NEED

- Piece of black scraperboard 30 x 22cm (12 x 8½in)
- White Conté pencil
- Curved cutter
- Pointed cutter
- Asymmetrical pointed cutter
- No.4 soft round brush
- Indian ink
- 6 coloured inks: Cobalt; Canary yellow; Nut brown; Viridian; Apple green; Brick red
- Distilled water

FIRST STEPS

1 ▼ Make a Conté sketch Your initial sketch needs to show clearly on the black surface of the scraperboard, so use a white Conté pencil to outline the main features of the landscape. Indicate the rounded trees and the conifers, the horizontal lines of the hedges and the pale foreground. Position the climbing plants on the left and the ornamental fence in the centre.

EXPERT ADVICE
Mask your composition

While you are building up your scraperboard picture, it is useful to have straight edges to work up to. A paper mask is a good way of isolating the picture area. Mark the picture size on a large sheet of white paper and cut out the centre. Then place the cut paper over the scraperboard and tape down the edges with masking tape.

2 ▲ Create a light lawn Begin by scraping away the black surface of the board to create the distant sunlit field. Use the wide blade of a curved cutter to remove solid white areas, and a pointed cutter for fine hatched lines. Work around the conifers, varying the direction of the hatching.

3 ▲ Work on the trees Continue scraping the field, leaving the thin tree trunk as a black shape against the white. Change back to the curved cutter to remove broad chunks across the sky, then return to the pointed cutter to draw the left-hand tree foliage with groups of hatched lines. The dark shapes left behind represent the tree's branches. Hatch some well-spaced lines on the right to suggest trees in the distant wood.

4 ▸ Continue the top part of the picture Build up the foliage on the remaining trees on the left with more hatched lines. With fine lines, mark the light tone on the sides of the conifers where they catch the sun. Describe the trees in the distant wood with more well-spaced hatching.

5 ▾ Draw the fence and hedges Using the tip of an asymmetrical pointed cutter, carefully draw the criss-cross lines of the fence, keeping them straight and parallel. Tilt the cutter on to its wider edge to draw the thicker line of the seat. Using the tip of the cutter once more, mark the sunlit tops of the hedges with a series of short lines.

BUILD UP THE MID TONES

Now that you have scraped away some of the main light-toned areas, it is time to work on the mid tones. Use widely spaced hatched lines so that the black background shows through – the optical effect of the alternate bands of white and black is to create a mid toned grey.

6 ▸ Make a mid tone Using the pointed cutter, draw long hatched lines diagonally across the trees in the wood, keeping the lines quite far apart. Where the long lines cross the shorter ones that you drew in step 4, lighter areas are built up, giving an effect of sunlight catching the tree-tops.

7 ▸ Add some texture Slightly lighten the tone on the trees in the wood with fine cross-hatching. Using the broad side of the asymmetrical cutter, make wider lines on the left of the field, working around the climbing plants. Then change to the tip of the blade to put textural marks on the plants. With the curved cutter, make a leafy texture in the trees with dots and dashes of white.

8 ▴ Move to the foreground Continuing with the curved cutter, scrape over the lawn in the foreground, working around the cast shadow. Create texture by working in different directions. Change to the pointed cutter and make a mid toned shadow with well-spaced cross-hatched lines, then add some finer texture to the lawn.

9▲ Put in final details Using a No.4 soft round brush, paint a shadow across the far field with Indian ink (see Trouble Shooter, below). Then, when the ink has dried, scrape fine lines across it to lighten its tone. Using the pointed cutter, break up the black hedges with a speckled texture. Draw the group of flowers behind the hedge on the left. Changing back to the curved cutter, scrape away more broad marks from the sky and the field.

TROUBLE SHOOTER

MAKING ADJUSTMENTS

If you have removed any of the black surface in error, you can restore dark areas using Indian ink and a fine, soft brush. Here, a long shadow is being painted across the white lawn. Wait for the ink to dry before you continue with the scraperboard work, in case you accidentally smudge it.

A FEW STEPS FURTHER

Although scraperboard work looks dramatic in its original black and white tonal form, it can also look very effective if you add a little colour. Here, brightly coloured inks give a sunny glow to the garden scene.

10▲ Begin painting with blue ink Thin some cobalt coloured ink with distilled water. Using the No.4 round brush, paint this blue shade over the sky. Brush cobalt across parts of the distant trees, too, leaving some areas unpainted so that yellow can be added later.

11▲ Paint the middle ground Water down some canary yellow ink and paint it over the field. Paint the trees on the left with undiluted yellow. Don't feel that you have to fill in every white mark with colour. The picture will look more lively if you leave patches of white showing here and there.

12 ▶ Introduce some greens Paint a little diluted canary yellow over the remaining white areas of the blue trees, and dab in some cobalt among the yellow trees. Add a touch of cobalt and nut brown ink to viridian ink to create a deep bluish green. Paint this across the dotted texture on the hedges and down the sides of the conifers.

13 ▲ Complete the picture Brush canary yellow over the hedge tops and the foreground lawn, using the ink more diluted in some areas than others. Put a touch of apple green on the climbing plants. Paint cobalt over the fence and the flowers. Finally, add a splash of brick red to the flowers.

THE FINISHED PICTURE

A Vertical lines
Black conifers stand out starkly against the light-coloured lawn, giving a strong vertical element to the composition, in contrast to the horizontal lines of the hedges.

B Hedge texture
Tiny dotted and dashed marks were used to convey the texture of the privet hedges, but were scattered well apart so as not to lighten the deep tone.

C Shades of yellow
The lawn was painted with both diluted and undiluted yellow ink. This varies the tone and colour across this broad band of the picture.

Painting in changing light

One subject painted several times from the same viewpoint can provide you with a series of entirely different images – it all depends on the effect of the light.

▲ Claude Monet's fascination with light led him to make 30 paintings of Rouen Cathedral from 1892 to 1894. In the examples here, you can see the radically different effects he achieved. On the left, the cathedral glitters in the sunlight, creating a rich canvas of golds, yellows and browns; on the right, it looks cool, pale and wintry in a hazy light.

The more you paint and draw, the more sensitive you become to the way light describes your subject matter. In some types of light your subject may come alive with exciting colours and tones; at other times it may appear more muted and moody.

Indeed, if you work outdoors a lot, it really pays to spend some time looking at how your subject changes in various lighting conditions – at different times of the day, in different seasons and in different weather. You might even find yourself drawn into making a series of paintings, such as the Houses of Parliament watercolours overleaf.

Depending on the conditions, you may need to adapt your palette to suit the lighting and the time of day. Indeed, a flexible approach really pays as it enables you to introduce different techniques to accommodate the changes in the subject.

Using photographs

Changes of light and colour are sometimes so gradual that the artist, engrossed in a painting, fails to notice the slow onset of an overcast sky or the arrival of dusk. It is therefore a good idea to take a photo before you start work, a reliable reference that can be checked later if the changes are so

MORNING GLORY

The artist made three paintings of the Houses of Parliament in London from three photos taken at various times of the day. Each photo makes a very different painting.

In the morning scene, above, the sun falls squarely on the buildings. This brings out the colour of the warm earthy stonework, which the artist captured with burnt sienna and touches of raw sienna. The sun and the shadows it throws also bring out the detail and texture of the buildings. The shadows were painted in burnt sienna and Payne's grey.

To preserve the crisp edges and straight lines of the buildings, the main shapes were blocked out with masking fluid before painting commenced. Doors, windows and ornamental stonework were picked out in detail using a small brush. For the darkest shadows under the bridge, a mix of Payne's grey and black was used.

Palette: Ultramarine, cerulean blue, burnt sienna, raw sienna, Payne's grey, black.

great that it becomes impossible to finish the painting.

Better still, if your subject is close at hand, take a series of photos over the course of one, or perhaps a few days. Photos are more reliable than the human memory, and you can compare the pictures to see precisely the difference made by the altered lighting and then decide which conditions you prefer.

The one problem with this is that automatic cameras and film processors are likely to compensate for changes in light, making dark colours paler and vice versa. So try to supplement your photos with some quick sketches on site so you have a record of the tones and colours as you actually saw them.

Sunny days

The vivid colours and stark shadows of a sunny day are very prevalent in the morning and evening, and during the winter. At these times the sun is low in the sky, throwing long shadows – and these strong, dark shapes will play a central and positive role in the composition.

As a general rule, you need both warm and cool colours on your palette – warm ones to capture the effect of sunlight, colder ones for the contrasting shadows that this creates. In addition, you need dark colours for the deepest shadows – Payne's grey or combinations of blue and brown are useful. It is also worth noting that faraway objects appear closer on a clear, sunny day. Distant hills and buildings are often surprisingly sharp, with clearly visible details.

In dull weather, light is diffused and evenly dispersed. There are no sharply defined shadows, and distant objects appear hazy and out of focus. Colours are generally cool, and even warm local colours like that of the stonework on the

MIDDAY CLOUD

In early afternoon, with the sun behind the clouds, the buildings have a completely different appearance. The bold yellow stonework has changed to a subtler range of browns; the architectural details are much less clearly defined; and the range of tones is much smaller.

Without sunlight and sharp shadows, the whole scene has a diffuse, misty appearance. To achieve blurred outlines and soft shadows, the artist worked wet-on-wet to capture the buildings, the clouds in the sky and in particular the murky shadows under the bridge. Architectural features were suggested in loose brush strokes rather than depicted in detail.

As the range of tones and colours in this scene is much more limited, the artist used just three colours. The darkest tones – the shadows under the bridge – are painted in Payne's grey and touches of cerulean blue without the addition of black.

Palette: Cerulean blue, raw sienna, Payne's grey.

Houses of Parliament look cool and grey in an afternoon mist.

Although the sky contains little or no blue in dull weather, you will probably need to use a considerable amount of blue in the rest of the painting. For example, our artist added cerulean to burnt sienna and raw sienna to create a cool colour for the stonework in the 'midday' picture.

A misty atmosphere generally obscures some of the distant detail. Make sure you paint only what you can see – not what you know to be there. Usually it is more effective to suggest distant objects with a few brush strokes than to make fine renderings, which work against the illusion of haze.

Against the light

Working against the light – or *contre jour* as it is sometimes called – is traditionally used in evening landscapes when the setting sun provides a dramatic background to darker foreground shapes.

In *contre jour* paintings, the emphasis is on tone – the relationship of lights and darks. However, this does not mean a total absence of colour. As can be seen in the evening view on the right, the sky is streaked with blue and the reflections in the river contain traces of sky colour and raw sienna.

DARKNESS FALLS

This watercolour captures the Houses of Parliament in late afternoon. The sun is now behind the buildings and although it is hidden by clouds it still throws a strong backlight.

In contrast to the morning view, the emphasis is no longer on colour and detail, but on the drama of light and dark and the silhouetted shape of the buildings. The artist has deliberately simplified and exaggerated the contrast of tones to heighten this effect.

Payne's grey is the dominant colour in the painting and – apart from splashes of blue in the sky, and raw sienna in the reflections – local colour is kept to a bare minimum.

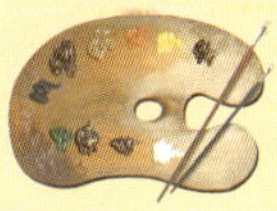

Palette: Ultramarine, cerulean blue, raw sienna, Payne's grey.

Scumbling techniques

One of the most interesting and versatile methods of applying broken colour to a surface is called scumbling. Used with oil or acrylic paints, this technique will add a new dimension to your work.

Despite its intriguing name, scumbling is simply an effective way of changing or breaking up an area of colour without completely covering it over. In practice, scumbling changes a colour while allowing the original colour to show through. Although the term traditionally refers to an opaque or semi-opaque pale colour which is applied in loose, uneven brush strokes over a darker one, it is also used in a more general way to describe any form of broken colour, including glazing and drybrush work.

Brush strokes

A scumbled colour is usually irregular; the scumbled brush strokes can be seen and the colour underneath shows through, usually in flecks or long streaks depending on your brush strokes. The strokes can be short and stippled, long and streaky, or entirely random. For streaky strokes, simply dip the brush into the paint and drag this across the dry undercolour using the tips of the bristles. Alternatively, you can roll a loaded brush in a more random manner to create more textural areas of modified colour.

Scumbling is especially useful when you have established the colour scheme in a painting, but then decide that you want to make one particular area lighter or darker without destroying the overall effect. Simply load your brush with a lighter or darker tone of the colour you have already used and scumble this over the relevant area.

▲ In this oil painting, *Still Life* by Brenda Holtam, scumbling is used extensively, especially in the background and the spaces between the objects. Small patches of opaque paint are built up using fine strokes until the tone and colour of each scumbled area is in complete harmony with the rest of the composition. Throughout the picture, undercolours and the warm tone of the support show through the subtly scumbled strokes.

SCUMBLED COLOUR MIXING

When one colour is scumbled across another the result is an optical mix – the illusion of a third colour, created by the merging of the two colours by the eye of the viewer. The examples below show what happens when one primary colour is scumbled over another. Red scumbled over yellow produces a more yellowy orange than yellow over red, for example. Although the brush marks are irregular, the tone of the scumbled area is even across the whole area.

Blue over yellow

Red over blue

Red over yellow

Yellow over red

Changing colours

One colour scumbled over another will create the impression of a third colour. For example, yellow over red will produce an optical orange – that is, the red and yellow marks are still visible as separate colours but they merge in the perception of the viewer to create orange.

Colours created in this way are more vibrant and shimmering than the flat version of the same colour. Try a few variations for yourself. The examples on page 190 are created from the three primary colours – red, yellow and blue. However, combined complementaries are equally effective and you could also experiment by using two similar colours, by overlaying earth colours, or by scumbling with black and white.

Suitable surfaces

Any type of painting surface is suitable for scumbling, including canvas, paper and board, although the rougher the texture the more effective the scumbling colour will be. On a coarse canvas, the scumbled paint catches on the raised fibres, and the weave of the fabric often features in the scumbled colour.

On a smooth surface, work with lively, irregular brush strokes, preferably with a fairly stiff brush. The surface itself will not contribute to the finished effect.

Oils or acrylics

Textural scumbling is normally done with oils or acrylics – this is because these are paints which can be used either completely undiluted or thickly enough to allow the brush marks to retain their shape. Colour can then be applied quite dryly over the surface of the paint, allowing flecks of the colour underneath to show through the strokes. This technique works best of all on a coarse or toothed surface, such as highly textured paper, acrylic board or canvas.

Watercolour and gouache

Another version of scumbling involves applying diluted colour, either with a dry brush or as a thin film (the latter is similar to a glaze but done with semi-opaque rather than transparent colour). These wet scumble effects can be achieved with all types of paint, including gouache and watercolour.

TEXTURE AND IRREGULAR COLOUR

Drybrush scumbling

The tips of the bristles of a stiff brush are dipped in thick colour and dragged lightly across a coarse canvas, or other textured surface. The paint is caught on the raised textures of the support allowing indentations of undercolour to show through. For a lighter effect, the bristles can be splayed apart with your finger, as seen below.

Atmospheric colour

Irregular strokes of pale opaque colour are traditionally used in landscapes to paint dappled light, reflections on water and atmospheric skies. In the picture below, the artist is rolling a round brush heavily loaded with white paint on to a darker blue background in order to suggest fluffy white clouds.

CREATING A RANDOM SCUMBLED EFFECT

For a loose, random effect, the brush is loaded with colour and then rolled lightly across the painting surface in short, irregular strokes. As you can see from the examples here, the texture of the surface affects the finished result. On canvas, the weave of the fabric contributes to the strong textural effect. This effect is particularly obvious on unprimed canvas and hessian. On paper, the uneven application of paint shows clearly, but the surface of the paper does not affect the surface of the paint.

On coarse unprimed canvas

On unprimed hessian

On paper

On primed canvas

Spattering effects

Random speckled patterns are ideal for suggesting textures in painting. Effects like this are quick and easy to achieve with the spattering technique.

Spattering or flicking fluid paint on to a support allows you to create a range of dappled, speckled and mottled effects. The appeal of these effects is their spontaneity, their randomness and the fact that they do not show any brush marks.

▶ Run your finger briskly across a toothbrush loaded with paint to create a shower of tiny droplets.

Showing texture

Textural effects can be introduced into your paintings for a variety of reasons. You can use them to imitate rough surfaces or perhaps to represent particular elements in a landscape. Areas of spattering provide an effective shorthand for pebbles on a beach, cobblestones, foliage in the distance, stone walls, turned earth and many other 'broken' surfaces.

Textures can also be used for purely decorative effects. With various spattering techniques, you can create delicate mists of a single colour or build up complex, random patterns using a rich, varied palette of colours. Use these effects to enrich surfaces or add interest to passages of otherwise flat colour.

Suitable media

Any liquid medium, including inks, acrylics, watercolour, gouache and thinned oil paint, can be used in spattering techniques. Spattering works best when the support is kept completely flat – if the surface is tilted, the droplets of paint might run, spoiling the effect you have created.

▼ A variety of tools can be used for spattering: (clockwise from far left) toothbrush, artist's soft brush, bristle brush, small stencil brush, large stencil brush, pump spray, mouth spray, nailbrush.

Methods of spattering

There are many different ways to create a spattered effect. One method is to use a stiff-bristled brush, such as a toothbrush or a stencilling brush. Mix a quantity of paint, dip the brush and shake off any surplus. Hold the brush over the support and draw your finger or something rigid, such as a metal ruler or brush handle, through the bristles. A fine spray of droplets will be deposited on the paper, creating a speckled effect. The further away you hold the brush, the larger the droplets will be.

Splashes and sprays

Another method of spattering is to load a paint brush with thinned paint and flick your wrist vigorously to deposit droplets of paint on the support. This introduces larger splashes and variation in size. Or you can load a brush with colour, hold it over the surface and then tap it across the handle of another brush. This technique allows you to cover a large area of paper and to build up dense layers of spattered colour.

A similar effect can be achieved by spraying paint, using a mouth spray or a container with a pump spray nozzle – many cosmetics and household products are supplied in such containers.

Diverse effects

A wide range of effects can be achieved with any of these spattering techniques. You can create a light stipple with a single application of colour, or build up a dense, granular surface by applying several layers of spatter, allowing the paint to dry between each application. For a subtly modulated surface, apply different tones of the same colour, or create a rich multi-coloured effect by overlaying different shades.

With soluble media, such as watercolour, you can spatter pure water on to a dry wash. The droplets of water will cause the paint to dissolve and the pigment will migrate to the outside of each splash, creating pale splodges within the wash. This effect is particularly dramatic if gum arabic is added to the base wash. To create a similar effect with oil paints, you should spatter some turpentine or methylated spirits on to the still-wet paint surface.

If you spatter watercolour paint on to a damp surface, the spatters bleed into the adjoining areas. This creates a softly diffused, mottled pattern.

Spend some time experimenting with the exciting and unpredictable effects created by spattering. You will find that you quickly build up a useful range of patterns and textures to add to your painting repertoire.

▶ **Heavy spattering fading to a lighter texture suggests pebbles on a beach stretching into the distance.**

EXPERIMENTING WITH SPATTERING TECHNIQUES

A wide range of results can be achieved using this simple technique. Explore the different effects you can create by experimenting with watercolours on scrap paper. Remember to protect the area surrounding your paper while you practise.

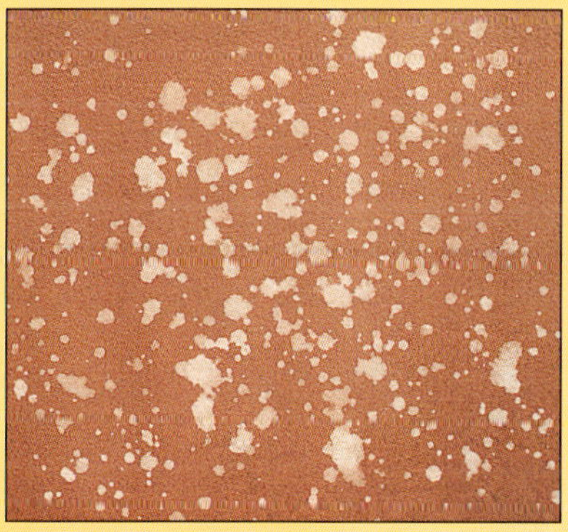

◀ **Blotting spattered water** A wash of alizarin crimson and gum arabic was applied to the support and left to dry. Water was spattered on, then blotted with kitchen paper to create irregularly shaped dapples of light tone.

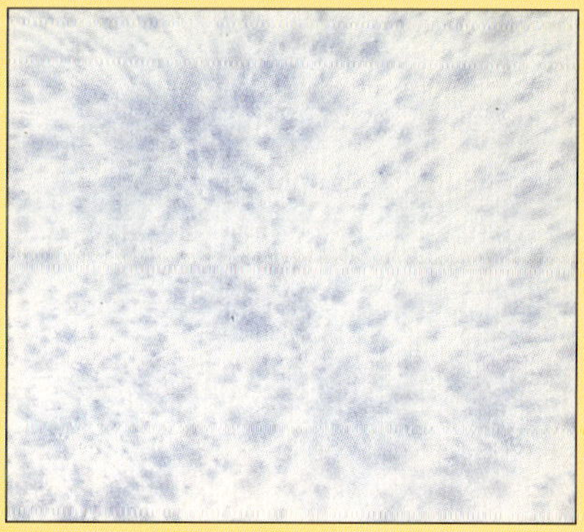

◀ **Spattering on damp paper** This softly diffused effect was created by spattering Winsor blue watercolour on to damp paper. The droplets of wash have bled across and into the paper.

▶ **Spattering water over a wash** A wash of Winsor blue mixed with gum arabic was applied to the support and allowed to dry. Water was spattered on and left to dry. This process was repeated several times, allowing the surface to dry thoroughly between each application.

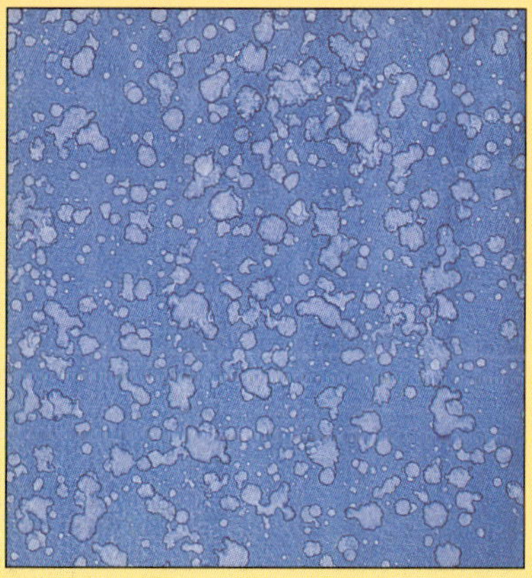

▶ **Spattering in layers** This subtly variegated effect was achieved by spattering green and yellow washes on to rough watercolour paper, leaving the support to dry between applications.

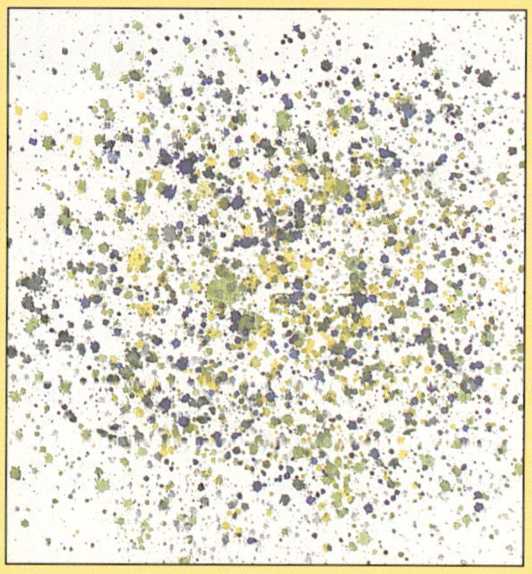

Using adhesives

The range of available glues and gums is now enormous, and you can have great fun using these to invent your own textures and patterns, and to create stunning collages.

The first adhesives were used by our prehistoric ancestors in the deepest recesses of limestone caves. They painted pictures of animals and hunting scenes on the cavern walls, working with only a handful of earth pigments plus soot and chalk. Paints were made by grinding and mixing the powdered ingredients with adhesives which bound the colours together and ensured they stuck firmly to the rocky cavern walls.

These early adhesives – gum from trees and plants, and glues made by boiling animal bones and skin – were so effective that many of the ancient cave paintings are still there, brilliant and intact, some 20,000 years later.

Adhesives today

Like the adhesives used by our painter ancestors, many modern products are still based on natural materials. These include starch, from potato and cereal; casein, from milk; latex, from rubber trees; and water-soluble gums, such as gum arabic, from the acacia plant. Other natural adhesives are obtained by boiling bones, hoofs and skin; resin, extracted from pine trees; and shellac, produced by a parasitic tree insect.

In addition, many more adhesives are made from the wide range of synthetic resins now available. These include all acrylic products; PVA; superglue; most contact glues; synthetic rubberised adhesive; and the 'two-tube' glues which consist of a resin and a hardener to be mixed just before use.

Cow gum

This sticky gum brings out translucent colour mixtures when two or more layers of tissue paper are stuck together so that they overlap.

1 ► Magenta tissue paper is stuck down on a sheet of thin white card using a plastic spreader, then more gum is spread on top of the magenta.

2 ◄ A piece of yellow tissue is laid on the gummed area and pressed firmly down to create a bright orange where the papers overlap.

A few of the many adhesives used in the artist's studio:

- **A** Double-sided tape
- **B** Woodworking glue
- **C** Rabbit-skin glue crystals
- **D** Prepared rabbit-skin glue
- **E** Cow gum
- **F** Spray adhesive
- **G** Plastic spreaders
- **H** Latex glue
- **I** Transparent adhesive tape
- **J** Invisible tape

◄ **Exploit the adhesive properties of acrylic to combine texture and colour. Silver flakes sprinkled over this wet acrylic surface produce an unusual collage effect.**

Adhesives for the artist

Artists use adhesives all the time. Apart from their role in collage and texture-making techniques, adhesives are an essential ingredient in most art materials. Paints, pastels and crayons are made with a binder which holds dry pigment particles together; papers are sized with a gum or resin to make them suitable for painting and drawing; and canvas is sealed and primed with size or an acrylic medium. Here are some of the adhesives most often used by artists:

Rabbit-skin glue is traditionally used for sizing canvas and boards prior to oil painting. The glue, made by boiling off-cuts of rabbit skin, is sold in granule or powder form. Prepare it by soaking in water overnight, then warming it in a double burner. The recipe for canvas size is about an ounce of glue to a pint of water. Real gesso is a combination of rabbit-skin glue and titanium white.

Rabbit-skin glue can go off, producing a putrid smell, especially in warm weather. Synthetic cellulose size (CMC), which is odourless and dissolvable in cold water, is an alternative.

Acrylic including gloss and matt mediums, and impasto and texture paste, has adhesive properties, making it excellent for combining collage with texture and colour. Acrylic mediums can be diluted and used to seal paper and canvas prior to acrylic painting.

PVA (polyvinyl acetate) is cheaper than acrylic but with the same adhesive properties. PVA medium is thick and viscous, similar to woodworking glue. It can be used as a binder with powder pigments to produce PVA paints; diluted with water to seal and size painting surfaces; and used in textural collages.

Latex adhesive remains flexible and rubbery when dry. It is good for sticking fabric, tissue and paper. Latex is also the basis of masking fluid – this is applied with a brush or pen and dries to form a rubbery film that protects the area underneath from overlaid colour.

Adhesive tapes have one or two sticky sides. For artists, masking tape is one of the most useful. It is strong with a low-tack adhesive on one side, and can be stuck to canvas, paper or a dry painted surface to protect the masked area from subsequent paint. The tape can be removed without damaging the surface. Double-sided tape is used for fixing works on paper to a card mount or backing.

Spray adhesives come in pressurised cans and are used mainly for sticking and mounting paper and thin card. Some have a delayed drying time, which allows you to remove and reposition the paper or card.

Cow gum is flexible, slow-drying and highly viscous – particularly effective in paper collage. To remove unwanted cow gum, roll some dried gum into a small ball and use this as an eraser.

Binders are used to bind dry ingredients in many artist's materials. Gum arabic is a common watercolour binder; egg is used to bind tempera colours; various gums, starches, resins and caseins are all used in manufacturing soft pastels.

WOODWORKING GLUE FOR COLLAGE

Similar to PVA or acrylic medium, woodworking glue offers a convenient and inexpensive alternative for creating texture in collage. Here, a piece of white tissue is used to create a rugged surface ready to be painted.

Spread the glue liberally on a sheet of stiff white card and lay the crumpled tissue on the wet glue.

With a clean stiff brush, apply more glue to the top of the tissue. Use the brush to create peaks and swirls.

When the glue is completely dry, brush acrylic colour on to the rigid textured surface.

The finished effect is a richly textured surface which artists might find useful for representing foliage or grass.

Using resists

Discover the range of textures you can achieve by using watercolours with different masking materials.

▲ **Masking off areas in this picture has created sparkling highlights and interesting textures.**

Watercolour paints are unique because they are transparent. The colours contain no white or chalky pigments to make them opaque or cloudy.

For this reason, the most effective watercolour painting is done without the addition of white paint. This means you must plan ahead, leaving areas of white paper unpainted so that they represent highlights and paler tones in the picture.

Mask out the whites

Although white paper is a crucial element in most watercolour painting, you are not restricted to simply leaving certain areas unpainted. In fact, as you might have discovered, it is quite difficult to retain patches of white paper simply by painting around them. Not only do you have to remember where the white areas are, but you also have to take care not to paint over them by mistake.

The trick is to protect, or mask, the white areas before you start painting. In this way, you can work quickly, applying colour freely over the masked areas which will eventually show through the paint as patches of pure white. Any substance that temporarily blocks out the paper is known as a resist.

Masking fluid

For sharply defined shapes with a hard edge, such as the crisp highlight on this shiny, ceramic plate, nothing is more effective than masking fluid. This can be applied to the paper with either a brush or pen, and dries to form a thin, rubbery film. You can then paint over it and rub it off when the colours are dry to reveal the white paper underneath.

Candles and wax crayons

For a textured or linear resist, try using candles, wax crayons or oil pastels. When watercolour is painted over the oily or waxy marks, it forms droplets, which run off the resist area. However, a few drops will usually dry on top of the resist to create an attractive speckled texture. Wax crayons or oil pastels will provide a touch of colour too.

FIRST STEPS

1 ▸ Draw the still life Start by making a simple line drawing of the bowl of fruit – a chunky carpenter's pencil will help you to keep the shapes broad and unfussy. Draw the plate as an ellipse and then establish each piece of fruit as an approximate circle. Take the spiky leaves over the edge of the plate to interrupt the elliptical shape.

YOU WILL NEED

Piece of 300gsm (140lb) Not watercolour paper 41 x 46cm (16 x 18in)

Carpenter's pencil

Brushes: 38mm (1½in) flat wash brush; Nos.8 and 7 soft rounds

9 watercolours: Burnt umber; Cadmium yellow; Ivory black; Lemon yellow; Viridian; Cadmium red; Alizarin crimson; Ultramarine; Yellow ochre

2 wax crayons: Lemon yellow; Orange

Household candle

Masking fluid and old round brush

2 ◂ Apply a wash over the background Using a 38mm (1½in) flat wash brush, paint the table top in a wash of burnt umber mixed with a little cadmium yellow. Apply the colour in broad, rapid strokes, working around the outlines of the bowl and fruit. A few drips and tidemarks will add interest to the flat table area, so don't worry if the paint looks uneven.

EXPERT ADVICE
Removing masking fluid

When removing areas of masking fluid, start rubbing from the centre of the masked shape and work outwards. In this way, the fluid should come away easily without tearing the surface of the paper.

3 ▸ Mask out the highlights While the wash dries, take the opportunity to mask out some of the highlights on the fruit, using wax crayons. Make loose, sketchy strokes, but indicate the approximate rounded contours of the fruits. Choose a yellow wax crayon for the lime and an orange one for the tangerines and the pomegranate.

4▼ Draw reflections with a candle Continuing with the orange wax crayon, scribble over the highlight area of the pomegranate. Then use a candle to establish the white reflections on the grapes and figs. The colourless wax preserves the whiteness of the paper

5▲ Apply masking fluid Paint the highlight around the rim of the bowl as a curved line, using masking fluid and an old round brush. Paint another line of fluid across the plate – this will be the grapes' stalk (see step 14).

DEVELOPING THE PICTURE

All the masked highlights have now been established, and it is time to start painting. Remember, the beauty of using resists is that it allows you to paint quite freely as the highlight areas are protected.

6▲ Apply a wash to the plate Using the 38mm (1½in) flat brush, paint the plate with a pale grey wash mixed from ivory black with lots of water. Follow the curved shape of the plate and use bold strokes to paint around the grapes and other fruit. Darken the tone of your wash to paint the shadow under the plate.

7▲ Paint the lime Change to a No.8 round brush to paint the lime in a mixture of lemon yellow and viridian, taking the brush strokes around the shape of the fruit and over the waxy crayon marks.

8 ▼ Continue painting the fruit Using the same technique, paint the tangerines in a mixture of cadmium red and cadmium yellow. Leave a tiny patch of white paper showing through at the centre of each fruit.

9 ▲ Complete the fruit Paint the pomegranate in alizarin crimson, and the figs and grapes in a mixture of alizarin crimson and ultramarine. You will find that the candle wax resists the colour and shows up on the fruit as white reflected highlights.

Express yourself

A sketch in wax crayons

The wax crayons used in the painting to mask out highlights on the fruit are an excellent drawing medium in their own right. They are perfect for chunky sketches in which bold line and colour are more important than a detailed rendering. This still life from the artist's sketch book was done using a basic set of 12 wax crayons. The highlights on the fruit are left as plain white paper or filled with lightly applied, smudged colour. The blue shadows on the plate echo the colour of the table.

10 ▲ Paint the leaves and plate Using viridian darkened with a little ivory black, paint each leaf as a single brush stroke of colour. Add a few darker shadows by overpainting in a darker tone of the same colour. Use the same green to paint the leaves on the ceramic plate design.

◄ **The table top is burnt umber and cadmium yellow; the foliage viridian with a touch of added black; and the plate a diluted wash of ivory black. Note the rough texture created by the candle resist.**

11 ▲ **Complete the bowl** Develop the leaf design on the painted ceramic plate, taking the pattern up to and around the curved shape of the pomegranate.

A FEW STEPS FURTHER

Local colours and the highlights are now in place. Shadows and dark tones need to be added – particularly on the plate, which looks a little flat at this stage.

12 ▲ **Add the bowl shadow** The shadow on the bowl is painted in a wash of ultramarine and burnt umber – the fruit shows up as lighter shapes against this dark colour. Put the paint on in broad strokes with a No.7 brush, redefining the round shapes. Flood extra colour into the darker areas.

Master Strokes

Jan van Os (1744-1808)
Fruit and Flowers

This lavish display by Jan van Os is typical of Dutch still life painting in the eighteenth century. Rather than being arranged in a formal way, the fruit and flowers spill in profusion across the table top. The light falls in a diagonal band across the centre of the picture from top right to bottom left, making this swathe of fruit stand out from the darker areas around it. In oil paintings, the highlights do not require forward planning as they do with watercolours – the bright reflected light can be added as final touches.

The highlights on the black grapes are restricted to single points of white paint; the green grapes, by contrast, are outlined in white.

Fruit of many different shapes and sizes, from tiny berries to a large melon, add variety and interest to the composition.

13▲ **Add detail to the patterned plate** Complete the rim of the plate in yellow ochre applied with the tip of a No.7 brush. Still using the tip of the brush, add dark green details to the leaves on the fruit and the plate design.

14▼ **Complete the grapes** Remove the masking fluid applied to the line of the grapes' stalk in step 5. Then paint the stalk with yellow ochre.

THE FINISHED PICTURE

A Textured fruit
Coloured wax crayon was used for the highlights on the citrus fruits. The slightly rough surface of the watercolour paper helped create the texture of the peel.

B Bowl highlight
The sharp linear highlight on the ceramic bowl was achieved with masking fluid, applied in a bold, unbroken line.

C White reflections
The wax from an ordinary household candle was applied in loose, sketchy strokes to create patches of reflected light on the purple grapes and the figs.

FURTHER TECHNIQUES

This chapter deals with those aspects of composition that require detailed explanation, showing how to perfect perspective, frame your subject and make light work. The section includes advice on judging tone, depth and distance as well as giving a convincing impression of solidity. To finish the chapter there is advice using these techniques in unusual ways, for unexpected results.

Choosing the best format

There are many ways to frame a scene – make sure you choose the best one before you start drawing.

One of the first decisions to make when planning a drawing is whether it should have a horizontal (landscape) format or vertical (portrait) one. In this scene of a tree-lined road in France, the artist saw the possibilities of both formats (right).

The vertical format was ideally suited to capturing the height and grandeur of the trees. These strong verticals help to create a rather dramatic mood. The artist, however, decided to use the horizontal format. This enlarges the scope of the view and the inclusion of the farm building helps to provide a balanced composition. The strong horizontals of this building make for a more serene, peaceful mood.

Whether you choose a horizontal or a vertical format, plan to offset the centre of interest in the composition. A useful rule of thumb is to divide your paper into thirds each way, either by eye or by marking it lightly in pencil, and then place the focal point at the crossing point of two of the dividing lines. The focal point of the drawing below – the distant hut with the cyclist in front of it – is positioned in this way.

▼ In the horizontal format, the farmhouse on the left balances the verticals of the trees, helping to create a tranquil, rural image.

YOU WILL NEED

Piece of Hot-pressed watercolour paper

7B pencil

15 coloured pencils: Light turquoise; Apple green; Lemon yellow; Olive green; Sap green; Pale grey; Venetian red; Yellow ochre; Dark grey; Prussian blue; Aubergine; Burnt sienna; Viridian; Vandyke brown; Burnt orange

FIRST STROKES

1 ▼ **Sketch the composition** Using a 7B pencil, sketch the main elements of the scene – the trees, buildings, road and cyclist. Notice how the negative sky shapes formed between the trees are roughly triangular. Also, look at how different parts of the scene relate to each other – the roof of the long building lines up with the distant tree-tops, for example.

2 ▶ **Establish dark and light tones** Add more spiky branches to the tree at the end of the avenue, tapering them off from the trunk towards the top of the paper. Hatch in the shaded parts of the trunks and also the shadows cast on the grass and road.

3 ▶ **Begin with the light colours** Complete the tonal pencil shading on the trunks and vegetation on the right of the picture. Now, using a light turquoise coloured pencil, fill in the sky, including all the shapes between the trees. Move on to the sunlit areas of foliage, using an apple green pencil. As with watercolour painting, you are working from light to dark, so that you gradually build up depth of colour.

CHANGING THE EMPHASIS

Quick pencil sketches are a great way of working out the best format and composition for your drawing. The vertical format emphasises the height of the avenue of trees, conjuring up a cathedral-like image. The horizontal format provides a 'quieter' image – the eye is still pulled down the road but it also has a place to rest on the farm building on the left.

ADDING COLOUR TO THE SCENE

Once you have roughed in the main shapes and tonal areas, work up the rest of the drawing in coloured pencil. Blend shades if necessary to capture the essence of the colours.

4 ▲ Introduce darker greens Put more apple green on the tree-tops and highlight the distant trees with a touch of lemon yellow. Now look for the areas of darker green in the distant trees and colour these with olive green and sap green, working over some of the graphite pencil tone.

5 ▲ Continue with dark greens Using vigorous strokes of sap green, hatch in the shadows on the grass and foliage to the left and right of the road. Changing to the olive green, hatch across the tree-tops and trunks. Block in a mid tone across the road with a pale grey pencil.

EXPERT ADVICE
Giving form to the trees

Shade in the tree trunks using mainly horizontal hatching lines. The eye reads them as curving around the trunks, which helps to suggest the cylindrical shapes. By leaving one side of the trunks pale where they catch the light, you can convey their form and solidity.

6 ▶ Work on the building and road Hatch the roof on the building with diagonal strokes of Venetian red and work loosely over the wall below it with yellow ochre and dark grey. Use Prussian blue for the figure on the bicycle, then strengthen the cast shadows on the road with Prussian blue, aubergine and dark grey.

7 ▶ Colour doors and windows Shade the hut doors in burnt sienna, dark grey and viridian, and the doors and windows of the building in Vandyke brown and burnt orange. Hatch over the trees with the 7B and olive green pencils, suggesting leaf texture with dashes of olive green. Use dark grey to put tone down the ochre wall and to strengthen the far left tree.

A FEW STEPS FURTHER

The drawing now successfully evokes the atmosphere of a sunny and tranquil rural scene. A touch of detail on the roof and tree-tops will add texture and interest.

8 ▼ **Complete the roof** A suggestion of terracotta roof tiles will give the left-hand building more character. Using the 7B pencil and Vandyke brown, draw the lines of tiles and their rounded ends.

9 ▲ **Hatch in more leaves** To enhance the effect of mottled colour in the tree-tops, use the olive green pencil to hatch dark clumps of leaves amidst the foliage. Press firmly to achieve a deep, rich shade.

THE FINISHED PICTURE

A Blended colours
To find the correct shade for the wall of the building, a darker colour was worked over a lighter one to tone down the brightness.

B Dappled effect
The shadows falling across the road create an interesting pattern on what would otherwise be a broad area of plain colour.

C Focal point
The eye is drawn down the avenue of trees towards the focal point – the brightly coloured doors in the distant building.

Creating emotional impact

Tonal key tells us about the overall lightness and darkness of a picture – and it's an invaluable tool for creating mood and atmosphere.

The tones and colours in a painting are like musical notes – when pitched to a particular key, they produce a result that is not only rich and harmonious but also emotionally expressive. Music that is composed mainly of high-key notes can sound either light and cheerful or poignant and romantic. Low-key notes tend to produce a more melancholy sound. In the same way, light and dark tones in a painting can be 'orchestrated' to express a particular mood or atmosphere.

Tonal key

The term 'tonal key' is used to describe the range of tones within a picture. It tells us about its overall lightness or darkness. Imagine a bright, sunny scene. This subject is well suited to the lighter range of the tonal scale – a high-key painting. A dimly lit interior or a stormy seascape are obvious examples of low-key subjects.

Look at any good painting and you will see how the artist has deliberately orchestrated the tones to express a mood, to convey the character of a sitter, or to capture the atmosphere created by light and weather on a landscape. In short, sensitive control of tonal values can enrich the mood of a scene and make it 'talk'.

The Impressionists, for example, captured the shimmering light and the exuberant feeling of summer days with

▼ In a *Game of Tennis* (*c.*1910), Spencer Gore (1878-1914) uses light tones to capture the carefree, sun-drenched atmosphere of summer in the park. Note how even the shadows are filled with light and colour.

brilliant high-key images. In contrast are the magnificent, low-key portraits by Rembrandt (1606-69) in which softly lit figures or faces emerge from the surrounding shadows.

High-key paintings

In a high-key painting, most of the tones are in the light-to-middle range. Depending on the intensity of the colours and the way you apply them, you can convey a mood that's cheerful and bright or quiet and restrained.

Take a beach scene, for instance. On a summer day, the light is intense and there is a lot of colour. To capture the bracing seaside atmosphere, you would use mostly light, bright colours, accentuated by a sprinkling of crisp, dark accents.

That same beach on a misty morning takes on a completely different mood. This time, let soft colours predominate. By keying most of your tonal values to the higher end of the scale, keeping contrasts to a minimum and blending edges wet-on-wet, you can convey a quiet, more poignant atmosphere.

In a high-key painting, watercolours can be applied in a series of transparent washes to create a delicate, subtle effect. Leaving flecks and patches of light-reflecting white paper breathes air into a watercolour painting – try it next time you paint a sunny beach scene.

Alternatively, try working on toned paper, using watercolours mixed with a little Chinese white; the colours take on a milky, semi-transparent quality that is well suited to romantic themes.

In oils and acrylics, colours can be lightened by adding lots of white to create delicate, high-key tones – as in the painting opposite. To keep the colours fresh and lively, don't overmix them on the palette, and try using broken colour effects. Small strokes and dabs of pure colour will blend in the viewer's eye and give a vibrant, joyful effect.

In a low-key painting, tones from the darker end of the scale predominate – though a few telling accents of light will enhance the drama. By choosing your subject carefully and picking colours in the mid to dark tonal range, you can use the psychological associations of darkness and shadow – mystery, suspense, sadness – to create powerful images.

As with high-key paintings, the effect depends on your choice of subject, composition and how you apply the paint. To convey a bleak winter landscape, you might accentuate the dramatic patterns of dark branches against a pale sky. But a low-key painting doesn't have to be sombre: an interior at evening, lit by a table lamp that casts a soft pool of light in a shadowy room, creates a low-key mood that is warm and intimate.

▲ Rembrandt was the undoubted master of the low-key portrait. In this image, entitled *An Oriental* (1635), the shadowy tones underline the sitter's mood of melancholic contemplation.

A change of mood

Try making a series of paintings of the same scene at different times of the day or under different weather conditions – similar to the Houses of Parliament series on pages 188-189. Choose a location that's convenient to get to – your own garden might be suitable as you can return to it quickly when the light changes. Notice the different moods created as the amount, direction and colour of the light changes, and communicate this observation by 'keying' your tonal values to fit the mood of the subject.

In the Houses of Parliament series, the evening scene is a low-key picture. The result is a rather ominous image that looks as if it could come from wartime. In contrast, the morning scene has a lot of pale tones, especially in the sky and water, creating a lighter, happier mood.

Blueprint for a painting

Like a play or film, a picture must be put together so that its component parts make a balanced, harmonious whole to hold the attention of the viewer. This important skill is called 'composition'.

Traditionally, artists have used the rectangle as the framework for paintings. When used horizontally, it is referred to as having a 'landscape' format, and when used upright as having a 'portrait' format (although, of course, you could paint a landscape in the 'portrait' format or use other shapes instead).

Getting the right fit

The shape and size of the rectangle has to be right for what you want to fit into it. If it is too small, the image looks squashed and this makes the viewer want to see past the edges; too large, and the eye wanders about trying to find something to hold its interest. Good composition is achieved when all the elements of the picture (colours, shapes, tones, textures and, vitally, the spaces between them) relate to each other in a balanced way.

The focal point

Imagine that you have just moved into an empty house and you are arranging the furniture in the living room. You will probably set out the armchairs and sofa so that they face the television, or perhaps a fireplace. These are 'focal points', and the angles and relative distances that you create in positioning the furniture is an important consideration.

Alternatively, the chairs might be arranged to face each other for conversation, in which case the focal point is actually a space.

In a painting, the focal point is the point to which the viewer's eye tends to be drawn most strongly. This is usually the main subject of the work – for example, the face in a portrait, or the

THE GEOMETRY OF COMPOSITION

This information is by no means essential to composing a successful picture, but you may find it interesting. Absorb as much, or as little, of it as you like.

Euclid noted that a sequence of numbers (3, 5, 8, 13, 21, etc) gave a series of ratios which Renaissance artists called the 'divine proportion', otherwise the 'Golden Section' or 'Golden Mean'. If a line is drawn by combining any two successive numbers (say 5 and 8, making 13), and divided into the two component lengths (i.e. one of 5 and one of 8), then the ratio of the smaller part to the larger (5:8) is the same as the ratio of the larger part to the whole (8:13).

This principle was used as the basis for many Classical buildings because the balance created by these divisions, either vertically or horizontally (or both), is very satisfying. In paintings, the points where the verticals and horizontals of the 'Golden Mean' intersect within the rectangle are often used as the focal point (or points) of the image. This is about a third of the way in and a third of the way up (or down).

AB is to BC (8:5) as
BC is to AC (13:8)

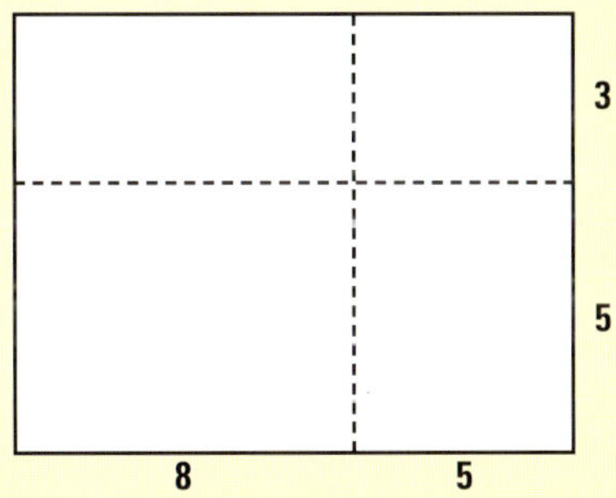

▶ **The Golden Section**
The diagram shows how a focal point within a rectangle is created by using the 'Golden' proportions. Giovacchino Toma (1838-91) used this principle for the main focal point in his painting *Luisa San Felice In Prison*, below.

▲ **Renaissance painters used the formal geometry of vertical, horizontal and diagonal lines to form triangular compositions within the rectangle. The portrait shown here, the *Madonna of the Goldfinch* by Raphael Sanzio (1483-1520), shows the principle clearly.**

Composition in practice

To understand the importance of composition, you will need to explore a little, observing how different elements relate to each other. Try these exercises.

1 Take a sheet of white paper and some coloured papers (say red and green). Cut up the colours into rectangular shapes of various sizes and practise arranging them in different ways on the white sheet, overlapping some of them if you like. Try to organise a focal point and to achieve a good balance between shapes, spaces and colours. Look at how your arrangements visually affect the rectangle. Is there a sense of space; are there 'busy' areas and 'quiet' ones; is there any sense of 'movement' or 'tension' between shapes? Try the same exercise with other colours, or with black and grey.

2 Find a reproduction of a well-known painting for this exercise. Using tracing paper, draw lines to connect up the main directions formed by the various objects, light, shadows and forms within the painting. Notice how diagonals are used to hold together different areas and create 'routes' for the eye to follow.

3 From a sheet of white paper measuring 8 x 5cm (3 x 2in), cut out a rectangle from the centre to leave a frame about 1cm (3/8in) wide all round. Hold this at arm's length and move it slowly around the room or the garden. The view you see inside the frame is your composition. Notice how a very small shift of the frame can make for a much more balanced composition.

church tower in a village scene. In more complex images, where no one element is more important than another, the artist has to guide the viewer's eye around the picture by the way the various elements are arranged. As in the living room, the balance of these and the 'dynamic' that is set up within the rectangle are what composition is all about.

Things to avoid

There are no firm rules, but some things are best avoided. Dividing the surface in half by placing a tall object in the centre, or positioning the horizon line exactly half-way up, makes the picture 'boring'.

Similarly, same-size objects equidistant on either side of the centre line, or a continuous row of trees running right across the middle of the picture, make for dull compositions. As a rule of thumb, remember to compose 'through' the picture as well as across the surface.

▼ **The compositions of Pieter Brueghel (the Elder) (c. 1515-69) are full of incident and usually contain lots of different focal points with plenty of space for the eye to wander about in. Notice the position of the flying bird in his painting *Hunters in the Snow*. Is it the first thing that caught your eye?**

Abstract painting

The great abstract artists of this century were innovators who explored radical approaches to materials and methods.

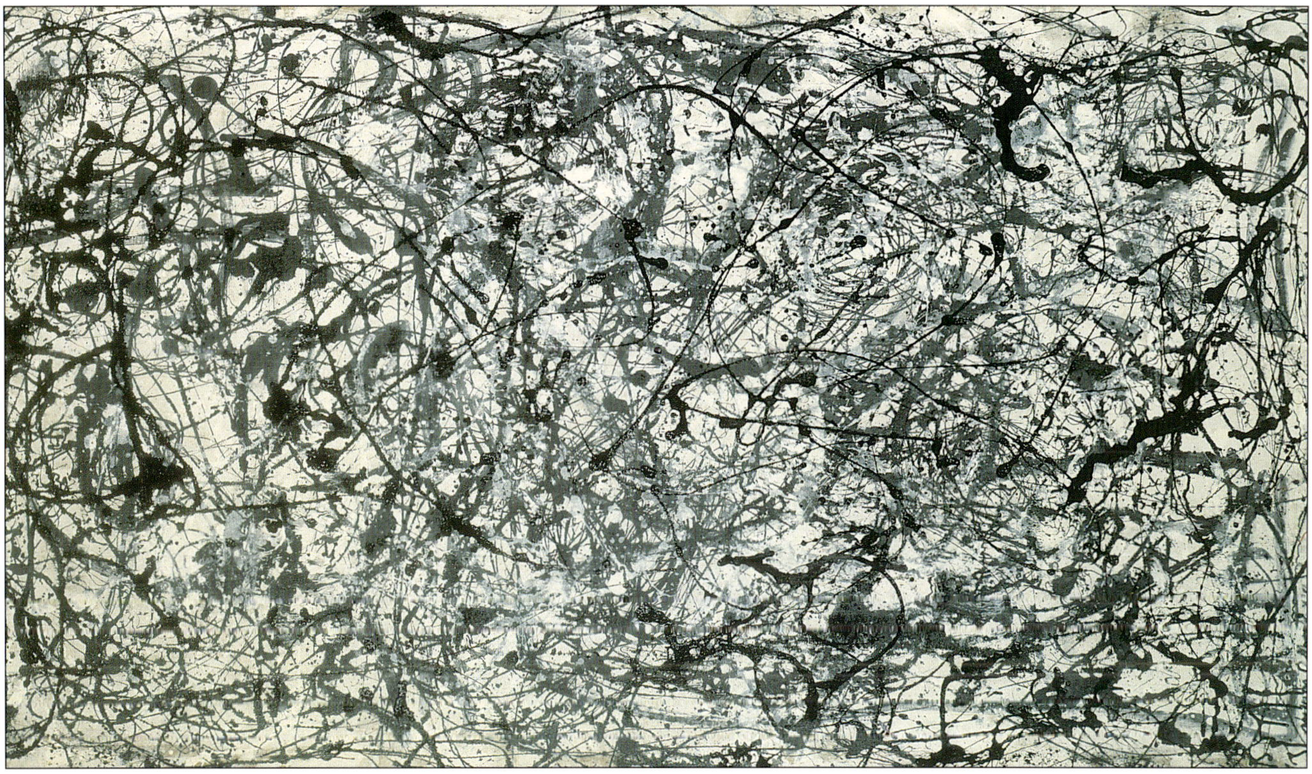

▲ ***Black and White*, painted in 1948 by Jackson Pollock, is an early example of the artist's revolutionary drip painting technique.**

The term 'abstract' describes art that is non-figurative and does not seek to represent the visible world literally. Abstract art began to emerge in Europe, Russia and the USA in the early twentieth century. The resulting explosion of creativity has affected the way we look at the world, and via film and advertising it has also affected the way the world looks to us.

Cubism, pioneered by Pablo Picasso (1881-1973) and Georges Braque (1882-1963) between 1907 and 1914, made the first moves towards abstract art. However, it depicted recognisable images and was a realist movement.

The roots of abstract art

Abstract Expressionism developed in New York, USA in the 1940s and 1950s. Primarily concerned with spontaneity and self-expression, it rejected traditional subjects and avoided figurative images. It was triggered by the presence in the USA of many European avant garde and Surrealist artists, many of whom were refugees escaping persecution.

With its emphasis on individualism, Abstract Expressionism was a diverse movement. Nevertheless, two broad strands can be detected: action painting and colour-field painting.

Action painting

This was a dynamic style of painting, which involved dripping and splashing paint in a spontaneous way. The canvas was described as 'an arena in which to act', and the picture was 'an event'. It took its inspirations from Surrealists like Max Ernst (1891-1976) who used techniques such as frottage (making an impression of a texture by rubbing over it) and automatic drawing – a technique which allows the subconscious to dictate the artist's actions.

The most famous exponent of action painting was Jackson Pollock (1912-56). His early works were naturalistic, but became freer and more expressive under the influence of Picasso and the Surrealist artists.

Pollock invented drip painting in 1946-47. Stretching huge canvases on the floor, he used objects such as twigs, sticks and trowels to splatter, dribble, drip and spill paint on to the canvas. The painting was built up layer upon layer as a series of intentional accidents, each mark determined by the swing of the arm, the energy of the movement and the amount of paint on the painting implement. The combination of the complexity of the all-over pattern and the lack of obvious focal points makes viewing these paintings face-to-face an overwhelming experience.

Colour-field painting

Abstract Expressionism's other strand, colour-field painting, was characterised by large expanses of saturated colour. Like all abstract painters, the colour-field artists rejected recognisable forms, but they also rejected the abstract linear form and painterly qualities of the action painters. Like the Minimalist painters who followed in the 1960s, they favoured large-scale works with little or no surface texture, concentrating on the experience of pure colour and the optical effects that could be achieved.

Mark Rothko (1903-70) was one of the most lyrical exponents of colour-field art. His works usually consisted of two or three large, hazily defined rectangles of delicate, glowing colour. The paintings have a compelling, incandescent presence which can only be experienced fully in front of the actual canvas.

◄ ***Blue Penumbra* (1957) by Mark Rothko is an example of colour-field Abstract Expressionism. Layers of scumbled paint give it a luminous quality.**

Exploiting chance

Use the random techniques of the action painters to introduce an element of chance into your work. The following monoprint exercises are especially useful if you find a blank sheet of paper intimidating. The abstract images they produce will free up your technique and stimulate your imagination.

1 Random image Squeeze blobs of acrylic, oil or gouache on to a sheet of paper, using as many colours as you like. Alternatively, you can drip and spatter the paint on to the paper. Lay another sheet of paper on top and press firmly. Remove the top sheet and see if the random shapes suggest an image. Use a brush and paint, or a drawing medium to develop the patterns on both sheets.

2 Symmetrical image Another method is to lay paint on the paper, then fold the sheet in half. When you open it out, you will find a symmetrical image, as shown below.

Seurat, Signac and the art of Pointillism

With their Pointist brushwork and highly structured compositions, Georges Seurat and Paul Signac changed the course of painting in the 1880s.

One of France's greatest painters, Georges Seurat (1859-91) revolutionised painting in the late nineteenth century. Reacting against the Impressionists' loose, spontaneous treatment of subject matter, he began taking a much more considered approach to painting.

Pioneering approach

In doing so, Seurat forged a new style, often called Neo-Impressionism, and helped invent Pointillism – the technique of using small touches of paint to create vibrant colour effects.

Amazingly, he did all this before his death (reputedly of meningitis) at the age of just 31. He was 24 years old when he exhibited his first masterpiece, *The Bathers, Asnières* (1884), and 27 when *A Sunday Afternoon on the Island of La Grande Jatte* (1884-86) was shown at the Eighth Impressionist Exhibition in May 1886, establishing him as the leader of a new avant-garde. In all, his working life lasted only ten years.

Seurat was born in Paris and trained at the École des Beaux-Arts where he drew from casts and from life, and studied the work of the Old Masters. In April 1879 Seurat visited the Fourth Impressionist Exhibition, where the paintings of Claude Monet (1840-1926)

▶ In Seurat's *Study for Le Chahut* (*c.* 1889), the vibrant colour effects of Pointillism appear ideally suited to the noisy, joyful cabaret (*chahut* means 'racket'). Note how carefully Seurat has constructed the composition, with the musical instrument parallel to the dancer's legs. He believed that diagonal lines represented emotional extremes, in contrast to horizontal ones, which signified calmness.

▶ *The Papal Palazzo, Avignon* (1900) is a classic example of the mosaic-like brushwork of Signac's later paintings. Look at the way the colours optically mix. The water in the bottom left corner, for instance, is made up of yellow, green, turquoise and blue patches which merge to form an overall green when seen from a distance.

and Camille Pissarro (1830-1903) in particular caused him 'an unexpected and profound shock'. Despite Seurat's academic training, his earliest subjects, perhaps inspired by the Impressionists, were taken from the lower classes – peasants and workers of the Paris suburbs.

The great works

After completing *The Bathers, Asnières* (see Seurat's Masterpiece, right), he began working on a companion piece *A Sunday Afternoon on the Island of La Grande Jatte*. This large canvas depicts about 50 figures strolling on the island opposite Asnières.

Like *The Bathers*, *La Grande Jatte* is similar to Impressionist paintings in subject matter. It shows ordinary people in an outdoor setting. However, the way it was painted was completely different. Rather than paint instinctively, as did the Impressionists, Seurat took pains over his brushwork. He first completed the work in March 1885, but then reworked the painting with Pointillist brush strokes.

Seurat exhibited *La Grande Jatte* at the Eighth Impressionist Exhibition. Other artists showing works in a Neo-Impressionist manner were Camille Pissarro, his son Lucien (1863-1944), and Paul Signac (1863-1935). Their paintings were hung in the same room as Seurat's, which highlighted the similarities in their approach.

In the time remaining to him, Seurat completed four other major paintings: *Les Poseuses* (*The Posers*), *Parade*, *Le Chahut* (*The Racket*), and *Le Cirque* (*The Circus*). In these late works (*c.* 1886-91), Seurat employed the theories of the art critic Charles Henry, concerning the expressive values of line, colour and tone. In *Parade*, for example, he used repeated horizontals and descending verticals to express a mood of calm and melancholy, while the upswept forms of the simplified gas jets and the warm light suggest a contrasting

The telling terms

The art of the late nineteenth century – like that of the twentieth century – is littered with 'isms'. Although these can seem a little intimidating, most of these terms have been coined for good reason. Here is an explanation of the 'isms' associated with Georges Seurat and Paul Signac.

Divisionism The use of pure colours applied in small strokes or patches to the canvas. Seen from a distance, these patches blend to produce an overall colour. Divisionism refers to the general principle of the separation of colour, unlike the term Pointillism, which refers specifically to the application of paint in tiny dots.

Pointillism The art critic Félix Fénéon used the term *Peinture au point* (Painting by dot) to describe Seurat's famous painting *La Grande Jatte*, and from this the term 'Pointillism' was coined. The size of the dots is adjusted to the size of the image and the distance at which it will be viewed.

Neo-Impressionism The school of painters led by Seurat, Signac and Camille Pissarro. Like the Impressionists, these artists were concerned with the representation of light and colour, but they evolved a less spontaneous, more considered approach to painting. Keenly interested in colour theory, they pioneered the technique of Pointillism.

happiness (see also the *Study for Le Chahut* (*c.* 1889) on page 213 to appreciate Seurat's use of line).

Seurat's legacy

While many later artists found Seurat's method of systematically applying dots too restricting, his ideas about colour, composition and subject were absorbed and reinterpreted by succeeding generations. In particular, his influence can be seen in van Gogh's use of colour and Divisionist brushwork, and in the work of the Fauves Henri Matisse (1869-1954) and André Derain (1880-1954).

Seurat also had a big influence on his contemporaries as well as his successors. Paul Signac first encountered Seurat's work at the Salon des Indépendants in 1884, where Seurat was exhibiting *The Bathers, Asnières*. Signac began collaborating with Seurat, persuading him to remove earth pigments from his palette, while Seurat had encouraged Signac to adopt a Divisionist technique. By 1886 they were both using the Pointillist dot.

Signac – the publicist

If Seurat was the founder of Neo-Impressionism, Signac was its publicist. Among Signac's friends were the critic Félix Fénéon (1861-1944), who coined the terms Pointillism and Neo-Impressionism, Camille Pissarro and Charles Henry. His book *The Neo-Impressionism of Eugène Delacroix* (1899) introduced the principles of Neo-Impressionism to a younger generation of artists. It provided a robust defence of the movement, although it did not necessarily give the most objective account of its history.

Around 1900, Signac moved away from strict Pointillism, opting instead for small squares of colour to create a mosaic-like effect as in *The Papal Palazzo, Avignon* (1900, above left) and *View of the Port of Marseilles* (1905).

SEURAT'S MASTERPIECE

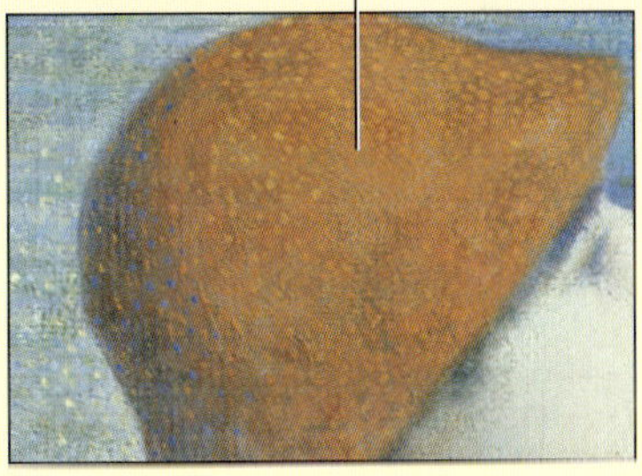

Perhaps Seurat's most famous work is *The Bathers, Asnières* (1884). This massive painting, measuring 300 x 200cm (118½ x 79in), depicts a group of workers relaxing by the Seine. Unlike Impressionist paintings, which were often completed on location, the painting was carefully constructed in the studio from a series of *plein air* sketches. The result is a more considered approach than the loose, immediate style of the Impressionists. Seurat has paid particular attention to his brushwork, rendering different surfaces with different types of strokes. These include criss-cross, or balaye, marks for the grass (see left detail), a Pointillist technique to render the back of the boy's cap (see right detail), and longer horizontal brush strokes for the slightly ruffled water.

Colour for colour's sake

When great artists at the end of the nineteenth century turned away from naturalistic painting, a whole new world of colour opened up.

The end of the nineteenth century saw many radical changes in painting. One of the most important was the use of decorative rather than realistic colour. 'Who cared if a landscape actually was green?' thought many avant-garde artists; they would paint it red if it tallied with their sense of beauty or emotional feelings. This philosophy was one of the major steps on the road to abstract art, where the artist's internal world becomes more important than the external one.

Gauguin's legacy

Paul Gauguin (1848-1903), with his use of bright, flat areas of colour, was one of the most important artists in this development. But perhaps the most influential painting was by one of Gauguin's disciples, a young French artist called Paul Sérusier (1863-1927).

While visiting Gauguin in 1888, he made a little painting (right) on the wooden lid of a cigar box that was to have far-reaching consequences. He claimed to have created it 'under the dictation' of Gauguin. With abstract yellow blobs and light blue for wood, the scene shows trees reflected in a river.

▲ **Paul Sérusier's *The Talisman* (1888), in which a river scene is rendered in bold blocks of colour, inspired a generation of artists.**

The Talisman

Sérusier came back to Paris describing Gauguin as his talisman to his friends, and the painting is commonly referred to as 'The Talisman'. He and his friends, including Maurice Denis (1870-1943), Pierre Bonnard (1867-1947) and Edouard Vuillard (1868-1940), the three of whom shared a studio, started painting in a similar style.

Colour, rather than being truthful to appearance, was the guiding force. In 1892 they formed a group called the 'Nabis', a Hebrew word meaning prophets. As apostles of Gauguin, they were both progressive and traditional, painting like their master but without the black brush-marked outlines. They believed in a work of art as a decorative object, using the expressive power of planes of intense colour. In 1890, Denis formulated a famous theory: 'Remember

▲ **In Maurice de Vlaminck's *Landscape with Dead Wood* (1906), the colours have been simplified and exaggerated to create a dance of energy and excitement.**

that a picture – before being a warhorse or a nude woman or an anecdote – is essentially a flat surface covered with colours assembled in a certain order.'

Reaching under the surface

While the Impressionists wanted to convey the objective appearance of scenes, the Nabis deliberately distorted colour and composition for dramatic effect. Denis was relatively conservative in the style and subject matter of his painting, but Bonnard and Vuillard forged a revolutionary path.

They kept the loose brushwork of the Impressionists to create mosaic-like patchworks of glittering colour. They were also great fans of Japanese art, with its simplicity and clarity of form. Bonnard, in particular, flattened perspective so that tables tilt alarmingly towards the viewer. Figures are closely cropped and seem to become part of the busy background pattern. Look, for instance, at Bonnard's 1932 painting *Breakfast*, page 218.

Bonnard and Vuillard also painted non-naturalistic theatre sets for the many experimental plays of the time. Even their paintings for private patrons took the form of large-scale, vertical, decorative panels. Absorbent canvases helped to give their paintings a matt appearance in which blobs of colour melted into one another.

In the 1890s, Bonnard was rather in the shadow of Vuillard. But as the Nabis were absorbed into the establishment, Vuillard became increasingly slick at painting bourgeois French lifestyle. Bonnard, by contrast, developed his use of colour. In the early 1900s, he returned to broken touches of glowing colour. His many pictures of his wife in the bath show how effectively he used colour to portray form.

Possibilities of colour

The Nabis never quite realised their own radical aims. In 1905, they were eclipsed by a group of artists known as the Fauves (literally the 'wild beasts').

The movement's central figure, Henri Matisse (1869-1954), transformed interior scenes into a colourful pattern.

Matisse and Bonnard were good friends and in tune with each other's work. Matisse bought and kept Bonnard's *Soirée in the Salon* in 1911, while Bonnard purchased Matisse's *Open Window, Collioure* in 1912. Like Bonnard, Matisse flattened perspective so that his paintings were as shallow as a pane of glass.

Playing with colour

Select a scene: indoors or outdoors, still life, landscape or portrait – it doesn't matter. Whether you are working in oils or watercolour, keep all your colours by you but leave out black and white. Exaggerate the colours in your subject as you paint, letting imagination rather than natural appearance govern your choice. Listen to what Gauguin said to his disciple Sérusier: 'What colour do you see that tree? Is it green? Then use green, the finest green on your palette. And that shadow? It's blue, if anything. Don't be afraid to paint it as blue as you possibly can.'

Take a tip from Bonnard as well. Keep a warm and a cool palette and mix the colours for each separately, so you have one predominantly red plate and one based on blues. Bonnard's pictorial ideas often developed out of his responses to the colours on his palette – try letting your paints be your guide rather than your tool. He kept a plate to record the palette used for each painting – a useful memory jogger if you have enough old plates at home!

Ideal colours

But Matisse went much further. Whereas Bonnard kept a sense of light and shade, Matisse dispensed with modelling. He created wonderful designs by simplifying his subject matter down to exciting, distorted shapes. The same went for the colours. He would merrily change them to fit his ideal of beauty. If his scheme was red, then wallpaper, table-cloth and surroundings were all red, with touches of cool complementaries serving to accentuate the warm glow.

Restless vitality

While Matisse used colour to create a sense of harmony and balance, his fellow Fauve, Maurice de Vlaminck (1876-1958), used it to instil a feeling of restless vitality. He favoured hot, fiery reds and oranges and would often apply paint straight from the tube. 'I try to paint with my heart and my loins,' he said.

The Nabis, and Bonnard in particular, may have laid down the rules of the game, but it was the Fauves who scored the goal and took decorative colour to its logical conclusion.

▼ Bonnard's expressive use of colour is evident in *Breakfast* (1932). Blues and lilacs are emphasised in the shadows and are played off against their complementaries, orange and yellow.

A sense of perspective

With a basic knowledge of perspective, you will find it much easier to recreate the often complex three-dimensional world around you on a flat painting surface.

▲ In *The Avenue at Middelharnis* (1689), Meindert Hobbema (1638-1709) used receding verticals to create the illusion of space in a landscape. The parallel lines of trees converge downwards towards a vanishing point on the horizon, as though the viewer is standing on the road.

Try this simple experiment: take two paperback books of the same size and hold one in each hand vertically at arm's length in front of you, level with your eyes. Gradually bring one of them towards you, moving it slightly across so that it overlaps the one in the outstretched hand. The book furthest away now appears to be about half the size of the other one. This effect, which is called foreshortening, demonstrates the first principle of perspective: distant objects appear smaller than those close to.

It wasn't until the early fifteenth century that Filippo Brunelleschi, a Florentine architect, devised precise mathematical rules to work out the scale of objects at different points in space. His discovery brought a new sense of reality into art, which had a great effect on its subsequent history – painters could now give objects depth on a flat surface.

How perspective works

The first thing to establish when looking at a scene is your eye-level – if you are sitting down, this will be lower than if you are standing. Assuming the ground is flat, the eye-level is also the horizon line.

Now look at any parallel lines that recede into the distance and you will see that they appear to taper towards a single point on the horizon. Look at a railway track from a bridge to see this effect.

If the parallel lines in the scene are below your eye-level (the base and top of a fence, perhaps), they will run upwards. If, however, the parallel lines are above eye-level (like the treetops in the painting above), they will run downwards.

The following exercise demonstrates how the principles of perspective affect what we see. Take a felt-tip watercolour pen (not an indelible one) and stand or sit in front of a window. Closing one eye, draw a horizontal line on the window, level with your eyes. Then trace on the window the outlines of the main objects you can see. Try to keep your head still, drawing only what is within range. The result will be a drawing in perfect perspective. The window, in this case, has become what is called the 'picture plane'.

One- and two-point perspective

On the left-hand side of the diagram on the right, the viewer is looking at two boxes placed on a flat surface below the eye-level (EL) directly in front of the line of vision so that they are exactly parallel (Row 1). The receding lines 'vanish' to a single point on the horizon (VP1), while the horizontal lines forming the other two sides of the boxes remain parallel to the picture plane.

When the boxes are moved along to the right of the viewer (Row 2), but drawn from the same position, the receding lines on the long sides vanish to the same point as before, but the lines that were horizontal now line up with a new vanishing point far to the right (VP2). This is known as two-point perspective.

Further to the right, the two original boxes are placed upright. Two others are added, one on top of the other (Row 3). Standing upright, the boxes happen to be exactly the same height as the eye-level – the tops of each box therefore lie along a straight line. The box balanced on top is above the eye-level, so its upper edges incline downwards to the two vanishing points. Notice how the boxes in this row rapidly reduce in height as they recede. This effect also means that the vertical centre line of a given plane appears to be closer to the vanishing point than the front edge. In the diagram of the house below, this effect is shown by the dotted line running from the highest point of each roof to the base of the house.

Bear in mind that the vanishing points do not have to be within the picture; in the diagram below, one is and one is not. Also, parallel lines never actually meet, even though they look as if they will, so the vanishing points are at infinity. Perspective implies the location and scale of objects, creating an illusion of space. In the diagram above, you 'read' the boxes as being about the same size. But if you measure them, you will see that they are actually very different in size on the paper. The brain operates an 'adjustment' factor so that the scene appears realistic.

Without any extra information, the actual size of the boxes is undefined. If the viewer is standing, the boxes could be packing cases in a warehouse. But the viewer could equally well be a child looking over a table-top at some matchboxes. More clues are needed to identify the scale: if a bowl and spoon were added in the right scale, you might assume that the boxes contained breakfast cereals.

One- and two-point perspective

This diagram illustrates how perspective alters according to the position of the objects relative to a given viewpoint.

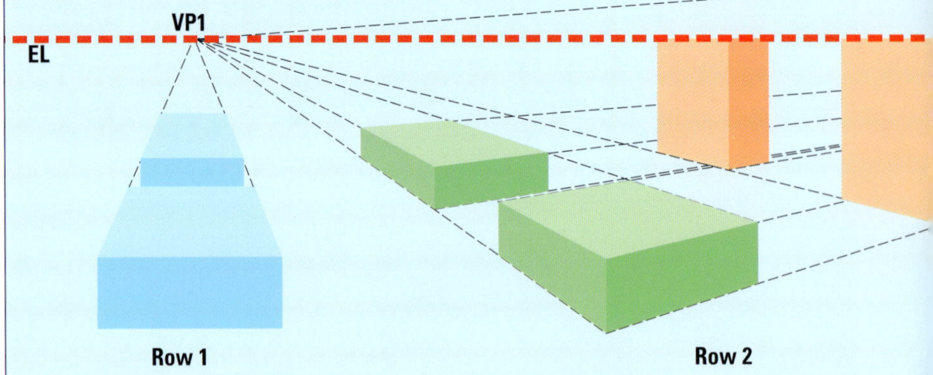

Drawing buildings

To help you draw a roof peak correctly, draw diagonal lines on the house wall from A to A and from B to B. Then draw a vertical line from the base of the house through the point where the lines cross. The peak lies somewhere on this line, depending on the slope of the roof. The ridge of the roof runs down towards the vanishing point on the right. To practise two-point perspective, try drawing doors and windows on to the house.

Key
EL Eye-level
VP Vanishing point
(The left-hand vanishing point is off the page.)

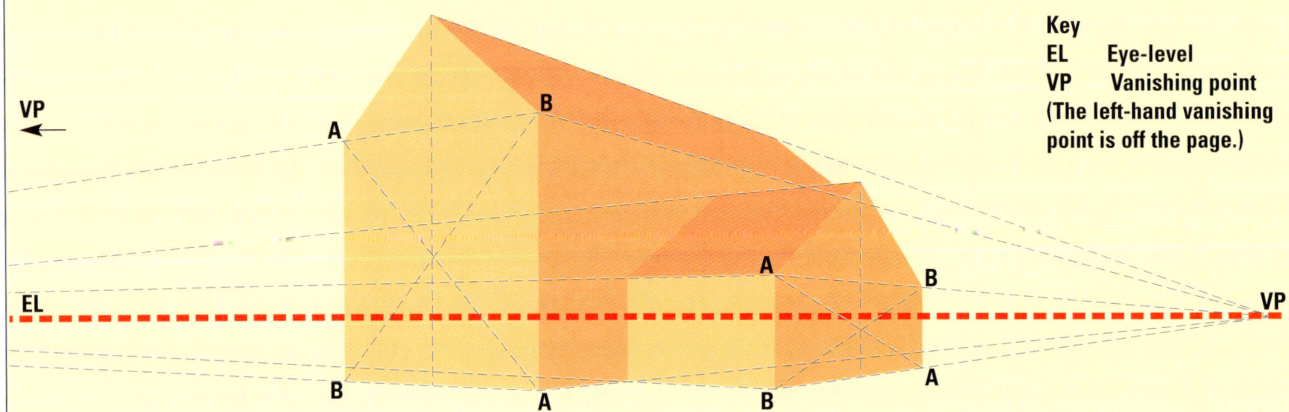

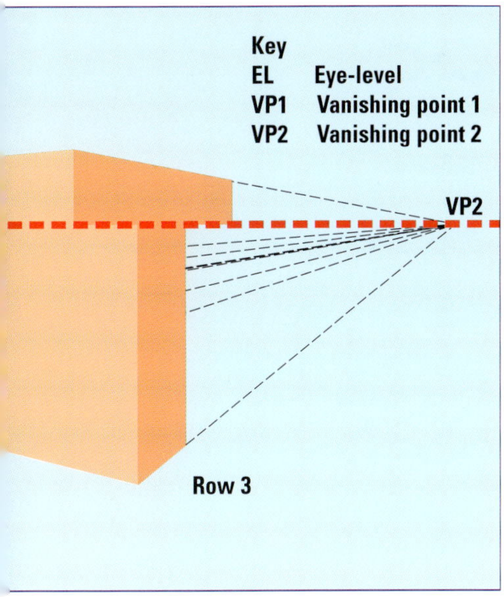

▼ **The battle scene in *The Rout of San Romano* by Paolo Uccello (*c.* 1396-1475) is one of the earliest examples of linear perspective. The strange foreshortening of the soldier's corpse in the left foreground shows the difficulties in applying what was, at that time, a very new idea.**

Getting it in perspective

Try this exercise to practise drawing a selection of rectangular objects, such as books and small boxes, in perspective. It will help if you draw 'sight-size', that is the size at which you actually see the objects. You can work this out by using a pencil as a measuring tool. Hold the pencil up at arm's length, locate the tip at one corner of an object and move your thumb along to the point on the pencil that lines up with the other corner. Draw a line of this length on to your paper.

You could also make a small viewfinder from a piece of perspex in the same proportions as your paper. Draw vertical and horizontal centre lines on it to help you assess the angles of the receding lines.

1 Set up the objects at random Place the objects at random angles on a table, with one or two on top of each other or standing upright. Position the biggest ones furthest away and the smallest ones nearest to you.

2 Draw the objects in perspective First establish your eye-level line on the paper, then make a careful line drawing of the objects. Draw those lying straightest first and remember to check the size of the spaces in between objects. As you draw each item, follow through all the receding lines to their vanishing points with the ruler. You will almost certainly be dealing with more than two of these vanishing points and some may extend beyond the page.

3 Put your skills to the test Show the drawing to a friend and ask if he or she can tell which are the largest and smallest books.

YOU WILL NEED

- Several boxes or books of different sizes
- Piece of cartridge paper
- Graphite pencil: B or 2B
- Ruler

Breaking the rules

A soundly constructed picture has its own logic that will always look convincing, even if the artist appears to have broken the conventional 'rules' of composition.

Composition is a slippery subject. Because the artist's intention and the context are so important, it is difficult to be too rigid, and for every 'rule' there is an example that contradicts it. So, although you are traditionally advised to avoid placing tall objects in the centre of the picture area, you will find plenty of cases where the artist has done just that – for example, in a portrait to make a sitter look imposing.

Taking risks

Painters sometimes deliberately distort spatial relationships, reverse dark and light tones to upset conventional perspective, or exaggerate colours. There are many reasons for this – they may want to create an effect, introduce ambiguity or play with your preconceptions of how things should appear and so force you look at the image afresh.

▼ Many of the compositional devices in the paintings of Paul Gauguin (1848-1903), such as *Vision after the Sermon: Jacob Wrestling with the Angel,* are derived from Oriental art, in particular Japanese prints.

The only real 'rule' worth following is that you should do whatever is necessary to create an image that has impact and holds together as a coherent whole. And if you need to take risks to achieve that end, then that is what you should do.

One of the best ways of improving or enlivening your own compositions is to study the work of artists like Edgar Degas (1834-1917), who explored the possibilities of composition. Borrowing ideas from photography and the art of Japan, Degas deliberately flouted the traditional rules.

Degas' 'snapshot' compositions

In the 1850s, Japan was opened up to the West after a period of isolation. Exhibitions in London in 1854 and 1862 fuelled a huge interest in Japanese art and crafts. Edgar Degas was inspired by the Japanese prints which flooded the market. There he found flat colours, emphatic outlines, cropped images, asymmetrical compositions, figures thrust dramatically into the foreground, pushed up to the top of the picture or sliced by the edge of the picture. He saw that floors were steeply tipped and interiors were often observed from a bird's eye view.

Photography was another major influence on Degas, and he borrowed from its apparent spontaneity, the 'accidental' cutting off, or cropping, of figures, unusual viewpoints, and frozen movement.

These novel art forms offered a vivid means of rendering contemporary life – very different from the painstaking realism of academic art. Cropped figures jutting into the front of the picture area created a sense of immediacy and involvement missing from most traditional painting. Yet in spite of the apparent spontaneity of his paintings Degas composed very deliberately in the studio rather than working directly from the subject as many of his contemporaries did. The careful process of composition enabled him to incorporate these non-Western effects into his art. His depictions of fleeting moments were usually carefully contrived. "I know nothing about inspiration, spontaneity, temperament . . . Nothing in art must be accidental, not even movement," he said.

Compositional devices

The pictures that leave a lasting impression and demand further study are those that force you to see the ordinary in a new light. *The Rehearsal* by Edgar Degas is an example of an everyday subject that has been rendered extraordinary by a series of compositional devices. The dancers – the ostensible

subject of the painting – are arbitrarily cropped by the edge of the picture area and by the spiral staircase which is such a dominant element in the composition.

A revolutionary approach

Degas' pictures of dancers are now so familiar to us that it is difficult to recapture their original impact. But even now, the idea of including fragments of figures – the disjointed legs at the top and base of the stairs – seems perverse. Furthermore, a great proportion of the picture consists of 'empty' or 'negative' space: the boarded floor is a large and emphatic shape which draws the eye up and into the studio space. Notice, too, the use of counterchange: figures seen light against a dark background in some places and dark against light in others. All these devices give an impression of incidents glimpsed in passing. But Degas' compositions are actually highly contrived, developed from individual and group studies, and the same figures often appear in several pictures.

▲ **The most rewarding pictures are full of surprises. In *The Rehearsal* by Edgar Degas, the unusual devices include the high horizon line, bold cropping of the dancers' figures and the sense of arrested movement.**

Experimenting with compositions

Successful compositions are only rarely found in real life. They are usually contrived – though a clever 'composer' makes them look inevitable and natural. Composition is a process of selecting, shifting and exaggerating the various components to create a convincing artifice.

1 'Borrow' compositions from artists such as Degas, Gauguin and Henri de Toulouse-Lautrec. Visit art galleries and study pictures in books. Decide which paintings you like, then try to discover what it is that makes them successful. And don't think you are cheating – throughout history artists have borrowed themes and compositions from other artists. Start with the images reproduced on these pages – you can copy the composition and change the subject.

2 Take a tip from Degas. In his late work, he acquired the habit of developing his pictures in series. Many of his drawings and pastels are made on tracing paper which allowed him to copy and then modify his own compositions. This constant repetition shows what you can do by pursuing a single theme.

3 Make two L-shaped masks from card. Take an image, sketch or photograph and, holding the L-shapes together so they form a central window, move them over the image to frame different compositions. Adjust the window to trap tall thin slivers and wide formats, crop right in to details and deliberately slice through figures and important subjects. See if these 'strange' compositions inspire you to develop a picture.

▶ **Degas' *Women on the Terrace of a Café* shows a group of gossiping prostitutes. The bold verticals of the columns disrupt the horizontal lines of the picture, cutting figures in an apparently random manner and emphasizing the picture surface.**

Outdoor composition

If you are confronted with a wide view when painting out of doors, a viewfinder can help you decide exactly what to paint.

▲ **In this oil painting of the *Rue de la Machine, Louveciennes,* by Alfred Sisley (1839-99), the artist uses a foreground expanse of road which sharpley recedes into the picture, drawing the viewers eye and creating a sense of depth.**

If, when looking at a potential painting site, you keep your head still and move only your eyes, your field of vision is relatively limited. This is why many artists have composed their pictures using more than one viewpoint, moving the head (panning) to see a broader vista. Selecting which areas of what you see to fit your painting surface is the first step in the process of composition.

The French artist Henri Matisse (1869-1954) often worked close to his subjects. He would pan across the scene, combining several viewpoints, and for some people the resulting paintings lack depth. Maurice Utrillo (1883-1955), a contemporary of Matisse, was much more interested in recording town-scapes from a middle or long-distance viewpoint, like a snapshot – indeed, he often worked from postcards. Utrillo's compositions are a good guide for the beginner working from observation out of doors, mainly because they always lead the viewer's eye into the picture and are generally well-balanced.

Making a viewfinder

A viewfinder helps to sort out the best balance for a composition in the same way as it is used on a camera. When taking a photograph, we use the viewfinder to select one particular area of the scene in front of us. But our eyes do not work in the same way as a camera lens, and we usually paint on a larger scale, so we need to make a viewfinder to do the same job.

A small 35mm transparency mount will serve the purpose, but it will isolate only a fraction of what you can see, and the range between foreground and background is limited. It is better to make a similar frame on a larger scale and, most importantly, in the same ratio as the painting surface you intend to work on. The A-size range of papers is in the ratio of either 2:3 (for example, A2 and A4) or 3:4 (A1 and A3, which is a comfortable size for water-colour pads and oil boards used outdoors).

Two home-made viewfinders, each with a central frame that matches these proportions, would therefore meet most of your needs. Use rectangles of stiff card and cut out central frames of about 9 x 12cm (a ratio of 3:4) and 8 x 12cm (2:3). Trim the card to create an even margin of two or three centimetres all round. If your paper is fairly small (say 15 x 20 cm), you could make the viewfinder actual size to avoid having to scale up. You can then draw centre lines (horizontal and vertical, as in the picture below) or 'thirds' lines on to a piece of acetate and tape it across the viewfinder frame. Sheets of acetate with a printed square grid are also commercially available. These provide an even more solid framework for your composition.

BEING PREPARED

Draw in the viewfinder's grid on your painting surface scaled up (or identical if it matches the painting size) before you go on location. This will ensure that the chosen arrangement will fit into your board and, with frequent checks, be accurate in proportion. The image that you see through the viewfinder is sight-size, and will need to be scaled up to fit the grid on the painting surface (if it is larger than the viewfinder).

The viewfinder in use

Before setting up your easel, move around your chosen view with your viewfinder held at arm's length in front of you to find the most balanced composition. Make a few thumbnail sketches of possible arrangements. You are making decisions about:

- potential focal points (not necessarily an object; it could be a space or a vanishing point), perhaps more than one, near and far, high and low.
- a balance of mass both across the surface and 'through' the space (large balancing small in visual terms – not evenly weighted like a pair of scales).
- a similar balance of colour and texture, and the positions of verticals, horizontals and diagonals.

◀ **Move closer to and further from your subject when looking for a balanced composition.**

▶ **Try using the viewfinder upright to explore the possibilities of a portrait composition.**

Optical effects

Some abstract artists deliberately avoid having a realistic subject in order to create an image that is a purely optical experience.

◄ *Movement in Squares* (1961) by Bridget Riley. As you contemplate this image, it appears to move continually. The pattern of black and white blocks gives the illusion of undulating before your eyes.

Although abstract art does not represent actual objects, it can nevertheless arouse intense emotions in the viewer. Abstract paintings can affect our sense of space and make us feel exhilarated, disconcerted or soothed. Using their knowledge of colour and optical effects, abstract artists are able to create luminous, shimmering work that can be rhythmic and harmonious, but may also be discordant and disorientating.

Provoking the eye

It is worth studying abstract images carefully, because they allow you to concentrate on colour relationships, shape and pattern. Without the distraction of a realistic subject, the incredible power of colour is revealed, and the lessons learned from this can be applied to any kind of art, whether it is figurative or purely abstract.

Pattern, as well as colour, plays a large part in creating the visual excitement of many abstract works. You may have found that you feel slightly dizzy when looking at wallpapers or floor coverings with particular geometric patterns, for example, rows of parallel lines, chequerboard squares and concentric circles. These simple repetitive forms, if arranged in certain ways, prevent the viewer's eye from resting long enough on any one area to be able to interpret it literally. When this happens, the repeating patterns create an illusion of shimmering movement.

This phenomenon, together with other optical illusions, such as after-image, border contrast and colour dominance, has been exploited in the work of artists such as Frank Stella (b. 1936) and Bridget Riley (b. 1931).

Colour and space

In the 1950s, American artists such as Helen Frankenthaler (b. 1928) and Morris Louis (1912-62) concentrated on exploring colour and space. Moving away from the spontaneity of the Action Painters and Abstract Expressionists, they created large areas of colour in

THE ART OF ILLUSION

If you concentrate on this geometric motif, you will find that it flips between two very different images. It can be read as an overhead view of a pyramid with the smallest square at the top. It can also be seen as a passageway leading to a small square door. As you look at it, it seems to shimmer.

which the mark of the brush was absent. They applied thin paint using a staining technique.

The Minimalists took this paring down of the image even further, often using a single colour and an all-over treatment so that there was no top, bottom or centre. As there is no pictorial image, the colour on the canvas becomes the visual experience.

Frank Stella

The American painter Frank Stella was a pioneer of hard-edged, flat geometric art. In his Minimalist paintings, he eliminated colour completely by using black and silver-coloured paint.

Later he combined brilliantly coloured, interrelating semicircles with rectangular shapes. His *Agbatana II* (1968) is a pattern of concentric and interlocking semicircles within a grid based on a square, and the canvas is shaped to the image. The contrast between the cartwheeling bands and the square grid sets up a tension across the picture surface.

The painting is carefully constructed and executed: precise geometry is achieved by the use of measurement and masking tape, and there is a constant gap of unprimed canvas showing between the lines of colour. The paint has been applied without any modulation of tone within each band of colour.

Op Art

Optical or Op Art was a movement in abstract art in the late 1950s and 1960s, in which colour and pattern were once again used to create optical effects, particularly the illusion of movement. The main exponents of Op Art were the Hungarian-born Victor de Vasarély (b. 1908) and Bridget Riley.

The precursors of the movement were the Post-Impressionists, such as Georges Seurat (1859-91). He created paintings made up of pure dots of colour, which, when viewed at a distance, appeared to blend together.

Another important influence on the development of Op Art was Josef Albers (1888-1976). In his experiments with colour, particularly in the *Homage to the Square* series, he showed how different colours can be made to look identical, or how the same colours can be read differently.

Bridget Riley

In her work, Bridget Riley explores the way that colours can generate light, mood and movement. She compares her work with music, 'another abstract art'. Her early paintings were black and white and 'based on a contrast between stability and instability'.

In the late 1960s, she began to paint long coloured stripes arranged edge to edge. Used like this, colours appeared to change their hue, shimmering, emanating light and flickering. Her use of colour became increasingly complex as she introduced sharp angles and twisted bands into her paintings.

◄ ***Agbatana II* by Frank Stella (1968) combines pure vibrant colours with a more muted palette on a shaped canvas. Although abstract, the painting has a lively, cartwheeling quality.**

Experimenting with colour

You can explore harmonious and discordant colours and optical effects in abstract and figurative images.

1 Optical effects with stripes Use coloured strips of paper to create your own optical images with stripes. See what happens when related colours such as blues and greens are laid beside each other, then explore the effects you can achieve with complementary colour pairs such as red and green.

2 Creating harmony The next exercise is based on colour dominance. Paint six sheets of paper in the three primaries (red, blue and yellow) and the three secondaries (orange, violet and green). Cut out squares of equal size from each sheet and arrange them in complementary pairs on a neutral background. Trim one square of each pair until you achieve a harmonious relationship between the two colours (below left). Notice the sense of discord that is generated if you allow the dominant colour – orange – more space than the other colour – blue (below right).

▲ **In this Futurist painting, *Red Cross Train Passing Through a Village* (1915), Gino Severini (1883-1966) creates the impression of speed by repeating and merging images of the train and the steam and by depicting the countryside in a semi-abstract style.**

Capturing movement

Take a look at the devices used by artists to convey a sense of movement on a static picture surface.

Any painting that sets out to tell a story or record an event will involve images that represent activity in some way. The problem for the artist has always been how best to convey this idea of movement in what is essentially a fixed, still environment, namely the painting surface.

Until the late nineteenth century, artists settled for what they called the frozen moment. They directed models to hold action poses, or made rapid sketches from direct observation of people working, dancing or going about everyday activities and then attempted to capture them in their paintings to convey a sense of motion. There are countless examples, well illustrated in the four story-series of satirical pictures by William Hogarth (1697-1764), such as *A Rake's Progress* (*c.* 1735). He aptly describes his concern with movement and its limitations within painting: '...my picture is my stage, and men and women my players, who by means of certain actions and gestures, are to exhibit a dumb show'.

The influence of photography

It is ironic that early photographers in the nineteenth century required their subjects to remain motionless for long periods because the film had a very slow exposure time. But it soon became obvious that the camera could also record movement, albeit seen as a blurred image and often recorded accidentally. This was to have a considerable influence on painters, together with innovative ideas about composition and the effects of light.

The contribution made by the photographer Eadweard Muybridge (1830-1904) to the depiction of movement is significant. In the 1870s, he produced a set of images of men and women photographed sequentially while they were walking, running, jumping and throwing. These not only paved the way for film-makers, but also showed the body in positions which could not be held as static poses by artists' models.

The pictures by Edgar Degas (1834-1917) of ballet dancers rehearsing in their class and on the stage show complex designs, with each dancer caught in an individual pose. These scenes of bustle and confusion, with movements overlapping and parts of the dancers' bodies cropped off the picture edges, look very much as a camera might have recorded them.

Power and speed

The Italian Futurist movement produced the first group of artists directly concerned with representing machines or figures actually in motion. 'Universal dynamism must be rendered as dynamic sensation where movement and light destroy the substance of objects,' stated the Futurist Manifesto in 1909. This was the age of invention – the motor-car, flight, automatic weapons – described collectively as 'a new beauty' by Filippo Marinetti, the Manifesto's author. Futurists Gino Severini (1883-1966) and Umberto Boccioni (1882-1916), in particular, produced several notable works, which attempted to show sequential movement and thus what could be described as a time scale within a single image. Their basic method was to use an echoing effect – in other words, to repeat a given shape or form across the canvas, a device that was later adopted by cartoonists, who use 'trail' lines behind or under a running or jumping character.

Energy in application

You can decide for yourself from the paintings on these pages whether the Futurists' technique is convincing. In many respects, you might feel that Degas conveys a stronger sense of the fleeting moment, and certainly the Futurist movement was very short-lived (apart from a brief excursion by the English artist Wyndham Lewis into Vorticism in 1912). But it did make us more conscious of the problems that artists face when attempting to record motion in paint. It also showed that the physical energy with which the paint has been applied can play a part in expressing movement – an idea to which the Abstract Expressionists returned later in the twentieth century.

▲ In ***Girl Running on the Balcony*** **(1912) one of the leading Futurist artists, Giacomo Balla (1871-1958), combines a pointillist technique with a repetition of forms to convey a figure in motion before the viewer's eyes.**

◄ **Movements of all kinds are captured in Edgar Degas' painting** ***The Rehearsal of the Ballet on Stage*** **(1873-74), ranging from the formal balletic poses of the dancers performing on the stage itself to the more relaxed gestures of the waiting ballerinas.**

Putting movement on paper

Try this exercise using any medium except watercolour – you will need to overpaint several times, so an opaque medium is best. Work on A3 boards or paper, using large brushes.

• On a windy day, peg a few shirts, tights, jeans and scarves on a washing line. Choose both dark and light-coloured clothes to give tonal contrast. Position yourself at right angles to the wind direction, so that the blowing clothes fly out to your right or left.

• Watch the clothes for five minutes before you begin. Look at the shapes they make, and at the way they move through an arc as the wind varies. Start with the darkest tones, making strong brush strokes to show the main movements. Build up to the lighter tones, painting over earlier marks, using 'echoes' and softening edges.

• After about 20 minutes' work, you should be able to see how easy it is to achieve a strong sense of movement in the clothes.

Frame within a frame

Doorways, window frames and overhanging trees – they can all help you guide the viewer's eye around your pictures.

Of all the compositional devices available to the artist, one of the most effective is that of creating a 'frame within a frame'.

The inclusion of a window or doorway in a painting, for example, creates a square or rectangle within the rectangle of the picture itself and this echoing of geometric shapes creates a satisfying harmony. Not only that, but placing a frame around the centre of interest in a picture can also be an effective means of focusing attention on it by isolating and enclosing it.

Illusion of depth

Frames within pictures are equally effective for breaking up the picture space in an interesting way, for creating an extra illusion of depth in the composition and for preventing the viewer's eye from wandering off the picture. A time-honoured device for directing the eye into the pictorial space has been to introduce a dark shadowy foreground and 'wings' of trees or buildings to the right and left to frame a pastoral scene.

▼ In *View of Salisbury Cathedral* (1823), John Constable (1776-1837) uses the classic framing device of overhanging trees. The change in tone – from dark to light – helps the movement of the eye through the trees.

▲ **In *The Love Letter* (*c.*1669) by Jan Vermeer (1632-75), the eye is led not only through the doorway but also to the maid's face which falls inside the picture frame behind.**

The distant trees and hills are made to look far off by the introduction of these tall foreground elements, which also provide verticals to offset the horizontals of the land.

This type of composition was typical of the great seventeenth-century landscape painter Claude Lorraine (1600-82) and is still used today, though in a less rigid way. You could, for instance, have a whole line of trees in the foreground, with the landscape glimpsed between them. Or there might be a tree just outside the picture, its overhanging branches breaking into the picture from one side; the gaps between the branches provide several small 'frames' for the sky and landscape beyond.

When painting buildings and townscapes, try using features such as doors, windows, arches or gateways to provide a ready-made frame for the focal point, be it a group of figures or a grand building in the distance. Architectural features like these also have strong shapes that can make a positive contribution to the foreground and edges of the picture.

New dimension

An interior scene takes on a whole new dimension when you include the space that can be viewed through a window or an open door. By depicting part of the inside of the room as well as offering a

▲ In *Conference at Night* (*c.*1949) Edward Hopper uses the light coming through the window to draw the eye to the figures. This is an effective alternative to using the window itself to frame the subject.

tantalising glimpse of a scene beyond the room, you create an intriguing double image – a 'picture within a picture'. This was a favourite device of the French artist Raoul Dufy (1877-1953), who painted many pictures of his studio in the south of France and invariably included an open door or window revealing a view of the Mediterranean Sea.

The inclusion of a distant view seen through a door or window increases the sensation of depth and recession, drawing the viewer deeper into the picture. It also provides a contrast of tone and colour – the cool, comparatively dark tones of the interior emphasising the warmer, lighter colours of the outdoor scene.

You can bring an extra dimension to your still lifes and portraits by placing them in front of a window. Not only does the geometric shape of the window strengthen the design of the picture, the light falling on the subject from behind creates a subtle *contre-jour* effect.

Mirrors can make unusual frames within frames and create an arresting contrast between the reflection itself and the mirror's surroundings. Try placing a mirror with an interesting frame behind the subject of a portrait, or using a mirror in an interior scene to reflect another part of the room.

Foreground shadows

Don't forget that shadows and passages of dark tone can also act as framing devices. For example, dramatic contrast is achieved by framing a sunlit street scene within a dark archway or between the shadowy walls of foreground buildings. If the foreground of a landscape or street scene lacks any obvious features, pretend that there's a tree or building just outside the picture and paint its cast shadow. This area of dark tone helps to break up an empty foreground, and provides an implied frame.

Hidden depths

Frames are not simply a visual device – they can also add an extra level of meaning to your pictures. In the Jan Vermeer image on page 1146, for instance, there is an air of mystery surrounding the content of the letter and the conversation between mistress and maid. The doorway seems to symbolise this fact – emphasising that we are on the outside looking in. Indeed it makes us feel almost as if we are prying on a personal moment.

In the twentieth century, frames and doors were a recurring motif in the work of American artist Edward Hopper (1882-1967). In many of his paintings, either the viewer looks at the subject through a window or a doorway or the subject is gazing at the world through them. This helps to convey the isolation and loneliness of modern city life.

Broadening your horizons

There are certain 'rules' about the best position for the horizon. However, the most successful paintings are often the result of breaking the conventions.

In any landscape, the standard place to put the horizon is at either a third of the way up or a third of the way down the picture. This division is restful and balanced, and yet keeps the eye on the move. However, there are other, more unusual options to consider – in the middle, very low, very high or indeed eliminated altogether.

Art teachers generally advise against putting the horizon in the middle because the half-and-half split of sky and land can lead to a dull, static composition. This is, after all, the position invariably favoured by young children.

Half-and-half division

However, all rules are made to be broken. One method of creating an effective composition around a half-and-half division of the picture area is to introduce verticals such as trees, figures or buildings that project from the ground plane into the sky area. These create a link between the two parts of the composition, and interrupt the dominant horizon.

The French artist Gustave Courbet (1819-77) uses this device to dramatic

▼ In *On the Beach* (1873), Edouard Manet uses a very high horizon – an innovative composition for its day. This allows him to emphasise the shapes of the foreground figures against a flattened background, creating a semi-abstract image.

JUGGLING THE HORIZON

In these watercolour studies of Battersea Power Station in London, the artist has explored different locations for the horizon. Putting the horizon on a third is probably most restful on the eye. But high and low horizons allow the artist to emphasise the exciting colours and patterns in the river and sky respectively.

HORIZON ON A THIRD

▶ Here the horizon is placed roughly one-third of the way up. This produces a well-balanced composition, but one which possibly lacks the drama of the other versions.

LOW HORIZON

▲ Here the greater part of the picture area is devoted to the sky. The power station sits four-square at the bottom of the picture, its towers set against a blustery sky. This solution places equal emphasis on the building and the background so that the eye wanders in a leisurely manner between the two.

HIGH HORIZON

◀ In this version, the eye is drawn up through the foreground, across the water to the power station, which is unmistakably the focus of the composition. If the foreground is filled with interesting detail, textures or – as here – reflections, consider using a high horizon.

effect in his famous painting *Bonjour, Monsieur Courbet* (1854), right. In Peter Blake's (b. 1932) homage to Courbet, *The Meeting or 'Have a nice day, Mr Hockney'* (1981-83), the artist protagonists – Howard Hodgkin (b. 1932), Peter Blake and David Hockney (b. 1937) – are seen from a higher viewpoint.

Although the poses and gestures have a mannered quality, the higher horizon means that they are seen against the ground plane rather than the sky. They are a part of their surroundings in a way that Courbet's more theatrical triumvirate are not.

Low horizon

When the horizon line is set low in the picture area, the greater part of the image can be devoted to the sky. This allows plenty of scope for atmospheric sky effects such as sunsets, or for depicting cloud or weather conditions. Indeed, a low horizon is often used to evoke the grandeur and immensity of nature. In a later Courbet painting entitled *The Immensity* (1869), the horizon is placed well into the bottom third so that the focus is on the colours and forms of the stormy clouds.

Light mood

In a short but prolific life, Richard Parks Bonnington (1802-1828) returned time and again to coastal studies in which boats, fisher folk and horses are set against a vast sky. In contrast to the brooding nature of Courbet's *The Immensity*, Bonnington usually conjures up a carefree mood. His low horizons, together with a high-key palette, contribute to the light, open and airy feel of the seaside.

A sense of recession is often sacrificed with a low horizon, especially when combined with a narrow, upright format. Choosing a wide format, or including tall trees, allows more scope for introducing perspective lines or other clues to scale. Meyndert Hobbema (1638-1709) achieved this in his famous painting *Avenue at Middleharnis* by using tall poplars receding in plunging perspective.

High horizon

With a high horizon, only a sliver of sky is visible, which limits the scope for depicting the effects of light and weather, and creates an enclosed feeling. Edvard Munch (1863-1944) often combined a high horizon and cropped figures for his claustrophobic and intensely psychological figure studies.

A high horizon can also be used to emphasise a towering mountain landscape. In the series of paintings of Mont Sainte-Victoire that French painter Paul Cézanne (1839-1906) produced from 1900 until his death, he often placed the mountain right at the top of the picture area. The sky becomes a negative shape around its brooding outline and the eye is swept up to its summit.

▼ In *Bonjour, Monsieur Courbet*, Gustave Courbet puts the horizon line halfway up the picture. This works because the figures link the top and bottom halves of the composition. Also, the symmetry is broken laterally, with two figures on the left balancing Courbet himself on the right.

Eliminating the horizon

Placing the horizon line right at the very top of the picture area, or omitting it altogether, removes an important clue to spatial relationships. This device is often used when the artist wants to flatten the picture and play up the abstract or decorative aspects of the painting.

This can be seen in many of the compositions of the French Post-Impressionist Paul Gauguin (1848-1903) – for example, *The Vision after the Sermon: Jacob Wrestling with the Angels* (see page 222). Here, the foreground figures are severely cropped and the wrestlers are seen against a bright red background. The advancing red emphasises the background so that figure and ground jostle for attention in a very shallow space.

Putting it into practice

One of the best ways of understanding this complex subject is to study the work of other artists, and analyse the choices they have made. Then try to apply these thought processes to your own work. When you next paint a landscape, explore different horizon locations in a series of quick thumbnail sketches. Remember, you can change the horizon position by taking a higher or lower viewpoint or simply by cropping out areas of sky or land.

Understanding tone

Whether you want to convey depth, model form or create mood, you need to pay attention to the arrangement of darks and lights.

The word 'tone' in painting is often misunderstood, but its meaning is actually very simple. The tone of an object describes its lightness or darkness, regardless of its colour. Some colours reflect more light than others, which is why we perceive them as being lighter in tone.

Colours can be graded on an imaginary tonal scale which runs from white to black, with infinite shades of grey in between; every colour has a tonal equivalent somewhere on that scale. Light colours such as lemon yellow would appear close to the white end of the scale, while dark colours such as burnt umber would appear near the black end. However, in judging tone you also have to take note of the lighting. A dark colour can have a high tonal value under strong light, and a light colour overcast by shadow may have a dark value.

An understanding of tonal values, and how to use them, is a key to success in painting and drawing. Although colour is obviously important, it is the arrangement of darks, lights and mid tones that forms the underlying foundation of an image. Outlined here are some of the ways in which you can use tonal values to increase the visual effectiveness of your pictures.

▼ ***Castle of Bentheim*, painted in the mid 1650s by Jacob van Ruisdael (1628/9-82), has a beautiful arrangement of tones. The pale diagonal path is echoed by the diagonal break in the clouds. In between, the sun illuminates the turret and the figures below.**

▲ **The contrast of tones in *Male Nude, Half-Length* by Théodore Géricault (1791-1824) helps to give the figure a real sense of solidity.**

When light falls on an object, its three-dimensional form becomes easy to 'read' thanks to the shadows created by the light. By learning to evaluate lights, mid tones and shadows accurately, it is possible to create the illusion of three-dimensional form on a flat surface.

Judging the tone of a colour can be difficult, especially if the subject is highly textured or patterned. The trick is simply to ignore the actual colour as much as possible and break the subject down into large, simple areas of light and shade. Then you can break down these large tonal masses into smaller, more subtle ones, developing and refining the image.

Depth and distance

You can make use of light and dark tones to reproduce the effects of atmospheric perspective and suggest space and depth in your landscapes. Use dark, advancing tones in the foreground, mid tones in the middle ground, and light, receding tones in the background to emphasise the feeling of distance. When working in colour, this effect is enhanced by using warm

CONVEYING FORM

To give a convincing impression of the solidity of your subject matter, it is vital to look closely at the tones. First, try to identify the line where the form turns out of the light and into shadow. In strongly lit subjects (such as the nude on the left) this is usually quite easy to see. However, in soft, diffuse light, you must look more carefully as it will be blurred.

Once you have located this line, pay attention to the tone on either side of it. For instance, don't think that the part of the subject in shadow will be just one uniform block of tone.

▼ **Look at the variation of tone on the dark side of the face. The shadowed side of the head, for example, is broken into three basic areas of tone – a very dark one for the hair and eyebrow (A), a middle shadow tone for most of flesh area (B), and a paler tone where light has bounced back off the upraised arm (C).**

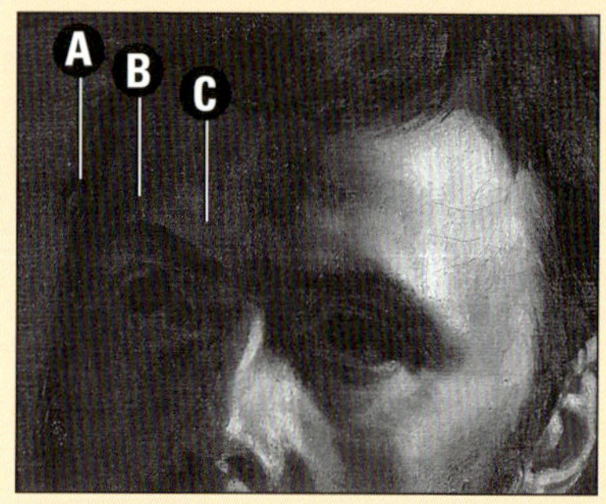

▼ **To give your subject an illusion of three dimensions, try to identify the line or lines where light turns to shadow (shown in red).**

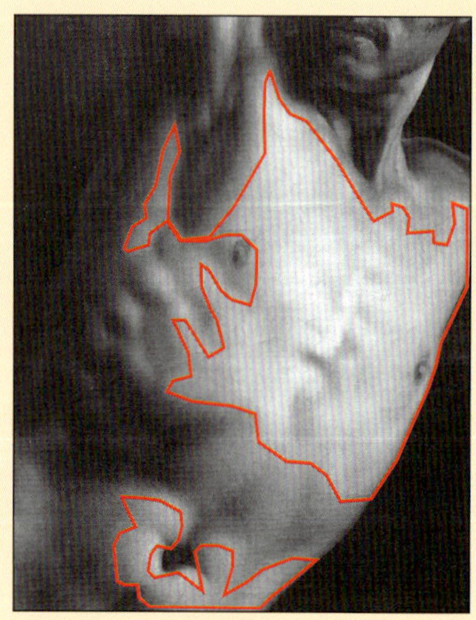

▲ **In *The Yellow Umbrella* (1996) by Ken Howard (b. 1932), note how the dark tones – in particular those used for the figures – become progressively paler in the distance to help give the illusion of depth.**

colours in the foreground and cool colours in the background.

The distribution of tones within the picture is an vital aspect of composition. Think of tonal values like keys on a piano: used together, they have the potential to produce an infinite variety of compositions. Without a pleasing arrangement of light, medium and dark tones, a painting can look flat and lack balance.

It is good advice to study master paintings and make sketches of them in pencil or charcoal. In this way you will discover how the great artists orchestrated their tones so as to produce striking images. For example, simplifying and massing together areas of similar tone helps to strengthen and unify a design, giving it more impact. Passages of light and dark tone help to move a viewer's eye through a painting, and the positioning of the lightest and darkest tones next to each other attracts attention and can be used to emphasise the focal point of the picture.

Creating mood

Tonal values also play a major role in expressing mood and emotion. The tonal 'key' of an image – that is, its overall lightness or darkness – is particularly important. The Impressionists, for example, often used pale, or high-key, tones to create a light-filled, joyous mood. In contrast, the paintings of the Dutch masters, such as Rembrandt (1606-69) and Jan Vermeer (1632-75), were low-key – the dark tones conveying a more quiet, contemplative mood.

Judging tone

It is not always easy to judge the tones of colours, as the eye is much more receptive to hue than to how light or dark a colour is.

The best way to judge the tones in the subject you are painting is to look for a neutral middle tone – say, the grey of a sky or soft green backcloth in a still life – and compare how much darker or lighter the rest of the tones appear in comparison. Keep your eyes on the move, looking at one tone in relation to another.

Try looking at your subject through half-closed eyes. This cuts out most of the colour and detail and reduces the scene to simple shapes of light and dark.

Sketching landscapes

Simplicity is the key to sketching outdoors. This allows you to work quickly, capture fleeting light effects and end up with the essence of the scene.

The landscape artist frequently has to contend with changing light. This means working quickly to record as much information as possible before the scene alters completely. In addition, materials and equipment must be portable – often a handful of watercolours and a small sketchbook.

Working on a small scale does not necessarily mean painting with a small brush or recording minute detail. On the contrary, the changing landscape allows no time to depict every branch on the tree, or every cloud in the sky.

The minimum of brush strokes

The best approach to landscape sketching is to use as large a brush as is practical, and to simplify what is in front of you. A sweeping expanse of grass or water can often be described in one or two strokes of colour; a tree or bush may be painted with a single brush mark.

The watercolour sketches here appear effortless because they contain very little detail. However, this impression is misleading. It is often more difficult to describe a scene in half a dozen strokes than it is to include every detail. You will need a little practice to gain the necessary skill and confidence.

Wet and wild

Working wet-on-wet, for instance, is a vital skill – it lets you work quickly (before the paper dries) and is ideal for capturing mist, clouds and reflections. However, to control the runs of colour, you must be able to judge the dampness of the paper.

If you have problems eliminating details, look at your subject through half-closed eyes. This excludes much of the detail and some of the local colour from your vision. You see only the main shapes and tones which, in turn, helps you to simplify the composition. Try to be selective – include only those elements in the subject that you either like or are essential to the painting. Is it the tones or colours that attract you? Make up your mind firmly and execute your ideas quickly.

Simplification need not be limited to sketches. Once you have mastered economic brushwork and minimal colour, there is no reason why these techniques should not be used in finished paintings. Many artists prefer to take this broad approach in all their work.

Scaling up

As a first step, try working on a large sheet of paper. You will then need to scale up the size of your brushes and strokes in proportion to the support. For example, use 50-75mm (2-3in) brushes on a sheet of A1 paper. These will seem ludicrously large compared with your usual brushes. But, for simple, suggestive marks and a 'no detail' approach, they are perfect.

▼ Working wet-on-wet can create visually stunning sketches. Here the technique was used for the mist over the mountaintops and the beautiful silvery surface of the water.

CAPTURING THE MOMENT

CHASING THE SUN

This sunset was as transient as it was beautiful. The artist had to work quickly to capture it, as the colours and the tonal relationship between the sky and the landscape were rapidly changing. The hills are rendered in Payne's grey and ultramarine; the sky is cerulean with cadmium orange and vermilion bleeding into it to capture the colour of the sun.

Palette: Cerulean, cadmium orange, vermilion, ultramarine, Payne's grey

A 'SNAPSHOT' SKETCH

Again, the light was changing rapidly in this scene. The clouds were scudding across the sky creating ever-changing shadows and patches of pale sunlight. As a result, the artist mixed up the washes of green, yellow and grey before starting to paint. The artist describes the resulting sketch as a watercolour 'snapshot', a moment frozen in time.

Palette: Payne's grey, ultramarine, raw sienna, indigo, burnt sienna

SPONTANEOUS CLOUDS

On this damp day at the seaside, the paint took forever to dry. However, the artist used this to his advantage. Working wet-on-wet, the colours of the sky and horizon immediately ran together to create the hazy effect of low clouds hanging over water. The rest of the sketch is painted wet-on-dry, with flecks of white paper left untouched to represent highlights.

Palette: Cerulean, Payne's grey, ultramarine, raw sienna, indigo

From darkness into light

Some of the greatest artists, including Leonardo da Vinci and Rembrandt, have added a sense of drama to their images by exaggerating the light and dark areas – a style of painting known as chiaroscuro.

Chiaroscuro is often misinterpreted as a particular technique of painting. In fact, it is used to describe any painting in which strong lights and darks have been used for dramatic effect. The term is made up from two Latin words: *chiara* meaning light or brightness and *obscura* meaning shadow or darkness.

An air of mystery

Often a chiaroscuro painting will contain just one, strong light source, leaving the shadow areas of the painting completely devoid of detail. This focuses the viewer's attention on the lit areas and can give the picture an air of mystery or drama.

The origins of this style can be traced back to the Renaissance and the development of oil painting at the turn of the fifteenth century. Previously, artists had worked with quick-drying, egg-based tempera paints which were unsuited to building up richly contrasting tones.

Perfectly balanced

The first great exponent of chiaroscuro was Leonardo da Vinci (1452-1519). The *Mona Lisa* (*c.* 1503), for instance, perfectly balances the areas of light, which reveal the face and hands of his subject, and dark, almost undefined areas of her clothing and the distant landscape.

The realism and remarkable softness of the portrait is enhanced by Leonardo's use of *sfumato*, whereby light and shade blend into one another gradually without any noticeable edge or border. Leonardo wrote in his notes

▶ In this detail from *The Virgin on the Rocks* (*c.* 1508), Leonardo directs the viewer's attention to the angel by using very pale tones to describe her face.

▲ **In Georges de la Tour's *Mary Magdalene with a Night-light*, the darkness surrounding the subject adds an air of awe and melancholy to the painting.**

Experiment with contrast

Extreme contrasts of light and dark tones are less apparent in more modern painting where the use of heightened colour has diminished the more obvious effects of chiaroscuro. Nevertheless, you could explore the possibilities in either a still-life or perhaps a self-portrait, working in oils on canvas.

You will need to bear in mind the following:

- Use a single light source trained only on the subject you are working from – you don't want it to light up the background.
- Restrict your palette to one half of the colour spectrum, so that the painting is almost monochrome. This way you can concentrate on the tonal contrast, rather than looking for colour.
- Start by painting the whole canvas with thin layers of dark tones of the background colour and gradually build up the lighter tones on top, finishing with highlights of almost pure white. Sometimes the tones might blend, and you will probably need to work over two or three sessions allowing the first layers to dry to achieve sharp contrasts.
- Remember to 'balance' the composition. This does not necessarily mean equal amounts of light and dark tones. The aim is to achieve a harmonious arrangement of light areas across the dark surface.

that he wanted to achieve an effect 'like smoke'. The mysterious smile of Mona Lisa is the result of the softening of the corners of the mouth and eyes using *sfumato* to blend them into shadow.

When chiaroscuro is taken to the extremes of intense light and shadow contrast, the result is very theatrical with the same dramatic effects as those of stage lighting. Michelangelo Caravaggio (1573-1610) also used this style to great effect in his paintings.

Larger-than-life character

Caravaggio was a larger-than-life character with a quick temper and some revolutionary ideas about painting. He chose to portray the characters in the Christian stories as peasants and ordinary people, which often upset the devout followers of the Church. And his dramatic illumination – in which backgrounds are obscured in deep shadow, and strongly lit foreground figures dominate the viewer's attention – certainly helped to bring these stories vividly to life.

In *Doubting Thomas* (*c.* 1600), Caravaggio shows St Thomas plunging a finger into one of Christ's crucifixion wounds to test its reality. The harsh lighting and dark shadows heighten the drama of the scene. Another example is the *Crucifixion of St. Peter* (1600-01) which shows a boldly lit St Peter struggling on the cross. His face is illuminated while the faces of his persecutors are either turned away or in deep shadow.

By the 1620s, several Dutch painters – including Gerrit van Honthorst (1590-1656) and Dirck van Baburen (1595-1624) – who had been working in Rome, returned to Holland with knowledge of Caravaggio's dramatic style. Indeed van Honthorst became known as 'Gerard of the Night Scenes' as a result of his chiaroscuro style.

Caravaggio's style influenced the French artist Georges de la Tour (1593-1652), whose reputation enjoyed something of a revival in the 1970s. La Tour often used candlelight to create dynamic chiaroscuro effects.

He made four paintings of the penitent Mary Magdalene lit by candles. In the version opposite, note how the light picks out her profile and white blouse but diminishes towards the edge of the frame. Significantly, the light also catches the skull in her lap – a symbol traditionally used to suggest mortality and the vanity of worldly goods.

Rembrandt's real people

Perhaps the greatest exponent of chiaroscuro was Rembrandt (1606-69). Many of his paintings are built up on dark-toned grounds – often warm brown in colour – with a few brightly illuminated and sometimes highly coloured light areas describing forms in dramatic fashion. Like Caravaggio, Rembrandt was interested in real people rather than idealised figures. He brought his subjects to life by using strong, directional illumination, which catches and highlights the most unexpected parts of the face. In *St. Matthew and the Angel* (*c.* 1655-60), for instance, the tip of the angel's nose is illuminated but not the rest of his face. As for St Matthew, his eye sockets are in deep shadow while there are bright highlights on his forehead.

Chiaroscuro is also evident in Rembrandt's self-portraits, where he ruthlessly illuminated his ageing flesh. Rembrandt differs from Caravaggio in that he used chiaroscuro to create a sense of meditation and sombre reflection rather than powerful drama.

▼ Bold use of chiaroscuro – as well as graphic poses and strong diagonals – contributes to the drama of Caravaggio's *The Flagellation of Christ* (*c.* 1605-07).

Painting reflected light

The use of reflected light in painting presents a challenge for the artist, but helps significantly with rendering form. Find out how you can exploit this kind of light to best advantage.

You will notice, when you are drawing or painting a cylindrical or spherical form, that the darkest area on the surface facing away from the light is not at the very edge of the form but a little way into it. Because there are no edges or corners on such forms, they usually pick up some light from those parts of their surroundings that lie behind them. This kind of light is known as 'reflected light'.

Reflected light is usually bounced back from the nearest reflecting surface and is particularly noticeable in still lifes, where the subject matter is enclosed in a relatively small space. In landscapes, the effect is less obvious, but can be seen on tree trunks, posts and cylindrical architecture.

Colour in reflected light

When light is reflected from a coloured surface, it takes on a hint of that colour. If this reflected light then falls on to an object in its path, it will alter the hue of that object.

One of the exciting aspects of using reflected light in your paintings is that sometimes rich, unexpected colours can be found, especially in the range of greens, where bright yellow light often bounces back from dark-coloured surfaces within the green spectrum. However, working out the exact colour that you can see in reflected light is complicated by the relationship between the colour which is reflected and the colour of the surface on to which the

◄ In his oil painting, *Girl Reading* (1874), Auguste Renoir (1841-1919) makes maximum use of reflected colour from the light bouncing back from the open book. The light on the girl's face has a beautifully diffused, flattering quality.

reflection falls. For example, if you place a brightly-coloured object, such as a vase against a white-painted window frame or wall in strong daylight, you can see very clearly that the reflected light from the vase produces a softer, paler and slightly fainter version of its colour on the surface of the wall or frame. But if you place the same vase against another reflective surface that is itself brightly coloured, the result is more complex. You will find there is a blending of the colours of the vase and the surface – an optical mix in a lower tone.

Tone in reflected light

Reflected colour is normally lower in tone than the original source from which it stems. This can be deceptive, because it can look quite bright; however, you have to remember that, because the reflected light appears on a surface shielded from the main source of light, it must by definition have a darker tone.

When you are mixing paints to find a suitable shade, a darkening agent therefore needs to be added to the colour of the reflection to lower its value without being so strong that it changes the identity of the original colour. Adding black is not recommended – your work can look flat and unsubtle if too much black is used in a painting. It is much better to mix in one of the umbers if the reflected colour is warm (red or yellow) or one of the blues if it is cool.

◄ In *A Portrait of Robin*, the painter Augustus John (1878-1961) has made subtle but effective use of reflected light and colour on the shaded cheek of his son, giving fullness to the form of the face.

▲ **Paul Cézanne (1839-1906) was skilled in using the various tones he observed to add form and atmosphere to his compositions. The reflected colour from the patterned jug gives a green cast to the dark tones on the shaded sides of the apples in this still life.**

Reflected light in portraiture

You need to consider lighting very carefully when deciding on a pose for a portrait. A full-face portrait can lack visual appeal; on the other hand, if you light a face strongly from one side, the shadowed part of the face can look very flat without any reflected light bounced back on to it to help define it – in the next issue, we will look at practical ways to tackle lighting a portrait. A portrait artist will generally try to light a subject from one side at a 45 degree angle. This is to ensure that some light is reflected up from the sitter's shoulders or is thrown back from a nearby surface in order to give form to the shaded side of the face. You can see this effect in the portrait by Augustus John opposite. Without this additional illumination, the appearance of solidity of the head and features is very difficult to convey.

Experiment with light

Experiment with capturing the colours of reflected light with acrylic paint. Use three snooker balls as props: one white and two in bright colours. Set the balls up on a white ground in a strong natural light – artificial light is not so effective for reflecting colour because it is generally more diffuse. If you don't have access to any snooker balls, you can conduct the same experiment with any brightly coloured, shiny plastic or metal objects. For example, the coloured tops of spray cans will give similar results.

- First place each coloured ball in turn next to the white ball. Then position one coloured ball beside the other one.
- The main reflected light that you will notice bounces from the ground up on to the undersurface of the balls. Echoes of the colours of the balls are evident in the cast shadows.
- Less obvious is the reflection of one coloured ball on to the other. Let's say, for example, that you can see pink reflected on to darkish green. To mix this shade, start with the reflecting colour (pink) and add a little of the receiving colour (darkish green). Go on adding a little more green until you hit the right tone – you might have to add a little crimson to keep the warmth of the colour within the lower tonal range.
- Remember that colours can be changed dramatically by their surroundings. The pink you are mixing might not look quite right when mixed on a white palette, but if it looks like a low tone of pink when you paint it on to the green ball, then you can begin to call yourself a real painter!

AND FINALLY...

This chapter shows you what to do when you've put the pencil down. There are tips on how to record and preserve your pictures so that, in time, you will have an extensive collection. There is also practical advice on photographing artwork and using fixatives and varnishes as well as techniques for carrying and storing your drawings and paintings.

Working with fixatives

When working with powdery media, such as charcoal, soft pastel or chalk, you will find it useful to have fixative to hand. You can apply this synthetic resin at stages as you go along or just spray it on to your final work.

Dusty, easily crumbled media, such as charcoal, pastel, chalk and Conté crayon, work by depositing loose particles of pigment on your sheet of paper. If the support does not have enough tooth, or if you are applying heavy layers of colour, the pigment won't bind to the surface. There is a danger of smudging, or the particles might simply fall off the paper when the picture is displayed, staining the mount and spoiling all your hard work. Treating the image with fixative binds the pigments to the ground and protects the fragile surface.

Fixative should be used sparingly because it can affect the qualities that make these delicate media so attractive. If a pastel painting is heavily treated with fixative, the pigment will become compacted and solid, losing its characteristic powdery bloom. Fixative also darkens the colour and can make some colours appear more transparent.

▼ The pastel picture below has been fixed above the diagonal red line only, to show how fixative can darken pastels. Notice how the clouds have become greyer, especially just above the windmill. The blue sky, the grey-green distant hills and the golden yellow fields in the foreground have also deepened in tone.

SPOT FIXING

Sometimes you need to fix just a small area of a pastel painting. Masking off the rest of the image will allow you to control the application of the fixative accurately.

1 ▶ Place a mask over a specific area In order to create the textures of the stamens in the centre of this anemone flower, you will need to build up layers of broken colour. Cut a hole in the centre of a sheet of paper. Make sure that the hole is the right size to fit around the stamens, and that the sheet of paper is large enough to protect the rest of the image. Lay the mask over the image and apply a light coating of fixative. Remove the mask and allow to dry.

2 ▲ Work over the fixed area Now that the centre is fixed, you can build up extra texture on this area. Repeat the masking and fixing process if necessary. Notice that the unfixed petals have kept their velvety bloom.

Applying fixative

Fixative should always be used in a well-ventilated space; avoid spraying it near delicate surfaces or equipment.

To apply fixative from an aerosol canister, lay your paper horizontally. Start to spray from the top, beginning outside the edge of the paper and working back and forth across the surface, going beyond the picture area each time. To avoid a build-up of fixative in one place, keep your hand moving and don't hold the spray too close. Try to keep the spray mist even, and lay a light film only – several light applications of fixative are better than a single heavy one.

▲ If you find yourself without fixative, you can use ordinary hairspray as an emergency measure to protect your drawing or painting in the same way.

If you are using a bottle of fixative with a spray diffuser, pin the paper to a vertical surface. Pour some fixative into a jar, insert one end of the diffuser into the liquid, then blow through the mouthpiece to produce a fine spray. It takes a while to master the technique, so practise on scrap paper before you start.

Aerosol canisters are better for use on large pieces of work, whereas mouth diffusers are convenient for small-scale work or for spot fixing. If you need to use fixative but don't want to affect the final appearance of the painting, apply it to the first layers of pigment only, then add a final layer and leave it unfixed.

Suitable papers

Pastel is the most friable (crumbly) medium, and often needs some fixing. If you use paper with the correct texture, however, you won't have to use very much fixative. A rough or a Not paper will hold the pigment particles in the recesses of the paper surface. The paper should be well sized so that it will not be damaged by vigorous application of the medium.

For very heavy pastel work, you should use one of the specialised pastel papers. Velour papers have a velvety surface rather like flock wallpaper and will hold a dense application of pigment. Sansfix papers are like fine sandpaper; again, you can build up the pastel surface. Even with these heavily textured surfaces, you might still need to fix small areas that will be heavily worked (see Spot Fixing above).

WHAT NEEDS FIXING?

Two sets of marks were made in different media; the top line was fixed and the lower line was left unfixed and smudged with a fingertip, in order to show how some media need fixing more than others.

A Chalk – loses texture without fixing

B Conté crayon – changes little

C Soft pastel – colour spreads easily

D Charcoal – rapidly loses definition

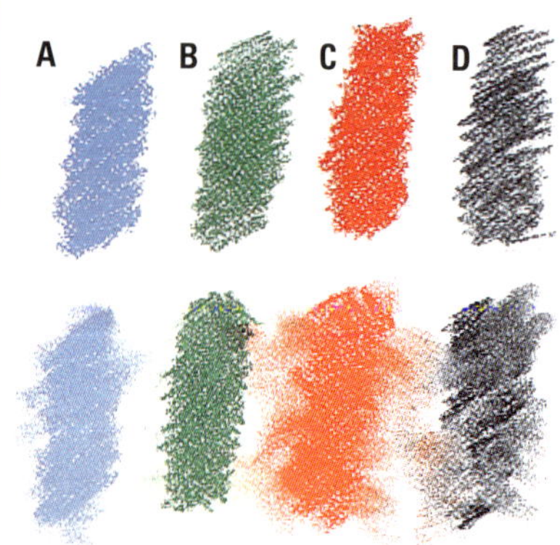

Using varnishes

Varnish your oil and acrylic paintings and you will get an even, uniform finish to your artwork. More importantly, the colours will still look fresh and vibrant for years to come.

There are two schools of thought about varnishes. One believes that the smooth, uniform surface of a varnish is the perfect finishing touch for a good oil painting. The other maintains that varnishing tends to kill the painterly qualities of the image – especially the subtle glazes and brush marks.

Whichever camp you fall in, one fact is for sure: if you want your paintings to last beyond your lifetime, you need to varnish them. Even when completely dry, an oil painting attracts air-borne moisture, dust and dirt. These impurities will inevitably impregnate the surface, causing the colours to dull for ever. A varnish, however, provides a hard, transparent protective coating.

The perfect varnish would never crack, cloud or turn yellow. Unfortunately, no varnish completely meets all these conditions. But even if the varnish itself dulls, a picture restorer can remove and replace it so that the painting is returned to its original splendour. This, of course, is not a possibility with an unvarnished painting.

Types of varnish

There are many types of varnish, both natural and synthetic. One of the most popular is mastic, made from Mediterranean pistachio trees. It gives a very fine, high-gloss finish, but tends to darken and cloud a little.

Damar varnishes, made from the resin of two kinds of conifer from South-east Asia, are not quite as easy to apply as mastic, but they do not cloud or darken quite so quickly. Copal varnish is known as a 'cooked oil' type, as it is prepared by heating a variety of resins with linseed oil. Once popular for its hard, shiny finish, copal varnish has been found to be prone to cracking and darkening.

Retouching varnish

Retouching varnish has a completely different role from conventional picture varnish. It is used during the painting process – not after it.

At the start of each new session of oil painting, artists use retouching varnish to restore dry, sunken-in paint to the colour it was when first applied. This enables them to continue painting from where they left off.

Although retouching varnish can help protect paintings from impurities, it doesn't provide a continuous layer for complete protection.

There are two types of varnish – ordinary varnish (A) (often called picture varnish) and retouching varnish (B) (see above). Picture varnishes can be made from mastic resin (C), damar resin (D), synthetic materials (E), or specially made for acrylic paintings (F). You can make your own varnish with the actual resin (G) or you can simply buy spray-on varnish (H).

MAKE YOUR OWN VARNISH

You can easily and inexpensively make your own varnish. Varnish resins – such as damar, mastic or ketone – are available from good art suppliers. Otherwise, all you need is some double-rectified turpentine, a muslin bag (or an old stocking) and a container.

1 ▲ Put 100g (3½oz) of your varnish resin in the middle of your piece of muslin. Gather the edges so that you create a bag and tie the top with a knot or piece of string.

2 ▲ Pour 300ml (10fl. oz) of double-rectified turpentine into the container and then immerse the bag of resin in it. Cover the container and leave for two or three days.

3 ▲ Once all the resin has dissolved, you have some varnish solution. To use, simply thin with turpentine and brush or spray it on to your picture (see Applying the varnish, below).

Synthetic varnishes are a relatively recent innovation. Ketone, the most common synthetic type, is thought not to yellow or cloud as much as natural resins, but it can become brittle and difficult to remove with age.

Check the paint is dry

To apply any of these varnishes, you must first make sure that the painting is completely dry. If the paint is still wet, the varnish might crack or even sink back into the paint. (To check this, follow the instructions in Applying the varnish, right.) Remember, an oil painting can take anything up to a year to dry, depending on the thickness of the paint and any mediums used.

You can, of course, varnish acrylic paintings as well as oils, but take note: it is highly questionable whether it is worth varnishing acrylic paintings to make them last longer. The actual paint on many acrylic works from the 1960s and 1970s has started to crack and deteriorate, and a varnish will not stop this process.

However, you may still want to varnish your acrylic paintings to attain a high-sheen finish. One of the best ways of doing this is to apply acrylic gel medium (see Using acrylic mediums, pages 44-45).

Applying the varnish

To apply the varnish, you need a varnishing brush or a spray gun. A varnishing brush has very fine bristles which don't leave brush marks. A spray gun should give you a thin, even layer, but don't try to use one with a mouth diffuser as you are bound to introduce some moisture. Whatever you use, make sure you work in a dry, well-ventilated and dust-free room – don't try it on a damp day.

Before you start, leave the varnish and the painting for several hours so both acclimatise to the atmosphere.

Once you've varnished the painting, wait for about 15 minutes for it to set and then prop the picture up to dry with the face inwards. Clean your brush in white spirit. If you are using a spray gun, pump white spirit through the nozzle.

1 ▲ Check that the painting is dry by dipping a soft rag in white spirit and rubbing it over the painting. If more than a trace of colour comes off, the painting is not ready.

2 ▲ With the painting lying flat, apply the varnish in two sets of parallel strokes – the second at right angles to the first. The aim is to achieve a thin, uniform covering.

Photographing your artwork

Every painting and drawing you do is unique and irreplaceable – so it really pays to make photographic copies of your work.

Almost all painters – whether they are keen amateurs or high-flying, full-time artists – need to copy their work at some time. Beginners might want to send photos of their paintings to friends and relatives. More advanced artists might want to keep a record of paintings they have sold and, as a consequence, are likely never to see again. Really committed artists might need to send photos of their work to galleries or art publications.

To achieve top-quality reproduction many artists will go to a professional photographer. However, unless you know a friendly photographer, this is not a cheap option. As long as you have a reasonably good camera, you can obtain perfectly acceptable results yourself with the most basic equipment.

What camera?

It is probably best not to use disposable cameras or a very cheap compact. These models have plastic lenses, which give very blurred photos, and they usually have a very basic control of exposure.

A compact camera (the type with a fixed lens, labelled A below) of reasonable quality will do, although it is worth noting that with this type of camera you do not actually look through the lens. As a result, what you see through the viewfinder might differ slightly from what you get in your final photo. If you are shooting something far away, such as a landscape, this effect is hardly noticeable, but when working up close (as you would if you were photographing most drawings and paintings), you need to make a little adjustment.

Adjusting for a compact camera

This is not a big problem. The viewfinder is always above and to the left of the lens – so when you have composed the photo with all the painting in the frame, compensate by moving the camera diagonally up to the left a little.

As this is not an exact science, you should also move back about 10cm (4in), so that you can see some space around the edge of your painting in the viewfinder. But don't get too far away – the smaller the painting is within the viewfinder, the poorer the quality of the final image.

You won't have this problem with a single-lens reflex (SLR) camera, labelled B below. With this type of camera, what you see is what you get. If you are thinking of buying a new camera, consider an SLR – the basic models are cheaper than the more advanced compacts and they have the advantage of interchangeable lenses.

▼ Whether you have a compact camera (A), a single-lens reflex (B) or a digital camera (C), you can take perfectly acceptable photos of your artwork. A digital camera also allows you to produce photos in a variety of sizes (D) on a PC.

HOW TO SET IT UP

It is best to photograph your artworks outside, on a cloudy day. This will provide an even lighting across the whole painting. If there is some sunlight, try positioning a piece of white card on the opposite side of the painting to the sun to throw some light back on to the darker side (see below).

On a very sunny day you might want to try a few shots in a shaded spot. However, if you do this you may get a bluish colour cast and there might not be quite enough light. If you are using an SLR you can attach a warm-up filter to eliminate cold casts, but make sure it's the right diameter for your lens. Don't use a flash, as you will probably get a bright area in the centre of the painting and a dark silhouette around the edges where the flash light falls off.

For minimum camera shake, it is best to set up the camera on something stable (below centre) and set the timer release. Alternatively, try using a cable release – you can attach this to most cameras.

When handholding the camera, if possible set a shutter speed of 1/125th or over to prevent camera shake. Consult your instruction booklet to see if you can change the shutter speeds.

▶ The easiest way to shoot your artwork is to stand over it and shoot down. This is particularly convenient if you have a zoom lens as you can frame tightly. If you are worried about camera shake, it's best to set your camera on a wall or stepladder (as below). You will have to use the same method when photographing a very large painting – you will not be able to get far enough away by bending over it.

◀ For precise framing and minimum camera shake, it pays to set up your camera on something solid – like a wall or a stepladder. Use the self-timer or, as here, a cable release to make sure the camera is absolutely still when you release the shutter. If your artwork is in portrait format, simply shoot it on its side: you can always turn the photo round!

▶ If you see that the lighting across your painting is uneven, get a friend to throw some light back on to the dark side by holding a piece of white card out of frame. Uneven lighting may occur if the sun begins to peek out from behind the clouds.

The digital route

The increasingly popular digital cameras provide another way of photographing your artwork. They really make sense if you have a computer and printer at home, because you can cut out the photo lab altogether. But take note, this is not a cheap option – if you want good-quality pictures above postcard size, you are going to have to make a big investment in computer equipment.

Film choice

As far as film goes, it's best to choose print film rather than slides. The problem with slides is in getting the exposure right. If you are slightly off, you'll either get a washed-out image or a dark one. Exposure is not as critical with print film since the processors compensate for mistakes when the negative is printed.

The only occasion for which you really need slides of your work is if you are going to have a painting reproduced in a book or a magazine. Most printers prefer to work from slides. However, if you are having your work published, it is probably worth having your paintings photographed professionally.

Prints and processing

For accurate colours, it is best to buy a well-known brand of film rather than cheaper types given away free when you have a film processed. And watch out for colour casts on your prints. If the processors have a machine that is not maintained properly, the reds and yellows in your painting can easily end up as purples and greens in your photos.

Don't be afraid to ask the processors to reprint the photos if there is a strong colour cast. If necessary, show them how the original painting differs from the photos.

Stay clear of black-and-white film – even if you are photographing a monochrome drawing. Most high-street processors do a very poor job of developing and printing black-and-white negatives, because most of their business is for colour films. If you want good quality black-and-white prints, you will have to go to a specialist printer, and that can be costly.

Carrying and storing your artworks

Your best drawings and paintings are irreplaceable, so it is important to find practical ways of transporting and storing them to avoid any damage.

Your pictures are probably at their most vulnerable when in transit after a drawing or painting trip. This is especially true of watercolours, drawings and other work on paper, as these might tear or become creased.

The simplest answer is to leave the artworks on the drawing board or pad and cover them with a sheet of clean paper. Alternatively, paintings can be rolled up and carried in a cardboard tube container. These are available in a range of sizes from many office supply stores and stationers, and are also excellent if you want to send drawings, prints or watercolours through the post. To carry wet oil paintings, you can use corks and pins to separate the canvases (see Portable art materials, pages 16-17).

At some point, you might need to show your work – perhaps at an interview or to a gallery – and this is the time to invest in an artist's portfolio. Rather like a large, flat briefcase, a portfolio enables you to transport a number of drawings and paintings easily. It also looks businesslike, especially if the work is presented attractively and in the order in which you want it to be seen.

Wide range of portfolios

Portfolios come in a range of sizes to fit all standard papers, so choose one that is suitable for your requirements. Simple card portfolios are light and inexpensive. They are normally flat and the work is retained by folding flaps, which are fastened with cord or ribbon.

For carrying a large amount of work, try a box-type portfolio secured with a zip, studs, buckles or Velcro. Those made of fluted plastic sheet are tough yet lightweight. Drawings and paintings can also be stored and displayed in transparent plastic sleeves, which fit inside zipped, ring-bound portfolios. Small work will fit into a shallow brief-case or similar compact case.

Artworks pile up very quickly, so try to plan a storage system at home before they

▼ The range of portfolios includes the box-type (A), the flat card (B) and the ring-bound (C). Soft briefcases (D) are ideal for carrying card portfolios or works on panels. Tube containers (E) are a less bulky alternative to the portfolio.

become damaged or dog-eared. A plan chest has shallow drawers designed to accommodate large-scale artworks. For smaller works, an ordinary desk with drawers might be adequate.

Drawings and watercolours should be stored flat. Before putting away artworks in soft pencil, charcoal or pastel, spray them with fixative. Also, secure a sheet of tracing paper over the top of the work with two masking tape hinges. This protects each drawing from loose particles of pigment and dust.

A practical way of storing boards and canvases is to stack them vertically in simple wooden racks – easily made by anyone with rudimentary carpentry skills. It is important that canvases of a similar size are stored together with the wooden stretchers resting against each other. If the wooden edge of one painting leans against the fabric of another, the edges of the smaller painting will make dents or holes in the larger one.

Small dents are sometimes permanent but they can often be remedied by restretching the painting or by brushing the reverse side of the dented surface with water to shrink the canvas.

Roll with it

Alternatively, you can remove the painted canvas from the stretcher altogether and store the painting rolled up. Always roll with the painted surface facing outwards – dried paint will stretch a little, but will not contract. Wrap the rolled painting in paper or cloth to protect it from dust.

MAKING YOUR OWN PORTFOLIO

This portfolio is made from sheets of A3 card – but you can make yours to whatever size you want.

YOU WILL NEED

- PVA glue
- Glue spreader or scrap of card
- Two A3 sheets of thick card, and one strip of the same card, 42cm x 1.5cm (16½in x ⅝in)
- Sheet of firm wrapping paper
- Scissors
- Gummed paper tape
- Bowl of water
- A2 and A3 sheets of thin coloured card
- 2m (2¼yd) of ribbon

1 ▲ Cover the card Spread PVA glue thinly over one side of each A3 card, and on one side of the card strip. Glue them to the back of the wrapping paper, with a 1cm (⅜in) gap between the strip and the A3 sheets on each side. Leave a 5cm (2in) border of paper around the edge. Fold in each paper corner and glue it in place, then fold in the borders and glue them to the card.

2 ▲ Strengthen the spine Cut a 42cm (16½in) length of gummed paper tape. Wet the glue on the tape, then stick it along the spine, pushing it down into the valleys on each side of the spine strip. Repeat with three more strips to make the spine really strong.

3 ▲ Prepare the envelope Fold the thin card around the largest sketch you wish to store. Unfold the card and remove the sketch. Then cut away the sides of the two end flaps, tapering the flaps slightly away from the central rectangle.

4 ▲ Finish the inside Strengthen the corners with strips of gummed paper tape. Then glue a rectangle of coloured card to the back of one panel of the portfolio. Glue the back of the envelope to the other panel. Tie the portfolio with coloured ribbon.

▲ Stylish and practical, the portfolio is the perfect place to store your art.